The Parousia

A Critical Inquiry into the New Testament Doctrine of Our Lord Christ's Second Coming

By James Stuart Russell

PANTIANOS
CLASSICS

Published by Pantianos Classics

ISBN-13: 978-1-78987-071-8

First published in 1878

Contents

Preface

No Attentive reader of the New Testament can fail to be struck with the prominence given by the evangelists and the apostles to the PAROUSIA, or 'coming of the Lord.' That event is the great theme of New Testament prophecy. There is scarcely a single book, from the Gospel of St. Matthew to the Apocalypse of St. John, in which it is not set forth as the glorious promise of God and the blessed hope of the church. It was frequently and solemnly predicted by our Lord; it was incessantly kept before the eyes of the early Christians by the apostles; and it was firmly believed and eagerly expected by the churches of the primitive age.

It cannot be denied that there is a remarkable difference between the attitude of the first Christians in relation to the Parousia and that of Christians now. That glorious hope, to which all eyes and hearts in the apostolic age were eagerly turned, has almost disappeared from the view of modern believers. Whatever may be the theoretical opinions ex- pressed in symbols and creeds, it must in candor be admitted that the 'second coming of Christ' has all but ceased to be a living and practical belief.

Various causes may be assigned in explanation of this state of things. The rash vaticinations of those who have too confidently undertaken to be interpreters of prophecy, and the discredit consequent on the failure of their predictions, have no doubt deterred reverent and soberminded men from entering upon the investigation of 'unfulfilled prophecy.' On the other hand, there is reason to think that rationalistic criticism has engendered doubts whether the predictions of the New Testament were ever intended to have a literal or historical fulfilment.

Between rationalism on the one hand, and irrationalism on the other, there has come to be a widely prevailing state of uncertainty and confusion of thought in regard to New Testament prophecy, which to some extent explains, though it may not justify, the consigning of the whole subject to the region of hopelessly obscure and insoluble problems.

This, however, is only a partial explanation. It deserves consideration whether there may not be a fundamental difference between the relation of the church of the apostolic age to the predicted Parousia and the relation to that event sustained by subsequent ages. The first Christians undoubtedly believed themselves to be standing on the verge of a great catastrophe, and we know what intensity and enthusiasm the expectation of the almost immediate coming of the Lord inspired; but if it cannot be shown that Christians now are similarly placed, there would be a want of truth and reality in affecting the eager anticipation and hope of the primitive church. The same event cannot be imminent at two different periods separated by nearly two thousand years. There must, therefore, be some grave misconception on the part of those who maintain that the Christian church of to-day occupies precisely the same relation, and should maintain the same attitude, towards the 'coming of the Lord' as the church in the days of St. Paul.

The present volume is an attempt, in a candid and reverent spirit, to clear up this misconception, and to ascertain the true meaning of the Word of God on a subject which holds so conspicuous a place in the teaching of our Lord and His apostles. It is the fruit of many years of patient investigation, and the Author has spared no pains to test to the utmost the validity of his conclusions. It has been his single aim to ascertain what saith the Scripture, and his one desire to be governed by a loyal submission to its authority. The ideal of Biblical interpretation which he has kept before him is that so well expressed by a German theologian - *'Explicatio plana non tortuosa, facilis non violenta, eademque et exegeticce et Chistanae conscientium pariter arridens.'* (1)

Although the nature of the inquiry necessitates a somewhat frequent reference to the original of the New Testament, and to the laws of grammatical construction and interpretation, it has been the object of the Author to render this work as popular as possible, and such as any man of ordinary education and intelligence may read with ease and interest. The Bible is a book for every man, and the Author has not written for scholars and critics only, but for the many who are deeply interested in Biblical interpretation, and who think, with Locke, 'an impartial search into the true meaning of the sacred Scripture the best employment of all the time they have.' (2) It will be a sufficient recompense of his labour if he succeeds in elucidating in any degree those teachings of divine revelation which have been obscured by traditional prejudices, or misinterpreted by an erroneous exegesis.

1. Donier's tractate, De Oratione Christi Eschatologica, p. 1.
2. Locke, Notes on Ephesians i. 10.

The Last Words of Old Testament Prophecy

The Book of Malachi

THE canon of the Old Testament Scriptures closes in a very different manner from what might have been expected after the splendid future revealed to the covenant nation in the visions of Isaiah. None of the prophets is the bearer of a heavier burden than the last. Malachi is the prophet of doom. It would seem that the nation, by its incorrigible obstinacy and disobedience, had forfeited the divine favour, and proved itself not only unworthy, but incapable, of the promised glories. The departure of the prophetic spirit was full of evil omen, and seemed to intimate that the Lord was about to forsake the land. Accordingly, the light of Old Testament prophecy goes out amidst clouds and thick darkness. The Book of Malachi is one long and terrible impeachment of the nation. The Lord Himself is the accuser, and sustains every charge against the guilty people by the clearest proof. The long indictment includes sacrilege, hypocrisy, contempt of God, conjugal infidelity, perjury, apostasy, blasphemy; while, on the other hand, the people have the effrontery to repudiate the accusation, and to plead ' not guilty ' to every charge. They appear to have reached that stage of moral insensibility when men call evil good, and good evil, and are fast ripening for judgment.

Accordingly, *coming judgment* is 'the burden if the word of the Lord to Israel by Malachi.'
Chap. iii. 5: 'I will come near to you to judgment; and I will be a swift witness against the sorcerers, and against the adulterers, and against false swearers, and against those that oppress the hireling in his wages, the widow, and the fatherless, and that turn aside the stranger from his right, and fear not me, saith the Lord of hosts.,
Chap. iv. 1: 'For, behold, the day cometh that shall burn as an oven [furnace]: and all the proud, yea, and all that do wickedly, shall be stubble: and the day that cometh shall burn them up, saith the Lord of hosts, that it shall leave them neither root nor branch.'

That this is no vague and unmeaning threat is evident from the distinct and definite terms in which it is announced. Everything points to an approaching crisis in the history of the nation, when God would inflict judgment upon His rebellious people. 'The day, was coming - 'the day that shall burn as a furnace;, 'the great and terrible day of the Lord., That this 'day' refers to a certain period, and a specific event, does not admit of question. It had already been foretold in precisely the same words by the Prophet Joel (ii. 31): 'The great and terrible day of the Lord;, and we shall meet with a distinct reference to it in the address of the Apostle Peter on the Day of Pentecost (Acts ii. 20). But the period is further more precisely defined by the remarkable statement of Malachi in chap. iv. 5: 'Behold, I will send you Elijah the prophet before the coming of the great and terrible day of the Lord.' The explicit declaration of our Lord that the predicted Elijah was no other than His own forerunner, John the Baptist (Matt. xi. 14), enables us to determine the time and the event referred to as 'the great and terrible day of the Lord., It must be sought at no great distance from the period of John the Baptist. That is to say, the allusion is to the judgment of the Jewish nation, when their city and temple were destroyed, and the entire fabric of the Mosaic polity was dissolved.

It deserves to be noticed, that both Isaiah and Malachi predict the appearance of John the Baptist as the forerunner of our Lord, but in very different terms. Isaiah represents him as the herald of the coming *Saviour:* 'The voice of him that crieth in the wilderness, Prepare ye the way of the Lord, make straight in the desert a highway for our God' (Isa. xl. 3). Malachi represents John as the precursor of the coming Judge: 'Behold, I will send my messenger, and he shall prepare the way before me; and the Lord, whom ye seek, shall suddenly come to his temple, even the messenger of the covenant whom ye delight in: behold, he shall come, saith the Lord of hosts' (Mal. iv. 1).

That this is a coming to judgment, is manifest from the words which immediately follow, describing tile alarm and dismay caused by His appearing: 'But who may abide the day of his coming? and who shall stand when he appeareth?' (Mal. iii. 2.)

It cannot be said that this language is appropriate to the first coming of Christ; but it is highly appropriate to His second coming. There is a distinct allusion to this passage in Rev. vi. 17, where 'the kings of the earth, and the great men, and the rich men, and the chief captains,' etc., are represented as 'hiding from the face of him that sitteth on the throne, and from tile wrath of the Lamb, and saying, *The great day of his wrath is come; and who shall be able to stand?*'. Nothing can be more clear than that the 'day of his coming', in Mal. iii. 1 is the same as 'the great and dreadful day of the Lord' in chap. iv. 5, and that both answer to 'the great day of his wrath' in Rev. vi. 17. We conclude, therefore, that the prophet Malachi speaks, not of the first advent of our Lord, but of the second.

This is further proved by the significant fact, that, in chap. iii. 1, the Lord is represented as 'suddenly coming to *his temple.*' To understand this as referring to the presentation of the infant Saviour in the temple by His parents, or to His in the courts of the temple, or to His of the buyers and sellers from the sacred edifice, is surely a most inadequate explanation. Those were not occasions of terror and dismay, such as is implied in the second verse, 'But who may abide the day of his coming?' The expression is, however, vividly suggestive of His final and judicial visitation of His Father's house, when it was to be 'left desolate,' according to His prediction. The temple was the centre of the nation's life, the visible symbol of the covenant between God and His people; it was the spot where 'judgment must begin,' and which was to be overtaken by *sudden destruction.'* Taking, then, all these particulars into account, the 'sudden coming of the Lord to his temple,' the dismay attending 'the day of his coming,' His coming as 'a refiner's fire,' His coming ' near to them to judgment,' 'the day coming that shall burn as a furnace,' 'burning up the wicked root and branch,' and the appearing of John the Baptist, the second Elijah, previous to the arrival of 'the great and dreadful day of the Lord,' it is impossible to resist the conclusion that the prophet here foretells that great national catastrophe in which the temple, the city, and the nation, perished together; and that this is designated, *'the day of his coming.'*

However strange, therefore, it may seem, it is undoubtedly the fact that the first coming of our Lord is not alluded to by Malachi. This is distinctly acknowledged by Hengstenberg, who observes: 'Malachi passes by the first coming of Christ in humiliation altogether and leaves the interval between his forerunner end the judgment of Jerusalem a perfect blank.' (1) This is to be accounted for by the fact, that the main object of the prophecy is to predict national destruction and not national deliverance.

At the same time, while judgment and wrath are the predominant elements of the prophecy, features of a different character are not wholly absent. The day of wrath is also a day of redemption. There is a faithful remnant, even among the apostate nation: there are gold and silver to be refined and jewels to be gathered, as well as dross to be rejected, and stubble to be burned. There are sons to be spared, as well as enemies to be destroyed; and the day which brought dismay and darkness to the wicked, would see 'the Sun of righteousness arise with healing in his wings' on the faithful. Even Malachi intimates that the door of mercy is not yet shut. If the nation would return unto God, He would return unto them. If they would make restitution of that which they had sacrilegiously withheld from the service of the temple, He would repay them with blessings more than they could receive. They might even yet be a 'delightsome land,' the envy of all nations. At the eleventh hour, if the mission of the second Elijah should succeed in winning the hearts of the people, tile impending catastrophe might after all be averted (chap. iii. 3, 16-18; iv. 2, 3, 5, 6).

Nevertheless, there is a foregone conclusion that expostulation and threatening will be unavailing. The last words sound like the knell of doom (Mal. iv. 6): 'Lest I come and smite the land with a *curse!'*

The full import of this ominous declaration is not at once apparent. To the Hebrew mind. it suggested the most terrible fate that could befall a city or a people. The 'curse' was the *anathema,* or *cherem* which denoted that the person or thing on which the malediction was laid was given over to utter destruction. We have an example of the *cherem,* or *ban,* in the curse pronounced upon Jericho (Josh. vi. 17); and a more particular statement of the ruin which it involved, in the Book of Deuteronomy (chap. xiii. 12-18). The city was to be smitten with the edge of the sword, every living thing in it to be put to death, the spoil was not to be touched, all was accursed and unclean, it was to be wholly consumed with fire, and the place given up to perpetual desolation. Hengstenberg remarks: 'All the things that can possibly be thought of are included in this *one* word;' (2) and he quotes the comment of Vitringa on this passage: ' There can be no doubt that God intended to say, that He would give up to certain destruction, both the obstinate transgressors of the law and also their city, and that they should suffer the extreme penalty of His justice, as *heads devoted to God,* without any hope of favour or forgiveness.'

Such is the fearful malediction suspended over the land of Israel by the prophetic Spirit, in the moment of taking its departure, and becoming silent for ages. It is important to observe, that all this has a distinct and specific reference to the land of Israel. The message of the prophet is to Israel; the sins which are reprobated are the sins of Israel; the coming of the Lord is to His temple in Israel; the land threatened with the curse is the land of Israel. (3) All this manifestly points to a specific local and national catastrophe, of which the land of Israel was to be the scene and its guilty inhabitants the victims. History records the fulfilment of the prophecy, in exact correspondence of time, place, and circumstance, in the ruin which overwhelmed the Jewish nation at the period of the destruction of Jerusalem.

The Interval Between Malachi and John the Baptist.

The four centuries which intervene between the conclusion of the Old Testament and the commencement of the New are a blank in Scripture history. We know, however, from the Books of the Maccabees and the writings of Josephus, that it was an eventful period in the Jewish annals. Judea was by turns the vassal of the great monarchies by which it was surrounded - Persia, Greece, Egypt, Syria, and Rome, - with an interval of independence under the Maccabean princes. But though the nation during this period passed through great suffering, and produced some illustrious examples of patriotism and of piety, we look in vain for any divine oracle, or any inspired messenger, to declare the word of the Lord. Israel might truly say: 'We see not our signs, there is no more any prophet: neither is there among us any that knoweth how long' (Psa. lxxiv. 9). Yet those four centuries were not without a powerful influence on the character of the nation. During this period, synagogues were established throughout the land, and the knowledge of the Scriptures was widely extended. The great religious schools of the Pharisees and Sadducees arose, both professing to be expounders and defenders of the law of Moses. Vast numbers of Jews settled in the great cities of Egypt, Asia Minor, Greece, and Italy, carrying with them everywhere the worship of the synagogue and the Septuagint translation of the Old Testament. Above all, the nation cherished in its inmost heart the hope of a coming deliverer, a scion of the royal house of David, who should be the theocratic king, the liberator of Israel from Gentile domination, whose reign was to be so happy and glorious that it might deserve to be called 'the kingdom of heaven.' But, for the most part, the popular conception of the coming king was earthly and carnal. There had not in four hundred years been any improvement in the moral condition of the people, and, between the formalism of the Pharisees and the scepticism of the Sadducees, true religion had sunk to its lowest ebb. There was still, however, a faithful remnant who had truer conceptions of the kingdom of heaven, and 'who looked for redemption in Israel.' As the time drew near, there were indications of the return of the prophetic spirit, and premonitions that the promised deliverer was at hand. Simeon received assurance that before his death ho should see 'the Lord's anointed;' a like intimation appears to have been made to the aged prophetess Anna. Such revelations, it is reasonable to suppose, must have awakened eager expectation in the hearts of many, and prepared them for the cry which soon after was heard in the wilderness of Judea: 'Repent; for the kingdom of heaven is at hand!' A prophet had again risen up in Israel, and 'the Lord had visited His people.'

1. See Hengst. Nature of Prophecy. Christ. vol. iv. p. 418
2. Hengst. Christology, vol. iv. p 227
3. The meaning of this passage (Mal. iv. 6) is obscured by the unfortunate translation earth instead of land. The Hebrew ch,a, like the Greek gh/, is very frequently employed in a restricted sense. The allusion in the text plainly is to the land of Israel. -See Hengst. Christology, vol. iv. p 224

Part One - The Parousia in the Gospels

THE PAROUSIA PREDICTED BY JOHN THE BAPTIST

THERE is nothing more distinctly affirmed in the New Testament than the identity of John the Baptist with the wilderness-herald of Isaiah and the Elijah of Malachi. How well the description of John agrees with that of Elijah is evident at a glance. Each was austere and ascetic in his manner of life; each was a zealous reformer of religion; each was a stern reprover of sin. The times in which they lived were singularly alike. The nation at both periods was degenerate and corrupt. Elijah had his Ahab, John his Herod. It is no objection to this identification of John as the predicted Elijah, that the Baptist himself disclaimed the name when the priests and Levites from Jerusalem demanded: 'Art thou Elias?' (John i. 21.) The Jews expected the reappearance of the literal Elijah, and John's reply was addressed to that mistaken opinion. But his true claim to the designation is expressly affirmed in the announcement made by the angel to his father Zacharias: 'He shall go before him in the spirit and power of Elias' (Luke i. 17); as well as by the declarations of our Lord: 'If ye will receive it, *this is Elias* which was for to come' (Matt.. xi. 14); 'I say unto you that Elias is come already, and they knew him not.... Then the disciples understood that he spake unto them of *John the Baptist*' (Matt.. xvii. 10-13). John was the second Elias, and exhaustively fulfilled the predictions of Isaiah and Malachi concerning him. To dream of an 'Elijah of the future,' therefore, is virtually to discredit the express statement of the word of God, and rests upon no Scripture warrant whatever.

We have already adverted to the twofold aspect of the mission of John presented by the prophets Isaiah and Malachi. The same diversity is seen in the New Testament descriptions of the second Elias. The benignant aspect of his mission which is presented by Isaiah, is also recognized in the words of the angel by whom his birth was foretold, as already quoted; and in the inspired utterance of his father Zacharias: 'Thou, child, shalt be called the prophet of the Highest, for thou shalt go before the face of the Lord to prepare his ways, to give knowledge of salvation unto his people by the remission of their sins , (Luke i. 76, 77). We find the same gracious aspect in the opening verses of the Gospel of St. John: 'The same came for a witness, to bear witness of the Light, that all men through him might believe, (John i. 7).

But the other aspect of his mission is no less distinctly recognized in the Gospels. He is represented, not only as the herald of the coming Saviour, but of the coming Judge. Indeed, his own recorded utterances speak far more of wrath than of salvation, and are conceived more in the spirit of the Elijah of Malachi than of the wilderness-herald of Isaiah. He warns the Pharisees and Sadducees, and the multitudes that crowded to his baptism, to 'flee from the coming wrath.' He tells them that 'the axe is laid unto the root of the trees.' He announces the coming of One mightier than himself, 'whose fan is in his hand, and who will thoroughly purge his floor, and gather his wheat into the garner, but who will burn up the chaff with unquenchable fire' (Matt. iii. 12).

It is impossible not to be struck with the correspondence between the language of the Baptist and that of Malachi. As Hengstenberg observes: 'The prophecy of Malachi is throughout the text upon which John comments." (1) In both, the coming of the Lord is described as a day of wrath; both speak of His coming with fire to purify and try, with fire to burn and consume Both speak of a time of discrimination and separation between the righteous and the wicked, the gold and the dross, the wheat and the chaff; and both speak of the utter destruction of the chaff, or stubble, with unquenchable fire. These are not fortuitous resemblances: the two predictions are the counterpart one of the other, and can only refer to the self-same event, the same 'day of the Lord,' the same coming judgment.

But what more especially deserves remark is the evident *nearness* of the crisis which John predicts. 'The wrath to come' is a very inadequate rendering of the language of the prophet. (2) It should be 'the *coming* wrath;' that is, not merely *future,* but *impending.* 'The wrath to come' may be indefinitely distant, but 'the coming wrath' is imminent. As Alford justly remarks: 'John is now speaking in the true character of a prophet foretelling *the wrath soon to be poured on the Jewish nation.*' (3) So with the other representations in the address of the Baptist; all is indicative of the swift approach of destruction. *'Already* the axe was lying at the root of the trees.' The 'winnowing shovel' was actually in the hands of the Husbandman; the sifting process was about to begin. These warnings of John the Baptist are not the vague and indefinite exhortations to repentance, addressed to men in all ages, which they are sometimes assumed to be; they are urgent, burning words, having a specific and present bearing upon the then existing generation, the living men to whom he brought the message of God. The Jewish nation was now upon its last trial; the second Elijah had come as the precursor of 'the great and dreadful day of the Lord:' if they rejected his warnings, the doom predicted by Malachi would surely and speedily follow; 'I will come and smite the land with the curse.' Nothing can be more obvious than that the catastrophe to which John alludes is *particular, national, local,* and *imminent,* and history tells us that within the period of the generation that listened to his warning cry, 'the wrath came upon them to the uttermost.'

1. Christol.. vol. iv. p.. 232.   *2. thj melloushj orghj*   *3. Greek Test. in loc.*

The Teaching of Our Lord Concerning the Parousia in the Synoptical Gospels

The close of John the Baptist's ministry, in consequence of his imprisonment by Herod Antipas, marks a new departure in the ministry of our Lord. Previous to that time, indeed, He had taught the people, wrought miracles, gained adherents, and obtained a wide popularity; but after that event, which may be regarded as indicating the failure of John's mission, our Lord retired into Galilee, and there entered upon a new phase of His public ministry. We are told that 'from that time Jesus began to preach, and to say, Repent; for the kingdom of heaven is at hand' (Matt. iv. 17). These are the precise terms in which the preaching of John the Baptist is described (Matt. iii. 2). Both our Lord and His forerunner called 'the nation to repentance,' and announced the approach of the 'kingdom of heaven.' It follows that John could not mean by the phrase, 'the kingdom of heaven is at hand,' merely that the Messiah was about to appear, for when Christ did appear, He made the same announcement. 'The kingdom of heaven is *at hand.*' In like manner, when the twelve disciples were sent forth on their first evangelistic mission, they were commanded to preach, not that the kingdom of heaven was come, but that it was *at hand* (Matt. x. 7). Moreover, that the kingdom did not come in our Lord's time, nor at the day of Pentecost, is evident from the fact that in His prophetic discourse on the Mount of Olives our Lord gave His disciples certain tokens by which they might know that the kingdom of God was nigh at hand (Luke xxi. 31).

We find, therefore, the following conclusions plainly deducible from our Lord's teaching:

1. That a great crisis, or consummation, called 'the kingdom of heaven, or of God,' was proclaimed by Him to be nigh. 2. That this consummation, though near, was not to take place in His own lifetime, nor yet for some years after His death. 3. That His disciples, or at least some of them, might expect to witness its arrival.

But the whole subject of 'the kingdom of heaven' must be reserved for fuller discussion at a future period.

PREDICTION OF COMING WRATH UPON THAT GENERATION.

There is another point of resemblance between the preaching of our Lord and that of John the Baptist. Both gave the clearest intimations of the near approach of a time of judgment which should overtake the existing generation, on account of their rejection of the warnings and invitations of divine mercy. As the Baptist spoke of 'the coming wrath,' so our Lord with equal distinctness forewarned the people of 'coming judgment.' He upbraided 'the cities wherein most of his mighty works were done, because they repented not,' and predicted that a heavier woe would overtake them than had fallen upon Tyre and Sidon, Sodom and Gomorrha (Matt. xi. 20-24). That all this points to a catastrophe which was not remote, but near, and which would actually overtake the existing generation, appears evident from the express statements of Jesus.

Matt. xii. 38-46 (compare Luke xi. 16, 24-36): 'Then certain of the scribes and of the Pharisees answered, saying, Master, we would see a sign from thee. But he answered and said unto them, An evil and adulterous generation seeketh after a sign: and there shall no sign be given unto it, but the sign of the prophet Jonas: for as Jonas was three days and three nights in the whale's belly, so shall the Son of man be three days and three nights in the heart of the earth. The men of Nineveh shall rise in the judgment with this generation, and shall condemn it, because they repented at the preaching of Jonas and, behold, a greater than Jonas is here. The queen of the south shall rise up in the judgment with generation, and condemn it, for sue came from the uttermost parts of the earth to hear the wisdom of Solomon; and, behold, a greater than Solomon is here. When the unclean spirit is gone out of a man, he walketh through dry places seeking rest, and findeth none. Then he saith, I will return into my house from whence I came out; and when he is come he findeth it empty, swept, and garnished. Then goeth he, and taketh with himself seven other spirits more wicked than himself, and they enter in and dwell there: and the last state of that man is worse than the first. Even so shall it be also unto this wicked generation.'

This passage is of great importance in ascertaining the true meaning of the phrase 'this generation' [genea]. It can only refer, in this place, to the people of Israel then living- the existing generation. No commentator has ever proposed to call 'genea' here the Jewish race in all ages. Our Lord was accustomed to speak of His contemporaries as *this generation:*

Whereunto shall I liken this generation?'- that is, the men of that day who would listen neither to His forerunner nor to Himself' (Matt. xi. 16; Luke vii. 31). Even commentators like Stier, who contend for the rendering of 'genea' by *race* or *lineage in* other passages, admit that the reference in these words is 'to the generation living in that then extant and most important age.' (1) So in the passage before us there can be no controversy respecting the application of the words exclusively to the then existing generation, the contemporaries of Christ. Of the aggravated and enormous wickedness of that period our Lord here testifies. The generation has just before been addressed by Him in the very words of the Baptist- ' O brood of vipers' (ver. 34). Its guilt is declared to surpass that of the heathen; it is likened to a demoniac, from whom the unclean spirit had departed for a while, but returned in greater force than before, accompanied by seven other spirits more wicked than himself, so that 'the last state of that man is worse than that first.' We have in the testimony of Josephus a striking confirmation of our Lord's description of the moral condition of that generation. 'As it were impossible to relate their enormities in detail, I shall briefly state that no other city ever endured similar calamities, and no generation ever existed more prolific in crime. They confessed themselves to be, what they were- slaves, and the very dregs of society, the spurious and polluted spawn of the nation.' (2) 'And here I cannot refrain from expressing what my feelings suggest. I am of opinion, that had the Romans deferred the punishment of these wretches, either the earth would have opened and swallowed up the city, or it would have been swept away by a deluge, or have shared the shun. defaults of the land of Sodom. For it produced a race far more ungodly than those who were thus visited. For through the desperate madness of these men the whole nation was involved in their ruin.' (3) 'That period had somehow become so prolific in iniquity of every description amongst the Jews, that no work of evil was left unperpetrated; ... so universal was the contagion, both in public and private, and such the emulation to surpass each other in acts of impiety towards God, and of injustice towards their neighbors.' (4)

Such was the fearful condition to which the nation was hastening when our Lord uttered these prophetic words. The climax had not yet been reached, but it was full in view. The unclean spirit had not yet returned to his house, but he was on the way. As Stier remarks, 'In the period between the ascension of Christ and the destruction of Jerusalem, especially towards the end of it, this nation shows itself, one might say, as if possessed by seven thousand devils.' (5) Is not this an adequate and complete fulfilment of our Saviour's prediction? Have we the slightest warrant or need for saying that it means something else, or something more, than this? What presence is there for supposing a further and future fulfilment of His words? Is it not a virtual discrediting of the prophecy to seek any other than the plain and obvious sense which points so distinctly to an approaching catastrophe about to befall that generation? Surely we show most reverence to the Word of God when we accept implicitly its obvious teaching, and refuse the unwarranted and merely human speculations which critics and theologians have drawn from their own fancy. We conclude, then, that, in the notorious profligacy of that age, and the signal calamities which before its close overwhelmed the Jewish people, we have the historical attestation of the exhaustive fulfilment of this prophecy.

FURTHER ALLUSIONS TO THE COMING WRATH.

Luke xiii. 1-9: 'There were present at that season some that told him of the Galileans, whose blood Pilate had mingled with their sacrifices. And Jesus answering said unto them, Suppose ye that these Galileans were sinners above all the Galileans, because they suffered such things? I tell you, Nay: but, except ye repent, ye shall all likewise perish. Or those eighteen, upon whom the tower in Siloam fell, and slew them, think ye that they were sinners above all men that dwelt in Jerusalem? I tell you, Nay: but, except ye repent, ye shall all likewise perish.'

How vividly our Lord apprehended the approaching calamities of the nation, and how clear and distinct His warnings were, may be inferred from this passage. The massacre of some Galileans who had gone up to Jerusalem to the feast of the Passover, either by the command, or with the connivance of the Roman governor; and the sudden destruction of eighteen persons by the fall of a tower near the pool of Siloam, were incidents which formed the topics of conversation among the people at the time. Our Lord declares that the victims of these calamities were not exceptionally wicked, but that a *like fate* would overtake the very persons now talking about them, unless they repented. The point of His observation, which is often overlooked, lies in the *similarity* of the threatened destruction. It is not 'ye *also* shall all perish,' but, 'ye shall all perish in *'the same manner'*. That our Lord had in view the final ruin, which was about to overwhelm Jerusalem and the nation, can hardly be doubted. The analogy between the cases is real and striking. It was at the feast of the Passover that the population of Judea had crowded into Jerusalem, and were there cooped in by the legions of Titus. Josephus tells us how, in the final agony of the siege, the blood of the officiating priests was shed at the altar of sacrifice. The Roman soldiers were the executioners of the divine judgment; and as temple and tower fell to the ground, they buried in their ruins many a hapless victim of impenitence and unbelief. It is satisfactory to find both Alford and Stier recognising the historical allusion in this passage. The former remarks: the force of which is lost in the English version "*likewise*," should be rendered "*in like manner,*" as indeed the Jewish people did perish by the sword of the Romans.' (6)

IMPENDING FATE OF THE JEWISH NATION.

The Parable of the Barren Fig-tree.

Luke xiii. 6-9: 'He spake also this parable: A certain man had a figtree planted in his vineyard: and he came and sought fruit thereon, and found none. Then said he to the dresser of his vineyard, Behold, these three years I come seeking fruit on this fig-tree, and find none: cut it down; why cumbereth it the ground? And he answering said unto him, Lord, let it alone this year also, till I shall dig about it, and dung it: and if it bear fruit, well: and if not, then after that thou shalt cut it down.'

The same prophetic significance is manifest in this parable, which is almost the counterpart of that in Isa. v., both in form and meaning. The true interpretation is so obvious as to render explanation scarcely necessary. Its bearing on the people of Israel is most distinct and direct, more especially when viewed in connection with the preceding warnings. Israel is the fruitless tree, long cultivated, but yielding no return to the owner. It was now on its last trial: the axe, as John the Baptist had declared, was laid to the root of the tree; but the fatal blow was delayed at the intercession of mercy. The Saviour was even then at His gracious work of nurture and culture; a little longer, and the decree would go forth- 'Cut it down; why cumbereth it the ground?'

No doubt there are general principles in this, as in other parables, applicable to all nations and all ages; but we must not lose sight of its original and primary reference to the Jewish people. Stier and Alford seem to lose themselves in searching for recondite and mystical meanings in the minor details of the imagery; but Neander gives a luminous explanation of its true import: 'As the fruitless tree, failing to realize the aim of its being, was destroyed, so the theocratic nation, for the same reason, was to be overtaken, after long forbearance, by the judgments of God, and shut out from His kingdom.' (7)

THE END OF THE AGE, OR CLOSE OF THE JEWISH DISPENSATION.

Parables of the Tares, and of the Drag-net.

Matt. xiii. 36-47: 'Then Jesus sent the multitude away, and went into the house: and his disciples came unto him, saying, Declare unto us the parable of the tares of the field. He answered and said unto them, He that soweth the good seed is the Son of man; the field is the world; the good seed are the children of the kingdom; but the tares are the children of the wicked one; the enemy that sowed them is the devil; the harvest is the end of the world [age]; and the reapers are the angels. As therefore the tares are gathered and burned in the fire; so shall it be at the end of this world [age]. The Son of man shall send forth his angels, and they shall gather out of his kingdom all things that offend, and them which do iniquity, and shall cast them into a [the] furnace of fire: there shall be wailing and gnashing of teeth. 'Then shall the righteous shine forth as the sun in the kingdom of their Father. Who hath ears to hear, let him hear.... Again, the kingdom of heaven is like unto a net, that was east into the sea, and gathered of every kind: which, when it was full, they drew to the shore, and sat down, and gathered the good into vessels, but cast the bad away. So shall it be at the end of the world [age]: the angels shall come forth, and sever the wicked from among the just, and shall cast them into the furnace of fire: there shall be wailing and gnashing of teeth.'

We find in the passages here quoted an example of one of those erroneous renderings which have done much to confuse and mislead the ordinary readers of our English version. It is probable, that ninety-nine in every hundred understand by the phrase, 'the end of the world,' the close of human history, and the destruction of the material earth. They would not imagine that the ' world ' in ver. 38 and the 'world' in ver. 39 40, are totally different words, with totally different meanings. Yet such is the fact. *Koinos* in ver. 38 is rightly translated *world*, and refers to the world of men, but *aeon* in ver. 39, 40, refers to a *period of time*, and should be rendered *age* or *epoch*. Lange translates it *aeon*. It is of the greatest importance to understand correctly the two meaning of this word, and of the phrase *'the end of the aeon*, or *age.' aion* is, as we have said, a period of time, or an age. It is exactly equivalent to the Latin word *aevum*, which is merely *aion* in a Latin dress; and the phrase, (Greek- coming), translated in our English version, 'the end of the world,' should be, 'the close of the age.' Tittman observes: (Greek - coming), as it occurs in the New Testament, does not denote the end, but rather the consummation, of the *aeon*, which is to be followed by a new age. So in Matt. xiii. 39, 40, 49; xxiv. 3; which last passage, it is to be feared, may be misunderstood in applying it to the destruction of the world.' (8) It was the belief of the Jews that the Messiah would introduce a new aeon: and this new aeon, or age, they called 'the kingdom of heaven.' The existing aeon: therefore, was the Jewish dispensation, which was now draw- ing to its close; and how it would terminate our Lord impressively shows in these parables. It is indeed surprising that expositors should have failed to recognize in these solemn predictions the reproduction and reiteration of the words of Malachi and of John the Baptist. Here we find the same final separation between the righteous and the wicked; the same purging of the floor; the same gathering of the wheat into the garner; the same burning of the chaff [tares, stub- ble] in the fire. Can there be a doubt that it is to the same act of judgment, the same period of time, the same historical event, that Malachi, John, and our Lord refer?

But we have seen that John the Baptist predicted a judgment which was then impending - a catastrophe so near that already the axe was lying at the root of the trees,- in accordance with the prophecy of Malachi, that 'the great and dreadful day of the Lord' was to follow on the coming of the second Elijah. We are therefore brought to the conclusion, that this discrimination between the righteous and the wicked, this gathering of the wheat into the garner, and burn- ing of the tares in the furnace of fire, refer to the same catastrophe, viz., the wrath which came upon that very genera- tion, when Jerusalem became literally 'a furnace of fire,' and the aeon of Judaism came to a close in 'the great and dreadful day of the Lord.'

This conclusion is supported by the fact, that there is a close connection between this great judicial epoch and the coming of 'the kingdom of heaven.' Our Lord represents the separation of the righteous and the wicked as the charac- teristic of the great consummation which is called 'the kingdom of God.' But the kingdom was declared to be *at hand*. It follows, therefore, that the parables before us relate, not to a remote event still in the future, but to one which in our Saviour's time was near.

An additional argument in favour of this view is derived from the consideration that our Lord, in His explanation of the parable of the tares, speaks of *Himself* as the sower of the good seed: 'He that soweth the good seed is the *Son of man.*' It is to *His own personal ministry* and its results that He refers, and we must therefore regard the parable as hav- ing a special bearing upon His contemporaries. It is in perfect harmony with His solemn warning in Luke xiii. 26, where He describes the condemnation of those who were privileged to enjoy *His personal presence and ministrations,* the pretenders to discipleship, who were tares and not wheat. 'Then shall ye begin to say, We have eaten and drunk in thy presence, and thou hast taught in our streets. But he shall say, I tell you, I know you not whence ye are; depart from me, all ye workers of iniquity. There shall be weeping and gnashing of teeth, when ye shall see Abraham, and Isaac, and Jacob, and all the prophets, in the kingdom of God; and you yourselves thrust out.' However applicable to men in general under the gospel such language may be, it is plain that it had a direct and specific bearing upon the contemporaries of our Lord - the generation that witnessed His miracles and heard His parables; and that it has a rela- tion to them such as it can have to none else.

We find at the conclusion of the parable of the tares an impressive *nota bene,* drawing special attention to the in- struction therein contained: 'Who hath ears to hear, let him hear.' We may take occasion from this to make a remark on the vast importance of a true conception of the period at which our Lord and His apostles taught. This is indispen- sable to the correct understanding of the New Testament doctrine respecting the 'kingdom of God,' the 'end of the age,' and the 'coming aeon,' or ' world to come. That period was near the close of the Jewish dispensation. The Mosaic economy, as it is called - the system of laws and institutions given to the nation by God Himself, and which had existed for more than forty generations,- was about to be superseded and to pass away. Already the last generation that was to possess the land was upon the scene,- the last and also the worst, -the child and heir of its predecessors. The long period, during which Jehovah had exhausted all the methods which divine wisdom and love could devise for the cul- ture and reformation of Israel, was about to come to an end. It was to close disastrously. The wrath, long pent up and restrained, was to burst forth and overwhelm *that generation*. Its 'last day' was to be a *dies irae* ' the great and terrible day of the Lord.' This is 'the end of the age,' so often referred to by our Lord, and constantly predicted by His apostles. Already they stood within the penumbra of that tremendous crisis, which was every day advancing nearer and nearer, and which was at last to come suddenly, 'as a thief in the night.' This is the true explanation of those constant exhorta- tions to vigilance, patience, and hope, which abound in the apostolic epistles. They lived expecting a consummation which was to arrive in their own time, and which they might witness with their own eyes. This fact lies on the very face of the New Testament writings; it is the key to the interpretation of much that would otherwise be obscure and unintelligible, and we shall see in the progress of this investigation how consistently this view is supported by the whole tenor of the New Testament Scriptures.

THE COMING OF THE SON OF MAN (THE PAROUSIA) IN THE LIFETIME OF THE APOSTLES.

Matt. x. 23: 'But when they persecute you in this city, flee ye into another: for verily I say unto you, Ye shall not have gone over the cities of Israel, till the Son of man be come.'

In this passage we find the earliest distinct mention of that great event which we shall find so frequently alluded to henceforth by our Lord and His apostles, viz., His coming again, or the Parousia. It may indeed be a question, as we shall presently see, whether this passage properly belongs to this portion of the gospel history. (9) But waiving for the moment this question, let us inquire what the *coming* here spoken of is. Can it mean, as Lange suggests, that Jesus was to follow so quickly on the heels of His messengers in their evangelistic circuit as to overtake them before it was completed? Or does it refer, as Stier and Alford think, to two different comings, separated from each other by thousands of years: the one comparatively near, the other indefinitely remote? Or shall we, with Michaelis and Meyer, accept the plain and obvious meaning which the words themselves suggest? The interpretation of Lange is surely inadmissible. Who can doubt that 'the coming of the Son of man' is here, what it is everywhere else, the formula by which the Parousia, the second coming of Christ, is expressed? This phrase has a definite and constant signification, as much as His crucifixion, or His resurrection, and admits of no other interpretation in this place. But may it not have a double reference: first, to the impending judgment of Jerusalem; and, secondly, to the final destruction of the world,- the former being regarded as symbolical of the latter? Alford contends for the double meaning, and is severe upon those who hesitate to accept it. He tells us what He thinks Christ *meant*; but on the other hand we have to consider what He *said*. Are the advocates of a double sense sure that He meant more than He said? Look at His words. Can anything be more specific and definite as to persons, place, time, and circumstance, than this prediction of our Lord? It is to the *twelve* that he speaks; it is the cities of *Israel* which they are to evangelize; the subject is His own *speedy coming;* and the *time* so near, that before their work is complete His coming will take place. But if we are to be told that this is not the meaning, nor the half of it, and that it includes another coming, to other evangelists, in other ages, and in other lands - a coming which, after eighteen centuries, is still future, and perhaps remote,- then the question arises: What may not Scripture mean? The grammatical sense of words no longer suffices for interpretation; Scripture is a conundrum to be guessed- an oracle that utters ambiguous responses; and no man can be sure, without a special revelation, that he understands what he reads. We are disposed, therefore, to agree with Meyer, that this twofold reference is 'nothing but a forced and unnatural evasion,' and the words simply mean what they' say - that before the apostles completed their life-work of evangelizing the land of Israel, the coming of the Lord should take place.

This is the view of the passage which is taken by Dr. E. Robinson.(10) 'The coming alluded to is the destruction of Jerusalem and the dispersion of the Jewish nation; and the meaning is, that the apostles would barely have time, before the catastrophe came, to go over the land warning the people to save themselves from the doom of an untoward generation; so that they could not well afford to tarry in any locality after its inhabitants had heard and rejected the message.'

THE PAROUSIA TO TAKE PLACE WITHIN THE LIFETIME OF SOME OF THE DISCIPLES.

Matt. xvi. 27,28	Mark viii. 38; ix. 1.	Luke ix. 26,27.
'For the Son of man shall come in the glory of his Father with his angels; and then he shall reward every man according to his works.	' Whosoever therefore shall be ashamed of me and of my words in this adulterous and sinful generation; of him also shall the Son of man be ashamed, when he cometh in the glory of his Father with the holy angels.	'For whosoever shall be ashamed of me and of my words, of him shall the Son of man be ashamed, when he shall come in his own glory, and in his Father's, and of the holy angels.
'Verily I say unto you, there be some standing here, which shall not taste of death, till they see the Son of man coming in his kingdom.'	'And he said unto them, Verily I say unto you, That there be some of them that stand here, which shall not taste of death, till they have seen the kingdom of God come with power.'	'But I tell you of a truth, there be some standing here, which shall not taste of death, till they see the kingdom of God.'

This remarkable declaration is of the greatest importance in this discussion, and may be regarded as the key to the right interpretation of the New Testament doctrine of the Parousia. Though it cannot be said that there are any special difficulties in the language, it has greatly perplexed the commentators, who are much divided in their explanations. It is surely unnecessary to ask what is the *coming of the Son of man* here predicted. To suppose that it refers merely to the glorious manifestation of Jesus on the mount of transfiguration, though an hypothesis which has great names to support it, is so palpably inadequate as an interpretation that it scarcely requires refutation. The same remark will apply to the comments of Dr. Lange, who supposes it to have been partially fulfilled by the resurrection of Christ. His exegesis is so curious an illustration of the shifts to which the advocates of a double- sense theory of interpretation are compelled to resort to, as to deserve quotation. 'In our opinion,' he says, 'it is necessary to distinguish between the advent of Christ in the glory of His kingdom within the circle of His disciples, and that same advent as applying to the world generally and for judgment. The latter is what is generally understood by the second advent: the former took place when the Saviour rose from the dead and revealed Himself in the midst of His disciples. Hence the meaning of the words of Jesus is: the moment is close at hand when your hearts shall be set at rest by the manifestation of My glory; nor will it be the lot of all who stand here to die during the interval. The Lord might have said that only two of that circle would die till then, viz., Himself and Judas. But in His wisdom He chose the expression, " Some standing here shall not taste of death," to give them exactly that measure of hope and earnest expectation which they needed.' (12)

It is enough to say that such an interpretation of our Saviour's words could never have entered into the minds of those who heard them. It is so far-fetched, intricate, and artificial, that it is discredited by its **very ingenuity.** But neither does the interpretation satisfy the requirements of the language. How could the resurrection of Christ be called His coming in the glory of His Father, with the holy angels, in His kingdom, and to judgment? Or how can we suppose that Christ, speaking of an event which was to take place in about twelve months, would say, 'Verily I say unto you, There be some standing here which shall not taste of death till they see' it? The very form of the expression shows that the event spoken of could not be within the space of a few months, or even a few years: it is a mode of speech which suggests that not *all* present will live to see the event spoken of; that not *many* will do so; but that *some* will. It is exactly such a way of speaking as would suit an interval of thirty or forty years, when the majority of the persons then present would have passed away, but some would survive and witness the event referred to.

Alford and Stier more reasonably understand the passage as referring 'to the destruction of Jerusalem and the full manifestation of the kingdom of Christ by the annihilation of the Jewish polity,' though both embarrass and confuse their interpretation by the hypothesis of an occult and ulterior allusion to another 'final coming,' of which the destruction of Jerusalem was the 'type and earnest.' Of this, however, no hint nor intimation is given either by Christ Himself, or by the evangelists. It cannot, indeed, be denied that occasionally our Lord uttered ambiguous language. He said to the Jews: 'Destroy this temple, and in three days I will raise it up' (John ii. 19); but the evangelist is careful to add: 'But he spate of the temple of his body.' So when Jesus spoke of 'rivers of living water flowing from the heart of the believer,' St. John adds an explanatory note: ' This spake he of the spirit,' etc. (John vii. 36). Again, when the Lord alluded to the manner of His own death, 'I, if I be lifted up from the earth,' etc., the evangelist adds: 'This he said, signifying what death he should die' (John ix. 33). It is reasonable to suppose, therefore that had the evangelists known of a deeper and hidden meaning in the predictions of Christ, they would have given some intimation to that effect; but they say nothing to lead us to infer that their apparent meaning is not their full and true meaning. There is, in fact; no ambiguity whatever as to the *coming* referred to in the passage now under consideration. It is not one of several possible comings; but the one, sole, supreme event, so frequently predicted by our Lord, so constantly expected by His disciples. It is His coming in glory; His coming to judgment; His coming in His kingdom; the coming of the kingdom of God. It is not a process, but an act. It is not the same thing as 'the destruction of Jerusalem,'- that is another event related and contemporaneous; but the two are not to be confounded. The New Testament knows of only one Parousia, one coming in glory of the Lord Jesus Christ. It is altogether an abuse of language to speak of several senses in which Christ may be said to come, -- as at His own resurrection; at the day of Pentecost; at the destruction of Jerusalem; at the death of a believer; and at various providential epochs. This is not the usage of the New Testament, nor is it accurate language in any point of view. This passage alone contains so much important truth respecting the Parousia, that it may be said to cover the whole ground; and, rightly used, will be found to be a key to the true interpretation of the New Testament doctrine on this subject.

We conclude then:

1. That the coming here spoken of is the Parousia, the second coming of the Lord Jesus Christ.

2. That the manner of His coming was to be *glorious* -' in his own glory; 'in the glory of his Father; " with the holy angels.'

3. That the object of His coming was to judge that 'wicked and adulterous generation ' (Mark viii. 38), and ' to reward every' man according to his works.'

4. That His coming would be the consummation of 'the kingdom of God;' the close of the aeon; 'the coming of the kingdom of God with power.'

5. That this coming was expressly declared by our Saviour to be *near.* Lange justly remarks that the words, are 'emphatically placed at the beginning of the sentence; not a simple future, but meaning, The event is impending that He shall come; He is about to come.' (14)

6. That some of those who heard our Lord utter this prediction were to live to witness the event of which He spoke, viz., His coming in glory.

The inference therefore is, that the Parousia, or glorious coming of Christ, was declared by Himself to fall within the limits of the then existing generation,- a conclusion which we shall find in the sequel to be abundantly justified.

THE COMING OF THE SON OF MAN CERTAIN AND SPEEDY.

Parable of the Importunate Widow.

Luke xviii. 1-8: 'And he spake a parable unto them to this end, that men ought always to pray and not to faint; saying, There was in a city a judge, which feared not God, neither regarded man: and there was a widow in that city; and she came unto him, saying, Avenge me of mine adversary. And he would not for a while: but afterward he said within himself, Though I fear not God, nor regard man; get because this widow troubleth me, I will avenge her, lest by her continual coming she weary me. And the Lord said, Hear what the unjust judge saith. And shall not God avenge his own elect, which cry day and night unto him, though he bear long with them? I tell you that he will avenge them speedily. Nevertheless, when the Son of man cometh, shall he find faith on the earth' [in the land]?

The intensely practical and *present-day* character, if we may so call it, of our Lord's discourses, is a feature of His teaching which, though often overlooked, requires to be steadily kept in view. He spoke to His own people, and to His own times. He was God's messenger to *Israel;* and, while it is most true that His words are for all men and for all time, yet their primary and direct bearing was upon His own generation. For want of attention to this fact, many expositors have wholly missed the point of the parable before us. It becomes in their hands a vague and indefinite prediction of a vindication of the righteous, in some period more or less remote, but having no special relation to the people and time of our Lord Himself. Assuredly, whatever the parable may be to us or to future ages, it had a close and bearing upon the disciples to whom it was originally spoken. The Lord was about to leave His disciples 'as sheep in the midst of wolves; ' they were to be persecuted and afflicted, hated of all men for their Master's sake; and it might well be that their courage would fail them, and their hearts would faint. In this parable the Saviour encourages them 'to pray always, and not to faint,' by the example of what persevering prayer can do even with man. If the importunity of a poor widow could constrain an unprincipled judge to do her right, how much more would God, the righteous Judge, be moved by the prayers of His own children to redress their wrongs. Without allegorising all the details of the parable, after the manner of some expositors, it is enough to mark its great moral. It is this. The persecuted children of God would he surely and *speedily* avenged. God will vindicate them, and that *speedily.* But when? The point of time is not left indefinite. It is 'when the Son of man cometh.' The Parousia was to be the hour of redress and deliverance to the suffering people of God.

The reflection of our Lord in the close of the eighth verse deserves particular attention. 'Nevertheless when the Son of man cometh, shall he find faith on the earth?' We must here revert to the facts already stated with respect to the ministry of John the Baptist. We have seen how dark and ominous was the outlook of the prophet who preached repentance to Israel. He was the precursor of 'the great and terrible day of the Lord;' he was the second Elijah sent to proclaim the coming of Him who would 'smite the land with a curse.' The reflection of our Lord suggests that He foresaw that the repentance which could alone avert the doom of the nation was not to be looked for. There would be no faith in God, in His promises, or in His threatenings. The day of His therefore, would be the 'day of vengeance (Luke xxi. 22).

Doddridge has well apprehended the scope of this parable, and paraphrases the opening verse as follows: 'Thus our Lord discoursed with His disciples of the approaching destruction of Jerusalem by the Romans; and for their encouragement under those hardships which they might in the meantime expect, from their unbelieving countrymen or others, He spake a parable, to them, which was intended to inculcate upon them this great truth, that how distressed soever their circumstances might be, they ought always to pray with faith and perseverance, and not to faint under their trials.' (15)

The following is his paraphrase of ver. 8: ' Yes I say unto you, He will certainly vindicate them; and when He once undertakes it, He will do it speedily too; and this generation of men shall see and feel it to their terror. Nevertheless, when the Son of man, having been put ill possession of His glorious kingdom, comes to appear for this important purpose, will He find faith in the land?' (16)

THE REWARD OF THE DISCIPLES IN THE COMING AEON, i.e. AT THE PAROUSIA

Matt. xix. 27-30.	Mark x. 18-31.	Luke xvii. 28-30.
'Then answered Peter and said unto him, Behold, we have forsaken all, and followed thee; what shall we have therefore?	'Then Peter began to say unto him, Lo, we have left all, and have followed thee.	'Then Peter said, Lo, we have left all, and followed thee.
And Jesus said unto them, Verily I say	'And Jesus answered and said, Verily I say unto you, There is no man that hath	'And he said unto them, Verily I say unto you, There is no

unto you, That ye which have followed me, in the regeneration when the Son of man shall site in the throne of his glory, ye also shall sit upon twelve thrones, judging the twelve tribes of Israel. And every one that hath forsaken houses, or brethren, or sisters, or father, or mother, or wife, or children, or lands, for my name's sake, shall receive an hundredfold, and shall inherit everlasting life.'	left house, or brethren, or sisters, of father, or mother, or wife, or children, or lands, for my sake, and the gospel's, but he shall receive an hundredfold now in this time, houses, and brethren, and sisters, and mothers, and children, and lands, with persecutions; and in the world to come eternal life.'	man that hath left house, or parents, or brethren, or wife, or children, for the kingdom of God's sake, who shall not receive manifold more in this present time, and in the world to come life everlasting.'

To what period are we to assign the event or state here called by our Lord the 'regeneration'? It is evidently contemporaneous with 'the Son of man sitting on the throne of his glory;' nor can there be any question that the two phrases, 'The Son of man coming in his kingdom,' and, 'The Son of man sitting on the throne of his glory,' both refer to the same thing, and to the same time. That is to say, it is to the Parousia that both these expressions point.

We have another note of time, and another point of coincidence between the 'regeneration ' and the Parousia, in the reference made by our Lord to the 'coming age or aeon' as the period when His faithful disciples were to receive their recompense (Mark x.30; Luke xviii. 30). But the 'coming age' was, as we have already seen, to succeed the existing age or aeon, that is to say, the period of the Jewish dispensation, the end of which our Lord declared to be at hand. We conclude, therefore, that the 'regeneration,' the 'coming age,' and the 'Parousia,' are virtually synonymous, or, at all events, contemporaneous. The coming of the Son of man in His kingdom, or in His glory, is distinctly affirmed to be a coming to judgment -- 'to reward every man according to his works (Matt. xvi. 27); and His sitting on the throne of His glory, in the regeneration, is as evidently a sitting in judgment. In this judgment the apostles were to have the honour of being assessors with the Lord, according to His declaration (Luke xxii. 29, 30)- 'I appoint unto you a kingdom, as my Father hath appointed unto me; that ye may eat and drink at my table in my kingdom, and sit on thrones judging the twelve tribes of Israel.' But this glorious coming to judgment is expressly affirmed by our Lord to fall within the limits of the generation then living: 'There be some standing here which shall not taste of death, till they see the Son of man coming in his kingdom' (Matt. xvi. 28). It was therefore no long-deferred and distant hope which Jesus held out to His disciples. It was not a prospect that is still seen afar off in the dim perspective of an indefinite futurity. St. Peter and his fellow-disciples were fully aware that 'the kingdom of heaven' was at hand. They had learned it from their first teacher in the wilderness; they had been reassured of it by their Lord and Master; they had gone through Galilee proclaiming the truth to their countrymen. When the Lord, therefore, promised, that in the coming aeon His apostles should sit upon thrones, is it conceivable that He could mean that ages upon ages, centuries upon centuries, and even millennium upon millennium must slowly roll away before they should reap their promised honours? Are the inheritance of 'everlasting life' and the 'sitting upon twelve thrones' still among 'the things hoped for but not seen ' by the disciples? Surely such a hypothesis refutes itself. The promise would have sounded like mockery to the disciples had they been told that the performance would be so long delayed. On the other hand, if we conceive of the 'regeneration' as contemporaneous with the Parousia, and the Parousia, with the close of the Jewish age and the destruction of the city and temple of Jerusalem, we have a definite point of time, not far distant, but almost within the sight of living men, when the predicted judgment of the enemies of Christ, and the glorious recompense of His friends, would come to pass.

1. Reden Jesu, in loc.
2. Jewish War, bk v. c. x sec. 5. Traill's translation.
3. Ibid. G. Xiii. sec. 6.
4. Ibid. bk. vii. c. viii. sec. I.
5. sec. Reden Jesu; Matt. xii, 43-45.
6. Greek Test. *in loc.*
7. Life of Christ, sec. 245.
8. Synonyms of the New Test. vol. i. a. 70; Bib. Cab. No. iii.
9. There is a real difficulty in this passage which ought not to be overlooked. It seems unaccountable that our Lord, on an occasion like this, when He was sending forth the twelve on a short mission, apparently within a limited district, and from which they were to return to Him in a short time, should speak of of His coming as overtaking them before the completion of their task. It seems scarcely appropriate to the particular period, and to belong more properly to a subsequent charge, viz., that recorded in the discourse spoken on the Mount of Olives (Matt. xxiv.; Mark xiii.; Luke xxi). Indeed, a comparison of these passages will go far to satisfy any candid mind that the whole paragraph Matt. x. 16-23) is transposed from its original connection, and inserted in our Lord's first charge to His disciples We find the very words relating to the persecution of the

apostles, their being delivered up to the councils, their being scourged in the synagogues, brought before governors and kings, etc., which are recorded in the tenth chapter of St. Matthew, assigned by St. Mark and St. Luke to a subsequent period, viz., the discourse on the Mount of Olives. There is no evidence that the disciples met with such treatment on their first evangelistic tour There is therefore as strong evidence as the nature of the case will admit, that ver. 23 and its context belong to the discourse on the Mount of Olives. This would remove the difficulty which the passage presents in the connection in which we here find it, and give a coherence and consistency to the language, which, as it stands, it is not easy to discover. It is an admitted fact that even the Synoptical Gospels do not relate all events in precisely the same order; there most therefore be greater chronological accuracy in one than in another. Stier says: 'Matthew is careless of chronology in details' (Reden Jesu, vol. iii. p. US). Neander, speaking on this very charge, says: 'Matthew evidently connects many things with the instructions given to the apostles in view of their first journey, which chronologically belong later; ' (Life of Christ, _ 174, note b); and again, speaking of the charge given to the seventy, as recorded by St. Luke: 'he says, 'The entire and characteristic coherency of everything spoken by Christ, according to Luke, with the circumstances (so superior to the collocation of Matthew),' etc. (Life of Christ, _ 204, note 1). Dr. Blaikie observes: 'It is generally understood that Matthew arranged his narrative more by subjects and places than by chronology' (Bible History, p. 372).

There seems, therefore, abundant warrant for assigning the important prediction contained in Matt. x .23 to the discourse delivered on the Mount of Olives.

10. See note In Harmony of the Four Gospels.

11. The training of the Twelve, p. 117

12. Large, Comm. on St. Matt. in loc.

13. Alford, Greek Test. in loc.

14. See Lange *in loc.*

15. Family Expos. on Luke xviii. 1-8

16. Doddridge teas the following note on 'Will he find faith in the land?' 'It is evident the word often signifies not the *earth* in general, but some particular *land* or country; as in Acts vii. 3, 4,11, and in numberless other places. And the context here limits it to the less extensive signification. The believing Hebrews were evidently in great danger of being wearied out with their persecutions and distresses. Comp. Heb. iii. 12-14; x. 23-39; xii. 1-4; James i. 1-4; ii. 6.'

The interpretation given by the judicious Campbell adds confirmation, if it were needed, needed, to this view of the passage. 'There is a close connection in all that our Lord says on any topic of conversation, which rarely escapes an attentive reader. If in this, as is very probable, He refers to the destruction impending over the Jewish nation, as the judgment of Heaven for their rebellious against God, in rejecting and murdering the Messiah. and in persecuting His adherents, (the Greek) must be understood to mean "this belief," or the belief of the particular truth He had been inculcating, namely, that God will in due time avenge His elect, and signally punish their oppressors; and (the Greek) must mean "the land," to wit, of Judea. The words may be translated either way -- earth or land; but the latter evidently gives them a more definite meaning, and unites them more closely with those which preceded, (Campbell on the Gospels, vol. ii. p. 384). The teaching of this instructive parable is by no means exhausted; and we shall find it throw an unexpected light on a very obscure passage, at a future stage of this investigation. Meantime we may refer to 2 Thess. i 4-10, as furnishing a striking commentary on the whole parable, and showing the connection between the Parousia and the avenging of the elect.

Prophetic Intimations of the Approaching Consummation of the Kingdom of God.

I. - *The Parable of the Pounds.*

Luke xix. 11-27: *'And as they heard these this, He added and spake a parable, because he was nigh to Jerusalem, and because they thought that the kingdom of God should immediately appear. He said therefore, A certain nobleman went into a far country to receive for himself a kingdom, and to return. And he called his ten servants, and delivered them ten pounds, and said unto them, Occupy till I come. But his citizens hated him, and sent a message after him, saying, We will not have this man to reign over us. And it came to pass, that when he was returned, having received the kingdom, then he commanded these servants to be called unto him, to whom he had given the money, that he might know how much every man had gained by trading. Then came the first, saying, Lord, thy pound hath gained ten pounds. And he said unto him, Well, thou good servant: because thou hast been faithful in a very little, have thou authority over ten cities. And the second came, Saying, Lord, thy pound hath gained five pounds. And he said likewise to him, Be thou also over five cities. And another came, saying, Lord, behold, here is thy pound, which I have kept laid up in a napkin: for I feared thee, because thou art all austere man: thou takest up that thou layedst not down, and reapest that thou didst not sow. And he saith Unto him, Out of thine own mouth will I judge thee, thou wicked servant. Thou knewest that I was all austere man, taking up that I laid not down, and reaping that I did not sow: wherefore then gavest not thou my money into the bank, that at* *my coming I might have required mine own with usury? And he said unto them that stood by, Take from him the pound, and give it to him that hath ten pounds. (And they said unto him, Lord, he hath ten pounds.) For I say unto you, That unto every one which hath shall be given; and from him that hath not, even that he hath shall be taken away from him. But those mine enemies, which would not that I should reign over them, bring hither, and stay them before me.'*

It cannot fail to strike every attentive reader of the Gospel history, how much the teaching of our Lord, as He approached the close of His ministry, dwelt upon the theme of coming judgment. When He spoke this parable, He was on His way to Jerusalem to keep His last Passover before He suffered; and it is remarkable how His discourses from this time seem almost wholly engrossed, not by His own approaching death, but the impending catastrophe of the nation. Not Only this parable of the pounds, but His lamentation over Jerusalem (Luke xix. 41); His cursing of the fig-tree (Matt. xxi. Mark xi.); the parable of the wicked husbandmen (Matt. xxi. Mark xii.; Luke xx.); the parable of the marriage of the king's son (Matt. xxii.); the woes pronounced) upon that generation' (Matt. xxiii. 29-36); the second lamentation over Jerusalem (Matt. xxiii. 37, 38); and the prophetic discourse on the Mount of Olives, with the parables and parabolic illustrations appended thereto by St. Matthew, all are occupied with this absorbing theme.

The consideration of these prophetic intimations will show that the catastrophe anticipated by our Lord was not a remote event, hundreds and thousands of years distant, but one whose shadow already fell upon that age and that nation; and that the Scriptures give us no warrant whatever to suppose that anything else, or anything more than this, is included in our Saviour's words.

The parable of the pounds was spoken by our Lord to correct a mistaken expectation on the part of His disciples, that 'the kingdom of God' was about to commence at once. It is not surprising that they should have fallen into this mistake. John the Baptist had announced, 'The kingdom of God is at hand.' Jesus Himself had proclaimed the same fact, and commissioned them to publish it throughout the cities and villages of Galilee. As patriotic Israelites they writhed under the yoke of Rome, and yearned for the ancient liberties of the nation. As pious sons of Abraham they desired to see all nations blessed in him. And there were other less noble sentiments that had a place in their minds. Was not their own Master the Son of David - the coming King? What might not they expect who were His followers and friends? This made them contest with. each other the place of honour in the kingdom. This made the sons of Zebedee eager to secure His promise of the most honourable seats, on His right hand and on His left, where he assumed the sovereignty. And now they were approaching Jerusalem. The great national festival of the Passover was at baud; all Israel was flocking, to the Holy City, and there was not a man there but would be eager to see Jesus of Nazareth. What more probable than that the popular enthusiasm would place their Master on the throne of His father David? As they wished, so they believed; and 'they thought that the kingdom of God would immediately appear.'

But the Lord checked their enthusiastic hopes, and intimated, in a parable, that a certain interval must elapse before the fulfillment of their expectations. Taking a well-known incident from recent Jewish history as the groundwork of the parable- viz., the journey of Archelaus to Rome, in order to seek from the emperor the succession to the dominions of his father, Herod the Great, he employed it as an apt illustration of His own departure from earth, and His subsequent return in glory. Meanwhile, during the period of His absence, He gave His servants a charge to keep-' Occupy till I come.' It was for them to be diligent and faithful, until their Lord's return, when the loyal servants should be applauded and rewarded, and His enemies utterly destroyed.

Nothing can be better than Neander's explanation of this parable, though, indeed, it may be said to explain itself. Nevertheless, it may be well to subjoin his observations. "In this parable, in view of the circumstances under which it was uttered, and of the approaching catastrophe, special intimations are given of Christ's departure from the earth, of His ascension, and return to judge the rebellious theocratic nation, and consummate His dominion. It describes a great man, who travels to the distant court of the mighty emperor, to receive from him authority over his countrymen, and to return with royal power. So Christ was not immediately recognised in His kingly office, but first had to depart from the earth. and leave His agents to advance His kingdom, to ascend into heaven and be appointed theocratic Ring, and return a 'gain to exercise His contested power." (1)

Such is the teaching of the parable of the pounds. But though the kingdom of God was not to appear at the precise. time which the disciples anticipated, it does not follow that it was postponed since he, and that the expected consummation would not take place for hundreds and thousands of years. This would be to falsify the most express declarations of Christ and of His forerunner. How could they have said that the kingdom was at hand, if it was not to appear for acres?

How could an event be said to be near, if it was actually further off than the whole period of the Jewish economy from Moses to Christ? The kingdom might still be at hand, though not so near as the disciples supposed. It was expedient that their Lord should 'go away,' but only for 'a little while,' when He would come again to them, and come 'in His kingdom.' This was the hope in which they lived, the faith which they preached; and we cannot think that their faith and hope were a delusion.

II.-Lamentation of Jesus over Jerusalem.

Luke xix. 41-44: ' And when he was come near, he beheld the city, and wept over it, saying, If thou hadst known, even thou, at least in this thy day, the things which belong unto thy peace I but now they are bid from thine eyes. For the days shall come upon thee, that thine enemies shall cast a trench about thee, and compass thee round, and keep thee in on every side, and shall lay thee even with the ground, and thy children within thee; and they shall not leave in thee one stone upon another; because thou knewest not the time of thy visitation.'

Here we are upon ground which is not debatable. This prophecy is clear and perspicuous as history. No advocate of the double-sense theory of interpretation has proposed to find here anything but Jerusalem and its approaching desolation.

It is not the conflagration of the earth, nor the dissolution of creation: it is the siege and demolition of the Holy City, and the slaughter of her citizens, as historically fulfilled in less than forty years-only this, and nothing more. But wily so? Why should not a double sense be possible here, as well as in the prediction delivered upon the Mount of Olives? The reply will doubtless be, Because here all is homogeneous and consecutive; the Saviour is looking on Jerusalem, and speaking of Jerusalem, and predicting an event which was speedily to come to pass. But this is equally the case with the prophecy in Matt. xxiv., where the expositors find, sometimes Jerusalem, and sometimes the world; sometimes the termination of the Jewish polity, and sometimes the conclusion of human history; sometimes the year A.D. 70, and sometimes a period as yet unknown. We shall yet see that the prophecy oil the Mount of Olives is no less consecutive, no less homogenous, no less one and indivisible, than this clear and plain prediction of the approaching destruction of Jerusalem. If the double-sense theory were good for anything, it would be found equally applicable to the prediction before us. Here, however, its own advocates discard it; for common sense refuses to see in this affecting lamentation anything else than Jerusalem, and Jerusalem alone.

III. - Parable of the Wicked Husbandmen.

MATT. XXI. 33-46.	MARK XII. 1-12.	LUKE XX. 9-19.
There was a certain house- holder, which planted a vineyard, and hedged it round about, and digged a winepress in it, and built a tower, and let it out to husbandman, and went into a far country: and when the time of the fruit drew near, be sent his servants to the husbandmen, that they might receive the fruits of it. And the husbandman took his servants, and beat one, and killed another, and stoned another. Again, be sent other servants more than the first: and they did unto them likewise.	'A certain man planted a vineyard, and set an hedge about it, and digged a place for the winefat, and built a tower, and let it out to husbandmen, and went into a far country. 'And at the season he sent to the husbandmen a servant, that he might receive from the husbandmen of the fruits of the vineyard. And they caught him, and beat him, and sent him away empty. 'And again he sent unto them another servant; and at him they cast stones, and wounded him in	A certain man planted a vineyard, and let it forth to husbandman, and went into a far country for a long time. 'And at the season he sent a servant to the husbandmen, that they should give him of the fruit of the vineyard: but the husbandmen beat him, and sent him away empty. 'And again he sent another servant: and they beat him also, and entreated him shamefully, and sent him away empty.
But last of all be sent unto them his son, saying, They will reverence my son. But when the husbandmen saw the son, they said among themselves, This is the heir; come, let us kill him, and let us seize on his inheritance, And they caught him, and cast him out of the vineyard, and slew him.	the head, and sent him away shamefully handled. And again he sent another, and him they killed, and many others; beating some, and killing some. 'Having yet therefore one son, his well-beloved, be sent him also last unto them, saying, They will reverence my son. But those husbandman said among themselves, This is the heir; come, let us kill him, and the inheritance shall be ours.	'And again he sent a third: and they wounded him also, and cast him out. Then said the lord of the vineyard, What shall I do? I will send my beloved son: it may be they will reverence him when they see him. 'But when the husbandmen saw him, they reasoned among themselves, saying, This is the heir; come, let us kill him, that the inheritance may be ours. ' So they cast him out of the vineyard, and killed him. What therefore shall the lord of the vineyard do unto them?
When the lord therefore of the vineyard cometh, what will he do unto those husbandmen?		He shall come and destroy these husbandmen, and shall give the vineyard to others. And when they heard it, they said, God forbid.
	'And they took him, and killed him, and cast him out of the vine-	

They say unto him, He will miserably destroy those wicked men and will let Out his vineyard unto other husbandmen, which shall render him the fruits in their seasons. Jesus saith unto them, Did ye never rend in the Scriptures, The stone which the builders, rejected, the same is become the head of the corner: this is the Lord's doing, and it is marvelous in our eyes? Therefore say I unto you, The kingdom of God shall be taken from you, and given to a nation bringing forth the fruits thereof. And whosoever shall fall on this stones shall be broken: but on whomsoever it shall fall, it will grind him to powder. And when the chief priests and Pharisees had heard his parables, they perceived that he spake of them. But when they sought to lay hands on him, they feared the multitude, because they took him for a prophet.'

yard. What shall therefore the lord of the vineyard do? He will come and destroy the husbandmen, and will give the vineyard un to others.

'And have ye not read this Scripture; The stone which the builders rejected is become the head of the corner: this was the Lord's doing, and it is marvellous in our eyes?

'And they sought to lay hold on him, but feared the people: for they knew that he bad spoken the parable against them: and they left him, and went their way.'

'And he beheld them, and said, What is this then that is written, The stone which the builders rejected, the same is become the head of the corner? 'Whosoever shall fall upon that stone shall be broken; but on whomsoever it shall fall, it will grind him to powder. 'And the chief priests and the scribes the same hour sought to lay hands on. him; and they feared the people; for they perceived that he had spoken this parable against them.'

This parable, recorded in almost identical terms by the Synoptists, scarcely requires an interpreter. Its local, personal, and national reference is too manifest to be questioned. The vineyard is the land of Israel; the lord of the vineyard is the Father; His messengers are His servants the prophets; His only and beloved Son is the Lord Jesus Himself; the husbandmen are the rebellious and wicked Jews; the punishment is the coming catastrophe at the Parousia, when, as Neander well expresses it, "the theocratic relation is broken, and the kingdom is transferred to other nations that shall bring forth fruits corresponding to it." (2)

The bearing of this parable on the people of our Saviour's time is so direct and explicit, that it might be supposed that no Critic would have to seek for a hidden meaning, or an ulterior reference. The chief priests and Pharisees felt that it was 'spoken against *them;'* and they winced under the lash. As it stands, all is perfectly clear and intelligible; but the exegesis of a theologian can render it turbid and obscure indeed. For example, Lange thus comments upon ver. 41

The Parousia of Christ is consummated in His last coming, but is not one with it. It begins *in principle* with the resurrection. (John xvi. 16); continues as a power through the New Testament period (John xiv. 3-19); and is *consummated* in the stricter sense in the final advent (I Cor. xv. 23; Matt. xxv. 31; 2 Thess. ii., etc.).' (3)

Here we have not a coming, nor *the* coming of Christ, but no less than three separate and distinct comings, or a coming of three different kinds- a continuous coming which has been going on for nearly two thousand years already, and may go on for two thousand more, for aught we know. But of all this not a hint is given in the text, nor anywhere else. It is a merely human gloss, without a particle of authority from Scripture, and invented in virtue of the double- and triplesense theory of interpretation.

Far more sober is the explanation of Alford. ' We may observe that our Lord makes " when the Lord cometh " *coincide with the destruction of Jerusalem,* which is incontestably the overthrow of the wicked husbandmen. This passage therefore forms an important key to our Lord's prophecies, and a decisive justification for those who, like myself, firmly hold that *the coming of the Lord* is, in many places, to be identified, primarily, with that overthrow." (4)

It is to be regretted that this otherwise sound and sensible note is marred by the phrases 'in many places ' and , 'primarily,' but it is, nevertheless, all important admission. Undoubtedly we do find here 'an important key to our Lord's prophecies; ' but the *master key* is that which we have already found in Matt xvi. 27, 28, and which serves to open, not only this, but many other dark sayings in the prophetic oracles.

iv.-Parable of the Marriage of the King's Son.

Matt. xxii. 1-14 -. 'And Jesus answered and spake unto them again by parables, and said, The kingdom of heaven is like unto a certain king, which made a marriage for his son, and sent forth his servants to call them that were bidden to the wedding: and they would not come. Again, he sent forth other servants, saying, Tell them which are bidden, Behold, I have prepared my dinner: my oxen and my fatlings are killed, and all things are ready: come unto the marriage. But they made light of it, and went their ways, one to his farm, another to his merchandise: and the remnant took his servants, and entreated them spitefully, and slew them. But when the king heard thereof, he was wroth: and he sent forth his armies, and destroyed those murderers, and burned up their city. Then saith he to his servants, The wedding is ready, but they which were bidden were not worthy. Go ye therefore into the highways, and as many as ye shall find, bid to the marriage. So those servants went out into the highways, and gathered together all as many as they found, both bad and good: and the wedding was furnished with guests. And when the king came in to see the guests, he saw there a man which had not on a wedding garment: and he saith unto him, Friend. how camest thou in hither not having a wedding garment? And he was speechless. Then said the king to the servants, Bind him band and foot, and take him away, and cast him into outer darkness there shall be weeping and gnashing of teeth. For many are called but few are chosen.'

This parable bears a strong resemblance to that of 'The Great Supper,' contained in Luke xiv. It is possible that the two parables may be only different versions of the same original. The question, however, does not affect the present discussion, and it cannot be proved that they were not spoken on different occasions. The moral of both is the same; but the character of the parable recorded by St. Matthew is more distinctively eschatological than that of St. Luke. It points clearly to the approaching consummation of the ' kingdom of heaven.' The vengeance taken by the king oil the murderers of his servants, and on their city fixes the application to Jerusalem and the Jews. The Roman armies were but the executioners of divine justice; and Jerusalem perished for her guilt and rebellion against her King.

Alford, in his notes on this parable, while recognising a partial and primary reference to Israel and Jerusalem, finds also that it extends far beyond its apparent scope, and is divided into two acts, the first of which is past, and closes with. ver. 10; while a new act opens with ver. 11, which is still in the future. This implies that the judgment of Israel and of Jerusalem does not supply a full and exhaustive fulfillment of our Lord's words. On the one hand we have the teaching of Christ Himself- simple, clear, and unambiguous; on the other hand, the conjectural speculation of the critic, without a scintilla of evidence or authority from the Word of God. To expound the parable according to its plain historic significance will be derided by some as shallow, superficial, unspiritual to find in it ulterior and hidden meanings, dark and profound riddles, mystical depths, which none but theologians can explore,- this is critical acumen, keen insight, high spirituality! In our opinion, all this foisting of human hypotheses and double senses into the predictions of our Lord is utterly incompatible with sober criticism, or with true reverence for the Word of God; it is not criticism, but mysticism; and obscures the truth instead of elucidating it. At the risk, then, of being considered superficial and shallow, we shall hold fast to the plain teaching of the words of Scripture, turning a deaf ear to all fanciful and conjectural speculations of merely human origin, no matter how learned or dignified the quarter from which they come.

v.- The Woes denounced on the Scribes and Pharisees.

MATT xxiii. 29-36.

Woe unto you, scribes and Pharisees, hypocrites I because ye build the tombs of the prophets, and garnish the sepulchres of the righteous, and say, If we had been in the days of our fathers, we would not have been partakers with them in the blood of the prophets. Wherefore ye be witnesses unto yourselves, that ye are the children of them which killed the prophets. Fill ye up then the measure of your fathers. Ye serpents, ye generation of vipers, how can ye escape the damnation of h ell? Wherefore, behold, I send unto you prophets, and wise men, and scribes: and some of them ye shall kill and crucify; and some of them shall ye scourge in your synagogues, and persecute them from city to city: That upon you may come all the righteous blood shed upon the earth, from the blood of righteous Abel unto the blood of Zacharias son of Barachias, whom ye slew between the temple and the altar. Verily, I say unto you, All these things shall come upon this generation.'

LUKE xi. 47-51.

'Woe unto you! for ye build the sepulchres of the prophets, and your fathers killed them.

'Truly ye bear witness that ye allow the deeds of your fathers: for they indeed killed them, and ye build their sepulchres.

'Therefore also said the wisdom of God, I will send them prophets and apostles, and some of them they shall slay and persecute:

'That the blood of all the prophets, which was shed from the foundation of the world, may be required of this generation; from the blood of Abel unto the blood of Zacharias, which perished between the altar and the temple: verily I say unto you, It shall be required of this generation.'

It will be seen that St. Luke gives this passage as spoken in a different connection, and on a different occasion, from those stated by St. Matthew Whether our Lord spoke the same words on two different occasions, or whether they have been transposed by St. Luke from their original connection, is a question not easy to determine. The former hypothesis does not seem probable, and does not commend itself to the critical mind. Apophthegms, and brief parabolic sayings, such as ' Many are called but few are chosen,' 'The last shall be first, and the first last,'-may have been repeated on several occasions; but connected and elaborate discourses, such as the Sermon on the Mount, the prophetic discourse upon Olivet, and this denunciation of the Scribes and Pharisees, can hardly be imagined to have been repeated verbatim on different occasions. It is a mistake, as we have already seen, to look for strict chronological order in the narratives of the Evangelists: it is admitted on all hands that they are accustomed sometimes to group together facts which have a natural relation, quite independently of the order of time in which they occurred.

Stier says of the chronology of St. Luke in general: 'Two things are sufficiently plain: First, that he mentions individual occurrences without strict regard to chronology, even repeating and Intercalating some things elsewhere recorded,' etc.

Neander makes the following observation oil the passage now before us: 'As this last discourse given by Matthew contains various passages given by Luke in the table conversation (chap. xi.), so Luke inserts *there* this prophetic announcement, whose proper position is found in Matthew.' (5) We cannot, however, agree with Neander's opinion, that 'this discourse, as given in Matt. xxiii., contains many passages uttered on other occasions.' (6) It seems to us impossible to read the twenty-third chapter of St. Matthew without perceiving that it is a continuous and connected discourse, spoken at one time, its different parts naturally growing out of and following one another. Its very structure consisting of seven woes (7) denounced against the hypocritical pretenders to sanctity, who were the blind guides of the people,- and the solemn occasion on which it was uttered being the filial public utterance of our Lord,- irresistibly compel the conclusion that it is a complete whole, and that St. Matthew gives us the original form of the discourse.

But the settlement of this question is not essential to this investigation. Far more important it is to observe how our Lord closes His public ministry in almost the identical terms in which His forerunner addressed the same class: 'Ye serpents, ye offspring of vipers, bow can ye escape the damnation of hell?' This is no fortuitous coincidence: it is evidently the deliberate adoption of the words of the Baptist, when he spoke of the 'coming wrath.' Israel had rejected alike the stern call to repentance of the second Elijah, and the tender expostulations of the Lamb of God. The measure of their guilt was almost full, and the 'day of wrath ' was swiftly coming.

But the point which deserves special attention is the particular application of this discourse to the Saviour's own times: ' Verily I say unto you, All *these things shall come upon this generation.' ' It* shall be required of *this generation.'* Surely there can be no pretense of a primary and a secondary reference here. No expositor will deny that these words have a sole and exclusive application to the generation of the Jewish people then living upon the earth. Even Dorner, who contends most strenuously for a great variety of meanings of the word *genea* [generation], frankly admits that it can only refer here to the contemporaries of our Lord: 'Hoc ipsum hominum aevum." (8) This is an admission of the greatest importance. It enables us to fix the true meaning of the phrase, ' This generation', Which plays so important a part in several of the predictions of our Lord, and notably in the great prophecy spoken on the Mount of Olives. In the passage before us, the words are incapable of any other application than to the *existing generation* of the Jewish nation, which is represented by our Lord as the heir of all the preceding generations, inheriting the depravity and rebelliousness of the national character, and fated to perish in the deluge of wrath which had been accumulating through the ages, and was at length about to overwhelm the guilty land.

vi. .-The (second) Lamentation of Jesus over Jerusalem.

MATT. xxiii, 37-39.	Luke xiii. 34, 35.
'0 Jerusalem, Jerusalem, thou that killest the prophets, and stonest them which are sent unto thee, how often would I have gathered thy children together, even as a hen gathereth her chickens under her wings, and ye would not! Behold, your house is left unto you desolate. For I say unto you, Ye shall not see me henceforth, till ye shall say, Blessed is he that cometh in the name of the Lord.'	0 Jerusalem, Jerusalem, which killest the prophets, and stonest them that are sent unto thee: how often would I have gathered thy children together, as a hen doth gather her brood under her wings, and ye would not I Behold, your house is left unto you desolate: and verily I say unto you, Ye shall not see me, until the time come when ye shall say, Blessed is he that cometh in the name of the Lord.'

Here, again, we have another example of those discrepancies in the Gospel history which perplex harmonists. St. Luke records this affecting apostrophe of our Lord in quite a different connection from St. Matthew. Yet we can scarcely suppose that these *ipsissima verba* were spoken on more than one occasion, namely, that specified by St. Matthew. Dorner says: ' That these words (" Behold, your house is left unto you desolate," etc.) were spoken by Christ, not where Luke, but where Matthew, places them, the words themselves show; for they were spoken when our Lord was departing from the temple to return to it no more till he came to judgment." (9) Lange says the passage is placed earlier by St. Luke 'for pragmatic reasons.' At all events, we may properly regard the words as spoken on the occasion indicated by St. Matthew.

As such their collocation is most suggestive. This pathetic expostulation mitigates the severity of the foregoing denunciations, and closes the public ministry of our Lord with a burst of human tenderness and divine compassion. As Dr. Lange well says: 'The Lord mourns and laments over His own ruined Jerusalem. . . . His whole pilgrimage on earth was troubled by distress for Jerusalem, like the hen which sees the eagle threatening in the sky, and anxiously seeks to gather her chickens under her wings. With such distress Jesus saw the Roman eagles approach for judgment upon the children of Jerusalem, and sought with the strongest solicitations of love to save them. but in vain. They were like dead children to the voice of maternal love!' (10)

Need it be said that here is Jerusalem, and Jerusalem alone? There is no ambiguity, no twofold reference, no proximate and ultimate fulfilments conceivable here. One thought, one feeling, one object, filled the heart of Jesus- Jerusalem, the city of God, the loved, the guilty, the doomed! Her fate was now all but sealed, and the heart of our Saviour was wrung with anguish as he bade her a last farewell.

But how are we to understand the closing words, 'Ye shall not see me henceforth, till ye shall say, Blessed is he that cometh in the name of the Lord'? This phrase, 'Blessed is he that cometh in the name of the Lord,' is the recognised formula which was employed by the Jews in speaking of the coming of Messiah- the Messianic greeting: equivalent to 'Hail to the anointed one of God.' It is generally supposed to have been adopted from Psa. cxviii. 26. There was a time coming, therefore, when such a salutation would be appropriate. The Lord who was leaving the temple would once more return to His temple. More than this, *that same generation would witness that return.* This is plainly implied in the form of our Saviour's language, ' Ye shall not see me again till ye shall say,' etc.-words which would be deprived of half their significance if the persons referred to in the first part of the sentence were not the same as those referred to in the second. Nothing can be more distinct and explicit than the reference throughout to the people of Jerusalem, the contemporaries of Christ. They and He were to meet again; and the Messiah, the Lord whom they professed to seek so eagerly, would suddenly come to his temple,' according to the saying of Malachi the prophet. They expected that coming as an event to be welcomed with gladness; but it was to be far otherwise. 'Who may abide the day of his coming? and who shall stand when he appeareth?' That day was to bring the desolation of the house of God, the destruction of their national existence, the outburst of the pent-up wrath of God upon Israel. This was the return, the meeting together again, to which our Saviour here alludes. And is not this the very thing that He had again and again declared? Had He not a little before said, that 'upon *this generation*' should come the sevenfold woes which He had just pronounced? (Ver.36.) Had He not solemnly affirmed, that some then living should see the Son of man coming in glory, with His angels, 'to reward every man according to his works' -- that is, coming to judgment? Is it possible to adopt the strange hypothesis of some commentators of note, that in these words our Lord means that He would never be seen again by those to whom He spoke, until a converted and Christian Israel, in some far distant era of time, was prepared to welcome Him as King of Israel? This would indeed be to take unwarrantable liberties with the words of Scripture. Our Lord does not say, Ye shall not see me until *they* shall say, or, until *another generation* shall say; but, 'until *ye* shall say,' etc. It by no means follows, that because the Messianic salutation is here quoted, the people who are supposed to use it were qualified to enter into its true significance. Those very words had been shouted by multitudes in the streets of Jerusalem only a day or two before, and yet they were changed into ' Crucify him! crucify him!' in a very brief space. They simply denote the fact of His coming. The unhappy men to whom our Saviour spoke could not adopt the Messianic greeting in its true and highest sense; *they* would never say, 'Blessed is he,' etc., but they would witness His coming- the coming with which that formula was indissolubly associated, viz., the Parousia.

We contend, then, that we are not only warranted, but compelled, to conclude, that our Lord here refers to His coming to destroy Jerusalem and to close the Jewish age, according to His express declarations, within the period of the then existing generation. History verifies the prophecy. In less than forty years from the time when these words were uttered, Jerusalem and her temple, Judea and her people, were overwhelmed by the deluge of wrath predicted by the Lord. Their land was laid waste; their house was left desolate; Jerusalem, and her children within her, were engulfed in one common ruin.

vii.-The Prophecy on the Mount of Olives.

THE COMING OF THE SON OF MAN [THE PAROUSIA] BEFORE THE PASSING AWAY OF THAT GENERATION. MATT. XXIV..; MARK XIII.; LUKE XXI.

We now enter upon the consideration of by far the most full and explicit of our Lord's prophetic utterances respecting His coming, and the solemn events connected therewith. The discourse or conversation on the Mount of Olives is the great prophecy of the New Testament, and may be not unfitly styled the Apocalypse of the Gospels. Upon the interpretation of this prophetic discourse will depend the right understanding of the predictions contained in the apostolic writings; for it may almost be said that there is nothing in the Epistles which is not in the Gospels. This prophecy of our Saviour is the great storehouse from which the prophetic statements of the apostles are chiefly derived.

The commonly received view of the structure of this discourse, which is almost taken for granted, alike by expositors and by the generality of readers, is, that our Lord, in answering the question of His disciples respecting the destruction of the temple, mixes up with that event the destruction of the world, the universal judgment, and the final consummation of all things. Imperceptibly, it is supposed, the prophecy slides from the city and temple of Jerusalem, and their impending fate in the immediate future, to another and infinitely more tremendous catastrophe in the far distant and indefinite future. So intermingled, however, are the allusions- now to Jerusalem and now to the world at large; now to Israel and now to the human race; now to events close at hand and now to events indefinitely remote; that to distinguish and allocate the several references and topics, is exceedingly difficult, if not impossible.

Perhaps it will be the fairest way of exhibiting the views of those who contend for a double meaning in this predictive discourse, to set forth the scheme or plan of the prophecy proposed by Dr. Lange, and adopted by many expositors of the greatest note.

' In harmony with apocalyptic style, Jesus exhibited the judgments of His coming in a series of cycles, each of which depicts the whole futurity, but in such a manner, that with every new cycle the scene seems to approximate to and more closely resemble the final catastrophe. Thus, the first cycle delineates the whole course of the world down to the end, in its general characteristics (ver. 4-14). The second gives the signs of the approaching destruction of Jerusalem, and paints this destruction itself as a sign and a commencement of the judgment of the world, which from that day onward proceeds in silent and suppressed days of judgment down to the last (ver. 15-28). The third describes the sudden end of the world, and the judgment which ensues (ver. 29-44). Then follows a series of parables and similitudes, in which the Lord paints the judgment itself, which unfolds itself in an organic succession of several acts. In the last act Christ reveals His universal judicial majesty. Chap. xxiv. 45-51 exhibits the judgment upon the servants of Christ, or the clergy. Chap. xxv. 1- 13 (the wise and foolish virgins) exhibits the judgment upon the Church, or the people. Then follows the judgment on the individual members of the Church (ver. 14-30). Finally, ver. 31-46 introduce the universal judgment of the world.' (11)

Not very dissimilar is the scheme proposed by Stier, who finds three different comings of Christ ' which perspectively cover each other: '

'1. The coming of the Lord to judgment upon Judaism. 2. His coming to judgment upon degenerate anti-Christian Christendom. 3. His coming to judgment upon all heathen nations- the final judgment of the world, all which together are the coming again of Christ, and in respect of their similarity and diversity are most exactly recorded from the mouth of Christ by Matthew.' (12)

Such is the elaborate and complicated scheme adopted by some expositors; but there are obvious and grave objections to it, which, the more they are considered, will appear the more formidable, if not fatal.

1. An objection may be taken, *in limine,* to the principles involved in this method of interpreting Scripture. Are we to look for double, triple, and multiple meanings, for prophecies within prophecies, and mysteries wrapt in mysteries, where we might reasonably have expected a plain answer to a plain question? Call any one be sure of understanding the Scriptures if they are thus enigmatical and obscure? Is this the manner in which the Saviour taught His disciples, leaving them to grope their way through intricate labyrinths, irresistibly suggestive of the Ptolemaic astronomy - 'Cycle and epicycle, orb in orb'? Surely so ambiguous and obscure a revelation can hardly be called a revelation at all, and seems far more befitting a Delphic Oracle, or a Cumaean Sibyl than the teaching of Him whom. the common people heard gladly. (13)

2. It will scarcely be pretended that, if the exposition of Lange, and Stier be correct, the disciples who listened to the sayings of Jesus on the Mount of Olives could have comprehended or followed the drift of His discourse. They were at all times slow to understand their Master's words; but it would be to give them credit for astonishing penetration to suppose that they were able to thread their way through such a maze of comings, extending through ' a series of cycles, each of which depicts the whole futurity, but in such a manner that with every new cycle the scene seems to approximate to, and more closely resemble, the final catastrophe.'

It is not easy for the ordinary reader to follow the ingenious critic through his convoluted scheme; but it is plain that the disciples must have been hopelessly bewildered amidst a rush of crises and catastrophes from the fall of Jerusalem to the end of the world. Perhaps we shall be told, however, that it does not signify whether the disciples understood our Lord's answer or not: it was not to them that He was speaking; it was to future ages, to generations yet unborn, who were destined, however, to find the interpretation of the prophecy as embarrassing to them as it was to the original bearers. There are no words too strong to repudiate such a suggestion. The disciples came to their Master with a plain, straightforward inquiry, and it is incredible that He would mock them with an unintelligible riddle for a reply. It is to be presumed that the Saviour meant His disciples to understand His words, and it is to be presumed that they did understand them.

3. The interpretation which we are considering appears to be founded upon a misapprehension of the question put to our Lord by the disciples, as well as of His answer to their question.

It is generally assumed that the disciples came to our Lord with three different questions, relating to different events separated from each other by a long interval of time; that the first inquiry, 'When shall *these things* be?'- had reference to the approaching destruction of the temple; that the second and third question-,, 'What shall be the sign of *thy coming,* and of the *end of the world? '- referred* to events long posterior to the destruction of Jerusalem, and, in fact, not yet accomplished. It is supposed that our Lord's reply conforms itself to this threefold inquiry, and that this gives the shape to His whole discourse. Now, lot it be considered how utterly improbable it is that the disciples should have had any such scheme of the future mapped out in their minds. We know that they bad just been shocked and stunned by their Master's prediction of the total destruction of the glorious house of God on which they had so recently been gazing with admiration. They had not yet had time to recover from their surprise, when they came to Jesus with the inquiry, 'When shall these things be?' etc. Is it not reasonable to suppose that *one* thought possessed them at that moment- the portentous calamity awaiting the magnificent structure, the glory and beauty of Israel? Was that a time when their minds would be occupied with a distant future? Must not their whole soul have been concentrated on the fate of the temple? and must they not have been eager to know what tokens would be given of the approach of the catastrophe? Whether they connected in their imagination the destruction of the temple with the dissolution of the creation, and the close of human history, it is impossible to say; but we may safely conclude, that the uppermost thought in their mind was the announcement which the Lord had just made, 'Verily I say unto you, there shall not be left here one stone upon another which shall not be thrown down.' They must have gathered from the Saviour's language that this catastrophe was imminent; and their anxiety was to know the time and the tokens of its arrival. St. Mark and St. Luke make the question of the disciples refer to on*e* event and *one* time- 'When shall these things be, and what shall be the sign when all these things shall be fulfilled? ' It is not only presumable, therefore, but indubitable, that the questions of the disciples only refer to *different aspects of the same great event.* This harmonises the statements of St. Matthew with those of the other Evangelists, and is plainly required by the circumstances of the case.

4. The interpretation which we are discussing rests also upon an erroneous and misleading conception of the phrase, end of the world' (age). It is not surprising that mere English readers of the New Testament should suppose that this phrase really means the destruction of the material earth; but such an error ought not to receive countenance from men of learning. We have already had occasion to remark that the true signification of (aion) is not world, but age; that, like its Latin equivalent *aevum,* it refers to a period of time: thus, 'the end of the age ' means the close of the epoch or Jewish age or dispensation which was drawing nigh, as our Lord frequently intimated. All those passages which speak of 'the end' 'the end of the age,' or, 'the ends of the ages' , refer to the same consummation, and always as nigh at hand. In I Cor. x. 11, St. Paul says The ends of the ages have stretched out to us implying, that he regarded himself and his readers as living near the conclusion of an aeon, or age.

So, in the Epistle to the Hebrews, we find the remarkable expression: 'Now, once, close upon the end of the ages' (erroneously rendered, The end of the world), 'hath be appeared to put away sin by the sacrifice of himself ' (Heb. ix. 26); clearly showing that the writer regarded the incarnation of Christ as taking place near the end of the aeon, or dispensational period. To suppose that he meant that it was close upon the end of the world, or the destruction of the material globe, would be to make him write false history as well as bad grammar. It would not be true in fact; for the world has already lasted longer since the incarnation than the whole duration of the Mosaic economy, from the exodus to the destruction of the temple. It is futile, therefore, to say that the 'end of the age' may mean a lengthened period, extending from the incarnation to our own times, and even far beyond them. That would be an aeon, and not the close of an men. The aeon, of which our Lord was speaking was about to close in a great catastrophe; and a catastrophe is not a protracted process, but a definitive and culminating act. We are compelled, therefore, to conclude that the 'end of the age,' or refers solely to the approaching termination of the Jewish age or dispensation.

5. It may indeed be objected, that even admitting the apostles to have been occupied exclusively with the fate of the temple and the events of their own time, there is no reason why the Lord should not overpass the limits of their vision, and extend a prophetic glance into the ages of a distant futurity. No doubt it was competent for Him to do so; but in that case we should expect to find some hint or intimation of the fact; some well-defined line between the immediate future and the indefinitely remote. If the Saviour passes from Jerusalem and its day of doom to the world and its judgment day, it would be only reasonable to look for some phrase such as, 'After many days,' or, ' It shall come to pass after these things,' to mark the transition. But we search in vain for any such indication. The attempts of expositors to draw transition lines in this prophecy, showing where it ceases to speak of Jerusalem and Israel and passes to remote events and unborn generations, are wholly unsatisfactory. Nothing can be more arbitrary than the divisions attempted to be set up; they will not bear a moment's examination, and are incompatible with the express statements of the prophecy itself. Will it be believed that some expositors find a mark of transition at Matt. xxiv. 29, where our Lord's own words make the very idea totally inadmissible by His own note of time 'Immediately'*! If,* in the face of such authority, so rash a suggestion can be proposed, what may not be expected in less strongly marked cases? But, in fact, all attempts to set up imaginary divisions and transitions in the prophecy signally fail. Let any fair and candid reader judge of the scheme of Dr. Lange, who may be taken as a representative of the school of double-sense expositors, in his distribution of this discourse of our Lord, and say whether it is possible to discern any trace of a natural division where he draws lines of transition. His first section, from ver. 4 to ver. 14, he entitles,

'Signs, and the manifestation of the end of the world in general.

What! is it conceivable that our Lord, when about to reply to the eager and palpitating hearts, filled with anxiety about the calamities which He told them were impending, should commence by speaking of the 'end of the world in general'? They were thinking of the temple and the immediate future: would He speak of the world and the indefinitely remote? But is there anything in this first section inapplicable to the disciples themselves and their time? Is there anything which did not actually happen in their own day? ' 'Yes'. it will be said; ' the gospel of the kingdom has not yet been preached in all the world for a witness unto all nations.' But we have this very fact vouched for by St. Paul (Col. i. 5, 6)-'The word of the truth of the gospel, which is come. unto you, as *it is in all the* world,' etc.; and, again (Col. i. 23)-' The gospel, which ye have heard, and which was preached to every creature which is under heaven.' There was, then, in the acre of the apostles, such a world- wide diffusion of the gospel as to satisfy the Saviour's predictions - 'The gospel of the kingdom shall be preached in all the word' (oikemene).

But the decisive objection to this scheme is, that the whole passage is evidently addressed to the *disciples,* and speaks of what *they* shall see, *they* shall do, *they* shall suffer; the whole falls within their own observation and experience, and cannot be spoken of or to an invisible audience in a far distant era of futurity, which even yet has not appeared upon the earth.

Lange's next division, comprising from ver. 15 to ver. 22, is entitled,
' *signs of the end of the world in particular: (a) The Destruction of Jerusalem.*

Without stopping to inquire into the relation of these ideas, it is satisfactory to find Jerusalem at last introduced. But how unnatural the transition from the 'end of the world' back to the invasion of Judea and the siege of Jerusalem! Could such a sudden and immense leap have possibly been made by the disciples? Could it have been intelligible to them, or is it intelligible now? But mark the point of transition, as fixed by Lange, at ver. 15: 'When ye, therefore, shall see the abomination of desolation,' etc. This, surely, is not *transition,* but *continuity:* all that precedes leads up to this point; the wars, and famines, and pestilences, and persecutions, and martyrdoms, were all preparatory and introductory to the *'end;' that* is, to the final catastrophe which was to overtake the city, and temple, and nation of Israel.

Next follows a paragraph from ver. 23 to ver. 28, which Lange calls,
' *(b) Interval of partial and suppressed judgment.'*

This title is itself an example of fanciful and arbitrary exposition. There is something incongruous and self-contradictory in the very words themselves. A day of judgment implies publicity and manifestation, not silence and suppression. But what can be the meaning of 'silent and suppressed days of judgment,' which go on from the destruction of Jerusalem to the end of the world? If it be meant that there is a sense in which God is always judging the world, that is a truism which might be affirmed of any period, before as well as after the destruction of Jerusalem. But the most objectionable part of this exposition is the violent treatment of the word ' then' (p. 62) [tote] (ver. 23). Lange says: 'Then (i.e., in the time intervening between the destruction of Jerusalem and the end of the world).' Surely, a prodigious *then! It* is no longer a point of time, but an aeon - a vast and indefinite period; and during all that time the statements in the paragraph, ver. 23 to ver. 28, are supposed to be in course of fulfilment. But when we turn to the prophecy itself we find no change of subject, no break in the continuity of the discourse, no hint of any transition from one epoch to another. The note of time, *'then'* [tote], is decisive against any hiatus or transition. Our Saviour is putting the disciples on their guard against the deceivers and impostors who infested the last days of the Jewish commonwealth; and says to them, ' *Then' (i.e.,* at that time, in the agony of the Jewish war) 'if any man shall say unto you, Lo, here is Christ, or there, believe it not,' etc. It is Jerusalem, always Jerusalem, and only Jerusalem, of which our Lord here speaks. At length we come to -
' *The Actual End of the World'* (ver. 24-31).

Having made the transition from the 'end of the world backwards to the destruction of Jerusalem, the process is now reversed, and there is another transition, from the destruction of Jerusalem to the ' actual end of the world.' This actual end is placed after the appearance of those false Christs and false prophets against whom the disciples were warned. This allusion to 'false Christs ' ought to have saved the critic from the mistake into which be has fallen, and to have distinctly indicated the period to which the prediction refers. But where is there any sign of a division or transition here? There is no trace or token of any: on the contrary, the express language of our Lord excludes the idea of any interval at all; for He says: 'Immediately after the tribulation of those days,' etc. This note of time is decisive, and peremptorily forbids the supposition of any break or hiatus in the continuity of His discourse.

But we have gone far enough in the demonstration of the arbitrary and uncritical treatment which this prophecy has received, and have been betrayed into premature exegesis of some portion of its contents. What we contend for, is the *unity and continuity of the whole discourse.* From the beginning of the twenty-fourth chapter of St. Matthew to the close of the twenty-fifth, it *is one* and *indivisible.* The theme is the approaching consummation of the age, with its attendant and concomitant events; the woes which were to overtake that 'wicked generation,' comprehending the invasion of the Roman armies, the siege and capture of Jerusalem, the total destruction of the temple, the frightful calamities of the people. Along with this we find the true Parousia, or the coming of the Son of man, the judicial infliction of divine wrath upon the impenitent, and the deliverance and recompense of the faithful. From beginning to end, these two chapters form one continuous, consecutive, and homogeneous discourse. So it must have been regarded by the disciples, to whom it 'was addressed; and so, in the absence of any hint or indication to the contrary in the record, we feel bound to it.

6. In. conclusion, we cannot help adverting to one other consideration, which we are persuaded has had much to do with the erroneous interpretation of this prophecy, viz., the inadequate appreciation of the importance and grandeur of the event which forms its burden- the consummation of the aeon age, and the abrogation of the Jewish dispensation.

That was an event which formed an epoch in the divine government of the world. The Mosaic economy, which had been ushered in with such pomp and grandeur amidst the thunders and lightenings of Sinai, and had existed for well nigh sixteen centuries, which had been the divinely instituted medium of communication between God and man, and which was intended to realise a kingdom of God upon earth,- had proved a comparative failure through the moral unfitness of the people of Israel, and was doomed to come to an end amid the most terrific demonstration of the justice and wrath of God. The temple of Jerusalem, for ages the glory and crown of Mount Zion,- the sacred shrine, in whose holy place Jehovah was pleased to dwell,- the holy and beautiful house, which was the palladium of the nation's safety, and dearer than life to every son of Abraham,- was about to be desecrated and destroyed, so that not one stone should be left upon another. The chosen people, the children of the Friend of God, the favoured *nation, with* whom the God of the whole earth deigned to enter into *covenant and* to be called their King, - were to be overwhelmed by the most terrible calamities that ever befell a nation; were to be expatriated, deprived of their nationality, excluded from their *ancient and* peculiar relation to God, and driven forth as wanderers on the face of the earth, a byword and hissing among all nations. But along with all this there were to be changes for the better. First, and chiefly, the close of the won would be the inauguration of the reign of God. There were to be honour and glory for the true and faithful servants of God, who would then enter into the full possession of the heavenly inheritance. (This will be more fully unfolded in the sequel of our investigation.) But there was also to be a glorious change in this world. The old made way for the new; the Law was replaced by the Gospel; Moses was superseded by Christ. The narrow and exclusive system, which embraced only a single people, was succeeded by a new and better covenant, which embraced the whole family of man, and knew no difference between Jew and Gentile, circumcised and uncircumcised. The dispensation of symbols and ceremonies, suited to the childhood of humanity, was merged in an order of things in which religion became a spiritual service, every place a temple, every worshipper a priest, and God the universal Father. This was a revolution greater far than any that bad ever occurred in the history of mankind. It made a new world; it was the 'world to come,' the [oikongenh mellonoa] of Hebrews ii. 5; and the magnitude and importance of the change it is impossible to overestimate. It is this that gives such significance to the overthrow of the temple and the destruction of Jerusalem: these are the outward and visible signs of the abrogation of the old order and the introduction of the new. The story of the siege and capture of the Holy City is not simply a thrilling historical episode, such as the siege of Troy or the fall of Carthage; it is not merely the closing scene in the annals of an ancient nation;- it has a supernatural and divine significance; it has a relation to God and the human race, and marks one of the most memorable epochs of time. This is the reason why the event is spoken of in the Scripture in terms which to some appear overstrained, or to require some greater catastrophe to account for them. But if it was fitting that the introduction of that economy should be signalised by portents and wonders, earthquakes, lightenings, thunders, and trumpet-blasts, -it was no less fitting that it should go out amid similar phenomena, fearful sights and great signs from heaven.' Had the true significance and grandeur of the event been better apprehended by expositors, they would not have found the language in which it is depicted by our Lord extravagant or overstrained. (14)

We are now prepared to enter upon the more particular examination of the contents of this prophetic discourse; which we shall endeavour to do as concisely as possible.

1. Life of Christ, sec. 239.
2. Life of Christ, sec. 256.
3. Lange on St. Matt. p. 388.
4. Alford, Greek Test. in loc.
5. Life of Christ, sec. 253, note n.
6. Life of Christ, sec. 253, note m.
7. Tischendorf rejects ver. 14, which is omitted by Cod. Sin. and Vat.
8. See Dorner's tractae, De Oratione Christi Eschatologica, p. 41.

9. Dorner, Orat. Chris. Esch. p. 43
10. Comm. on Matt. p. 416
11. Lange, Comm. on Matt. p. 418
12. Stier. Red. Jes. vol. iii. 251.
13. See Note A, Part I., on the Double-sense Theory of Interpretation
14. The termination of the Jewish aion in the first century, and of the Roman in the fifth and sixth, were each marked by the same concurrence of calamities, wars,

tumults, pestilences, earthquakes, &c., all marking the time of one of God's peculiar seasons of visitation.' 'For the same belief in the connexion of physical with moral convulsion-, see Niebuhr, Leben's Nachrichten, ii. p. 672 Dr. Arnold: See ' Life by Stanley,' vol. i. p. 311.

vii.-The Prophecy on the Mount of Olives.
THE COMING OF THE SON OF MAN [THE PAROUSIA] BEFORE THE PASSING AWAY OF THAT GENERATION. MATT. XXIV..; MARK XIII.; LUKE XXI.

We now enter upon the consideration of by far the most full and explicit of our Lord's prophetic utterances respecting His coming, and the solemn events connected therewith. The discourse or conversation on the Mount of Olives is the great prophecy of the New Testament, and may be not unfitly styled the Apocalypse of the Gospels. Upon the interpretation of this prophetic discourse will depend the right understanding of the predictions contained in the apostolic writings; for it may almost be said that there is nothing in the Epistles which is not in the Gospels. This prophecy of our Saviour is the great storehouse from which the prophetic statements of the apostles are chiefly derived.

The commonly received view of the structure of this discourse, which is almost taken for granted, alike by expositors and by the generality of readers, is, that our Lord, in answering the question of His disciples respecting the destruction of the temple, mixes up with that event the destruction of the world, the universal judgment, and the final consummation of all things. Imperceptibly, it is supposed, the prophecy slides from the city and temple of Jerusalem, and their impending fate in the immediate future, to another and infinitely more tremendous catastrophe in the far distant and indefinite future. So intermingled, however, are the allusions- now to Jerusalem and now to the world at large; now to Israel and now to the human race; now to events close at hand and now to events indefinitely remote; that to distinguish and allocate the several references and topics, is exceedingly difficult, if not impossible.

Perhaps it will be the fairest way of exhibiting the views of those who contend for a double meaning in this predictive discourse, to set forth the scheme or plan of the prophecy proposed by Dr. Lange, and adopted by many expositors of the greatest note.

' In harmony with apocalyptic style, Jesus exhibited the judgments of His coming in a series of cycles, each of which depicts the whole futurity, but in such a manner, that with every new cycle the scene seems to approximate to and more closely resemble the final catastrophe. Thus, the first cycle delineates the whole course of the world down to the end, in its general characteristics (ver. 4-14). The second gives the signs of the approaching destruction of Jerusalem, and paints this destruction itself as a sign and a commencement of the judgment of the world, which from that day onward proceeds in silent and suppressed days of judgment down to the last (ver. 15-28). The third describes the sudden end of the world, and the judgment which ensues (ver. 29-44). Then follows a series of parables and similitudes, in which the Lord paints the judgment itself, which unfolds itself in an organic succession of several acts. In the last act Christ reveals His universal judicial majesty. Chap. xxiv. 45-51 exhibits the judgment upon the servants of Christ, or the clergy. Chap. xxv. 1- 13 (the wise and foolish virgins) exhibits the judgment upon the Church, or the people. Then follows the judgment on the individual members of the Church (ver. 14-30). Finally, ver. 31-46 introduce the universal judgment of the world.' (11)

Not very dissimilar is the scheme proposed by Stier, who finds three different comings of Christ ' which perspectively cover each other: '

'1. The coming of the Lord to judgment upon Judaism. 2. His coming to judgment upon degenerate anti-Christian Christendom. 3. His coming to judgment upon all heathen nations- the final judgment of the world, all which together are the coming again of Christ, and in respect of their similarity and diversity are most exactly recorded from the mouth of Christ by Matthew.' (12)

Such is the elaborate and complicated scheme adopted by some expositors; but there are obvious and grave objections to it, which, the more they are considered, will appear the more formidable, if not fatal.

1. An objection may be taken, *in limine,* to the principles involved in this method of interpreting Scripture. Are we to look for double, triple, and multiple meanings, for prophecies within prophecies, and mysteries wrapt in mysteries, where we might reasonably have expected a plain answer to a plain question? Call any one be sure of understanding the Scriptures if they are thus enigmatical and obscure? Is this the manner in which the Saviour taught His disciples, leaving them to grope their way through intricate labyrinths, irresistibly suggestive of the Ptolemaic astronomy - 'Cycle and epicycle, orb in orb'? Surely so ambiguous and obscure a revelation can hardly be called a revelation at all, and seems far more befitting a Delphic Oracle, or a Cumaean Sibyl than the teaching of Him whom. the common people heard gladly. (13)

2. It will scarcely be pretended that, if the exposition of Lange, and Stier be correct, the disciples who listened to the sayings of Jesus on the Mount of Olives could have comprehended or followed the drift of His discourse. They were at all times slow to understand their Master's words; but it would be to give them credit for astonishing penetration to suppose that they were able to thread their way through such a maze of comings, extending through ' a series of cycles, each of which depicts the whole futurity, but in such a manner that with every new cycle the scene seems to approximate to, and more closely resemble, the final catastrophe.'

It is not easy for the ordinary reader to follow the ingenious critic through his convoluted scheme; but it is plain that the disciples must have been hopelessly bewildered amidst a rush of crises and catastrophes from the fall of Jerusalem to the end of the world. Perhaps we shall be told, however, that it does not signify whether the disciples understood our Lord's answer or not: it was not to them that He was speaking; it was to future ages, to generations yet unborn, who were destined, however, to find the interpretation of the prophecy as embarrassing to them as it was to the original bearers. There are no words too strong to repudiate such a suggestion. The disciples came to their Master with a plain, straightforward inquiry, and it is incredible that He would mock them with an unintelligible riddle for a reply. It is to be presumed that the Saviour meant His disciples to understand His words, and it is to be presumed that they did understand them.

3. The interpretation which we are considering appears to be founded upon a misapprehension of the question put to our Lord by the disciples, as well as of His answer to their question.

It is generally assumed that the disciples came to our Lord with three different questions, relating to different events separated from each other by a long interval of time; that the first inquiry, 'When shall *these things* be?'- had reference to the approaching destruction of the temple; that the second and third question-,, 'What shall be the sign of *thy coming,* and of the *end of the world?* '- *referred* to events long posterior to the destruction of Jerusalem, and, in fact, not yet accomplished. It is supposed that our Lord's reply conforms itself to this threefold inquiry, and that this gives the shape to His whole discourse. Now, lot it be considered how utterly improbable it is that the disciples should have had any such scheme of the future mapped out in their minds. We know that they bad just been shocked and stunned by their Master's prediction of the total destruction of the glorious house of God on which they had so recently been gazing with admiration. They had not yet had time to recover from their surprise, when they came to Jesus with the inquiry, 'When shall these things be?' etc. Is it not reasonable to suppose that *one* thought possessed them at that moment- the portentous calamity awaiting the magnificent structure, the glory and beauty of Israel? Was that a time when their minds would be occupied with a distant future? Must not their whole soul have been concentrated on the fate of the temple? and must they not have been eager to know what tokens would be given of the approach of the catastrophe? Whether they connected in their imagination the destruction of the temple with the dissolution of the creation, and the close of human history, it is impossible to say; but we may safely conclude, that the uppermost thought in their mind was the announcement which the Lord had just made, 'Verily I say unto you, there shall not be left here one stone upon another which shall not be thrown down.' They must have gathered from the Saviour's language that this catastrophe was imminent; and their anxiety was to know the time and the tokens of its arrival. St. Mark and St. Luke make the question of the disciples refer to on*e* event and *one* time- 'When shall these things be, and what shall be the sign when all these things shall be fulfilled? ' It is not only presumable, therefore, but indubitable, that the questions of the disciples only refer to *different aspects of the same great event.* This harmonises the statements of St. Matthew with those of the other Evangelists, and is plainly required by the circumstances of the case.

4. The interpretation which we are discussing rests also upon an erroneous and misleading conception of the phrase, end of the world' (age). It is not surprising that mere English readers of the New Testament should suppose that this phrase really means the destruction of the material earth; but such an error ought not to receive countenance from men of learning. We have already had occasion to remark that the true signification of (aion) is not world, but age; that, like its Latin equivalent *aevum,* it refers to a period of time: thus, 'the end of the age ' means the close of the epoch or Jewish age or dispensation which was drawing nigh, as our Lord frequently intimated. All those passages which speak of 'the end' 'the end of the age,' or, 'the ends of the ages' , refer to the same consummation, and always as nigh at hand. In I Cor. x. 11, St. Paul says The ends of the ages have stretched out to us implying, that he regarded himself and his readers as living near the conclusion of an aeon, or age.

So, in the Epistle to the Hebrews, we find the remarkable expression: 'Now, once, close upon the end of the ages' (erroneously rendered, The end of the world), 'hath be appeared to put away sin by the sacrifice of himself ' (Heb. ix. 26); clearly showing that the writer regarded the incarnation of Christ as taking place near the end of the aeon, or dispensational period. To suppose that he meant that it was close upon the end of the world, or the destruction of the material globe, would be to make him write false history as well as bad grammar. It would not be true in fact; for the world has already lasted longer since the incarnation than the whole duration of the Mosaic economy, from the exodus to the destruction of the temple. It is futile, therefore, to say that the 'end of the age' may mean a lengthened period, extending from the incarnation to our own times, and even far beyond them. That would be an aeon, and not the close of an men. The aeon, of which our Lord was speaking was about to close in a great catastrophe; and a catastrophe is not a protracted process, but a definitive and culminating act. We are compelled, therefore, to conclude that the 'end of the age,' or refers solely to the approaching termination of the Jewish age or dispensation.

5. It may indeed be objected, that even admitting the apostles to have been occupied exclusively with the fate of the temple and the events of their own time, there is no reason why the Lord should not overpass the limits of their vision, and extend a prophetic glance into the ages of a distant futurity. No doubt it was competent for Him to do so; but in that case we should expect to find some hint or intimation of the fact; some well-defined line between the immediate future and the indefinitely remote. If the Saviour passes from Jerusalem and its day of doom to the world and its judgment day, it would be only reasonable to look for some phrase such as, 'After many days,' or, ' It shall come to pass after these things,' to mark the transition. But we search in vain for any such indication. The attempts of expositors to draw transition lines in this prophecy, showing where it ceases to speak of Jerusalem and Israel and passes to remote events and unborn generations, are wholly unsatisfactory. Nothing can be more arbitrary than the divisions attempted to be set up; they will not bear a moment's examination, and are incompatible with the express statements of the prophecy itself. Will it be believed that some expositors find a mark of transition at Matt. xxiv. 29, where our Lord's own words make the very idea totally inadmissible by His own note of time 'Immediately'! *If,* in the face of such authority, so rash a suggestion can be proposed, what may not be expected in less strongly marked cases? But, in fact, all attempts to set up imaginary divisions and transitions in the prophecy signally fail. Let any fair and candid reader judge of the scheme of Dr. Lange, who may be taken as a representative of the school of double-sense expositors, in his distribution of this discourse of our Lord, and say whether it is possible to discern any trace of a natural division where he draws lines of transition. His first section, from ver. 4 to ver. 14, he entitles,

'Signs, and the manifestation of the end of the world in general.

What! is it conceivable that our Lord, when about to reply to the eager and palpitating hearts, filled with anxiety about the calamities which He told them were impending, should commence by speaking of the 'end of the world in general'? They were thinking of the temple and the immediate future: would He speak of the world and the indefinitely remote? But is there anything in this first section inapplicable to the disciples themselves and their time? Is there anything which did not actually happen in their own day? ' 'Yes'. it will be said; ' the gospel of the kingdom has not yet been preached in all the world for a witness unto all nations.' But we have this very fact vouched for by St. Paul (Col. i. 5, 6)-'The word of the truth of the gospel, which is come. unto you, as *it is in all the* world,' etc.; and, again (Col. i. 23)-' The gospel, which ye have heard, and which was preached to every creature which is under heaven.' There was, then, in the acre of the apostles, such a world- wide diffusion of the gospel as to satisfy the Saviour's predictions - 'The gospel of the kingdom shall be preached in all the word' (oikemene).

But the decisive objection to this scheme is, that the whole passage is evidently addressed to the *disciples,* and speaks of what *they* shall see, *they* shall do, *they* shall suffer; the whole falls within their own observation and experience, and cannot be spoken of or to an invisible audience in a far distant era of futurity, which even yet has not appeared upon the earth.

Lange's next division, comprising from ver. 15 to ver. 22, is entitled,

' signs of the end of the world in particular: (a) The Destruction of Jerusalem.

Without stopping to inquire into the relation of these ideas, it is satisfactory to find Jerusalem at last introduced. But how unnatural the transition from the 'end of the world' back to the invasion of Judea and the siege of Jerusalem! Could such a sudden and immense leap have possibly been made by the disciples? Could it have been intelligible to them, or is it intelligible now? But mark the point of transition, as fixed by Lange, at ver. 15: 'When ye, therefore, shall see the abomination of desolation,' etc. This, surely, is not *transition,* but *continuity:* all that precedes leads up to this point; the wars, and famines, and pestilences, and persecutions, and martyrdoms, were all preparatory and introductory to the *'end;'* that is, to the final catastrophe which was to overtake the city, and temple, and nation of Israel.

Next follows a paragraph from ver. 23 to ver. 28, which Lange calls,

' (b) Interval of partial and suppressed judgment.'

This title is itself an example of fanciful and arbitrary exposition. There is something incongruous and self-contradictory in the very words themselves. A day of judgment implies publicity and manifestation, not silence and suppression. But what can be the meaning of 'silent and suppressed days of judgment,' which go on from the destruction of Jerusalem to the end of the world? If it be meant that there is a sense in which God is always judging the world, that is a truism which might be affirmed of any period, before as well as after the destruction of Jerusalem. But the most objectionable part of this exposition is the violent treatment of the word ' then' (p. 62) [to,te] (ver. 23). Lange says: 'Then (i.e., in the time intervening between the destruction of Jerusalem and the end of the world).' Surely, a prodigious *then! It* is no longer a point of time, but an aeon - a vast and indefinite period; and during all that time the statements in the paragraph, ver. 23 to ver. 28, are supposed to be in course of fulfilment. But when we turn to the prophecy itself we find no change of subject, no break in the continuity of the discourse, no hint of any transition from one epoch to another. The note of time, *'then'* [to,te], is decisive against any hiatus or transition. Our Saviour is putting the disciples on their guard against the deceivers and impostors who infested the last days of the Jewish commonwealth; and says to them, ' *Then' (i.e.,* at that time, in the agony of the Jewish war) 'if any man shall say unto you, Lo, here is Christ, or there, believe it not,' etc. It is Jerusalem, always Jerusalem, and only Jerusalem, of which our Lord here speaks. At length we come to -

' The Actual End of the World' (ver. 24-31).

Having made the transition from the 'end of the world backwards to the destruction of Jerusalem, the process is now reversed, and there is another transition, from the destruction of Jerusalem to the ' actual end of the world.' This actual end is placed after the appearance of those false Christs and false prophets against whom the disciples were warned. This allusion to 'false Christs ' ought to have saved the critic from the mistake into which be has fallen, and to have distinctly indicated the period to which the prediction refers. But where is there any sign of a division or transition here? There is no trace or token of any: on the contrary, the express language of our Lord excludes the idea of any interval at all; for He says: 'Immediately after the tribulation of those days,' etc. This note of time is decisive, and per-emptorily forbids the supposition of any break or hiatus in the continuity of His discourse.

But we have gone far enough in the demonstration of the arbitrary and uncritical treatment which this prophecy has received, and have been betrayed into premature exegesis of some portion of its contents. What we contend for, is the *unity and continuity of the whole discourse.* From the beginning of the twenty-fourth chapter of St. Matthew to the close of the twenty-fifth, it *is one* and *indivisible.* The theme is the approaching consummation of the age, with its at-tendant and concomitant events; the woes which were to overtake that 'wicked generation,' comprehending the inva-sion of the Roman armies, the siege and capture of Jerusalem, the total destruction of the temple, the frightful calami-ties of the people. Along with this we find the true Parousia, or the coming of the Son of man, the judicial infliction of divine wrath upon the impenitent, and the deliverance and recompense of the faithful. From beginning to end, these two chapters form one continuous, consecutive, and homogeneous discourse. So it must have been regarded by the disciples, to whom it 'was addressed; and so, in the absence of any hint or indication to the contrary in the record, we feel bound to it.

6. In. conclusion, we cannot help adverting to one other consideration, which we are persuaded has had much to do with the erroneous interpretation of this prophecy, viz., the inadequate appreciation of the importance and grandeur of the event which forms its burden- the consummation of the aeon age, and the abrogation of the Jewish dispensa-tion.

That was an event which formed an epoch in the divine government of the world. The Mosaic economy, which had been ushered in with such pomp and grandeur amidst the thunders and lightenings of Sinai, and had existed for well nigh sixteen centuries, which had been the divinely instituted medium of communication between God and man, and which was intended to realise a kingdom of God upon earth,- had proved a comparative failure through the moral un-fitness of the people of Israel, and was doomed to come to an end amid the most terrific demonstration of the justice and wrath of God. The temple of Jerusalem, for ages the glory and crown of Mount Zion,- the sacred shrine, in whose holy place Jehovah was pleased to dwell,- the holy and beautiful house, which was the palladium of the nation's safety, and dearer than life to every son of Abraham,- was about to be desecrated and destroyed, so that not one stone should be left upon another. The chosen people, the children of the Friend of God, the favoured *nation, with* whom the God of the whole earth deigned to enter into *covenant and* to be called their King, - were to be overwhelmed by the most ter-rible calamities that ever befell a nation; were to be expatriated, deprived of their nationality, excluded from their *an-cient and* peculiar relation to God, and driven forth as wanderers on the face of the earth, a byword and hissing among all nations. But along with all this there were to be changes for the better. First, and chiefly, the close of the won would be the inauguration of the reign of God. There were to be honour and glory for the true and faithful servants of God, who would then enter into the full possession of the heavenly inheritance. (This will be more fully unfolded in the se-quel of our investigation.) But there was also to be a glorious change in this world. The old made way for the new; the Law was replaced by the Gospel; Moses was superseded by Christ. The narrow and exclusive system, which embraced only a single people, was succeeded by a new and better covenant, which embraced the whole family of man, and knew no difference between Jew and Gentile, circumcised and uncircumcised. The dispensation of symbols and cere-monies, suited to the childhood of humanity, was merged in an order of things in which religion became a spiritual service, every place a temple, every worshipper a priest, and God the universal Father. This was a revolution greater far than any that bad ever occurred in the history of mankind. It made a new world; it was the 'world to come,' the [oikongenh mellonoa] of Hebrews ii. 5; and the magnitude and importance of the change it is impossible to over-estimate. It is this that gives such significance to the overthrow of the temple and the destruction of Jerusalem: these are the outward and visible signs of the abrogation of the old order and the introduction of the new. The story of the siege and capture of the Holy City is not simply a thrilling historical episode, such as the siege of Troy or the fall of Car-thage; it is not merely the closing scene in the annals of an ancient nation;- it has a supernatural and divine signifi-cance; it has a relation to God and the human race, and marks one of the most memorable epochs of time. This is the reason why the event is spoken of in the Scripture in terms which to some appear overstrained, or to require some greater catastrophe to account for them. But if it was fitting that the introduction of that economy should be signalised by portents and wonders, earthquakes, lightenings, thunders, and trumpet-blasts, -it was no less fitting that it should go out amid similar phenomena, fearful sights and great signs from heaven.' Had the true significance and grandeur of the event been better apprehended by expositors, they would not have found the language in which it is depicted by our Lord extravagant or overstrained. (14)

We are now prepared to enter upon the more particular examination of the contents of this prophetic discourse; which we shall endeavour to do as concisely as possible.

11. Lange, Comm. on Matt. p. 418
12. Stier. Red. Jes. vol. iii. 251.
13. See Note A, Part I., on the Double-sense Theory of Interpretation

14. The termination of the Jewish aion in the first century, and of the Roman in the fifth and sixth, were each marked by the same concurrence of calamities, wars, tumults, pestilences, earthquakes, &c., all marking the time of one of God's peculiar seasons of visitation.' 'For the same belief in the connexion of physical with moral convulsion-, see Niebuhr, Leben's Nachrichten, ii. p. 672 Dr. Arnold: See ' Life by Stanley,' vol. i. p. 311.

The Prophecy on the Mount examined:-

I. - The Interrogatory of the Disciples.

Matt. xxiv. 1-3.

'And Jesus went and departed from the temple: with his disciples came to join for to shew him all the buildings of the temple.

' And Jesus said unto them, See ye not all these things? verily I say **unto** you, There shall not be left here one stone upon another that shall not be thrown down.

'And as he sat upon the mount of Olives, the disciples came unto him privately, saying, Tell us, when shall these thins be? and what shall be the sign of thy coming, and of the end of the world' [age]?

Mark xiii. 1-4.

'And as he went out of the temple, one of his disciples saith unto him, Master, what manner of stones and what buildings are here!

' And Jesus answering said unto them, Seest thou these great buildings? there shall not be left one stone upon another, that shall not be thrown down.

'And as he sat upon the mount of Olives over against the temple, Peter and James and John and Andrew asked him privately, 'Tell us, when shall these things be? and what shall be the sign when all these things shall be fulfilled?

Luke xxi. 5-7.

'And as some spake of the temple, how it was adorned with goodly stones, and gifts, he said,

'As for these things which ye behold, the days will come, in the which there shall not be left one stone upon another, that shall not be thrown down.

' 'And they asked Him, saying, , Master, but when shall these things be,? and what sign will there be when these things shall come to pass?'

We may conceive the surprise and consternation felt by the disciples when Jesus announced to them the utter destruction which Was coming upon the temple of God, the beauty and splendour of which had excited their admiration. it is no marvel that four of their number, who seem to have been admitted to more intimate familiarity than the rest, sought for fuller information On a subject so intensely interesting. The only point that requires elucidation here refers to the extent of their interrogatory. St. Mark and St. Luke represent it as having reference to the *time* of the predicted catastrophe and the sign of As fulfilment coming to pass. St. Matthew varies the form of the question, but evidently gives the same sense, -- ' Tell us, when shall these things be? and what shall be the sign of thy coming, and of the end of the age?' Here again it is the time and the sign which form the subject of inquiry. There is no reason whatever to suppose that they regarded in their own minds the destruction of the temple, the coming of the Lord, and the end of the age, as three distinct or widely separated events; but, on the contrary, it is most natural to suppose that they regarded them as coincident and contemporaneous. What precise idea-, they entertained respecting the end of the age and the events therewith connected, we do not know; but we do know that they had been accustomed to hear their Master speak of His coming again ill His kingdom, coming in His glory, and that within the lifetime of some among themselves. They hall also heard Him speak of the 'end of the age; ' and they evidently connected His ' coming ' with the end of the three points embraced in file form of their question, is given by St. Matthew, were therefore in their view contemporaneous; and thus we find no practical difference in the terms of the question of the disciples as recorded by the three Synoptists.

II. -- Our Lord's Answer to the Disciples.

(a) Events which more remotely were to precede the consummation.

Matt. xxiv. 4-14.

'And Jesus answered and said unto the, Take heed that no man deceive you. For many shall come in my name, saying, I am Christ; and shall deceive many. And ye shall hear of wars and rumours of wars: see that ye be not troubled: for all these things must

Mark xiii. 5- 13.

'And Jesus answering them began to say, Take heed lest any man deceive you: for many shall come in my name, saying, I am Christ; and shall deceive many.

And when ye shall hear of wars and rumours of wars, be ye not troubled:

Luke xxi. 8-19.

And he said, Take heed that ye be not deceived: for many shall come in my name, saying, I am Christ; and the time draweth near: go ye not therefore after them. But when ye shall hear of wars and commotions, be not terrified: for these things must first come to come to pass, but the end is not yet. For nation shall rise against nation, and kingdom against kingdom: and there shall be famines, and pestilences, and earthquakes, in divers places. All these are the beginning of sorrows. Then shall they deliver you up to be afflicted, and shall kill you: and ye shall be hated of all nations for my name's sake. And then shall many be offended, and shall betray on another, and shall hate one another. And many false prophets shall rise, and shall deceive many. And because iniquity shall abound, the love of many shall wax cold. But he that shall endure unto the end, the same shall be saved. And this gospel of the kingdom shall be preached in all the world for a witness unto all nations; and then shall the end come.'

for such things must needs be; but the end shall not be yet. For nation shall rise against nation, and kingdom against kingdom: and there shall be earthquakes in divers places, and there shall be famines and troubles: these are the beginnings of sorrows. But take heed to yourselves: for they shall deliver you up to councils; and in the synagogues ye shall be beaten: and ye shall be brought before rulers and kings for my sake, for a testimony against them. And the gospel must first be published among all nations. But when they shall lead you, and deliver you up, take no thought beforehand what ye shall speak, neither do ye premeditate: but whatsoever shall be given you in that hour, that speak ye: for it is not ye that speak, but the Holy Ghost.
Now the brother shall betray the brother to death, and the father the son; and children shall rise up against their parents, and shall cause them to be put to death. And ye shall be hated of all men for my name's sake: but he that shall endure unto the end, the same shall be saved.

pass; but the end is not by and by. Then said he unto them, Nation shall rise against nation, and kingdom against kingdom: And great earthquakes shall be in divers places, and famines, and pestilences; and fearful sights and great signs shall there be from heaven. But before all these, they shall lay their hands on you, and persecute you, delivering you up to the synagogues, and into prisons, being brought before kings and rulers for my name's sake. And it shall turn to you for a testimony. Settle it therefore in your hearts, not to meditate before what ye shall answer: For I will give you a mouth and wisdom, which all your adversaries shall not be able to gainsay nor resist. And ye shall be betrayed both by parents, and brethren, and kinsfolks, and friends; and some of you shall they cause to be put to death. And ye shall be hated of all men for my name's sake. But there shall not an hair of your head perish. In your patience possess ye your souls.

It is impossible to read this section and fail to perceive its distinct reference to the period between our Lord's crucifixion and the destruction of Jerusalem. Every word is spoken to the disciples, and to them alone. To imagine that the 'ye' and 'you ' in this address apply, not to the disciples to whom Christ wits speaking, but to some unknown and yet non-existent persons in it far distant age, is so preposterous a supposition is not to deserve serious notice.

That our Lord's words were fully verified during- the interval, between His crucifixion and the end of the age, we have the most ample testimony. False Christs and false prophets began to make their appearance at it very early period of the, Christian era, and continued to infest the land down to the very close, of Jewish history. In the procuratorship of Pilate (A.D. 36), one such appeared in Samaria, and deluded great multitudes. There was another in the procuratorship of Cuspius Fadus (A.D. 45). During the government of Felix (53-60), Josephus tells us 'the country was full of robbers, magicians, false prophets, false Messiahs, and impostors' who deluded the People with promises of great events." (1) The same authority informs its that civil commotions and international feuds, were rife in those days, especially between the Jews and their neighbours. In Alexandria, in Selucia, in Syria, in Babylonia, there were violent tumults between the Jews and the Greeks, the Jews and the Syrians, inhabiting, the same cities. 'Every city was divided,' says Josephus, 'into two camps.' In the reign of Caligula great apprehensions were entertained in Judea of war with the Romans, in consequence of that tyrant's proposal to place his statue in the temple. In the reign of the Emperor Claudis (A.D. (41-54), there were four seasons of great scarcity. In the fourth year of his reign the famine in Judea was so severe, that the price of food became enormous and great numbers perished. Earthquakes occurred in each of the reigns of Caligula and Claudius. (2)

Such calamities, the Lord gave His disciples to understand, would precede the 'end.' But they were not its immediate antecedents. They were the 'beginning of the end; ' but 'the end is not yet.'

At this point (ver. 9-13), our Lord passes from the general to the particular; from the public to tile personal; from the fortunes of nations and kingdoms to the fortunes of the disciples themselves. While these events were proceeding, the apostles were to become objects of suspicion to tile ruling powers. They were to be brought before councils, rulers, and kings, imprisoned, beaten in the synagogues, and hated of all men for Jesus' sake,

How exactly all this was verified in the personal experience of the disciples we may read in the Acts of the Apostles and in the Epistles of St. Paul. Yet the divine promise of protection ill the hour of peril was remarkably fulfilled. With the single exception of 'James the brother of John,' no apostle seems to have fallen a victim to the malignant persecution of their enemies tip to the close of the apostolic history, as recorded in the Acts (A.D. 63).

One other sign was to precede and usher in the consummation. 'The gospel of the kingdom shall be preached in all the world [oi.koume,ne] for a witness unto all nations and then shall the end come.' We have already adverted to the fulfilment of this prediction within the apostolic age. We have the authority of St. Paul for such a universal diffusion Of tile gospel in his days as to verify the saying of Our Lord. (See Col. 1. 6, 23.) But for this explicit testimony ' from all apostle if, would have been impossible to persuade some expositors that our Lord's words had been in any sense fulfilled previous to the destruction of Jerusalem, it would have been regarded as mere extravagance, and rhodomontade. -Now, however, the objection cannot reasonably be urged.

Here it may be proper to call to mind the note of time, given on a previous occasion to the disciples as indicative of our Lord's coming: 'Verily I say unto you, Ye shall not have gone over the cities of Israel, till the Son of man be come' (Matt. x. 23). Comparing this declaration with the prediction before us (Matt. xxiv. 14), we may see the perfect consistency of the two statements, and also the 'terminus ad quem ' in both. In the one ease it is the evangelisation of the land of Israel, in the other, the evangelisation of the Roman empire that is referred to as the precursor of the Parousia. Both statements are true. It might well occupy the space of a generation to carry the glad tidings into every city in the land of Israel. The apostles had not too much time for their home mission, though they had upon their hands so vast a foreign mission. Obviously, we must take the language employed by Paul, as well as by our Lord in a popular sense and it would be unfair to press it to the extremity of the letter. The wide diffusion of the gospel both in the land of Israel and throughout the Roman empire, is sufficient to justify the prediction of our Lord.

Thus far Own we have one continuous discourse, relating to a particular event, and spoken of and to particular persons. We find four signs, or sets of signs, which were to portend the approach of the great catastrophe.

1. The appearance of false Christs and false prophets.
2. Great social disturbances and natural calamities and convulsions.
3. Persecution of the disciples and apostasy of professed believers.
4. The general publication of the gospel throughout the Roman empire.

This last sign especially betokened the near approach of the 'end.'

(b) Further indications of the approaching doom of Jerusalem

Matt. xxiv. 15-22	**Mark xiii. 14-20.**	**Luke xxi. 20-20.**
'When ye therefore shall see the abomination of desolation, spoken of by Daniel the prophet, stand in the holy place, (whoso readeth, let him understand:) Then let them which be in Judaea flee into the mountains: Let him which is on the housetop not come down to take any thing out of his house: Neither let him which is in the field return back to take his clothes.	'But when ye shall see the abomination of desolation, spoken of by Daniel the prophet, standing where it ought not, (let him that readeth understand,) then let them that be in Judaea flee to the mountains: And let him that is on the housetop not go down into the house, neither enter therein, to take any thing out of his house: And let him that is in the field not turn back again for to take up his garment.	'And when ye shall see Jerusalem compassed with armies, then know that the desolation thereof is nigh.

'Then let them which are in Judaea flee to the mountains; and let them which are in the midst of it depart out; and let not them that are in the countries enter thereinto. For these be the days of vengeance, that all things which are written may be fulfilled. |
| 'And woe unto them that are with child, and to them that give suck in those days! But pray ye that your flight be not in the winter, neither on the sabbath day: For then shall be great tribulation, such as was not since the beginning of the world to this time, no, nor ever shall be. And except those days should be shortened, there should no flesh be saved: but for the elect's sake those days shall be shortened. ' | 'But woe to them that are with child, and to them that give suck in those days! And pray ye that your flight be not in the winter. For in those days shall be affliction, such as was not from the beginning of the creation which God created unto this time, neither shall be. And except that the Lord had shortened those days, no flesh should be saved: but for the elect's sake, whom he hath chosen, he hath shortened the days. ' | 'But woe unto them that are with child, and to them that give suck, in those days! for there shall be great distress in the land, and wrath upon this people. And they shall fall by the edge of the sword, and shall be led away captive into all nations: and Jerusalem shall be trodden down of the Gentiles, until the times of the Gentiles be fulfilled. ' |

No argument is required to prove the strict and exclusive reference of this section to Jerusalem and Judea. Here we can detect no trace of it double meaning, of primary and ulterior fulfilments, of underlying and typical senses. Everything is national, local, and near:- 'the land ' is the land of Judea,-' this people ' is the people of Israel,-and the ' time the lifetime of the disciples,--' *When* YE *therefore Shall See.'*

Most expositors find an allusion to the standards of the Roman legions in the expression, "the abomination of desolation" and the explanation is highly probable. The eagles were the objects of religious worship to the soldiers; and the parallel passage in St. Luke is all but conclusive evidence that this is the true meaning. We know from Josephus that the attempt of a Roman general (Vitellius), in the reign of Tiberius, to march his troops through Judea, was resisted by the Jewish authorities, on the ground that the idolatrous images on their ensigns would be a profanation of the law. (3) How much greater the profanation when those idolatrous emblems were displayed in full view of the temple and the Holy City! This was the last token which portended that the hour of doom for Jerusalem had come. Its appearance was to he the. signal to all in Judea to escape beyond the mountains for then would ensue a period of misery and horror without a parallel in the annals of time.

That the 'great tribulation' (Matt. xxiv. 21) has express reference to the dreadful calamities attending the siege of Jerusalem, which bore With such peculiar severity on the female sex, is too evident to be questioned. That those calamities were literally unparalleled, can easily be believed by al1 who have read the ghastly narrative in the pages of Josephus. It is remarkable that the historian begins his account of the Jewish war with the affirmation, 'that the aggregate of human woes from the beginning of the world, would, in his opinion, be light in comparison with those of the Jews., (4)

The following graphic description introduces the tragic story of the wretched mother, whose horrible repast may have been in our Saviour's thoughts when he uttered the words recorded in Matt, xxiv. 19:
'Incalculable was the multitude of those who perished in famine in the city -, and beyond description the sufferings they endured. In every house, if anywhere there appeared but the shadow of food, a conflict ensued; those united by the tenderest ties fiercely contending, and snatching from one another the miserable supports of life. Nor were even the dying allowed the credit of being in want; nay, even those. who were just expiring the brigands would search, lest, any, with food concealed under a fold of his garment, should feign death. Gaping with hunger, as maddened dogs, they went staggering to and fro and prowling about assailing the doors like drunken men, and in bewilderment rushing into the same house twice, or thrice in one hour. The cravings of nature led them to gnaw anything, and what would be rejected by the Very filthiest or the brute creation they were fain to collect and eat. Even from their belts and shoes they were at length unable to refrain, and they tore off find chewed the very leather of their shields. To some, wisps of old hay served for food; for the fibres were gathered, and the smallest quantities sold for four Attic pieces.
' But why speak of the famine as despising restraint in the use of inanimate, When I am about to state an instance of it to which, in the history of Greeks or Barbarians, no parallel is to be found, and which is horrible to relate, and is incredible to hear? Gladly , indeed would I have omitted to mention the occurrence, lest I Should be thought by future generations to deal in the marvellous, had I not innumerable witnesses among my contemporaries. I should, besides, pay my country but a cold compliment, were I to suppress the narration of the woes which she actually suffered.' (5)

That our Lord had in view the horrors which were to befall the Jews in the siege, and not any subsequent events it the end of time, is perfectly clear from the closing words of ver. 21-' No, nor ever shall be.'
(c) The disciples warned against false prophets.

MATT. xxiv. 23-28.
Then if any man shall say unto you, Lo, here is Christ, or there; believe it not. For there shall arise false Christs, and false prophets, and shall shew great signs and wonders; insomuch that, if it were possible, they shall deceive the very elect. Behold, I have told you before. Wherefore if they shall say unto you, Behold, he is in the desert; go not forth: behold, he is in the secret chambers; believe it not. For as the lightning cometh out of the east, and shineth even unto the west; so shall also the coming of the Son of man be. For wheresoever the carcase is, there will the eagles be gathered together.

Mark xiii. 21-23.
And then if any man shall say to you, Lo, here is Christ; or, lo, he is there; believe him not: For false Christs and false prophets shall rise, and shall shew signs and wonders, to seduce, if it were possible, even the elect. But take ye heed: behold, I have foretold you all things.

As yet we have found no break in the continuity of the discourse, - not the faintest indication that any transition has taken place to any other subject or any other period. The narrative is perfectly homogeneous and consecutive, and flows on without diverging to the right hand or to the left.

The same is equally true with respect to the section now before us. The very first word is indicative of continuity Then [To,te] rid every succeeding word is plainly addressed to the disciples themselves, for their personal warning and guidance. It is clear that our Lord gives them intimation of what would shortly come to pass, or at least what they might live to witness with their own eyes. It is a vivid representation of what actually occurred in the last days of the

Jewish commonwealth. The unhappy Jews, and especially the people of Jerusalem, were buoyed up with false hopes by the specious impostors who infested the land and brought ruin upon their miserable dupes. Such was the infatuation produced by the boasting pretensions of these impostors, that, as we learn from Josephus, when the temple was actually in flames a vast multitude of the deluded people fell victims to their credulity. The Jewish historian states:
' Of so great a multitude, not one escaped. Their destruction Was caused by a false prophet, who hall on that day proclaimed to those remaining in the city, that "God commanded them to go up to the temple, there to receive the signs of their deliverance." There were at this time many prophets suborned by the tyrants to delude the people, by bidding them wait for help from God, in order that there might be less desertion, and that those who were above fear and control might be encouraged by hope. Under calamities man readily yields to persuasion but when the deceiver pictures to him deliverance from pressing evils, then the sufferer is wholly influenced by hope. Thus it was that the impostors and pretended messengers of heaven at that **time beguiled the** wretched people., (6)

Our Lord forewarns His disciples that His coming to that judgment- scene would be conspicuous and sudden as the lightning-flash, which reveals itself and seems to be everywhere at the, same moment. 'For,' He adds, ' wheresoever the carcase is, there will the eagles be gathered together; that is, wherever the guilty and devoted children of Israel were found, there the destroying ministers of wrath, the Roman legions, -would overwhelm them.
(d) The arrival of the 'end,' or the catastrophe of Jerusalem.

MATT. xxiv. 29 31.	Mark xiii. 24-27	Luke x xi. 25-28.
Immediately after the tribulation of those days shall the sun be darkened, and the moon shall not give her light, and the stars shall fall from heaven, and the powers of the heavens shall be shaken:	But in those days, after that tribulation, the sun shall be darkened, and the moon shall not give her light, And the stars of heaven shall fall, and the powers that are in heaven shall be shaken.	And there shall be signs in the sun, and in the moon, and in the stars; and upon the earth distress of nations, with perplexity; the sea and the waves roaring; Men's hearts failing them for fear, and for looking after those things which are coming on the earth: for the powers of heaven shall be shaken.
And then shall appear the sign of the Son of man in heaven: and then shall all the tribes of the earth mourn, and they shall see the Son of man coming in the clouds of heaven with power and great glory. And he shall send his angels with a great sound of a trumpet, and they shall gather together his elect from the four winds, from one end of heaven to the other.	And then shall they see the Son of man coming in the clouds with great power and glory.	And then shall they see the Son of man coming in a cloud with power and great glory. And when these things begin to come to pass, then look up, and lift up your heads; for your redemption draweth nigh.
	And then shall he send his angels, and shall gather together his elect from the four winds, from the uttermost part of the earth to the uttermost part of heaven.	

Here also the phraseology absolutely forbids the idea of any transition from the. subject in hand to another. There is nothing to indicate that the scene has shifted, or a new topic been introduced. The section before, us connects itself most distinctly with the ' great tribulation' spoken of in ver. 21 of Matt. xxiv., and it is inadmissible to suppose any interval of time in the face of the adverb ' immediately ' But the scene of the 'great tribulation' is undeniably Jerusalem and Judea (ver. 15, 16), so that no break in the subject of the discourse is allowable. Again, in ver. 30, we read that *'all the tribes of the land* shall mourn,' referring evidently to the population of the land of Judea; and nothing can be more forced and unnatural than to make it include, as Lange does, 'all the races and peoples' of the globe. The restricted sense of the word (gh) [=land] in the New Testament is common; and when connected, as it is here, with the word *'tribes'*, its limitation to the land of Israel is obvious. This is the view adopted by Dr. Campbell and Moses Stuart, and it is indeed self- evident. We find a similar expression in Zech. xii. 12--'All the families [tribes] of the land,'- where its restricted sense is obvious and undisputed. The two passages are in fact exactly parallel, and nothing could be more misleading than to understand the phrase as including 'all the races of the earth.' The structure of the discourse, then, inflexibly resists the supposition of a change of subject. Time, place, circumstances, all continue the same. It is therefore with unfeigned wonder that we find Dean Alford commenting in the following fashion: ' All the difficulty which this word [immediately - e.uqe,wj] has been supposed to involve has arisen from confounding, the fulfillment of the prophecy with it's ultimate one. The important insertion ver. 23,24, in Luke xxi.. shows us that be " tribulation " [qliyij] includes o.rgh. e,n tw/ law tou,tw (wrath upon this people), which is yet being inflicted, and the treading down of Jerusalem by the Gentiles, still going on; and immediately after *that tribulation,* which shall happen *when the cup of Gentile iniquity is full,* and *when this gospel shall have hem preached it all the world for a witness, and rejected by the Gentiles,* shall the coming of the, Lord Himself happen. . . . (The expression in Mark is equally indicative of a considerable interval -- in those days after that tribulation.) The fact of His coming and its attendant circumstances being known to Him, but the exact time unknown, He speaks *without regard to the interval,* which would be, employed in His waiting till all things are put under His feet,' etc. (7)

It may be said that in this comment there are almost as many errors as words. Indeed, it is not the explanation of a prophecy so much as an independent prophecy of the commentator himself. First, there is the groundless hypothesis of it double sense, it *partial* and an *ultimate* fulfilment, for which there is no foundation in the text, but which is a mere arbitrary and gratuitous supposition. Next, we have it 'tribulation,' not *'shortened,'* as the Lord declares, but *protracted* so as be 'still going on' in the present day. Then the word 'immediately ' is made to refer to a period not yet come, so that between ver. 28 and ver. 29, where the unassisted eye can perceive no trace of any line of transition, the critic intercalates an immense period of more than eighteen centuries, with the possibility of an indefinite duration in addition. Still further we have an implied contradiction of St. Paul's statement that the gospel was preached 'in all the world' (Col. i. v. 23), and the assumption that the gospel is to be rejected by the Gentiles. Then the commentator finds that St. Mark suggests a 'considerable interval,' whereas he expressly says In *those very days* after that tribulation' [en ekeinaij taij hmeraij meta thn qliyin ekeinhn] -precluding the possibility of any interval at all, and lastly we have what appears like an apology for the veracity of the prediction, on the ground that our Lord, not, knowing the exact time when His coming would take place, ' speaks without regard to the, interval,' etc.

It is obvious, that if this is the way in which Scripture is to be interpreted, the ordinary laws of exegesis must be thrown aside as useless. He is the best interpreter who is the boldest guesser. Is there any ancient book which a grammarian would treat after this fashion? Would it not be pronounced intolerable and uncritical if such liberties were taken with Homer or Plato? Would it not have been a mockery to propound such riddles to the disciples as an answer to their question, 'When shall these things be?

How could they know of *partial* and *ultimate* fulfilments, and double senses? and what effect could be produced in their minds, but titter perplexity and bewilderment? We cannot help protesting against such treatment of the words of Scripture, as not only unscholarly and uncritical, but in the highest degree presumptuous and irreverent.

But, it is answered, the character of our Lord's language in this passage necessitates. As application to a grand and awful catastrophe which is still future, and can be properly understood of nothing less than the total dissolution of the fabric of the universe, and the mid of all things. How can any one pretend it is said, that the sun has been darkened, that the moon has withdrawn her light, that the stars have fallen from heaven, that the Son of man has been seen coming in the clouds of heaven with power and great glory? Did such phenomena occur at the destruction of Jerusalem, or can they apply to anything else than the Enid consummation of all things?

To argue in this strain is to lose sight of the very nature and genius of prophecy. Symbol and metaphor belong to the grammar of prophecy, as every reader of the Old Testament prophets must know. Is it not reasonable that the doom of Jerusalem should be depicted in language as glowing and rhetorical as the destruction of Babylon, or Bozrah, or Tyre? How then does the prophet Isaiah de scribe the downfall of Babylon?

'Behold the day of the Lord cometh, cruel tooth with wrath and fierce anger, to lay the land desolate: and he shall destroy the sinners thereof out of a. For Me skin of heaven and the constellations thereof shall not their light: the sun shall be darkened in his going forth, awl /he moon shall not cause her light to shine. . . . I will shake the heavens, and the earth shall remove out of her place' (Isa. xiii. 9. 10, 13).

It will at once be seen that the imagery employed in this passage is almost identical with that of our Lord. If these symbols therefore were proper to represent the fall of Babylon why should they be improper to set forth a still greater catastrophe -- the destruction of Jerusalem?

Take another example. The prophet Isaiah announces the desolation of Bozrah, the capital of Edom, in the following language:

' The mountains shall be melted with the blood of the slain. . . . All the host of heaven shall be dissolved and the heavens shall be rolled together as a scroll: and all their host shall fall down, as the leaf falleth off from my vine, and as a falling fig from the fig-tree. For my sword shall be bathed in heaven: behold it - shall come down upon Idumea,' etc. (Isa. xxxiv. 4, 5.)

Here again we have the very imagery **used by our Lord in His** prophetic discourse; And if the fate of Bozrah might properly be described in language so lofty, why should it be thought extravagant to employ similar terms in describing the fate of Jerusalem?

Again, the prophet Micah speaks of a 'coming of the Lord ' to judge and punish Samaria and Jerusalem -- a coming to judgment which had unquestionably taken place long before our Saviour's time, -- and in what magnificent diction does he represent this scene!

'Behold, *the Lord cometh* forth out of his place, *and* will *come down,* and tread upon the high Oar, of the earth. And *the mountains shall be molten under him, and the valleys shall be as wax before the fire, and as Me waters that arc poured down a steep place' (Micah i. 3, 4).*

It would be easy to multiply examples of this characteristic quality of prophetic diction. Prophecy is of the nature of poetry, and depicts events, not in the prosaic style of the historian, but in the glowing imagery of the poet. Add to this that the Bible does not speak with the cold logical correctness of the Western peoples, but with the tropical fervour of the, gorgeous East. Yet it would be improper to call such language extravagant or overcharged. The moral grandeur of the events which such symbols represent may be most fitly set forth by convulsion; and cataclysms in the natural world. Nor is it necessary to construct a grammar of symbolology and End an analogue for every sacred hieroglyphic, by which to translate each particular metaphor into its proper equivalent, for this would be to turn prophecy into allegory. The following observations on the figurative language of Scripture are judicious. What is grand in nature is used to express what is dignified and important among men, ---the heavenly bodies, mountains, stately trees, kingdoms or those in authority. . . . Political changes are represented by earthquakes, tempests, eclipses, the turning of waters and seas into blood.' (8)

The conclusion then to which we are irresistibly led, is, that the imagery employed by our lord in His prophetic discourse is not inappropriate to the dissolution of the Jewish state and polity which took place at the destruction of Jerusalem. It is appropriate, both as it is in keeping with the acknowledged style of the ancient prophets, and also because the moral grandeur of the event is such as to justify the use of such language in this particular case.

But we may go further than this, and affirm that it is not only appropriate as applied to the destruction of Jerusalem, but that this is its true and exclusive application. We find no vestige of an intimation that our Lord had any ulterior and occult signification in view. But we do find that there is scarcely a feature in this sublime and awful description which He Himself had not already anticipated, and fixed in its application to a particular event and a particular time. Let the reader carefully compare the description in the passage before us, of 'the Son of man coming in the clouds of heaven, with power and great glory' (Matt. xxiv. 30) (9), with our Lord's declaration (Matt. xvi. 27)- 'For the Son of man shall come in the glory of his Father with his angels,'- an event which He expressly affirms would be witnessed by some of His disciples then living. Again, the sending forth of His angels to gather together His elect, corresponds exactly with the representation of what would take place in the 'harvest,' at the end of the won, as described in the parables of the tares and the dragnet (Matt. xii. 41-50)- 'The Son of man shall send forth his angels, and they shall gather out of his kingdom all things that offend, and them which do iniquity.' 'So shall it be at the end of the age [won]: the angels shall come forth, and sever the wicked from among the just, and shall cast them into the furnace of fire.' Here the prophecy and the parable represent the self- same scene, the self-same period: they alike speak of the close of the won or age, not of the end of the world, or material universe; and they alike speak of that great judicial epoch as *at hand.* How plainly does St. Luke, in his record of the prophecy on the Mount of Olives, represent the great catastrophe as falling within the lifetime of the disciples: 'And when these things begin to come to pass, then look up, and lift up your heads; for your redemption draweth nigh' (Luke xxi. 28). Were not these words spoken to the disciples, who listened to the discourse? Did they not apply to them? Is there anywhere even a suspicion that they were meant for another audience, thousands of years distant, and not for the eager group who drank in the words of Jesus? Surely such a hypothesis carries its own refutation in its very front.

But, its if to preclude even the possibility of misconception or mistake, our Lord in the next paragraph draws around His prophecy a line so plain and palpable, shutting it wholly within a limit so definite and distinct, that it ought to be decisive of the whole question.

(e) The Parousia to take place before the passing away of the existing generation.

MATT. xxiv. 32-31.	MARK xiii. 28-30.	LUKE xxi. 29-32.
Now learn a parable of the fig tree; When his branch is yet tender, and putteth forth leaves, ye know that summer is nigh: So likewise ye, when ye shall see all these things, know that it is near, even at the doors.	Now learn a parable of the fig tree; When her branch is yet tender, and putteth forth leaves, ye know that summer is near: So ye in like manner, when ye shall see these things come to pass, know that it is nigh, even at the doors.	And he spake to them a parable; Behold the fig tree, and all the trees; When they now shoot forth, ye see and know of your own selves that summer is now nigh at hand. So likewise ye, when ye see these things come to pass, know ye that the kingdom of God is nigh at hand.
Verily I say unto you, This generation shall not pass, till all these things be fulfilled.	Verily I say unto you, that this generation shall not pass, till all these things be done.	Verily I say unto you, This generation shall not pass away, till all be fulfilled.

Words have no meaning if this language, uttered on so solemn an occasion, and so precise and express in its import, does not affirm the near approach of the great event which occupies the -whole discourse of our Lord. First, the parable of the fig-tree intimates that as the buds on the trees betoken the near approach of summer, so the signs which He had just specified would betoken that the predicted consummation was at hand. They, the disciples to whom He was speaking, were to see them, and when they saw them to recognise that the end *was ' near, even at the doors.'* Next, our Lord sums up with an affirmation calculated to remove every vestige of doubt or uncertainty,

'VERILY I SAY UNTO YOU, THIS GENERATION SHALL NOT PASS, TILL ALL THESE THINGS BE FULFILLED.'

One would reasonably suppose that after a note of time so clear and express there could not be room for controversy. Our Lord Himself has settled the question. Ninety-nine persons in every hundred would undoubtedly understand His words as meaning that the predicted catastrophe would fall within the limits of the lifetime of the existing generation. Not that *all* would probably live to witness it, but that *most* or many would. There can be no question that this would be the interpretation which the disciples would place upon the words. Unless, therefore, our Lord intended to mystify His disciples, He gave them plainly to understand that His coining, the judgment of the Jewish nation, and the close of the age, would come to pass before the existing generation had -wholly passed away, and within the limits of their own lifetime. This, as we have already seen, was no new idea, but one which on several occasions He had previously expressed.

Far, however, from accepting this decision of our Lord as final, the commentators have violently resisted that which seems the natural and common-sense meaning of His words. They have insisted that because the events predicted did Hot so come, to pass in that generation, therefore the word *generation (genea.)* cannot possibly mean, what it is usually understood to mean, the people of that particular age or period, the contemporaries of our Lord. To affirm that these things did not conic to pass is to beg the question, and something more.

But we submit that it is the business of grammarians not to be apprehensive of possible consequences, but to settle the true meaning of words. Our Lord's predictions may be safely left to take care of themselves; it is for us to try to understand them.

It is contended by many that in this place the word *genea.* should be rendered 'race, or *nation; '* and that our Lord's words mean no more than that the Jewish race or nation Should Hot pass away, or perish, until the predictions which He had just uttered had come to pass. This is the meaning which Lange, Stier, Alford, and many other expositors attach to the word, and it is maintained with conspicuous ability and copious learning by Dorner in his tractate, ' Do Oratione Christi Eschatologica.' It is true, no doubt, that the word *genea,* like most others, has different shades of meaning, and that sometimes, in the Septuagint and in classic authors it may refer to a nation or a race. But we think that it is demonstrable without any shadow of doubt that the expression ' this *generation,'* so often employed by our Lord, always refers solely and exclusively to *His contemporaries, the Jewish people of His own period.* It might safely be left to the candid judgment of every reader, whether a Greek Scholar or not, whether this is Hot so: but as the point is one of great importance, it may be desirable to adduce the proofs of this assertion.

1. In our Lord's final address to the people, delivered on the same day as this discourse on the Mount of Olives, He declared, ' All these things shall come upon *this generation* ' (Matt xxiii. 36). No commentator has ever proposed to understand this as referring to any other than the *existing* generation.

2. 'Whereunto shall I liken this generation?' (Matt. xi. 16.) Here it is admitted by Lange and Stier that the word refers to ' the *then existing last generation of Israel ' (Lange, in loc.* Stier, vol ii. 98).

3. 'An evil and adulterous *generation* seeketh after a sign.' 'The men of Nineveh shall rise up in the judgment with *this generation.' ' The* Queen of the South shall rise up in the judgment with *this generation.' '* Even so shall it be also unto *this* wicked *generation ' (Matt.* xii. 39, 41, 42, 45).

In these four passages Dorner endeavours to make out That our Lord is not speaking of His contemporaries, the men of His own period, ' For,' be says, 'the Gentiles ' (the Ninevites and the Queen of the South) 'are opposed to the Jews; therefore *"this generation "' [h, genea.* a[uth] 'must signify the *nation* or *race* of the Jews' (Dorner, Orat. Chr. Esch., p. 81). His argument, however, is not convincing. Surely the generation which sought after a sign was the *then existing generation; and* can it be supposed that it was against any other generation than that which had resisted such preaching as that of John the Baptist and of Christ that the Gentiles were to rise up in the judgment? There is only one interpretation of our Lord's language possible, and it is that which refers His words to His own perverse and unbelieving contemporaries.

4. 'That the blood of all the prophets . . . may be required of *this generation.' ' It* shall be required of *this generation ' (Luke* xi. 50, 51).

Here Dorner himself admits that it is of *the existing generation (hoc ipsum hominum avum)* that these words are spoken (p. 41).

5. 'Whosoever shall be ashamed of me in *this* adulterous and sinful *generation'* (Mark viii. 38).

6. ' The Son of man must be rejected of *this generation* (Luke xvii. 25). It is only necessary to quote these passages in order to determine their sole reference to the particular generation that rejected the Messiah.

These are all the examples in which the expression 'this *generation*' occurs in the sayings of our Lord, and they establish beyond all reasonable question the reference of the words in the important declaration now before us. But suppose that we were to adopt the rendering proposed, and take genea as meaning a *race,* what point or significance would there be in the prediction then? Can any one believe that the assertion so solemnly made by our Lord, 'Verily I say unto you,' etc., amounts to no more than this, 'The Hebrew race shall not become extinct till all these things be fulfilled '? Imagine a prophet in our own times predicting a great catastrophe in which London would be destroyed, St. Paul's and the Houses of Parliament levelled with the ground, and a fearful slaughter of the inhabitants be perpetrated; and that when asked, 'When shall these things come to pass? ' he should reply, 'The Anglo-Saxon race shall not become extinct till all these things be fulfilled'! Would this be a satisfactory answer? Would not such an answer be considered derogatory to the prophet, and an affront to his hearers? Would they not have reason to say, 'It is safe prophesying when the event is placed at an interminable distance! ' But the bare supposition of such a sense in our Lord's prediction shows itself to be a *reductio ad absurdum.* Was it for this that the disciples were to wait and watch? Was this the lesson son that the budding fig- tree taught? Was it not until the Jewish race was about to become extinct that they were to 'look up, and lift up their beads '? Such a hypothesis is its own refutation.

We fall back, therefore, upon the only tenable and possible interpretation, and understand our Lord to mean, what in so many words He says, that *the events specified in His prediction would assuredly come to pass before the existing generation had wholly passed away.* This is the only interpretation which the words will bear; every other involves a wresting of language, and a violence to the understanding. Besides, it is in harmony with the uniform teaching of our Saviour. He had long before assured His disciples that some of them should live to witness His return in glory (Matt. xvi. 27, 28).

He had told them that before they had completed their apostolic mission to the cities of Israel the Son of man should come (Matt. x. 23). H**e had declared that all** the blood shed upon the earth, from the blood of Abel to the blood of Zacharias, should be required of *that generation* (Matt. xxiii. 35, 36). It was, therefore, of *that generation* that He spoke. It should never be forgotten that there was a specialty about that generation. It was the last and worst of all the generations of Israel, inheriting the guilt of all its predecessors, and was about to be visited with signal and unparalleled judgments. Whether the predicted catastrophe came to pass is another question, which will come to be considered in its proper place. (10)

Other interpretations which have been suggested, as 'the human race,' 'the generation of the righteous,' and 'the generation of the wicked,' do not require consideration.

A word or two may be needful respecting the length of time covered by a generation. Of course, it is not an exact measure of time, like a decade or a century, but has a certain indefiniteness or elasticity, yet within certain limits, say between thirty and forty years. In the book of Numbers we find that the generation which provoked the Lord to exclude them from the land of Canaan, and were doomed to fall in the wilderness, were to die out in the space of forty years. In the ninety-fifth psalm we read, ' Forty years long was I grieved with this generation.' In the genealogical table given by St. Matthew we have data for estimating the length of a generation. We there find that 'from the carrying" away into Babylon unto Christ are fourteen generations' (Matt. 1. 17). Now the date of the captivity, in the reign of Zedekiah, is said to be circa B.C. 586, which, divided by fourteen, gives forty-one years and a fraction as the average length of each generation. The Jewish war under Nero broke Out A.D. 66, and assuming our Lord to have been about thirty-three years of age at the time of His crucifixion, this would give a space of about thirty-three years when the signs betokening the approach of 'the end' would ' begin to come to pass.' The destruction of the temple and city of Jerusalem took place in September A.D. 70, that is, about thirty-seven years after the prophecy of the Mount of Olives, a space of time that amply satisfies the requirements of the case. It is neither so short as to make it inappropriate to say, 'This generation shall not pass away,' etc., nor so long as to throw it beyond the lifetime of many who might have seen and heard the Saviour, or of the disciples themselves.

'That generation' would indeed be then passing away, but it would not have wholly passed.

(f) Certainty of the consummation, yet uncertainty of its precise date.

MATT. xxiv. 35, 36.	MARK xiii. 31, 32.	Luke xxi. 33.
Heaven and earth shall pass away, but my words shall not pass away. But of that day and hour knoweth no man, no, not the angels of heaven, but my Father only.	Heaven and earth shall pass away: but my words shall not pass away. But of that day and that hour knoweth no man, no, not the angels which are in heaven, neither the Son, but the Father.	Heaven and earth shall pass away: but my words shall not pass away.

Although our Lord has defined the limits of the time within which the predicted consummation would take place, yet a certain amount of indefiniteness remains respecting the moment of its arrival. He does not specify the exact date, the 'hour, or the day,' or even the month or the year. This does not mean that the whole question of time is left unsettled: it refers merely to the precise date. The consummation was to fall within the term of the existing generation, but the particular hour when the knell of doom should sound was not revealed to man, nor angel, nor (what is stranger still) to the Son of man Himself. It was the secret which the Father kept 'in His own power.' There were doubtless sufficient reasons for this reserve. To have specified 'the day and the hour'-to have said, 'In the seven and-thirtieth year, in the sixth month and the eighth day of the month, the city shall be taken and the temple burnt with fire '-would not only have been inconsistent with the manner of prophecy, but would have taken away one of the strongest inducements to constant watchfulness and prayer-the uncertainty of the precise time.

(g) Suddenness of the Parousia, and calls to watchfulness.

Matt. xxiv. 37-42.	Luke xvii. 26-37.
But as the days of Noe were, so shall also the coming of the Son of man be. For as in the days that were before the flood they were eating and drinking, marrying and giving in marriage, until the day that Noe entered into the ark, And knew not until the flood came, and took them all away; so shall also the coming of the Son of man be. Then shall two be in the field; the one shall be taken, and the other left. Two women shall be grinding at the mill; the one shall be taken, and the other left.	And as it was in the days of Noe, so shall it be also in the days of the Son of man. They did eat, they drank, they married wives, they were given in marriage, until the day that Noe entered into the ark, and the flood came, and destroyed them all. Likewise also as it was in the days of Lot; they did eat, they drank, they bought, they sold, they planted, they builded; But the same day that Lot went out of Sodom it rained fire and brimstone from heaven, and destroyed them all. Even thus shall it be in the day when the Son of man is revealed. In that day, he which shall be upon the housetop, and his stuff in the house, let him not come down to take it away: and he that is in the field, let him likewise not return back. Remember Lot's wife. Whosoever shall seek to save his life shall lose it; and whosoever shall lose his life shall preserve it. I tell you, in that night there shall be two men in one bed; the one shall be taken, and the other shall be left. Two women shall be grinding together; the one shall be taken, and the other left. Two men shall be in the field; the one shall be taken, and the other left. And they answered and said unto him, Where, Lord? And he said unto them, Wheresoever the body is, thither will the eagles be gathered together.

MATT. xxiv. 42.	Mark xiii. 33-5.	Luke xxi. 34-6.
	' Take ye heed, watch and pray: for ye know not when the time is.	'And take heed to yourselves, lest at any time your hearts be overcharged with surfeiting, and drunkenness, and cares of this life, and so that day come upon you unawares. For as a snare shall it come on all them that dwell on the face of the whole earth. [land].
'Watch therefore: for ye know not what hour your Lord doth come. '	'Watch ye therefore: for ye know not when the master of the house cometh, at even, or at midnight, or at the cockcrowing, or in the morning: lest coming suddenly he find you sleeping. And what I say unto you, I say unto all, Watch.'	'Watch ye therefore, and pray always, that ye may be accounted worthy to escape all these things that shall come to pass, and to stand before the Son of man. '

All the representations given by our Lord of the coming catastrophe and its concomitant events imply that it would take men by surprise. As the deluge came suddenly upon the antediluvians, and the storm of fire and brimstone on the cities of the plain, so the final catastrophe would overtake Jerusalem and Judea at an unexpected hour, when the business and the pleasure of life occupied men's hands and hearts. In Luke xvii. we have the fullest record of our Lord's discourse on this point. Whether the passage in St. Luke has been transposed by him from its original connection, or whether our Lord uttered the same words on separate occasions, does not particularly concern us here. Neander is of opinion that 'Luke gives the natural connection of these words,' and that in St. Matthew 'they are placed with many other similar passages referring to the last crisis.' [11] We doubt this; but, waiving this question, one thing is indubitable, viz., that both St. Matthew and St. Luke describe the same thing, the self-same period, the self-same catastrophe.

It is surprising to find Alford asserting, in regard to the passage in St. Luke, ' There is not a word in all this of the destruction of Jerusalem.' It would be more correct to say,' ' Every word here is of the destruction of Jerusalem. Observe the note of *time* so distinctly marked by our Lord: ' But first must he suffer many things, and be rejected of *this generation'* (Luke xvii. 25). What other catastrophe belongs to the period of that generation which could fitly be compared with the destruction of the antediluvian world by a flood of water, and the destruction of Sodom and Gomorrah by a deluge of fire?

From the certainty and suddenness of the approaching consummation our Lord draws the lesson which He impresses on His disciples, -the necessity for vigilance. Here He first utters the admonition which from that time never ceased to be the watchword of His disciples throughout the apostolic age, 'Watch and pray! ' We shall find how constantly and urgently this call was addressed by the Apostles to the faithful in their day, and how it is continually repeated, down to the latest moment that we catch the sound of an apostolic -voice. This watchfulness was essential to the safety of the followers **of Christ, for so sudden would be the catastrophe** that it would overtake the unready and unwary, as birds that are caught in a net. 'For as a snare shall it come on all them that dwell on the face of the whole land (pashj thj ghj) - words which plainly intimate the local character of the event.

We have a striking commentary on this passage in the history of Josephus. Accounting for the prodigious numbers slaughtered in the siege of Jerusalem, -one million one hundred thousand, -he says, 'Of these the greater proportion were of Jewish blood, though not natives of the place. Having assembled from the whole country for the feast of unleavened bread, *they were suddenly hemmed in by the war.* On this occasion *the whole nation had been shut up as in a prison, by fate; and the war encircled the city when it was crowded with,* men.' (12) A more exact verification of our Lord's prediction (Luke xxi. 35) it is impossible to conceive.

In all this we observe the continuation of that direct personal address which proves that our Lord was speaking to His disciples of that in which they were personally concerned. There is not the faintest hint that there was an undercurrent of meaning in His words, and that when He said 'Jerusalem,' and 'this generation,' and 'ye,' He meant ' the world,' and ' distant ages,' and 'disciples yet unborn.'

At this point St. Mark and St. Luke close their record of the prophecy on the Mount of Olives, and it cannot be denied that their ending here is natural and appropriate. We have in the Gospel of St. Matthew, however, a series of parables appended to our Lord's discourse, such as He was accustomed to employ in teaching the people. It strikes us as somewhat singular that our Lord should speak in parables to His disciples, especially on such an occasion; and there is not a little to be said for the opinion of Neander, that ' it was peculiar to the editor of our Greek Matthew to arrange together congenial sayings of Christ, though uttered at different times and in different relations. We need not therefore wonder if we find it impossible to draw the lines of distinction in this discourse with entire accuracy; nor need such It result lead us to forced interpretations, inconsistent with truth, and with the love of truth. It is much easier to make such distinctions in Luke's account (chap. xxi.), though even that is not without its difficulties. In comparing Matthew and Luke together, however, we can trace the origin of most of these difficulties to the blending of different portions together, when the discourses of Christ were arranged in collections.' (13)

But without discussing this question, it is very evident that the parables recorded by St. Matthew in connection with this discourse, even if not originally spoken on this particular occasion, are strictly germane to the subject; while, if this be their true place in the narrative, their bearing on the matter in hand is still more close and intimate.

We now proceed to consider the parables and parabolic sayings of our Lord recorded in connection with this prophecy, chiefly by St. Matthew.

(h) The disciples warned of the suddenness of the Parousia.
Parable of the Goodman of the House.

Matt. xxiv. 43-51.	Mark xiii. 34-37.	Luke xii. 39-46.
But know this, that if the goodman of the house had known in what watch the thief would come, he would have watched, and would not have suffered his house to be broken up. Therefore be ye also ready: for in such an hour as ye think not the Son of man cometh. Who then is a faithful and wise servant, whom his lord hath made ruler over his household, to give them meat in due season? Blessed is that servant, whom his lord when he cometh shall find so doing. Verily I say unto you, That he shall make him ruler over all his goods.	'For the Son of man is as a man taking a far journey, who left his house, and gave authority to his servants, and to every man his work, and commanded the porter to watch.	'And this know, that if the goodman of the house had known what hour the thief would come, he would have watched, and not have suffered his house to be broken through. Be ye therefore ready also: for the Son of man cometh at an hour when ye think not. Then Peter said unto him, Lord, speakest thou this parable unto us, or even to all? And the Lord said, Who then is that faithful and wise steward, whom his lord shall make ruler over his household, to give them their portion of meat in due season? Blessed is that serv-

'But and if that evil servant shall say in his heart, My lord delayeth his coming; And shall begin to smite his fellowservants, and to eat and drink with the drunken; The lord of that servant shall come in a day when he looketh not for him, and in an hour that he is not aware of, And shall cut him asunder, and appoint him his portion with the hypocrites: there shall be weeping and gnashing of teeth.

'Watch ye therefore: for ye know not when the master of the house cometh, at even, or at midnight, or at the cock-crowing, or in the morning: Lest coming suddenly he find you sleeping. And what I say unto you I say unto all, Watch.

ant, whom his lord when he cometh shall find so doing. Of a truth I say unto you, that he will make him ruler over all that he hath.

'But and if that servant say in his heart, My lord delayeth his coming; and shall begin to beat the menservants and maidens, and to eat and drink, and to be drunken; The lord of that servant will come in a day when he looketh not for him, and at an hour when he is not aware, and will cut him in sunder, and will appoint him his portion with the un-believers.

It will be seen that this parabolic saying of our Lord is recorded in quite different connections by St. Matthew and St. Luke. The verbal resemblance, however, is too exact to render it probable that it was spoken on two different occasions. The slightest attention will satisfy the reader that St. Luke's report is the more full and circumstantial, and that be assigns to it its true chronological position. This appears from the fact that the question of St. Peter, recorded only by St. Luke, gave rise to the concluding remarks of our Lord, which, as given by St. Matthew without this connecting link, seem somewhat incoherent and abrupt. Besides, we can scarcely suppose that St. Peter, conversing in private with only three other disciples in company with the Lord, would ask, 'Speakest thou this parable to us, or even to all? ' --a question which was most natural when, as St. Luke tells us, Jesus was speaking to His disciples in the presence of a great multitude (Luke xii. 1). It is worthy of notice also that in Mark xiii. 34-37, where we can detect evident traces of this parable, the question of St. Peter is distinctly answered, 'What I say unto you, I say unto all, Watch;' a statement which would be out of place when our Lord was speaking to four persons, but quite appropriate when speaking to a multitude.

There is no impropriety, therefore, in supposing that St. Matthew, perceiving the words of Jesus, spoken on another occasion, to be admirably illustrative of the necessity for watchfulness in view of the Lord's coming, inserted them in this eschatological discourse. Stier suggests that St. Mark gives a short abridgment of Matt. xxiv. 43, with the two parables of the servant, Matt. xxiv. 45-51 and xxv. 14, and even with a slight echo of the parable of the virgins.' [14] We have no more reason to require strict chronological arrangement in the Evangelists than strictly -verbatim reports: neither the one nor the other entered into their plan.

But what is chiefly important for us is the bearing of this parable, if it may be so called, of the goodman of the house watching against the midnight thief, on the preceding discourse of our Lord. Nothing can be more evident than that it is wrought into the very warp and woof of that discourse. There is Do introduction of a new topic at the forty- third verse of the twenty-fourth chapter of St. Matthew: no transition to another catastrophe, or another coming different from those of which He had all along been speaking. There is no hiatus, no break, in the continuity of the discourse; no indication of passing away from the grand event which engrossed the thoughts of the disciples to another in the far distant futurity. It seems incredible that any critical judgment should select Matt. xxiv. 43 as the commencement of a new subject of discourse. Yet this is done by Dr. Ed. Robinson, who says, ' Our Lord here makes a transition, and proceeds to speak of his final coming at the day of judgment. This appears from the fact that the matter of these sections is added by Matthew after Mark and Luke have ended their parallel reports relative to the Jewish catastrophe; and Matthew here commences, with ver. 43, the discourse which Luke has given on another occasion, Luke xii. 39, &c." [15] But there is not the faintest shadow of any transition. The finest instrument cannot draw a dividing line between the parts of the discourse, and assign one portion to the judgment of the Jewish nation and another to the judgment of the human race. There is not transition, but continuation, at ver. 43. Nothing can be more consecutive and concatenated. 'Watch therefore,' says our Lord to His disciples in ver. 42, 'for ye know not what hour your Lord doth come.' 'Therefore, be ye also ready,' He says in ver. 44, ' for in such an hour as ye think not the Son of man cometh.' The suggestion that a new topic, having reference to a totally different event, in a far distant age of time, is introduced here, is altogether arbitrary and groundless.

1. Jos. Antiq. bk. xx. x. xiii. § 5, 6.
2. Conybeare and Howson, Life and Epist. of St. Paul, c. iv
3. Jos. Antiq. bk. xviii. c. v, § 3
4. Traill's Jos. Jewish War, pref. ~ 4.
5. Traill's Jos. Jewish War, bk. vi. c. v. § 3

6. Traill's Jos. Jewish War, bk. vi. c. v. § 2
7. See Alford Gr. Test, Matt. xxiv. 29,
8. Angus's Bible Handbook p. 20 § i.
9. The phenomena described by our Lord as accompanying the Parousia (ver. 29), cannot be explained by the portents slid

prodigies alleged by Josephus to have preceded the capture of Jerusalem (Jewish War, bk. vi. c. v. § 3). That some at least of those portents actually appeared there seems no reason to doubt, and they serve to verify the prediction in Luke xxi. 11, -- 'Fearful sights and great signs shall there be from heaven.'

10. The note in Robinson's Harmony of the Four Gospels, part vii. § 128, is excellent. 'This generation,' etc. These words (genea) cannot be understood (as some have explained them) of the Jewish nation or the human race. The meaning is, that the men of that age should not all die (See Matt. xvi. 28, in § 74) before the prophecy would be accomplished, which began to come to pass thirty-seven years after its utterance in the destruction of Jerusalem,' etc. -

11. Life of Christ, c. xii. § 214, note.

12. Traill's Josephus, Jewish War, b. -vi. ch. ix. § § 3, 4

13. Life of Christ, § 254, Note.

14. Reden Jesu, vol. iii. p. 304

15. Harmony of the Four Gospels, § 129.

II. Our Lord's Answer to the Disciples, cont.:-

(i) The Parousia a time of judgment alike to the friends and the enemies of Christ.
Parable of the Wise and Foolish Virgins.

MATT. xxv. *Then shall the kingdom of heaven be likened unto ten virgins, which took their lamps, and went forth to meet the bridegroom. And five of them were wise, and five were foolish. They that were foolish took their lamps, and took no oil with them: but the wise took oil in their vessels with their lamps. While the bridegroom tarried, they all slumbered and slept. And at midnight there was a cry made, Behold, the bridegroom cometh; go ye out to meet him. Then all those virgins arose, and trimmed their lamps. And the foolish said unto the wise, Give us of your oil; for our lamps are gone out. But the wise answered, saying, Not so; lest there be not enough for us and you: but go ye rather to them that sell, and buy for yourselves. And while they went to buy, the bridegroom came; and they that were ready went in with him to the marriage; and the door was shut. Afterwards came also the other virgins, saying, Lord, Lord, open to us. But he answered and said, Verily I say unto you, I know you not. Watch therefore, for ye know neither the day nor the hour' [wherein the Son of man cometh].*

Almost all expositors suppose that Jerusalem and Israel now disappear wholly from the scene, and that our Lord refers exclusively to the final consummation of all things and the judgment of the human race. This supposed transition is rendered more easy to the English reader by a new chapter commencing at this point.

But has our Lord really dropped the subject with which He and His disciples had been hitherto occupied? Has He passed from the near and imminent to a far distant era, separated from His own time by hundreds and thousands of years? If it were so, we might surely expect some very distinct indication of the change of subject. But there is absolutely none. On the contrary, the supposition of a new theme being introduced by this parable is entirely forbidden by the express terms in which the parable opens and closes. it opens with a very explicit note of time,- *then, at that time.* There is no hiatus between the end of chap. xxiv. and the commencement of chap. xxv. The connecting link ' *then*' carries forward the discourse, and knits it into close connection as regards theme, time, and the persons addressed. This is further confirmed by the fact that the *moral* of the parable of the ten virgins is precisely the same as that of the good man of the house in the preceding chapter, viz. the necessity of watchfulness. The closing words,- 'Watch therefore, for ye know neither the day nor the hour,'- so evidently addressed to the disciples, are the very same which our Lord had already spoken in chap. xxiv. 42; so that in both passages the reference must be to the self-same event.

It does not come within our province to give a detailed exposition of this parable. There are theologians who find a mystery in every word: in the number ten, in the number five, in virginity, in lamps, in oil, etc. (See Lange *in loc.*) As Calvin sarcastically observes, 'Multum se torquent quidam, in lucernis, in vasis, in oleo.' Suffice it here to note the great lesson of the parable. It is the necessity for constant readiness and watchfulness for the sudden and speedy return of the Son of man. Unwatchfulness and unreadiness would involve the penalty which befell the foolish virgins, viz. exclusion from the marriage supper of the Lamb.

We find therefore in this parable an organic connection with the whole previous discourse of our Lord. It is still the same great theme of which He is speaking,- the consummation which was to take place within the limits of the existing generation, -- and concerning which the disciples expressed so natural an anxiety.

(k) The Parousia a time of judgment.
Parable of the Talents.

MATT. xxv. 14-30. -- ' For [the kingdom of heaven is] as a man travelling into a far country, who called his own servants, and delivered unto them his goods. And unto one he gave five talents, to another two, and to another one; to every man according to his several ability; and straightway took his journey. Then he that had received the five talents went and traded with the same, and made them other five talents. And likewise he that had received two, he also gained other two. But he that had received one went and digged in the earth, and hid his lord's money. After a long time the lord of those servants cometh, and reckoneth with them. And so he that had received five talents came and brought other five talents, saying, Lord, thou deliveredst unto me five talents: behold, I have gained beside them five talents more. His lord said unto him, Well done, thou good and faithful servant: thou hast been faithful over a few things, I Will make thee ruler over many things; enter thou into the joy of thy lord. He also that had received two talents came and said, Lord, thou deliveredst unto me two talents: behold, I have gained two other talents beside them. His lord said unto him, Well clone, good and faithful servant: thou hast been faithful over a few things, I win make thee ruler over many things; enter thou into the joy of thy lord. Then he which had received the one talent came and said, Lord, I knew thee that thou art an hard mail, reaping where thou hast not sown, and gathering where thou hast not strewed: and I was afraid, and went and hid thy talent in the earth: lo, there thou hast that is thine. His lord answered and said unto him, Thou wicked and slothful servant, thou knewest that I reap where I sowed not, and gather where I have not strewed; thou oughtest therefore to have put my money to the exchangers, and then at my coming I should have received mine own with usury. Take therefore the talent from him, and give it unto him which hath ten talents. For unto every one that hath shall be given, and he shall have abundance: but from him that hath not shall be taken away even that which he hath. And cast ye the. unprofitable servant into outer darkness: there shall be weeping and gnashing of teeth.'

In this parable we find an evident continuation of the same sub though presented in a somewhat different aspect. The moral of the preceding parable was *vigilance;* that of the present is *diligence.* It can hardly be said that a new element is introduced in this parable, for the representation of the coming of Christ as a time of judgment runs through the whole prophetic discourse of our Lord. It is this fact which gives point and urgency to the oft-reiterated call to watchfulness. Not only was it to be a time of judgment for Jerusalem and Israel, but even for the disciples of Christ themselves. They too were 'to stand before the Son of man.' There was danger lest 'that day' should come upon them unprepared and unaware. This association of judgment with the Parousia comes out in the parable of the good man of the house, and still more in that of the good and the evil. servants. It is yet more vividly expressed in the parable of the wise and foolish virgins, has greater prominence still in the parable of the talents; but it reaches the climax in the concluding parable, if it may be so called, of the sheep and the goats.

It is not necessary to enter into the details of the parable of the talents. Its leading features are simple and obvious. It contains a solemn warning to the servants of Christ to be faithful and diligent in the absence of their Lord. It points to a day when He would return and reckon with them. It sets forth the abundant recompense of the good and faithful, and the punishment of the unfaithful servant.

The point, however, which chiefly concerns us in this investigation is the relation of this parable to the preceding discourse. What can be more plain than the intimate connection between the one and the other? The connective particle 'for' in ver. 14 distinctly marks the continuation of the discourse. The theme is the same, the time is the same, the catastrophe is the same. Up to this point, therefore, we find no break, no change, no introduction of a different topic; all is continuous, homogeneous, one. Never for a moment has the discourse swerved from the great, all absorbing theme,- the approaching doom of the guilty city and nation, with the solemn events attendant thereon, all to take place within the period of that generation, and which the disciples, or some of them, would live to witness.

(1) The Parousia a time of judgment.

The Sheep and the Goats.

MATT. XXV. 31-46-' When the Son of man shall come in his glory and all the holy angels with him, then shall he sit upon the throne of his glory: and before him shall be gathered all [the] nations; and he shall separate them one from another, as a shepherd divideth his sheep from the goats; and he shalt set the sheep on his right hand, but the goats on the left.

'Then shall the King say unto them on his right hand, Come, ye blessed of my Father, inherit the kingdom prepared for you from the foundation of the world: for I was an hungered, and ye gave me meat: I was thirsty, and ye gave me drink: I was a stranger, and ye took Die in: naked, and ye clothed Die: I was sick, and ye visited me: I was in prison, and ye came unto me. Then shall the righteous answer him, saying, Lord, when saw we thee ,in hungered, and fed thee? or thirsty, and gave thee drink? When saw we thee a stranger, and took thee in? or naked, and clothed thee? Or when saw we thee sick, or in prison, and came unto thee? And the King shall answer and say unto them, Verily I say unto you, Inasmuch as ye have done it unto one of the least of these my brethren, ye have done it unto me.

'Then shall he say also unto them on the left hand Depart from me, ye cursed, into everlasting fire., prepared for the devil and his angels: for I was an hungered, and ye gave me no meat: I was thirsty, and ye gave me no drink: I was a stranger, and ye took me not in: naked, and ye clothed me not: sick, and in prison, and ye visited me not. Then shall they also answer him, saying, Lord, when saw we thee an hungered, or athirst, or a stranger, or naked, or sick, or in prison, and did not minister unto thee? Then shall he answer them, saying, Verily I say unto you, Inasmuch as ye did it not to one of the least of these, ye did it not to me. And these shall go away into everlasting punishment: but the righteous into life eternal.'

Up to this point we have found the discourse of Jesus on the Mount of Olives one connected and continuous prophecy, having sole reference to the great catastrophe impending over the Jewish nation, and which was to take place, according(, to our Lord's prediction, before the existing generation should pass away. Now, however, we encounter a passage which, in the opinion of almost all commentators, cannot be understood as referring to Jerusalem or Israel, but to the whole human race and the consummation of all things. If the *consensus* of expositors can establish an interpretation, no doubt this passage must be regarded as wholly quitting the subject of the disciples' interrogatory, and describing the last scene of all in this world's history.

It may be freely admitted that this parable, or parabolic description, has many points of difference from the preceding portion of our Lord's discourse. It seems to stand separate and distinct from the rest, without the connecting links which we have found in other sections. Still more, it seems to take a wider range than Jerusalem and Israel; it reads like the judgment, not of a nation, but of all nations; not of a city or a country, but of a world; not a passing crisis, but final consummation.

It is therefore with a deep sense of the difficulty of the task that we venture to impugn the interpretation of so many wise and good men, and to contend that the passage is not only an integral part of the prophecy, but also belongs wholly to the subject of our Lord's discourse,-- the judgment of Israel and the end of the [Jewish] age.

1. This parable, though in our English version standing apart and unconnected with the context, is really connected by a very sufficient link with what goes before. This is a parent in the Greek, where we find the particle, the force of which is to indicate transition and connection, -- transition to a new illustration, and connection with the foregoing Context. Alford, in his revised New Testament, preserves the continuative particle-- 'But when the **Son of man shall have** come in his glory,' etc. It might with equal propriety be rendered -- And when,' etc.

2. This 'coming of the Son of man' has already been predicted by our Lord (Matt. xxiv. 30, and parallel passages, and the time expressly defined, being included in the comprehensive declaration, 'Verily I say unto you, This generation shall not pass, till all these things be fulfilled' (Matt. xxiv. 34).

3. It deserves particular notice that the description of the coming of the Son of man in his glory' given in this parable tallies in all points with that in Matt. xvi. 27, 28, of which it is expressly affirmed that it would be witnessed by some then present when the prediction was made.

It may be well to compare the two descriptions

MATT. xvi. 27, 28.
For the Son of man shall come in the glory of his Father with his angels; and then he shall reward every man according to his works.

MATT. XXV. 31-33.
When the Son of man shall come in his glory, and all the holy angels with him, then shall he sit upon the throne of his glory: And before him shall be gathered all nations,' etc.

'Verily I say unto you, There be some standing here, which shall not taste of death, till they see the Son of man coming in his kingdom.

Here the reader will note
(a) That in both passages the subject referred to is the same, *viz. the coming of the Son of* man- the Parousia.
(b) In both passages He is described as coming in *glory.*
(c) In both He is attended by *the holy angels.*
(d) In both He comes as a *King. ' Coming* in his kingdom; ' He shall sit upon his *throne;* Then shall the *King,'* etc.
(e) 'In both He comes *to judgment.*
(f) In both the judgment is represented as in some sense *universal.* 'He shall reward *every man* 'Before him shall be gathered *all the nations.'*
(g) In Matt. xvi. 28 it is expressly stated that this coming in glory, etc., was to take place *in the lifetime* of some then present. This fixes the occurrence of the Parousia within the limit of a human life, thus being in perfect accord with the period defined by our Lord in His prophetic discourse. 'This generation shall not pass,' etc.

We are fully warranted, therefore, in regarding the coming of the Son of man in Matt. xxv. as identical with that referred to in Matt. xvi., which some of the disciples were to live to witness.

Thus, notwithstanding the words ' all the nations ' in Matt. xxv. 32, we are brought to the conclusion that it is not the 'final consummation of all things ' which is there spoken of, but the judgment of Israel at the close of the [Jewish] ,aeon or age.

4. But it will still be objected that a very formidable difficulty remains in the expression 'all the nations.' The difficulty, however, is more apparent than real; for

(1) It is not at all uncommon to find in Scripture universal propositions which must be understood in a qualified or restricted sense.

There is a case in point in this very discourse of our Lord. In Matt. xxiv. 22, speaking of the 'great tribulation,' He Says, ' Except those days should be shortened *there should no* flesh be saved.' Now it is evident that this 'great tribulation' was limited to Jerusalem, or, at all events, to Judea, and yet we have an expression used in regard to the inhabitants of a city or country -which is wide enough to include the whole human race, in which sense Lange and Alford actually understand it.

(2) There is great probability in the opinion that the phrase ' all the nations ' is equivalent to 'all the tribes of the land' (Matt. xxiv. 30). There is no impropriety in designating the *tribes* as *nations.* The promise of God to Abraham was that he should be the father of many nations (Gen. xvii. 5; Rom. iv. 17, 18).

In our Lord's time it was usual to speak of the inhabitants of Palestine as consisting of several nations. Josephus speaks of ' the nation of the Samaritans,' 'the nation of the Batanaeans,' ' the nation of the Galileans,'-- using the very word (etnoj) which we find in the passage before us. Judea, was a distinct nation, often with a king of its own; so also was Samaria; and so with Idumea, Galilee, Paraea, Batanea, Trachonitis, Ituraea, Abilene,-- all of which had at different times princes with the title of *Ethnarch,* a name which signifies the ruler of a nation. It is doing no violence, then, to the language to understand as referring, to 'all the nations' of Palestine, or ' all the tribes of the land.'

(3) This view receives strong confirmation from the fact that the same phrase in the apostolic commission (Matt. xxviii.19), 'Go and teach *all the nations,'* does not seem to have been understood by the disciples as referring to the whole population of the globe, or to any nations beyond Palestine. It is commonly supposed that the apostles knew that they had received a charge to evangelise the world. If they did know it, they were culpably remiss in not acting upon it. But it is presumable that the words of our Lord (lid not convey any such idea to their mind. The learned Professor Burton observes: "It was not until fourteen years after our Lord's ascension that St. Paul travelled -for the first time, and preached the gospel to the Gentiles. Nor is there any evidence that during that period the other apostles passed the confines of Judea.' (1)

The fact seems to be that the language of the apostolic commission did not convey to the minds of the apostles any such ecumenical ideas. Nothing more astonished them than the discovery that 'God had granted to the Gentiles also repentance unto life' (Acts xi. 18). When St. Peter was challenged for going in 'to men uncircumcised, and eating with them,' it does not appear that he vindicated his conduct by an appeal to the terms of the apostolic commission. If the phrase ' all the nations' had been understood by the disciples in its literal and most comprehensive sense, it is difficult to imagine bow they could have failed to recognise ,it once the universal character of the gospel, and their commission to preach it alike to Jew and Gentile. It required a distinct revelation from heaven to overcome the Jewish prejudices of the apostles, and to make known to them the mystery 'that the Gentiles should be fellow-heirs, and of the same body, and partakers of the promise in Christ by the gospel ' (Ephes. iii. 6).

In view of these considerations we hold it reasonable and warrantable to give the phrase ' all the nations' a restricted signification, and to limit it to the nations of Palestine. In this sense it harmonises well with the words of our Lord, " Ye shall not have gone over the cities of Israel till the Son of man be come' (Matt. x. 23).

5. Once more, the peculiar test of character which is applied by the Judge in this parabolic description is strongly opposed to the notion that this scene represents the final judgment of the whole human race. It will be observed that the destiny of the righteous and the wicked is made to turn on the treatment which they respectively offered to the suffering disciples of Christ. All moral qualities, all virtuous conduct, all true faith, are apparently thrown out of the reckoning, and acts of charity and beneficence to distressed disciples are alone taken into account. It is not surprising that this circumstance should have occasioned much perplexity both to theologians and general readers. Is this the doctrine of St. Paul? Is this the ground of justification before God set forth in the New Testament? Are we to conclude that the everlasting destiny of the whole human race, from Adam to the last man, will finally turn on their charity and sympathy towards the persecuted and suffering disciples of Christ?

The difficulty is a grave one, on the supposition that we have here a description of 'the general judgment at the last day,' and ought not to be slurred over, as commonly it is. How could the nations which existed before the time of Christ be tried by such a standard? How could the nations which never heard of Christ,-- or those which flourished in the ages when Christianity was prosperous and powerful, be tried by such a standard? It is manifestly inappropriate and inapplicable. But the difficulty is easily and completely solved if we regard this judicial transaction as the judgment of Israel at the close of the Jewish aeon. It is the rejected King of Israel who is the judge: it is the hostile and unbelieving generation, the last and worst of the nation, that is arraigned before His tribunal. Their treatment of His disciples, especially of His apostles, might most fitly and justly be made the criterion of character in ' discerning between the righteous and the wicked.' Such a test would be most appropriate in an age when Christianity was a persecuted faith, and this is evidently supposed by the very terms of the King's address: -- 'I was hungry, thirsty, a stranger, was naked, sick, and in prison.' The persons designated as *'these my brethren,'* and who are taken as the representatives of

Christ Himself, are evidently the apostles of our Lord, in whom He hungered, and thirsted, was naked, sick, and in prison. All this is in perfect harmony with the words of Christ to His disciples, when He sent them forth to preach-- 'He that receiveth you receiveth me, and he that receiveth me receiveth him that sent me. He that receiveth. a prophet in the name of a prophet shall receive a prophet's reward; and he that receiveth a righteous man in the name of a righteous man, shall receive a righteous man's reward. And whosoever shall give to drink unto one of these little ones a cup of cold water only in the name of a disciple, verily I say unto you, he shall in no wise lose his reward' (Matt. x. 40-42).

We are thus brought to the conclusion, the **only one which in** all respects suits the tenor of the entire discourse, that we have here, not the final judgment of the whole human race, but that of the guilty nation or nations of Palestine, who rejected their King, despitefully treated and slew His messengers (Matt. xxii. 1-14), and whose day of doom was now near at hand.

This being so, the entire prophecy on the Mount of Olives is seen to be one homogeneous and connected whole: 'simplex duntaxat et unum.' It is no longer a confused and unintelligible medley, baffling all interpretation, seeming to speak with two voices, and pointing in different directions at the same time. It is a clear, consecutive, and historically truthful representation of the judgment of the Theocratic nation at the close of the age, or Jewish period. The theory of interpretation which regards this discourse as typical of the final judgment of the human race, and of a world-wide catastrophe attendant upon that event,-- really finds no countenance in the prediction itself, while it involves inextricable perplexity and confusion. If, on the one hand, it could be shown that the prophecy, *as a whole,* is in every part equally applicable to two different and widely separated events; or, on the other hand, that at a certain point it quits the. one subject, and takes tip the other, then the double sense, or twofold reference, would stand upon some intelligible basis. But we have found no dividing line in the prophecy between the near and the remote, and all attempts to draw such a line are unsatisfactory and arbitrary in the extreme. Still more untenable is the hypothesis of a double meaning running through the whole; a hypothesis which supposes a 'verifying faculty ' in the expositor or reader, and gives so large a discretionary power to the ingenious critic that it seems utterly incompatible with the reverence due to the Word of God.

The perplexity which the double-sense theory involves is placed in a. strong light by the confession of Dean Alford, who, at the close of his comments on this prophecy, honestly expresses his dissatisfaction with the views which he had propounded. ' I think it proper,' he says, ' to state, in this third edition, that, having now entered upon the deeper study of the prophetic portions of the New Testament, I do not feel by any means that full confidence which I once did in the exegesis, *quoad* prophetical interpretation, here given of the three portions of this chap. xxv. But I have no other system to substitute, and some of the points here dwelt on seem to me as weighty as ever. I very much question whether the thorough study of Scripture prophecy will not make me more and more distrustful of all human systematising, and less willing to hazard strong assertion on any portion of the subject.' (July 1855.) In the fourth edition Alford adds, 'Endorsed, October 1858.' This is candour highly honourable to the critic, but it suggests the reflection, --if, with all the light and experience of eighteen centuries, the prophecy on the Mount of Olives still remains an unsolved enigma, bow could it have been intelligible to the disciples who eagerly listened to it as it fell from the lips of the Master? Can we suppose that at such a moment he would speak to them in inexplicable riddles?-that when they asked for bread He would give them a stone? Impossible. There is no reason for believing that the disciples were unable to comprehend the words of Jesus, and if these words have been misapprehended in subsequent times, it is because a false and unnatural method of interpretation has obscured and distorted what in itself is luminous and simple enough. It is matter for just surprise that such disregard should have been shown by expositors to the express limitations of time laid down by our Lord; that forced and unnatural meanings should have given to such words as ai,w.n genea. entew.j, &C.; that arbitrary lines of division should have been drawn in the discourse where none exist,-- and generally that the prophecy should have been subjected to a treatment which would not be tolerated in the criticism of any Greek or Latin classic. Only let the language of Scripture be treated with common fairness, and interpreted by the principles of grammar and common sense, and much obscurity and misapprehension will be removed, and the very form and substance of the truth will come forth to view. (2)

Before passing away from this deeply interesting prophecy it may be proper to advert to the marvellously minute fulfilment which it received, as testified by an unexceptionable witness,-- the Jewish historian Josephus. It is a fact of singular interest and importance that there should have been preserved to posterity a full and authentic record of the times and transactions referred to in our Lord's prophecy; and that this record should be from the pen of a Jewish statesman, soldier, priest, and man of letters, not only having access to the best sources of information, but himself an eye-witness of many of the events which he relates. It gives additional weight to this testimony that it does not come from a Christian, who might have been suspected of partisanship, but from a Jew, indifferent, if not hostile, to the cause of Jesus.

So striking is the coincidence between the prophecy and the history that the old objection of Porphyry against the Book of Daniel, that it must have been written after the event, might be plausibly alleged, were there the slightest pretense for such an insinuation.

Though the Jewish people were at all times restless and uneasy under the yoke of Rome, there were no urgent symptoms of disaffection at the time when our Lord delivered this prediction of the approaching destruction of the temple, the city, and the nation. The higher classes were profuse in their professions of loyalty to the Imperial government: 'We have no king but Caesar' was their cry. It was the policy of Rome to grant the free exercise of their own religion to the subject provinces. There was, therefore, no apparent reason why the new and splendid temple of Jerusalem should not stand for centuries, and Judea enjoy **a greater tranquillity** and prosperity under the aegis of Caesar than she had ever known under her native princes. Yet before the generation which rejected and crucified the Son of David had wholly passed away, the Jewish nationality was extinguished: Jerusalem was a desolation; ' the holy and beautiful house' on Mount Zion was razed to the ground; and the unhappy people, who knew not the time of their visitation, were overwhelmed by calamities without a parallel in the annals of the world.

All this is undeniable; and yet it would be too much, to expect that this will be regarded as an adequate fulfilment of our Saviour's words by many whom prejudice-or traditional interpretations have taught to see more in the prophecy than ever inspiration included in it. The language, it is said, is too magnificent, the transactions too stupendous to be satisfied by so inadequate an event as the judgment of Israel and the destruction of Jerusalem. We have already endeavoured to point out the real significance and grandeur of that event. But the one sufficient answer to all such objections is the express declaration of our Lord, which covers the whole ground of this prophetic discourse, ' Verily I say unto you, This generation shall not pass till all these things are fulfilled.' No doubt there are some portions of this prediction which are capable of verification by human testimony. Does any one expect Tacitus, or Suetonius, or Josephus, or any other historian, to relate that 'the Son of man was seen coining in the clouds of heaven with power and great glory; that He summoned the nations to his tribunal, and rewarded every man according to his works '? There is a region into which witnesses and reporters may not enter; flesh and blood may not gaze upon the mysteries of the spiritual and immaterial. But there is also a large portion of the prophecy which is capable of verification, and which has been amply verified. Even an assailant of Christianity, who impugns the supernatural knowledge of Christ, is compelled to admit that ' the portion relating to the destruction of the city is singularly definite, and corresponds very closely with the actual event.' (4) The punctual fulfilment of that part of the prophecy which comes within the field of human observation is the guarantee for the truth of the remainder, which does not fall within that sphere. We shall find in the sequel of this discussion that the events which now appear to many incredible were the confident expectation and hope of the apostolic age, and that the early Christians were fully persuaded of their reality and nearness. We are placed, therefore, in this dilemma -- either the words of Jesus have failed, and the hopes of His disciples have been falsified; or else those words and hopes have been fulfilled, and the prophecy in all its parts has been fully accomplished. One thing is certain, the veracity of our Lord is committed to the assertion that the whole and every part of the events contained in this prophecy were to take place before the close of the existing generation. If any language may claim to be precise and definite, it is that which our Lord employs to mark the limits of the time within which all His words were to be fulfilled. Whatever other catastrophes, of other nations, in other ages, there may be in the future, concerning them our Lord is silent. He speaks of His own guilty nation, and of His judicial coming at the close of the age, as had been often and clearly foretold by Malachi, by John the Baptist, and by Himself. (5) For this His words are to be bold responsible; but beyond this all is mere human speculation, the hypothesis of theologians, grounded upon no warranty of Scripture.

We have thus endeavoured to rescue this great prophecy from the loose and uncritical method of interpretation by which it has been so much obscured and perplexed; to let it speak the same distinct and definite meaning to us as it did to the disciples. Reverence for the Word of God, and due regard to the principles of interpretation, forbid us to impose non-natural constructions and double senses, which in effect would be 'to add to the words of this prophecy.' We dare not play fast and loose with the express and precise statements of Christ. We find but one Parousia; one end of the age; one impending catastrophe; one *terminus ad quem,* -- *'this* generation.' We protest against the exegesis which handles the Word of God in such free fashion as commends itself to many. 'The Lord,' it is said, 'is always coming to those who look for His appearing. We see His coming on a large scale in every crisis of the great human story. In revolutions, in reformations, and in the crises of our individual history. For each one of us there is an advent of the Lord, as often as new and larger views of truth are presented to us, or we are called to enter on new and perchance more laborious and exciting duties.' (6) In this way it might be difficult to say what is not a 'coming of the Lord.' But by making it anything and everything we make it nothing. It is evacuated -of all precision and reality. There is no reason why the incarnation, the crucifixion, and the resurrection should not Similarly become common and everyday transactions as well as the Parousia. It is one thing to say that the principles of the divine government are eternal and immutable, and therefore what God does to one people, or to one age, He will do in similar circumstances to other nations and other ages; and it is quite another thing to say that this prophecy has two meanings: one for Jerusalem and Israel, and another for the world and the final consummation of all things. We hold, with Neander, that 'the words of Christ, like His works, contain within them the germ of an infinite development, reserved for future ages to unfold.' (7) But this does not imply that prophecy is anything that an ingenious fancy can devise, or hag occult and ulterior senses underlying the apparent and natural signification of the language. The duty of the interpreter and student of Scripture is not to try what Scripture may be made to say, but to submit his understanding to 'the true sayings of God,' which are usually as simple as they are profound. (8)

*1.*Professor Burton's Bampton Lecture, p. 20.

2. The following extract is taken from an excellent article in the first volume of the Bibliotheca Sacra (1843), by Dr. E. Robinson, entitled 'The coming of Christ.' Up to ver. 42 of chap. xxiv. of St. Matthew, Dr. Robinson maintains the exclusive reference of the prediction to Jerusalem, and thus notices the interpretations which refer it to the 'end of the world:'
'The question now arises whether, under these limitations of time, a reference of our Lord's language to the day of judgment and the end of the world, in our sense of these terms, is possible. Those who maintain this view attempt to dispose of the difficulties arising from these limitations in different ways. Some assign to (genea) the meaning suddenly, as it is employed by the LXX in Job v. 3, for the Hebrew. But even in this passage the purpose of the writer is simply to mark an immediate sequence -- to intimate that another and consequent event happens forthwith. Nor would anything be gained even could the word (genea) be thus disposed of, so long as the subsequent limitation to 'this generation' remained. And in this again others have tried to refer genea to the race of the Jews, or to the disciples of Christ, not only without the slightest ground, but contrary to all usage and all analogy. All these attempts to apply force to the meaning of the language are in vain, and are now abandoned by most commentators of note.'
After so luminous an exposition it is disappointing to find Dr. Robinson failing to carry out the principles with which he started consistently to the end. Embarrassed by the foregone conclusion that the 'final judgment' and 'the end of the world' are somewhere to be found in the prophecy, and unable to see where the theme of Jerusalem ends, and the other and greater theme of the world's catastrophe begins, he adopts the following method. Starting with the assumption that the parable of the sheep and the goats must describe the latter event, he feels his way backwards to the preceding parable of the talents, in which he finds the same subject, the doctrine of final retribution. Going still further back, to the parable of the tell virgins, he finds the object of that parable to be the inculcation of the same important truth. The twenty-fifth chapter of St. Matthew must therefore, he concludes, refer wholly to the transactions of the last great day.
'But,' he continues, 'the latter portion of chap. xxiv., viz. from ver. 43 to 51, is intimately connected with the opening parable of chap. xxv.,' which seems to furnish a sufficient ground for regarding this passage also as referring to the future judgment. At ver. 43 of Matthew xxiv., therefore, Dr. Robinson conceive that our Lord leaves the subject of Jerusalem altogether and takes up a new topic, the judgment of the world.
It will at once be apparent that the whole of this reasoning is vitiated by the false premise with which it starts, viz., the assumption that the parable of the sheep and the goats refers to the judgment of the human race. We have already shown that there is no new departure at Matt. xxiv. 48.

4. Contemporary Review, Nov. 1876. See Note B, Part I

5. Jonathan Edwards says, referring to the destruction of Jerusalem, -' Thus there was a final end to the Old Testament world: all was finished with a kind of day of judgment, in which the people of God were saved, and His enemies terribly destroyed.' -- History story of Redemption, vol. i. p. 445

6. Evang. Meg. Feb. 1877, p. 69

7. Life of Christ, 165

8. See Note A, Part I.

Our Lord's declaration before the High Priest.

MATT. xxvi. 61.

'Jesus saith unto him, Thou hast said: nevertheless I say unto you, Hereafter shall ye see the Son of man sitting on the right hand of power, and coming in the clouds of heaven.'

MARK xiv. 62.

'And Jesus said, I am: and ye shall see the Son of man sitting on the right hand of power, and coming in the clouds of heaven.'

Luke xxii. 69.

'Hereafter shall the Son of man sit on the right hand of the power of God.'

The reply of our Saviour to the solemn adjuration of the high priest is the almost verbatim repetition of what He had declared to the disciples on the Mount of Olives,-- 'They shall see the Son of man coming in the clouds of heaven with power and great glory ' (Matt. xxiv. 30). It is evidently the same event and the same period that are referred to. The language implies that the persons addressed, or some of them, would witness the event predicted. The expression 'Ye shall see' would not be proper if spoken of something which the hearers would none of them live to witness, and which would not take place for thousands of years. Our Lord therefore told His judges that they, or some of them, would live to see Him coming to judgment, or coming in His kingdom. This declaration is in harmony with what our

Saviour said to His disciples,-' The Son of man shall come in the glory of his Father with his angels. . . . Verily I say unto you, There be some standing here which shall not taste of death, till they see the Son of man in his kingdom' (Matt. xvi. 27, 28). Some of His disciples, and some of His judges, would live long enough to witness that great consummation, less than forty years distant, when the Son of man would come in His kingdom, to execute the judgments of God on the guilty nation. This is precisely what the prophecy on the Mount of Olives asserts: 'This generation shall not pass,' etc. Here again we have neither obscurity nor ambiguity. But can as much be said for the interpretation which makes our Lord's words refer to a time still future, and an event which has not yet taken place? Can as much be said for the interpretation which finds in this scene, which the Jewish Sanhedrim were to witness, no one distinct and particular event, but a prolonged and continuous process, which began at the resurrection of Christ, is still going on, and will continue to go on to the end of the world?

This strange interpretation, which is that of Lange and Alford, is based partly on the assumption that our Lord's prediction has never yet been fulfilled, and partly on the word 'henceforth,' which is held to indicate a continuous process. (1) But is such an explanation credible, or even conceivable? Is it true that the high priest and the Sanhedrim began from that time to see the Son of man coming in the clouds of heaven? etc. How could such an apparition be a continuous process? Plainly, the words can only refer to a definite and specific event; and we can be at no loss to determine what that event is. It can be no other than the Parousia, so often predicted before. That was not a protracted process, but a summary act,-- sudden, swift, conspicuous as the lightning. The sense is well expressed by the editors of the 'Critical English Testament: ' The meaning cannot be, that immediately after the moment of His answer He should so come, and they so see Him; but rather that He would now depart from them, and that when they *next* saw Him, after His rejection by them, it would be at His coming in glory, as foretold by the prophet Daniel.' (2)

We find, then, in this declaration of our Lord an additional confirmation of His previous statements that His coming again would take place within the period of the existing generation. Some of His judges, as well as some of His disciples, were to witness it; and there would be no meaning in such an assertion if it did not imply that they were to witness it 'in the flesh.'

Prediction of the Woes coming on Jerusalem.

LUKE xxiii. 27-31.-- 'And there followed him a great company of people, and of women, which also bewailed and lamented him. But Jesus turning unto them, said, Daughters of Jerusalem, weep not for me, but weep for yourselves, and for your children. For, behold, the (lays are coming in the which they shall say, Blessed are the barren, and the wombs that never bare, and the paps which never gave suck. Then shall they begin to say to the mountains, Fall on us; and to the hills, Cover us. For if they do these things in a green tree, what shall be done in the dry?'

Here we have a statement so clear, so definite in every point that can fix its reference, -time, place, persons, circumstances,-- that no room is left for uncertainty. It points to a time which was not far distant, but at hand-' the days are coming; '-a time which the persons addressed and their children would live to see; -- a time of great tribulation, which would fall with peculiar severity upon womanhood and childhood; -- a time when, in the agony of their terror, despairing multitudes would cry to the mountains and the hills to fall on them and cover them.

Those memorable details will be found most valuable in the elucidation of Scripture prophecy at a subsequent stage of this investigation. Meanwhile it is clear that this pathetic description can refer only to the catastrophe of Jerusalem in the last days of her history. We have only to turn to the pages of Josephus for the facts which illustrate and confirm our Saviour's language. The horrors of that tragic history culminate in the episode of Mary of Peraea, whose Thyestean banquet horrified even the merciless banditti who prowled like famished wolves through the city. It is in the light of an incident like this that we see the full meaning of the words, 'Blessed are the barren, and the wombs that never bare.'

It is with a movement of something like impatience that we listen to Stier, beguiled by the *ignis fatuus* of a double sense, insisting on a hidden meaning in our Saviour's words: 'He spoke expressly and primarily of the judgment of Jerusalem and Israel, yet He contemplated and refers to that which was shadowed out in this historical type,-the judgment of all the impenitent, and of all unbelievers in common, down to the last." (3) So also Alford, following Stier. It is only in the imagination of the expositor, however, that this ulterior reference exists: there is no suggestion of it in the text; and it is with a degree of wonder that we find a scholarly critic so far forgetting his true vocation as to pronounce 'the historical and actual specific fulfilment' to be 'the least thing: the meaning of the word reaches much further.' If ever there was a case in which double meanino's and typical fulfilments are not to be thought of, surely it is here. At such an hour of anguish, there could be but one thought present to the heart of Jesus. He saw the gathering storm of wrath in which the devoted city was soon to be enveloped, and which would burst with such violence on the tender and delicate, the children and the mothers of Jerusalem. , and He reciprocated the pity which He received from those compassionate hearts,-- more touched in that moment by their anticipated woes, than by His own. What need is there to go beyond that tragical catastrophe, and seek for another concerning which the context is altogether silent?

The Prayer of the Penitent Thief.

Luke xxiii. 42.-- 'And He said unto Jesus, Lord, remember me when thou comest in thy kingdom.'

The single point which concerns us in this memorable incident is the reference made by the malefactor to our Lord's *coming* in his kingdom.' In whatever way he had come by the knowledge, He recognised in the rejected Prophet by his side the King of Israel, the Son of God. He believed that, notwithstanding His rejection and crucifixion by Israel, He would one day 'come again in his kingdom.' Marvellous faith in such a man and at such a moment! If the thief on the cross had listened to the testimony of Jesus before the high priest, or if he had known what He said to the disciples, that 'some of them should not taste of death till they had seen the Son of man coming in his kingdom,' we could better account for his faith and his prayer. At any rate, there could not have been more intelligence and precision in the language of a disciple than in the words of this 'brand plucked out of the fire.' What notion the malefactor entertained respecting the *time* of that coming,-- whether he conceived it to be near or distant, we have no means of knowing; but it is presumable that he thought of it as near. A dying man would scarcely pray to be remembered in some distant age, after centuries and millenniums had rolled away. In such a crisis it could only be the imminent, or the immediate, that could be in his thoughts. One thing seems certain: the most incredible of all interpretations is that which would represent his prayer as still unanswered, and the coming' of which he spoke as still among the events of an unknown futurity.

The Apostolic Commission.

MATT. xxviii. 19, 20.	MARK Xvi. 15, 20.	Luke xxiv. 47.
'Go ye therefore, and teach all [the] nations, baptizing them in the name of the Father, and of the Son, and of the Holy Ghost. Teaching them to observe all things whatsoever I have commanded you; and, lo, I am with you alway, even unto the end of the age.'	'And he said unto them, Go ye into all the world, and preach the gospel to every creature. 'And they went forth, and preached everywhere, the Lord working with them, and confirming the word with signs following.'	'And that repentance and remission of sins should be preached in his name among all [the] nations, beginning at Jerusalem.'

It is usual to regard this commission as if it were addressed to the whole Christian Church in all ages. No doubt it is allowable to infer from these words the perpetual obligation resting upon all Christians in all times, to propagate the Gospel among all nations; but it is important to consider the words in their proper and original reference. It is Christ's commission to His chosen messengers, designating them to their evangelistic work, and assuring them of His constant presence and protection. It has a special application to the apostles which it cannot have to any others. We have already adverted to the fact that the disciples, to whom this charge was given, do not seem to have understood it as directing them to extend their evangelistic labours beyond the bounds of Palestine, or to preach the Gospel to Jews and Gentiles indiscriminately. It is certain that they did not immediately, nor yet for years, act upon this commission in its largest sense; nor does it seem probable that they would ever have done so without an express revelation. As Dr. Burton has shown, no less than fifteen years elapsed between the conversion of St. Paul and his first apostolic journey to preach among the Gentiles. "Nor is there any evidence that during that period the other apostles passed the confines of Judaea." (4) There is much probability therefore in the opinion that the language of the apostolic commission did not convey to their minds the same idea that it does to us, and that, as we have already seen, the phrase 'all the nations ' is really equivalent to 'all the tribes of the land.'

But what especially deserves notice is the remarkable limitation of time, the *'terminus ad quem,'* here specified by our Saviour. 'Lo, **I am with you always [all the days],** even to the close of the age'. Nothing can be more misleading to the English reader than the rendering 'the end of the world; ' which inevitably suggests the close of human history, the end of time, and the destruction of the earth,-- a meaning which the words will not bear. Lange, though far from apprehending the true significance of the phrase, rightly gives the sense, 'the consummation of the secular won, or the period of time which comes to an end with the Parousia.' What can be more evident than that the promise of Christ to be with His disciples to the close of the age, implies that they were to live to the close of the age? That great consummation Was Dot far off; the Lord had often spoken of it, and always as an approaching event, one which some of them would live to see. It was the winding up of the Mosaic dispensation; the end of the long probation of the Theocratic nation; when the whole frame and fabric of the Jewish polity were to be swept away, and 'the kingdom of God to come with power.' This great event, our Lord had declared, was to fall within the limit of the existing generation. The 'close of the age' coincided with the Parousia, and the outward and visible sign by which it is distinguished is the destruction of Jerusalem. This is the *terminus by* which in the Now Testament the field is bounded. To Israel it was 'the end,' 'the end of all things,' 'the passing away of heaven and earth,' the abrogation of the old order, the inauguration of the new. Of this great providential epoch, history tells us much, but prophecy more. History shows us the predicted Signs Coming to pass; the premonitory symptoms of the approaching catastrophe --the false Christs, the wars and rumours of wars, the insurrections and commotions, the earthquakes, famines, and pestilences; the persecutions and tribulations; the invading legions of Rome; the besieged and captured city; the burning temple; the slaughtered myriads; the extinguished nation. But history cannot lift the veil which hangs over the spirit world; it leads us up to the very border, and bids us guess the rest. But we have a more sure word of prophecy which, instead of conjecture, gives us assurance. It reveals 'the Son of man coming in his glory; ' the King seated on the throne; the judgment set, and the books opened. It reveals the sheep and the goats separated the one from the other; the righteous entering into everlasting life; the wicked sent away into everlasting punishment. If we have not the historical verification of the unseen and spiritual, as we have of the visible and material elements of this consummation, it is because they are not in the nature of things equally cognizable by the senses. But we accept them on the faith of His word who declared, 'Verily I say unto you, All these things shall come upon this generation; ' and again, ' Verily I say unto you, This generation shall not pass away until all these things be fulfilled.' ' Heaven and earth shall pass away, but my words shall not pass away.' The literal fulfilment of all that falls within the sphere of human observation is the voucher for the credibility of the remainder, which belongs to the realm of the unseen and the spiritual.

1..(a/rti) in later Greek came to signify soon,' 'presently:' see Liddell and Scott; and thus our translators, correctly, Here-after,' which leaves the actual time of the event future, but not necessarily immediate,'-- Critical English Test. vol. iii. P. 860, note.
2. Critical English Test. vol. iii. p. 860, note
3. Reden Jesu, vol. vii. p. 426

The Parousia in the Gospel of St. John.

In the Synoptical Gospels we have generally been able to compare the allusions to the Parousia, recorded by the Evangelists, one with another; and have often found it advantageous to do so. It is not easy, however, to interweave the Fourth Gospel with the Synoptics, and it is somewhat remarkable that not one allusion to the Parousia in the latter is to be found in the former. It is therefore preferable on all accounts to consider the Gospel of St. John by itself, and we shall find that the references to the subject of our inquiry, though not many in number, are very important and full of interest.

Th*e Parousia and the Resurrection of the Dead.*
John v. 25-29.-- 'Verily, verily, I say unto you, The hour is coming, and now is, when the dead shall bear the voice of the Son of God: and they that hear shall live. For as the Father hath life in himself; so hath he given to the Son to have life in himself; and hath given him authority to execute judgment also, because lie is the Son of man.
' Marvel not at this: for the hour is coming, in the which all that are in the graves shall hear his voice, and shall come forth; they that have done good, unto the resurrection of life; and they that have done evil, unto the resurrection of damnation.'

In the references to the approaching consummation which we have found in the Synoptical Gospels, it is impossible not to be struck with the constant association of the Parousia with a great act of judgment. From the very first notice of this great event to the last, the idea of judgment is put prominently forward. John the Baptist warns the nation of 'the coming wrath.' The men of Nineveh and the queen of the south are to appear *in the judgment with this generation.* In the harvest at the close of the age the tares were to be burned, and the wheat gathered into the barn. The Son of man was to come in His glory to reward every man according to his works. The judgment of Capernaum and Chorazin was to be heavier than that of Tyre and Sidon. The closing parables in our Lord's ministry are nearly all declaratory of coming judgment -the pounds, the wicked husbandman, the marriage of the king's son, the ten virgins, the talents, the sheep and the goats. The great prophecy on the Mount of Olives is wholly occupied with the same subject.

It is remarkable that the first allusion which St. John makes to this event recognises its *judicial* character. But we now find a new element introduced into the description of the approaching consummation. It is connected with *the resurrection of the dead;* of 'all that are in the graves.' ' The hour is coming when all that are in the graves shall hear his voice, and shall come forth,' etc.

There can be no doubt that the passage just quoted (ver. 28, 29) refers to the literal resurrection of the dead. It may also be admitted that the preceding verses (25, 26) refer to the communication of spiritual life to the spiritually dead.(1) The time for this life-giving process had already commenced,-' The hour is coming, and now is.' The dead in trespasses and sins were about to be made alive by the quickening power of the divine Spirit acting upon men's souls in the preaching of the gospel of Christ. This lifegiving power belonged by divine appointment to the Son of God, to whom also wag committed, in virtue of His humanity, the office of supreme Judge (ver. 27).

Anticipating that this claim to be the Judge of mankind would stagger His hearers, our Lord proceeds to strengthen His assertion and heighten their admiration by declaring that at His voice the buried dead would ere long come forth from their graves to stand before His judgment throne.

The reader will particularly note the indications of time specified by our Lord in these important passages. First we have 'the hour is coming, and now is: ' this intimates that the action spoken of, viz. the communication of spiritual life to the spiritually dead, has already begun to take effect. Next we have 'the hour is coming,' without the addition of the words 'and now is:' intimating that the event specified, viz., the raising of the dead from their graves, is at a greater distance of time, although still not far off. The formula ' the hour is coming' always denotes that the event referred to is not far distant. It does not indeed define the time, but it brings it within a comparatively brief period. We find these two expressions, 'the hour is coming,' and 'the hour is coming, and now is,' employed by our Lord in His conversation with the woman of Samaria (John iv. 21, 23), and their use there may help us to determine their force in the passage before us. When our Lord says, 'the hour cometh, and now is, when the true worshippers shall worship the Father in spirit and in truth,' He intimates that the time was already present, for had He not begun to collect the materials of that spiritual Church of true worshippers of which He spoke? When, however, He says, 'Woman, believe me, the hour cometh when ye shall neither in this mountain, nor yet at Jerusalem, worship the Father,' He speaks of a time which, though not distant, was not yet come. He foresaw the period of which He spoke, when the worship of the temple would cease,-- when Mount Zion would be 'ploughed as a field,' and Mount Gerizirn also be overwhelmed in the deluge of wrath. But the abrogation of the local and material was necessary to the inauguration of the universal and spiritual; and therefore it was that the temple with its ritual must be swept away to make room for the nobler worship 'in spirit and in truth.'

Of course, it cannot be absolutely proved that the phrase 'the hour is coming' refers to precisely the same point of time in these two instances, though the presumption is strong that it does. Let it suffice, at this stage, to note the fact that our Lord here speaks of the resurrection of the dead and the judgment as events which were not distant, but so near that it might properly be said, 'The hour is coming,' etc.

The Resurrection, the Judgment, and the Last Day.
JOHN vi. 39.-- ' This is the Father's will which hath sent me, that of all which lie hath given me I should lose nothing, but should raise it up again at the last day.'
JOHN vi. 40.-'1 will raise him up at the last day.'
JOHN vi. 44-- ' 1 will raise him up at the last day.'
JOHN ix. 24.-' He shall rise again in the resurrection at the last day.'
JOHN xii. 48.-- 'The word that I have spoken, the same shall judge him in the last day.'

We have in these passages another new phrase in connexion with the approaching consummation, which is peculiar to the Fourth Gospel. We never find in the Synoptics the expression 'the last day,' although we do find its equivalents, 'that day,' and 'the day of judgment.' It cannot be doubted that these expressions are synonymous, and refer to the same period. But we have already seen that the judgment is contemporaneous with the 'end of the age ' (sonteleia ton aiwnoj), and we infer that ' the last day' is only another form of the expression 'the end of the age or Aeon.' The Parousia also is constantly represented as coincident in point of time with the ' end of the age,' so that all these great events, the Parousia, the resurrection of the dead, the judgment, and the last day, are contemporaneous. Since, then, the end of the age is not, as is generally imagined, the *end of the world,* or total destruction of the earth, but the close *of the Jewish economy;* and since our Lord Himself distinctly and frequently places that event within the limits of the existing generation, we conclude that the Parousia the resurrection, the judgment, and the last day, all belong to the **period of the destruction of** Jerusalem.

However startling or incredible such a conclusion may at first sight **appear, it is what the teachings of the New Testament** are absolutely committed to, and as we advance in this inquiry, we shall find the evidence in support of it accumulating to such a degree as to be irresistible. We shall meet with such expressions as ' the *last times,' ' the last days,'* and ' the *last hour,'* evidently denoting the same period as *the last* day,'-- yet spoken of as being not far off, and even as already come. Meanwhile we can only ask the reader to reserve his judgment, and calmly and impartially to weigh the evidence, derived, not from human authority, but from the word of inspiration itself.

The Judgment of this World, and of the Prince of this World.
JOHN xii. 31-- ' Now is - the judgment of this world: now shall the prince of this world be cast out.'
JOHN xvi. 11.-- 'Of judgment, because the prince of this world is judged.'

It is usual to explain these words as meaning that a great crisis in the spiritual history of the world was now at hand: that the death of Christ upon the cross was the turning-point, so to speak, of the great conflict between good and evil, between the living and true God and the false usurping god of this world- that the result of Christ's death would be the ultimate overthrow of Satan's power and the final establishment of the kingdom of truth and righteousness on the ruins of Satan's empire.

No doubt there is much important truth in this explanation, but it fails to satisfy all the requirements of the very distinct and emphatic language of our Lord with respect to the *nearness* and *completeness* of the event to which He refers: 'Now is the judgment of this world; *now* shall the prince of this world be cast out.' It is not enough to say that, to the prophetic foresight of our Saviour, the distant future was as if it were present; nor, that by His approaching death the judgment of the world and the expulsion of Satan would be virtually secured, and might therefore be re-garded as accomplished facts. Nor is it enough to say, that from the moment when the great sacrifice of the Cross was offered, the power and influence of Satan began to ebb, and must continually decrease until it is finally annihilated. The language of our Lord manifestly points to a great and final *judicial* transaction, which was soon to take place. But *judgment is* an act which can hardly be conceived as extending over an indefinite period, and especially when it is re-stricted by the word now, to a distinct and imminent point of time. The phrase *'cast out,'* also, is evidently an allusion to the expulsion of a demon from a body possessed by an unclean spirit. But this suggests a sudden, violent, and al-most instantaneous act, and not a gradual and protracted process. No figure could be less appropriate to describe the slow ebbing and ultimate exhaustion of Satanic power than the *casting out* of a demon. We are compelled, therefore, to set aside the explanation which makes our Lord's words refer to a judgment which, after the lapse of many ages, is still going on; or to an expulsion of Satan which has not yet been effected. He would not speak of a judgment which was not to take place for thousands of years as 'now,' nor of a 'casting out' of Satan as *imminent,* which was to be the result of a slow and protracted process.

We conclude, then, that when our Lord said, ' Now is the judgment of this world,' etc., He had reference to an event which was near, and in a sense *immediate:* that is to say, He had in view that great catastrophe which seems to have been scarcely ever absent from His thoughts- the solemn judicial transaction when 'the Son of man was to sit upon the throne of his glory '-the great ' harvest' at the end of the age, when the angel reapers were to 'gather out of his king-dom all things that offend, and them that do iniquity.' If it be objected to this that the word kosmos (world) is too comprehensive to be restricted to one land or one nation, it may be replied that kosmos is employed here, as in some other passages, especially in the writings of St. John, rather in an ethical sense than as a geographical expression. (See John vii. 7; viii. 23; 1 John ii. 15; v. 14.)

But it may be said, How could this judgment of Israel be spoken of as 'now,' any more than a judgment which is still in the future? Forty years hence is no more now than four thousand years. To this it may be replied, That event was now imminent which more than any other would precipitate the day of doom for Israel. The crucifixion of Christ was the climax of crime,-- the culminating act of apostasy and guilt which filled the cup of wrath, and sealed the fate of 'that wicked generation.' The interval between the crucifixion of Christ and the destruction of Jerusalem was only the brief space between the passing of the sentence and the execution of the criminal; and just as our Lord, when. quitting the temple for the last time, exclaimed, 'Behold, your house is left unto you desolate!' though its desolation did not actually take place till nearly forty years after, so He might say, 'Now is the judgment of this world'-- though a like space of time would elapse between the utterance and the accomplishment of His words.

In like manner the ' casting out of the prince of this world' is represented as coincident with 'the judgment of this world,' and both are manifestly the result of the death of Christ. But how can it be said that Satan was cast out at the period referred to, viz. the judgment at the close of the age? That event marked a great epoch in the divine administra-tion. It was the inauguration of a new order of things: the 'coining of the kingdom of God' in a high and special sense, when the peculiar relation subsisting between Jehovah and Israel was dissolved, and He became known as the God and Father of the whole human race. Thenceforth Satan was no longer to be the god of this world, but the Most High was to take the kingdom to Himself. This revolution was effected by the atoning death of Christ upon the cross, which is declared to be 'the reconciliation of all *things* unto God, whether they be things in earth, or things in heaven' (Col. i. 20). But the formal inauguration of the new order is represented as taking place at ' the end of the age,' the period when 'the kingdom of God was to come with power,' and the Son of man was to sit as Judge 'on the throne of his glory.' What, then, could be more appropriate than the 'casting out ' of the prince of this world at the period when his king-dom, 'this world,' was judged?

It may be objected that if any such event as the casting out of Satan did then take place, it ought to be marked by some very palpable diminution of the power of the devil over men. The objection is reasonable, and it may be met by the assertion that such evidence of the abatement of Satanic influence in the world does exist. The history of our Sav-iour's own times furnishes abundant proof of the exercise of a power over the souls and bodies of men then possessed by Satan which happily is unknown in our days. The mysterious influence called 'demoniacal possession' is always ascribed in Scripture to Satanic agency; and it was one of the credentials of our Lord's divine commission that He, 'by the finger of God, cast out devils.' At what period did the subjection of men to demoniacal power cease to be manifest-ed? It was common in our Lord's days: it continued during the age of the apostles, for we have many allusions to their casting out of unclean spirits; but we have no evidence that it continued to exist in the post-apostolic ages. The phenomenon has so completely disappeared that to many its former existence is incredible, and they resolve it into a popular superstition, or ,in unscientific theory of mental disease,-- an explanation totally incompatible with the representations of the New Testament.

It is worthy of remark that our Lord, on a previous occasion, made a declaration closely resembling that now under consideration.

When the severity disciples returned from their evangelistic mission they reported with exultation their success in casting out demons through the name of their Master:

Lord, even the demons are subject unto us through thy name' (Luke x. 17).

In His reply, Jesus said, I beheld Satan ,is lightening fall from heaven; ' an expression nearly equivalent to the words, ' Now shall the prince of this world be cast out,' and on which Neander makes the following suggestive remarks:

'As Christ had previously designated the cure of demoniacs wrought by Himself as a sign that the kingdom of God had come upon the earth, so now he considered what the disciples reported as a token of the conquering power of that kingdom, before which every evil thing must yield: "I beheld Satan as lightning fall from heaven," *i.e.* from the pinnacle of power which he had thus far held among men. Before the intuitive glance of His spirit lay open the results which were to flow from His redemptive work after His ascension into heaven. he saw, in spirit, the kingdom of God advancing in triumph over the kingdom of Satan. He does not say, " I see now," but, "I saw." He saw it before the disciples brought their report of their accomplished wonders. While they were doing these isolated works he saw the *one* great work, of which theirs were only particular and individual signs -- the victory over the mighty power of evil which had ruled mankind completely achieved.' (2)

In comparing these two remarkable sayings of our Lord there are three points that deserve particular notice:

1. They are both uttered on occasions when the approaching triumph of His cause was vividly brought before Him.

2. In both, the casting out of Satan is represented as an accomplished fact.

3. In both it is regarded as a swift and summary act, not a slow and protracted process: in the one case Satan falls ' as lightning from heaven,' in the other he is 'cast out' as an unclean spirit from a demoniac.

Neander, therefore, has somewhat missed the real point of the expression, in his otherwise admirable remarks. We think the words plainly point to a great judicial transaction, taking place at a particular point of time, that time very near, and as the consequence and result of the Saviour's death upon the cross. Such a transaction and such a period we can find only in the great catastrophe so vividly depicted by our Lord in His prophetic discourse, and we can therefore have no hesitation in understanding His words to refer to that memorable event.

No other explanation satisfies the requirements of the declaration: 'Now is the judgment of this world; now shall the prince of this world be cast out.'

CHRIST'S RETURN [THE PAROUSIA] SPEEDY.
JOHN xiv. 3-- 'And if I go and prepare a place for you, I will come again, and receive you unto myself.'

JOHN xiv. 18. -- ' 1 will not leave you orphans, I will come to you.'

John xiv. 28.-- 'l go away, and come again unto you.'

JOHN xvi. 16.-- ' A little while, and ye shall not see me: and again, a little while, and ye shall see me, because I go to the Father.'

JOHN Xvi. 22.-- ' 1 will see you again, and your heart shall rejoice.'

Simple as these words may seem they have occasioned great perplexity to commentators. Their very simplicity maybe the chief cause of their difficulty: for it is so hard to believe that they mean what they seem to say. It has been Supposed that our Lord refers in some of these passages to His approaching departure from earth, and His final return at the 'end of all things,' the consummation of human history; and that in the others He refers to His temporary absence from His disciples during the interval between His crucifixion and His resurrection.

A careful examination of our Lord's allusions to His departure and His coming again will satisfy every intelligent reader that His coming,' or coming again,' always refers to one particular event and one particular period. No event is more distinctly marked in the New Testament than the Parousia, the 'second coming' of the Lord. It is always spoken of as an act, and not a process; a great and auspicious event; a ' blessed hope,' eagerly anticipated by His disciples and confidently believed to be at hand. The apostles and the early believers knew nothing of a Parousia spread over a vast and indefinite period of time; nor of several 'comings,' all distinct and separate from one another; but of only one coming,-- the Parousia, 'the glorious appearing of the great God even our Saviour Jesus Christ' (Titus ii. 13). If anything is clearly written in the Scriptures it is this. It is therefore with astonishment that we read the comments of Dean Alford on our Lord's words in John xiv. 3

The *coming again of the Lord is* not one single act, as His resurrection, or the descent of the Spirit, or His second personal advent, or the final coming to judgment, but the *great complex of* all these, the result of which shall be His taking

His people to Himself to where He is. This ercomai *is begun* (ver. 18) in His resurrection; *carried on* (ver. 23) in the spiritual life, making them ready for the place prepared; *farther advanced* when each by death is fetched away to be with Him (Phil. i. 23); fully *completed* at His coming in glory, when they shall ever be with Him (I Thess. iv. 17) in the perfected resurrection state.' (3)

This is all evolved out of the single word ercomai! But if ercomai has such a variety and complexity of meaning, why not npayw and porenomai? Why should not the 'going away' have as many parts and processes as the 'coming again?' It may be asked likewise, How could the disciples have understood our Lord's language, if it had such a 'great complex' of meaning? Or how can plain men be expected ever to come to the apprehension of the Scriptures if the simplest expressions are so intricate and bewildering?

This comment is not conceived in the spirit of lucid English common sense, but in the mystical jargon of Lange and Stier. What can be more plain than that the 'coming again' is as definite an act as the 'going away,' and can only refer to that one coming which is the great prophecy and promise of the New Testament, the Parousia? That this event was not to be long deferred is evident from the language in which it is announced: 'Ercomai -- 'I am coming.' The whole tenor of our Lord's address supposes that the separation between His disciples and Himself is to be brief, and their reunion speedy and perpetual. Why does He go away? To prepare a place for them. Is it, then, not yet prepared? Has he not yet received them to Himself? Are they not yet where he is? If the Parousia be still in the future these hopes are still unfulfilled.

That this anticipated return and reunion was not a far-off event, many centuries distant, but one that was at hand, is shown in the subsequent references made to it by our Lord. ' A little while, and ye shall not see me: and again, a little while, and ye shall see me, because I go to the Father' (John xvi. 16). He was soon to leave them; but it was not for ever, nor for long,-- 'a little while,' a few short years, and their sorrow and separation would be at an end; for 'I will see you again, and your heart shall rejoice, and your joy no man taketh from you' (chap. xvi. 22). It will be observed that our Lord does not say that *death* will reunite them, but His coming to them. That coming, therefore, could not be distant.

That it is to this interval between His departure and the Parousia that our Lord refers when He speaks of 'a little while' is evident from two considerations: First, because he distinctly states that He is going to the Father, which shows that His absence relates to the period subsequent to the ascension; and, secondly, because in the Epistle to the Hebrews this same period, viz. the interval between our Lord's departure and His coming again, is expressly called ' a little while.' ' For yet *a little while,* and be that is coming shall come, and will not tarry' (Heb. x. 37).

Here again we are constrained to protest against the forced and unnatural interpretation of this passage (John xvi. 16) by Dr. Alford:

'The mode of expression,' he observes, 'is purposely enigmatical; the qewreite and oesqe not being co-ordinate: the first referring to physical, the second also to spiritual sight. The odesqj (ye shall see) *began to be* fulfilled at the resurrection; then received its main *fulfilment* at the day of Pentecost; and shall have its *final* completion at the great return of the Lord hereafter. Remember, again, that in all these prophecies we have a perspective of continually unfolding fulfilments presented to us.' (4)

Conceive of an act of vision, 'ye shall see,' divided into three distinct operations, each separated from the other by a long interval, and the last still uncompleted after the lapse of eighteen centuries, and this in the face of our Lord's express declaration that it was to be 'in *a little while.'* This is not criticism, but mysticism. So artificial and intricate an explanation could never have occurred to the disciples, and it is surprising that it should have occurred to any sober interpreter of Scripture. But even the disciples, though at first perplexed about I the little while,' soon fully comprehended our Lord when He said,

' I came forth from the Father, and am come into the world: again, I leave the world, and go to the Father' (John xvi. 28).

Supplement this by three other words of Jesus, and we have the substance of His teaching respecting the Parousia: I will come again, and receive you unto myself; that where I am there ye way be also ' (John xiv. 3).

I will not leave you orphans; I will come to you' (John xiv. 18).

A little while, and ye shall not see me; and again, a little while, and ye shall see me John xvi. 16).

Language is incapable of conveying thought with accuracy if these words do not affirm that the return of our Saviour to His disciples was to be speedy.

ST. JOHN TO LIVE TILL THE PAROUSIA.

John xxi. 22.-- ' Jesus said unto him, If I will that he tarry till I come, what is that to thee?'

It would serve no purpose to specify and discuss the various - interpretations of this passage which learned men have conjectured. Had it been a riddle of the ancient Sphinx, it could not have been more perplexing and bewildering. Those who wish to see some of the numerous opinions which have been broached on the subject will find them referred to in Lange. (5)

The words themselves are sufficiently simple. All the obscurity and difficulty have been imported into them by the reluctance of interpreters to recognise in the ' coming' of Christ a distinct and definite point of time within the space of the existing generation. Often as our Lord reiterates the assurance that he would come in His kingdom, come in glory, come to judge His enemies and reward His friends, before the generation then living on earth -bad wholly passed away, there seems an almost invincible repugnance on the part of theologians to accept His words in their plain and obvious sense. They persist in supposing that He must have meant something else or something more. Once admit, what is undeniable, that our Lord Himself declared that His coming was to take place in the lifetime of some of His disciples (Matt. xvi. 27, 28), and the whole difficulty vanishes. He had just revealed to Simon Peter by what death he was to glorify God, and Peter, with characteristic impulsiveness, presumed to ask what should be the destiny of the beloved disciple, who at that moment caught his eye. Our Lord did not give an explicit answer to this question, which savoured somewhat of intrusiveness, but his reply was understood by the disciples to mean that John would live to see the Lord's return. 'If I will that he tarry till I come.' This language is very significant. It assumes as *possible* that John might live till the Lord's coming. It does more, it suggests it as *probable,* though it does not affirm it as *certain.* The disciples put the interpretation upon it that John was not to die at all. The Evangelist himself neither affirms nor denies the correctness of this interpretation, but contents himself with repeating the actual words of the Lord,-- 'If I will that he tarry till I come.' It is, however, a circumstance of the greatest interest that we know how the words of Christ were generally understood at the time in the brotherhood of the disciples. They evidently concluded that John would live to witness the Lord's coming; and they inferred that in that case he would not die at all. It is this latter inference that John guards against being committed to. That he would live till the coming of the Lord he seems to admit without question. Whether this implied further that he would not die at all, was a doubtful point which the words of Jesus did not decide.

Nor was this inference of 'the brethren' so incredible a thing or so unreasonable as it may appear to many. To live till the coming of the Lord was, according to the apostolic belief and teaching, tantamount to enjoying exemption from death. St. Paul taught the Corinthians,-' We shall not all Sleep [die], but we shall all be changed' (I Cor. xv. 51). He spoke to the Thessalonians of the possibility of their being alive at the Lord's coming: ' We which are alive and remain unto the coming of the Lord' (I Thess. iv. 15). He expressed his own personal preference 'not to be unclothed [of the bodily vesture], but to be clothed upon' [with the spiritual vesture]-- in other words, not to die, but to be changed (2 Cor. v. 4). The disciples might be justified in this belief by the words of Jesus on the evening of the paschal supper: 'I will come again, and receive you unto myself.' How could they suppose that this meant death? Or they may have remembered His saying on the Mount of Olives, 'The Son of man Shall send his angels with a great sound of a trumpet, and they shall gather together his elect,' etc. (Matt. xxiv. 31). This, He had assured them, would take place before the existing generation passed away. They were, therefore, not wholly unprepared to receive such an announcement as our Lord made respecting St. John.(6)

We may therefore legitimately draw the following inferences from this important passage:
1. That there was nothing incredible or absurd in the supposition that John might live till the coming of the Lord.
2. That our Lord's words suggest the probability that he would actually do so.
3. That the disciples understood our Lord's answer as implying besides that John would not die at all.
4. That St. John himself gives no sign that there was anything incredible or impossible in the inference, though he does not commit himself to it.
5. That such an opinion would harmonise with our Lord's express teaching respecting the nearness and coincidence of His own coming, the destruction of Jerusalem, the judgment of Israel, and the close of the aeon or age.
6. That all these events, according to Christ's declarations, lay within the period of the existing generation.

Having thus gone through the four gospels, and examined all the passages which relate to the Parousia, or coming of the Lord, it may be useful to recapitulate and bring into one view the general teaching of these inspired records on this important subject.

SUMMARY OF THE TEACHING OF THE GOSPELS RESPECTING THE PAROUSIA.
1. We have the link between Old and New Testament prophecy in the announcement by John the Baptist (the Elijah of Malachi) of the near approach of the coming wrath, or the judgment of the Theocratic nation.
2. The herald is closely followed by the King, who announces that the kingdom of God is at hand, and calls upon the nation to repent.
3. The cities which were favoured with the presence, but rejected the message, of Christ are threatened with a doom more intolerable than that of Sodom and Gomorrah.
4. Our Lord expressly assures His disciples that His coming would take place before they should have completed the evangelisation of the cities of Israel.
5. He predicts a judgment at the 'end of the age ' or aeon [sunteleia ton aiwnos], a phrase which does not mean the destruction of the earth, but the *consummation of the age, i.e.* the Jewish dispensation.

6. Our Lord expressly declares that He would *speedily* come [mellei epcesqai] in glory, in His kingdom, with His angels, and that some among His disciples should not die until His coming took place.

7. In various parables and discourses our Lord predicts the doom impending over Israel at the period of His coming. (See Luke xviii., *parable of the importunate widow.* Luke xix., *parable of the pounds.* Matt. xxi., *parable of the wicked husbandmen.* Matt. xxii., *parable of the marriage feast.*)

8. Our Lord frequently denounces the wickedness of the generation to which He preached, and declares that the crimes of former ages and the blood of the prophets would be required at their bands.

9. The resurrection of the dead, the judgment of the world, and the casting out of Satan are represented as coincident with the Parousia, and near at hand.

10. Our Lord assured His disciples that He would come again *to them,* and that His coming would be in *'a little while.'*

11. The prophecy on the Mount of Olives is one connected and continuous discourse, having exclusive reference to the approaching doom of Jerusalem and Israel, according to our Lord's express statement (Matt. xxiv. 34; Mark xiii. 30; Luke xxi. 32.)

12. The parables of the ten virgins, the talents, and the sheep and the goats all belong to this same event, and are fulfilled in the judgment of Israel.

13. The disciples are exhorted to watch and pray, and to live in the continual expectation of the Parousia, because it would be sudden and speedy.

14. After His resurrection our Lord gave St. John reason to expect that He would live to witness His coming.

1. Some interpreters prefer to understand 'the dead' in verse 25 as having reference to such cases as the daughter of Jairus, the son of the widow of Nain, and Lazarus of Bethany, persons literally raised from the dead and restored to life by our Lord. They understand the argument of our Lord to be something like this: 'You are astonished at the wonderful work which I have wrought upon this impotent man, but you will yet see far greater wonders. The moment is at hand when I will recall even the dead to life; and if this appear incredible to you, a still mightier work will one day be accomplished by my power: for the hour is coming when all that are in the grave shall come forth at my call, and stand before me in judgment.' (Dr. J. Brown. Discourses and Sayings of our Lord vol. i. p. 98.)   This explanation has the advantage of consistency, in giving the same sense of the word 'dead' throughout the whole passage; but it seems impossible to admit that our Lord in verse 24 is speaking of literal death. To say that the believer has already 'passed from death unto life' obviously is the same thing as to say that he has passed from condemnation to justification. We feel compelled, therefore, to adopt the generally received interpretation, which regards verses 24 and 25 as referring to the spiritually dead, and verses 28 and 29 to the corporeally dead.
2. Life of Christ, chap. xii. 205.
3. Greek Test., in loc..
4. Alford, Greek Test., in loc..
5. Commentary of St. John.
6. It is scarcely necessary to point out that, on the hypothesis that the 'coming' of Christ was not to take place until the 'end of the world,' in the popular acceptation of the phrase, the answer of our Lord would involve an extravagance, if not an absurdity. It would have been equivalent to saying, ' Suppose I please that he should live a thousand years or more, what is that to you? ' But it is evident that the disciples took the answer seriously.

Appendix to Part I.

NOTE A.

On the Double-sense Theory of Interpretation.

THE following extracts, from theologians of different ages, countries, and churches, exhibit a powerful consensus of authorities in opposition to the loose and arbitrary method of interpretation adopted by many German and English commentators:

' Unam quandam ac certam et simplicem sententiam ubique quaerendam esse.'- **Melanethon.**

('One definite and simple meaning of [Scripture] is in every case to be sought.')

'Absit a nobis ut Deum faciamus o,.i,glwtton, aut multiplices sensus affingamus ipsius verbo, in quo potius tanquarn in speculo limpidissimo sui autoris simplicitatem contemplari debemus. (Ps. xii. 6; xix. B.) *Unicus* ergo *sensus* scripturae, nempe *grammaticus,* est admittendus, quibuscunque demum terminis, vel propriis vel tropicis et figuratis exprimatur.' **-Maresius.**

(Far be it from us to make God speak with two tongues, or to attach a variety of senses to His Word, in which we ought rather to behold the simplicity of its divine author reflected as in a clear mirror (Ps. xii. 6; xix. 8.) Only one meaning of Scripture, therefore, is admissible: that is, the *grammatical,* in whatever terms, whether proper or tropical and figurative, it may be expressed.)

'Dr. Owen's remark is full of good sense-" If the Scripture has more than one meaning, it has no meaning at all: " and it is just as applicable to the prophecies as to any other portion of Scripture.'- **Dr. John Brown, Sufferings and Glories of the Messiah, p. 5, note.**

The consequences of admitting such a principle should be well weighed.

What book on earth has a double sense, unless it is a book of designed *enigmas?* And even this has but one real meaning. The heathen oracles indeed could say, "*Aio te, Pyrrhe, Romanos vincere posse; " but* can such an *equivoque* be admissible into the oracles of the living God? And if a *literal* sense, and an *occult* sense, can at one and the same time, and by the same words, be conveyed, who that is uninspired shall tell us what the occult sense is? By what laws of interpretation is it. to be judged? By none that belong to human language; for other books than the Bible have not a double sense -attached to them.

'For these and such-like reasons, the scheme of attaching a double sense to the Scriptures is inadmissible. It sets afloat all the fundamental principles of interpretation by which we arrive at established conviction and certainty and casts us on the boundless ocean of imagination and conjecture without rudder or compass.'- **Stuart on the Hebrews, Excurs. xx.**

'First, it may be laid down that Scripture has one meaning, -the meaning which it had to the mind of the prophet or evangelist who first uttered or wrote to the hearers or readers who first received it.'

' Scripture, like other books, has one meaning, which is to be gathered from itself, without reference to the adaptations of fathers or divines, and without regard to a *priori* notions about its nature and origin.'

' The office of the interpreter is not to add another [interpretation], but to recover the original one: the meaning, that is, of the words as they struck on the ears or flashed before the eyes of those who first heard and read them.' - **Professor Jowett, Essay on the Interpretation of Scripture, § i. 3, 4.**

'I hold that the words of Scripture were intended to have one definite sense, and that our first object should be to discover that sense, and adhere rigidly to it. I believe that, as a general rule, the words of Scripture are intended to have, like all other language, one plain definite meaning, and that to say that words do mean a thing merely because they can be tortured into meaning it, is a most dishonourable and dangerous way of handling Scripture.'- -**Canon Ryle, Expository Thoughts on St. Luke, vol. i. P. 383.**

NOTE B.

On the Prophetic Element in the Gospels.

Let us proceed to the predictions of the destruction of Jerusalem. These predictions, as is well known, in all the gospel narratives (which, by the way, are singularly consentaneous, implying that all the Evangelists drew from one consolidated tradition) are inextricably mixed up with prophecies of the second coming of Christ and the end of the world -a confusion which Mr. Hutton fully admits. The portion relating to the destruction of the city is singularly definite, and corresponds very closely with the actual event. The other portion, on the contrary, is vague and grandiloquent, and refers, chiefly to natural phenomena and catastrophes. From the precision of the one portion, most critics infer that the gospels were compiled after or during the siege and conquest of Jerusalem. From the confusion of the two portions Mr. Hutton draws the opposite inference -- namely, that the prediction existed in the present recorded form before that event. It is in the greatest degree improbable, he argues, that if Jerusalem had fallen, and the other signs of Christ's coming showed no indication of following, the writers should not have recognised and disentangled the confusion, and corrected their records to bring them into harmony with what it was then beginning to be seen might be the real meaning of Christ or the actual truth of history.

'But the real perplexity lies here. The prediction, as we have it, makes Christ distinctly affirm that His second coming shall follow "immediately," --"in those days," after the destruction of Jerusalem, and that "this generation" (the generation he addressed) should not pass away till all "these things are fulfilled." Mr. Hutton believes that these last words were intended by Christ to apply only to the destruction of the Holy City. He is entitled to his opinion; and in itself it is not an improbable solution. But it is, under the circumstances, a somewhat forced construction, For it must be remembered, first, that it is rendered necessary only by the assumption which Mr. Hutton is maintaining --namely, that the prophetic powers of Jesus could not be at fault; secondly, it assumes or implies that the gospel narratives of the utterances of Jesus are to be relied upon, even though in these especial predictions he admits them to be essentially confused and, thirdly (what at we think he ought not to have overlooked), the sentence he quotes is by no means the only one indicating that Jesus Himself held the conviction, *which He undoubtedly communicated to His followers,* that His Second coming to judge the world would take place at a very early date. Not only was it to take place "immediately" after the destruction of the city (Matt. xxiv. 29), but it would be witnessed by many of those who heard Him. And *these* predictions *are in no way mixed up with those of the destruction of Jerusalem*: " There be some standing here that shall not taste of death till they see the Son of man coming in his kingdom " (Matt. xvi. 28); " Verily I say unto you, Ye shall not have gone over the cities of Israel till the Son of man be come (Matt. x. 23); " If I will that he tarry till I come, what is that to thee 2 (John xxi. 23): and the corresponding passages in the other Synoptics.

'If, therefore, Jesus did not say these things, the gospels must be strangely inaccurate. If He did, His prophetic faculty cannot have been what Mr. Hutton conceives it to have been. That His disciples all confidently entertained this erroneous expectation, and entertained it on the supposed authority of their Master, there can he no doubt whatever. (See 1 Cor. x. 11, xv. 51; Phil. iv. 5; I Thess. iv. 15; James v. 8; I Peter iv. 7; 1 John ii. 18; Rev. i. 13, xxii. 7, 10, 12.) Indeed, Mr. Hutton recognises this at least as frankly and fully as we have stated it.'- W. R. Greg, in Contemporary Review, Nov. 1876.

To those who maintain that our Lord predicted the end of the world before the passing away of that generation, the objections of the sceptic present a formidable difficulty --insurmountable, indeed, without resorting to forced and unnatural evasions, or admissions fatal to the authority and inspiration of the evangelical narratives. We, on the contrary, fully recognise the common-sense construction put by Mr. Greg upon the Language of Jesus, and the no less obvious acceptance of that meaning by the apostles. But we draw a conclusion directly contrary to that of the critic, and appeal to the prophecy on the Mount of Olives as a signal example and demonstration of our Lord's supernatural foresight.

Part Two - The Parousia in the Acts of The Apostles

THE 'GOING AWAY' AND THE 'COMING AGAIN.'

ACTS i. 11. -' This same Jesus, which is taken up from you into heaven, shall so come in like manner as ye have seen him go unto heaven.'

THE last conversation of Jesus with His disciples before His crucifixion was concerning His coming to them again, and the last word left with them at His ascension was the promise of His coming again.

The expression 'in like manner' must not be pressed too far. There are obvious points of difference between the manner of the Ascension and the Parousia. He departed alone, and without visible splendour; He was to return in glory with His angels. The words, however, imply that His coming was to be visible and personal, which would exclude the interpretation which regards it as *providential, or spiritual.* The visibility of the Parousia is supported by the uniform teaching of the apostles and the belief of the early Christians: 'Every eye shall see him' (Rev. i. 7).

There is no indication of *time* in this parting promise, but it is only reasonable to suppose that the disciples would regard it as addressed *to them,* and that they would cherish the hope of soon seeing Him again, according to His own saying, 'A little while, and ye shall see me.' This belief sent them back to Jerusalem with great joy. Is it credible that they could have felt this elation if they had conceived that His coming would not take place for eighteen centuries? Or can we suppose that their joy rested upon a delusion? There is no conclusion possible but that which holds the belief of the disciples to have been well founded, and the Parousia nigh at hand.

THE LAST DAYS COME.

ACTS ii. 16-20-- ' This is that which is spoken by the prophet Joel: It shall come to pass in the last days, saith God, I will pour out of my Spirit upon all flesh: and your sons and your daughters shall prophesy, and your young men shall see visions, and your old men shall dream dreams; moreover on my servants and on my handmaidens I will pour out in those days of my Spirit; and they shall prophesy: and I will shew wonders in heaven above, and signs on the earth beneath; blood, and fire, and vapour of smoke: the sun shall be turned into darkness, and the moon into blood, before that great and notable day of the Lord come.'

In these words of St. Peter, the first apostolic utterance spoken in the power of the divine afflatus of Pentecost, we have an authoritative interpretation of the prophecy which he quotes from Joel. He expressly identifies the time and the event predicted by the prophet with the time and the event then actually present on the day of Pentecost. The ' *last days ' of* Joel are *these days* of St. Peter. The ancient prediction was in part fulfilled; it was receiving its accomplishment before their eyes in the copious effusion of the Holy Spirit.

This outpouring of the Spirit was introductory to other events, which would in like manner come to pass. The day of judgment for the Theocratic nation was at hand, and ere long the presages of 'that great and notable day of the Lord' would be manifested.

It is impossible not to recognise the correspondence between the phenomena preceding the day of the Lord as foretold by Joel, and the phenomena described by our Lord as preceding His coming, and the judgment of Israel (Matt. xxiv. 29). The words of Joel can refer only to the *last days* of the Jewish age or aeon, the ounteleia ton aiwnoj, which was also the theme of our Lord's prophecy on the Mount of Olives. In like manner the words of Malachi as evidently refer to the same event and the same point of time,-- 'the day of his coming,' ' the day that shall burn as a furnace,' ' the great and dreadful day of the Lord' (Mal. iii. 2; iv. 1-5).

We have here a consensus of testimonies than which nothing can be conceived more authoritative and decisive,-- Joel, Malachi, St. Peter, and the great Prophet of the new covenant Himself. They all speak of the same event and of the same period, the great day of the Lord, the Parousia, and they speak of them as *near.* Why encumber and embarrass a prediction so plain with supposititious double references and ulterior fulfilments? Nothing else will fit this prophecy save that event to which alone it refers, and with which it corresponds as the impression with the seal and the lock with the key. The catastrophe of Israel and Jerusalem was at hand, long foreseen, often predicted, and now imminent. The self-same generation that had seen, rejected, and crucified the King would witness the fulfilment of His warnings when Jerusalem perished in 'blood and fire, and vapour of smoke.'

THE COMING DOOM OF THAT GENERATION.

ACTS ii. 40.-'And with many other words did he testify and exhort them, saying, Save yourselves from this untoward generation.'

This verse fixes the reference of the apostle's address. It was the existing generation whose coming doom he foresaw, and it was from participation in its fate that he urged his hearers to escape. It was but the echo of the Baptist's cry,

'Flee from the coming wrath.' Here, again, there can be no question about the meaning of 'genea',-it is that 'wicked generation' which was filling up the measure of its predecessor; the perverse and incorrigible nation over which judgment was impending.

Before leaving this address of St. Peter we may point out another example of a universal proposition which must be taken in a restricted sense. ' I will pour out of my Spirit upon *all flesh.'* The effusion of the Holy Spirit on the day of Pentecost was not literally universal, but it was indiscriminate and general in comparison of former times. The necessarily qualified use of so large a phrase shows how a similar limitation may be justifiable in such expressions as 'all the nations,' ' every creature,' and ' the whole world.'

THE PAROUSIA AND THE RESTITUTION OF ALL THINGS.

ACTS iii. 19-21- 'Repent ye therefore, and be converted, that your sins may be blotted out, that the times of refreshing may come from the presence of the Lord, and that he may Send Jesus Christ, who was before appointed unto you; whom the heavens must receive until the times of. the restoration of all things, of which God hath spoken by the mouth of all his holy prophets since the world began.'

It is scarcely possible to doubt that in this address the apostle speaks of that which be conceived his bearers might and would experience, if they obeyed his exhortation to repent and believe. Indeed, any other supposition would be preposterous. Neither the apostle nor his auditory could possibly be thinking of ' times of refreshing' and 'times of restoration' in remote ages of the world; blessings which were at a distance of centuries and millenniums would hardly be powerful motives to immediate repentance. We must therefore conceive of the times of refreshing and of restoration as, in the view of the apostle, near, and within the reach of that generation.

But if so, what are we to understand by 'the times of refreshing and of restoration'? Are they the same, or are they different, things? Doubtless, virtually the Same; and the one phrase will help us to understand the other. The restitution, or rather restoration [apokatustasij] of all things, is said to be the theme of all prophecy; then it can only refer to what Scripture designates 'the kingdom of God,' the end and purpose of all the dealings of God with Israel. It was a phrase well understood by the Jews of that period, who looked forward to the days of the Messiah, the kingdom of God, as the fulfilment of all their hopes and aspirations. It was the coming age or aeon, aiwn o mellwn, when all wrongs were to be redressed, and truth and righteousness were to reign. The whole nation was pervaded with the belief that this happy era was about to dawn. What was our Lord's doctrine on this subject? He Said to His disciples, 'Elias indeed cometh first, and *restoreth all things'* (Mark ix. 12). That is to say, the second Elijah, John the Baptist, had already commenced the restoration which He Himself was to complete; had laid the foundations of the kingdom which He was to consummate and crown. For the mission of John was, in one aspect, restorative, that is in *intention,* though not in effect. He came to recall the nation to its allegiance, to renew its covenant relation with God: he went before the Lord, 'in the spirit and power of Elias, to turn the hearts of the fathers to the children, and the disobedient to the wisdom of the just; to make ready a people prepared for the Lord' (Luke i. 17). What is all this but the description of 'the times of refreshing from the presence of the Lord,' and 'the times of restoration of all things,' which were held forth as the gifts of God to Israel?

But have we any clear indication of the period at which these proffered blessings might be expected? Were they in the far distant future, or were they nigh at baud? The note of time is distinctly marked in verse 20. The coming of Christ is specified as the period when these glorious prospects are to be realized. Nothing can be more clear than the connection and coincidence of these events, the coming of Christ, the times of refreshing, and the times of restoration of all things. This is in harmony with the uniform representation given in the eschatology of the New Testament: the Parousia, the end of the age, the consummation of the kingdom of God, the destruction of Jerusalem, the judgment of Israel, all synchronise. To find the date of one is to fix the date of all. We have already seen how definitely the time was fixed for the fulfilment of some of these events. The Son of man was to come in His kingdom before the death of some of the disciples. The catastrophe of Jerusalem was to take place before the living generation bad passed away. The great and notable day of the Lord is represented by St. Peter in the preceding chapter as overtaking that 'untoward generation.' And now, in the passage before us, he as clearly intimates that the arrival of the times of refreshing, and of the restoration of all things, was contemporaneous with the 'sending of Jesus Christ' from heaven.

But it may be said, How can so terrible a catastrophe as the destruction of Jerusalem be associated with times of refreshing or of restoration? There were two Bides to the medal: there was the reverse as well as the obverse. Unbelief and impenitence would change 'the times of refreshing' into 'the days of vengeance.' If they ' despised the riches of the goodness and forbearance and long- suffering of God, 'then, instead of restoration, there would be destruction; and instead of the day of salvation there would be 'the day of wrath, and revelation of the righteous judgment of God' (Rom. ii. 4, 5).

We know the fatal choice that Israel made; how 'the wrath came upon them to the uttermost;' and we know how it all came to pass at the appointed and predicted period, at the 'close of the age,' within the limits of that generation.

We are thus enabled to define the period to which the apostle makes allusion in this passage, and conclude that it coincides with the Parousia.

We are conducted to the same conclusion by another path. In Matt. xix. 20 our Lord declares to His disciples, 'Verily I say unto you, that ye which have followed me, in the regeneration, when the Son of man shall sit in the throne of his glory,' etc. We have already commented upon this passage, but it may be proper again to notice that the 'regeneration' [paliggenesia] of St. Matthew is the precise equivalent of the 'restoration' [apokatastasij] of the Acts. What is meant by the regeneration is clear beyond the shadow of a doubt, for it is the time 'when the Son of man shall sit upon the throne of his glory.' But this is the period when He comes to judge the guilty nation (Matt. xxv. 31). There is no possibility of mistaking the time; no difficulty in identifying the event: it is the end of the age, and the judgment of Israel.

We thus arrive at the same conclusion by another and independent route, thus immeasurably strengthening the force of the demonstration.

CHRIST SOON TO JUDGE THE WORLD.

ACTS xvii. 31.-- ' Because he hath appointed day in the which he will judge the world in righteousness by the man whom he hath ordained.'

We have already seen that the Lord Jesus Christ is declared to be constituted the Judge of men (John v. 22, 27). As clearly it is declared that the time of judgment is the Parousia. With equal distinctness we are taught that the Parousia was to fall within the term of the generation then living. The judgment was therefore viewed by St. Paul as being near. We have in the passage now before us an incidental but unnoticed confirmation of this fact. The words 'he will judge' do not express a simple future, but a speedy future, mellei krinein, *He is about to judge,* or will soon judge. This shade of meaning is not preserved in our English version, but it is not unimportant.

Here, then, we are again met by the oft-recurring association of the Parousia and the judgment, both of *which were* evidently regarded by the apostle as nigh at hand.

The Parousia in the Apostlotic Epistles

INTRODUCTION

WE have seen how the Parousia, or coming of Christ, pervades the Gospels from beginning to end. We find it distinctly announced by John the Baptist at the very commencement of his ministry, and it is the last utterance of Jesus recorded by St. John. Between these two points we find continual references to the event in various forms and on various occasions. We have seen also that the Parousia is generally associated with judgment,- that is, the judgment of Israel and the destruction of the temple and city of Jerusalem. The reason of this association of the coming of Christ with the judgment of Israel is very apparent. The Parousia was the culminating event in what may be called Messianic history, or the Theocratic government of the Jewish people. The incarnation and mission of the Son of God, though they had a general relation to the whole human race, had at the same time an especial and peculiar relation to the covenant nation, the children of Abraham. Christ was indeed the 'second Admit,' the new Head and Representative of the race, but before that, He was the Son of David and the King of Israel. His own declared view of His mission was, that it was first of all special to the chosen people,-- 'I am not sent but to the lost sheep of the house of Israel ' (Matt. xv. 24). The very title which He claimed, 'Christ,' the Messiah, or Anointed One, was indicative of His relation to Judaism and the Theocracy, for it recognised Him as the rightful King, come in the fulness of time 'to His own,' to take possession of the throne of His father David. This special Judaic character of the mission of the Lord Jesus is constantly recognised in the New Testament, though it is often ignored by theologians and almost forgotten by Christians in general. St. Paul lays great stress upon it.

'Now I say that Jesus Christ was *a minister of the circumcision,* to confirm the promises made unto the fathers'(Rom. xv. 8); and we might well add, 'to fulfil the threatenings' as well. The phrase 'the kingdom of God' is distinctly a Messianic and Theocratic idea, and has a special and unique reference to Israel, over whom the Lord was King in a sense peculiar to that nation alone (Deut. vii. 6; Amos iii. 2). We shall see that 'the kingdom of God' is represented as arriving at its consummation at the period of the destruction of Jerusalem.

That event marks the denouement of the great scheme of divine providence, or economy, as it is called, which began with the call of Abraham and ran a course of two thousand years. We may regard that scheme, the Jewish dispensation, not only as an important factor in the education of the world, but also as an experiment, on a large scale and under the most favourable circumstances, whether it were possible to form a people for the service, and fear, and love of God; a model nation, the moral influence of which might bless the world. In some respects, no doubt, it was a failure, and its end was tragic and terrible; but what is important for us to notice, in connection with this inquiry, is that the relation of Christ, the Son of David and King of Israel, to the Jewish nation explains the prominence given in the Gospels to the Parousia, and the events which accompanied it, as having a special bearing upon that people. Inattention to this has misled many theologians and commentators:-they have read 'the earth,' when only 'the land' was meant; ' the human race,' when only 'Israel' was intended; 'the end of the world,' when 'the close of the age, or dispensation,' was alluded to. At the same time it would be a serious mistake to undervalue the importance and magnitude of the event which took place at the Parousia. It was a great era in the divine government of the world: the close of an economy which had endured for two thousand years; the termination of one aeon and the commencement of another; the abrogation of the 'old order' and the inauguration of the new. It is, however, its special relation to Judaism which gives to the Parousia its chief significance and import.

Passing from the Gospels to the Epistles we find that the Parousia occupies a conspicuous place in the teaching and writings of the apostles. It is natural and reasonable that it should be so. If their Master taught them in His lifetime that He was soon to come again; that some of themselves would live to see Him return; if in His farewell conversation with them at the Paschal supper He dwelt upon the shortness of the interval of His absence, and called it ' a little while;' and if at His ascension divine messengers bad assured them that He would come again even as they had seen Him go; it would be strange indeed if they could have forgotten or lost sight of the inspiring hope of a speedy reunion with the Lord. They certainly often express their expectation of His coming. That hope was the day-star and dawn that cheered them in the gloomy night of tribulation through which they had to pass: they comforted one another with the familiar watchword, 'The Lord is at hand.' They felt that at any moment their hope might become a reality. They waited for it, looked for it, longed for it, and exhorted one another to watchfulness and prayer. So the Lord had commanded them, and so they did. Could they be mistaken? Is it possible that they cherished illusions on this subject? May they not have misunderstood the teachings of the Lord? If this were possible, it would shake the foundations of our faith. If the apostles could have been in error respecting a matter of fact about which they had the most ample means of information, and on which they professed to speak with authority as the organs of a divine inspiration, what confidence could be reposed in them on other subjects, in their nature obscure, abstruse, and mysterious? No one who has any faith in the assurance which the Saviour gave His disciples that He would send the Holy Spirit to ' guide them into all the truth,' to ' teach them all things,' and to ' bring all things to their remembrance that he had said unto them,' can doubt that the authority with which the apostles speak concerning the Parousia is equal to that of our Lord Himself. The hypothesis that a distinction may be made between what they believed and taught on this subject, and what they believed and taught on other subjects, will not bear a moment's examination. The whole of their teaching rests upon the same foundation, and that foundation the same on which rests the doctrine of Christ Himself.

We now proceed to examine the references to the Parousia contained in the Epistles of St. Paul,-- taking them in their chronological order, so far as this may be said to be ascertained.

The Parousia In the Epistles to The Thessalonians.

THE FIRST EPISTLE TO THE THESSALONIANS

It is generally agreed that this is the earliest of all the apostolic epistles, and its date is assigned to the year A.D. 52, sixteen years after the conversion of St. Paul, [1] and twenty-two Years after the crucifixion of our Lord. It is evident, therefore, that any suggestions of inexperience, or new-born enthusiasm, being visible in this epistle, afterwards toned down by the riper judgment of subsequent years, are quite out of place. We can detect no difference in the faith and hope of 'Paul the aged' and that of the 'weighty and powerful' writer of this epistle. It is, therefore, most instructive to observe the Sentiments and beliefs which were manifestly current and prevalent in the minds of the early Christians.

Bengel remarks: 'The Thessalonians were filled with the expectation of Christ's advent. So praiseworthy was their position, so free and unembarrassed was the rule of Christianity among them, that they were able to look each hour for the coming of the Lord Jesus.' [2] This is strange reasoning. It is true the Thessalonians were filled with the expectation of Christ's speedy coming, but if in this expectation they were deceived, where is the praiseworthiness of labouring under a delusion? If it was an amiable weakness, 'sancta simplicitas,' to expect the speedy return of Christ, it seems a poor compliment to praise their credulity at the expense of their understanding.

We shall find, however, that the Christians of Thessalonica stand in no need of any apology for their faith.

EXPECTATION OF THE SPEEDY COMING OF CHRIST.

1 THESS. i. 9, 10-- 'Ye turned to God from your idols, to serve the living and true God; and to wait for his Son from the heavens, whom he raised from the dead, even Jesus, who delivereth us from the coming wrath.'

This passage is interesting as showing very clearly the place which the expected coming of Christ held in the belief of the apostolic churches. It was in the front rank; it was one of the leading truths of the Gospel. St. Paul describes the new attitude of these Thessalonian converts when they 'turned from their idols to serve the living and true God;' it was the attitude of 'waiting for his Son.' It is very significant that this particular truth should be selected from among all the great doctrines of the Gospel, and should be made the prominent feature which distinguished the Christian converts of Thessalonica. The whole Christian life is apparently summed up under two heads, the one general, the other particular: the former, the service of the living God; the latter, the expectation of the coming of Christ. It is impossible to resist the inference, (1) That this latter doctrine constituted an integral part of apostolic teaching. (2) That the expectation of the speedy return of Christ was the faith of the primitive Christians. [3] For, how were they to wait? Not Surely, in their graves; not in Heaven; nor in Hades; plainly while they were alive on the earth. The form of the expression, 'to wait for his Son from the heavens,' manifestly implies that they, *while on earth,* were waiting for the coming of Christ from heaven. Alford observes 'that the especial aspect of the faith of the Thessalonians was *hope;* hope of the return of the Son of God from heaven;' and he adds this singular comment: 'This hope was evidently entertained by them as pointing to an event more immediate than the church has subsequently believed it to be. Certainly these words would give them an idea of the *nearness* of the coming of Christ; and perhaps the misunderstanding of them may have contributed to the notion which the apostle corrects, 2 Thess. ii. 1.' This is a suggestion that the Thessalonians were mistaken in expecting the Saviour's return in their own day. But whence did they derive this expectation? Was it not from the apostle himself? We shall presently see that the Thessalonians erred, not in *expecting* the Parousia, or in *expecting it in their own day,* but in supposing that the time had actually arrived.

The last clause of the verse is no less important,-' Jesus, who delivereth us from *the coming wrath.'* These words carry us back to the proclamation of John the Baptist,-- 'Flee from the coming wrath.' It would be a mistake to suppose that St. Paul here refers to the retribution which awaits every sinful soul in a future state; it was a particular and predicted catastrophe which he bad in view. 'The coming wrath' [h orgh h ercomenh] of this passage is identical with the 'coming wrath' [*orgh* mellousa] of the second Elijah; it is identical with 'the days of vengeance,' and 'wrath upon this people,' predicted by our Lord, Luke xxi. 23. It is 'the day of wrath, and revelation of the righteous judgment of God,' spoken of by St. Paul, Rom ii. 5. That coming *'dies irae'* always stands out distinct and visible throughout the whole of the New Testament. It was now not far off, and though Judea might be the centre of the storm, yet the cyclone of judgment would sweep over other regions, and affect multitudes who, like the Thessalonians, might have been thought beyond its reach. We know from Josephus how the outbreak of the Jewish war was the signal for massacre and extermination in every city where Jewish inhabitants had settled. It was to this ubiquity of 'the coming Wrath' that our Lord referred when He said, 'Wheresoever the body is, thither will the eagles be gathered together' (Luke xvii. 37). Here again, as we have so frequently had occasion to remark, the Parousia is associated with the judgment.

'THE WRATH' COMING UPON THE JEWISH PEOPLE.

I Thess. ii. 16 -- ' But the wrath is come upon them to the uttermost.'

Here the apostle represents the 'coming wrath' as already come. Now it is certain that the judgment of Israel, that is, the destruction of Jerusalem and the extinction of the Jewish nationality, had not yet taken place. Bengel seems to think that the apostle alludes to a fearful massacre of Jews that bad just occurred at Jerusalem, where 'an immense multitude of persons (some say more than thirty thousand) were slain.' [4] Alford's explanation is: ' He looks *back* on the fact in the divine counsels as a thing in past time, *q.d.* " was appointed to come;" not "has come." Jonathan Edwards, in his sermon on this text, refers it to the approaching destruction of Jerusalem. "The wrath is come," i.e. it is just at hand; it is at the door: as it proved with respect to that nation: their terrible destruction by the Romans was soon after the apostle wrote this epistle." [5] Either Bengel's supposition is correct, or the final catastrophe was, in the apostle's view, so *near* and so sure that he spoke of it as an accomplished fact.

We may trace a very distinct allusion in the language of the apostle in verses 15 and 16 to our Lord's denunciations of 'that wicked generation' (Matt. xxiii. 31, 32, 36).

THE BEARING OF THE PAROUSIA ON THE DISCIPLES OF CHRIST.

I Thess. ii. 19.-- ' For what is our hope, or joy, or crown of rejoicing? Are not even ye in the presence of our Lord Jesus at his coming?'

The uniform teaching, of the New Testament is, that the event which was to be so fatal to the enemies of Christ was to be an auspicious one to His friends. Everywhere the most malignant opposers and persecutors of Christianity were the Jews; the annihilation of the Jewish nationality, therefore, removed the most formidable antagonist of the Gospel and brought rest and relief to suffering Christians. Our Lord had said to His disciples, when speaking of this approaching catastrophe, 'When these things begin to come to pass, then look up, and lift up your heads, for your redemption draweth nigh' (Luke xxi. 28). But this explanation is far from exhausting the whole meaning of such passages. It cannot be doubted that the Parousia is everywhere represented as the crowning day of Christian hopes and aspirations; when they would 'inherit the kingdom,' and 'enter into the joy of their Lord.' Such is the plain teaching both of Christ and His apostles, and we find it clearly expressed in the words of St. Paul now before us. The Parousia was to be the consummation of glory and felicity to the faithful, and the apostle looked for 'his crown' at the Lord's 'coming.'

CHRIST TO COME WITH ALL HIS HOLY ONES.

I Thess. iii. 13. -- ' To the end that he may stablish ' your hearts unblameable in holiness before God, even our Father, at the coming of our Lord Jesus with all his holy' [ones].

This passage furnishes another proof that the apostle regarded the period of our Lord's coming as the consummation of the blessedness of His people. He here represents it as a judicial epoch when the moral condition and character of men would be scrutinised and revealed. This is in accordance with I Cor. iv. 5: ' Judge nothing before the time, *until the Lord come,* who both will bring to light the hidden things of darkness, and will make manifest the counsels of the hearts: and then shall every man have praise of God.' Similarly in Col. i. 22 we find an almost identical expression,-'To present you holy, and unblameable, and unreproveable in his sight,' words which can only be understood as referring to a judicial investigation and approval.

That this prospect was not distant, but, on the contrary, very near, the whole tenor of the apostle's language implies. Is St. Paul still without his crown of rejoicing? Are his Thessalonian converts Still waiting for the Son of God from heaven? Are they not yet ' stablished in holiness before God'? not yet presented holy, and unblameable, and unreproveable in His sight? For this was to be their felicity 'at the coming of the Lord Jesus,' and not before. If that event therefore has never yet taken place, what becomes of their eager expectation and hope? If they could have known that hundreds and thousands of years must first Slowly run their course, could St. Paul and his children in the faith have been thus filled with transport at the thought of the coming glory? But on the supposition that the Parousia was close at hand; that they might all expect to witness its arrival, then how natural and intelligible all this eager anticipation and hope become. That both the apostle and the Thessalonians believed that 'the coming of the Lord was drawing nigh,' is so evident that it scarcely requires any argument to prove it. The only question is, were they mistaken, or were they not?

A remark may be added on the concluding word of the passage. 'Agioi, holy, may refer to angels, or men, or to both. There is nothing in the text to determine the reference. It is true that in the next chapter (ver. 14) we are told that them also which sleep in Jesus will God bring with him but this seems to refer rather to the raising of the sleeping saints from their graves, than of their coming from heaven with Him. We are therefore precluded from referring agioi to the dead in Christ. The more so that Christ at His coming is always represented as attended by His angels.

'He shall come with his angels' (Matt. xvi. 27); 'with the holy angels' (Mark viii. 38); 'with his mighty angels' (2 Thess. i. 7); 'all his holy angels with him' (Matt. xxv. 1).

This is in accordance also with Old Testament usage. The royal state of Jehovah when He came to give the law at Mount Sinai is thus described,-- 'He came with ten thousands ' *i.e. ,* of saints, angels (Dent. xxxiii. 2). 'The chariots of God are twenty thousand, even thousands of angels; the Lord is among them as in Sinai' (Ps. lxviii. 17). 'Ye received the law by the disposition [at the injunction, - Alford] of angels' (Acts vii. 53). We may therefore take it as probable that the reference in this passage is to the angels.

EVENTS ACCOMPANYING THE PAROUSIA.

1. The Resurrection of the Dead in Christ.

2. The Rapture of the Living Saints to Hearen.

I Thess. iv. 13-17 -- ' But I would not have .you to be ignorant, brethren, concerning them which are asleep, that ye sorrow not, even ,is others which have no hope. For if we believe that Jesus died and rose again, even so them also which sleep in Jesus will God bring with him. For this we say unto you by [in] the word of the Lord, that we which are alive and remain unto the coming of the Lord, shall not prevent [come before, take precedence of] them which are asleep. For the Lord himself shall descend from heaven with a shout, with the voice of the archangel and with the trump of God: and first the dead in Christ shall rise then we which are alive and remain shall be caught up together with them in the clouds, to meet the Lord in the air: and so shall we ever be with the Lord.'

These explanations of St. Paul are evidently intended to meet a state of things which had begun to manifest itself among the Christians of Thessalonica, and which had been reported to him by Timotheus. Eagerly looking for the coming of Christ, they deplored the death of their fellow Christians as excluding them from participation in the triumph and blessedness of the Parousia. ' They feared that these departed Christians would lose the happiness of witnessing their Lord's second coming, which they expected soon to behold.' [6]- To correct this misapprehension the apostle makes the explanations contained in this passage.

First, be assures them that they had no reason to regret the departure of their friends in Christ, as if they bad sustained any disadvantage by dying before the coming of the Lord; for as God had raised up Jesus from the dead, so He would raise u His sleeping disciples from their graves, at His return in glory.

Secondly, he informs them, on the authority of the Lord Jesus, that those of themselves who lived to see His coming would not take precedence of, or have any advantage over, the faithful who had deceased before that event.

Thirdly, he describes the order of the events attending the Parousia: --

1. The descent of the Lord from heaven with a shout, with the voice of the archangel, and the trump of God.

2. The raising up of the dead who had departed in the Lord.

3. The simultaneous rapture of the living saints, along with the resuscitated dead, into the region of the air, there to meet their coming Lord.

4. The everlasting reunion of Christ and His people in heaven.

The legitimate inference from the words of St. Paul in ver. 15, 'we who are alive and remain unto the coming of the Lord,' is that he anticipated it as possible, and even probable, that his readers and himself would be alive at the coming of the Lord. Such is the natural and obvious interpretation of his language. Dean Alford observes, with much force and candour, -

' Then, beyond question, he himself expected to be alive, together with the majority of those to whom he was writing, at the Lord's coming. For we cannot for a moment accept the evasion of Theodoret and the majority of ancient commentators (viz. that the apostle does not speak of himself personally, but of those who should be living at the period), but we must take the words in their only plain grammatical meaning, that "we which are alive and remain" are a class distinguished from "they that sleep" by being yet in the flesh when Christ comes, in which class by prefixing " we " he includes his readers and himself. That this was his expectation we know from other passages, especially from 2 Cor. v.' [7]

But while thus admitting that the apostle held this expectation, Alford treats it as a mistaken one, for he goes on to say:

"Nor need it surprise any Christian that the apostles should in this matter of detail have found their personal expectation liable to disappointment respecting a day of which it is so solemnly said that no man knoweth its appointed time, not the angels in heaven, not the Son, but the Father only (Mark xiii. 32).'

In like manner we find the following remarks in Conybeare and Howson (chap. xi.):

' The early church, and even the apostles themselves, expected their Lord to come again in that very generation. St. Paul himself shared in that expectation, but, being under the guidance of the Spirit of truth, he did not deduce therefrom any erroneous practical conclusion.'

But the question is, had the apostles sufficient grounds for their expectation? Were they not fully justified in believing as they did? Had not the Lord expressly predicted His own coming within the limit of the existing generation? Had He not connected it with the overthrow of the temple and the subversion of the national polity of Israel? Had He not assured His disciples that in 'a *little while*' they should see Him again? Had He not declared that some of them should live to witness His return? And after all this, is it necessary to find excuses for St. Paul and the early Christians, as if they had laboured under a delusion? If they did, it was not they who were to blame, but their Master. It would have been strange indeed if, after all the exhortations which they bad received to be on the alert, to watch, to live in continual expectancy of the Parousia, the apostles had not confidently believed in His speedy coming, and taught others to do the same. But it Would seem that St. Paul rests his explanations to the Thessalonians on the authority of a special divine communication made to himself, ' This I say unto you *by the word of the Lord,*' etc. This can hardly mean that the Lord had so predicted in His prophetic discourse on the Mount of Olives, for no such statement is recorded; it must therefore refer to a revelation Which he had himself received. How, then, could he be at fault in his expectations? It is strange that so great incredulity should exist in this day respecting the plain sense of our Lord's express declarations on this subject. Fulfilled or unfulfilled, right or wrong, there is no ambiguity or uncertainty in His language. It may be said that we have no evidence of such facts having occurred as are here described,-- the Lord descending with a shout, the sounding of the trumpet, the raising of the sleeping dead, the rapture of the living saints. True; but is it certain that these are facts cognisable by the senses? is their place in the region of the material and the visible? As we have already said, we know and are sure that a very large portion of the events predicted by our Lord, and expected by His apostles, did actually come to pass at that very crisis called 'the end of the age.' There is no difference of opinion concerning the destruction of the temple, the overthrow of the city, the unparalleled slaughter of the people, the extinction of the nationality, the end of the legal dispensation. But the Parousia is inseparably linked with the destruction of Jerusalem; and, in like manner, the resurrection of the dead, and the judgment of the 'wicked generation,' with the Parousia. They are different parts of one great catastrophe; different scenes in one great drama. We accept the facts verified by the historian on *the word of man; is* it for Christians to hesitate to accept the facts which are vouched *by the word of the Lord?*

EXHORTATIONS TO WATCHFULNESS IN PROSPECT OF THE PAROUSIA.

I Thess. v. 1-10.-- 'But of the times and the seasons, brethren, ye have no need that I write unto you. For yourselves know perfectly that the day of the Lord so cometh as a thief in the night. For when they shall ray, Peace and safety; then sudden destruction cometh upon them, as travail upon a woman with child; and they shall not escape. But ye, brethren, are not in darkness, that that day should overtake you as a thief. Ye are all the children of light, and the children of the day: we are not of the night, nor of darkness. Therefore let us not sleep as do others; but let us watch and be sober. For they that sleep, sleep in the night; and they that be drunken are drunken in the night. But let us, who axe of the day, be sober, putting on the breastplate of faith and love; and for an helmet, the hope of salvation. For God hath not appointed us to wrath, but to obtain salvation by our Lord Jesus Christ, who died for us, that, whether we wake or sleep, we should live together with Him.'

It is manifest that there would be no meaning in these urgent calls to watchfulness unless the apostle believed in the nearness of the coming crisis. Was it to the Thessalonians, or to some unborn generation in the far distant future, that St. Paul was penning these lines? Why urge men in A.D. 52 to watch, and be on the alert, for a catastrophe which was not to take place for hundreds and thousands of years? Every word of this exhortation supposes the crisis to be impending and imminent.

To say that the apostle writes not for any one generation, nor to any persons in particular, is to throw an air of unreality into his exhortations from which reverent criticism revolts. He certainly meant the very persons to whom he wrote, and who read this epistle, and he thought of none others. We cannot accept the Suggestion of Bengel that the 'we which are alive and remain' are only imaginary personages, like the names Caius and Titius (John Doe and Richard Roe); for no one can read this epistle without being conscious of the warm personal attachment and affection to individuals which breathe in every line. We conclude, therefore, that the whole bad a direct and present bearing upon the actual position end prospects of the persons to whom the epistle is addressed.

PRAYER THAT THE THESSALONIANS MIGHT SURVIVE UNTIL THE COMING OF CHRIST.

1 THESS. v. 23 -- ' Now may the God of peace himself sanctify you wholly, and may your spirit, and soul, and body, all together be preserved blameless at the appearing of our Lord Jesus Christ.' [8]

If any shadow of a doubt still rested on the question whether St. Paul believed and taught the incidence of the Parousia in his own day, this passage would dispel it. No words can more clearly imply this belief than this prayer that the Thessalonian Christians might not die before the appearing of Christ. Death is the dissolution of the union between body, soul, and spirit, and the apostle's prayer is that spirit, soul, and body might 'all together' be preserved in sanctity till the Lord's coming. This implies *the continuance of their corporeal life until that event.*

1. Conybeare and Howson.

2. Gnomon, in loc.

3. ' It is known to every reader of Scripture that the First Epistle to the Thessalonians speaks of the coming of Christ in terms which indicate an expectation of His speedy appearance: "For this we say unto you by the word of the Lord, that we," etc. (chap. iv. 15-17; v. 4). Whatever other construction these texts may bear, the idea they leave upon the mind of an ordinary reader is that of the author of the epistle looking for the day of judgment to take place in his own time, or near to it.'-- Paley's Horae Paulinae, chap. ix.

*'If we were asked for the distinguishing characteristic of the first Christians of Thessalonica, we should point to their overwhelming sense of the nearness of the second advent, accompanied with melancholy thoughts concerning those who might die before it, and with gloomy and un practical views of the shortness of life and the vanity of the world. Each chapter in the First Epistle to the Thessalonians ends with an allusion to this subject; and it was evidently the topic of frequent conversations when the apostle was in Macedonia. But St. Paul never spoke or wrote of the future as though the present was to be forgotten. When the Thessalonians were admonished of Christ's advent, he told them also of other coming events, full of practical warning to all ages, though to our eyes still they are shrouded in mystery,-- of " the falling away," and of " the man of sin." " These awful revelations," he said, " must precede the revelation of the Son of God. Do you not remember," he adds, with emphasis, in his letter, " that when I was still with you, I often told you this! You know therefore the hindrance why he is **not revealed, as he** will be in his own season." He told them, in the words of Christ Himself, that " the times and the seasons of the coming revelations were known only to God; " and he warned them, as the first disciples had been warned in Jude, that the great day would come suddenly on men unprepared, .. as the pangs of travail on her whose time is full," and "as a thief in the night; " and he showed them both by precept and example that though it be true that life is short and the world is vanity, yet God's work must be done diligently and to the last.'-- Conybeare and Howson, Life and Epistles of St. Paul, chap. ix*

*4. **Gnomon,** in loc.*

5. Works, vol. iv. p. 281

6. Conybeare and Howson ch. xi.

7. Greek Testament, in loc.

8. Conybeare and Howson's Translation

The Parousia In the Epistles to the Thessalonians - The Second Epistle to the Thessalonians

The Second Epistle to the Thessalonians appears to have been written shortly after the First, to correct the misapprehension into which some had fallen respecting the time of the Parousia, whether through an erroneous interpretation of the apostle's former letter, or in consequence of some pretended communication circulated among them purporting to be from him. We learn from this epistle the precise nature of the mistake which some of the Thessalonians had committed. I was that the time of the Parousia had *actually arrived.* In consequence of this opinion some had begun to neglect their secular employments and subsist upon the charity of others. To check the evils which might arise, or had arisen, from such erroneous impressions, St. Paul wrote this second epistle, reminding them that certain events, which had not yet taken place, must precede the 'day of the Lord.' There is nothing, however, in the epistle to suggest that the Parousia was a distant event, but the contrary.

THE PAROUSIA A TIME OF JUDGMENT TO THE ENEMIES OF CHRIST, AND OF DELIVERANCE TO HIS PEOPLE

2 THESS i.7-10. - 'And to you who are troubled rest with us, when the Lord Jesus shall be revealed from heaven with his mighty angels, in flaming fire, taking vengeance on them that know not God, and that obey not the gospel of our Lord Jesus Christ: who shall be punished with everlasting destruction from the presence of the Lord and from the glory of his power: in that day when he shall come to be glorified in his saints, and to be admired in all them that believed.'

It is obvious from the allusions in the commencement of this epistle that the Thessalonians were at this time suffering severely from the malice of their Jewish persecutors, and those 'lewd fellows of the baser sort,' who were in league with them (Acts xvii.5). The apostle comforts them with the prospect of deliverance at the appearing of the Lord Jesus, which would bring rest to them and retribution to their enemies. This is in perfect accordance with the representations constantly made with respect to the Parousia,---that it would be the time of judgment to the wicked, and the reward to the righteous. The apostle seems not to anticipate the 'rest' of which he speaks until the Parousia, 'when the Lord Jesus shall be revealed from heaven,' etc. It follows that the rest was conceived by St. Paul to be very near; for if the revelation of the Lord Jesus be an event still future, then we must conclude that neither the apostle nor the suffering Christians have yet entered into that rest. It will be observed that it is not said that *death* is to bring them rest, but 'the apocalypse' of the Lord Jesus from heaven: a clear proof that the apostle did not regard that apocalypse as a distant event.

That this approaching 'apocalypse,' or revelation of the Lord Jesus from heaven, is identical with the Parousia predicted by our Saviour, is so evident that it needs no proof. It is 'the day of the Lord' (Luke xvii. 24); '*the* day when the Son of man is revealed' (Luke xvii. 30); 'the day which shall be revealed in fire' (1 Cor. iii. 13); 'the day which shall burn as a furnace' (Mal. iv. 1); 'the great and dreadful day of the Lord' (Mal. iv. 5). It is the day when 'the Son of man shall come in the glory of his Father with his angels, to reward every man according to his works' (Matt. xvi. 27). And once more, it is that day concerning which our Lord declared, 'Verily I say unto you, There be some standing here which shall not taste of death till they see the Son of man coming in his kingdom' (Matt. xvi. 28).

We are thus brought back to the same truth which everywhere meets us in the New Testament, that the Parousia, the day of Israel's judgment, and the close of the Jewish dispensation, was not a distant event, but within the limit of the generation which rejected the Messiah.

The objection will be urged, What had that to do with Thessalonica and the Christians there? How could the destruction of Jerusalem, or the extinction of the Jewish nationality, or the close of the Mosaic economy, affect persons at so great a distance from Judea as Thessalonica? Even if it were impossible to give a satisfactory answer to this objection, it would not alter the plain and natural meaning of words, or make it incumbent upon us to force an interpretation upon them which they will not bear. The Scriptures must be allowed to speak for themselves --- a liberty which many will not concede. But with regard to the bearing of the Parousia on Christians in Thessalonica, or outside of Judea in general, it cannot be denied that the language of this passage, as of many others, intimates that it was an event in which all had a deep and personal interest. Nor is it enough to say that the most bitter antagonists of the Gospel in Thessalonica were Jews, and that the Jewish revolt was the signal for the massacre of the Jewish inhabitants in almost every city of the Empire. This may be true, but it is not the whole truth, according to apostolic teaching. We must admit, therefore, that as the eschatological scheme of the New Testament unfolds itself, it becomes apparent that the Parousia, and its accompanying events, did not relate to Judea exclusively, but had an ecumenical or world-wide aspect, so that Christians everywhere might look and long for it, and hail its coming as the day of triumph and of glory. As we proceed we shall find ample evidence of this larger aspect of 'the day of Christ,' as a great epoch in the divine administration of the world.

EVENTS WHICH MUST PRECEDE THE PAROUSIA

1. The Apostasy

2. The Revelation of the Man of Sin

2 THESS. ii. 1-12.---'But, as concerning the coming of our Lord Jesus Christ, and our gathering together unto him, we beseech you, brethren, that ye be not soon shaken from your mind, nor be troubled, neither by spirit, nor by word, nor by letter, as from us, to the effect that the day of the Lord is come. Let no man deceive you by any means; for [that day shall not come] unless there shall have come the apostasy first, and the man of sin shall have been revealed, the son of perdition: who opposeth and exalteth himself above all that is called God, or an object of worship: so that he seateth himself in the temple of God, and openly declareth himself a god. Remember ye not that, when I was yet with you, I told you these things? And now ye know what hindereth his being revealed in his own time. For the mystery of lawlessness is already working, only he who now hindereth will hinder until he be taken out of the way. And then shall the lawless one be revealed, whom the Lord Jesus shall slay with the breath of his mouth, and shall destroy with the appearance of his coming: whose coming is after the working of Satan in all power and signs and wonders of falsehood, and in all deceit of unrighteousness for them that are perishing, because they received not the love of the truth, that they might be saved. And for this cause God is sending them the working of delusion, that they should believe the lies: that they all may be condemned who believed not the truth, but had pleasure in unrighteousness'

Few passages have more exercised and baffled commentators, or are regarded to this day as involved in deeper obscurity, than the one before us. There is no reason, however, to suppose that it was unintelligible to the Thessalonians, for it refers to matters which had formed the topic of frequent conversation between them and the apostle, and possibly not a little of the obscurity of which expositors complain may arise from the fact that, to the Thessalonians, it was only necessary to give hints, rather than full explanations.

The apostle begins by distinctly stating the subjects on which he is desirous of setting the Thessalonians right. They are, (1) 'the coming of Christ,' and (2) 'our gathering together unto him.' These are evidently regarded by the apostle as simultaneous, or, at all events, closely connected. What are we to understand by this 'gathering together unto Christ' at the Parousia? There is no doubt a reference here to our Lord's own words, Matt. xxvi. 31: 'He shall send his angels with a great sound of a trumpet, and they shall gather together his elect from the four winds,' etc. The [shall gather together] in the gospel in evidently the [the gathering together] of the epistle; and we have another reference to the same event and the same period in 1 Thess. iv. 16,17: 'For the Lord himself shall descend from heaven with a shout, with the voice of the archangel, and with the trump of God,' etc. This can be nothing else, then, than the summoning of the living and the dead to the tribunal of Christ.

That great and solemn 'gathering' the Thessalonians had been taught to 'wait for;' but it appears they were labouring under some misapprehension concerning the time of its arrival. Some of them had formed the opinion that 'the day of Christ' had actually arrived []. It is important to observe that our English version does not give the correct rendering of this word. The apostle does not say, 'as that the day of Christ is *at hand*,' but 'as that the day of Christ *is present*, or, *is actually come*,' The constant teaching of St. Paul was, that the day of Christ was *at hand*, and it would have been to contradict himself to tell Christians of Thessalonica that that day was *not* at hand. Yet nothing is more common than to find some of our most respectable scholars and critics deny that the apostles and early Christians expected the Parousia in their own day, on the strength of the erroneous rendering of this word . Even so eminent an authority as Moses Stuart says, in reply to Tholuck:---

'This interpretation (viz. The speedy advent of Christ) was formally and strenuously corrected in 2 Thess. ii. Is it not enough that Paul has explained his own words? Who can safely venture to give them a meaning different from what he gives?'

So, too, Albert Barnes:---

'If Paul here refers to his former epistle, ---which might easily be understood as teaching that the end of the world was near,---we have the authority of the apostle himself that he meant to teach no such thing.'

Most singular of all is the explanation of Dr. Lange:---

'The first epistle [to the Thessalonians] is pervaded by the fundamental thought, *"the Lord will come speedily:"* the second, by the thought, *"the Lord will not yet come speedily."* Both of these are in accordance with the truth; because, in the first part, the question is concerning the coming of the Lord in His dynamic rule in a religious sense; and, in the second part, concerning the coming of the Lord in a definite historical and chronological sense.'

What can be more arbitrary and whimsical than such a distinction? What more empirical than such treatment of Scripture, by which it is made to say Yes and No; to affirm and to deny; to declare that an event is nigh and distant, in the same breath? Who would presume to interpret Scripture if it spoke in such ambiguous language as this?

We hold by the 'definite historical and chronological sense' of the Parousia, and by no other. It is the only sense which is respectful to the Word of God and satisfactory to sober criticism. The apostle does not correct himself, nor does he refer to two different 'comings,' but he corrects the mistake of the Thessalonians, who affirmed that the day of Christ had actually *come*. In every instance in which the word occurs in the New Testament it refers to what is *present*, and not to what is future. To Greek scholars it is unnecessary to point this out, but to English readers it may be satisfactory to refer to competent authorities.

Dr. Manton, comparing the force of the words and [draweth nigh] (Jas. v. 8; 1 Pet. iv. 17), observes:---

'There is some difference in the words, for signifies *it draweth near*, , it is begun already.'

Bengel says:---

'Extreme proximity is signified by this word; for is *present.*'

Whiston, the translator of Josephus, has the following note:---

' is here, and in many other places of Josephus, *immediately* at hand; and is to be so expounded 2 Thess. ii. 2, where some falsely pretended that St. Paul had said, either by word of mouth or by an epistle, or by both, "that the day of Christ was immediately at hand;" for still St. Paul did then plainly think that day not many years future.

Dr. Paley observes:---

'It should seem that the Thessalonians, or some however amongst them, had from this passage (1 Thess. iv. 15-17) conceived an opinion (and that not very unnaturally) that the coming of Christ was to take place instantly: and that persuasion had produced, as it well might, much agitation in the church.'

Conybeare and Howson translate,---

"That the day of the Lord is come;" adding the following note:---'Literally, "is present." So the verb is always used in New Testament.'

Dean Alford comments thus:---

'The day of the Lord is present (not is at hand), occurs six time besides in the New Testament, and always in the sense of being *present*. Besides which, St. Paul could not have so written, nor could the Spirit have so spoken by him. The teaching of the apostles was, and of the Holy Spirit in all ages has been, that the day of the Lord is *at hand*. But these Thessalonians imagined it to be already come, and accordingly were deserting their pursuits in life, and falling into other irregularities, as if the day of grace were closed.'

The very general misconception which prevails respecting the meaning of this verse renders it of the utmost importance that it should be correctly apprehended.

It is easy to understand how the erroneous opinion of the Thessalonians should have 'troubled and shaken' their minds. It was calculated to produce panic and disorder. History tells us that a general belief prevailed in Europe towards the close of the tenth century that the year 1000 would witness the coming of Christ, the day of judgment, and the end of the world. As the time drew near, a general panic seized the minds of men. Many abandoned their homes and their families, and repaired to the Holy Land; others made over their lands to the Church, or permitted them to be uncultivated, and the whole course of ordinary life was violently disturbed and deranged. A similar delusion, though on a smaller scale, prevailed in some parts of the United States in the year 1843, causing great consternation among multitudes, and driving many persons out of their senses. Facts like these show the wisdom which 'hid the day and the hour' of the Son of man's coming, so that, while all might be watchful, none should be thrown into agitation.

In the third verse the apostle intimates that 'the day of Christ' must be preceded by two events:---(1) The coming of *'the apostasy,'* and (2) the manifestation of *'the man of sin.'*

Could we place ourselves in the situation and circumstances of the Christians of Thessalonica when this epistle was written; could we call up the hopes and fears, the expectations and apprehensions, the social and political agitations of that period, we might be better able to enter into the explanations of St. Paul. Doubtless the Thessalonians understood him perfectly. As Paley justly observes, 'No man writes unintelligibly on purpose,' and we cannot suppose that he would tantalise them with enigmas which could only perplex and bewilder them more than ever.

The first question that presents itself is, Are the 'apostasy' and the 'man of sin' identical? Do they both point to the same thing? It is the opinion of many, perhaps of most, expositors that they are virtually one and the same. But evidently they are distinct and separate things. The apostasy represents a *multitude,* the man of sin a *person;* so that though they may be in some respects *connected,* they are not to be *confounded;* they may exist *contemporaneously,* but they are not *identical.*

The Apostasy

St. Paul does not at present dwell upon 'the apostasy,' but, having simply named it as to come, passes on to the description of 'the man of sin.' We may here, however, refer to the fact that 'the falling away' was no new idea to the disciples of Christ. The Saviour had expressly predicted its coming in His prophetic discourse, Matt. xxiv. 10,12, and St. Paul elsewhere gives as full a delineation of the apostasy as he here does of the man of sin. (See 1 Tim. iv. 1-3; 2 Tim. iii. 1-9.) It can only refer to that *defection from the faith* so clearly predicted by our Lord, and described by His apostles, as indicative of 'the last days.' But this topic will come to be considered in its proper place.

The Man of Sin

It is of utmost importance in entering upon this field of inquiry to find some principle which may guide and govern us in the investigation. We find such a principle in the very simple and obvious consideration that the apostle is here referring to circumstances which lay within the ken of the Thessalonians themselves. If the Parousia itself, to which the development of the apostasy and the appearing of the man of sin were antecedent, was declared by the word of the Lord to fall within the period of the existing generation, it follows that 'the apostasy' and 'the man of sin' lay *nearer* to them than the Parousia. Besides, if we suppose 'the apostasy' and 'the man of sin' to lie far beyond the times of the Thessalonians, what would be the use of giving them explanations and information about matters which were not at all urgent, and which, in fact, did not concern them at all? Is it no obvious that whoever the man of sin may be, he must be someone with whom the apostle and his readers had to do? Is he not writing to living men about matters in which they are intensely interested? Why should he delineate the features of this mysterious personage to the Thessalonians if he was one with whom the Thessalonians had nothing to do, from whom they had nothing to fear, and who would not be revealed for ages yet to come? It is clear that he speaks of one whose influence was already beginning to be felt, and whose unchecked and lawless fury would ere long burst forth. All this lies on the very surface, obvious and unquestionable. But this is not all. It appears certain that the Thessalonians were not ignorant what person was intended by the man of sin. It was not the first time that the apostle had spoken with them on the subject. He says, 'Remember ye not, that when I was yet with you, I kept telling you these things? and now *ye know* what hindereth his being revealed in his own time.' This language plainly indicates that the apostle and his readers were well acquainted with the name 'man of sin,' and knew who was designated thereby. If so, and it seems unquestionable, the area of investigation becomes greatly contracted, and the probabilities of discovery proportionately increased. What the Thessalonians had *'talked about,' 'remembered,'* and *'knew,'* must have been something of living and present interest; in short, must have belonged to *contemporary history.*

But why does not the apostle speak out frankly? Why this reserve and reticence in darkly hinting what he does not name? It was not from ignorance; it could not be from the affectation of mystery. There must have been some strong reason for this extreme caution. No doubt; but of what nature? Why should he have been in the habit, as he says, of *speaking* so freely on the subject in private, and then *write* so obscurely in his epistle? Obviously, *because it was not safe to be more explicit.* On the one hand, a hint was enough, for they could all understand his meaning; on the other, more than a hint was dangerous, for to name the person might have compromised himself and them.

From what quarter, then, was danger to be apprehended from too great freedom of speech? There were only two quarters from which the Christians of the apostolic age had just cause for apprehension, --- Jewish bigotry and Roman jealousy. Hitherto the Gospel had suffered most from the former: the Jews were everywhere the instigators in 'stirring up the Gentiles against the brethren.' But the power of Rome was jealous, and the Jews knew well how to awaken that jealousy; in Thessalonica itself they had got up the cry, 'These all do contrary to the decrees of Cæsar.' Which of these causes, then, may have sealed the lips of the apostle? Not fear of the Jews, for nothing that he could say was likely to make their hostility more bitter; nor had the Jews any direct civil authority by which they could inflict injury upon the Christian cause. We conclude, therefore, that it was from the *Roman power* that the apostle apprehended danger, and that his reticence was occasioned by the desire not to involve the Thessalonians in the suspicion of disaffection and sedition.

Let us now turn to the description of 'the man of sin' given by the apostle, and endeavour to discover, if possible, whether there was any individual then existing in the Roman Empire to whom it will apply.

1. The description requires that we should look, not for a system or abstraction, but an *individual,* a *'man'.*

2. He is evidently not a private, but a *public person.* The powers with which he is invested imply this.

3. He is a personage holding the highest rank and authority in the State.

4. He is heathen, and not Jewish.

5. He claims divine names, prerogatives, and worship.

6. He pretends to exercise miraculous power.

7. He is characterised by enormous wickedness. He is 'the man of sin,' *i.e.* the incarnation and embodiment of evil.

8. He is distinguished by lawlessness as a ruler.

9. He had not yet arrived at the fulness of his power when the apostle wrote; there existed some hindrance or check to the full development of his influence.

10. The hindrance was a person; was known to the Thessalonians; and would soon be taken out of the way.

11. The 'lawless one,' the 'man of sin,' was doomed to destruction. He is 'the son of *perdition,*' 'whom the Lord shall *slay.*'

12. His full development, or 'manifestation,' and his destruction are immediately to precede the Parousia. 'The Lord shall destroy him with the brightness of his coming.'

With these descriptive marks in our hands can there be any difficulty in identifying the person in whom they all are found? Were there three men in the Roman Empire who answered this description? Were there two? Assuredly not. But there was *one*, and only one. When the apostle wrote he was on the steps of the Imperial throne---a little longer and he sate on the throne of the world. It is NERO, the first of the persecuting emperors; the violator of all laws, human and divine; the monster whose cruelty and crimes entitle him to the name 'the man of sin.'

It will at once be apparent to every reader that all the features in this hideous portraiture belong to Nero; but it is remarkable how exact is the correspondence, especially in those particulars which are more recondite and obscure. He is an individual---a public person---holding the highest rank in the State; heathen, and not Jewish; a monster of wickedness, trampling upon all law. But how striking are the indications that point to Nero in the year when this epistle was written, say A.D.52 or 53. At that time Nero was not yet 'manifested;' his true character was not discovered; he had not yet succeeded to the Empire. Claudius, his step-father, lived, and stood in the way of the son of Agrippina. But that hindrance was soon removed. In less than a year, probably, after this epistle was received by the Thessalonians, Claudius was 'taken out of the way,' a victim to the deadly practice of the infamous Agrippina; her son also, according to Suetonius, being accessory to the deed. But 'the mystery of lawlessness was already working;' the influence of Nero must have been powerful in the last days of the wretched Claudius; the very plots were probably being hatched that paved the way for the accession of the son of the murderess. A few months more would witness the advent to the throne of the world of a miscreant whose name is gibbeted in everlasting infamy as the most brutal of tyrants and the vilest of men.

The remaining notes of the description are no less true to the original. The claim to divine honours; the opposing and exalting himself above all that is called God, or an object of worship; his seating himself in the temple of God, showing himself to be a god; all are distinctive of Nero.

The assumption of divine prerogatives, indeed, was common to all Roman Emperors. 'Divus,' god, was inscribed on their coins and statues. The Emperor might be said to 'exalt himself above all that is called God, or an object of worship,' by monopolising to himself all worship. This fact is placed in a striking light in the following remarks of Dean Howson:---

'The image of the Emperor was at that time the object of religious reverence; he was a deity on earth; and the worship paid to him was a real worship. It is a striking thought, that in those times (setting aside effete forms of religion) the only two genuine worships in the civilised world were the worship of a Tiberius or a Nero on the one hand, and the worship of Christ on the other.'

The attempt of Caligula to set up his statue in the temple of God in Jerusalem had driven the Jews to the brink of rebellion, and it is just possible that this fact may have given their peculiar form to the description of the apostle. Certainly it suggested to Grotius that Caligula must be the person intended to be portrayed; but the date of the epistle renders this opinion untenable. Nero, however, came behind none of his predecessors in his impious assumption of divine prerogatives. Dio Cassius informs us that when he returned victorious from the Grecian games, he entered Rome in triumph, and was hailed with such acclamations as these, 'Nero the Hercules! Nero the Apollo! Thou August, August! Sacred voice! *Eternal One.*' In all this we see sufficient evidence of the assumption of divine honours by Nero.

The same is true with respect to another note in this delineation,---the pretension to miraculous powers. 'Whose coming is after the working of Satan with all power and signs and lying wonders' (ver. 9). This pretension follows almost as a matter of course from the assumption of the prerogatives of deity.

It is to be supposed that the Imperial *Divus* would be credited with the possession of supernatural powers; and we find a very remarkable side-light thrown upon this subject in Rev. xiii. 13-15. At this stage of the investigation, however, it would not be desirable to enter into that region of symbolism, though we shall fully avail ourselves of its aid at the proper time.

Further, 'the man of sin' is doomed to perish. He is 'the son of *perdition*,' a name which he bears in common with Judas, and indicative of the certainty and completeness of his destruction. 'The Lord is to slay him with the breath of his mouth, and to destroy him with the appearance of his coming.' In this significant expression we have a note of the *time* when the man of sin is destined to perish, marked with singular exactitude. It is the coming of the Lord, the Parousia, which is to be the signal of his destruction; yet not the full splendour of that event so much as the first appearance or dawn of it. Alford (after Bengel) very properly points out that the rendering 'brightness of his coming' should be 'the appearance of his coming,' and he quotes the sublime expression of Milton,---'far off His coming shone.' Bengel, with fine discrimination, remarks, 'Here the appearance of His coming, or, at all events, *the first glimmerings of His coming, are prior to the coming itself.*' This evidently implies that the man of sin was destined to perish, not in the full blaze of the Parousia, but at its first dawn or beginning. Now what do we actually find? Remembering how the Parousia is connected with the destruction of Jerusalem, we find that the death of Nero preceded the event. It took place in June A.D.68, in the very midst of the Jewish war which ended in the capture and destruction of the city and the temple. It might therefore be justly said that 'the appearance, or dawn, of the Parousia' [ ] was the signal for the tyrant's destruction.

It does not follow that the death of Nero was to be brought about by immediate supernatural agency because it is said that 'the Lord shall slay him with the breath of his mouth,' etc. Herod Agrippa was smitten by the angel of the Lord, but this does not exclude the operation of natural causes: 'he was eaten of worms, and gave up the ghost' (Acts xii.23). So Nero was overtaken by the divine judgment, though he received his death-blow from the sword of the assassin, or from his own hand.

Lastly, it is scarcely necessary to make good the title of Nero to the appellation 'the man of sin.' It will be observed that it is the profligacy of his personal character that stamps him with this distinctive epithet, as if he were the very impersonation and embodiment of vice. Such, indeed, was Nero, whose name has become a synonym for all that is base, cruel, and vile; the highest in rank and the lowest in Character in the Roman world: a monster of wickedness even among Pagans, who were not squeamish about morality and who were familiar with the most corrupt society on the face of the earth. The following graphic delineation of the character of Nero is taken from Conybeare and Howson:---

'Over this distinguished bench of judges presided the representative of the most powerful monarchy which has ever existed,---the absolute ruler of the whole civilised world. But the reverential awe which his position naturally suggested was changed into contempt and loathing by the character of the sovereign who now presided over that supreme tribunal. For Nero was a man whom even the awful attribute of "power equal to the gods" could not render august, except in title. The fear and horror excited by his omnipotence and his cruelty, were blended with contempt for his ignoble lust of praise and his shameless licentiousness. He had not as yet plunged into that extravagance of tyranny which, at a later period, exhausted the patience of his subjects and brought him to destruction. Hitherto his public measures had been guided by sage advisers, and his cruelty had injured his own family rather than the State. But already, at the age of twenty-five, he had murdered his innocent wife and his adopted brother, and had dyed his hands in the blood of his mother. Yet even these enormities seem to have disgusted the Romans less than the prostitution of the Imperial purple by publicly performing as a musician on the stage and a charioteer in the circus. His degrading want of dignity and insatiable appetite for vulgar applause drew tears from the councillors and servants of his house, who could see him slaughter his nearest relatives without remonstrance.'

But there is probably another reason why Nero is branded with this epithet. The name 'man of sin' was not unknown to Hebrew history. It had already been given to one who was not only a monster of cruelty and wickedness, but also a bitter enemy and persecutor of the Jewish people. It would not have been possible to pronounce a name more hateful to Jewish ears than the name of *Antiochus Epiphanes.* He was the Nero of his age, the inveterate enemy of Israel, the profaner of the temple, the sanguinary persecutor of the people of God. In the first Book of Maccabees we find the name *'the man the sinner'* given to Antiochus (1 Macc. ii. 48, 62), and it seems highly probable that the character and destined to a similar fate with Antiochus, the relentless tyrant and persecutor who became a monument of the wrath of God.

The parallel between 'the man of sin' and Antiochus Epiphanes is particularly noticed by Bengel, who points out that the description of the former in ver. 4 is borrowed from the description of the latter in Dan. xi. 36. The comment of Bengel is well worthy of quotation:---

'This, then, is what Paul says: The day of Christ does not come, unless there be fulfilled (in the man of sin) what Daniel predicted of Antiochus; the prediction is more suitable to the man of sin, who corresponds to Antiochus, and is worse than he.'

We shall find in the sequel that this is not the only passage in which Antiochus Epiphanes is referred to as the prototype of Nero.

But the question may be asked, Why should the revelation of Nero in his true character be a matter of such concern to the apostle and the Christians of Thessalonica? The answer is not far to seek. It was the ferocity of this lawless monster that first let loose all the power of Rome to crush and destroy the Christian name. It was by him that torrents of innocent blood were to be shed and the most exquisite tortures inflicted upon unoffending Christians. It was before his sanguinary tribunal that St. Paul was yet to stand and plead for his life, and from his lips that the sentence was to come that doomed him to a violent death. But more than this, it was under Nero, and by his orders, that the final Jewish war was commenced, and that darkest chapter in the annals of Israel was opened which terminated in the siege and capture of Jerusalem, the destruction of the temple, and the extinction of the national polity. This was the consummation predicted by our Lord as the 'end of the age' and the 'coming of his kingdom.' The revelation of the man of sin, therefore, as antecedent to the Parousia, was a matter that deeply concerned every Christian disciple.

We can now understand why the apostle should use such caution in writing on a subject like this. It was from no affection of oracular obscurity, but from prudential motives of the most intelligible kind. There were many prying eyes and calumnious tongues in Thessalonica, that only waited an opportunity to denounce the Christians as disaffected and seditious men, secret plotters against the authority of Caesar. To write openly on such subjects would be in the highest degree indiscreet and perilous. Nor was it necessary; for they had discussed these matters before in many a private conversation. 'Do you not recollect,' he asks, 'that when I was with you *I was often telling* you these things?' More than hints were unnecessary to the Thessalonians, for they had a key to his meaning which subsequent readers had not. Nor is it greatly to be wondered at if obscurity has gathered round the teaching of the apostle on this subject. Events which to contemporaries are full of intense interest often become not only uninteresting but unintelligible to posterity. Yet it is somewhat strange that the very obvious reference to contemporary history, and to Nero, should have been so generally overlooked. This is the most ancient interpretation of the passage relating to the man of sin. Chrysostom, commenting on the *mystery of iniquity,* says, 'He (St. Paul) speaks here of *Nero* as being the type of the Antichrist; for he also wished to be thought a god.' This opinion is also referred to by Augustine, Theodoret, and others. Bengel, referring to the obstacle to the manifestation of the man of sin, says: 'The ancients thought that Claudius

74

was this check: hence it appears they deemed Nero, Claudius' successor, the man of sin. Moses Stuart has collected a great number of authorities for the identification of Nero with the man of sin. He remarks: 'The idea that Nero was *the man of sin* mentioned by Paul, and the *Antichrist* spoken of so often in the epistles of St. John, prevailed extensively and for a long time in the early church.' And again: 'Augustine says: What means the declaration, that the mystery of iniquity already works? . . . Some suppose this to be spoken of the Roman emperor, and therefore Paul did not speak in plain words, because he would not incur the charge of calumny for having spoken evil of the Roman emperor: although he always expected that what he had said would be understood as applying to Nero.'

We consider it a fact of peculiar importance that a conclusion arrived at on quite independent grounds should be found to have the sanction of some of the greatest names of antiquity. We are, however, not at all disposed to rest this interpretation upon external authority; we are inclined to think that the internal evidence in favour of the identification of Nero as the man of sin amounts almost, if not altogether, to demonstration. But we have yet to deal with the confirmation of this fact furnished by the Apocalypse, which we presume to think will produce conviction in every candid mind.

It would be improper to pass from the consideration of this deeply interesting passage without some notice of what may be called the popular Protestant interpretation, which finds here the rise and development of Popery and identifies the Pope as the man of sin. The interpretation is in may respects so plausible, and the points of correspondence so numerous, that it is not surprising that it should have found favour with perhaps the majority of commentators. There is a certain family likeness among all systems of superstition and tyranny, which makes it probable that some of the features which distinguish one may be found in all. But few expositors of any note or weight will now contend that all the descriptive notes of the man of sin are to be found in the Pope. Dean Alford justly observes:---

'In the characteristic of ver. 4, the Pope does not, and never did, fulfil the prophecy. Allowing all the striking coincidences with the latter part of the verse which have been so abundantly adduced, it never can be shown that he fulfils the former part; so far is he from it, that the abject adoration and submission to and has ever been one of his most notable peculiarities. The second objection, of an external and historical character, is even more decisive. If the papacy be Antichrist, then has the manifestation been made, and endured now for nearly fifteen hundred years, and yet that day of the Lord is not come which, by the terms of our prophecy, such manifestations is immediately to precede.'

The Parousia In the Apostlotic Epistles – Corinthians

The two epistles to the church in Corinth are believed to have been written in the same year (A.D.57). The contents are more varied than those of the Epistles to the Thessalonians, but we find many allusions to the anticipated coming of the Lord. That was the consummation to which, in St. Paul's view, all things were hastening, and that for which all Christians were eagerly looking. It is represented as the decisive day when all the doubts and difficulties of the present would be resolved and all its wrongs redressed. That this great event was regarded by the apostle as at hand is implied in every allusion to the subject, while in several passages it is expressly affirmed in so many words.

THE FIRST EPISTLE TO THE CORINTHIANS.

ATTITUDE OF THE CHRISTIANS OF CORINTH IN RELATION TO THE PAROUSIA.

1 Cor. i. 7.---'Waiting [looking earnestly] for the coming of our Lord Jesus Christ, who shall also confirm you unto the end, that ye may be blameless in the day of our Lord Jesus Christ.'

The attitude of expectation is which the Corinthians stood is here distinctly indicated, although it is feebly expressed by the rendering 'waiting.' The phrase used by the apostle is the same as in Romans viii. 19, where the whole creation is represented as 'groaning and travailing in pain *waiting for the revelation* of the sons of God' [ ]. Conybeare and Howson translate,---'looking earnestly for the time when our Lord Jesus Christ shall be revealed to sight.' Such an attitude plainly implies that the object expected was understood to be near; for it is obvious that if it were a great way off, the earnest looking and longing would end only in bitter disappointment. It may be said, Did not the Old Testament saints wait for the day of Christ? Did not Abraham rejoice to see His day, and was not that a distant prospect? True; but the Old Testament saints were nowhere given to understand that the first coming of Christ would take place in their own day, or within the limits of their own generation, nor were they urged and exhorted to be continually on the watch, waiting and looking for His coming. We have no reason whatever to suppose that their minds were constantly on the stretch, and their eyes eagerly straining in expectation of the advent, as was the case with the Christians of the apostolic age. The case of the aged Simeon is the proper parallel to the early Christians. It was revealed to him that he should not see death till he had seen the Lord's anointed: he *waited* therefore 'for the consolation of Israel.' In like manner it was revealed to the Christians of the apostolic age that the Parousia would take place in their own day; the Lord had over and over again distinctly assured His disciples of this fact, they therefore cherished the hope of living to see the longed-for-day, and all the more because of the sufferings and persecutions to which they were exposed.

Like the Thessalonians they regarded death as a calamity, because it seemed to disappoint the hope of seeing the Lord 'coming in his kingdom.' They wished to be 'alive and remain unto the coming of the Lord.' Billroth remarks: 'The [revelation] refers to the visible advent of Christ, an event which Paul and the believers of that day imagined would take place within the term of an ordinary life, so that many of them would be then alive. Paul here commends the Corinthians for expecting or waiting for it.' The critic evidently regards the opinion as a delusion. But whence did the early Christians derive their expectation? Was it not from the teaching of the apostles and the words of Christ? To say that it was a mistaken opinion is to strike a blow at the authority of the apostles as trustworthy reporters of the sayings of Christ and competent expounders of His doctrine. If they could be so egregiously mistaken as to a simple matter of fact, what confidence can be placed in their teaching on the more difficult questions of doctrine and duty?

The confidence expressed by the apostle that the Christians of Corinth would be confirmed unto *the end,* and be blameless *in the day of our Lord Jesus Christ,* recalls his prayer for the Thessalonians: 'That he may stablish your hearts unblameable in holiness at the coming of our Lord Jesus Christ' (1 Thess. iii. 13). The two passages are exactly parallel in signification, and refer to the same point of time, 'the end,' the 'Parousia.' Obviously, by *'the end'* the apostle does not mean the *'end of life;'* it is not a general sentiment such as we express when we speak of being *'true to the last;'* it has a definite meaning, and refers to a particular time. It is 'the end' [ ] spoken of by our Lord in His prophetic discourse on the Mount of Olives (Matt. xxiv. 6, 13, 14). It is 'the end of the age' [ ] of Matt. xiii. 40, 49. It is 'the end' [then cometh the end] (1 Cor. xv. 24. See also Heb. iii. 6, 14, vi. 11, ix. 26; 1 Pet. iv. 7). All these forms of expression [, ,] refer to the same epoch---viz., the close of the aeon or Jewish age, *i.e.* the Mosaic dispensation. This is pointed out by Alford in his note on the passage before us: 'To the end,' *i.e.* to the , not merely 'to the end of your lives.' It refers, therefore, no to *death,* which comes to different individuals at a different time, but to one specific event, not far off, the Parousia, or coming of the Lord Jesus Christ.

No less definite is the phrase, 'the *day* of our Lord,' etc. The allusions to this period in the apostolic writings are very frequent, and all point to one great crisis which was quickly approaching, the day of redemption and recompense to the suffering people of God, the day of retribution and wrath to their enemies and persecutors.

THE JUDICIAL CHARACTER OF 'THE DAY OF THE LORD.'

1 Cor. iii. 13.---'Every man's work shall be made manifest: for the day shall declare it, because it [the day] shall be revealed with fire; and the fire shall try every man's work of what sort it is.'

In this passage, again, there is a distinct allusion to the 'day of the Lord' as a day of discrimination between good and evil, between the precious and the vile. The apostle likens himself and his fellow-labourers in the service of God to workmen employed in the erection of a great building. That building is God's church, the only foundation of which is Jesus Christ, that foundation which he (the apostle) had laid in Corinth. He then warns every labourer to look well what kind of material he built up on that one foundation: that is to say, what sort of characters he introduced into the fellowship of God's church. A day was coming which would test the quality of every man's work: it must pass through a fiery ordeal; and in that scorching scrutiny the flimsy and worthless must perish, while the good and true remained unscathed. The unwise builder indeed might escape, but his work would be destroyed, and he would forfeit the reward which, if he had builded with better materials, he would have enjoyed.

There can be no doubt what day is here referred to. It is the day of Christ, the Parousia. This is said to be revealed 'with *fire,'* and the question arises, Is the expression literal or metaphorical? The whole passage, it will be perceived, is figurative: the building, the builders, the materials; we may therefore conclude that the *fire* is figurative also. Moral qualities are not tested in the same way as material substances. The apostle teaches that a judicial scrutiny of the life-work of the Christian labourer is at hand. He 'who hath his eyes like unto a flame of fire' is coming to 'search the reins and hearts, and to give every man according to his work' (Rev. ii. 18, 23). How clearly these representations of 'the day of the Lord' connect themselves with the prophetic words of Malachi, 'Who may abide the day of his coming? For he is like a refiner's fire.' 'For, behold, the day cometh that shall burn as a furnace, and all the proud, yea and all that do wickedly, shall be as stubble' (Mal. iii. 2, 3; iv. 1). In like manner John the Baptist represents the day of Christ's coming as 'revealed with fire,' 'He will burn up the chaff with unquenchable fire' (Matt. iii. 12). See also 2 Thess. i. 7, 8, etc.

Yet, if any should be disposed to maintain that the fire here is not wholly metaphorical, a not improbable case might easily be made out. In the central spot where that revelation took place, the city and the temple of Jerusalem, the Parousia was accompanied with very literal fire. In that glowing furnace in which perished all that was most venerable and sacred in Judaism, men might well see the fulfilment of the apostle's words, 'that day will be revealed in fire.'

Since, then, the Parousia coincides in point of time with the destruction of Jerusalem, it follows that the period of sifting and trial here alluded to,---the day which shall be revealed in fire---is also contemporaneous with that event. Otherwise, on the hypothesis that this day has not yet come, we are led to the conclusions that 'the proving of every man's work' has not yet taken place: that no judgment has yet been pronounced on the work of Apollos, or Cephas, or Paul, or their fellow-labourers; it has still to be ascertained with what sort of material every man built up the temple of God; that the labourers have not yet received their reward. For the great proving day has not yet come, and the fire has not tried every man's work of what sort it is. But this is a *reductio ad absurdum,* and shows that such a hypothesis is untenable.

THE JUDICIAL CHARACTER OF THE DAY OF THE LORD.

1 Cor. iv. 5.---'Therefore judge nothing before the time, until the Lord come, who shall both bring to light the hidden things of darkness, and make manifest the counsels of the hearts: and then shall every man have [his] praise from God.'

1 Cor. v. 5.---'That the spirit may be saved in the day of the Lord Jesus.'

In both these passages the Parousia is represented as a time of judicial investigation and decision. It is the time when characters and motives shall be disclosed, and every man receive his appropriate meed of praise or blame. The apostle deprecates hasty and ill-informed judgments, apparently not without some personal reason, and exhorts them to wait 'till the Lord come,' etc. Does not this manifestly imply that he thought they would not have long to wait? Where would be the reasonableness of his exhortation if there were no prospect of vindication or retribution for ages to come? It is the very consideration that the day is at hand that constitutes the reason for patience and forbearance now.

In like manner the case of the offending member of the Corinthian church points to a speedily approaching time of retribution. St. Paul argues that the effect of present discipline exercised by the church may prove the salvation of the offender 'in the day of the Lord Jesus.' That day, therefore, is the period when the condemnation or salvation of men is decided. But on the supposition that the day of the Lord Jesus is not yet come, it follows that the day of salvation has not come either for the apostle himself or for the Christians of Corinth, or for the offender whom he calls upon the church to censure. All this clearly shows that the apostle believed and taught the speedy coming of the day of the Lord.

NEARNESS OF THE APPROACHING CONSUMMATION.

1 Cor. vii. 29-31.---'But this I say, brethren, the time henceforth is short [the time that remains is short]: in order that both they that have wives be as though they had none: and they that weep as though they wept not; and they that rejoice as though they rejoiced not; and they that buy, as though they possessed not; and they that use this world as not abusing it: for the fashion of this world is passing away.'

No words could more distinctly show the deep impression on the mind of the apostle that a great crisis was near, which would powerfully affect all the relations of life, and all the possessions of this world. There is a significance in this language, as spoken at that time, very different from that which it has in these days. These are not the ordinary platitudes about the brevity of time and the vanity of the world, the stock common-places of moralists and divines. Time is always short, and the world always vain; but there is an emphasis and an urgency in the declaration of the apostle which imply a speciality in the time then present: he knew that they were on the verge of a great catastrophe, and that all earthly interests and possessions were held by a slight and uncertain tenure. It is not necessary to ask what that expected catastrophe was. It was the coming of the day of the Lord already alluded to, and the near approach of which is implied in all his exhortations. Alford correctly expresses the force of the expression, 'the time is shortened henceforth, *i.e.* the interval between now and the coming of the Lord has arrived at an extremely contracted period.' But, unhappily, he goes on to treat the opinion of St. Paul as a mistaken one: 'Since he wrote, the unfolding of God's providence has taught us more of the interval before the coming of the Lord than it was given even to an inspired apostle to see.' What the private opinion of St. Paul might be respecting the date of the Parousia, or what would take place when it did arrive, we do not know, and it would be useless to speculate; but we have a right to conclude that in his official teaching (save when he expressly states that he speaks his private opinion) he was the organ of a higher intelligence than his own. We are really not competent to say how far the shock of the tremendous convulsion that took place at 'the end of the age' may have extended, but every one can see that the exhortations of the apostle would have been peculiarly appropriate within the bounds of Palestine. As we pursue this investigation, the area affected by the Parousia seems to grow and expand: it is more than a national, it becomes an ecumenical, crisis. Certainly we must infer from the representation of the apostles, as well as from the sayings of the Master, that the Parousia had a significance for Christians everywhere, whether within or without the boundaries of Judea. It is more seemly to inquire into the true import of the doctrine of the apostles on this subject than to assume that they were mistaken, and invent apologies for their error. If it be an error, it is common to the whole teaching of the New Testament, and will meet us in the writings of St. Peter and St. John, for they, no less than St. Paul, declare that 'the end of all things is at hand,' and that 'the world is passing away, and the lust thereof' (1 Pet. iv. 7; 1 John ii. 17).

THE END OF THE AGES ALREADY ARRIVED.

1 Cor. x. 11.---'Now all these things happened unto them for ensamples, and they are written for our admonition, upon whom the ends of the world are come.' [to whom the ends of the ages have arrived].

The phrase 'the end of the ages' [ ] is equivalent to 'the end of the age' [ ], and 'the end' [ ]. They all refer to the same period, viz. the close of the Jewish age, or dispensation, which was now at hand. It will be observed that in this chapter St. Paul brings together some of the great historical incidents which took place at the *commencement* of that dispensation, as affording warning to those who were living near its close. He evidently regards the early history of the dispensation, especially in so far as it was supernatural, as having a typical and educational character. 'These things happened unto them by way of ensample; and they were written for our admonition, upon whom the ends of the ages are come.' This not only affirms the typical character of the Jewish economy, but shows that the apostle regarded it as just about to expire.

Conybeare and Howson have the following note on this passage:---'The coming of Christ was "the end of the ages," *i.e.* the commencement of a new period of the world's existence. So, nearly the same phrase is used Heb. ix. 26. A similar expression occurs five times in St. Matthew, signifying *the coming of Christ to judgment.*' This note does not distinguish with accuracy which coming of Christ was the end of the age. It is the Parousia, the second coming which is always so represented. That event was, therefore, believed to be at hand when the end of the age, or ages, was declared to have arrived.

It is sometimes said that the whole period between the incarnation and the end of the world is regarded in the New Testament as 'the end of the age.' But this bears a manifest incongruity in its very front. How could the *end* of a period be a long protracted duration? Especially how could it be longer than the period of which it is the end? More time has already elapsed since the incarnation than from the giving of the law to the first coming of Christ: so that, on this hypothesis, the end of the age is a great deal longer than the age itself. Into such paradoxes interpreters are led by a false theory. But as in a true theory in science every fact fits easily into its place, and lends support to all the rest, so in a true theory of interpretation every passage finds an easy solution, and contributes its quota to support the correctness of the general principle.

EVENTS ACOMPANYING THE PAROUSIA.

The Resurrection of the Dead; the Change of the Living; the Delivering up of the Kingdom.

In entering upon this grand and solemn portion of the Word of God we desire to do so with profound reverence and humility of spirit, dreading to rush in where angels might fear to tread; and anxiously solicitous 'to bring out of the inspired words what is really in them, and to put nothing into them that is not really there.'

We venture also to bespeak the judicial candour of the reader. A demand may be made upon his forbearance and patience which he may scarcely at first be prepared to meet. Old traditions and preconceived opinions are not patient of contradiction, and even truth may often be in danger of being spurned as foolishness merely because it is novel. Let him be assured that every word is spoken in all honesty, after every effort to discover the true meaning of the text has been exhausted, and in the spirit of loyalty and submission to the supreme authority of Scripture. It is no part of the business of an interpreter to vindicate the sayings of inspiration; his whole care should be to find out what those sayings are.

---

1 Cor. xv. 22-28.---'For as in Adam all die, even so in Christ shall all be made alive. But every man in his own order. Christ the first-fruits; afterwards they that are Christ's, at his coming. Then the end, when he shall deliver up the kingdom to God, even the Father: when he shall have put down all rule and all authority and power. For he must reign, till he hath put all enemies under his feet. The last enemy, death, shall be destroyed. For, he hath put all things under his feet. But when he saith, all things are put under him, it is manifest that he is excepted, which did put all things under him. And when all things shall be subdued unto him, then shall the Son also himself be subject unto him that put all things under him, that God may be all in all.'

Although it does not fall within the scope of this investigation to enter into any detailed exposition of passages which do not directly affect the question of the Parousia, yet it seems necessary to refer to the state of opinion in the church of Corinth which gave occasion to the argument and remonstrance of St. Paul.

The resurrection of Jesus Christ from the dead is one of the great vouchers for the truth of Christianity itself. If this be true, all is true; if this be false, the whole structure falls to the ground. In the brief summary of the fundamental truths of the Gospel given by the apostle in the commencement of this chapter, special stress is laid upon the fact of Christ's resurrection, and the evidence on which it rested. It was 'according to the scripture.' It was attested by the positive testimony of eye-witnesses: 'He was *seen* of Cephas, then of the twelve: after that he was *seen* of above five hundred brethren at once,' most of whom are still living at the writing of the apostle. After that he was *seen* of James; then of all the apostles. 'Last of all he was *seen* of me also.' The emphasis laid upon the words *'he was seen'* cannot fail to be remarked. The evidence is irresistible; it is ocular demonstration, testified not by one or two, but by a multitude of witnesses, men who would not lie, and who could not be deceived.

Yet, it appears, there were some among the Corinthians who said, 'that there is no resurrection of the dead.' It seems incomprehensible to us how such a denial should be compatible with Christian discipleship. It is not said, however, that they question the fact of Christ's resurrection, though the apostle shows that their principles led to that conclusion. His argument with them is a *reductio ad absurdum.* He lands them in a state of blank negation, in which there is no Christ, no Christianity, no apostolic veracity, no future life, no salvation, no hope. They have cut away the ground under their own feet, and they are left, without a Saviour, in darkness and despair.

But, as we have said, they do not seem to have denied the fact of Christ's resurrection; on the contrary, this is the argument by means of which the apostle convicts them of absurdity. Had they not admitted this, the apostle's argument would have had no force, neither could they have been regarded as Christian believers at all.

Some light, however, is thrown upon this strange scepticism by the Epistles to the Thessalonians. An opinion not very dissimilar appears to have prevailed at Thessalonica. So at least we may infer from 1 Thess. iv. 13, etc. They had given themselves up to despair on account of the death of some of their friends previous to the coming of the Lord. They appear to have regarded this as a calamity which excluded the departed from a participation in the blessedness which they expected at the revelation of Jesus Christ. The apostle calms their fears and corrects their mistake by declaring that the departed saints would suffer no disadvantage, but would be raised again at the coming of Christ, and enter along with the living in to the presence and joy of the Lord.

This shows that there had been doubts about the resurrection of the dead in the Thessalonian church as well as in the Corinthian; and it is highly probable that they were of the same nature in both. The anxious desire of all Christians was to be alive at the Lord's coming. Death, therefore, was regarded as a calamity. But it would not have been a calamity had they been aware that there was to be a resurrection of the dead. This was the truth which they either did not know, or did not believe. St. Paul treats the doubt in Thessalonica as *ignorance,* in Corinth as *error;* and it is highly probable that, among a people so conceited and pragmatical as the Corinthians, the opinion would assume a more decided and dangerous shape. It may be observed, also, that the apostle meets the case of the Thessalonians with much the same reasoning as that of the Corinthians, viz. by an appeal to the fact of the resurrection of Christ: 'If we believe that Jesus died and rose again,' etc. (1 Thess. iv. 14). The two cases, therefore, are very similar, if not precisely parallel. We can easily imagine that to the early Christians, often smarting under bitter persecution, and watching eagerly for the expected coming of the Lord, it must have been a grievous disappointment to be taken away by death before the fulfilment of their hopes. Add to this the difficulty which the idea of the resurrection of the dead would naturally present to the Gentile converts (1 Cor. xv. 35). It was a doctrine at which the philosophers of Athens mocked; which made Festus exclaim, 'Paul, thou art mad,' and which the scientific men of the time declared to be preposterous, a thing 'impossible even to God.'

So much for the probable nature and origin of this error of the Corinthians. The apostle in combating it ascribes the glorious boon of the resurrection to the mediatorial interposition of Christ. It is part of the benefits arising from His redemptive work. As the first Adam brought death, so the second Adam brings life; and, as the pledge of the resurrection of His people, He himself rose from the dead, and became the first-fruits of the great harvest of the grave.

But there is a due order and succession in this new life of the future. As the first-fruits precede and predict the harvest, so the resurrection of Christ precedes and guarantees the resurrection of His people: 'Christ the first-fruits, afterwards they that are Christ's AT HIS COMING.'

This is a most important statement, and unambiguously affirms, what is indeed the uniform teaching of the New Testament, that the Parousia was to be immediately followed by the resurrection of the sleeping dead. He comes 'that he may awake them out of sleep.' The First Epistle to the Thessalonians supplies the hiatus which the apostle leaves here: 'For the Lord himself shall descend from heaven with a shout, with the voice of the archangel and the trump of God: and first, the dead in Christ shall arise: then we who are alive and remain shall be caught up all together with them in the clouds, to meet the Lord in the air: and so shall we ever be with the Lord' (1 Thess. iv. 16, 17).
In the passage before us the apostle does not enter into those details; he is arguing for the resurrection, and he stops short for the present at that point, adding only the significant words, *'Then the end'* [ ], as much as to say, 'That is the end;' 'Now it is done;' 'The mystery of God is finished.'

But we may venture to ask, What is this 'end,' this; It is no new term, but a familiar phrase which we have often met before, and shall often meet again. If we turn to our Lord's prophetic discourse we find almost the self-same significant words, 'Then shall *the end* come' [ ] (Matt. xxiv. 14), and they furnish us with the key to their meaning here. Answering the question of the disciples, 'Tell us, when shall these things be; and what shall be the sign of thy coming, and of the end of the age?' our Lord specifies certain signs, such as the persecution and martyrdom of some of the disciples themselves; the defection and apostasy of many; the appearance of false prophets and deceivers; and, lastly, the general proclamation of the Gospel throughout the nations of the Roman Empire; and *'then,'* he declares, 'shall come *the end.'* Can there be the slightest doubt that the of the prophecy is the of the epistle? Or can there be a doubt that both are identical with the of the disciples? (Matt. xxiv. 3.) But we have seen that the latter phrase refers, not to 'the end of the world,' or the destruction of the material earth, but to the close of the age, or dispensation , then about to expire. We conclude, therefore, that 'the end' of which St. Paul speaks in 1 Cor. xv. 24 is the same grand epoch so continually and prominently kept in view both in the gospels and the epistles, when the whole civil and ecclesiastical polity of Israel, with their city, their temple, their nationality, and their law, were swept out of existence by on tremendous wave of judgment.

This view of 'the end,' as having reference to the close of the Jewish economy or age, seems to furnish a satisfactory solution of a problem which has greatly perplexed the commentators, viz. *Christ's delivering up of the kingdom.* It is stated twice over by the apostle, as one of the great events attending the Parousia, that the Son, having then put down all rule and all authority and power, 'shall deliver up *the kingdom* to God, even the Father' (vers. 24, 28). What kingdom? No doubt the kingdom which *the Christ,* the *Anointed* King, undertook to administer as the representative and vicegerent of His Father: that is to say, the Theocratic kingdom, with the sovereignty of which He was solemnly invested, according to the statement in the second Psalm, 'Yet have I set my king upon my holy hill of Zion. I will declare the decree: the Lord hath said unto me, Thou art my Son; this day have I begotten thee' (Ps. ii. 6, 7). This Messianic sovereignty, or Theocracy, necessarily came to its termination when the people who were its subjects ceased to be the covenant nation; when the covenant was in fact dissolved, and the whole framework and apparatus of the Theocratic administration were abolished. What more reasonable than that the Son should then 'deliver up the kingdom,' the purposes of its institution having been answered, and its limited, local, and national character being superseded by a larger and universal system, the ' ,' or new order of a 'better covenant.'

This surrender of the kingdom to the Father at the Parousia---at the end of the age---is represented as consequent on the subjugation of all things to Christ, the Theocratic King. This cannot refer to the gentle and peaceful conquests of the Gospel, the *reconciliation* of all things to Him: the language implies a violent and victorious conquest affected over hostile powers,---'He must reign till he hath put all enemies under his feet.' Who those enemies are may be inferred from the closing history of the Theocracy. Unquestionably the most formidable opposition to the King and the kingdom was found in the heart of the Theocratic nation itself, the chief priests and rulers of the people. The highest authorities and powers of the nation were the bitterest enemies of the Messiah. It was a domestic, and not a foreign, antagonism---a Jewish, and not a Gentile, enmity---that rejected and crucified the King of Israel. The Roman procurator was only the reluctant instrument in the hands of the Sahedrin. It was the Jewish rule, the Jewish authority, the Jewish power that incessantly and systematically pursued the sect of the Nazarenes with the persistent malignity, and this was 'the rule and authority and power' which, by the destruction of Jerusalem and the extinction of the Jewish State, was 'put down' and annihilated. The terrible scenes of the final war, and especially of the siege and capture of Jerusalem, show us what this subjugation of the enemies of Christ implies. 'But those mine enemies, which would not that I should reign over them, bring hither, and slay them before me' (Luke xix. 27).

But what shall we say of the destruction of 'the last enemy, death?' Is it not fatal to this interpretation that it requires us to place the abolition of the dominion of death, and the resurrection, in the past, and not the future? Does not this contradict fact and common sense, and consequently expose the fallacy of the whole explanation? Of course, if the language of the apostle can only mean that at the Parousia the dominion of death over all men was everywhere and for ever brought to an end, it follows either that he was in error in making such an assertion, or that the interpretation which makes him say so is an erroneous one. That he does affirm that at the Parousia (the time of which is incontrovertibly defend in the New Testament as contemporaneous with the destruction of Jerusalem) death will be destroyed, is what no one can with any fairness deny; but it does not follow that we are to understand that expression in an absolutely unlimited and universal sense. The human race did not cease to exist in its present earthly conditions at the destruction of Jerusalem; the world did not then come to an end; men continued to be born and to die according to the law of nature. What, then, did take place? We are to conceive of that period as the end of an aeon, or age; the close of a great era; the winding up of a dispensation, *and the judgment of those who were placed under that dispensation.* The whole of the subjects of that dispensation (the kingdom of heaven), both the living and the dead, were, according to the representation of Christ and His apostles, to be convoked before the Theocratic King seated on the throne of His glory. That was the predicted and appointed period of that great judicial transaction set before us in the parabolic description of the sheep and the goats (Matt. xxv. 31, etc.), the outward and visible signs of which were indelibly stamped on the annals of time by the awful catastrophe which effaced Israel from its place among the nations of the earth. True, the spiritual and invisible accompaniments of that judgment are not recorded by the historian, for they were not such as the human senses could apprehend or verify; yet what Christian can hesitate to believe that, contemporaneously with the outward judgment of the seen, there was a corresponding judgment of the unseen? Such, at least, is the inference fairly deducible from the teachings of the New Testament. That at the great epoch of the Parousia the dead as well as the living---not of the whole human race, but of the subjects of the Theocratic kingdom---were to be assembled before the tribunal of judgment, is distinctly affirmed in the Scriptures; the dead being raised up, and the living undergoing an instantaneous change. *In this recall of the dead to life---the resuscitation of those who throughout the duration of the Theocratic kingdom had become the victims and captives of death---we conceive the 'destruction' of death referred to by St. Paul to consist.* Over them death lost his dominion; 'the spirits in prison' were released from the custody of their grim tyrant; and they, being raised from the dead, 'could not die anymore;' 'Death had no more dominion over them.' That this is in perfect harmony with the teaching of the Scriptures on this mysterious subject, and in fact explains what no other hypothesis can explain, will more fully appear in the sequel. Meantime, it may be observed that much expressions as the 'destruction' or 'abolition' of death do not always imply the total and final termination of its power. WE read that 'Jesus Christ had abolished death' (2 Tim. i. 10). Christ Himself declared, 'If a man keep my saying, he shall never see death' (John viii. 51); 'Whosoever liveth and believeth in me shall never die' (John xi. 26). We must interpret Scripture according to the analogy of Scripture. All that we are fairly warranted in affirming respecting the 'destruction of death' in the passage before us is, that it is co-extensive with all those who at the Parousia were raised from the dead. This seems to be referred to in our Lord's reply to the Sadducees: 'They which shall be accounted worthy to attain that period [ ], and the resurrection from among the dead, neither marry nor are given in marriage; for neither can they die any more: for they are equal unto the angels,' etc. (Luke xx. 35, 36). For *them* death is destroyed; for *them* death is swallowed up in victory. So, the apostle's argument in the 26th, 54th, and following verses really affirms no more than this,---To those who are raised from the dead there is no more liability to death; their deliverance from his bondage is complete; his sting is taken away; his power is at an end; they can shout, O death, where is thy sting? O grave, where is thy victory? Even as 'Christ, being raised from the dead, dieth no more, death hath no more dominion over him,' so, at the Parousia, His people were emancipated for ever from the prison-house of the grave: *'the last enemy, death, to them was destroyed.'*

THE LIVING (SAINTS) CHANGED AT THE PAROUSIA.

1 Cor. xv. 51.---'Behold, I shew you a mystery; we shall not all sleep, but we shall all be changed, in a moment, in the twinkling of an eye, at the last trump: for the trumpet shall sound, and the dead shall be raised incorruptible, and we shall be changed.'

This declaration supplies what was lacking in the statement made at ver. 24, and brings the whole into accordance with 1 Thess. iv. 17. The language of St. Paul implies that he was communicating a revelation which was new, and presumably made to himself. It cannot be said that it is derived from any recorded utterance of the Saviour, nor do we find any corresponding statement in any other apostolic writing. But the question for us is, To whom does the apostle refer when he says, '*We* shall not all sleep,' etc.? Is it to some hypothetical persons living in some distant age of time, or is it of the Corinthians and himself that he is thinking? Why should he think of the distant future when it is certain that he considered the Parousia to be imminent? Why should he not refer to himself and the Corinthians when their common hope and expectation was that they should live to witness the Parousia? There is no conceivable reason, then, why we should depart from the proper grammatical force of the language. When the apostle says '*we,*' he no doubt means the Christians of Corinth and himself. This conclusion Alford fully endorses: 'We which are alive and remain unto the coming of the Lord,---in which number the apostle firmly believed that he himself should be. (See 2 Cor. v. 1 ff. And notes).'

The revelation, then, which the apostle here communicates, the secret concerning their future destiny, is this: That they would not all have to pass through the ordeal of death, but that such of them as were privileged to live until the Parousia would undergo a change by which they would be qualified to enter into the kingdom of God, without experiencing the pangs of dissolution. He had just before (ver. 50) been explaining that material and corruptible bodies of flesh and blood could not, in the nature of things, be fit for a spiritual and heavenly state of existence: 'Flesh and blood cannot inherit the kingdom of God.' Hence the necessity for a transformation of the material and corruptible into that which is immaterial and incorruptible. Here it is important to observe the representation of the true nature of 'the kingdom of God.' It is not 'the gospel;' nor 'the Christian dispensation;' nor any *earthly* state of things at all, but a *heavenly state,* into which flesh and blood are incapable of entering.

The sum of all is, that the apostle evidently contemplates the event of which he is speaking as nigh at hand: it is to come to pass in their own day, before the natural term of life expires. And is not this precisely what we have found in all the references of the New Testament to the time of the Parousia? That event is never spoken of as distant, but always as imminent. It is looked for, watched for, hoped for. Some even leap to the conclusion that it has arrived, but their precipitancy is checked by the apostle, who shows that certain antecedents must first take place. We conclude, therefore, that when St. Paul said, 'We shall not all sleep,' he referred to himself and the Christians of Corinth, who, when they received this letter and read these words, could put only one construction upon them, viz. that many, perhaps most, possibly all of them, would live to witness the consummation which he predicted.

But the objection will recur, How could all this take place without notice or record? First, as regards the resurrection of the dead, it is to be considered how little we know of its conditions and characteristics. Must it come with observation? Must it be cognizable by material organs? 'It is raised a spiritual body.' Is a spiritual body one which can be seen, touched, handled? We are not certain that the eye can see the spiritual, or the hand can grasp the immaterial. On the contrary, the presumption and the probability are that they cannot. All this resurrection of the dead and transmutation of the living take place in the region of the spiritual, into which earthly spectators and reporters do not enter, and could see nothing if they did. A miracle may be necessary to empower the 'unassisted eye' to see the invisible. The prophet at Dothan saw the mountain full of 'chariots of fire, and horses of fire,' but the prophet's servant saw nothing until Elisha prayed, 'Lord, open his eyes, that he may see' (2 Kings vi. 17). The first Christian martyr, full of the Holy

Ghost, 'saw the glory of God, and Jesus standing on the right hand of God,' but none of the multitude that surrounded him beheld the vision (Acts vi. 56). Saul of Tarsus on the way to Damascus saw 'that Just One,' but his fellow-travellers saw no man (Acts ix. 7). It is not improbable that traditional and materialistic conceptions of the resurrection,--- opening graves and emerging bodies, may bias the imagination on this subject, and make us overlook the fact that our material organs can apprehend only material objects.

Secondly, as regards the change of the living saints, which the apostle speaks of as instantaneous,---'in a moment, in the twinkling of an eye;'---it is difficult to understand how so rapid a transition could be the subject of observation. The only thing we know of the change is its inconceivable suddenness. We know nothing of what residuum it leaves behind; what dissipation or resolution of the material substance. For aught we know, it may realise the fancy of the poet,---

'Oh, the hour when this material
Shall have vanished as a cloud.'

All we know is that 'in a moment, in the twinkling of an eye,' the change is completed; 'the corruptible puts on incorruption, the mortal puts on immortality, and death is swallowed up in victory.'

What, then, hinders the conclusion that such events might have taken place without observation, and without record? There is nothing unphilosophical, irrational, or impossible in the supposition. Least of all is there anything *unscriptural,* and this is all we need concern ourselves about. 'What saith the Scripture?' Does the language of St. Paul plainly affirm or imply that all this is just about to take place, within the lifetime of himself and those to whom he is writing? No fair and dispassionate mind will deny that it is so. Right or wrong, the apostle is committed to this representation of the coming of Christ, the resurrection of the dead, and the transmutation of the living saints, within the natural lifetime of the Corinthians and himself. We are placed therefore in this dilemma,---

1. Either the apostle was guided by the Spirit of God, and the events which he predicted came to pass; or,
2. The apostle was mistaken in his belief, and these things never took place.

THE PAROUSIA AND 'THE LAST TRUMP.'

There is still one circumstance in this description which requires notice, as bearing upon the question of time. The change which is said to pass upon 'us who are alive and remain unto the coming of the Lord' follows immediately on the signal of 'the last trump.' It is remarkable that there are two other passages which connect the great event of the Parousia, and its concomitant transactions, with the sound of a trumpet. 'He shall send his angels with *a great sound of a trumpet,* and they shall gather together his elect,' etc. (Matt. xxiv. 31). So also St. Paul in 1 Thess. iv. 16: 'The Lord himself shall descend from heaven with a shout, with the voice of the archangel, and with *the trump of God,'* etc. But the questions arises, Why the *last* trumpet? This epithet necessarily suggests other preceding trumpets or signals, and we are irresistibly reminded of the apocalyptic vision, in which seven angels are represented as sounding as many trumpets, each of which is the signal for the outpouring of judgments and woes upon the earth. Of course the seventh trumpet is the last, and it becomes an interesting question what connection there may be between the revelation in the Epistle and the vision in the Apocalypse. Alford (in opposition to Olshausen) considers that it is a refining upon the word *last* to identify it with the seventh trumpet of the Apocalypse; but his own suggestion, that it is the last 'in a wide and popular sense,' seems much less satisfactory. We refrain at this stage from entering upon any discussion of the apocalyptic symbols, but content ourselves with the single observation, that the sounding of the seventh trumpet in the Apocalypse is actually connected with *the time of the judgment of the dead* (Rev. xi. 18). The whole subject will come before us at a subsequent stage of the investigation, and we now pass on, merely taking note of the fact that we here find an undoubted link of connection between the prophetic element in the Epistles and that in the Apocalypse.

THE APOSTOLIC WATCHWORD, MARAN-ATHA,---THE LORD IS AT HAND.

1 Cor. xvi. 22.---'Maran-atha.' [The Lord cometh.]

The whole argument for the anticipated near approach of the Parousia is clenched by the last word of the apostle, which comes with the greater weight as written with his own hand, and conveying in one word the concentrated essence of his exhortation,---*'Maran-atha. The Lord is coming.'* This one utterance speaks volumes. It is the watchword which the apostle passes along the line of the Christian host; the rallying cry which inspired courage and hope in every heart. 'The Lord is coming!' It would have no meaning if the event to which it refers were distant or doubtful; all its force lies in its certainty and nearness. 'A weighty watchword,' says Alford, 'tending to recall to them the nearness of His coming, and the duty of being found ready for it.' Hengstenberg sees in it an obvious allusion to Mal. iii. 1: 'The Lord, whom ye seek, shall suddenly come to his temple,. . . behold, he shall come, saith the Lord of hosts.' 'The word Maran-atha, which is so striking in an epistle written in Greek, and to Greeks, is in itself a sufficient indication of an Old Testament foundation. The retention of the Aramean form can only be explained on the supposition that it was *a kind of watchword common to all the believers in Israel;* and no expression could well have come to be so used if it had not been taken from the Scriptures. There can hardly be any doubt that it was taken from Mal. iii. 1.' We may add that the occurrence of this Aramaic word in a Greek epistle suggests the existence of a strong Jewish element in the Corinthian church. This was probably true of all Gentile churches: the synagogue was the nucleus of the Christian congregation, and we know that in Corinth especially it was so: Justus, Crispus, and Sosthenes all belonged to the synagogue before they belonged to the church; and this fact explains what might otherwise appear a difficulty,---the direct interest of the church of Corinth in the great catastrophe the seat and centre of which was Judea.

THE SECOND EPISTLE TO THE CORINTHIANS.

ANTICIPATION OF 'THE END' AND 'THE DAY OF THE LORD.'

2 Cor. i. 13, 14.---'Even to the end;'. . . 'the day of the Lord Jesus.'

'The end' (ver. 13) does not mean 'to the end of my life,' as Alford says. It is the great consummation which the apostle ever keeps in view, the goal to which they were so rapidly advancing. has a definite and recognised signification in the New Testament, as may be seen by reference to such passages as Matt. xxiv. 6, 14; 1 Cor. xv. 24; Heb. iii. 16; vi. 11, etc.

In ver. 14 we find St. Paul anticipating the coming of the Lord as the time of joyful recompense to the faithful servants of God, and which was so near that, as he had told them in his former epistle, human judgments and censures might well be adjourned till its arrival. (1 Cor. iv. 5.) When that day came, the apostle and his converts would rejoice in each other. Can it be supposed that he could think of that day as otherwise than very near? Have those mutual rejoicings yet to begin? For if the day of the Lord be still future, so also must be the rejoicing.

THE DEAD IN CHRIST TO BE PRESENTED ALONG WITH THE LIVING AT THE PAROUSIA.

2 Cor. iv. 14.---'Knowing that he which raised up the Lord Jesus shall raise up us also by Jesus, and shall present us with you.'

We now enter upon a most important statement, which deserves special attention. Perhaps its true meaning has been somewhat obscured by regarding it as a general proposition, instead of something personal to the apostle himself. Conybeare and Howson observe:---

'Great confusion is caused in many passages by not translating, according to his true meaning, in the first person *singular;* for thus it often happens that what St. Paul spoke of himself individually, appears to us as if it were meant for a general truth; instances of this will repeatedly occur in the Epistle to the Corinthians, especially the Second. We propose, therefore, to change the pronouns *we* and *us* in this passage into *I* and *me.*'

We have already seen (1 Thess. iv. 15, and 1 Cor. xv. 51) that the apostle cherished the hope that he himself would be among those 'who would be alive, and remain unto the coming of the Lord.' In this epistle, however, it would seem as if this hope regarding himself were somewhat shaken. His experience in the interval between the First Epistle and the Second had been such as to lead him to apprehend speedy death. (See chap. i. 8, etc.) His 'trouble in Asia' had made him despair of life, and he probably felt that he could not calculate on escaping the malignant hostility of his enemies much longer. He had now 'the sentence of death in himself;' he bore about 'in his body the dying of the Lord Jesus,' and felt that he was 'always delivered unto death for Jesus' sake.'

But this anticipation did not diminish the confidence with which he looked forward to the future; for even should he die before the Parousia, he would not on that account lose his part in the triumphs and glories of that day. He was assured that 'he which raised up the Lord Jesus would raise up *him* also by Jesus, and would present him along with the living saints who might survive to that period. He would not be absent from the great at the coming of the Lord (2 Thess. ii. 1), but would be 'presented,' along with his friends at Corinth and elsewhere, 'before the presence of his glory.' In fact, the apostle now comforts himself with the same words with which he had comforted the bereaved mourners in Thessalonica. He appears to have relinquished the hope that he would himself live to witness the glorious appearing of the Lord; but not the less was he persuaded that he would suffer no loss by having to die; for, as he had taught the Thessalonians, 'them also which sleep in Jesus God would bring with him;' and the living saints would in that day have no advantage above those who slept (1 Thess. iv. 14, 15).

EXPECTATION OF FUTURE BLESSEDNESS AT THE PAROUSIA.

2 Cor. v. 1-10,---'For we know that if our earthly house of this tabernacle were dissolved, we have a building from God, a house not made with hands, eternal in the heavens. For in this we groan, earnestly desiring to be clothed upon with our house which is from heaven: if so be that being clothed we shall not be found naked. For we that are in this tabernacle do groan, being burdened: not for that we would be unclothed, but clothed upon, that mortality might be swallowed up of life. Now he that hath wrought us for the selfsame thing is God, who also hath given unto us the earnest of the Spirit. Therefore we are always confident, knowing that whilst we are at home in the body, we are absent from the Lord: (for we walk by faith, not by sight:) we are confident, I say, and willing rather to be absent from the body, and to be present with the Lord. Wherefore we labour, that whether present or absent, we may be accepted of him. For we must all appear before the judgment seat of Christ, that every one may receive the things done in his body, according to that he hath done, whether it be good or bad.'

This is the most complete account that we possess of the mysterious transition which the human spirit experiences when it quits its earthly tenement and enters the new organism prepared for its reception in the eternal world. It comes to us vouched by the highest authority,---it is the profession of his faith made by an inspired apostle,---one who could say 'I know.' It is the declaration of that hope which sustained St. Paul, and doubtless also the common faith of the whole Christian church. Nevertheless, the passage ought to be studied from the standpoint of the apostle, as his personal expectation and hope.

Observe the form of the statement---it is rather hypothetical than affirmative: *"If* my earthly tabernacle be dissolved,' etc. This is not the way in which a Christian now would speak respecting the prospect of dying; there would be no *'if'* in his utterance, for what more certain than death? He would say, *"When* this earthly tabernacle shall be taken down;" not, *'if* it should be,' etc. But not so the apostle; to him death was a problematical event; he believed that many, perhaps most, of the faithful of his day would never suffer the change of dissolution; would not be *unclothed,* that is disembodied, but would 'be alive and remain unto the coming of the Lord.' Perhaps at this time he had begun to have misgivings about his own survival; but what then? Even if the earthly tenement of his body were to be dissolved, he knew that there was provided for him a divinely prepared habitation, or vehicle of the soul; an indestructible and celestial mansion, not made with hands; not a material, but a spiritual body. His present residence in the body of flesh and blood he found to be attended with many sorrows and sufferings, under the burden of which he often groaned, and for deliverance from which he longed, earnestly desiring to be endued with the heavenly vesture which was awaiting him above (ver. 2). The Pagan conception of a disembodied spirit, a naked shivering ghost, was foreign to the ideas of St. Paul; his hope and wish were that he might be found 'clothed, and not naked;' 'not to be unclothed, but clothed upon.' Conybeare and Howson have, of all commentators, best caught and expressed the idea of the apostle: 'If indeed I shall be found still clad in my fleshly garment.' It was not *death,* but *life*, that the apostle anticipated and desired; not to be divested of the body, but invested with a more excellent organism, and endued with a nobler life. There is an unmistakable allusion in his language to the hope which he cherished of escaping the doom of mortality, 'not for that we (I) would be unclothed,' etc., *i.e.* 'not that I wish to put off the body by dying,' but to merge the mortal in the immortal, 'that mortality might be swallowed up of life.'

The following comment of Dean Alford well conveys the sentiment of this important passage:---

'The feeling expressed in these verses was one most natural to those who, like the apostles, regarded the coming of the Lord as *near*, and conceived the possibility of their living to behold it. It was no terror of death as to its *consequences,* but a natural reluctance to undergo *the mere act of death as such,* when it was written possibility that this mortal body might be superseded by the immortal one, *without it.'*

In the succeeding verses the apostle intimates his full confidence that in either alternative, living or dying, all was well. 'To be at home in the body was to be absent from the Lord; to be absent from the body was to be present with the Lord.' In either case, whether present or absent, his great concern was to be accepted by the Lord at last; 'For,' he adds, 'we must all be made manifest before the judgment seat of Christ; that every on may receive the things done in the body, according to that which he hath done, whether it be good or bad' (verses 6-10).

Thus the apostle brings the whole question to a personal and practical issue. All were alike on their way to the judgment seat of Christ, and there they would all meet at last. Some might die before the coming of the Lord, and some might live to witness that event; but there, at the judgment seat, all would be gathered together; and to be accepted and approved there was, after all, a greater matter than living or dying, 'falling asleep in the Lord,' or being 'changed' without passing through the pangs of dissolution. The judgment seat was the goal before them all, and we have seen how near and imminent that solemn appearing was believed to be. That all this heartfelt faith and hope, cherished and taught by the inspired apostles of Christ, was after all a mere fallacy and delusion appears an intolerable supposition, fatal to the credit and authority of apostolic doctrine.

The Parousia in The Apostlotic Epistles - Galatians

We find no direct allusion to the Parousia in the Epistle to the Galatians. It contributes, however, indirectly to the elucidation of the subject, by furnishing an illustration of the early appearance and rapid growth of that defection from the faith predicted by our Lord, and designated by St. Paul 'the apostasy,' or 'falling away,' which was a sign and precursor of the Parousia. (See Matt. xxiv. 12; 2 Thess. ii. 3; 1 Tim. iv.; 2 Tim. iii. Iv. 3, 4.) The plague had already broken out in the churches of Galatia, and we see in this epistle how earnestly the apostle endeavoured to check its progress, vehemently protesting against this perversion of the Gospel, and denouncing its originators and propagandists as enemies of the cross of Christ. The evil arose from the arts of the Judaising teachers, who were everywhere the inveterate opponents of St. Paul, and who seem to have been possessed with the same spirit of proselytism which distinguished the Pharisees, who 'compasses sea and land to make one proselyte.' In this manifestation of the predicted apostasy we have a marked indication of the approach of the 'last times,' or 'the end of the age.'

'THIS PRESENT EVIL AGE, OR AEON.'

Gal. i. 4.---'Who gave himself for our sins, that he might deliver us from this present evil world.'

The apostle here speaks of the existing state of things as evil, and of the Lord Jesus Christ as the deliverer therefrom. The word age [aion] does not of course refer to the material world, the earth; but to the moral world, or age. It is equivalent to the phrase so often occurring in the gospels, 'this wicked generation' (Matt. xii. 45, etc.). 'The present evil age' is regarded as passing away, and about to be succeeded by a new order, the . (Heb. ii. 5.)

THE TWO JERUSALEMS---THE OLD AND THE NEW.

Gal. iv. 25, 26.---'For this Agar is mount Sinai in Arabia, and answereth to Jerusalem which now is, and is in bondage with her children. But the Jerusalem which is above is free, which is our mother.'

It is not our intention at present to do more than simply take note of this remarkable contrast between the two cities, the new and the old Jerusalem. We purposely refrain at this stage from entering upon symbols and their significance, until the whole subject comes before us in the Book of Revelation.

In the meantime the reader is requested to not well the contrast here presented. The Jerusalem which now is, and the Jerusalem which is to be; the earthly Jerusalem, and the heavenly Jerusalem; the Jerusalem which is in bondage, and the Jerusalem which is free; the Jerusalem which is beneath, and the Jerusalem which is above, the Jerusalem which is the mother of slaves; and the Jerusalem which is *our* mother. We shall yet find this contrast of no little use in determining the meaning of some of the symbols in the Apocalypse.

The Parousia In the Apostlotic Epistles - Romans

The allusion to the coming of the Lord in this epistle are not many in number, but they are very important and instructive. It is spoken of as a thing most surely believed and eagerly expected by the Christians of the apostolic age; and the fact of its *nearness* is either implied or affirmed in every allusion to the event.

THE DAY OF WRATH.

Rom. ii. 5, 6,---'But after thy hardness and impenitent heart treasurest up unto thyself wrath against the day of wrath and revelation of the righteous judgment of God; who will render to every man according to his deeds.'

Rom. ii. 12, 16,---'As many as have sinned in the law shall be judged by the law; in the day when God shall judge the secrets of men by Jesus Christ according to my gospel.'

There can be no doubt concerning this 'day of wrath' and 'revelation of the righteous judgment of God.' It is the same which was predicted by Malachi as 'the great and dreadful day of the Lord' (Mal. iv. 5); by John the Baptist as 'the coming wrath' (Matt. iii. 7); and by the Lord Jesus Christ as 'the day of judgment' (Matt. xi. 22, 24). It was the closing act of the aeon, the . It is scarcely necessary to repeat that this 'end' is declared to fall within the period of the existing generation, when the Son of man, the appointed Judge, would render to every man according to his deeds' (Matt. xvi. 27).

THE ESCHATOLOGY OF ST. PAUL.

Rom. viii. 18-23.---'For I reckon that the sufferings of this present time are not worthy to be compared with the glory which shall be revealed [*which is about to be revealed*] in us. For the earnest expectation of the creature [] waiteth [is looking eagerly] for the revelation of the sons of God. For the creature was made subject to vanity, not willingly, but by reason of him who hath subjected the same in hope. Because the creature groaneth and travaileth in pain together until now. And not only they, but ourselves also, who have the first-fruits of the Spirit, even we ourselves groan within ourselves, waiting for the adoption, to wit, the redemption of our body.'

There are some things in this passage which are, and must probably remain, obscure from the nature of the subject; but there is also much that is plain and clear. We cannot mistake the exulting anticipation expressed by St. Paul of a coming day of deliverance from the sufferings and miseries of the present; a deliverance which was at hand, and not far off. There was a day of redemption coming which would bring freedom and glory to the sons of God, in the benefits of which the whole creation would participate. The arrival that hoped-for consummation was eagerly expected and desired, not only by those who like the apostle himself had the prospect of an endless and glorious inheritance above, but by the burdened and groaning creation at large, by whom they were surrounded. So exhilarating was the prospect of the coming emancipation that in the view of it the apostle could say, 'I reckon that the sufferings of this present time are not worthy to be compared with the glory which is about to be revealed in us;' or, as in a similar passage, 'our light affliction, which is but for a moment, worketh for us a far more exceeding and eternal weight of glory' (2 Cor. iv. 17).

We now proceed to examine the whole passage more particularly.

The first point that demands attention is the distinct indication of the *nearness* of this coming glory. This is entirely lost sight of in our Authorised Version; and it has been similarly ignored by almost all commentators. Even Alford, who is usually so careful in his attention to tenses, passes by this glaring instance without remark, though nothing can be more grammatically emphatic than the indication of the *nearness* of the expected revelation. Tholuck notices that the apostle speaks of the time as near,---'In joyful exultation the apostle conceives its commencement at hand,'---but regards him as mistaken, and carried away by his feelings. Conybeare and Howson give the proper force of the language,---'the glory *which is about to be revealed, which shall soon be revealed.'* [ ]. *'The coming glory'* is the counterpart or antithesis of *'the coming wrath;'* different aspects of the same great event; for the Parousia, which was the revelation of glory to the sons of God, was the revelation of the day of wrath to His enemies (Rom. ii. 5, 7).

Thus, it will be perceived it is not to *death* that the apostle looks as the period of deliverance from present evils; still less to some far distant epoch in the future. It would indeed have been cold comfort to men writhing under the anguish their sufferings to tell them of a period in some future age which would bring them compensation for their present distress. The apostle does not so mock them with hope deferred. The day of deliverance was *at hand;* the glory was just *about to be revealed;* and so *near* and so *great* was that 'weight of glory' that it reduced to insignificance the passing inconveniences of the present hour.

The next point that deserves notice is the statement which the apostle proceeds to make respecting the interest felt in that approaching consummation beyond the limits of the suffering people of God. These indeed were to be the chief gainers by the coming redemption, but its benefits were to extend far beyond them.

This is a most important and interesting topic, and requires very careful consideration.

'For the earnest expectation of the creature waiteth for the manifestation of the sons of God.'

Whatever meaning we attach to the word 'creature' it will make no difference to the eager and expectant attitude in which it is represented as waiting for the coming consummation. Lange observes that as the word means *to expect with raised head,* implies *intense expectation,* and intense longing, waiting for satisfaction. But this very attitude implies the nearness, or a persuasion of the nearness, of the wished-for deliverance. Taking, then, these two statements together, first, that the glory is *'soon* to be revealed;' secondly, that the is 'waiting with intense longing for its manifestation,' we have as strong demonstration as it is possible to conceive that the event in question is represented by the apostle as *nigh at hand.*

But what is meant by the creature or creation? Some commentators regard it as embracing the whole universe, or the material creation, animate and inanimate, rational and irrational,---the whole frame of nature. They speak of the earthquake, the storm, and the volcano as symptoms of the sore distemper of the natural world. But this seems far too vague and general for the argument of the apostle. It is evident that the can only refer to conscious, voluntary, rational, and moral beings. It has 'intense longings;' it has 'its own will;' it has 'hope;' it is capable of being 'made subject to vanity;' of being 'set free from corruption;' of participating in 'the glory of the children of God.' These characters *exclude* the inanimate and irrational creation, and *include* the human race in its totality. Besides, the antithesis in verse 23 between the as a whole, and 'ourselves who have the first-fruits of the Spirit,' would be very unnatural and imperfect if it did not differentiate Christians, not from beasts and plants, *but from other men.* The true contrast lies between those *who have the first-fruits of the Spirit* and *those who have not the first-fruits of the Spirit;* and it would be manifestly incongruous to speak of the irrational and inanimate creation as 'not having the Spirit.' To make the apostle refer here to universal nature may be admissible perhaps as poetry, but would be quite out of place in a sober and serious argument. We understand, then, by ---the *human race, mankind* generally; the meaning which the word bears in such passages as Mark xiv. 15, 'Preach the gospel to every *creature'*; Col. i. 23, 'Which was preached to every *creature* which is under heaven'.

This brings us to the question, Can the human race be said to be in this eager and expectant attitude, groaning and travailing in pain, waiting and longing for deliverance and freedom? Undoubtedly it may; and never more truly so than in the very period when the apostle wrote. It was an age of the deepest social corruption and degradation; humanity might be said to groan under the burden of its misery and bondage; and yet there was a strange and mysterious feeling in the minds of men that, somehow and somewhere, deliverance was at hand. How accurately the description of the apostle suits the moral and social condition of the *Jewish* people at this period needs no proof. They groaned under the yoke of Roman bondage. They eagerly panted for the promised Deliverer. The case of the *Greeks* and the *Romans* was not very dissimilar, as the following passages from Conybeare and Howson strikingly prove; indeed, they might have been written as a commentary on the passage before us:---

'The social condition of the Greeks had been falling, during this period, into the lowest corruption;... but the very diffusion and development of this corruption was preparing the way, because it showed the necessity, for the interposition of a gospel. The disease itself seemed to call for a *Healer.* And if the prevailing evils of the Greek population presented obstacles on a large scale to the progress of Christianity, yet they showed to all future time the weakness of man's highest powers if unassisted from above; and there must have been many who groaned under the bondage of a corruption which they could not shake off, and who were ready to welcome the voice of Him "who took our infirmities and bare our sicknesses."'

So much for the state of the Greeks: the condition of the Roman world is thus described:---

'It would be a delusion to imagine that when the world was reduced under one sceptre, any real principle of unity held its different parts together. The emperor was deified because men were enslaved. There was no true peace when Augustus closed the temple of Janus. The Empire was only the order of external government, with a chaos both of opinions and morals within. The writings of Tacitus and Juvenal remain to attest the corruption which festered in all ranks, alike in the Senate and the family. The old soverity of manners, and the old faith in the better part of the Roman religion, were gone. The licentious creeds and practices of Greece and the East had inundated Italy and the West, and the Pantheon was only the monument of a compromise among a multitude of effete superstitions. It is true that a re-markable toleration was produced by this state of things, and it is probable that for some short time Christianity itself shared the advantage of it. But, still, the temper of the times was essentially both cruel and profane, and the apostles were soon exposed to its bitter persecution. The Roman Empire was destitute of that unity which the Gospel give to mankind. It was a kingdom of this world, and the human race were groaning for the better peace of a "kingdom not of this world."

'Thus in the very condition of the Roman Empire, and the miserable state of its mixed population, we can recognise a negative preparation for the Gospel of Christ. This tyranny and oppression called for a *Consoler* as much as the moral sickness of the Greeks called for a *Healer.* A Messiah was needed by the whole Empire as much as by the Jews, though not looked for with the same conscious expectation. But we have no difficulty in going much further than this, and we cannot hesitate to discover in the circumstances of the world at this period significant traces of a positive preparation for the Gospel.'

It is certainly remarkable that a description of the social and moral condition of the world in the apostolic age, writ-ten apparently without any view to the illustration of the passage now before us, should unwittingly adopt not merely the spirit, but to a great extent the very words, in which St. Paul sets forth the misery, the bondage, the groaning, and the yearning for deliverance of the creation as it appeared to his apprehension. But, it may be said, Was there anything in the immediate future to respond to and satisfy this eager longing of the enslaved and groaning world? What is this *'terminus ad quem?'* this revelation of the sons of God? And in what sense could it, or did it, bring deliverance and con-solation to oppressed humanity?

The answer to this question is found in almost every page of the apostle's writings. To his view a great event ap-peared just at hand; the Lord was about to come, according to His promise, to exercise His kingly power, to give rec-ompense and salvation to His people, and to tread His enemies under His feet. But the Parousia was to bring more than this. It marked a great epoch in the divine government of man. It terminated the period of exclusive privilege for Israel. It dissolved the covenant-bond between Jehovah and the Jewish people, and made way for a new and better covenant which embraced all mankind. Christianity is the proclamation of the universal Fatherhood of God, but the new era was not fully inaugurated until the narrow and local theocratic kingdom was superseded, and the Theocratic King resigned His jurisdiction into the Father's hands. Then the national and exclusive relation between God and one single people was dissolved, or merged in the all-comprehensive and world-wide system in which 'there is neither Jew nor Greek, circumcised nor uncircumcised, barbarian, Scythian, bond nor free, but only *Man.* Christ had made all men *One,* 'that God might be All in all.'

Surely, this was an adequate response to the groans and travail of suffering and down-trodden humanity; the pro-spect of such a consummation may well be represented as the dawn of a day of redemption. It was nothing less than opening the gates of mercy to mankind; it was the emancipation of the human race from the hopeless despair which was crushing them down into ever deeper corruption and degradation; it was introducing them 'into the glorious lib-erty of the children of God;' investing Gentiles, 'aliens from the commonwealth of Israel and strangers from the cove-nants of promise,' with the privileges of 'fellow-citizenship with the saints and membership of the household of God.'

It is this admission of the whole human race into [adoption of sons] which had hitherto been the exclusive privilege of the chosen people, of which the apostle speaks in such glowing language in Rom. viii. 19-21. It was a theme on which he was never weary of expatiating, and which filled his whole soul with wonder and thanksgiving. He speaks of it as 'the mystery that was hid from ages and from generations'---the manifold wisdom of God' (Ephes. iii. 10; Col. i. 26). The first three chapters of the Epistle to the Ephesians are occupied with an animated description of the revolu-tion which had been brought about by the redemptive work of Christ in the relation between God and the uncove-nanted Gentiles. 'The dispensation of the fulness of times' had arrived, in which God meant 'to gather together in one all things in Christ, making him head over all things,' breaking down the barriers of separation between Jew and Gen-tile, making both one; abolishing the ceremonial law, fusing the heterogeneous elements into one homogeneous whole, reconciling the mutual antipathy, and bringing both to unite as one family at the feet of the common Father.

But it may be said, Had not all this been already accomplished by the atoning death of the cross? And is it not a revelation of a future and approaching glory, to which the apostle here alludes? No doubt it is so. Yet the New Testa-ment always speaks of the work of redemption being incomplete till the Parousia. It will be observed that the apostle, in the twenty-third verse, represents himself and his fellow-believers as still waiting for the . Even the sons of God had only received the earnest and first-fruits, and not the full harvest of their sonship. That was not to be completely theirs until the coming of the Lord, when 'the saints who were alive and remained,' would exchange the present mortal and corruptible body for a house not made with hands, eternal in the heavens. The Parousia was the public and formal proclamation that the Messianic or Theocratic dispensation had come to an end; and that the new order, in which God was All in all, was inaugurated. Until the judgment of Israel had taken place, all things were not put under Christ the Theocratic King; His enemies even were not yet made His footstool. Until that time the adoption [] might still be said, 'to pertain to Israel.' When the apostle wrote this epistle Christ was 'expecting till his enemies should be made his footstool.' There was still an incompleteness in His work until the whole visible fabric and frame of Judaism were swept away. This fact is clearly brought out in the Epistle to the Hebrews. The writer states that 'the way into the holy place has not yet been made manifest, so long as the first, or outer, tabernacle is still standing.' He says that this tabernacle is 'a figure or parable for the present time'---serving a temporary purpose---'until a time of reformation,' that is, the introduction of a new order (Heb. ix. 8, 9). This passage is of very great importance in connection with this discussion, and the following observations of Conybeare and Howson set forth its meaning very clearly:---

'It may be asked, How could it be said, after Christ's ascension, *that the way into the holy place was not made fully manifest?* The explanation is, that while the temple-worship, with its exclusion of all but the high priest from the holy of holies, still existed, the way of salvation would not be *fully manifest* to those who adhered to the outward and typical observances, instead of being thereby led to the antitype.'---Life and Epistles of St. Paul, chap. xxviii.

There was a fitness and fulness of time at which the old covenant was to be superseded by the new; the old and the new were permitted to subsist for a time together; the goodness and forbearance of God delaying the final stroke of judgment. Although, therefore, the great barriers to the introduction of all men, without distinction, into the privileges of the children of God were virtually removed by the death of Christ upon the cross, yet the formal and final demonstration that 'the way into the holiest of all' was not thrown open to all mankind, was not made until the whole framework of the Mosaic economy, with its ritual, and temple, and city, and people, was publicly and solemnly repudiated; and Judaism, with all that pertained to it, was for ever swept away.

There is still one portion of this deeply interesting passage on which much obscurity rests. In the twentieth verse the apostle states that 'the creature was made subject to vanity, not willingly, but by reason of him who had subjected the same in hope,' etc. The common interpretation put upon these words is, that 'the visible creation has been laid under the sentence of decay and dissolution, not by its own choice, but by the act of God, who has not, however, left it without hope.

This no doubt gives a good sense to the passage, though we venture to think not exactly the sense which the apostle intended. It fails to apprehend the nature of the evil to which 'the creation' was made subject; and consequently the nature of the deliverance from that evil which is hoped for.

Understanding by [creature] the human race, for the reasons already specified, we observe that it is said to have been made subject to vanity. What is this vanity? The word is a very significant one, especially in the lips of a Jew. To such an one 'vanity' was a synonym for *idolatry.* It is the word which the Septuagint employs to denote the folly of idol-worship. Idols are 'lying vanities' (Ps. xxxi. 6; Jonah ii. 8); 'the stock is a doctrine of *vanities;*' idols are '*vanity,* and the work of errors' (Jer. x. 8, 15). 'They that make a graven image are all of them *vanity*' (Isa. xliv. 9). The word is almost set apart for this special use. The same may be said of the New Testament usage. At Lystra St. Paul besought the people 'to turn from those *vanities* [] *i.e.* idolatrous worship, to serve the living God (Acts xiv. 15). In this very epistle (Rom. i. 21) we have a remarkable instance of the use of the word, where St. Paul, accounting for the apostasy of the human race from God, explains it by the fact that 'they became *vain*' in their imaginations []; a passage in which Alford, with Bengel, Locke, and many others, recognises the allusion to idolatrous worship. It is only necessary to look at the passage to see its bearing upon the origin and prevalence of idolatry (see also Ephes. iv. 17). here looks back upon in chap. i. 21, and thus furnishes us with the key to the true interpretation. *Idolatry* was the 'vanity' to which the human race was subjected; idolatry, the religion of the Gentiles, the degradation of man, the dishonour of God.

But can it be said that man was made subject to this evil by the act of God---('by reason of him who hath subjected the same')? Undoubtedly, such a statement would be in harmony with the Word of God. In the first chapter of the Epistle to the Romans the significant fact is thrice stated, 'God gave them up,' in reference to this very apostasy (Rom. i. 24, 26, 28). This abandonment can only be regarded as a judicial act. We find a still stronger expression in Rom. xi. 32 'God hath *concluded* [] them all in unbelief;' which Alford makes equivalent to 'subjected to.' Indeed, the doctrine that God delivers over the contumacious and rebellious to the fatal consequences of their sin pervades in Scriptures. Thus it may be said that the subjection of the human race to the evil of idolatry was not simply the will of man himself, but the judicial act of divine justice.

Yet it was not a hopeless decree. 'The preservation of one nation from the universal apostasy had in it a germ of hope for mankind. In the fulness of the time God's purpose of mercy and redemption for the human race was manifested, and 'the adoption of sons,' which had been the exclusive privilege of one people, was now declared to be open to all without distinction. For this high privilege the race is represented as waiting with eager expectation, and now the Gospel, which was the divinely appointed means of rescuing men from the moral corruption and degradation of heathenism, was proclaiming deliverance and salvation 'to Gentile and Jew, barbarian, Scythian, bond and free.'

In what sense this proclamation of the new era may be said to be made in the most public and formal manner at the Parousia has been already shown.

THE NEARNESS OF THE COMING SALVATION.

Rom. xiii. 11, 12.---'And that, knowing the time, that now it is high time to awake out of sleep: for now is our salvation nearer than when we believed. The night is far spent, the day is at hand,' etc.

It is not possible for words more clearly to express the apostle's conviction that the great deliverance was at hand. It would be preposterous to regard this language, with Moses Stuart, as referring to the near approach of death and eternity. In that case the apostle would have said, 'The day is far spent, the night is at hand.' But this is not the manner of the New Testament; it is never death and the grave, but the Parousia, the 'blessed hope, and the glorious appearing of Jesus Christ,' to which the apostles look forward. Professor Jowett justly observes that 'in the New Testament we find no exhortation grounded on the shortness of life. It seems as if the end of life had no practical importance for the first believers, because it would surely be anticipated by the day of the Lord.' This undoubtedly true; but what then? Either the apostle was in error, or our confidence must be withheld from him as an authoritative expounder of divine truth; or else he was under the guidance of the spirit of God, and what he taught was unerring truth. To this dilemma those expositors are shut up who cannot bring themselves even to imagine the possibility of the Parousia having come to pass according to the teaching of St. Paul. It is curious to see the shifts to which they resort in order to find some way of escape from the inevitable conclusion.

Tholuck frankly admits the expectation of the apostle, but at the sacrifice of his authority:---

'From the day when the faithful first assembled around their Messiah until the date of this epistle, a series of years had elapsed; the full daybreak, as Paul deemed, was already close at hand. We find here corroborated, what is also evident from several other passages, that the apostle expected the speedy advent of the Lord. The reason of this lay, partly in the general law that man is fond to imagine the object of his hope at hand, partly in the circumstance that the Saviour had often delivered the admonition to be every moment prepared for the crisis in question, and had also, according to the *usus loquendi* of the prophets, described the period as fast approaching.'

Stuart protests against Tholuck's surrender of the correctness of the apostle's judgment, but adopts the untenable position that St. Paul is here speaking of---

'The spiritual salvation which believers are to experience when transferred to the world of everlasting life and glory.'

Alford, on the other hand, admits that---

'A fair exegesis of this passage can hardly fail to recognise the fact that the apostle here, as well as elsewhere (1 Thess. iv. 17; 1 Cor. xv. 51), speaks of the coming of the Lord as *rapidly approaching.* To reason, as Stuart does, that because Paul corrects in the Thessalonians the mistake of imagining it to be *immediately at hand* (or even actually come), therefore he did not himself expect it soon, is surely quite beside the purpose.'

The American editor of Lange's Commentary on the Romans has the following note:---

'Dr. Hodge objects at some length to the reference to the second coming of Christ. On the other hand most modern German commentators defend this reference. Olshausen, De Wette, Philippi, Meyer, and others, think no other view in the least degree tenable; and Dr. Lange, while careful to guard against extreme theories on this point, denies the reference to eternal blessedness, and admits that the *Parousia* is intended. This opinion gains ground among Anglo-Saxon exegetes.'

There are some interpreters who evade the difficulty by denying that such terms as *near* and *distant* have any reference to time at all. For example, we are told that---

'This is in line of all our Lord's teaching, which represents the decisive day of Christ's second appearing as at hand, to keep believers ever in the attitude of wakeful expectancy, *but without reference to the chronological nearness or distance of that event.'*

This is a non-natural method of interpretation, which simply evacuates words of all meaning. There is only one way out of the difficulty, and that is to believe that the apostle says what he means, and means what he says. He was the inspired apostle and ambassador of Christ, and the Lord let none of his words fall to the ground. His continual watchword and warning cry to the churches of the primitive age was, 'The Lord is at hand.' He believed this; he taught this; and it was the faith and hope of the whole church.

Was he mistaken? Did the whole primitive church live and die in the belief of a lie? Did nothing corresponding to their expectation come to pass? Where is the temple of God? Where is the city of Jerusalem? Where is the law of Moses? Where is the Jewish nationality? But all these things perished at the same moment; and all these were predicted to pass away at the Parousia. The fulfilment of those other events in the region of the spiritual and unseen which were indissolubly connected therewith, but of which, in the nature of things, there can be no record in the pages of human history.

PROSPECT OF SPEEDY DELIVERANCE.
Rom. xvi. 20.---'And the God of peace shall bruise Satan under your feet shortly.'

We have here another unmistakable reference to the near approach of the day of deliverance. The bruising of the serpent's head is the victory of Christ, and that victory was shortly to be won. Among the enemies who were to be made His footstool was death, and he that had the power of death, that is, the Devil.

In the prospect of His crucifixion, the Lord declared, 'Now is the judgment of this world, now shall the prince of this world be cast out,' and we have already endeavoured to show in what sense and how truly that prediction was fulfilled. In like manner a day was approaching when suffering and persecuted Christians would be delivered by the Parousia from the enemies by whom they were surrounded, and when the malignant instigator and abettor of all that enmity would lie prostrate beneath their feet.

The Parousia in the Apostlotic Epistles - Colossians

In none of St. Paul's Epistles do we find less a direct mention of the Parousia, and yet it may be said there is none which is more pervaded by the idea of that event. The thought of it underlies almost every expression of the apostle; it is implied in 'the hope which is laid up for you in heaven;' 'the inheritance of the saints in light;' 'the kingdom of his dear Son;' 'the reconciliation of all things to God;' 'the presentation of his people holy, and unblameable, and unreproveable in his sight.'

But there is a least one very distinct allusion to the Parousia in which the apostle speaks of the expected consummation.

THE APPROACHING MANIFESTATION OF CHRIST.
Col. iii. 4.---'When Christ who is our life, shall appear [shall be made manifest], then shall you also appear [be made manifest] with him in glory.'

We find here a distinct allusion to the same event and the same period as in Rom. viii. 19, viz. 'the manifestation of the sons of God.' In both passages it is evidently conceived to be *near*. In Rom viii. 19, indeed, it is expressly affirmed to be so; the glory is *'about to be revealed;'* while here the Colossian disciples are represented as 'dead,' and waiting for the life and glory which would be brought to them at the revelation of Jesus Christ, *i.e.* at the Parousia. It is inconceivable that the apostle could speak in such terms of a far-off event; its nearness is evidently one of the elements in his exhortation that they should 'set their heart on things above, and not on things on the earth.' Are we to suppose that they are still in a state of death---that their life is still hidden? Yet their life and glory are represented as contingent on the 'manifestation of Jesus Christ.'

THE COMING WRATH.
Col. iii. 6.---'On account of which [idolatry] the wrath of God is coming.'

The foregoing conclusion (respecting the nearness of the coming glory) is confirmed by the apostle's reference to the nearness of the coming wrath. The clause 'on the children of disobedience' is not found in some of the most ancient MSS. and is omitted by Alford. It has probably been added from Ephes. v. 6. Taking the passage as thus read, there is something very suggestive as well as emphatic in its declaration, 'The wrath of God is coming.' There is an unmistakable contrast between 'the coming glory of the people of God' and 'the coming wrath' upon His enemies. No less distinct is the allusion to 'the coming wrath' predicted by John the Baptist, and so frequently referred to by our Lord and His apostles. Both the *glory* and the *wrath* are 'about to be revealed;' they were coincident with the Parousia of Christ; and of the speedy manifestation of both the apostolic churches were in constant expectation.

The Parousia In the Epistle to The Ephesians.

THE ECONOMY OF THE FULNESS OF THE TIMES.
Ephes. i. 9, 10.---'Having made known unto us the mystery of his will, according to his good pleasure, which he hath purposed in himself: that in the dispensation [] of the fulness of the times he might gather together in one all things in Christ, both which are in heaven, and which are in the earth,' etc.

Though this passage does not affirm anything directly respecting the nearness of the Parousia, yet it has a very distinct bearing upon the event itself. The field of investigation which it opens is indeed far too wide for us now to explore, yet we cannot wholly pass it by. The theme is one on which the apostle loves to expatiate, and nowhere does he dwell upon it more rapturously than in this epistle. It may be presumed therefore that, however obscure it may seem to us in some respects, it was not unintelligible to the Christians of Ephesus, or those to whom this epistle was sent, for, as Paley well observes, no man write unintelligibly on purpose. We may also expect to find allusions to the same subject in other parts of the apostle's writings, which may serve to elucidate dark sayings in this.

There are two questions which are raised by the passage before us: (1) What is meant by the 'gathering together in one of all things in Christ?' (2) What is the period designated 'the economy of the fulness of the times,' in which this 'gathering together in one' is to take place?

1. With regard to the first point we are greatly assisted in determination by the expression which the apostle employs in relation to it, viz. *'the mystery* of his will.' This is a favourite word of St. Paul in speaking of that new and wonderful discovery which never failed to fill his soul with adoring gratitude and praise,---the admission of the Gentiles into all the privileges of the covenant nation. It is difficult for us to form a conception of the shock of surprise and incredulity which the announcement of such a revolution in the divine administration excited in the Jewish mind. We know that even the apostles themselves were unprepared for it, and that it was with something like hesitation and suspicion that they at length yielded to the overpowering evidence of facts,---'Then hath God also to the Gentiles granted repentance unto life' (Acts xi. 18). But to the apostle of the Gentiles this was the glorious charter of universal emancipation. Of all men he saw its divine beauty and glory, its transcendent mystery and marvelousness, most clearly. He saw the barriers of separation between Jew and Gentile, the antipathies of races, 'the middle wall of partition,' broken down by Christ, and one great family of brotherhood formed out of all nations, and kindreds, and peoples, and tongues, under the all-reconciling and uniting power of the atoning blood. We cannot be mistaken, then, in understanding this mystery of the 'gathering together in one all things in Christ' as the same which is more fully explained in chap. iii. 5,6, 'the mystery which in other ages was not made known unto the sons of men, as it is now revealed unto his holy apostles and prophets by the Spirit; that the Gentiles should be fellow-heirs, and of the same body, and partakers of his promise in Christ by the gospel.' This is the *unification,* 'the summing up,' or consummation [], to which the apostle makes such frequent reference in this epistle: 'the making of both *one*,' 'the making of twain *one* new man;' 'reconciling both unto God in *one* body' (Ephes. ii. 14, 15, 16). This was the grand secret of God, which had been hidden from past generations, but was now disclosed to the admiration and gratitude of heaven and earth.

But it may be said, How can the reception of the Gentiles into the privileges of Israel be called the comprehension of *all things,* both which are in *the heavens,* and in *the earth?*

Some very able critics have supposed that the words *heaven* and *earth* in this, and in several other passages, are to be understood in a *limited* and, so to speak, *technical* sense. To the Jewish mind, the covenant nation, the peculiar people of God might fitly be styled *'heavenly,'* while the degraded and uncovenanted Gentiles belonged to an inferior, an *earthly,* condition. This is the view taken by Locke in his note on this passage:---

'That St. Paul should use "heaven" and "earth" for Jews and Gentiles will not be thought so very strange if we consider that Daniel himself expresses the nation of the Jews by the name of "heaven" (Dan. viii. 10). Nor does he want an example of it in our Saviour Himself, who (Luke xxi. 26) by "powers of heaven" plainly signifies the great men of the Jewish nation. Nor is this the only place in this Epistle of St. Paul to the Ephesians which will bear this interpretation of heaven and earth. He who shall read the first fifteen verses of chap. iii. and carefully weigh the expressions, and observe the drift of the apostle in them, will not find that he does manifest violence to St. Paul's sense if he understand by "the family in heaven and earth" (ver. 15) the united body of Christians, made up of Jews and Gentiles, living still promiscuously among those two sorts of people who continued in their unbelief. However, this interpretation I am not positive in, but offer it as matter of inquiry to those who think an impartial search into the true meaning of the Sacred Scriptures the best employment of all the time they have.'

It is in favour of such an interpretation of 'heaven and earth' that these expressions must apparently be taken in a similar restricted sense in other passages where they occur. For example, 'Till heaven and earth pass' (Matt. v. 18); 'Heaven and earth shall pass away' (Luke xxi. 33). In the first of these passages the context shows that it cannot possibly refer to the final dissolution of the material creation, for that would assert the perpetuity of every jot and tittle of that which has long ago been abrogated and annulled. We must, therefore, understand the 'passing away of heaven and earth' in a tropical sense. A judicious expositor makes the following observations on this passage:---

'A person at all familiar with the phraseology of the Old Testament Scriptures knows that the dissolution of the Mosaic economy and the establishment of the Christian, is often spoken of as the removing of the old earth and heavens, and the creation of a new earth and new heavens. (See Isa. lxv. 17, and lxvi. 22.) The period of the close of the one dispensation and the commencement of the other, is spoken of as "the last days," and "the end of the world," and is described as such a shaking of the earth and heavens, as should lead to the removal of the things which were shaken (Hag. ii. 6; Heb. xiv. 26, 27).'

There seems, therefore, to be Scripture warrant for understanding 'things in heaven and things in earth' in the sense indicated by Locke, as meaning *Jew and Gentiles.* It is possible, however, that the words point to a still wider comprehension and a more glorious consummation. They may imply that the human race, separated from God and all holy beings, and divided by mutual enmity and alienation, was destined by the gracious purpose of God to be reclaimed, restored, and reunited under one common Head, the Lord Jesus Christ, to the one God and Father of mankind, and to all holy and happy beings in heaven. The whole intelligent universe, according to this view, was to be brought under one dominion, the dominion of God the Father, through His Son, Jesus Christ. This is the great consummation presented to us in so many forms in the New Testament. It is the 'regeneration' of Matt. xix. 28; the 'times of refreshing'; and the 'times of restoration of all things' of Acts. iii. 19, 21; the 'subjection of all things to Christ' of 1 Cor. xv. 28; the 'reconciliation of all things to God' [] of Col. i. 20; the 'time of reformation' of Heb. ix. 10; the ' '---'the new age'---of Ephes. i. 21. All these are only different forms and expressions of the same thing, and all point to the same great coming era; and to this category we may unhesitatingly assign the phrase, 'the economy of the fulness of the times,' and 'the gathering together in one of all things in Christ.'

Before this universal dominion of the Father could be publicly assumed and proclaimed, it was necessary that the exclusive and limited relation of God to a single nation should be superseded and abolished. The Theocracy had therefore to be set aside, in order to make way for the universal Fatherhood of God: 'that God might be All in all.'

2. The next question for consideration is, Have we any indication of the period at which this consummation was to take place?

We have the most explicit statements on this point; for almost every on of those equivalent designations of the event enables us to fix the time. The regeneration is 'when the Son of man shall sit on the throne of his glory;' the times of 'restitution of all thing' are when 'God shall send Jesus Christ;' the 'subjection of all things to Christ' is 'at his coming' and 'the end.' In other words, all these events coincide with the Parousia; and this, therefore, is the period of 'the reuniting of all things' under Christ.

We arrive at the same conclusion from the consideration of the phrase, 'the economy of the fulness of the times.' An economy is an arrangement or order of things, and appears to be equivalent to the phrase , or *covenant.* The Mosaic dispensation or economy is designated the 'old covenant' (2 Cor. iii. 14), in contrast to the 'new covenant,' or the 'Gospel dispensation.' The 'old covenant' or economy is represented as 'decaying, waxing old, and ready to vanish away,'---that is to say, the Mosaic dispensation was about to be abolished, and to be superseded by the Christian dispensation' (Heb. viii. 13). Sometimes the old, or Jewish, economy is spoken of as *this* aeon, the present aeon; and the Christian, or Gospel, dispensation as 'the coming aeon,' and the 'world to come' (Ephes. i. 21; Heb. ii. 5). The close of the Jewish age or economy is called 'the end of the age', and it is reasonable to conclude that the end of the old is the beginning of the new. It follows, therefore, that the economy of the fulness of the times is that state or order of things which immediately succeeds and supersedes the old Jewish economy. The economy of the fulness of the times is the final and crowning dispensation; the 'kingdom which cannot be moved;' 'the better covenant, established upon better promises.' Since, then, the old economy was finally set aside and abrogated at the destruction of Jerusalem, we conclude that the new aeon, or 'economy of the fulness of times,' received its solemn and public inauguration at the same period, which coincides with the Parousia.

THE DAY OF REDEMPTION.

Ephes. i. 13, 14.---'The holy Spirit of promise, which is the earnest of our inheritance until [for] the redemption of the purchased possession.'

Ephes. iv. 30.---'The holy Spirit of God, whereby we are sealed unto the day of redemption.'

These two passages obviously point to the same act and the same period. What is the redemption here referred to---the redemption of the *purchased possession?* Ancient Israel is called the Lord's inheritance (Deut. xxxii. 9); and the people of God are said to be His inheritance (Ephes. i. 11, Alford's translation). Here, however, it is not *God's* inheritance, but *our* inheritance, that is referred to; and that inheritance is not yet in possession, but in prospect; the pledge or earnest of it only (viz. the Holy Spirit) having been received. We are therefore compelled to understand by the inheritance the future glory and felicity awaiting the Christian in heaven. This, then, is the inheritance, and also the purchased possession, for they both refer to the same thing. Obviously it is something future, yet not distant, for it is already purchased, though not yet possessed. It stood in the same relation to the Ephesian Christians as the land of Canaan to the ancient Israelites in the wilderness. It was the promised rest, into which they hoped to live to enter. The day when the Lord Jesus should be revealed from heaven was the day of redemption to which the apostolic churches were looking forward. Our Lord had foretold the tokens of that day's approach. 'When these things begin to come to pass, then look up, and lift up your heads, for your *redemption* draweth nigh.' He had also declared that the existing generation should not pass away till all was fulfilled' (Luke xxi. 28, 32). The day of redemption, therefore, was in their view drawing nigh.

In the same manner St. Paul, writing to the Christians in Rome, speaks of the eager longing with which they were 'waiting for the adoption, or redemption of their body from the bondage of corruption' (Rom. viii. 23). This passage is precisely parallel with Ephes. i. 14 and iv. 30. There is the same *inheritance*, the same *earnest* of it, the same *full redemption* in prospect. The change of the material and mortal body into an incorruptible and spiritual body was an important part of the inheritance. This was what the apostle and their converts expected at the Parousia. The day of redemption, therefore, is coincident with the Parousia.

THE PRESENT AEON AND THAT WHICH IS COMING.

Ephes. i. 21.---'Not only in this world [aeon], but also in that which is to come' [which is coming].

We have often had occasion to remark upon the true sense of the word , so often mistranslated 'world,' Locke observes: 'It may be worth while to consider whether hath not ordinarily a more natural signification of the New Testament by standing for a considerable *length of time,* passing under some one remarkable dispensation.' There were in the apostle's view at least two great periods or aeons: the one present, but drawing to a close; the other future, and just about to open. The former was the present order of things under the Mosaic law; the latter was the new and glorious epoch which was to be inaugurated by the Parousia.

'THE AGES [AEONS] TO COME.'

Ephes. ii. 7.---'That in the ages to come he might show the exceeding riches of his grace.' etc.

On this passage the following observation is made by Conybeare and Howson:---
'"In the ages which are coming;" viz. the time of Christ's perfect triumph over evil, always contemplated in the New Testament as *near at hand.'*

It would be perhaps be more proper to say that it refers to the approaching salvation of these Gentile believers, and their glorification with Christ; for this is the consummation always contemplated in the New Testament as near at hand (Rom. xiii. 11).

The Parousia In the Epistle to the Philippians.

THE DAY OF CHRIST.

Phil. i. 6.---'He which hath begun a good work in you, will perform it until the day of Jesus Christ.'
Phil. i. 10.---'That ye may be sincere and without offence until the day of Christ.'

The day of Christ is evidently regarded by the apostle as the consummation of the moral discipline and probation of believers. There can be no doubt that he has in view the day of the Lord's coming, when He would 'render to every man according to his works.' On the supposition that the day of Christ is still future, it follows that the moral discipline of the Philippians is not yet completed; that their probation is not finished; and that the good work begun in them is not yet perfected.

Alford's note on this passage (chap. i. 6.) deserves notice. 'The assumes the nearness of the coming of the Lord. Here, as elsewhere, commentators have endeavoured to escape from this inference,' etc. This is just; but Alford's own inference, that St. Paul was mistaken, is equally untenable.

THE EXPECTATION OF THE PAROUSIA.

Phil. iii. 20, 21.---'For our conversation is in heaven, from whence also we look for a Saviour, the Lord Jesus Christ; who shall change our vile body that it may be fashioned like unto his glorious body,' etc.

These words bear decisive testimony to the expectation cherished by the apostle, and the Christians of his time, of the speedy coming of the Lord. It was not death they looked for, and waited for, as we do; but that which would swallow up death in victory: the change which would supersede the necessity of dying. Alford's notes on this passage is as follows:---
'The words assume, as St. Paul always does when speaking incidentally, his surviving to witness the coming of the Lord. The change from the dust of death in the resurrection, however we may *accommodate* the expression to it, was not originally contemplated by it.'

NEARNESS OF THE PAROUSIA.

Phil. iv. 5.---'The Lord is at hand.'

Here the apostle repeats the well-known watchword of the early church, 'The Lord is at hand:'---equivalent to the 'Maran-atha' of 1 Cor. xvi. 22. To doubt his full conviction of the nearness of Christ's coming is incompatible with a due respect for the plain meaning of words; to set down this conviction as a mistake is incompatible with a due respect for his apostolic authority and inspiration.

The Parousia In the First Epistle to Timothy.

THE APOSTASY OF THE LAST DAYS.

1 Tim. iv. 1-3.---'Now the Spirit speaketh expressly that in the latter times some shall depart [apostatize] from the faith, giving heed to seducing spirits, and doctrines of devils [demons] speaking lies in hypocrisy; having their conscience seared as with a hot iron, forbidding to marry, and commanding to abstain from meats, which God hath created to be received with thanksgiving of them which believe and know the truth.'

One of the signs which our Lord predicted as among the precursors of the great catastrophe which was to overwhelm the Jewish polity and people was a wide-spread and portentous defection from the faith, manifesting itself among the professed disciples of Christ. Our Lord's reference to this defection, though distinct and pointed, is not so minute and detailed as the description of it which we find in the Epistles of St. Paul; hence we infer, as the language of the first verse of this chapter also suggests, that subsequent revelations of its nature and features had been made to the apostles. It is designated by St. Paul, in 2 Thess. ii. 3, *'the apostasy,'*---but he does not there stay to delineate its characteristic features, hastening on to portray the lineaments of 'the man of sin.' We have already pointed out the distinction between 'the apostasy' and 'the man of sin,' to confound which has been a common but egregious mistake. We shall find in the sequel that St. Paul's description of the apostasy is as minute as that of the 'man of sin,' so as to enable us to identify the one as readily as the other.

The first point which it will be well to determine is the *period* of the apostasy; *i.e.* the *time* when it was to declare itself. It is said to be *'in the latter times'*, an expression which, taken by itself, might seem somewhat indefinite, but when compared with other similar phrases will undoubtedly be found to denote a specific and definite period, well understood by Timothy and all the apostolic churches. It will be convenient to bring together into one view all the passages which refer to this momentous and critical epoch, which is the goal and terminus to which, by New Testament showing, all things were rapidly hastening.

ESCHATOLOGICAL TABLE, OR CONSPECTUS OF PASSAGES RELATING TO THE LAST TIMES.

The End of the Age

Matt. xiii. 39.---'The harvest is the end of the age.'
Matt. xiii. 40.---'So shall it be in the end of this age.'
Matt. xiii. 49.---'So shall it be at the end of the age.'
Matt. xxiv. 3.---'What shall be the sign of thy coming [p a r o u s i a] and of the end of the age?'
Matt. xxviii. 20.---'Lo, I am with you alway, even unto the end of the age.'
Heb. ix. 26.---'But now once in the end of the ages' [t v n a i w n w n]

The End

Matt. x. 22.---'He that endureth to *the end* shall be saved.'
Matt. xxiv. 6.---'But *the end* is not yet' (Mark xiii. 9; Luke xxi. 9).
Matt. xxiv. 13.---'But he that shall endure unto *the end*, the same shall be saved' (Mark xiii. 13).
Matt. xxiv. 14.---'Then shall *the end* come.'
1 Cor. i. 8.---'Who shall also confirm you unto *the end*.'
1 Cor. x. 11.---'Upon whom *the ends of the ages* are come.'
1 Cor. xv. 24.---'Then cometh *the end*.'
Heb. iii. 6.---'Firm unto *the end*.'
Heb. iii. 14.---'Stedfast unto *the end*.'
Heb. vi. 11.---'Diligence unto *the end*.'
1 Pet. ii. 7.---'*The end* of all things is at hand.'
Rev. ii. 26.---'He that keepeth my works unto *the end*.'

The Last Times, Days, etc.

1 Tim. iv. 1.---'In the *latter times* some shall apostatise'
2 Tim. iii. 1.---'In the *last days* perilous times shall come'.
Heb. i. 2.---'In *these last days* [God] hath spoken to us'.
James v. 3.---'Ye have heaped up treasure in *the last days*'.
1 Peter i. 5.---'Salvation, ready to be revealed in *the last*.

1 Peter i. 20.---'Who was manifest in *these last times* for .
2 Peter iii. 3.---'There shall come in *the last days* scoffers' .
1 John ii. 18.---'It is the last time' [hour].
Jude, ver. 18.---'That there should be mockers in the *last time*'

EQUIVALENT PHRASES REFERRING TO THE SAME PERIOD.

The Day.

Matt. xxv. 13.---'Ye know neither *the day* nor the hour when the Son of man cometh.'
Luke xvii. 30.---'*The day* when the Son of man is revealed.'
Rom. ii. 16.---'In *the day* when God shall judge the secrets of men.'
1 Cor. iii. 13.---'*The day* shall declare it.'
Heb. x. 25.---'Ye see *the day* approaching.'

That Day.

Matt. vii. 22.---'Many shall say unto me in *that day*, Lord, Lord.'
Matt. xxiv. 36.---'But of *that day* and that hour knoweth no man.'
Luke x. 12.---'It shall be more tolerable in *that day* for Sodom.'
Luke xxi. 34.---'And so *that day* come upon you unawares.'
1 Thess. v. 4.---'That *that day* should overtake you as a thief.'
2 Thess. ii. 3.---'*That day* shall not come except there come the apostasy.'
2 Tim. i. 12.---'Which I have committed unto him against *that day*.'
2 Tim. i. 18.---'That he may find mercy of the Lord in *that day*.'

94

2 Tim. iv. 8.---'A crown . . . which the Lord . . . shall give me at *that day.*'
The Day of the Lord.
1 Cor. i. 8.---'That ye may be blameless in *the day of our Lord Jesus Christ.*'
1 Cor. v. 5.---'That the spirit may be saved in *the day of the Lord Jesus.*'
2 Cor. i. 14.---'Ye are ours in the *day of the Lord Jesus.*'
Phil. ii. 16.---'That I may rejoice in the *day of Christ.*'
1 Thess. v. 2.---'The *day of the Lord* so cometh as a thief in the night.'
The Day of God.
2 Peter iii. 12.---'Looking for and hasting unto the coming of *the day of God.*'
The Great Day.
Acts ii. 20.---'That great and notable day of the Lord.'
Jude, ver. 6.---'The judgment of the great day.'
Rev. vi. 17.---'The great day of his wrath is come.'
Rev. xvi. 14.---'The battle of the great day.'
The Day of Wrath.
Rom. ii. 5.---'Treasurest up wrath against the day of wrath.'
Rev. vi. 17.---'The great day of his wrath is come.'
The Day of Judgment.

Matt. x. 15.---'It shall be more tolerable in the day of judgment' (Mark vi. 11).
Matt. xi. 22.---'It shall be more tolerable . . . in the day of judgment.'
Matt. xi. 24.---'It shall be more tolerable . . . in the day of judgment.'
Matt. xii. 36.---'They shall give account thereof in the day of judgment.'
2 Peter ii. 9.---'To reserve the unjust unto the day of judgment.'
2 Peter iii. 7.---'The day of judgment and perdition of ungodly men.'
1 John iv. 17.---'That we may have boldness in the day of judgment.'
The Day of Redemption.
Ephes. iv. 30.---'Sealed unto the day of redemption.'
The Last Day.
John vi. 39.---'That I should raise it up at the last day.'
John vi. 40.---'I will raise him up at the last day.'
John vi. 44.---'And I will raise him up at the last day.'
John vi. 54.---'And I will raise him up at the last day.'
John xi. 24.---'He shall rise again in the resurrection at the last day.'

From the comparison of these passages it will appear,---
1. That they all refer to *one and the same period*---a certain definite and specific time.
2. That they all either assume or affirm that the period in question is not far distant.
3. The limit beyond which it is not permissible to go in determining the period called 'the last times' is indicated in the New Testament scriptures, viz. the lifetime of the generation which rejected Christ.
4. This brings us to the period of the *destruction of Jerusalem,* as marking 'the close of the age,' 'the day of the Lord,' 'the end.' That is to say, the coming of the Lord, or the Parousia.

DESCRIPTION OF THE APOSTASY.

Having thus brought into one view the passages which speak of the *period* of the apostasy, it will be proper to follow a similar method with respect to the passages which describe the features and character of the apostasy itself. This fatal defection throws its dark shadow over the whole field of New Testament history, from our Lord's prophetic discourse on the Mount of Olives, and even earlier, to the Apocalypse of St. John. It is instructive to observe how, as the time of its development and manifestation approaches, the shadow becomes darker and darker, until it reaches its deepest gloom in the revelation of the Antichrist.

CONSPECTUS OF PASSAGES RELATING TO THE APOSTASY OF THE LAST TIMES.

1. *The Apostasy, predicted by our Lord.*

False Prophets.	Matt. vii. 15.	'Beware of false prophets, which come to you in sheep's clothing, but inwardly they are ravening wolves.'
Ditto.	Matt. vii. 22.	'Many will say to me in that day, Lord, Lord, have we not prophesied in thy name,' etc.
False Christs.	Matt. xxiv. 5	'Many will come in my name, and shall deceive many.'
False Prophets.	Matt. xxiv. 11.	'And many false prophets shall rise, and shall deceive many.'
False Christs and false Prophets	Matt. xxiv. 24.	'For there shall arise false Christs, and false prophets, and shall shew great signs and wonders.'
General defection.	Matt. xxiv. 10.	'And then shall many be offended, and shall betray one another, and shall hate one another.'
	Matt. xxiv. 12.	'And because iniquity shall abound, the love of many shall wax cold.'

2. *The Apostasy, predicted by St. Paul.*

False Teachers.	Acts xx. 29, 30.	'For I know this, that after my departing shall grievous wolves enter in among you, not sparing the flock. Also of your own selves shall men arise, speaking perverse things, to draw away disciples after them.'
The Apostasy.	2 Thess. ii. 3	'That day shall not come, except there come first the apostasy.'
False Apostles.	2 Cor. xi. 13, 14.	'For such are false apostles, deceitful workers, transforming themselves into the apostles of Christ. And no marvel: for Satan himself is transformed into an angel of light.'
False Teachers.	Gal. i. 7.	'But there be some that trouble you, and would pervert the gospel of Christ.'
False Brethren.	Gal. ii. 4.	'False brethren unawares brought in.'
Deceivers and Schismatics.	Rom. xvi. 17, 18.	'Mark them which cause divisions and offences contrary to the doctrine which ye have learned, and avoid them. For they that are such serve not our Lord Jesus Christ, but their own belly; and by good words and fair speeches deceive the hearts of the simple.'
False Teachers.	Col. ii. 8.	'Beware, lest any man spoil you through philosophy and vain deceit,' etc.
Ditto.	Col. ii. 18.	'Let no man beguile you of your reward in a voluntary humility and worshipping of angels.'
Judaising Teachers.	Phil. iii. 2.	'Beware of dogs; beware of evil workers; beware of the concision.'
Enemies of the Cross.	Phil. iii. 18.	'For many walk, of whom I have told you often . . . that they are the enemies of the cross of Christ.'
Sensualists.	Phil. iii. 19.	'Whose end is destruction: whose god is their belly.'
False Teachers.	1 Tim. i. 3, 4.	'That thou mightest charge some that they teach no other doctrine; neither give heed to fables and endless genealogies.'
Judaisers.	1 Tim. i. 6, 7.	'Some having swerved, have turned aside into vain jangling; desiring to be teachers of the law,' etc.
Apostates.	1 Tim. i. 19.	'Some have put away (faith and a good conscience) concerning faith have made shipwreck.'
Ditto. Liars and Hypocrites.	1 Tim. iv. 1, 2.	'Now the spirit speaketh expressly that in the latter times some shall depart from the faith, giving heed to seducing spirits, and doctrines of demons; speaking lies in hypocrisy: having their conscience seared with a hot iron.'
False Teachers.	1 Tim. iv. 3.	'Forbidding to marry, and commanding to abstain from meats,' etc.
Ditto.	1 Tim iv. 20, 21.	'Avoiding profane and vain babblings, and oppositions of science falsely so called: which some professing have erred concerning the faith.'
Ditto.	2 Tim. ii. 16-18.	'But shun profane and vain babblings: for they will increase unto more ungodliness. And their word will eat as doth a canker: of whom is Hymenaeus and Philetus; who concerning the truth have erred, saying that the resurrection is past already; and overthrow the faith of some.'
Immorality of the Apostasy.	2 Tim. iii. 1-6, 8.	'This know also, that in the last days perilous times shall come. For men shall be lovers of their own selves, covetous, boasters, proud, blasphemers, disobedient to parents, unthankful, unholy, without natural affection, trucebreakers, false accusers, incontinent, fierce, despisers of those that are good, traitors, heady, highminded, lovers of pleasures more than lovers of God; having a form of godliness, but denying the power thereof: . . . they creep into houses, and lead captive silly women laden with sins,' etc. 'Men of corrupt minds, reprobate concerning the faith.'
False Teachers.	2 Tim. iii. 13.	'Evil men and seducers wax worse and worse, deceiving and being deceived.'
Ditto.	2 Tim. iv. 3, 4.	'For the time will come when they will not endure sound doctrine, but after their own lusts shall they heap to themselves teachers, having itching ears; and they shall turn away their ears from the truth, and shall be turned unto fables.'
Judaising Teachers.	Titus i. 10.	'For there are many unruly and vain talkers and deceivers, specially they of the circumcision.'

| Ditto. | Titus i. 14. | 'Not giving heed to Jewish fables, and commandments of men, that turn from the truth.' |
| Immoral. | Titus i. 16. | 'They profess that they know God; but in works they deny him, being abominable, and disobedient, and unto every good work reprobate.' |

3. *The Apostasy, predicted by St. Peter.*

False Teach-ers.	2 Peter ii. 1.	'But there were false prophets also among the people, even as there shall be false teach-ers among you, who privily shall bring in damnable heresies, even denying the Lord that bought them, and bring upon themselves swift destruction.'
Immorality of the Apostasy.	2 Peter ii. 10, 13, 14.	'They walk after the flesh in the lust of uncleanness, and despise government. Presump-tuous are they, self-willed, they are not afraid to speak evil of dignities. Spots they are and blemishes, sporting themselves with their own deceivings, while they feast with you: having eyes full of adultery, and that cannot cease from sin,' etc.
Scoffers.	2 Peter iii. 3.	'Knowing this first, that there shall come in the last days scoffers, walking after their own lusts.'

4. *The Apostasy, predicted by St. Jude.*

False Teachers.   Jude.   Passim. See 2 Peter ii.

5. *The Apostasy, predicted by St. John.*

Antichrist, Apos-tates.	1 John ii. 18, 19.	'Little children, it is the last time: and as ye have heard that antichrist shall come, even now there are many antichrists; whereby we know that it is the last time. They went out from us, but they were not of us,' etc.
Antichrist.	1 John ii. 22.	'Who is a liar but he that denieth that Jesus is the Christ? He is antichrist that denieth the Father and the Son.'
False Teachers.	1 John ii. 26.	'These things have I written unto you concerning them that seduce you.'
False Prophets.	1 John iv. 1.	'Many false prophets are gone out into the world.'
Antichrist.	1 John iv. 3.	'Every spirit that confesseth not that Jesus Christ is come in the flesh is not of God: and this is that spirit of antichrist, whereof ye have heard that it should come; and even now already is in the world.'
Deceivers and Antichrists.	2 John, ver. 7.	'For many deceivers are entered into the world, who confess not that Jesus Christ is come in the flesh. This is a deceiver and an antichrist.'

CONCLUSIONS RESPECTING THE APOSTASY.

From a consideration and comparison of these passages it will appear,---

1.   That they all refer to the same great defection from the faith, designated by St. Paul 'the apostasy.'
2.   That this apostasy was to be very general and widespread.
3.   That it was to be marked by an extreme depravity of morals, particularly by sins of the flesh.
4.   That it was to be accompanied by pretensions to miraculous power.
5.   That it was largely, if not chiefly, Jewish in its character.
6.   That it rejected the incarnation and divinity of the Lord Jesus Christ,---*i.e.* was the predicted Antichrist.
7.   That it was to reach its full development in the 'last times,' and was to be the precursor of the Parousia.

Having thus taken a general survey of the New Testament doctrine concerning the apostasy, it only remains to no-tice some objections which may possibly be made to the foregoing conclusions.

1. It may be asked, What evidence have we that such errors and heresies prevailed in apostolic times? The answer is, The New Testament itself furnishes the proof. The evils which are described by St. Paul as future, are represented by St. Peter and St. John as actually present. The characteristics of the apostasy as set forth by the one are precisely those which are described by the others. Asceticism and immorality are conspicuous in the prophetic delineations of the apostasy by St. Paul, and we find the same features in the historical descriptions by St. Peter and St. John.

2. It may be objected that the period called 'the latter times,' or 'the last times,' is not strictly defined, and may, for aught we know, be still future.

But, in the first place, the injunctions given by St. Paul to Timothy clearly imply that it was not a distant, but a present, or at all events an impending, evil of which he was speaking. It is manifest that the symptoms of the apostasy had already begun to show themselves, and the whole tenor of the apostle's exhortation implies that the evils specified would come under the notice of Timothy (1 Tim. vi. 20, 21).

Nothing can be more certain than that the apostles considered themselves to be living in 'the last times.' We shall have occasion in the sequel to see this distinctly proved. Meanwhile it may be observed that the passages arranged under the heading *the Last Times'* in our Eschatological Table, all refer to the same great crisis. It was 'the close of the age' [s u n t e l e i a t o u a i v n o z], of which our Lord so often spoke. The apostasy was the predicted precursor of that end.

TIMOTHY AND THE PAROUSIA.

1 Tim. vi. 14.---[I give thee charge] 'that thou keep this commandment without spot, unrebukable, until the appearing of our Lord Jesus Christ: which in his times he shall show,' etc.

This implies that Timothy might expect to live until that event took place. The apostle does not say, 'Keep this commandment as long as you live;' nor, 'Keep it until death;' but 'until the appearing of Jesus Christ.' These expressions are by not means equivalent. The 'appearing' [e p i f a n e i a] is identical with the Parousia, an event which St. Paul and Timothy alike believed to be at hand.

Alford's note on this verse is eminently unsatisfactory. Alford's note on this verse is eminently unsatisfactory. After quoting Bengel's remark 'that the faithful in the apostolic age were accustomed to look forward to the day of Christ as approaching; whereas *we* are accustomed to look forward to the day of *death* in like manner,' he goes on to observe:---

'We may fairly say that whatever impression is betrayed by the words that the coming of the Lord would be in Timotheus's life-time, is chastened and corrected by the k a i r o i z i d i o i z [his own times]of the next verse.'
In other words, the erroneous opinion of one sentence is corrected by the cautious vagueness of the next! Is it possible to accept such a statement? Is there anything in k a i r o i z i d i o i z to justify such a comment? Or is such an estimate of the apostle's language compatible with a belief in his inspiration? It was no 'impression' that the apostle 'betrayed,' but a conviction and an assurance founded on the express promises of Christ and the revelations of His Spirit.

No less exceptionable is the concluding refection:---
'From such passages as this we see that the apostolic age maintained that which ought to be the attitude of all ages,---constant expectation of the Lord's return.'

But if this expectation was nothing more than a false impression, is not their attitude rather a caution than an example? We now see (assuming that the Parousia never took place) that they cherished a vain hope, and lived in the belief of a delusion. And if they were mistaken in this, the most confident and cherished of their convictions, how can we have any reliance on their other opinions? To regard the apostles and primitive Christians as all involved in an egregious delusion on a subject which had a foremost place in their faith and hope, is to strike a fatal blow at the inspiration and authority of the New Testament. When St. Paul declared, again and again, 'The Lord is at hand,' he did not give utterance to his private opinion, but spoke with authority as an organ of the Holy Ghost. Dean Alford's observations may be best answered in the words of his own rejoinder to Professor Jowett:---

'Was the apostle or was he not writing in the power of a spirit higher than his own? Have we, in any sense, God speaking in the Bible, or have we not? If we have, then of all passages it is in these which treat so confidently of futurity that we must recognise His voice: if we have it not in these passages, then where are we to listen for it all?'

We find the same apologetic tone in Dr. Ellicott's remarks on this passage:--
'It may, perhaps, be admitted that the sacred writers have used language in reference to the Lord's return which seems to show that the longings of hope had *almost* become the convictions of belief.'

Strange that the plainest, strongest, most oft-repeated affirmations of his faith and hope by St. Paul should produce in the mind of a reader so faint an impression of his convictions as this. But there is not faltering in the declaration of the apostle; it is no peradventure that he utters; it is with a firm and confident tone that he raises the exulting cry, 'The Lord is at hand.' He does not express his own surmises, or hopes, or longings, but delivers the message with which he was charged, and, as a faithful witness for Christ, everywhere proclaims the speedy coming of the Lord.

THE APOSTASY ALREADY MANIFESTING ITSELF.

1 Tim. vi. 20, 21.---'O Timothy, keep that which is committed to thy trust, avoiding profane and vain babblings, and oppositions of science falsely so-called; which some professing have erred concerning the faith.'

It is important to notice that from several intimations in this epistle it appears that the defection from the faith which was to characterise the latter days had already set in. St. Paul warns Timothy against 'false teachers,' with their 'fables and endless genealogies,'---against those 'who concerning the faith had made shipwreck;' against others 'who doted about questions, and strifes of words,---men of corrupt minds, and destitute of the truth.' These 'wolves in sheep's clothing' were evidently already devouring the flock. To place the apostasy therefore in a post-apostolic age is to overlook the obvious teaching of the epistle. It was a present and not a distant evil which the apostle deprecated: the plague had begun in the camp.

The Parousia In the Second Epistle to Timothy.

'THAT DAY'---VIZ. THE PAROUSIA---ANTICIPATED.

2 Tim. i. 12.---'He is able to keep that which I have committed unto him against *that day.'*

2 Tim. i. 18.---'The Lord grant unto him that he may find mercy of the Lord in *that day.'*

2 Tim. iv. 8.---'The crown of righteousness, which the Lord, the righteous Judge, shall give me at *that day.'*

The allusion in all these passages is to 'the day of the Lord;' *the* day *par excellence;* the day of His appearing; the Parousia.

The whole tenor of these passages indicates that St. Paul regarded 'that day' as now very near. In the anticipation of it he breaks forth into a burst of triumphant exultation, as if he were just about to receive the crown of victory,---'I have fought the good fight; I have finished my course; I have kept the faith. Henceforth is laid up for me the crown of righteousness, which the Lord, the righteous Judge, shall give me in that day; and not to me only, but to all who love his appearing.' How evidently all these events,---his own departure, his crown, 'that day,' and the Lord's appearing, are anticipated as at hand! Shall we say that his anticipations were too sanguine? That the day has not yet come? That his crown is still 'laid up'? that Onesiphorus has not yet found mercy? The supposition is incredible.

THE APOSTASY OF THE 'LAST DAYS' IMMINENT.

2 Tim. iii. 1-9.---'This know also, that in the last days perilous times shall come. For men shall be lovers of their own selves, covetous, boasters, proud, blasphemers, disobedient to parents, unthankful, unholy, without natural affection, trucebreakers, false accusers, incontinent, fierce, despisers of those that are good, traitors, heady, highminded, lovers of pleasures more than lovers of God; having a form of godliness, but denying the power thereof: from such turn away. For of this sort are they which creep into houses, and lead captive silly women laden with sins, led away with divers lusts, ever learning, and never able to come to the knowledge of the truth. Now as Jannes and Jambres withstood Moses, so do these also resist the truth: men of corrupt minds, reprobate concerning the faith.'

The 'last days' of this passage are evidently identical with the 'latter times' of 1 Tim. iv. 1. This is so obvious as to need no proof. The attempt to make a distinction between the 'latter' times and the 'last' times, which Bengel seems to sanction, is therefore futile. It is scarcely necessary to add that 'the last days' were the apostle's own days---the time then present. He is speaking, not of the distant future, but of a time already commencing; for it is plain that he draws the picture of the characters described from the life. Indications of the coming apostasy were already apparent,---'of this sort are they,' etc. (ver. 6). It is assumed that Timothy would encounter those times, and those evil men from whom he is exhorted to turn away. The following note from Conybeare and Howson comes very near the truth, though it falls short of the whole truth:---

'This phrase (e s c a t a i z h m e r a i z, used without the article, as having become a familiar expression) generally denotes the termination of the Mosaic dispensation. (See Acts ii. 17; 1 Pet. i. 5, 20; Heb. i. 2.) Thus the expression generally denotes (in the apostolic age) the time present; but here it points to a future immediately at hand, which is, however, blended with the present (see vers. 6, 8), and was in fact the end of the apostolic age. (Compare 1 John ii. 18, 'It is the last hour.') The *long duration* of this last period of the world's development was not revealed to the apostles: they expected that their Lord's return would end it, in their own generation; and thus His words were fulfilled, that none should foresee the time of His coming.

This closing explanation is what no one who believes that the apostles spoke and wrote by the power of the Holy Ghost can admit; and, notwithstanding the almost unanimous opinion of their critics that they were certainly mistaken, we hold by the apostles rather than by their critics.

Alford's comment on this passage is painfully self-contradictory, and shows to what shifts learned men are reduced in order to save the credit of the apostles when they cannot believe their plain declarations. He says:---

'The apostle for the most part wrote and spoke of it (the coming of the Lord) as soon to appear, not however without many and sufficient hints, furnished by the Spirit, of an interval, and that no short one, first to elapse.'

But how could and event be '*soon* to appear' and yet a long period first to elapse? Or, are we to suppose that the Holy Spirit taught one thing while the apostles wrote and spoke quite another? If they said what they did respecting the nearness of the Parousia when they really had no knowledge and no revelation on the subject, they clearly exceeded their commission, and committed what the Word of God pronounces on of the most presumptuous sins,---added to the words of the prophecy which they were commissioned to convey. We reject the explanation *in toto.* It is not only a non-natural interpretation, but wholly inconsistent with any theory of inspiration of the word of God.

The passage before us is most important as delineating the character of 'the apostasy.' The dreaded apparition had already begun to reveal itself, and the apostle evidently describes it from actual observation. Phygellus and Hermogenes, who deserted the apostle; Hymenaeus and Philetus, with their profane and vain babbling; the fawning deceivers, who made proselytes of weak-minded women; the men of corrupt minds, reprobate concerning the faith, who resisted the truth; these were the vanguard of the locust army of errorists and apostates which was coming up to overspread and devastate the fair face of early Christianity. Their appearance indicated that 'the last times' had arrived, and that the Parousia was at hand. We might at first suppose that the hideous catalogue of reprobates contained in the opening verses of chapter iii. describes the general corruption of society outside the Christian church, but it is too evident that the apostle is alluding to men who had once professed the faith of Christ. They had 'a form of godliness;' they had 'made shipwreck of faith,' they were truly 'apostates.'

That this 'falling away' from the truth had already set in is evident from the reiterated exhortations and warning which the apostle addresses to Timothy. Why should he speak with such impassioned earnestness if the evil was not to make its appearance for twenty or forty centuries? It is absurd to say that St. Paul was writing for the benefit of future ages. He was as truly a man living in his own age, and writing to a man of his own time concerning matters of present and personal interest to both, as any of us who now pour out our thoughts in a letter to an absent friend. There is an utter unreality in any other view of the apostolic epistles. It is impossible to read them without feeling the heart-throbs that beat in every line; all is vivid, intense, alive,. It is not a distant danger, seen through the haze of centuries, but one that is instant and urgent: the enemy was at the gate, and the veteran warrior, about to sink on the field of conflict, cheers on the young soldier to fidelity, and resistance to the end.

ANTICIPATIONS OF THE APPROACHING END.

2 Tim. iv. 1, 2.---'I adjure thee before God, and Jesus Christ, who is about to judge the living and the dead; and by his appearing and his kingdom, Preach the word; be instant in season, out of season; reprove, rebuke, exhort with all long-suffering and doctrine.'

We find associated together in this passage as contemporaneous events the Parousia, the judgment, and the kingdom of Christ. These are all connected and related in their nature and in the time of their occurrence. We find the same collocation of events in Matt. xxv. 31, 'When the Son of man shall come in his glory, then shall he sit upon the throne of his glory, and before him shall be gathered all the nations,' etc.

The nearness of this consummation is distinctly affirmed. It is not, as in our Authorised Version, 'who shall judge,' but 'who is about to judge'. One statement like this might suffice to settle the question both as to the fact and the apostle's belief of the fact, that the time of the Parousia was at hand. But, instead of a single affirmation, we have the constant and uniform tenor of the whole New Testament doctrine on the subject. Those who say the apostles were in error on this point must have 'a verifying faculty' to distinguish between their inspired and their uninspired utterances. If St. Paul was inspired to write k r i n e i n , was he not equally inspired to write m e l l o n t o z?

This imminency of the Parousia explains the fervour with which the apostle urges Timothy to put forth every effort in discharging the duties of his office: 'Preach the word; be instant in season, out of season; reprove, rebuke, exhort with all long-suffering and doctrine.' These injunctions are sometimes employed to set forth the normal intensity and urgency with which the pastoral function should be discharged (and we do not condemn the application); but it is plain that St. Paul is not speaking of ordinary times and ordinary efforts. It is the agony of a tremendous crisis; the time is short; it is now or never; victory or death. These are not the common-place phrases about the diligent discharge of duty, but the alarm of the sentinel who sees the enemy at the gates, and blows the trumpet to warn the city.

The Parousia In the Epistle to Titus.

ANTICIPATION OF THE PAROUSIA.

'Titus ii. 13.---'Looking for that blessed hope, and the revelation of the glory of the great God, and our Saviour Jesus Christ.'

We again find here, what we have long come to recognise, the habitual attitude of the Christians of the apostolic age, the expectation of the Lord's coming. It is inculcated as one of the primary Christian duties, and ranks with sober, righteous, and godly living. This implies that the event was regarded as at hand, for how could a powerful motive to watchfulness be derived from a remote and unknown contingency lying in the distant future? Or, how could it be the duty of Christians to be 'looking' for that which was not to happen for hundreds and thousands of years? The apostle evidently regards the present aeon, t o n n u n a i v n a , as drawing to a close, and exhorts Christians to live in the attitude of expectancy of the Parousia, which was to introduce the new order, 'the aiwno mellwn .'

The Parousia In the Epistle to the Hebrews.

It does not fall within the scope of this investigation to discuss the question of the authorship of the Epistle to the Hebrews. Even if it do not come from the same pen which wrote the Epistle to the Romans, and few who are familiar with the style of St. Paul will affirm that it does, yet its spirit and teaching are essentially Pauline, and we may justly regard it as one of the most precious legacies of the apostolic age. Its value as a key to the meaning of the Levitical economy, and as a contribution to Christian doctrine and living, is inestimable; and whether we ascribe its authorship to Barnabas or Apollos, or any other fellow-labourer with St. Paul, we may unhesitatingly accept it, 'not as the word of man, but, as it is in truth, the word of God.'

We now enter still more deeply into the dark shadow of the predicted apostasy. It was to combat this formidable antagonist of the Gospel that this epistle was written; and the *Judaic* character of the anti-Christian movement is apparent from the line of argument which the author adopts. We find ourselves at once in 'the last days.'

THE LAST DAYS ALREADY COME.

Heb. i. 1, 2.---'God, who at sundry times and in divers manners spake in time past unto the fathers by the prophets, hath in these last days spoken unto us by his Son.'

The phrase 'in these last days,' or 'in the end of these days,' shows that the writer regarded the time of Christ's incarnation and ministry as the closing period of a dispensation or aeon. We fin a somewhat similar expression in chap. ix. 26, 'Now, in the end of the ages' where the reference is to the time of our Saviour's incarnation and atoning sacrifice. And old era, call it Mosaic, Judaic, or Old Testament, was now running out; many things that had seemed immovable and eternal were about to vanish away; and 'the end of the age,' or 'the last times,' had arrived

THE AEONS, AGES, OR WORLD-PERIODS.

Heb. i. 2.---'By whom also he made the worlds' [aeons].

Much confusion has arisen from the indiscriminate use of the word 'world' as the translation of the different Greek words a i w n , k o z m o z , o i k o u m e n h , and g h . The unlearned reader who meets with the phrase 'the end of the world,' inevitably thinks of the destruction of the material globe, whereas if he read 'conclusion of the age, or aeon,' he would as naturally think of the close of a certain period of time---which is its proper meaning. We have already had occasion to observe that a i w n is properly a designation of *time,* an *age;* and it is doubtful whether it ever has any other signification in the New Testament. Its equivalent in Latin is *aevum,* which is really the Greek a i w n in a Latin dress. The proper word for the *earth,* or *world,* is k o s m o z , which is used to designate both the material and the moral world. O i k o u m e n h is properly the *inhabited* world, 'the *habitable,*' and in the New Testament refers often to the *Roman Empire,* sometimes to so small a portion of it as *Palestine.* G h , though it sometimes signifies the earth generally, in the gospels more frequently refers to the *land* of Israel. Much light is thrown upon many passages by a proper understanding of these words.

It is certain that the Jews in our Saviour's time were accustomed to make a division of time into two great periods or aeons, *the present aeon*, and *the coming*. The coming aeon was that of the Messiah, or 'the kingdom of God.' The same division is recognised in the New Testament, and we have already seen that, in the view of the writer of this epistle, the close of the present aeon was approaching. (See Stuart's Comm. on Heb. *in loc.;* Alford's Greek Testament; Wahl's Lexicon, *voc. a i w n*).

It may be said, however, that though the word does primarily signify an *age,* yet in this instance the sense of the passage obviously requires us to translate a i w n a z , *worlds.* It must be acknowledged that it seems uncouth to our ears to say, 'God made the ages by Jesus Christ,' and very simple and natural to say, 'He made the world;' yet when we consider that the writer of this epistle had no conception of *worlds* in the sense in which we now use that expression, it may perhaps modify our opinion. We are very apt to credit the author with our astronomical ideas, and suppose that he is referring to the sun, moon, and stars as so many *worlds.* But we have no reason to believe that he had any such notion. The heavenly bodies were to him lights, but not worlds. With aeons, however, the author of this epistle, as a man of letters, must have been perfectly familiar. What, then, did he mean by God making the aeons? These were the great eras, or epochs of time, which the Supreme Wisdom had ordained and arranged; world-periods, as we may call them, which constituted acts in the great drama of Providence. There seems to be an allusion to this ordering of the ages, or world-periods, in Acts xvii. 26: 'Having determined the times before appointed'; as also in Ephes. i. 10: 'The dispensation of the fulness of the times.' It is strongly in favour of this view that it is substantially that which is adopted by the Greek Fathers.

THE WORLD TO COME, OR THE NEW ORDER.

Heb. ii. 5.---'For unto the angels hath he not put in subjection the world to come whereof we speak.'

This passage elucidates the subject still more. We have here one of the aeons---the world to come---*i.e.* not a material world, but a system or order of things analogous to the Mosaic dispensation. There is an evident comparison or contrast between the Mosaic economy and the new, or Christian, state. The former was placed under the administration of angels; it was 'the word spoken by angels;' it was given by 'the disposition of angels' (Acts vii. 53); it was ordained by angels in the hand of a mediator (Gal. iii. 19). But the new aeon, the kingdom of heaven, was administered by one greater than the angels, the Son of God Himself; a proof of the superiority of the Christian over the Jewish dispensation.

It is certainly somewhat singular that we should find the word o i k o u m e n h here, where we should have expected to find a i w n a . Had it been o i k o n o m i a n , as in Ephes. i. 10, it would have been more in accordance with our ideas of the true purport; but there is no warrant for supposing that the one word has been substituted for the other. That the allusion is to the system or order of things inaugurated by Christ there can be no doubt, and the phrase is equivalent to 'the kingdom of heaven.' It may be added that it is said to be *'coming,'* m e l l o u s a , a word which implies *nearness,* like 'the coming wrath,' 'the coming glory,' 'the coming age.'

THE END, *i.e.* OF THE AGE, OR AEON.

Heb. iii. 6.---'If we hold fast the confidence and the rejoicing of the hope firm unto *the end.'*

Heb. iii. 14.---'If we hold the beginning of our confidence stedfast unto *the end.'*

Heb. vi. 11.---'The full assurance of hope unto *the end.'*

We have already had occasion to remark upon the significant phrase 'the end,' as it is used in the New Testament. It does not mean *to the last,* or to the *end of life;* but to the close of the aeon. Alford correctly observes,---
'The end thought of, is not the death of each individual, but the coming of the Lord, which is constantly called by this name.'

THE PROMISE OF THE REST OF GOD.

Heb. iv. 1-11.---'Let us therefore fear, since a promise still remaineth of entering into his rest, lest any of you should seem to come short of it. For unto us good tidings have been brought as well as unto them, but the report which they heard did not profit them, because it met with no belief in those that heard it. For we that have believed are entering into the (promised) rest, even as he hath said, So I sware in my wrath, they shall not enter into my rest. (Although his works were finished ever since the foundation of the world. For he hath spoken in a certain place of the seventh day on this wise, And God did rest on the seventh day from all his works. And in this place again, They shall not enter into my rest.) Since, therefore, it still remaineth that some must enter therein, and they who first received the glad tidings entered not in because of disobedience, he again limiteth a certain day, saying in David, After so long a time, to-day; as it hath been said before, To-day, if ye hear his voice, harden not your hearts. For if Joshua had given them rest, then God would not afterwards speak of another day. There still remaineth a rest [sabbath keeping] for the people of God. For he that is entered into his rest, hath himself also rested from his own works, as God did from his. Let us therefore strive to enter into that rest, lest any man fall after the same example of disobedience.'

This is an exceedingly important and interesting passage, not without its obscurities and difficulties, which have occasioned much diversity of interpretation. Some have found in it an argument for the perpetuity of the Fourth Commandment, and the observance of the first day of the week as the Christian sabbath. Others have interpreted the whole argument in an ethical and subjective sense, as if the writer exhorted to the attainment of a certain state of mind called *the rest of faith:* a ceasing from doubt and from self-dependence, and obtaining perfect repose of mind by full trust in God. Such interpretations, however, wholly miss the point of the argument, and are rather ingenious glosses than legitimate deductions.

What is the drift of the argument? It is very evident that the object of the writer is to warn Hebrew Christians against unbelief and disobedience by setting before them, on the one hand, the reward of obedience, and, on the other, the penalty of disobedience. There was ready to his hand a signal example, memorable to all Israelites, viz. the forfeiture of the land Canaan by their fathers in consequence of their unbelief. They had provoked the Lord to swear in His wrath, 'They shall not enter into my rest.'

In the view of the writer there was a remarkable correspondence between the situation of the Israelites approaching the land of promise and the situation of Christians expecting the fulfilment of their hope, the promise of rest. To make this correspondence more clear he shows that the *rest* promised to ancient Israel, and that promised to the people of God now, were really one and the same thing. The entrance into the land of Canaan was by no means the whole, nor even the principal part, of the promised rest of God. This he proves by showing that long after the settlement of the Israelites in Canaan, the Lord, by the mouth of David, in Psalm xcv., virtually repeats the promise made to the Israelites in the wilderness, and says to the people, *'To-day,* if ye will hear his voice, harden not your hearts.' The repetition of the command implies the repetition of the promise, and also of the threatening; as if God were saying, 'Believe, and ye shall enter into my rest. Disbelieve, and ye shall not enter into my rest.' Hence it follows that there is a *rest* besides and beyond the rest of Canaan.

Then follows the explanation of the *rest* referred to, viz. the 'rest of God,' that which He calls 'My rest.' Certainly that name was never given to the land of Canaan, nor can it be applied to any other than that 'rest' of which we read in the account of the creation, when God did *rest* from all 'his work which he had made' (Gen. ii. 2, 3). This was God's sabbath, the rest which He hallowed and called His own. It must be to this rest therefore---the holy, sabbatic, heavenly repose---that the promise chiefly refers. Of that rest of God Canaan was no doubt the type, for that was the rest of the Israelites after the perils and fatigues of the wilderness; but the possession of Canaan was far from exhausting the full meaning of the promise, and therefore it still remained, and was kept in reserve for the people of God. 'There remaineth therefore a rest for the people of God.'

The writer of the Epistle to the Hebrews evidently regarded the 'rest of God' as a consummation not far distant. He says of it, 'We that have believed *are entering* into that rest.' This does not mean 'going to heaven at death,' but the expectation of the speedily coming kingdom of God, the hope so strongly cherished by the first Christians (Rom. viii. 18-25). To regard these exhortations and appeals as the ordinary commonplaces of religious teaching, is to rob them of half their significance. True, there is a sense in which they may be applicable to all times, but they had a meaning and a force at that particular juncture which it is difficult for us now to comprehend. The Christians of that epoch stood, as it were, on the border-line between the old and the new, between the aeon that was closing and that which was opening. They believed that the day of the Lord was just at hand,---that Christ would soon return, and that they would enter along with Him into the kingdom of heaven, the rest of God. Hence the duty of 'exhorting one another; and so much the more as they saw the day approaching;' of holding the beginning of their confidence stedfast unto the end; of 'striving to enter into that rest, lest any many should fall,' or 'seem to come short of it.'

The writer of this epistle, in verses 9 and 10 of this chapter, shows the propriety of calling this promised rest a 'sabbatism,' or sabbatic rest. 'There remaineth therefore a sabbatism for the people of God. For he that is entered into his rest, he also hath rested from his own works, as God did from his.' There is an ambiguity in this language both in the Greek and in the English. It may mean that all the faithful departed have ceased from the toils of earth, and now enjoy the repose and reward of heaven. This is the sense usually attached to the words. (See Stuart's Commentary on Hebrews, *in loc.;* Conybeare and Howson, etc.) It must be confessed, however, that the relevance of this language so interpreted, to the matter in hand, is not very apparent, and that the grammatical construction will hardly warrant such an explanation. The argument affirms, not that Christians have entered into that rest, but just the contrary. The writer states, as Conybeare and Howson very properly show, *'that God's people have never yet enjoyed that perfect rest, therefore its enjoyment is still future.'* Who, then, is 'he that entered in'? Evidently it is *Christ*, the Forerunner, who *entered* on our behalf within the veil; our great High Priest, who *is passed* into the heavens; the New Testament Joshua, the Captain of our salvation, who *'entered* into his rest,' ceasing from His work of redemption, even as His Father did from His own work of creation. This shows the fitness of heaven being called a 'sabbatism,' a 'rest of God,' for there both the Father and the Son keep eternal sabbath. It may be added that this interpretation relieves us from the sense of incongruity which is felt in comparing a Christian's ceasing from his labours to God's ceasing from the work of creation; it is also perfectly relevant to the argument in the context.

Not only will the words bear this sense, but they will not bear any other, as Alford very well shows. (See Greek Testament, *in loc.*) We can now see the force of the argument as a whole. The writer shows the fatal consequences of unbelief and disobedience by the example of the ancient Israelites (chap. iii. 7-19). They had a great promise of entering into the rest of God, which they forfeited by their unbelief (chap. iii. 7-19). But that promise of rest is still offered, and my be still forfeited. It was offered to Israel again in the time and by the mouth of David; it was therefore not exhausted by the entrance of the Israelites into Canaan (chap. iv. 4-8). The promise, then had reference to the heavenly state, the rest of God Himself, when He kept sabbath after the work of creation (chap. iv. 3-5). But Christ also keeps His sabbath, having ceased from the work of redemption, as His Father did from that of creation (chap. iv. 10). There still remains therefore a sabbath, or heavenly rest for the people of God (chap. iv. 9). Let us, therefore, strive to enter into that rest of Christ and of God, warned against unbelief and disobedience by the example of ancient Israel (chap. iv. 11).

We shall find in the sequel much light thrown upon this whole subject of entrance into the heavenly state, and the relation in which the saints stood to it both before and since the coming of Christ.

THE END OF THE AGES.

Heb. ix. 26.---'For then must he often have suffered since the foundation of the world [k o s m o u]: but now once, in the end of the world [a i w n w n], hath he appeared to put away sin by the sacrifice of himself.'

In this verse we have a striking instance of the confusion arising from the translation of the two different words kosmos and aion by the same word 'world.'

The expression s u n t e l e i a t w n a i w n w n has precisely the same meaning as s u n t e l e i a t o u a i w n o z , and refers to the Jewish age which was about to close. Moses Stuart renders the passage thus: 'But now, at the close of the [Jewish] dispensation, He has once for all made His appearance,' etc. This is another decisive proof that 'the end of the age' was regarded by the apostolic churches as at hand.

EXPECTATION OF THE PAROUSIA.

Heb. ix. 28.---'And unto them that look for him shall he appear a second time, without sin, unto salvation.'

The attitude of expectation maintained by the Christians of the apostolic age is here incidentally shown. They waited in hope and confidence for the fulfillment of the promise of His coming. To suppose that they thus waited for an event which did not happen is to impute to them and to their teachers an amount of ignorance and error incompatible with respect of their beliefs on any other subject.

THE PAROUSIA APPROACHING.

Heb. x. 25.---'Exhorting one another, and so much more as ye see the day approaching.'

'The day' means, of course, 'the day of the Lord,' the time of His appearing,---the Parousia. It was now at hand; they could *see* it approaching. Doubtless the indications of its approach predicted by our Lord were apparent, and His disciples recognised them, remembering His words, 'When ye shall see these things come to pass, know that it is nigh, even at the doors' (Mark xiii. 29). It is not fair to palter with these words in a non-natural or double sense, and say with Alford,---

'That day, in its great and final sense, is always near, always ready to break forth upon the church; but these Hebrews lived actually close upon one of those great types and foretastes of it, the destruction of the Holy City.'

To the same effect is his note on Heb. ix. 26:---

'The first Christians universally spoke of the second coming of the Lord as close at hand, and indeed it ever was and is.'

The Hebrew Christians lived close upon the actual Parousia which our Lord predicted, and His church expected before the passing away of that generation. It is not true that the Parousia 'is always near, and always ready to break forth upon the church,' any more than that the birth of Christ, His crucifixion, or His resurrection, is always ready to break forth. The Parousia was as distinctly a specific event, with its proper place in time, as the incarnation or the crucifixion; and it is to evacuate the word of all meaning to make it a phantom shape, appearing and disappearing, always coming and never come, distant and near, past and future. We believe that Christ in his prophetic discourse had a real event full in his view; an event with a place in history and chronology; an event the period of which He Himself distinctly indicated,---not indeed the hour, nor the day, nor even the precise year, yet within limits well defined,---the period of the existing generation. Such was manifestly the belief of the writer of this epistle. To him the Parousia was a very definite event, and one the approach of which he could see; nor can any trace be detected in his language, or in the language of any of the epistles, of a double sense, or of a partial and preliminary Parousia and a great and final one.

The comment of Conybeare and Howson is far more satisfactory:

'"The day" of Christ's coming was seen approaching at this time by the threatening prelude of the great Jewish war, wherein He came to judge that nation.'

THE PAROUSIA IMMINENT.

Heb. x. 37.---'For yet a little while, and he that shall come will come, and will not tarry.'

This statement looks in the same direction as the preceding. The phrase, 'he that shall come' [o e r c o m e n o z] is the customary designation of the Messiah,---'the coming One.' That coming was now at hand. The language to this effect is far more expressive of the nearness of the time in the Greek than in English: 'Yet a very, very little while;' or, as Tregelles renders it, 'A little while, how little, how little!' The reduplication of the thought in the close of the verse,---'will come, and will not tarry,' is also indicative of the certainty and speed of the approaching event. Moses Stuart's comment on this passage is,---

'The Messiah will speedily come, and, by destroying the Jewish power, put an end to the sufferings which your persecutors inflict upon you.'

This is only part of the truth; the Parousia brought much more than this to the people of God, if we are to believe the assurances of the inspired apostles of Christ.

THE PAROUSIA AND THE OLD TESTAMENT SAINTS.

Heb. xi. 39, 40.---'And these all, having obtained a good report through faith, obtained not the promise: God having provided some better thing for us, that they without us should not be made perfect.'

The argument which is here brought to a conclusion is one of great importance, and deserves very careful consideration. It will be found to lend a powerful indirect support to the views propounded in this investigation, which in fact afford the true key to its explanation.

Having in this eleventh chapter illustrated his main position,---that faith in God was the distinguishing characteristic of the worthies whose names adorn the annals of the Old Testament, the writer draws attention to the fact that Abraham, Isaac, and Jacob were never actually put in possession of the inheritance which had been promised them. They did not obtain the land of Canaan; they never saw the earthly Jerusalem: 'These all died in faith, not having received the promises' (ver. 13). He then goes on to state that these fathers of Israel were aware of a deeper significance in the promise of God than a mere temporal and earthly inheritance. Abraham, while dwelling as a stranger and sojourner in the land of promise, looked beyond to 'the city which hath the foundations, whose builder and maker is God' (ver. 10). It is evident that this cannot refer to the earthly Jerusalem, and yet the language seems to point to some *well-known city so described.* But to what other city can the allusion be than to the city described in the Apocalypse as 'having *twelve foundations,*' 'the city of the living God,' the heavenly Jerusalem? The correspondence cannot be accidental, and affords more than a presumption that whoever wrote the Epistle to the Hebrews had read the description

104

of the New Jerusalem in the Apocalypse. It is not *a* city, but *the* city; not which hath foundations, but *'the* foundations;' a particular and well-known city.

But to return. The confession of the fathers that they were strangers and pilgrims in the land, was a declaration of their faith in the existence of a 'better country,' 'for they that say such things declare plainly that they seek a country,' not indeed any earthly country, but 'a *better,* that is, a *heavenly'* (vers. 14, 16). This faith in a future and heavenly inheritance, which they saw only 'afar off,' was true not only of Abraham, Isaac, and Jacob, but of the whole company of the ancient believers (ver. 39). Not one of them received the fulfilment of that divine promise which their faith had embraced: *'these all, being borne witness to through faith, received not the promise'* (ver. 39).

This is a fact worthy to be pondered. Up to that time, according to the author of this epistle, the Old Testament saints had been kept waiting, and were waiting still, for the fulfilment of the great promise of God made to Abraham and his seed, and had not yet received the inheritance, nor entered into the better country, nor seen the God-built city with the foundations. How was this? What could be the cause of the long delay? What obstacle stood in the way of their entrance upon the full enjoyment of the inheritance? The question has been anticipated and answered. 'The way into the holiest of all was not yet made manifest,' as was signified by the continued existence of the temple and its services (chap. ix. 8). Access into the place of sanctity and privilege was not permitted until the way had been opened by the atoning sacrifice of Christ, the great High Priest, the Mediator of the new covenant; it could not give a perfect title to its subjects by which they might be admitted to enter on the possession of the inheritance (chap. ix. 9). Mere ritual could not remove the barriers which sin had created between God and man; and therefore there was not admission even for the faithful under the old covenant into the full privileges of saintship and sonship. But this barrier was removed by the perfect sacrifice of the great High Priest. 'The Mediator of the new covenant,' by the offering of himself to God, redeemed the transgressions committed under the old covenant, or Mosaic economy, thus freeing the subjects of that covenant from their disabilities, and making it competent for the chosen 'to receive the promise of the eternal inheritance' (chap. ix. 11-15).

The argument of the epistle, then, requires us to suppose that until the atoning sacrifice of the cross was offered, the blessedness of the Old Testament saints was incomplete. In this respect they were at a disadvantage as compared with believers under the new covenant. The latter were at once put in possession of that for which the former had to wait a long time. The superiority of believers now, under the Christian dispensation, over believers under the former dispensation, is a strong point in the argument. We, says the writer, have no lengthened period of delay interposed between us and the promised inheritance,---we are near it; 'we are come unto it;' 'we are entering into it.' 'God hath provided *some better thing for us,* that they *without us* should not be made perfect' (ver. 40). That is to say, the ancient believers had not only no precedence in the enjoyment of the promised inheritance over Christians, but had to wait long, until the fulness of the time should come when, Christ having opened the way into the holiest of all, they might enter, *along with us,* into the possession of the promised inheritance.

It is scarcely necessary to ask, What is this *promised inheritance* of which so much is here spoken, and to which the Old Testament saints looked forward in faith? Unquestionably it is that thing which God promised to Abraham, Isaac, and Jacob (ver. 9); that which the patriarchs saw afar off (ver. 13); that which their illustrious successors believed, but never obtained (ver. 19). It is 'the promise of eternal inheritance' (chap. ix. 15); 'the hope set before us' (chap. vi. 18); 'the city which hath the foundations' (chap. xi. 10); 'a better, even a heavenly country' (chap. xi. 16); 'a kingdom which cannot be moved' (chap. xii. 28). It is, in fact, the true Canaan; the promised land; the 'rest of God;' 'the sabbath-keeping which remaineth for the people of God' (chap. iv.9). It is one thing of which the writer speaks all the way through. Let the reader carry his thoughts back to the fourth chapter, where the discussion respecting the promised rest first begins. Evidently that 'promised rest' is identical with the 'promised land,' and the 'promised land' is identical with the 'promised inheritance;' and all these different designations---city, country, kingdom, inheritance, promise,---all mean one and the same thing. The earthly Canaan was not the whole, was not the reality, but only the symbol of the inheritance which God gave by promise to Abraham and his seed. That promise, far from having been exhaustively fulfilled by the possession of the land under Joshua, was still kept in reserve for the people of God. But now the time was come when the inheritance was about to be actually entered and enjoyed, and the believers of the old covenant, with those of the new, were to enter at once and together into the promised rest.

There is a remarkable correspondence between the argument contained in this passage and the statements of St. Paul in his epistles to the Galatians and Romans, serving not only to throw additional light upon the whole subject, but also to prove how entirely *Pauline* is the argument in Hebrews. We select a few of the leading thoughts in Gal. iii. by way of illustration:---

Ver. 16.---'Now to Abraham and his seed were the promises made. He saith not, And to seeds, as of many; but as of one, And to thy seed, which is Christ.'

Ver. 18.---'For if the inheritance is of the law, it is no more of promise: but God gave it to Abraham by promise.'

Ver. 19.---'Wherefore then serveth the law? It was added because of transgressions, till the seed should come to whom the promise was made,' etc.

Ver. 22.---'Howbeit, the scripture shut up all under sin, that the promise by faith of Jesus Christ might be given to them that believe.'

Ver. 23.---'But before faith came, we were kept in ward, shut up under the law unto the faith which was afterward to be revealed.'

Ver. 29.---'And if ye be Christ's, then are ye Abraham's seed, and heirs according to the promise.'

Now, making allowance for the difference in the object which St. Paul has in view in writing to the Galatians, it will be seen how remarkably his statements support those in the Epistle of Hebrews.

1.   In both we find the same subject,---the *promised inheritance.*

2.   In both it is admitted that the inheritance was not actually possessed and enjoyed by those to whom it was first promised.

3.   In both it is shown that the fulfilment of the promise was suspended until the coming of Christ.

4.   In both it is shown that this event (the coming of Christ) produced a change in the situation of those who expected this inheritance.

5.   In both it is argued that faith is the condition of inheriting the promise.

6.   In both it is asserted that the time has at length arrived when the actual possession of the inheritance is about to be realised.

Very similar is the scope of the argument in the Epistle to the Romans:---

Rom. iv. 13.---'For the promise that he should be the heir of the world [land, k o s m o z = g h] was not to Abraham, or to his seed, through the law, but through the righteousness of faith.'

Ver. 16.---'For this cause it was of faith that it might be by grace; to the end the promise might be sure to all the seed; not to that only which is of the law, but to that also which is of the faith of Abraham; who is the father of us all.'

Rom. v. 1.---'Therefore being justified by faith we have peace with God through our Lord Jesus Christ. By whom also we have access by faith into this grace wherein we stand, and rejoice in hope of the glory of God.'

In these verses we find,---

1.   The same *promised inheritance* (ver. 13).

2.   The same condition of its possession, viz. faith (ver. 2).

3.   The suspension of the fulfilment of the promise during the period of the law (vers. 14, 16).

4.   The entrance of believers under the Christian dispensation into the state of privilege and heirship (chap. v. 2).

5.   The expectation of the full possession of the inheritance: 'We rejoice in hope of the glory of God' (chap. v. 1).

Taking all these passages together, we may deduce from them the following conclusions:---

1.   That the great object of faith and hope so constantly set forth in the Scriptures as the consummation of the happiness of believers both under the Old Testament and under the New, is one and the same; and, whether called by the name of 'the promised land,' 'the promised inheritance,' 'the kingdom of God,' 'the glory to be revealed,' 'the rest of God,' 'the hope which is set before us,'---they all mean the same thing, and point to a heavenly, and not an earthly , reward.

2.   That this was the true meaning of the promise made to Abraham.

3.   That the fulfilment of this promise could not take place until the true 'seed' of Abraham appeared and the sacrifice of the cross was offered.

4.   That the Old Testament saints had to wait until then before they could receive the promised inheritance,---that is, enter into the full possession and enjoyment of the heavenly state.

5.   That the New Testament saints had this advantage over their predecessors,---that they had not to wait for the realisation of their hope.

6.   That the Old Testament saints, and believers under the New Testament, were to enter at the same period into the possession of the inheritance; not 'they without us,' nor 'we without them,' but simultaneously (Heb. xi. 40).

It is evident, however, that the writer of the Epistle to the Hebrews did not consider that as yet either the Old Testament or the New Testament saints had actually entered upon the possession of the inheritance. The very purpose and aim of all his exhortations and appeals to the Hebrew believers is to warn them against the danger of forfeiting the inheritance by apostasy, and to encourage them to stedfastness and perseverance, that they might receive the promise. 'Let us therefore fear lest, a promise being left us of entering into his rest, any of you should seem to come short of it' (Heb. iv. 1); 'Ye have need of patience that ye may receive the promise' (Heb. x. 36). It was not theirs as yet, then, in actual possession; but the whole tenor of the argument implies that it was very near, so near that it might almost be said to be within reach. 'We which believe *are entering* into the rest' (Heb. iv. 3); 'Yet a very, very little while, and he that is coming shall come, and shall not tarry' (chap. x. 37). This clearly indicates the period of the expected entrance on the inheritance: it is the Parousia; 'the coming of the Lord;' the long looked-for day; the fulness of the time, when the saints of the old covenant and those of the new should enter simultaneously into the possession of the promised inheritance; the land of rest; the city with the foundations; the better country, that is, the heavenly; the kingdom which cannot be moved; 'the inheritance incorruptible, undefiled, and unfading, ready to be revealed in the last time.'

But it may be objected, If the seed has come 'to whom the promise was made; 'if the sacrifice of Calvary has been offered; if the great High Priest has rent the veil and removed the barrier; if the way into the holiest has thus been opened up,---does it not follow that the possession of the inheritance would be immediately bestowed upon the Old Testament believers, and that they would at once, along with the risen and triumphant Redeemer, enter into the promised rest?

This is the view which many theologians have adopted, who fix the resurrection of Christ as the period of advancement and glory for the Old Testament saints. But it is clear that the apostolic doctrine fixes that period at the Parousia, and that for the reason given in the Epistle to the Hebrews (chap. x. 12, 13). Though the great High Priest had offered His one sacrifice for sin; though He had sate down on the right hand of God; yet His triumph had not fully come. He was 'henceforth expecting till his enemies be made his footstool.' To the same effect is the statement of St. Paul in 1 Cor. xv. 22. The consummation is reached by successive steps; first, the resurrection of Christ; afterwards, they that are Christ's at His coming; then 'then end.' The edifice was not crowned until the Parousia, when the Son of man came in His kingdom, and His enemies were put under His feet. That was the consummation, the end, when the Messianic delegated government was to cease; the ceremonial, local, and temporary to be merged in the spiritual, universal, and everlasting; when God was to be revealed as the Father not of a nation, but of man; when all sectional and national distinctions were to be abolished, and 'God to be All in all.'

Meantime, when this epistle was written, the Mosaic system seemed to be unimpaired; 'the outer tabernacle' was still standing; Judaism, though a hollow trunk, out of which the heart had utterly decayed, still had a semblance of vigour; but the hour was at hand when the whole economy was to be swept away. A deluge of wrath was about to burst on the land, and overwhelm the city, the temple, and the nation; the judgment of the impenitent and the apostate people would then take place, and the Old Testament saints, along with the believers in Christ, would together 'enter into rest,' and 'inherit the kingdom prepared for them from the foundation of the world.'

When we remember that this epistle was written, according to some expositors, on the verge of the great Jewish war which ended in the destruction of Jerusalem; or, according to others, after its actual outbreak, we may conceive what an intense expectancy such an approaching crisis must have produced in Christian hearts. The long looked-for consummation was now not a question of years, but of months or days.

Before quitting this very interesting passage it may be proper to advert to the opinions of some of the most eminent expositors regarding it.

Professor Stuart wholly misses his way. He pronounces Heb. xi. 40 'an exceedingly difficult verse, about the meaning of which there have been a multitude of conjectures;' and expresses his opinion that *the better thing* reserved for Christians is not a reward in heaven; for such a reward was proffered also to the ancient saints.

'I must therefore,' he adds, 'adopt another exegesis of the whole passage, which refers e p a g g e l i a n [the promise] to the promised blessing of the Messiah. I construe the whole passage, then, in this manner:---The ancient worthies persevered in their faith, although the Messiah was known to them only by *promise*. We are under greater obligations than they to persevere; for God has fulfilled His promise respecting the Messiah, and thus placed us in a condition better adapted to perseverance than theirs. So much is our condition preferable to theirs that we may even say, without the blessing which we enjoy their happiness could not be completed. In other words, the coming of the Messiah was essential to the consummation of their happiness in glory, *i.e.* was necessary to their t e l e i o s i z.'

It will be seen that Stuart entirely mistakes the meaning of the writer. The e p a g g e l i a is not the Messiah, but the *inheritance,* the promise of entering into the rest. He fails also to apprehend the bearing of the subject on the time then present, and that the whole force of the argument lies in the fact that the moment was at hand when the great promise of God was to be fulfilled.

Dr. Alford apprehends the argument much more clearly, yet fails to grasp the precise sense of the whole. How nearly he approaches the true solution of the difficulty may be seen from the following note:---

'The writer implies, as indeed chap. x. 14 seems to testify, that the advent and work of Christ have changed the state of the Old Testament fathers and saints into greater and more perfect bliss, an inference which is forced on us by many other places in Scripture. So that their perfection was dependent on our perfection: their and our perfection were all brought in at the same time, when Christ "by one offering perfected for ever them that are sanctified." So that the result with regard to them is, that their spirits, from the time when Christ descended into Hades and ascended up into heaven, enjoy heavenly blessedness, and are waiting, with all who have followed their glorified High Priest within the veil, for the resurrection of their bodies, the regeneration, the renovation of all things.'

This explanation, though in some respects not far from the truth, is inconsistent with the statements in the epistle, for it supposes the Old Testament saints to be *still waiting* for their complete felicity, and it reduces even the New Testament believers to the same condition of *waiting* for a consummation still future. What becomes, then, of the k r e i t t o n t i , the 'some better thing,' which God (according to the writer) had provided for Christians? The advantage of which he makes so much wholly disappears. And if the Parousia never took place, the New Testament believers have no advantage whatever over the ancient saints.

Dr. Tholuck has the following remarks on the state of the departed saints previous to the advent of Christ:---

'The Old Testament saints were gathered with the fathers, and perhaps partly translated into a higher sphere of life; but as complete salvation is only to be attained through union with Christ, the indwelling Spirit of whom shall also quicken our newly glorified bodies, so the fathers gathered to God had to wait for the advent of Christ, as He said of Abraham himself, that he rejoiced to see His day.'

It is curious to find very similar opinions expressed by Dr. Owen, in his treatise on Hebrews (vol. v. p. 311):---

'I think that the fathers who died under the Old Testament had a nearer admission into the presence of God upon the ascension of Christ than they had enjoyed before. They were in heaven before the sanctuary of God, but were not admitted within the veil, into the most holy place, where all the counsels of God are displayed and represented.'

Much that is true is here blended with something erroneous. All these opinions agree in the conclusion that the redemptive work of Christ had a powerful influence on the state of the Old Testament believers; but none of them apprehend the fact, so legibly written on the face of this epistle, that until the external fabric of Judaism had been swept away, and Christ had come in His kingdom, the way to the promised inheritance was not open either to the Old or the New Testament believers, and that the Parousia was the appointed time for both to enter together into the possession of the 'rest of God.'

THE GREAT CONSUMMATION NEAR.

Contrast between the Situation of the Hebrew Christians and that of the Israelites at Sinai.

Heb. xii. 18-24.---'For ye are not come unto the mount that might be touched, and that burned with fire. . . . But ye are come unto mount Sion, and unto the city of the living God, the heavenly Jerusalem, and to an innumerable company of angels, to the general assembly and church of the first-born, which are written in heaven, and to God the Judge of all, and to the spirits of just men made perfect, and to Jesus the mediator of the new covenant, and to the blood of sprinkling, that speaketh better things than that of Abel.'

We have in this passage a powerful exhortation to stedfastness in the faith, enforced by a vivid parallel, or rather contrast, between the situation of their Hebrew ancestors as they stood quaking before Mount Sinai and the position occupied by themselves standing, as it were, in full view of Mount Sion and all the glories of the promised inheritance. There are, indeed, in this representation both a parallel and a contrast. The resemblance lies in the *nearness* of the object---the meeting with God. Like the Israelites at Mount Sinai, the Hebrew Christians had *drawn near* [p r o s e l h l u q a t e] to the Mount Sion; like their fathers, they were come face to face with God. But in other respects there was a striking contrast in their circumstances. At Mount Sinai all was terrible and awful; at Mount Sion all was inviting and attractive. And this was the prospect now full in their view. A few more steps and they would be in the midst of these scenes of glory and joy, safe in the promised land. There can be no question respecting the identity of the scene here described: it is a near view of the 'inheritance,' 'the rest of God,' so constantly set forth in this epistle as the ultimatum of the believer,---once beheld, afar off, by patriarchs, prophets, and saints of olden time, but now visible to all and within a few days' march,---'the city with the foundations,' the 'better country, that is the heavenly.'

Here an interesting question presents itself. From what source did the writer draw this glowing description of the heavenly inheritance? It is of course easy to say, It is an original and independent utterance of the Spirit which spake by the prophets. But the author of the epistle evidently writes as if the Hebrew Christians knew, and were familiar with, the things of which he speaks. The picture of Mount Sinai and its attendant circumstances is evidently derived from the book of Exodus; and if we find the materials for the picture of Mount Sion ready to our hand in any particular book of the New Testament, if is not unfair to presume that the description is borrowed from thence. Now we actually find every element of this description in the Book of Revelation; and when the reader compares every separate feature of the scene depicted in the epistle with its counterpart in the Apocalypse, it will be easy for him to judge whether the correspondence can be undesigned or not, and which is the original picture:---

Mount Sion . . . . Rev. xiv.1.
The city of the living God . . . . Rev. iii. 12; xxi. 10.
The heavenly Jerusalem . . . . Rev. iii. 12, xxi. 10.
The innumerable company of angels . . . . Rev. v. 11; vii. 11.
The general assembly and church of the first-born, etc. . . . . . Rev iii. 12; vii. 4; xiv. 1-4.
God the Judge of all . . . . Rev. xx. 11, 12.
The spirits of just men made perfect . . . . Rev. xiv. 5.

Jesus the mediator of the new covenant . . . . Rev. v. 6-9.
The blood of sprinkling . . . . Rev. v. 9.

Looking at the exact correspondence between the representations in the epistle and those in the Apocalypse, it seems impossible to resist the conclusion that the writer of this epistle had the descriptions of the Apocalypse in his mind; and his language presupposes the knowledge of that book by the Hebrews Christians. This conclusion involves the inference that the Apocalypse was written before the Epistle to the Hebrews, and consequently before the destruction of Jerusalem. The subject will come before us again when we enter upon the consideration of the Book of Revelation; meantime, let it suffice to observe that both in this epistle and in the Apocalypse the events spoken of are regarded as so near as to be described as actually present; in the epistle the church militant is viewed as already come to the inheritance, and in the Apocalypse the things which are shortly to come to pass are viewed as accomplished facts.

THE NEARNESS AND FINALITY OF THE CONSUMMATION.

Heb. xii. 25-29.---'See that ye refuse not him that speaketh. For if they escaped not who refused him that spake on earth, much more shall not we escape, if we turn away from him that speaketh from heaven: whose voice then shook the earth: but now he hath promised, saying, Yet once more I shake not the earth only, but also heaven. And this word, Yet once more, signifieth the removing of those things that are shaken, as of things that are made, that those things which cannot be shaken may remain. Wherefore we receiving a kingdom which cannot be moved, let us have grace, whereby we may serve God acceptably with reverence and godly fear: for our God is a consuming fire.'

The parallel, or rather contrast, between the situation of the ancient Israelites drawing near to God at Mount Sinai and that of the Hebrew Christians expecting the Parousia is here further carried out, with the view of urging the latter to endurance and perseverance. If it was perilous to disregard the words spoken from Mount Sinai---the voice of God by the lips of Moses; how much more perilous to turn away from Him who speaks from heaven---the voice of God by His Son? That voice at Sinai shook the earth (Exod. Xix. 18; Ps. lxviii. 8); but a more terrible convulsion was at hand, by which, not only earth, but also heaven, were to be finally and fore ever removed.

But what is this impending and final 'shaking and removing of earth and heaven'? According to Alford,---

'It is clearly wrong to understand, with some interpreters, by this shaking the mere breaking down of Judaism before the Gospel, or of anything else which shall be fulfilled *during* the Christian economy, short of its glorious end and accomplishment.'

At the same time he admits that---

'The period which shall elapse [before this shaking takes place] shall be but one, not admitting of being broken into many; and that one but short.'

But if so, surely the catastrophe must have been an immediate one; for, on the supposition that it belongs to the distant future, the *interval* must necessarily be very long, and divisible into many periods, as years, decades, centuries, and even millenniums.

Moses Stuart's comment is far more to the point:---

'That the passage has respect to the changes which would be introduced by the coming of the Messiah, and the new dispensation which He would commence, is evident from Haggai ii. 7-9. Such figurative language is frequent in the Scriptures, and denotes great changes which are to take place. So the apostle explains it here, in the very next verse. (Comp. Isa. xiii. 13; Haggai ii. 21, 22; Joel iii. 16; Matt. xxiv. 29-37.)'

The key to the interpretation of this passage is to be found in the prophecy of Haggai. On comparing the prophetic symbols in that book it will be seen that 'shaking heaven and earth' is evidently emblematic of, and synonymous with, 'overthrowing thrones, destroy kingdoms,' and similar social and political revolutions (Haggai ii. 21, 22). Such tropes and metaphors are the very elements of prophetic description, and it would be absurd to insist upon the literal fulfilment of such figures. Prodigies and convulsions in the natural world are constantly used to express great social or moral revolutions. Let those who find it difficult to believe that the abrogation of the Mosaic dispensation could be shadowed forth in language of such awful sublimity consider the magnificence of the language employed by prophets and psalmists in describing its inauguration. (See Ps. lxviii. 7, 8, 16, 17; cxiv. 1-8; Habak. iii. 1-6).

What, then, is the great catastrophe symbolically represented as the shaking of the earth and heavens? No doubt it is the overthrow and abolition of the Mosaic dispensation, or old covenant; the destruction of the Jewish church and state, together with all the institutions and ordinances connected therewith. There were 'heavenly things' belonging to that dispensation: the laws, and statutes, and ordinances, which were divine in their origin, and might be properly called the *'spiritualia'* of Judaism---these were the *heavens*, which were to be shaken and removed. There were also 'earthly things:' the literal Jerusalem, the material temple, the land of Canaan- these were the *earth*, which was in like manner to be shaken and removed. The symbols are, in fact, equivalent to those employed by our Lord when predicting the doom of Israel. 'Immediately after the tribulation of those days [the horrors of the siege of Jerusalem] shall the sun be darkened, and the moon shall not give her light, and the powers of the *heavens shall be shaken*' (Matt. xxiv. 29). Both passages refer to the same catastrophe and employ very similar figures; besides which we have the authority of our Lord for fixing the event and the period of which He speaks within the limits of the generation then in existence; that is to say, the references can only be to the judgment of the Jewish nation and the abrogation of the Mosaic economy at the Parousia.

That great event was to clear the way for a new and higher order of things. A kingdom which cannot be moved was to supersede the material and mutable institutions which were imperfect in their nature and temporary in their duration; the material would give place to the spiritual; the temporary to the eternal; and the earthly to the heavenly. This was by far the greatest revolution the world had ever witnessed. It far transcended in importance and grandeur even the giving of the law from Mount Sinai; and as that was accompanied by fearful signs and wonders, physical convulsions, and portentous phenomena, it was fitting that similar, and still more awful, prodigies should attend its abrogation and the opening of a new era. That such portents did actually precede the destruction of Jerusalem we have no difficulty in believing, first, on the ground of analogy; secondly, from the testimony of Josephus; and, above all, on the authority of our Lord's prophetic discourse.

But it is not so much to any new era here upon the earth as to the glorious rest and reward of the people of God in the heavenly state, that the author of the epistle directs the hope of the Hebrew Christians. Into that eternal kingdom the faithful servants of Christ believed they were just about to enter, and no consideration was more calculated to strengthen the weak and confirm the wavering. 'Since therefore we are receiving a kingdom which cannot be shaken, let us be filled with thankfulness, whereby we may offer acceptable worship unto God with reverent fear: for our God is a consuming fire.'

EXPECTATION OF THE PAROUSIA.
Heb. xiii. 14.---'For here have we no continuing city, but we seek for that which is coming.'

Alford well says:---

'This verse comes with a solemn tone on the reader, considering how short a time the m e n o u s a p o l i z [abiding city] did actually remain, and how soon the destruction of Jerusalem put an end to the Jewish polity, which was supposed to be so enduring.'

This is unexceptionable, and we may say, 'O si sic omnia!' The commentator sees clearly in this instance the relation of the writer's language to the actual circumstances of the Hebrews. This principle would have been a safe guide in other instances in which he seems to us to have entirely missed the point of the argument. The Christians to whom the epistle was written were come to the closing scene of the Jewish polity; the final catastrophe was just at hand. They heard the call, 'Come out of her, my people, that ye be not partakers of her plagues.' Jerusalem, the holy city, with her sacred temple, her towers and palaces, her walls and bulwarks, was no longer 'a continuing city;' it was on the eve of being 'shaken and removed.' But the Hebrew saint could see through his tears another Jerusalem, the city of the living God; an enduring and heavenly home, drawing very near, and 'coming down,' as it were 'from heaven.' This was the coming city [t h n m e l l o u s a n = the city *soon* to come] to which the writer alludes, and which he believed they were just about to receive. (Heb. xxi. 28.)

The Parousia in the Epistle of James.

There is a special interest attached to this epistle inasmuch as it manifestly belongs to the 'last days,' the closing period of the dispensation. It is a voice to the scattered Israel of God from within the doomed city whose catastrophe was now at hand. It is the last testimony of a faithful witness to the nation both within and without the bounds of Palestine. Though addressed to believing Hebrews, it contains evidences of the degeneracy in the Christian church and the extreme corruption of the nation. Iniquity abounds, and the love of many has waxed cold. But James of Jerusalem, like one of the old prophets of Israel, bears his testimony for truth and righteousness with unfaltering fidelity, till he wins the crown of martyrdom. The direct allusions to the Parousia in this epistle are few in number, but distinct and decisive in character; and it is plain that the whole epistle is written under the deep impression of the approaching consummation.

THE LAST DAYS COME.
Jas. v. 1, 3.---'Go to now, ye rich men, weep and howl for your miseries that are coming . . . . Ye laid up treasure in the last days.'

This bold denunciation of the powerful oppressors and robbers of the poor in the last days of the Jewish State recalls to our minds the warnings of the prophet Malachi: 'I will come near to you to judgment, and I will be a swift witness against the sorcerers, and against the adulterers, and against false swearers, and against those that oppress the hireling in his wages, the widow and the fatherless; and them that turn aside the stranger from his right, and fear not me, saith the Lord of hosts' (Mal. iii. 5). That judgment was now drawing nigh, and 'the judge was at the door.'

Nothing can be more frank than the recognition which Alford give of the historical significance of this combination, and its express reference to the times of the apostle. Accounting for the absence of any direct exhortation to penitence in this denunciation, he says,---

'That such does not here appear is owing chiefly to the close proximity of judgment which the writer has before him.' Again he observes, '"Howl" [o l o l u x e i n] is a word in the Old Testament confined to the prophets, and used, as here, with reference to the near approach of God's judgments.' Again: 'These miseries are not to be thought of as the natural and determined end of all worldly riches, but are the judgments connected with the coming of the Lord: *cf.* ver. 8,---"the coming of the Lord draweth nigh." It may be that this prospect was as yet intimately bound up with the approaching destruction of the Jewish city and polity, for it must be remembered that they are Jews who are here addressed.'

The only drawback to this explanation is the unfortunate 'may be' in the last sentence. How could a peradventure be thought of in a case so plain? Our concern is with what was in the mind of the apostle, and surely no words can convey a stronger testimony to his conviction that 'the last days' and 'the end' were all but come.

In his note on ver. 3, Alford gives the apostle's meaning with perfect accuracy:---

'The last days (*i.e. in these, the last days before the coming of the Lord),* etc.'

It is interesting to find Dr. Manton, a theologian who lived in days when rigorous exegesis was not much practised and Scripture exposition was whatever Scripture might be made to mean, has with great perspicacity discerned the historical significance of this and other allusions of St. James to the Parousia. For example, on the clause, 'The rust of them shall eat your flesh as it were fire,' Monton says,---

'Possibly there may be here some latent allusion to the manner of Jerusalem's ruin, in which many thousands perished by fire.' Again, on the clause, 'Ye heaped treasure together for the last days,' he remarks: 'There is no cogent reason why we should take this in a metaphorical sense, especially since, with good leave from the context, scope of the apostle, and the state of those times, the literal may be retained. I should, therefore, simply understand the words as an intimation of their approaching judgments; and so the apostle seemeth to me to tax their vanity in hoarding and heaping up wealth when those scattering and fatal days to the Jewish commonwealth were even ready to overtake them.'

NEARNESS OF THE PAROUSIA.

Jas. v. 7.---'Be patient therefore, brethren, unto the coming of the Lord.'

Jas. v. 8.---'The coming of the Lord draweth nigh.'

Jas. v. 9.---'Behold, the judge standeth before the door.'

Three distinct utterances, short, sharp, startling, all significant of the imminent arrival of 'the day of the Lord.'

Manton's comment on these passages, though he is haunted by the phantom of the double sense, is, on the whole, excellent:---

'What is meant here? (Jas. v. 7.) Any particular coming of Christ, or His solemn coming to general judgment? I answer, Both may be intended; the primitive Christians thought both would fall out together. 1. It may be meant of Christ's particular coming to judge these wicked men. This epistle was written about thirty years after Christ's death, and there was but a little time between that and Jerusalem's last, so that *unto the coming of the Lord* is until the overwhelming of Jerusalem, which is also elsewhere expressed by coming, if we may believe Chrysostom and Oecumenius on John xxi. 22: "If I will that he tarry till I come," that is, say they, come to Jerusalem's destruction.'

He then goes on to give an alternative meaning, according to the usage of double-sense expositors.

On the eighth verse, 'For the coming of the Lord draweth nigh,' Manton observes:---

'Either, first, to them by a particular judgment; for there were but a few years, and then all was lost; and probably that may be it which the apostles mean when they speak so often of the nearness of Christ's coming. But you will say, How could this be propounded as an argument of patience to the godly Hebrews that Christ would come and destroy the temple and city? I answer, (1) The time of Christ's solemn judiciary process against the Jews was the time when He did acquit Himself with honour upon His adversaries, and the scandal and reproach of His death was rolled away. (2) The approach of His general judgment ended the persecution; and when the godly were provided for at Pella, the unbelievers perished by the Roman sword,' etc.

On ver. 9, 'Behold, the judge standeth before the door,' Manton entirely discards the double sense, and gives the following unexceptionable explanation:-

'He had said before, "The coming of the Lord draweth nigh;" now he addeth that "he is at the door," a phrase that doth not only imply the sureness, but the suddenness, of judgment. See Matt. xxiv. 33: "Know that it is near, even at the door;" so that this phrase intendeth also the speediness of the Jewish ruin.'

It is easy to see that the pardonable anxiety to find a present didactic and edifying use in all Scripture lies at the foundation of much of the exposition of such divines as Manton, and inclines them to adopt alternative meanings and accommodations, which a strict exegesis cannot admit. But the language of the apostle in this instance stands in need of no elucidation, it speaks for itself. It shows the attitude of expectation and hope in which the apostolic churches waited for the manifestation of their returning Lord. A persecuted church had need of patience under the wrongs inflicted by their oppressors. Their cry was, 'O Lord, how long?' They were comforted by the assurance that the day of deliverance was at hand; 'the judge,' the avenger of their wrongs was already 'at the door;' 'Yet a very, very little while, and he who is coming shall come, and shall not tarry.' How is it possible to reconcile this confident expectation of almost immediate deliverance with a consummation still future after eighteen centuries have passed away? There are but two alternatives possible: either St. James and his fellow-apostles were grossly deceived in their expectation of the Parousia, or that event did come to pass, according to their expectation and the Lord's prediction, at the close of the aeon, or Jewish age. If we adopt the latter alternative, the only one compatible with Christian faith, we must accept the inference that the Parousia was the glorious appearing of the Lord Jesus Christ to abolish the Mosaic dispensation, execute judgment on the guilty nation, and receive His faithful people into His heavenly kingdom and glory.

The Parousia In the Epistles of St. Peter

THE PAROUSIA IN THE FIRST EPISTLE OF ST. PETER.

It is evident that this epistle, like that of St. James, belongs to the period called 'the last times.' Like his fellow-witness and brother-apostle James, St. Peter addresses his exhortations to Hebrew Christians of the dispersion; for this is the only natural interpretation of the title give to them in the first verse. The contents sufficiently evince that the epistle was written in a time of suffering for the sake of Christ. The disciples were 'in heaviness through manifold temptations;' but a far severer time of trial was approaching, and for this they are exhorted to prepare: 'Beloved, think it not strange concerning the fiery trial which is to try you, as though some strange thing happened unto you' (1 Pet. iv. 12). They are comforted, moreover, with the prospect of final and speedy deliverance.

It is necessary to read this epistle in the light of the actual circumstances of the time when, and of the persons to whom, it was written. Whatever may be its uses and lessons for other times and persons, its primary and special bearing upon the Jews of the dispersion in the apostolic age must not be lost sight of.

SALVATION READY TO BE REVEALED IN THE LAST TIME.

1 Pet. i. 5.---'You, who are kept by the power of God through faith unto salvation ready to be revealed I the last time.'

Every word in this opening address is full of meaning, and implies the near approach of a great and decisive crisis. In ver. 4 we have a very distinct allusion to the 'inheritance,' which is the theme of so large a portion of the Epistle to the Hebrews, that is to say, the true Canaan, 'the rest remaining for the people of God.' In very similar language St. Peter styles it 'the inheritance reserved in heaven,' and represents the entering upon it by believers as now very near. Salvation is *'ready to be revealed.'* What this *'salvation'* means is very evident; it is not the personal glorification of individual souls at death, but a great and collective deliverance, in which the people of God generally are to participate: such a salvation as God wrought for Israel on the shores of the Red Sea. In the same way St. Paul uses the same word with reference to this same approaching consummation: 'Now is our salvation nearer than when we believed' (Rom. xiii. 11).

This great general deliverance was not a *distant* event, it was now 'ready to be revealed,' on the very eve of being made manifest. As Alford remarks, the word e t o i m h n [ready] is stronger than m e l l o u s a n . To understand this as referring to individual believers entering into heaven one by one at the hour of death, or as an admission into a heavenly state which has not yet been granted, is utterly repugnant to the plain sense of the words.

The salvation is ready to be revealed in *'the last time,'* that is to say, *'now,'* the time then present. We have already had occasion to notice that the apostles call their own time *'the last time.'* They believed and they taught that they were living in the last times, and this must be reconcilable with fact, if their credit as faithful and authorised witnesses for Christ is to be maintained. They were justified in their belief: they were living in the last times, in the closing period of the Jewish aeon or age. In the twentieth verse of this chapter we find the same designation given to the time of Christ's incarnation: 'Who was manifested in these last times [at the last of the times] for you.' To say that the apostle regards the whole period from the beginning of the New Testament dispensation till Christ's coming in glory, in some future and possibly still distant age, as one short time called the last days, is a most unnatural and forced interpretation. The apostle is evidently speaking of a period of *crisis*, and to make a crisis extend over thousands of years is to do violence not only to the grammatical sense of words but to the nature of things.

At the risk of repetition we may here observe, that, according to New Testament usage, we are to conceive of the period between the incarnation of Christ and the destruction of Jerusalem as the close of an epoch or aeon. It was in the end of the age [e p i s u n t e l i a t w n a i w n w n = close upon the end of the ages] that 'Christ appeared to put away sin, by the sacrifice of himself' (Heb. ix. 26). This whole period of about seventy years is regarded as 'the last time;' but it is natural that the phrase should have a sharper accentuation when the Jewish war, the beginning of the end, was on the eve of breaking out, if it had not already begun.

THE APPROACHING REVELATION OF JESUS CHRIST.

1 Pet. i. 7.---'That the trial of your faith . . . may be found unto praise, and honour, and glory, at the revelation of Jesus Christ.'

1 Pet. i. 13.---'Hope conclusively for the grace which is being brought unto you at the revelation of Jesus Christ.'

Everything in the apostle's exhortation conveys the idea of eager expectancy and preparation. The salvation is ready to be revealed; the tried and persecuted believers are to 'gird up the loins of their mind;' the expected boon, the grace, is on its way,---it is *being brought* unto them. Alford properly remarks that the word f e r o m e n h n [being brought] signifies 'the near impending of the event spoken of; *q.d.* which is even now bearing down on you.' Does not this plainly prove that St. Peter understood, and wished his readers to understand, that this apocalypse of Jesus Christ was just at hand? It would have been mockery to tell suffering and persecuted men to get ready to receive a salvation which was not due for hundreds and thousands of years.

THE RELATION OF THE REDEMPTION OF CHRIST TO THE ANTEDILUVIAN WORLD.

1 Pet. iii. 18-20.---'For Christ also hath once suffered for sins, the just for the unjust, that he might bring us to God, being put to death in the flesh, but made alive in the Spirit: in which he also went and preached unto the spirits in prison; which were once disobedient, when the longsuffering of God waited in the days of Noah, while the ark was preparing.' etc.

The common interpretation of this difficult passage given by the majority of Protestant expositors is, that Christ, in effect, preached to the antediluvians by His Holy Spirit through the ministry of Noah. This no doubt asserts a truth, and has besides the advantage of keeping within the lines of well-known historical facts, and avoiding what seems dark and doubtful speculation. Nevertheless, as a question of grammar, this interpretation is wholly untenable. First, it is reasonable to expect a chronological sequence in the various parts of the apostle's statement, describing what Christ did after 'being put to death in the flesh.' What would be more harsh and abrupt than the sudden transition from the narrative of what Christ did and suffered in the flesh to what He had done, in a sense, some thousands of years before, in the days of Noah? Further, the rendering 'being quickened *by* the Spirit,' and '*by* which also,' implying that the Holy Spirit was the agent by whom Christ was made alive, and by whom He preached, etc., is clearly wrong. It ought to be, 'Being put to death *in* [his] flesh, but made alive in [his] spirit,'---the *flesh* being His body, and the *Spirit* His soul. Then the apostle adds, '*in which* also,' viz. in his soul, or human spirit. Further, as Ellicott has pointed out, p o r e u q e i z [having gone] 'suggests a literal and local descent.'

There seems no escape therefore, according to the true and natural sense of words, from the interpretation---that our Lord, after His death on the cross, went in His disembodied state into Hades, the place of departed spirits, and there made proclamation [preached] to the spirits in prison, viz. the antediluvians, who in the days of Noah disbelieved the prophet's warnings and perished in the flood. This, which is the most ancient interpretation, is now generally conceded by the most eminent critics. It is that which is embodied in the Apostle's Creed; it has the sanction of Luther and Calvin; and it seems to be supported by other passages in Scripture which are in harmony with this explanation. In St. Peter's sermon on the day of Pentecost (Acts ii. 27-31) there is a distinct allusion to the soul of Christ having been in Hades; also in Ephes. iv. 9,---'Now that he ascended, what is it but that he also descended first into the lower parts of the earth?' It is difficult to suppose that the burial of the body is all that is meant by His descending into the lower parts of the earth.

The more important question remains,---What was the object of our Lord's descent into Hades? It can hardly be doubted that it was a gracious one. The apostle says, 'He *preached* to the spirits in prison,'---and what could He preach but glad tidings? This fact gives a new and larger significance to the terms of our Lord's commission: 'He hat sent me to proclaim liberty to the captives, and the opening of the prison to them that are bound' (Isa. lxi. 1). The hypothesis of Bishop Horsley and others that those spirits in prison were in fact saints, or at least penitents, awaiting the period of their full salvation, scarcely requires refutation. If any thing is clear on the face of the question, it is that they were the spirits of those who had perished for their disobedience, and in their disobedience. As Bishop Ellicott remarks, a p e i q h s a s i n means, not 'who were disobedient,' but '*inasmuch* as they were disobedient.'

But it may be said, Why should the disobedient antediluvians have been selected as the objects of a gracious mission? Were there no other lost souls in Hades, and why should these find grace beyond others? Bishop Horsley owns this to be a difficulty, and the greatest by which his interpretation is embarrassed. Alford finds a reason, if we rightly apprehend him, in the manner of their death. 'The reason of mentioning here these sinners above other sinners, appears to be their connection with the type of baptism which follows;' but surely this is to ascribe an efficacy to that institution beyond the boldest theories of baptismal regeneration. We venture to suggest that the true reason lies in the nature of that great judicial act which took place at the deluge. That was the close of an age or aeon, and ended in a catastrophe, as the aeon then in progress was just about to terminate. The two cases were analogous. As the deluge was the close and consummation of a former aeon, or world-period, so the destruction of Jerusalem and the abrogation of the Jewish economy were about to close the existing world-period or aeon. What more natural on the eve of such a catastrophe as the apostle anticipated, than to advert to the catastrophe of a former aeon? What more pertinent than to note the fact that the 'coming salvation' had a retrospective effect upon those bygone ages? It is not difficult to see the connection of the ideas in the apostle's train of thought. The deluge was the s u n t e l e i a t o u a i w n o z of Noah's time; another s u n t e l e i a was just at hand. The 'old world, that then was,' perished in the baptismal waters of the flood; the 'world which now is'---the Mosaic order, the Jewish polity and people---was about to be submerged in a baptism of fire (Mal. iv. 1; Matt. iii. 11, 12; 1 Cor. iii. 13; 2 Thess. i. 7-10). Was it not appropriate to show that the redemptive work of Christ joined, and indeed covered, both these aeons, and looked backward on the past as well as forward to the future?

Notwithstanding, then, the mystery and obscurity which confessedly overhand the subject, we are led to the conclusion that the apostle in this passage does plainly teach that our blessed Lord, after His death upon the cross, descended as a disembodied spirit into Hades, the place of departed spirits, and there proclaimed the glad tidings of His accomplished redemption to the multitudes of the lost who perished at the catastrophe or final judgment of the former aeon; and though we have in the present passage no express affirmation that those who heard the announcement made by our Saviour were in consequence delivered from their prison-house, and introduced into 'the glorious liberty of the sons of God,' yet it seems not incredible, it is even presumable, that this emancipation was both the object and result of Christ's interposition. We have already referred to Ephes. iv. 9 as lending support to this view. 'Now that he ascended, what is it but that he also descended first into the lower parts of the earth?' Bishop Hersley shows that the phrase 'the lower parts of the earth' in the proper and customary designation of *Hades.* In the same passage the apostle speaks of the triumphant ascension of Christ in these words: 'When he ascended up on high, he led captivity captive, and gave gifts unto men.' Does not the teaching of St. Peter with reference to 'the spirits in prison' throw light on this 'leading of captivity captive?' Does it not suggest that the returning Saviour, having fought the fight and won the victory, enjoyed also the triumph---that He brought back with Him to heaven a great multitude whom He had rescued from captivity; the spirits in prison to whom He carried the glad tidings of redemption achieved; and who, being brought out of their prison-house, accompanied the returning conqueror to His Father's house, at once the ransomed by His blood and the trophies of His power?

Before quitting this subject it may be well to quote some opinions of Biblical critics in reference to it.

Steiger, who treats the whole passage in a most candid and scholarly manner, says,---

'The plain and literal sense of the words in this verse (19), viewed in connection with the following one, compels us to adopt the opinion that Christ manifested Himself to *the unbelieving dead.*' 'We must admit that the discourse here is of a proclamation of *the Gospel* among those who had died in unbelief, but we know not whether it found an entrance into many or few.' 'The expression e n f u l a k h (which the Syriac renders by *Sheol;* the fathers use it as synonymous with Hades) shows that the discourse can only be respecting *unbelievers.*' 'He who lay under death, entered into the empire of the dead as a conqueror, proclaiming freedom to its imprisoned subjects.'

Dean Alford's opinion is very decided:---

'From all, then, that has been said, it will be gathered that, with the great majority of commentators, ancient and modern, I understand these words to say that our Lord, in His disembodied state, did go to the place of detention of departed spirits, and did there announce His work of redemption, preach salvation, in fact, to the disembodied spirits of those who refused to obey the voice of God when the judgment of the flood was hanging over them. Why these rather than others are mentioned---whether merely as a sample of like gracious work on others, or for some special reason unimaginable by us,---we cannot say.'

In an interesting discourse on 'The Intermediate State,' by the Rev. J. Stratten, the following observations occur:---

'If this passage mean no more than that the Holy Spirit assisted Noah in preaching to the antediluvians, it is a most obscure, entangled, and unaccountable manner of expressing a most clear and simple principle. Would any of us employ this language, or any at all like it, to express that sentiment? I think not, and it seems to be only the refuge of a mind that does not understand the apostle, or seeks to misinterpret him.'

We may here, in passing, notice that such a deliverance from Hades serves vividly to illustrate the saying of St. Paul in 1 Cor. xv. 26: 'The last enemy, death, shall be destroyed.'

NEARNESS OF JUDGMENT AND OF THE END OF ALL THINGS.

1 Pet. iv. 5, 7.---'Who shall give an account to him that is ready to judge the quick and the dead. . . . But the end of all things is at hand, be ye therefore sober, and watch unto prayer.'

In these passages we find again, what we have so often found before, the clear apprehension of the judgment and of the end as nigh at hand.

In ver. 5 the apostle intimates that God was about to sit in judgment upon the living and the dead. This cannot possibly refer to that particular act of judgment which is, as we believe, always near to every man, in the same sense as death and eternity are always near. It is obviously a solemn, public, general adjudication, in which *the living* and *the dead* were together to answer for themselves before the tribunal of God. This approach of judgment follows course from the approach of the Parousia, which is so distinctly intimated in chap. i. 5. All that has been stated in regard to that passage applies with equal force to this; e t o i m w z e c o n t i = having it in readiness to judge, is a stronger expression than m e l l o n t i , and can by no means refer to any but an almost immediate event.

No less decisive is the statement in ver. 7, 'The end of all things is *at hand.*' Whatever that end may mean it is certain that the apostle conceives of it as near, for he urges it as a motive to vigilance and prayer. To comprehend the full force of the exhortation we must place ourselves in the situation of these apostolic Christians. As year after year lessened the distance to the passing away of the generation that saw and rejected the Son of man, the anticipation of the arrival of the great predicted consummation must have become more and more vivid in the minds of Christian believers. What their conceptions were as to the nature and extent of that consummation; whether they imagined that it involved the dissolution of the whole frame and fabric of the material world or not, it is not for us to determine. What we have to do with is not the private opinions of the apostles, but their public utterances. But that the consummation designated by our Lord 'the end,' and 'the end of the age,' was rapidly approaching, is not an open question, but a point of faith involving the truth of all His claims. There can be no doubt that in a Judaic or religious sense, that is, so far as the national polity and ecclesiastical system of Judaism were concerned, 'the end of all things was at hand.' All that lay beneath the eye of our Lord as He sate on the brow of Olivet was swiftly hurrying to destruction. This is the key to the meaning of St. Peter in this passage, and furnishes the only tenable and scriptural explanation.

We quote with entire satisfaction and approval the observations of a judicious expositor on the passage now before us:---

'After some deliberation I have been led to adopt the opinion of those who hold that "the end of all things" here is the entire and final end of the Jewish economy in the destruction of the city and the temple of Jerusalem, and the dispersion of the holy people. That was at hand; for this epistle seems to have been written a very short while before these events took place, not improbably after the commencement of the "wars and rumours of wars" of which our Lord spake. This view will not appear strange to any one who has carefully weighed the terms in which our Lord had predicted these events, and the close connection which the fulfilment of these predictions had with the interests and duties of Christians, whether in Judea or in Gentile countries.

'It is quite plain that in our Lord's predictions the expressions "the end," and probably "the end of the world," are used in reference to the entire dissolution of the Jewish economy. The events of that period were very minutely foretold, and our Lord distinctly stated that the existing generation should not pass away till all things respecting "this end" should be fulfilled. This was to be a season of suffering to all; of trial, severe trial, to the followers of Christ; of dreadful judgment on His Jewish opposers, and of glorious triumph to His religion. To this period there are repeated references to the apostolical epistles. "Knowing the time," says the Apostle Paul, "that now it is high time to awake out of sleep, for now is our salvation nearer than when we believed. The night is far spent, the day is at hand." "Be patient," says the Apostle James; "stablish your hearts: for the coming of the Lord draweth nigh." "The Judge standeth before the door." Our Lord's predictions must have been very familiar to the minds of Christians at the time this was written. They must have been looking forward with mingled awe and joy, fear and hope, to their accomplishment: "looking for the things which were coming upon the earth;" and it was peculiarly natural for Peter to refer to these events, and to refer to them in words similar to those used by our Lord, as he was one of the disciples who, sitting with his Lord in full view of the city and temple, heard these predictions uttered.

'The Christians inhabiting Judea had a peculiar interest in these predictions and their fulfilment. But all Christians had a deep interest in them. The Christians of the regions in which those to whom Peter wrote resided were chiefly converted Jews. As Christians they had cause to rejoice in the prospect of the accomplishment of the predictions, as greatly confirming the truth of Christianity and removing some of the greatest obstructions in the way of its progress, such as persecutions by the Jews, and the confounding of Christianity with Judaism on the part of the Gentiles, who were accustomed to view its professors as a Jewish sect. But while they rejoice, they cause to "rejoice with trembling," as their Lord had plainly intimated that it was to be a season of severe trial to His friends, as well as of fearful vengeance against His enemies. "The end of all things," which was at hand, seems to be the same thing as the judgment of the quick and the dead, which the Lord was ready to enter on---the judgment, the time for which was come, which was to begin with the house of God, the unbelieving Jews, in which the righteous should scarcely be saved, and the ungodly and wicked should be fearfully punished.

'The contemplation of such events as just at hand was well fitted to operate as a motive to sobriety and vigilance unto prayer. These were just the tempers and exercises peculiarly called for in such circumstances, and they were just the dispositions and employments required by our Lord when He speaks of those days of trial and wrath: "Take heed to yourselves," says our Lord, "lest at any time your hearts be overcharged with surfeiting, and drunkenness, and the cares of this life, and so that day come on you unawares; for as a snare shall it come upon all who dwell on the earth.

Watch, therefore, and pray always, that ye may be accounted worthy to escape all these things that are about to come to pass, and to stand before the Son of man." It is difficult to believe that the apostle had not these very words in his mind when he wrote the passage now before us.'---Expository Discourses on 1 Peter, by Dr. John Brown, Edinburgh, vol. ii. pp. 292-294.

THE GOOD TIDINGS ANNOUNCED TO THE DEAD.

1 Pet. iv. 6.---'For, for this cause was the gospel preached to the dead also, that they might be judged according to men in the flesh, but live according to God in the spirit.'

Perhaps the passage above cited can scarcely be said to fall within the scope of this discussion, as it does not seem to have any direct bearing upon the time of the Parousia; and its extreme difficulty might be a good reason for avoiding its examination altogether. Nevertheless, as it manifestly belongs to the eschatology of the New Testament, and as we have no right to look upon it as hopelessly insoluble, it seems better not to pass it by in silence.

There can be little doubt that the present is one of a class of difficult passages which, though obscure to us, were intelligible and easy to the original readers of the epistles. (See 1 Cor. xi. 10; xv. 29.) A passing allusion might bring up a whole train of thought in their minds, so that they easily comprehended what hopelessly embarrasses us. Paley, in his Horae Paulinae, chap. x. No. 1, adverts to this difficulty in a real correspondence falling into the hands of a third party.

The general scope of the argument is sufficiently plain. The apostle begins the chapter by calling upon the suffering and persecuted disciples to imitate the example of their once suffering but now victorious Lord: 'Arm yourselves with the same resolution,' i.e. suffer as He did, even unto death, if need be. In the next verses he alludes to their former godless and sensual life, and the offence which the change to the purity of a Christian behaviour gave to their heathen neighbours (vers. 2, 3, 4). This silent but living protest against the immorality of heathenism appears to have been one cause of the general antipathy to the Gospel which found vent in slanderous imputations against the unoffending Christians,---'Speaking evil of you'. But these calumniators and persecutors would soon be called to account by Him who was about to judge both the living and the dead (ver. 5).

It will be found very important to bear in mind this opening of the apostle's argument, as leading up to the statement in ver. 6.

Let us now look at that statement. 'For, for this cause was the gospel preached also to them that are dead, that they might be judged according to men in the flesh, but live according to God in the spirit.'

It may be truly said that there are here as many difficulties as there are words. When, where, and by whom was the Gospel preached to the dead? Who were the dead to whom the Gospel was preached? Why was it preached to them? How could the dead be judged according to men in the flesh? How could they live according to God in the spirit? And how did the preaching of the Gospel to the dead bring about this result,---'that they should live according to God in the spirit'?

It would answer no good purpose to pass in review the multitude of explanations of this obscure passage proposed by different commentators. Let is suffice to look at one or two of the most plausible.

To the question, Who were the dead to whom the Gospel is said to have been preached? some think it a sufficient answer to reply, They are those, now dead, who were alive in the flesh when the Gospel was preached unto them. This would be an easy solution if it were permissible so to construe the words of the apostle; but it is a fatal objection to this explanation that it makes the apostle state a very simple and obvious fact in an unaccountably obscure and ambiguous way. The words themselves reject such an explanation. Alford does not speak too strongly when he says,---

'If kai nekroiz euhggelisqh may mean "the gospel was preached to some during their lifetime who are now dead," exegesis has no longer any fixed rule, and Scripture may be made to prove anything.'

Others suppose that by the 'dead' in ver. 6 are to be understood the *spiritually* dead; but to this there are two insurmountable objections: first, this does not discriminate a particular class, for all men are spiritually dead when the Gospel is first preached to them; and, secondly, it gives to the word nekroi [the dead] in ver. 6 a different meaning from the same word in ver. 5---'the living and the dead.' According to this interpretation, the word 'dead' is used in a literal sense in ver. 5, and in an ethical sense in ver. 6. But, as Alford justly says,---

'All interpretations must be false which do not give nekroiz in ver. 6 the same meaning as nekrouz in ver. 5, *i.e.* that of *dead men,* literally and simply so called; men who have died, and are in their graves.'

But probably the most common opinion is that the apostle here alludes again to the preaching of Christ to the spirits in prison referred to in chap. iii. 19, 20; and at first this seems the most natural explanation. That was, no doubt, a preaching of the Gospel to the dead, and also to a particular class of the dead, the antediluvians who formerly were disobedient in the days of Noah, and who were overtaken by the judgment of God.

But when we come to examine more closely the statement of the apostle we find that this application of his words will by no means suit the persons designated 'the spirits in prison.' How could the antediluvians be said to be 'judged according to men in the flesh'? They perished by the visitation of God, and not by the judgment or act of man; and it appears evident that the succeeding clause---'that they might live according to God in the spirit'---implies the reversal of the human condemnation which had been passed upon the dead while still in the body.

None of the ordinary explanations, therefore, seems to meet the requirements of the case. Those requirements are, to find a class of the dead to whom the Gospel was preached after their death; who were condemned to death when in the flesh by the judgment of men, but who are destined to live in the spirit, according to the judgment of God, and this is consequence of the Gospel being preached to them after death.

We are at once led to conclude that this particular class, judged or condemned by human judgment, must refer to *persecuted disciples of Christ.* It is to such and of such that the apostle is speaking, as is evident from the opening verses of the chapter. It would be quite proper to say of such, that though (unjustly) condemned by man they would be vindicated by God. It is also proper to say of such (especially, if *martyrs for the faith*) that they had 'suffered in the flesh'---had been put to death by human judgment, but were made alive in spirit, or as to their spirits, and this according to God, or by the divine judgment. But there still remains the formidable difficulty presented by the words 'the gospel was preached to them that are dead.' We have no account in the New Testament of any such preaching to Christian martyrs after their death. But are we necessarily obliged to give this sense to the word euhggelisqh? It is here, we believe, that the key to the true explication of this passage will be found; and it is the wrong interpretation of this word that has misled commentators. Though it is very commonly used in the technical sense of preaching the Gospel, this is by no means its invariable use in the New Testament. It is employed to signify the announcement of any good news, and not exclusively the glad tidings of the Gospel. Thus in Heb. iv. 2, improperly rendered in our Authorized Version 'to us was the gospel preached, as well as unto them,' there is no allusion to the preaching of the Gospel in the technical sense of the phrase, but simply to the fact that 'to us as well as to the ancient Israelites *good news* have been brought', the good news in both cases being the promise of entering into God's rest. So in a still more general sense the word is used to denote any pleasing intelligence, as in 1 Thess. iii. 6: 'When Timotheus *brought us good tidings* of your faith,' etc. So also in Rev. x. 7: 'As he hath declared [euhggelisen = made a comforting declaration] to his servants the prophets.' (See also Gal. iii. 8).

But the question still recurs, Where have we in the New Testament any allusion to such good news, pleasing intelligence, or comforting declarations, made to any Christian confessors or martyrs after their death? The apostle seems to speak of some fact familiarly known to the persons to whom he wrote, and which he had only to allude to in order that they should at once recognise his meaning. Now, we actually have a historical representation in the New Testament in which we find all these circumstances present. We have a scene depicted in which Christian martyrs, who had been condemned and put to death in the flesh by the judgment of man, appeal to the justice of God against their persecutors, and a comforting declaration is brought to them, after their death, giving them the assurance of speedy vindication and of a glorious heavenly recompense.

We allude of course to the striking representation given in the Apocalypse of the martyred souls under the alter, appealing to God for the vindication of their cause against their persecutors and murderers---'them that dwell in the land'---and which is thus described in Rev. 9-11:---

'And when he had opened the fifth seal, I saw under the alter the souls of them that were slain for the word of God, and for the testimony which they held; and they cried with a loud voice, saying, How long, O Lord, holy and true, dost thou not judge and avenge our blood on them that dwell on the earth [the land]? And a white robe was given to every one of them; and it was said unto them [erreqh = euhggelisqh] that they should rest yet for a little season, until their fellow-servants also, and their brethren, that should be killed as they were, should be fulfilled.'

This seems exactly to meet all the requirements of the case. Here we find the nekroi, the Christian dead; they were judged or condemned in the flesh, by man's judgment, or 'according to men;' they had been put to death 'for the word of God, and for the testimony which they held.' We find a comforting declaration made to them in their disembodied state, and we have the lacuna in the epistle filled up in the apocalyptic vision, for we are informed what led to this eu-aggelion being brought to them; they are assured that in a little while their cause should be vindicated, according to their prayer; meanwhile 'a white robe,' the symbol of purity and victory, 'is given unto every one of them,' which is surely equivalent to their being justified by the divine judgment.

But this correspondence, striking as it is, is not the whole; the apostle's statement is not only elucidated by the Apocalypse on the one hand, but by the gospel on the other. Most commentators have noticed the obvious relation between the scene of the martyrs' souls under the alter in the apocalyptic vision and the remarkable parable of our Lord in Luke xviii.; but, so far as we have observed, none of them have seized the true analogy between the parable and the vision. In the seventh and eighth verses of that chapter we find the moral of the parable, 'And shall not God avenge his own elect, which cry day and night unto him, though he bear long with them? I tell you that he will avenge them speedily. Nevertheless, when the Son of man cometh, shall he find faith on the earth [in the land]?' The parable and the vision are, in fact, counterparts of each other, and both serve to explain the passage in this epistle of St. Peter. As in the Apocalypse, so in the parable, we find all the elements of the statement in the epistle. We have Christian disciples suffering unjustly; condemned in the flesh by man's judgment; appealing to God to judge their cause; we have the assurance of their speedy vindication by God, and we find in the gospel an additional feature which brings it into more perfect correspondence with the statement in the epistle; for it is evidently suggested that this vindication is to take place at the Parousia,---'when the Son of man cometh.'

Lastly, we may point out the intimate connection between the statement of the apostle as thus interpreted and the argument which he is carrying on. It was appropriate to assure persecuted believers that their cause was safe in the hands of God; that, even if called to suffer unto blood and unto death by the unjust sentence of men, God would vindicate them speedily, for He was about to summon their persecutors before His tribunal. This was the lesson of the parable of the importunate widow, and perhaps still more of the vision of the martyrs' souls under the altar, to which the language of the apostle seems more particularly to allude,---*'For to this end a comforting declaration was brought even to the dead, that though they had been condemned in the flesh by the unjust judgment of men, yet they should in their spirit enjoy eternal life, according to the righteous judgment of God.'*

This interpretation assumes that the Apocalypse was written and widely circulated before the destruction of Jerusalem. It is a reflection upon the critical acumen of many eminent English commentators that they should have leaned so long upon the broken reed of tradition in regard to the date of the Apocalypse. The internal evidence of that book ought to have prevented the possibility of their being misled by the authority of Irenaeus. But we must reserve any further remarks on this subject until we come to the consideration of the Apocalypse.

THE FIERY TRIAL AND THE COMING GLORY.

1 Pet. iv. 12, 13.---'Beloved, think it not strange concerning the fiery ordeal which is taking place for a trial to you, as though some strange thing were happening unto you; but rejoice, inasmuch as ye are partakers of Christ's sufferings, that when his glory shall be revealed, ye may be glad also with exceeding joy.'

These words clearly indicate that Christians everywhere were at this time passing through a severe sifting and testing---'a fiery ordeal.' And not merely *a* fiery trial, but *the* trial, long predicted and expected, viz. *the great tribulation* which was to precede the Parousia. The apostles warned the disciples that the 'must, through much tribulation, enter into the kingdom of God' (Acts xiv. 22). They had themselves been taught this by the Lord Himself, especially in His prophetic discourse.

The predicted tribulation had evidently set in; they were actually passing through the fire. It is impossible here not to be reminded of the words of St. Paul,---'It shall be revealed by fire; and the fire shall try every man's work, of what sort it is' (1 Cor. iii. 13). It is highly probable that the fierce persecution under Nero was raging at this juncture, and we have good authority for believing that it extended beyond Rome to the provinces of the Empire.

Another indication of time is found in ver. 13,---'That when his glory shall be revealed.' The Parousia is always represented as bringing relief from persecution, and recompense to the suffering people of God. We have already seen that the glory was 'ready to be revealed,' and we shall find the same assurance repeated in chap. v. 1.

THE TIME OF JUDGMENT ARRIVED.

1 Pet. iv. 17-19.---'For the time is come when the judgment must begin at the house of God: and if it first begin at us, what shall the end be of them that obey not the gospel of God? And if the righteous scarcely be saved, where shall the ungodly and the sinner appear? Wherefore let them suffer according to the will of God, commit the keeping of their souls to him in well-doing, as unto a faithful Creator.'

It is worthy of remark how different the tone of St. Peter in speaking of the day of the Lord is from St. Paul's in the Second Epistle to the Thessalonians. That day of which St. Paul speaks as not yet present, and as not possible until the apostasy first appeared, is declared by St. Peter to be come. The catastrophe was now imminent. 'God was ready to judge the quick and the dead;' 'the time was come for judgment to begin.' The significance of these words will be apparent if we consider that this epistle was written close upon the outbreak of the Jewish war, if not after its actual commencement.

That this is 'the judgment which must begin at the house of God' there can scarcely be a doubt. There is a manifest allusion in the language of the apostle to the vision seen by the prophet Ezekiel (chap. ix.). The prophet sees a band of armed men commissioned to go through the city (Jerusalem), and to slay all, whether old or young, who had not the seal of God upon their foreheads. The ministers of vengeance are commanded to begin the work of judgment at the house of God,---'Begin at my sanctuary.' The apostle sees this vision as about to be fulfilled in reality. The judgment must begin at the House of God, and the time is come. It may be a question whether by 'the house of God' the apostle intends the temple of Jerusalem, as the prophecy in Ezekiel would suggest, or the spiritual house of God, the Christian church. It may be that both ideas were present to his mind, as well they might, for both were being verified at the moment. The persecution of the church of Christ had already begun, as the epistle testifies, and the circle of blood and fire was narrowing around the doomed city and temple of Jerusalem.

It is perfectly clear that all this is spoken with reference to a particular and impending event, a catastrophe which was on the eve of taking place; and there is not other explanation possible than that which lies visible and palpable on the page of history, the judgment of the guilty covenant nation, with the destruction of the house of God and the dissolution of the Jewish economy.

The following remarks of Dr. John Brown well express the sense of this passage:---

'There seems here a reference to a particular judgment or trial, that the primitive Christians had reason to expect. When we consider that this epistle was written within a short time of the commencement of that awful scene of judgment which terminated in the destruction of the ecclesiastical and civil polity of the Jews, and which our Lord had so minutely predicted, we can scarcely doubt of the reference of the apostle's expression. After having specified wars and rumours of wars, famines, pestilences, and earthquakes, as symptoms of "the beginning of sorrows," our Lord adds, "Then shall they deliver you up to be afflicted, and shall kill you; and ye shall be hated of all nations for my name's sake." "They shall deliver you up to councils and to synagogues, and shall be beaten," etc. (Matt. xxiv. 9-13, 22).

'This is *the* judgment which, though to fall most heavily on the Holy Land, was plainly to extend to wherever Jews and Christians were to be found, "for where the carcase was, there were the eagles to be gathered together;" which was to begin at the house of God, and which was to be so severe that "the righteous should scarcely," *i.e.* not without difficulty, "be saved." They only who stood the trial should be saved, and many would not stand the trial. All the truly righteous should be saved; but many who seemed to be righteous would not endure to the end, and so should not be saved, etc. Some have supposed the reference to be to the Neronian persecution, which by a few years preceded the calamities connected with the Jewish wars and destruction of Jerusalem.---Dr. John Brown on 1 Peter, vol. ii. p. 357.

THE GLORY ABOUT TO BE REVEALED.

1 Pet. v. 1.---'The elders which are among you I exhort, who am also an elder, and a witness of the sufferings of Christ, and also a partaker of the glory *about to be revealed.*'

1 Pet. v. 4.---'And when the chief Shepherd is manifested, ye shall receive the unfading crown of glory.'

Everything in this chapter is indicative of the *nearness* of the consummation. This is the motive to every duty, to fidelity, to humility, to vigilance, to endurance. The glory is *soon* to be revealed; the unfading crown is to be received by the faithful undershepherds when the chief Shepherd is manifested; the sufferings of the persecuted church are to continue only *'a little while'* (ver. 10). All is suggestive of a great and happy consummation which is on the very eve of arriving. Would the apostle speak of an expected crown of glory as a motive to present faithfulness if it were contingent on an uncertain and possibly far distant event? Yet if the chief Shepherd has not yet been manifested, the crown of glory has not yet been received. It is quite clear that to the apostle's view the revelation of the glory, the manifestation of the chief Shepherd, the reception of the unfading crown, the end of suffering, were all in the immediate future. If he was mistaken in this, is he trustworthy in anything?

On this passage (ver. 11) Alford observes:---

'It would not be clear from this passage alone whether St. Peter regarded the coming of the Lord as likely to occur in the life of these his readers or not; but as interpreted by the analogy of his other expressions on the same subject, it would appear that he did.'

Doubtless he did; and so did St. Paul, and St. James, and St. John, and all the apostolic church; and they believed it on the highest authority, the word of their divine Master and Lord.

THE PAROUSIA IN THE SECOND EPISTLE OF ST. PETER.

It is no part of our plan to discuss the difficult and still unsettled questions respecting the genuineness and authenticity of the Second Epistle of Peter and the unsolved problem of the second chapter. We might perhaps, in view of the difficulties which it presents in its eschatological teaching, decline to accept its authority, but we accept it as it stands, honestly believing that it bears indubitable internal evidence of apostolic origin. It appears to have been written at no great interval after the first epistle, and very shortly before the death of the apostle (chap. i. 14). Alford gives the date conjecturally, A.D. 68.

SCOFFERS IN 'THE LAST DAYS.'

2 Pet. iii. 3, 4.---'Knowing this first, that there shall come in the last days scoffers, walking after their own lusts, and saying, Where is the promise of his coming? For since the fathers fell asleep, all things continue as they were from the beginning of the creation.'

The *scoffers* referred to in this passage are no doubt the same persons whose character is described in the preceding chapter. Disbelief of God's promises and threatenings, and especially of His coming judgment, is the characteristic of these evil men of 'the last times.' We are reminded by this description of these unbelievers, of our Lord's prediction with reference to the same period,---'Nevertheless, when the Son of man cometh, shall he find faith in the land?' (Luke xviii. 8.) It is worthy of notice also that the apostle, in replying to their argument derived from the stability of the creation, refers to the catastrophe of the deluge as an illustration of the power of God to destroy the wicked: the very same illustration employed by our Lord in referring to the state of things at the Parousia (Matt. xxiv. 37-39.)

It must not be forgotten that St. Peter is speaking, not of a distant, but of an impending, catastrophe. The 'last days' were the days then present (1 Pet. i. 5, 20), and the scoffers are spoken of as actually existing (chap. iii. 5),---'This they willingly are ignorant of,' etc.

ESCHATOLOGY OF ST. PETER.

2 Pet. iii. 7, 10-12.---'But the heavens and the earth, which are now, by the same word are kept in store, reserved unto fire against the day of judgment and perdition of ungodly men . . . . But the day of the Lord will come as a thief in the night; in the which the heavens shall pass away with a great noise, and the elements shall melt with fervent heat, the earth also and the works that are therein shall be burnt up. Seeing then that all these things shall be dissolved, what manner of persons ought ye to be in all holy conversation and godliness, looking for and hasting unto the coming of the day of God, wherein the heavens being on fire shall be dissolved, and the elements shall melt with fervent heat? Nevertheless we, according to his promise, look for new heavens and a new earth wherein dwelleth righteousness.'

The imagery here employed by the apostle naturally suggests the idea of the total dissolution by fire of the whole substance and fabric of the material creation, not the earth only but the system to which it belongs; and this no doubt is the popular notion of the final consummation which is expected to terminate the present order of things. A little reflection, however, and a better acquaintance with the symbolic language of prophecy, will be sufficient to modify such a conclusion, and to lead to an interpretation more in accordance with the analogy of similar descriptions in the prophetic writings. First, it is evident on the face of the question that this universal conflagration, as it may be called, was regarded by the apostle as on the eve of taking place,---'The end of all things is at hand' (1 Pet. iv. 7). The con-summation was so near that it is described as an event to be 'looked for, and hastened unto' (ver. 12.) It follows, there-fore, that it could not be the literal destruction or dissolution of the globe and the created universe concerning which the spirit of prophecy here speaks. But that there was at the moment when this epistle was written an awful and al-most immediate catastrophe impending; that the long-predicted 'day of the Lord' was actually at hand; that the day did come, both *speedily* and *suddenly;* that it came 'as a thief in the night;' that a fiery deluge of wrath and judgment overwhelmed the guilty land and nation of Israel, destroying and dissolving its earthly things and its heavenly things, that is to say, its temporal and spiritual institutions,---is a fact indelibly imprinted on the page of history. The time for the fulfillment of these predictions was now come, and when the apostle wrote it was to declare that it was the 'last time,' and the very taunts of the scoffers were verifying the fact. We are therefore brought to the inevitable conclusion that it was the final catastrophe of Judea and Jerusalem, predicted by our Lord in His prophecy on the Mount of Olives and so frequently referred to by the apostles, to which St. Peter alludes in the symbolic imagery which seems to imply the dissolution of the material universe.

Secondly, we must interpret these symbols according to the analogy of Scripture. The language of prophecy is the language of poetry, and is not to be taken in a strictly literal sense. Happily there is no lack of parallel descriptions in the ancient prophets, and there is scarcely a figure here used by St. Peter of which we may not find examples in the Old Testament, and thus be furnished with a key to the meaning of like symbols in the New.

THE CERTAINTY OF THE APPROACHING CONSUMMATION.

2 Pet. iii. 8, 9.---'But, beloved, be not ignorant of this one thing, that one day is with the Lord as a thousand years, and a thousand years as one day. The Lord is not slack concerning his promise, as some men count slackness; but is long-suffering to us-ward, not willing that any should perish, but that all should come to repentance.'

Few passages have suffered more from misconstruction than this, which has been made to speak a language incon-sistent with its obvious intention, and even incompatible with a strict regard to veracity.

There is probably an allusion here to the words of the psalmist, in which he contrasts the brevity of human life with the eternity of the divine existence,---'A thousand years in thy sight are but as yesterday when it is past' (Ps. xc. 4). It is a grand and impressive thought, and quite in unison with the sentiment of the apostle,---'One day is with the Lord as a thousand years.' But surely it would be the height of absurdity to regard this sublime poetic image as a calculus for the divine measurement of time, or as giving us a warrant for wholly disregarding definitions of time in the predictions and promises of God.

Yet it is not unusual to quote these words as an argument or excuse for the total disregard of the element of time in the prophetic writings. Even in cases where a certain time is specified in the prediction, or where such limitations as *'shortly,'* or *'speedily,'* or *'at hand'* are expressed, the passage before us is appealed to in justification of an arbitrary treatment of such notes of time, so that *soon* may mean *late,* and *near* may mean *distant,* and *short* may mean *long,* and *vice versa.* When it is pointed out that certain predictions must, according to their own terms, be fulfilled within a lim-ited time, the reply is, 'One day is with the Lord as a thousand years, and a thousand years as one day.' Thus we find an eminent critic committing himself to such a statement as the following: 'The apostles for the most part wrote and spoke of [the Parousia] as *soon to appear,* not, however, without many and sufficient hints of an interval, and that *no short one,* first to elapse.' Another, alluding to St. Paul's prediction in 2 Thess. ii., remarks that 'it tells us that while the coming of the Lord was then *near,* it was also *remote.'* These are specimens of what passes for exegesis in not a few commentators of high repute.

It is surely unnecessary to repudiate in the strongest manner such a non-natural method of interpreting the language of Scripture. It is worse than ungrammatical and unreasonable, it is immoral. It is to suggest that God has two weights and two measures in His dealings with men, and that in His mode of reckoning there is an ambiguity and variableness which makes it impossible to tell 'what manner of time the Spirit of Christ in the prophets may signify.' It seems to imply that a day may not mean a day, nor a thousand years a thousand years, but that either may be the other. If this were so, there could be no interpretation of prophecy possible; it would be deprived of all precision, and even of all credibility; for it is manifest that if there could be such ambiguity and uncertainty in respect to *time*, there might be no less ambiguity and uncertainty in respect to everything else.

The Scriptures themselves, however, give no countenance to such a method of interpretation. Faithfulness is one of the attributes most frequently ascribed to the 'covenant-keeping God,' and the divine *faithfulness* is that which the apostle in this very passage affirms. To taunt of the scoffers who impugn the faithfulness of God, and ask, 'Where is the promise of His coming?' he answers, 'The Lord is not slack concerning his promise as some men count slackness;' there is no fickleness nor forgetfulness in Him; the lapse of time does not invalidate His word; His promise stands sure whether for the near or the distant, for to-day or to-morrow, or a thousand years to come. To Him on day and a thousand years are alike: that is to say, the promise which falls due in a day will be performed punctually, and the promise which falls due in a thousand years will be performed with equal punctuality. Length of time makes no difference to Him. He will not falsify the promise which has only a day to run, nor forget the promise which has reference to a thousand years hence. Long or short, a day or an age, does not affect His faithfulness. 'The Lord is not slack concerning his promise;' He 'keepeth truth for ever.' But the apostle does not say that when the Lord promises a thing for *to-day* He may not fulfill His promise for *a thousand years: that would be slackness;* that would be a breach of promise. He does not say that because God is infinite and everlasting, therefore He reckons with a different arithmetic from ours, or speaks to us in a double sense, or uses two different weights and measures in His dealings with mankind. The very reverse is the truth. As Hengstenberg justly observes: 'He who speaks to men must speak according to human conceptions, or else state that he has not done so.'

It is evident that the object of the apostle in this passage is to give his readers the strongest assurance that the impending catastrophe of the last days was on the very eve of fulfillment. The veracity and faithfulness of God were the guarantees for the punctual performance of the promise. To have intimated that time was a variable quantity in the promise of God would have been to stultify his argument and neutralise his own teaching, which was, that 'the Lord is not slack concerning his promise.'

SUDDENNESS OF THE PAROUSIA.

2 Pet. iii. 10.---'But the day of the Lord will come as a thief' [in the night].

This statement fixes with precision the event to which the apostle refers as 'the day of the Lord.' It is familiar to us from the frequent allusions made to it in other parts of the New Testament. Our Lord had declared, 'In such an hour as ye think not the Son of man cometh.' He had cautioned His disciples to watch, saying, 'If the goodman of the house had know in what watch the thief would come, he would have watched;' implying that His own coming would be stealthy and unexpected as a thief in the night (Matt. xxiv. 43). St. Paul had said to the Thessalonians, 'Yourselves know perfectly that the day of the Lord so cometh as a thief in the night' (1 Thess. v. 2). And again, St. John, in the Apocalypse, had written, 'Behold, I come as a thief' (Rev. xvi. 15). Since, then the allusions in these passages undoubtedly refer to the impending catastrophe of Judea and Jerusalem, we conclude that this also is the event referred to in the passage before us.

ATTITUDE OF THE PRIMITIVE CHRISTIANS IN RELATION TO THE PAROUSIA.

2 Pet. iii. 12.---'Looking for and hasting into the coming of the day of God.'

That 'the day of God,' 'the day of Christ,' and 'the day of the Lord,' are synonymous expressions, having reference to the selfsame event, is too obvious to require proof. Here we find again what we have so often found before---the attitude of expectancy and that sense of the imminent nearness of the Parousia which are so characteristic of the apostolic age. It is incredible that all this was based on a mere delusion, and that the whole Christian church, with the apostles, and the divine Founder of Christianity Himself, were all involved in one common error. Words have no meaning if a statement like this may refer to some event still future, and perchance distant, which cannot be 'looked for' because it is not within view, nor 'hasted unto,' because it is indefinitely remote.

THE NEW HEAVENS AND NEW EARTH.

2 Pet. iii. 13.---'Nevertheless we, according to his promise, look for new heavens and a new earth, wherein dwelleth righteousness.'

The catastrophe about to take place was to be succeeded by a new creation. The death-pangs of the old are the birth-throes of the new. The old Jerusalem was to give place to the new Jerusalem; the kingdom of this world to the kingdom of our Lord and of His Christ. It may be a question whether by the new heavens and a new earth the apostle means a new order of things here among men or a holy and perfect heavenly state? It may also be asked, To what promise does the apostle refer when he says, 'According to his promise'? Alford suggests Isa. lxv. 17, 'For, behold, I create new heavens and a new earth,' etc., and this may be correct. But we are rather disposed to think that the apostle has in his mind 'the new heaven and the new earth' of the Apocalypse, where we find righteousness set forth as the distinguishing characteristic of the new aeon. The new Jerusalem is the *holy* city, into which 'there shall in no wise enter anything that defileth, neither whatsoever worketh abomination, or maketh a lie.' It is no more improbable that St. Peter should refer to the writings of the Apostle John than to those of the Apostle Paul.

THE NEARNESS OF THE PAROUSIA A MOTIVE TO DILIGENCE.

2 Pet. iii. 14.---'Wherefore, beloved, seeing that ye look for such things be diligent that ye may be found of him in peace, without spot, and blameless.'

This exhortation clearly indicates the expectation of the Parousia as at hand. Its nearness is a motive to diligence, preparedness to meet the Lord. It is not *death* that is here anticipated, but to be found by the Lord watching, 'with their loins girt, and their lamps burning.'

BELIEVERS NOT TO BE DISCOURAGED ON ACCOUNT OF THE SEEMING DELAY OF THE PAROUSIA.

2 Pet. iii. 15.---'And account that the long-suffering of our Lord is salvation.'

The apparent long delay of the anxiously looked-for coming of the Lord must have been disquieting to persecuted Christians longing for the expected hour of relief and redress. Their cry went up to heaven, 'How long, O Lord, holy and true?' Yet this very delay had a gracious aspect; it was 'long-suffering,' makroqumia; not 'slackness,' but 'unwillingness that any should perish.' Exactly in accordance with this is our Lord's parable of the importunate widow, which has relation to this very case. There were have the same delay in the execution of judgment through the long-suffering [makroqumia] of God; the consequent trial of the faith and patience of the saints; their appeal to the judgment of God for redress; and the exhortation to diligence: 'Men ought always to pray, and not to faint' (Luke xviii. 1-8).

ALLUSION OF ST. PETER TO ST. PAUL'S TEACHING CONCERNING THE PAROUSIA

2 Pet. iii. 15, 16.---'Even as our beloved brother Paul also, according to the wisdom given unto him, hath written unto you; as also in all his epistles, speaking in them of these things; in which are some things hard to be understood, which they that are unlearned and unstable wrest, as they do also the other scriptures, unto their own destruction.'

This allusion to the epistles of St. Paul suggests several important inferences.

1.   It proves the existence and general circulation of many epistles written by St. Paul.
2.   It recognizes their inspiration and co-ordinate authority with the scriptures of the Old Testament.
3.   It adverts to the fact that St. Paul, in all his epistles, speaks of the coming of the Lord.
4.   It specifies one epistle in particular in which distinct allusion is made to the subject.
5.   It acknowledges certain difficulties connected with the eschatology of the New Testament, and the perversion of the apostolic teaching by some ignorant and fickle-minded persons.

We may consider briefly one or two questions,---

1.   To which epistle of St. Paul is reference here made as specially bearing upon the subject of the Parousia? (Ver. 15.)

We are disposed to concur with Dr. Alford in the opinion that the reference is to the Epistles to the Thessalonians. The only difficulty lies in the statement 'hath written unto *you*,' for there is no reason to think that St. Peter addressed this epistle to the Thessalonians. But perhaps the expression means no more than that all the epistles of St. Paul were the common property of the church at large; otherwise the Epistles to the Thessalonians answer well to this description of their contents by St. Peter. We find in them allusions to the coming of the Lord; to the suddenness of His coming; to the nearness of His coming; to the deliverance and rest which His coming would bring to the suffering disciples of Christ; and to the duty of diligence and vigilance in the prospect of the event.

2.   What are the 'things hard to be understood,' either in the epistles or in the matters now under consideration?

It has often been pointed out that the proper antecedent to *which* in the second clause of the sixteenth verse is not 'epistles,' but 'things;' en oiz agreeing, not with epistoluz, but with toutwn. Now, however, it appears, since Tischendorf's discovery of the Codex Sinaiticus, that the reading of the three most ancient MSS. is aiz and not oiz, making epistles the proper antecedent to *'which.'* It does not, however, greatly affect the sense which of the two readings we may adopt. It is quite clear that the difficulties alluded to by St. Peter were in those portions of St. Paul's epistles which treated of the Parousia. We know how much the subject was misapprehended by the Thessalonians themselves; and we have abundant experience since then to prove how much the whole eschatology of the New Testament has been 'hard to be understood,' and has been 'wrested' by many even to this day. It is no marvel, then, that much difficulty should have been felt by the primitive Christians as to the true interpretation of many of the prophetic declarations respecting the coming of the Lord, the close of the age, the changing of the living, the resurrection of the dead, the end of all things, etc. That *some* should distort and pervert the apostolic teaching on such subjects was only too probable, and we know as a matter of fact that they did. It was needful, therefore, to exhort believers to beware of being 'led away with the error of the wicked.'

The Parousia in the First Epistle of John

Commentators are much divided on the questions, When, where, by whom, and to whom, this epistle was written. There is no evidence on the subject except that which may be found in the epistle itself, and this gives ample scope for difference in opinion. Lange, who doubts the authenticity of the epistle, says that it 'has quite the air of having been composed before the destruction of Jerusalem;' and Lücke, who maintains its authenticity, is also of the opinion 'that it may gave been written *shortly before* that event.' We think any candid mind will be satisfied, after a careful study of the internal evidence, first, that the epistle is a genuine production of St. John; and, secondly, that it was written on the very eve of the destruction of Jerusalem. It is impossible to overlook the fact, which everywhere meets us in the epistle, that the writer believes himself on the verge of a solemn crisis, for the arrival of which he urges his readers to be prepared. This is in harmony with all the apostolic epistles, and proves incontestably that their authors all alike shared in the belief of the near approach of the great consummation.

THE WORLD PASSING AWAY: THE LAST HOUR COME.

1 John ii. 17, 18.---'And the world passeth away, and the lust thereof. . . . Little children, it is the last time' [hour].

We have frequently in the course of this investigation had occasion to remark how the New Testament writers speak of *'the end'* as fast approaching. We have also seen what that expression refers to. Not to the close of human history, nor the final dissolution of the material creation; but the close of the Jewish aeon or dispensation, and the abolition and removal of the order of things instituted and ordained by divine wisdom under that economy. This great consummation is often spoken of in language which might seem to imply the total destruction of the visible creation. Notably this is the case in the Second Epistle of St. Peter; and the same might also be said of our Lord's prophetic language in Matt. xxiv. 24.

We find the same symbolic form of speech in the passage now before us: 'the world passeth away'. To the apprehension of the apostle it was already 'passing away;' the very expression used by St. Paul in 1 Cor. vii. 31, with reference to the same event [paragei gar to schma tou kosmou toutou] 'the fashion of this world is passing away.'

The impression of the Apostle John of the nearness of 'the end' seems, if possible, more vivid than of the other apostles. Perhaps when he wrote he stood still nearer to the crisis than they. In this view it is worthy of notice that there is a marked gradation in the language of the different epistles. The last *times* become the last *days,* and now the last *days* become the last *hour* [escath wra esti]. The period of expectation and delay was now over, and the decisive moment was at hand.

THE ANTICHRIST COME, A PROOF OF ITS BEING THE LAST HOUR.

1 John ii. 18.---'And as ye have heard that [the] antichrist cometh, even now are there many antichrists; whereby we know it is the last hour' [wra].

In this passage for the first time 'the dreaded name' of *antichrist* rises before us. This fact of itself is sufficient to prove the comparatively late date of the epistle. That which appears in the epistles of St. Paul as a shadowy abstraction has now taken a concrete shape, and appears embodied as a person,---'the antichrist.'

It is certainly remarkable, considering the place which this name has filled in theological and ecclesiastical literature, how very small a space it occupies in the New Testament. Except in the epistles of St. John, the name antichrist never occurs in the apostolic writings. But though the *name* is absent, the *thing* is not unknown. St. John evidently speaks of 'the antichrist' as an idea familiar to his readers,---a power whose coming was anticipated, and whose presence was an indication that 'the last hour' had come. 'Ye have heard that the antichrist cometh; even now are there many antichrists; whereby we know that it is the last hour.'

We expect, then, to find traces of this expectation---predictions of the coming antichrist---in other parts of the New Testament. And we are not disappointed. It is natural to look, in the first place, to our Lord's eschatological discourse on the Mount of Olives for some intimation of this coming danger and the time of its appearance. We find notices in that discourse of 'false christs and false prophets' (Matt. xxiv. 5, 11, 24), and we are ready to conclude that these must mean the same evil power designated by St. John the antichrist. The resemblance of the name favours this supposition; and the period of their appearance,---on the eve of the final catastrophe, seems to increase the probability almost to certainty.

There is, however, a formidable objection to this conclusion, viz. that the false christs and false prophets alluded to by our Lord seem to be mere Jewish impostors, trading on the credulity of their ignorant dupes, or fanatical enthusiasts, the spawn of that hot-bed of religious and political frenzy which Jerusalem became in here last days. We find the actual men vividly portrayed in the passages of Josephus, and we cannot recognise in them the features of the antichrist as drawn by St. John. They were the product of Judaism in its corruption, and not of Christianity. But the antichrist of St. John is manifestly of Christian origin. This is certain from the testimony of the apostle himself: 'They went out from us, but they were not of us,' etc. (ver. 19). This proves that the antichristian opponents of the Gospel must at some time have made a profession of Christianity, and afterwards have become apostates from the faith.

It cannot indeed be said to be impossible that the false christs and false prophets of the last days of Jerusalem could have been apostates from Christianity; but there is no evidence to show this either in the prophecy of our Lord or in the history of the time.

On the other hand, in the apostolic notices of the predicted apostasy this feature of its origin is distinctly marked. We have already seen how St. Paul, St. Peter, and St. John all agree in their description of 'the falling away' of the last days. (See Conspectus of passages relating to the Apostasy, p. 251). Nor can there be any reasonable doubt that the *apostates* of the two former apostles are identical with the *antichrist* of the last. They are alike in character, in origin, and in the time of their appearing. They are the bitter enemies of the Gospel; they are apostates from the faith; they belong to the last days. These are marks of identity too numerous and striking to be accidental; and we are therefore justified in concluding that the antichrist of St. John is identical with the apostasy predicted by St. Paul and St. Peter.

ANTICHRIST NOT A PERSON, BUT A PRINCIPLE.

1 John ii. 18.---'Even now are there many antichrists.'

In the opinion of some commentators the name 'the antichrist' is supposed to designate a particular individual, the incarnation and embodiment of enmity to the Lord Jesus Christ; and as no such person has hitherto appeared in history, they have concluded that his manifestation is still future, but that the personal antichrist may be expected immediately before the 'end of the world.' This seems to have been the opinion of Dr. Alford, who says:---

'According to this view we still look for the man of sin, in the fulness of the prophetic sense, to appear, and that immediately before the coming of the Lord.'

There is here, however, a strange confounding of things which are entirely different,---'the man of sin' and 'the apostasy;' the former undoubtedly a *person,* as we have already seen; the latter a *principle,* or *heresy,* manifesting itself in a multitude of persons. It is impossible, with this declaration of St. John before us,---'Even now are there *many* antichrists,'---to regard the antichrist as a single individual. It is true that in every individual who held the antichristian error, antichrist might be said to be personified; but this is a very different thing from saying that the error is incarnate and embodied in one particular persona as its head and representative. The expression 'many antichrists' proves that the name is not the exclusive designation of any individual.

But the most common and popular interpretation is that which makes the name antichrist refer to the Papacy. From the time of the Reformation this has been the favourite hypothesis of Protestant commentators; nor is it difficult to understand why it should have been so. There is a strong family likeness among all systems of superstition and corrupt religion; and no doubt much of the Papal system may be designated antichristian; but it is a very different thing to say that the antichrist of St. John is intended to describe the pope or the Papal system. Alford decidedly rejects this hypothesis:---

'It cannot be disguised,' he remarks, in treating of this very point, 'that in
several important particulars the prophetic requirements are very far from being fulfilled. I will only mention two,---one subjective, the other objective. In the characteristic of 2 Thess. ii. 4 ("who opposeth and exalteth himself above all that is called God," etc.) the pope does not, and never did, fulfil the prophecy. Allowing all the striking coincidences with the latter part of the verse which have been so abundantly adduced, it never can be shown that he fulfils the former part---nay, so far is he from it, that the abject adoration of and submission to legomenoi qeoi and sebasmata (all that is called God and that is worshipped) has ever been one of his most notable peculiarities. The second objection, of an external and historical character, is even more decisive. If the Papacy be antichrist, then has the manifestation been made, and endured now for nearly 1500 years, and yet that day of the Lord is not come which, by the terms of our prophecy, such manifestation is immediately to precede.

But the language of the apostle himself is decisive against such an application of the name antichrist. Indeed, it is difficult to understand how such an interpretation could have taken root in the face of his own express declarations. The antichrist of St. John is not a *person,* nor a *succession* of persons, but a *doctrine,* or *heresy,* clearly noted and described. More than this, it is declared to be *already existing and manifested* in the apostle's own days: 'Even NOW are there many antichrists;' 'this is that *spirit of antichrist,* whereof ye have heard that it should come; and *even now already is it in the world'* (1 John vi. 18; iv. 3). This ought to be decisive for all who bow to the authority of the Word of God. The hypothesis of an antichrist embodied in an individual still to come has not basis in Scripture; it is a fiction of the imagination, and not a doctrine of the Word of God.

MARKS OF THE ANTICHRIST.

1 John ii. 19.---'They went out from us, but they were not of us; for if they had been of us, they would no doubt have continued with us; but they went out, that they might be made manifest that they were not all of us.'

1 John ii. 22.---'Who is a [the] liar but he that denieth that Jesus is the Christ? He is [the] antichrist, that denieth the Father and the Son.'

1 John iv. 1.---'Beloved, believe not every spirit, but try the spirits whether they are of God: because many false prophets are gone out into the world.'

1 John iv. 3.---'Every spirit that confesseth not that Jesus Christ is come in the flesh is not of God; and this is that spirit of antichrist whereof ye have heard that it should come: and even now already is it in the world.'

2 John, ver. 7.---'Many deceivers are entered into the world, who confess not that Jesus Christ is come in the flesh. This is [the] deceiver and [the] antichrist.'

Here we may be said to have a full-length portrait of the antichrist, or, as we should rather say, the antichristian heresy or apostasy. From this description it distinctly appears,---

1.   That the antichrist was not an individual, or a person, but a principle, or heresy, manifesting itself in many individuals.

2.   That the antichrist or antichrists were apostates from the faith of Christ (ver. 19).

3.   That their characteristic error consisted in the denial of the Messiahship, the divinity, and incarnation of the Son of God.

4.   That the antichristian apostates described by St. John may possibly be the same as those denominated by our Lord 'false christs and false prophets' (Matt. xxiv. 5, 11, 24), but certainly answer to those alluded to by St. Paul, St. Peter, and St. Jude.

5.   All the allusions to the antichristian apostasy connect its appearance with the 'Parousia,' and with 'the last days' or close of the aeon or Jewish dispensation. That is to say, it is regarded as near, and almost already present.

Doubtless, if we possessed fuller historical information concerning that period we should be better able to verify the predictions and allusions which we find in the New Testament; but we have quite enough of evidence to justify the conclusion that all came to pass according to the Scriptures. Whether the false prophets spoken of by Josephus as infesting the last agonies of the Jewish commonwealth are identical with the false prophets of our Lord's prediction and the antichrist of St. John, it is not easy to determine. But the testimony of the apostle himself is decisive on the question of the antichrist. Here he is at the same time both prophet and historian, for he records the fact that 'even now are there many antichrists;' 'many false prophets are gone out into the world.'

ANTICIPATION OF THE PAROUSIA.

1 John ii. 28.---'And now, little children, abide in him, that when he shall appear we may have confidence, and not be ashamed before him at his coming.'

1 John iii. 2.---'We know that when he shall appear we shall be like him, for we shall see him as he is.'

1 John iv. 7.---'That we may have boldness in the day of judgment.'

In these exhortations and counsels St. John is in perfect accord with the other apostles, whose constant admonitions to the Christian churches of their time urged the habitual expectation of the Parousia, and therefore fidelity and constancy in the midst of danger and suffering. The language of St. John proves,---

1.   That the apostolic Christians were exhorted to live in the constant expectation of the coming of the Lord.

2.   That this event was regarded by them as the time of the revelation of Christ in His glory, and the beatification of his faithful disciples.

3.   That the Parousia was also the period of 'the day of judgment.'

The Parousia in the Epistle of St. Jude

Into the questions which relate to the genuineness and authenticity of this epistle it does not devolve upon us to enter. We have to consider it only in relation to the Parousia. Internal evidence shows that it belongs to 'the last days.' The faith and love of the early church had declined, and error, division, and corruption had come in like a flood, so that it became necessary for the apostle to exhort the brethren 'earnestly to contend for the faith which was once delivered to the saints.'

As in 2 Peter ii., so we have in this brief epistle a photograph of the heresiarchs denominated by St. John 'the antichrist' and by St. Paul 'the apostasy.' The resemblance cannot be mistaken.

1.   They were apostates from the faith (ver. 4).

2.   Their error consists in the denial of God and of Christ.

3.   They are marked by the following characteristics:---

Ungodliness, Sensuality, Denial of God and of Christ, Animalism	Lawlessness and Insubordination, Hypocrisy, Murmuring, Boasting	Scoffing, Schismatical separation, Destitution of the Holy Spirit.

It is quite evident that this description, which tallies so closely with that of 2 Peter ii. must have been derived from the same common source. But the mournful fact stands forth plain and palpable, that a fearful degeneracy and corruption of morals had infected the social life of 'the last days.' It is most suggestive to compare the moral state of the chosen people in this closing period of their national history with that described in the words of the last of the Old Testament prophets. The nation was now in that very condition which is there declared to be ripe for judgment. The second Elijah had failed to turn the people to righteousness, and now the Lord, the Messenger of the covenant, was about to come suddenly to His temple; the great and dreadful day of the Lord was at hand; and God was about to smite the land with the curse. (Mal. iv. 5, 6.)

Appendix to Part Two

NOTE A
The Kingdom of Heaven, or of God.

There is no phrase of more frequent occurrence in the New Testament than 'the kingdom of heaven,' or 'the kingdom of God.' We meet with it everywhere---in the beginning, the middle, and the end of the Book. It is the first thing in Matthew, the last in Revelation. The Gospel itself is called 'the gospel of the kingdom;' the disciples are the 'heirs of the kingdom;' the great object of hope and expectation is 'the coming of the kingdom.' It is from this that Christ Himself derives His title of 'King.' The kingdom of God, then, is the very kernel of the New Testament.

But while thus pervading in the New Testament, the idea of the kingdom of God is not peculiar to it; it belongs no less to the Old. We find traces of it in all the prophets from Isaiah to Malachi; it is the theme of some of the loftiest psalms of David; it underlies the annals of ancient Israel; its roots run back to the earliest period of Jewish national existence; it is, in fact the *raison d'etre* of that people; for, to embody and develop this conception of the kingdom of God, Israel was constituted and kept in being as a distinct nationality.

Going back to the primordial germ of the Jewish people we find the earliest intimation of the purpose of God to 'form a people for himself' in the original promise made to their great progenitor, Abraham: 'I will make of thee a great nation, and I will bless thee, and make thy name great; and thou shalt be a blessing; and I will bless them that bless thee, and curse him that curseth thee; and in thee shall all families of the earth be blessed' (Gen. xii. 2, 3). This promise was soon after solemnly renewed in the *covenant* made by God with Abraham: 'In the same day the Lord made a covenant with Abraham, saying, Unto thy seed have I given this land, from the river of Egypt unto the great river, the river Euphrates' (Gen. xv. 18). This covenant relation between God and the seed of Abraham is renewed and more fully developed in the declaration subsequently made to Abraham: 'I will establish my covenant between me and thee, and thy seed after thee, in their generations, for an everlasting covenant, to be a God unto thee, and to thy seed after thee. And I will give unto thee, and to thy seed after thee, the land wherein thou art a stranger, all the land of Canaan, for an everlasting possession, and I will be their God' (Gen. xvii. 7, 8). As a token and seal of this covenant the rite of circumcision was imposed upon Abraham and his posterity, by which every male of that race was marked and signed as a subject of the God of Abraham (Gen. xvii. 9-14).

More than four centuries after this adoption of the children of Abraham as the covenant people of God, we find them in a state of vassalage in Egypt, groaning under the cruel bondage to which they were subjected. We are told that God 'heard their groaning, and remembered his covenant with Abraham, with Isaac, and with Jacob.' He raised up a champion in the person of Moses, and instructed him to say to the children of Israel, 'I am the Lord, and I will bring you out from under the burdens of the Egyptians; . . . and I will take you to me for a people, and I will be to you a God,' etc. (Exod. vi. 6, 7). After the miraculous redemption from Egypt, the covenant relation between Jehovah and the children of Israel was publicly and solemnly ratified at Mount Sinai. We read that 'in the third month, when the children of Israel were gone forth out of the land of Egypt, . . . Israel camped before the mount. And Moses went up unto God, and the Lord called to him out of the mountain, saying, Thus shalt thou say to the house of Jacob, and tell the children of Israel: Ye have seen what I did unto the Egyptians, and how I bare you on eagles' wings, and brought you unto myself. Now therefore, if ye will obey my voice indeed, and keep my covenant, then ye shall be a peculiar treasure unto me above all people: for all the earth is mine, and ye shall be unto me a kingdom of priests, and an holy nation' (Exod. xix. 3-6).

It is at this period that we may regard the Theocratic kingdom as formally inaugurated. A horde of liberated slaves were constituted a nation; they received a divine law for their government, and the complete frame of their civil and ecclesiastical polity was organised and constructed by divine authority. Every step of the process by which a childless old man grew into a nation reveals a divine purpose and a divine plan. Never was any nationality so formed; none ever existed for such a purpose; none ever bore such a relationship to God; none ever possessed such a miraculous history; none was ever exalted to such glorious privilege; none ever fell by such a tremendous doom.

There can be no doubt that the nation of Israel was designated to be the depository and conservator of the knowledge of the living and true God in the earth. For this purpose the nation was constituted, and brought into a unique relation to the Most High, such as not other people ever sustained. To secure this purpose the Lord Himself became their King, and they became His subjects; while all the institutions and laws which were imposed upon them had reference to God, not only as the Creator of all things, but as the Sovereign of the nation. To express and carry out this idea of the kingship of God over Israel is the manifest object of the ceremonial apparatus of worship set up in the wilderness: 'Jehovah caused a royal tent to be erected in the centre of the encampment (where the pavilions of all kings and chiefs were usually erected), and to be fitted up with all the splendour of royalty, as a moveable palace. It was divided into three apartments, in the innermost of which was the royal throne, supported by golden cherubs; and the footstool of the throne, a gilded ark containing the tables of the law, the Magna Charta of church and state. In the anteroom a gilded table was spread with bread and wine, as the royal table; and precious incense was burned. The exterior room or court might be considered the royal culinary apartment, and there music was performed, like the music at the festive tables of Eastern monarchs. God made choice of the Levites for His courtiers, state officers, and palace guards; and of Aaron for the chief officer of the court and first minister of state. For the maintenance of these officers He assigned one of the tithes which the Hebrews were to pay as rent for the use of the land. Finally, He required all the Hebrew males of a suitable age to repair to His palace every year, on the three great annual festivals, with presents, to render homage to their King; and as these days of renewing their homage were to be celebrated with festivity and joy, the second tithe was expended in providing the entertainments necessary for those occasions. In short, every religious duty was made a matter of political obligation; and all the civil regulations, even the most minute, were so founded upon the relation of the people to God, and so interwoven with their religious duties, that the Hebrew could not separate his God and his King, and in every law was reminded equally of both. Consequently the nation, so long as it had a national existence, could not entirely lose the knowledge, or discontinue the worship, of the true God.'

Such was the government instituted by Jehovah among the children of Israel---a true Theocracy; the only real Theocracy that ever existed upon earth. Its intense and exclusive national character deserves particular notice. It was the distinctive privilege of the children of Abraham, and of them alone: 'The Lord thy God hath chosen thee to be a special people unto himself, above all people that are upon the face of the earth' (Deut. vii. 6). 'You only have I known of all the families of the earth' (Amos iii. 2). 'He hath not dealt so with any nation' (Ps. cxlvii. 20). The Most High was the Lord of the whole earth, but He was the King of Israel in an altogether peculiar sense. He was their covenanted Ruler; they were His covenanted people. They came under the most sacred and solemn obligations to be loyal subjects to their invisible Sovereign, to worship Him alone, and to be faithful to His law (Deut. xxvi. 16-18). As the reward of obedience they had the promise of unbounded prosperity and national greatness; they were to be 'high above all nations in praise and in name and in honour' (Deut. xxvi. 19); while, on the other hand, the penalties of disloyalty and unfaithfulness were correspondingly dreadful; the curse of the broken covenant would overtake them in a signal and terrible retribution, to which there should be no parallel in the history of mankind, past or to come. (Deut. xxviii.)

It is only reasonable to presume that this marvellous experiment of a Theocratic government must have had for its object something worthy of its divine author. That object was moral, rather than material; the glory of God and the good of men, rather than the political or temporal advancement of a tribe or nation. It was no doubt, in the first place, an expedient to keep alive the knowledge and worship of the One true God in the earth, which otherwise might have been wholly lost; and, secondly, notwithstanding its intense and exclusive spirit of nationalism, the Theocratic system carried in its bosom the germ of a universal religion, and thus was a great and important stage in the education of the human race. It is instructive to trace the growth and progressive development of the Theocratic idea in the history of the Jewish people, and to observe how, as it loses its political significance, it becomes more and more moral and spiritual in its character.

The people on whom this unequalled privilege was conferred showed themselves unworthy of it. Their fickleness and faithlessness neutralised at every step the favour of their invisible Sovereign. Their demand for a king, 'that they might be like all the nations,' was a virtual rejection of their heavenly Ruler. (1 Sam. viii. 7, 19, 20.) Nevertheless their request was granted, provision for such a contingency having been made in the original framing of the Theocracy. The human king was regarding as the viceroy of the divine King, and thus he became a type of the real, though unseen, Sovereign to whom he, as well as the nation, owed allegiance.

It is at this point that we note the appearance of a new phase in the Theocratic system. If we regard David as the author of the second Psalm, it was as early as his time that a prophetic announcement was made concerning a King, the Lord's Anointed, the Son of God, against whom the kings of the earth were to set themselves and the rulers to take counsel together, but to whom the Most High was to give the heathen for His inheritance and the uttermost parts of the earth for His possession. From this period the *mediatorial* character of the Theocracy begins to be more clearly indicated:---there is a distinction made between the Lord and His Anointed, between the Father and the Son. We meet with the titles Messiah, Son of God, Son of David, King of Zion, given to One to whom the kingdom belongs, and who is destined to triumph and to reign. The psalms called Messianic, especially the 72nd and 110th, are sufficient to prove that in the time of David there were clear prophetic announcements of a coming King, whose rule was to be beneficent and glorious; in whom all nations were to be blessed; who was to unite in Himself the twofold offices of Priest and King; who is declared to be David's Lord; and is represented as sitting at the right hand of God 'until his enemies be made his footstool.'

Henceforth through all the prophecies of the Old Testament we find the character and person of the Theocratic King more and more fully delineated, though in the description are blended together diverse and apparently inconsistent elements. Sometimes the coming King and His kingdom are depicted in the most attractive and glowing colours,---'a Rod is to spring from the stem of Jesse, and a Branch to grow out of his roots,' and under the conduct of this scion of the house of David all evil is to disappear and all goodness to triumph. The wolf is to dwell with the lamb and the leopard to lie down with the kid: 'They shall not hurt nor destroy in all God's holy mountain, for the earth shall be full of the knowledge of the Lord, as the waters cover the sea' (Isa. xi. 1-9). The loftiest names of honour and dignity are ascribed to the coming Prince; He is the 'Wonderful, Counseller, The mighty God, The everlasting Father, The Prince of Peace. Of the increase of his government and peace there is to be no end.' He is to sit upon the throne of David, and to govern his kingdom with judgment and with justice for ever (Isa. ix. 6, 7).

But side by side with these brilliant prospects lie dark and gloomy scenes of sorrow and suffering, of judgment and wrath. The coming King is spoken of as a 'root out of a dry ground;' as 'despised and rejected;' as 'a man of sorrows, and acquainted with grief;' as 'wounded for our transgressions and bruised for our iniquities;' 'brought like a lamb to the slaughter;' 'dumb like a sheep in the hand of the shearers;' 'cut off out of the land of the living' (Isa. liii.). He is described as coming to Jerusalem 'lowly' and riding upon an ass, and upon a colt the foal of an ass' (Zech. ix. 9); Messiah is to be cut off, but not for Himself (Dan. ix. 26); and among the latest prophetic utterances are some of the most ominous and sombre of all. The Lord, the Messenger of the covenant, the expected King, is to come: 'But who may abide the day of his coming? That day shall burn as a furnace; it is the great and dreadful day of the Lord' (Mal. iii. 1, 2; iv. 1, 5). This seeming paradox is explained in the New Testament. There actually was this twofold aspect of the King and the kingdom: 'The King of glory' was also 'the Man of sorrows;' 'the acceptable year of the Lord' was also 'the day of vengeance of our God.'

Ancient prophecy had given abundant reason for the expectation that the invisible Theocratic King would one day be revealed, and would dwell with men upon the earth; that He would come, in the interests of the Theocracy, to set up His kingdom in the nation, and to rally His people around His throne. The opening chapters of St. Luke's gospel indicate the views entertained by pious Israelites respecting the coming kingdom of the Messiah. It was understood by them to have a special relation to Israel. 'He shall be great,' said the angel of the annunciation, 'and shall be called the Son of the Highest, and the Lord God shall give unto him the house of his father David; and he shall reign over the house of Jacob for ever.' 'Rabbi!' exclaimed the guileless Nathanael, as the God suddenly flashed upon him through the disguise of the young Galilean peasant, 'thou are the Son of God, thou are the King of Israel!' (John i. 44) It is no less certain that His coming was then believed to be near, and it was eagerly expected by such holy men as Simeon, who 'waited for the consolation of Israel,' and to whom it had been revealed that he should not 'see death before he had seen the Lord's anointed' (Luke ii. 25, 26). There was indeed a wide-spread belief, not only in Judea, but throughout the Roman Empire, that a great prince or monarch was about to appear in the earth, who was to inaugurate a new epoch. Of this expectation we have evidence in the Annals of Tacitus and the Pollio of Virgil. Doubtless the cherished hope of Israel had diffused itself, in a more or less vague and distorted form, throughout the neighbouring lands.

But when, in the fulness of time, the Theocratic King appeared in the midst of the covenant nation, it was not in the form which they had expected and desired. He did not fulfil their hopes of political power and national pre-eminence. The kingdom of God which He proclaimed was something very different from that of which they had dreamed. Righteousness and truth, purity and goodness, were only empty names to men who coveted the honours and pleasures of this world. Nevertheless, though rejected by the nation at large, the Theocratic King did not fail to announce His presence and His claims. He was preceded by a herald, the predicted Elias, John the Baptist, whom the people were constrained to acknowledge as a true prophet of God. The second Elijah announced the kingdom of God as at hand, and called upon the nation to repent and receive their King. Next, His own miraculous works, unexampled even in the history of the chosen people for number and splendour, gave conclusive evidence of His divine mission; added to which the transcendent excellence of His doctrine, and the unsullied purity of His life, silenced, if they did not shame, the enmity of the ungodly. For more than three years this appeal to the heart and conscience of the nation was incessantly presented in every variety of method, but without success; until at length the chief men in the Jewish church and state, bitterly hostile to His pretensions, impeached Him before the Roman governor on the charge of making Himself a King. By their persistent and malignant clamour they procured His condemnation. He was delivered up to be crucified, and the title upon His cross bore this inscription,---

'THIS IS THE KING OF THE JEWS.'

This tragic event marks the final breach between the covenant nation and the Theocratic King. The covenant had often been broken before, but now it was publicly repudiated and torn in pieces. It might have been thought that the

Theocracy would now be at an end; and virtually it was; but its formal dissolution was suspended for a brief space, in order that the twofold consummation of the kingdom, involving the salvation of the faithful and the destruction of the unbelieving, might be brought about at the appointed time. This twofold aspect of the Theocratic kingdom is visible in every part of its history. It was at once a success and a failure---a victory and a defeat; it brought salvation to some and destruction to others. This twofold character had been distinctly set forth in ancient prophecy, as in the remarkable oracle of Isaiah xlix. The Messiah complains, 'I have laboured in vain, and spent my strength for nought and in vain,' etc. The divine answer is, 'Thus saith the Lord, Though Israel be not gathered, yet shall I be glorious in the eyes of the Lord, and my God shall be my strength. And He said, It is a light thing that thou shouldest be my servant to raise up the tribes of Jacob, and to restore the preserved of Israel: I will also give thee for a light to the Gentiles, that thou mayest be my salvation to the ends of the earth.' To take only one other example: we find in the Book of Malachi this twofold aspect of the coming kingdom, for while 'the day that cometh' is to 'burn as a furnace,' and to 'consume the wicked as stubble,' 'unto you that fear my name shall the Sun of righteousness arise with healing in his wings' (Mal. iv. 1, 2). Notwithstanding, therefore, the rejection of the King, and the forfeiture of the kingdom by the mass of the people, there was yet to be a glorious consummation of the Theocracy, bringing honour and happiness to all who owned the authority of the Messiah and proved dutiful and loyal to their King.

Have we any data by which to ascertain the period of this consummation? At what time may the kingdom be said to have fully come? Not at the *incarnation,* for the proclamation of Jesus ever was, 'The kingdom of God is *at hand.'* Not at the *crucifixion,* for the petition of the dying thief was, 'Lord, remember me when thou comest in thy kingdom.' Not at the *resurrection,* for after the Lord had risen the disciples were looking for the restoration of the kingdom to Israel. Not at the *ascension,* nor on the day of *Pentecost,* for long after these events we are told, in the Epistle to the Hebrews, that Christ, 'after he had offered one sacrifice for sins for ever, sate down on the right hand of God: from henceforth *expecting* till his enemies be made his footstool' (Heb. x. 12, 13). The consummation of the kingdom, therefore, is not coincident with the ascension, nor with the day of Pentecost. It is true that the Theocratic King was seated on the throne, 'on the right hand of the Majesty on high,' but He had not yet 'taken his great power.' His enemies were not yet put down, and the full development and consummation of His kingdom could not be said to have arrived until by a solemn and public judicial act the Messiah had vindicated the laws of His kingdom and crushed beneath His feet His apostate and rebellious subjects.

There is one point of time constantly indicated in the New Testament as the consummation of the kingdom of God. Our Lord declared that there were some among His disciples who should live to see Him *coming in His kingdom.* This coming of the King is of course synonymous with the coming of the kingdom, and limits the occurrence of the event to the then existing generation. That is to say, the consummation of the kingdom synchronises with the judgment of Israel and the destruction of Jerusalem, all being parts of one great catastrophe. It was at that period that the Son of man was to come in the glory of His Father, and to sit upon the throne of His glory; to render a reward to His servants and retribution to His enemies (Matt. xxv. 31). We find these events uniformly associated together in the New Testament,---the coming of the King, the resurrection of the dead, the judgment of the righteous and the wicked, the consummation of the kingdom, the end of the age. Thus St. Paul, in 2 Tim. iv. 5, says, 'I charge thee therefore, before God and the Lord Jesus Christ, who is about to judge the living and the dead at his appearing and His kingdom.' The *coming,* the *judgment,* the *kingdom,* are all coincident and contemporaneous, and not only so, but also *nigh at hand;* for the apostle says, 'Who is about to judge; . . . who shall *soon* judge' [mellontoz krinein].

It is perfectly clear, then, according to the New Testament, that the consummation, or winding up, of the Theocratic kingdom took place at the period of the destruction of Jerusalem and the judgment of Israel. The Theocracy had served its purpose; the experiment had been tried whether or not the covenant nation would prove loyal to their King. It had failed; Israel had rejected her King; and it only remained that the penalties of the violated covenant should be enforced. We see the result in the ruin of the temple, the destruction of the city, the effacement of the nation, and the abrogation of the law of Moses, accompanied with scenes of horror and suffering without a parallel in the history of the world. That great catastrophe, therefore, marks the conclusion of the Theocratic kingdom. It had been from the beginning of a strictly national character---it was the divine Kingship over Israel. It necessarily terminated, therefore, with the termination of the national existence of Israel, when the outward and visible symbols of the divine Presence and Sovereignty passed away; when the house of God, the city of God, and the people of God were effaced from existence by one desolating and final catastrophe.

This enables us to understand the language of St. Paul when, speaking of the coming of Christ, he represents that event as marking 'the end' [to teloz = h sunteleia tou aiwnoz], 'when he shall deliver up the kingdom to God, even the Father' (1 Cor. xv. 24). This has caused much perplexity to many theologians and commentators, who have seemed to regard it as derogatory to the divinity of the Son of God that He should resign His mediatorial functions and His kingly character, and sink, as it were, into the position of a private person, becoming a subject instead of a sovereign. But the embarrassment has arisen from overlooking the nature of the kingdom which the Son had administered, and which

He at length surrenders. It was the *Messianic kingdom:* the kingdom over Israel: that peculiar and unique government exercised over the covenant nation, and administered by the mediatorship of the Son of God for so many ages. That relation was now dissolved, for the nation had been judged, the temple destroyed, and all the symbols of the divine Sovereignty removed. Why should the Theocratic kingdom be continued any longer? There was nothing to administer. There was no longer a covenant nation, the covenant was broken, and Israel had ceased to exist as a distinct nationality. What more natural and proper, therefore, than at such a juncture for the Mediator to resign His mediatorial functions, and to deliver up the insignia of government into the hands from which He received them? Ages before that period the Father had invested the Son with the viceregal functions of the Theocracy. It had been proclaimed, 'I have set my King upon my holy hill of Zion: I will declare the decree; the Lord hath said unto me, Thou art my Son, this day have I begotten thee' (Ps. ii. 6, 7). The purposes for which the Son had assumed the administration of the Theocratic government had been effected. The covenant was dissolved, its violation avenged, the enemies of Christ and of God were destroyed; the true and faithful servants were rewarded, and the Theocracy came to an end. This was surely the fitting moment for the Mediator to resign His charge into the hands of the Father, that is to say, 'to deliver up the kingdom.'

But there is in all this nothing derogatory to the dignity of the Son. On the contrary, 'He is the Mediator of a better covenant.' The termination of the Theocratic kingdom was the inauguration of a new order, on a wider scale, and of a more enduring nature. This is the doctrine of the Epistle to the Hebrews: 'the throne of the Son of God is for ever and ever' (Heb. i. 8). The priesthood of the Son of God 'abideth continually' (chap. viii. 3); Christ 'hath now obtained a more excellent ministry, by how much also he is the mediator of a better covenant' (chap. viii. 6). The Theocracy, as we have seen, was limited, exclusive, and national; yet it bore within it the germ of a universal religion. What Israel lost was gained by the world. Whilst the Theocracy subsisted there was a favoured nation, and the Gentiles, that is to say all the world minus the Jews, were outside the kingdom, holding a position of inferiority, and, like dogs, permitted as a matter of grace to eat the crumbs that fell from the master's table. The first coming of Christ did not wholly do away with this state of things; even the Gospel of the grace of God flowed at first in the old narrow channel. St. Paul recognises the fact that 'Jesus Christ was a minister of the circumcision,' and our Lord Himself declared, 'I am not sent but to the lost sheep of the house of Israel.' For years after the apostles had received their commission they did not understand it was sending them to the Gentiles; nor did they at first regard heathen converts as admissible into the church, except as Jewish proselytes. It is true that after the conversion of Cornelius the centurion the apostles became convinced of the larger limits of the Gospel, and St. Paul everywhere proclaimed the breaking down of the barriers between the Jew and the Gentile; but it is easy to see that so long as the Theocratic nation existed, and the temple, with its priesthood and sacrifices and ritual, remained, and the Mosaic law continued, or seemed to continue, in force, the distinction between Jew and Gentile could not be obliterated. But the barrier was effectually broken down when law, temple, city, and nation were swept away together, and the Theocracy was visibly brought to a final consummation.

That event was, so to speak, the formal and public declaration that God was no longer the God of the Jews only, but that He was now the common Father of all men; that there was no longer a favoured nation and a peculiar people, but that the grace of God 'which bringeth salvation to *all* men was now made manifest' (Titus ii. 11); that the local and limited had expanded into the ecumenical and universal, and that in Christ Jesus 'all are one' (Gal. iii. 29). This is what St. Paul declares to be the meaning of the surrender of the kingdom by the Son of God into the hands of the Father: thenceforth the exclusive relations of God to a single nation ceases, and He becomes the common Father of the whole human family,---

'THAT GOD MAY BE ALL IN ALL' (1 Cor. xv. 28).

NOTE B

On the 'Babylon' of 1 Peter 5:13

'The *church* in Babylon [she in Babylon] elected together (with you) saluteth you; and Marcus my son.'

It is not easy to convey in so many words in English the precise force of the original. Its extreme brevity causes obscurity. Literally it reads thus: 'She in Babylon, co-elect, saluteth you; and Marcus my son.'

The common interpretation of the pronoun *she* refers it to 'the church in Babylon;' though many eminent commentators---Bengel, Mill, Wahl, Alford, and others---understand it as referring to an individual, presumably the *wife* of the apostle. 'It is hardly probable,' remarks Alford, 'that there should be joined together in the same message of salutation an *abstraction,* spoken of thus enigmatically, and a *man* (Marcus my son), by name.' The weight of authority inclines to the side of *church,* the weight of grammar to the side of *wife.*

But the more important question relates to the identity of the place here called Babylon. It is natural at first sight to conclude that it can be no other than the well-known and ancient metropolis of Chaldea, or such remnant of it as existed in the apostle's days. We are ready to think it highly probable that St. Peter, in his apostolic journeyings rivalled the apostle to the Gentiles, and went everywhere preaching the Gospel to the Jews, as St. Paul did to the Gentiles.

There appear, however, to be formidable objections to this view, natural and simple as it seems. Not to mention the improbability that St. Peter in his old age, and accompanied by his wife (if we accept the opinion that she is referred to in the salutation), should be found in a region so remote from Judea, there is the important consideration that Babylon was not at that time the abode of a Jewish population. Josephus states that so long before as the reign of Caligula (A.D. 37-41) the Jews had been expelled from Babylonia, and that a general massacre had taken place, by which they had been almost exterminated. This statement of Josephus, it is true, refers rather to the whole region called Babylonia than to the city of Babylon, and that for the sufficient reason that in the time of Josephus Babylon was as much an uninhabited place as it is now. Rosenmüller, in his Biblical Geography, affirms that in the time of Strabo (that is, in the reign of Augustus) Babylon was so deserted that he applies to that city what an ancient poet had said of Megalopolis in Arcadia, viz. that it was 'one vast wilderness.' Basnage, also, in his History of the Jews, says, 'Babylon was declining in the days of Strabo, and Pliny represents it in the reign of Vespasian as one vast unbroken solitude.'

Other cities have been suggested as the Babylon referred to in the epistle: a fort so called in Egypt, mentioned by Strabo; Ctesiphon on the Tigris; Seleucia, the new city which drained ancient Babylon of its inhabitants: but these are mere conjectures, unsupported by a particle of evidence.

The improbability that the ancient capital of Chaldaea should be the place referred to may account in great measure for the general consent which from the earliest times has attached a symbolical or spiritual interpretation to the name Babylon. If the question were to be decided by the authority of great names, Rome would no doubt be declared to be the mystic Babylon so designated by the apostle. But this involves the vexed question whether St. Peter ever visited Rome, into the discussion of which we cannot here enter. The gospel history is totally silent on the subject, and the tradition, unquestionably very ancient, of St. Peter's episcopate there, and of his martyrdom under Nero, is embarrassed with so much that is certainly fabulous, that we are justified in setting the whole aside as a legend or myth. There is an *a priori* argument against the probability of St. Peter's visit to Rome, which, in the absence of any evidence to the contrary, we hold to be insurmountable. St. Peter was the apostle of the *circumcision;* his mission was to the Jews, his own nation; we cannot conceive it possible that he should quit his appointed sphere of labour and 'enter into another man's line of things,' and 'build upon another man's foundation.' St. Paul was in Rome in the days of Nero, and nothing can be more improbable that that St. Peter, the apostle of the circumcision, in extreme old age, and 'knowing that shortly he must put off his earthly tabernacle,' should undertake a voyage to Rome without any special call, and without leaving any trace of so remarkable an event in the history of the Acts of the Apostles.

But if Rome be not the symbolical Babylon referred to, and if the literal Babylon be inadmissible, what other place can be suggested with any show of probability? Is there no other city which might not as fitly be called the mystical Babylon as Rome? No other which has not similar symbolical names attached to it, both in the Old Testament and in the New? It seems unaccountable that the very city with which the life and acts of St. Peter are more associated than any other should have been entirely ignored in this discussion. Why might not the city which is called *Sodom* and *Gomorrah* be just as reasonably styled Babylon? Now *Jerusalem* has these mystic names affixed to it in the Scriptures, and no city had a better claim to the character which they imply. Jerusalem also seems undoubtedly to have been the fixed residence of the apostle; Jerusalem, therefore, is the place from which we might expect to find him writing and dating his epistles to the churches.

Whatever the city may be which the apostle styles Babylon, it must have been the *settled abode* of the person or the church associated with himself and Marcus in the salutation. This is proved by the form of the expressions h en babulwni, which, as Steiger shows, signifies '*a fixed abode* by which one may be designated.' If we decide that the reference is to a person, it will follow that Babylon was the place where she was domiciled, her settled place of abode, and this, in the case of Peter's wife, could only be Jerusalem. The apostolic history, so far as it can be gleaned from the documentary evidence in the New Testament, distinctly shows that St. Peter was habitually resident in Jerusalem. It is nothing else than a popular fallacy to suppose that all the apostles were evangelists like St. Paul, travelling through foreign countries and preaching the Gospel to all nations. Professor Burton has shown that 'it was not until fourteen years after our Lord's ascension that St. Paul traveled for the first time, and preached the Gospel to the Gentiles. Nor is there any evidence that during this period the other apostles passed the confines of Judea.' But what we contend for is, that St. Peter's habitual or settled abode was in Jerusalem. This will appear from a variety of circumstantial proofs.

1.   When the Jerusalem church was scattered abroad after the persecution which arose at the time of Stephen's martyrdom, St. Peter and the rest of the apostles remained in Jerusalem. (Acts viii. 1.)
2.   St. Peter was in Jerusalem when Herod Agrippa I. apprehended and imprisoned him. (Acts xii. 3.)
3.   When St. Paul, three years after his conversion, goes up to Jerusalem, his errand is *'to see Peter;'* and he adds, 'I abode with him fifteen days' (Gal. i. 18). This implies that St. Peter's place of abode was Jerusalem.
4.   Fourteen years after this visit to Jerusalem, St. Paul again visits that city in company with Barnabas and Titus; and on this occasion, also, we find St. Peter there (Gal. ii. 1-9). (A.D.50---Conybeare and Howson.)

5.   It is worthy of notice that it was the presence in Antioch of certain persons who came from *Jerusalem* that so intimidated St. Peter as to lead him to practise an equivocal line of conduct, and to incur the censure of St. Paul. (Gal. ii. 11.) Why should the presence of Jerusalem Jews intimidate St. Peter? Presumably because, on his return to Jerusalem, he would be called to account by them: thus implying that Jerusalem was his usual residence.

6.   If we suppose, which is most probable, that Marcus, named in this salutation, is John Mark, sister's son to Barnabas, we know that he also abode in *Jerusalem*. (Acts xii. 12.)

7.   Silvanus, or Silas, the writer or bearer of this epistle, is known to us as a prominent member of the church of *Jerusalem*: 'a chief man among the brethren' (Acts xv. 22-32).

We thus find all the persons named in the concluding portion of the epistle habitual residents in Jerusalem.

Lastly, we infer from an incidental expression in chap. iv. 17 that St. Peter was in Jerusalem when he wrote this epistle. He speaks of judgment having begun at the *'house of God;'* that is, as we have seen, the sanctuary, the temple; and he adds, 'if it first begin at *us,'* etc. Now, would he have expressed himself so if at the time of his writing he had been in Rome, or in Babylon on the Euphrates, or in any other city than Jerusalem? It certainly seems most natural to suppose that if the judgment begins at the *sanctuary,* and also at *us*, both the place and the persons must be *together*. The vision of Ezekiel, which gives the prototype of the scene of judgment, fixes the locality where the slaughter is to commence, and it appears highly probable that the coming doom of the city and temple was in the mind of the apostle, as well as the afflictions which were to befall the disciples of Christ. Wiesinger remarks: 'It is hardly possible that the destruction of Jerusalem was *past* when these words were written; if that had been so, it would hardly have been said, o kairoz tou arxasqai.' No; it was not past, but the beginning of the end was already present; the judgment seems to have commenced, as the Lord said it would, with the disciples; and this was the sure prelude to the wrath which was coming upon the ungodly 'to the uttermost.'

But it may be objected, If St. Peter meant Jerusalem, why did he not say so without any ambiguity? There may have been, and doubtless were, prudential reasons for this reserve at the time of St. Peter's writing, even as there were when St. Paul wrote to the Thessalonians. But, probably, there was no such ambiguity to his readers as there is to us. What if Jerusalem were already known and recognised among Christian believers as the mystical Babylon? Assuming, as we have a right to do, that the Apocalypse was already familiarly known to the apostolic churches, we consider it in the highest degree probable that they identified the 'great city' whose fall is depicted in that book, 'Babylon the great,' as the same whose fall is depicted in our Lord's prophecy on the Mount of Olives.

This, however, belongs to another question, the discussion of which will come in its proper place,---the identity of the Babylon of the Apocalypse. Let it suffice for the present to have made out a probable case, on wholly independent grounds, for the Babylon of St. Peter's first epistle being no other than *Jerusalem.*

NOTE C

On the Symbolism of Prophecy, with special reference to the Predictions of the Parousia.

The slightest attention to the language of the Old Testament prophecy must convince any sober-minded man that it is not to be understood according to the letter. First of all, the utterances of the prophets are poetry; and, secondly, they are Oriental poetry. They may be called hieroglyphic pictures representing historical events in highly metaphorical imagery. It is inevitable, therefore, that hyperbole, or that which to us appears such, should enter largely into the descriptions of the prophets. To the cold prosaic imagination of the West, the glowing and vivid style of the prophets of the East may seem turgid and extravagant; but there is always a substratum of reality underlying the figures and symbols, which, the more they are studied, commend themselves the more to the judgment of the reader. Social and political revolutions, moral and spiritual changes, are shadowed forth by physical convulsions and catastrophes; and if these natural phenomena affect the imagination more powerfully still, they are not inappropriate figures when the real importance of the events which they represent is apprehended. The earth convulsed with earthquakes, burning mountains cast into the sea, the stars falling like leaves, the heavens on fire, the sun clothed in sackcloth, the moon turned to blood, are images of appalling grandeur, but they are not necessarily unsuitable representations of great civil commotions,---the overturning of thrones and dynasties, the desolations of war, the abolition of ancient systems, and great moral and spiritual revolutions. In prophecy, as in poetry, the material is regarded as the type of the spiritual, the passions and emotions of humanity find expression in corresponding signs and symptoms in the inanimate creation. Does the prophet come with glad tidings? He calls upon the mountains and the hills to break forth into song, and the trees of the forest to clap their hands. Is his message one of lamentation and woe? The heavens are draped in mourning, and the sun is darkened in his going down. No one, however anxious to keep by the bare letter of the word, would think of insisting that such metaphors should be literally interpreted, or must have a literal fulfilment. The utmost that we are entitled to require is, that there should be such historical events specified as may worthily correspond with such phenomena; great moral and social movements capable of producing such emotions as these physical phenomena seem to imply.

It may be useful to select some of the most remarkable of these prophetic symbols as found in the Old Testament, that we may note the occasions on which they were employed, and discover the sense in which they are to be understood.

In Isaiah xiii. we have a very remarkable prediction of the destruction of ancient Babylon. It is conceived in the highest style of poetry. The Lord of hosts mustereth the host of the battle; the tumultuous rush of the nations is heard; the day of the Lord is proclaimed to be at hand; the stars of the heaven and the constellations withhold their light; the sun is darkened in his going forth; the moon ceases to shine; the heavens are shaken, and the earth removed out its place. All this imagery, it will be observed, which if literally fulfilled would involve the wreck of the whole material creation, is employed to set forth the destruction of Babylon by the Medes.

Again, in Isaiah xxiv. we have a prediction of judgments about to come upon the land of Israel; and among other representations of the woes which are impending we find the following: 'The windows from on high are open; the foundations of the earth do shake. The earth is utterly broken down; the earth is clean dissolved; the earth shall reel to and fro like a drunkard, and shall be removed like a cottage; it shall fall, and not rise again,' etc. All this is symbolical of the civil and social convulsion about to take place in the land of Israel.

In Isaiah xxxiv. the prophet denounces judgments on the enemies of Israel, particularly on Edom, or Idumea. The imagery which he employs of the most sublime and awful description: 'The mountains shall be melted with the blood of the slain. All the host of heaven shall be rolled together as a scroll, and all their host shall fall down, as the leaf falleth off from the vine, and as a falling fig from the fig-tree.' 'The streams thereof shall be turned into pitch, and the dust thereof into brimstone, and the land thereof shall become burning pitch. It shall not be quenched night nor day; the smoke thereof shall go up fore ever; from generation to generation it shall be waste; none shall pass through it for ever and ever.'

It is not necessary to ask, Have these predictions been fulfilled? We know they have been; and the accomplishment of them stands in history as a perpetual monument of the truth of Revelation. Babylon, Edom, Tyre, the oppressors or enemies of the people of God, have been made to drink the cup of the Lord's indignation. The Lord has let none of the words of His servants the prophets fall to the ground. But no one will pretend to say that the symbols and figures which depicted their overthrow were literally verified. These emblems are the drapery of the picture, and are used simply to heighten the effect and to give vividness and grandeur to the scene.

In like manner the prophet Ezekiel uses imagery of a very similar kind in predicting the calamities which were coming upon Egypt: 'And when I shall put them out, I will cover the heaven, and make the stars thereof dark. I will cover the sun with a cloud, and the moon shall not give her light. All the bright lights of heaven will I make dark over them, and set darkness upon the land, saith the Lord God' (Ezek. xxxii. 7, 8).

Similarly the prophets Micah, Nahum, Joel, and Habakkuk describe the presence and interposition of the Most High in the affairs of nations as accompanied by stupendous natural phenomena: 'Behold, the Lord cometh forth out of his place, and will come down, and tread upon the high places of the earth, and the mountains shall be molten under him, and the valleys shall be cleft as wax before the fire, and as the waters that are poured down a steep place' *(Micah i. 3, 4).*

'The Lord hath his way in the whirlwind and in the storm, and the clouds are the dust of his feet. He rebuketh the sea, and maketh it dry, and drieth up all the rivers. The mountains quake at him, and the hills melt, and the earth is burned at his presence: yea, the world, and all that dwell therein. His fury is poured out like fire, and the rocks are thrown down by him' (Nahum i. 3-6).

These examples may suffice to show, what indeed is self-evident, that in prophetic language the most sublime and terrible natural phenomena are employed to represent national and social convulsions and revolutions. Imagery, which if literally verified would involve the total dissolution of the fabric of the globe and the destruction of the material universe, really may mean no more than the downfall of a dynasty, the capture of a city, or the overthrow of a nation.

The following are the views expressed by Sir Isaac Newton on this subject, which are substantially just, though perhaps carried somewhat too far in supposing an equivalent in fact for every figure employed in the prophecy:---

'The figurative language of the prophets is taken from the analogy between the world natural and an empire or kingdom considered as a world politic. Accordingly, the world natural, consisting of heaven and earth, signifies the whole world politic, consisting of thrones and people, or so much of it as is considered in prophecy; and the things in that world signify analogous things in this. For the heavens and the things therein signify thrones and dignities, and those who enjoy them: and the earth, with the things thereon, the inferior people; and the lowest parts of the earth, called Hades or Hell, the lowest or most miserable part of them. Great earthquakes, and the shaking of heaven and earth, are put for the shaking of kingdoms, so as to distract and overthrow them; the creating of a new heaven and new earth, and the passing of an old one; or the beginning and end of a world, for the rise and ruin of a body politic signified thereby. The sun, for the whole species and race of kings, in the kingdoms of the world politic; the moon, for the body of the common people considered as the king's wife; the stars, for subordinate princes and great men; or for bishops and rulers of the people of God, when the sun is Christ. Setting of the sun, moon, and stars; darkening the sun, turning the moon into blood, and falling of the stars,---for the ceasing of a kingdom.'

We will only quote in addition the excellent remarks of a judicious expositor---Dr. John Brown of Edinburgh:---

'"Heaven and earth passing away," understood literally, is the dissolution of the present system of the universe; and the period when that is to take place is called "the end of the world." But a person at all familiar with the phraseology of the Old Testament scriptures knows that the dissolution of the Mosaic economy and the establishment of the Christian, is often spoken of as the removing of the old earth and heavens, and the creation of a new earth and new heavens. For example, "Behold, I create new heavens and a new earth, and the former shall not be remembered, nor come into mind." "For as the new heavens and the new earth, which I will make, shall remain before me, saith the Lord, so shall your seed and your name remain" (Isa. lxv. 17; lxvi. 22). The period of the close of the one dispensation and the commencement of the other is spoken of as "the last days," and "the end of the world," and is described as such a shaking of the earth and heavens as should lead to the removal of the things which were shaken. (Hagg. ii. 6; Heb. xiv. 26, 27.)'

It appears, then, that if Scripture be the best interpreter of Scripture, we have in the Old Testament a key to the interpretation of the prophecies in the New. The same symbolism is found in both, and the imagery of Isaiah, Ezekiel, and the other prophets helps us to understand the imagery of St. Matthew, St. Peter, and St. John. As the dissolution of the material world is not necessary to fulfilment of Old Testament prophecy, neither is it necessary to the accomplishment of the predictions of the New Testament. But though symbols are metaphorical expressions, they are not unmeaning. It is not necessary to allegorise them, and find a corresponding equivalent for every trope; it is sufficient to regard the imagery as employed to heighten the sublimity of the prediction and to clothe it with impressiveness and grandeur. There are, at the same time, a true propriety and an underlying reality in the symbols of prophecy. The moral and spiritual facts which they represent, the social and ecumenical changes which they typify, could not be adequately set forth by language less majestic and sublime. There is reason for believing that an inadequate apprehension of the real grandeur and significance of such events as the destruction of Jerusalem and the abrogation of the Jewish economy lies at the root of that system of interpretation which maintains that nothing answering to the symbols of New Testament prophecy has ever taken place. Hence the uncritical and unscriptural figments of double senses, and double, triple, and multiple fulfilments of prophecy. That physical disturbances in nature and extraordinary phenomena in the heavens and in the earth may have accompanied the expiring throes of the Jewish dispensation we are not prepared to deny. It seems to us highly probable that such things were. But the literal fulfilment of the symbols is not essential to the verification of the prophecy, which is abundantly proved to be true by the recorded facts of history.

The apostle makes a distribution of the world into *heaven* and *earth*, and saith they were destroyed with water, and perished. We know that neither the fabric nor substance of the one or other was destroyed, but only men that liveth on the earth; and the apostle tells us (ver. 7) of *the heaven and earth that were then, and were destroyed by water*, distinct from *the heavens and the earth that were now, and were to be consumed by fire*; and yet as to the visible fabric of heaven and earth they were the same both before the flood and in the apostle's time, and continue so to this day; when yet it is certain that the heavens and earth, whereof he spake, were to be destroyed and consumed by fire in that generation. We must, then, for the clearing of our foundation a little, consider what the apostle intends by the heavens and the earth in these two places.

NOTE D

' 1. It is certain that what the apostle intends by the world, with its heaven, and earth (vers. 5, 6), which was destroyed; the same, or some-what of that kind, he intends by the heavens and the earth that were to be consumed and destroyed by fire (ver. 7); otherwise there would be no coherence in the apostle's discourse, nor any kind of argument, but a mere fallacy of words.

' 2. It is certain that by the flood, the world, or the fabric of heaven and earth, was not destroyed, but only the inhabitants of the world; and therefore the destruction intimated to succeed by fire is not of the substance of the heavens and the earth, which shall not be consumed until the last day, but of person or men living in the world.

'3. Then we must consider in what sense men living in the world are said to be the world, and the heavens and earth of it. I shall only insist on one instance to this purpose among many that may be produced: Isa. li. 15, 16. The time when the work here mentioned, of planting the heavens and laying the foundation of the earth, was performed by God was when He *divided the sea* (ver. 15) and *gave the law* (ver. 16), and said to Zion, *Thou art my people*; that is, when He took the children of Israel out of Egypt, and formed them in the wilderness into a church and state; then He planted the heavens and laid the foundation of the earth: that is, brought forth order, and government, and beauty from the confusion wherein before they were. This is the planting of the heavens and laying the foundation of the earth in the world. And since it is that when mention is made of the destruction of a state and government, it is in that language which seems to set forth the end of the world. So Isa. xxxiv. 4, which is yet but the destruction of the state of Edom. The like also is affirmed of the *Roman* Empire (Rev. vi. 14), which the Jews constantly affirm to be intended by

Edom in the prophets. And in our Saviour Christ's prediction of the destruction of Jerusalem (Matt. xxiv.) He sets it out by expressions of the same importance. It is evident, then, that in the prophetical idiom and manner of speech, by heavens and earth, the civil and religious state and combination of men in the world, and the men of them, were often understood. So were the heavens and earth that world which then was destroyed by the flood.

' 4. On this foundation I affirm that the heavens and earth here intended in this prophecy of Peter, the coming of the Lord, the day of judgment and perdition of ungodly men, mentioned in the destruction of that heaven and earth, do all of them relate, not to the last and final judgment of the world, but to that utter desolation and destruction that was to be made of the Judaical church and state; for which I shall offer these two reasons, of many that might be insisted on from the text:-

'(1.) Because whatever is here mentioned was to have its peculiar influence on the men of that generation. He speaks of that wherein both the profane scoffers and those scoffed at were concerned, and that as *Jews*, some of them believing, others opposing, the faith. Now there was no particular concernment of that generation, nor in that sin, nor in that scoffing, as to the day of judgment in general; but there was a peculiar relief for the one and a peculiar dread for the other at hand, in the destruction of the Jewish nation; and, besides, an ample testimony both to the one and the other of the power and dominion of the Lord Jesus Christ, which was the thing in question between them.

'(2.) Peter tells them, that after the destruction and judgment that he speaks of (vers. 7-13), " We, according to his promise, look for new heavens and a new earth,' etc. They had this expectation. But what is that promise? Where may we find it? Why, we have it in the very words and letter, Isa. lxv. 17. Now, when shall this be that God shall create these new heavens and new earth, wherein dwelleth righteousness? Saith Peter, " It shall be after the coming of the Lord, after that judgment and destruction of ungodly men, who obey not the gospel, that I foretell." But now it is evident from this place of Isaiah, with chap. lxvi. 21, 22, that this is a prophecy of Gospel times only; and that the planting of these new heavens is nothing but the creation of Gospel ordinances to endure for ever. The same thing is so expressed Heb. xii. 26-28.

This being the design of the place, I shall not insist longer on the context, but briefly open the words proposed, and fix upon the truth continued in them.

First, There is the foundation of the apostle's inference and exhortation, seeing that all these things, however precious they seem, or what value soever any put upon them, shall be dissolved, that is, destroyed; and that in that dreadful and fearful manner before mentioned, in a day of judgment, wrath, and vengeance, by fire and sword; let others mock at the threats of Christ's coming: He will come- He will not tarry; and then the heavens and earth that God Himself planted, -the sun, moon, and stars of the Judaical polity and church, -the whole old world of worship and worshippers, that stand out in their obstinancy against the Lord Christ, shall be sensibly dissolved and destroyed: this we know shall be the end of these things, and that shortly.

There is no outward constitution nor frame of things in government or nations, but it is subject to a dissolution, and may receive it, and that in a way of judgment. If any might plead exemption, that, on many accounts, of which the apostle was discoursing in prophetical terms (for it was not yet time to speak it openly to all) might interpose for its share.' (Dr. Owen's Sermon on 2 Peter iii. 11. Works, folio, Reprinted 1721.)

NOTE E

The Rev. F. D. Maurice on 'the Last Time.' (1 John ii. 18)

'How could St. John say that his time was the last time? Has not the world lasted nearly one thousand eight hundred years since he left it? May it not last yet many years more?

'You will be told by many that not only St. John, but St. Paul, and all the apostles, laboured under the delusion that the end of all things was approaching in their day. People say so who are not in general disposed to undervalue their authority; some adopt the opinion practically, though they may not express it in words, who hold that the writers of the Bible were never permitted to make a mistake in the most trifling point. I do not say that; it would not shake my faith in them to find that they had erred in names or points of chronology. But if I supposed they had been misled themselves, and had misled their disciples, on so capital a subject as this of Christ's coming to judgment, and of the latter days, I should be greatly perplexed. For it is a subject to which they are constantly referring. It is a part of their deepest faith. It mingles with all their practical exhortations. If they were wrong here, I cannot myself see where they can have been right.

'I have found their language on this subject of the greatest possible use to me in explaining the method of the Bible; the course of God's government over nations and over individuals; the life of the world before the time of the apostles, during their time, and in all the centuries since. If we will do them the justice which we owe to every writer, inspired or uninspired,---if we will allow them to interpret themselves, instead of forcing our interpretations upon them, we shall, I think, understand a little more of their work, and of ours. If we take their words simply and literally respecting the judgment and the end which they were expecting in their day, we shall know what position they were occupying with respect to their forefathers and to us. And in place of a very vague, powerless, and artificial conception of the judgment which we are to look for, we shall learn what our needs are by theirs; how God will fulfil all His words to us by the way in which He fulfilled His words to them.

'It is not a new notion, but a very old and common one, that the history of the world is divided into certain great periods. In our days the conviction that there is a broad distinction between ancient and modern history has been forcing itself more and more upon thoughtful men. M. Guizot dwells especially upon the unity and universality of modern history, as contrasted with the division of ancient history into a set of nations which had scarcely any common sympathies. The question is, where to find the boundary between these two periods. About these, students have made many guesses; most of them have been plausible and suggestive of truths; some very confusing; none, I think, satisfactory. One of the most popular,---that which supposes modern history to begin when the barbarous tribes settled themselves in Europe, would be quite fatal to M. Guizot's doctrine. For that settlement, although it was a most important and indispensable event to modern civilisation, was the temporary breaking up of a unity which had existed before. It was like the re-appearance of that separation of tribes and races, which he supposes to have been the especial characteristic of the former world.

'Now, may we expect any light upon this subject in the Bible? I do not think it would fulfil its pretensions if we might not. It professes to set forth the ways of God to nations and to mankind. We might be well content that it should tell us very little about physical laws; we might be content that it should be silent about the courses of the planets and law of gravitation. God may have other ways of making *these* secrets known to His creatures. But that which concerns the moral order of the world and the spiritual progress of human beings falls directly within the province of the Bible. No one could be satisfied with it if it was dumb respecting these. And accordingly all who suppose it is dumb here, however much importance they may attach to what they call its religious character,---however much they may suppose their highest interests to depend upon a belief in its oracles, are obliged to treat it as a very disjointed fragmentary volume. They afford the best excuse for those who say that it is not a whole book, as we have thought it, but a collection of the sayings and opinions of certain authors, in different ages, not very consistent with each other. On the other hand, there has been the strongest conviction in the minds of ordinary readers, as well as of students, that the book does tell us how the ages past, and the ages to come, are concerned in the unveiling of God's mysteries,---what part one country and another has played in His great drama,---to what point all the lines in His providence are converging. The immense interest which has been taken in prophecy,---an interest not destroyed, nor even weakened, by the numerous disappointments which men's theories about it have had to encounter, is a proof how deep and widely-spread this conviction is. Divines endeavour in vain to recall simple and earnest readers from the study of the prophecies by urging that they have not leisure for such a pursuit, and that they ought to busy themselves with what is more practical. If their consciences tell them that there is some ground for they warning, they yet feel as if they could not heed it altogether. They are sure that they have an interest in the destinies of their race, as well as in their own individual destiny. They cannot separate the one from the other; they must believe that there is light somewhere about both. I dare not discourage such an assurance. If we hold it strongly, it may be a great instrument of raising us out of our selfishness. I am only afraid lest we should lose it, as we certainly shall if we contract the habit of regarding the Bible as a book of puzzles and conundrums, and of looking restlessly for certain outward events to happen at certain dates that we have fixed upon as those which the prophets and apostles have set down. The cure for such follies, which are very serious indeed, lies not in the neglect of prophecy, but in more earnest meditation upon it; remembering that prophecy is not a set of loose predictions, like the sayings of the fortune-teller, but an unfolding of Him whose going forth are from everlasting; who is the same yesterday, and to-day, and for ever; whose acts in one generation are determined by the same laws as His acts in another.

'If I should ever speak to you of the Apocalypse of St. John I shall have to enter much more at large on this subject. But so much I have said to introduce the remark that the Bible treats the downfall of the Jewish polity as the winding-up of a great period in human history and as the commencement of another great period. John the Baptist announces the presence of One "whose fan is in his hand; and he will thoroughly purge his floor, and gather his wheat into the garner; but he will burn up the chaff with unquenchable fire." The evangelists say, that by these words he denoted that Jesus of Nazareth, who afterwards went down into the waters of Jordan, and as He came out of it was declared to be the Son of God, and on whom the Spirit descended in a bodily shape.

'*We* are wont to separate Jesus the Saviour from Jesus the King and the Judge. They do not. They tell us from the first that He came preaching a kingdom of heaven. They tell us of His doing acts of judgment as well as acts of deliverance. They report the tremendous words which He spoke to Pharisees and Scribes, as well as the Gospel which He preached to publicans and sinners. And before the end of His ministry, when His disciples were asking Him about the buildings of the temple, He spoke plainly of a judgment which He, the Son of man, should execute before that generation was over. And to make it clear that He meant us to understand Him strictly and literally, He added,---"Heaven and earth shall pass away, but my words shall not pass away." This discourse, which is carefully reported to us by St. Matthew, St. Mark and St. Luke, does not stand aloof from the rest of His discourses and parables, nor from the rest of His deeds. They all contain the same warning. They are gracious and merciful,---far more gracious and merciful than we have even supposed them to be; they are witnesses of a gracious and merciful Being; but they are witnesses that those who did not like that Being just because this was His character,---who sought for another being like themselves, that is, for an ungracious and unmerciful being---would have their houses left to them desolate.

'When, therefore, the apostles went forth after our Lord's ascension, to preach His Gospel and baptize in His name, their first duty was to announce that that Jesus whom the rulers of Jerusalem had crucified was both Lord and Christ; their second was to preach remission of sins and the gift of the Spirit in His name; their third was to foretell the coming of a great and terrible day of the Lord, and to say to all who hear, "Save yourself from this untoward generation." It was the language which St. Peter used on the day of Pentecost,; it was adopted with such variations as befitted the circumstances of the hearers by all who were entrusted with the Gospel message. It was no doubt peculiarly applicable to the Jews. They had been made the stewards of God's gifts to the world. They had wasted their Master's goods, and were to be no longer stewards. But we do not find the apostles confining their language to the Jews. St. Paul, speaking at Athens,---speaking in words specially appropriate to a cultivated, philosophical, heathen city,---declares that God "has appointed a day in the which he will judge the world by that Man whom he hath ordained," and points to the resurrection from the dead as determining who that Man is. Why was this? Because apostles believed that the rejection of the Jewish people was the manifestation of the *Son of Man*; a witness to all nations who their King was; a call to all nations to cast away their idols and confess Him. The Gospel was to explain the meaning of the great crisis which was about to occur; to tell the Gentiles as well as the Jews what it would imply; to announce it as nothing less than the commencement of a new era in the world's history, when the crucified Man would claim an universal empire, and would contend with the Roman Caesar as well as with all other tyrants of the earth who should set up their claims against His.

'This Scriptural view of the ordering of times and seasons entirely harmonizes with that conclusion at which M. Guizot has arrived by an observation of facts. Our Lord's birth nearly coincided with the establishment of the Roman Empire in the person of Augustus Caesar. That empire aspired to crush the nations and to establish a great world supremacy. The Jewish nation had been the witness against all such experiments in the old world. It had fallen under the Babylonian tyranny, but it had risen again. And the time which followed its captivity was the great time of the awakening of national life of Europe,---the time in which the Greek republics flourished,---the time in which the Roman Republic commenced its grand career.

'The Jewish nation had been overcome by the armies of the Roman Republic; still it retained the ancient signs of its nationality, its law, its priesthood, its temple. These looked ridiculous and insignificant to the Roman emperors, even to the Roman governors who ruled the little province of Judea, or the larger province of Syria, in which it was often reckoned. But they found the Jews very troublesome. Their nationality was of a peculiar kind, and of unusual strength. When they were most degraded they could not part with it. They would stir up endless rebellions, in the hope of recovering what they had lost, and of establishing the universal kingdom which they believed was intended for them, and not for Rome. the preaching of our Lord declared to them that there was such an universal kingdom,---that He, the Son of David, had come to set it up on the earth. The Jews dreamed of another kind of kingdom, with another kind of king. They wanted a Jewish kingdom, which should trample upon the nations, just as the Roman Empire was trampling upon them; they wanted a Jewish king who should be in all essentials like the Roman Caesar. It was a dark, horrible, hateful conception; it combined all that is narrowest in the most degraded exclusive form of nationality, with all that is cruellest, most destructive of moral and personal life in the worst form of imperialism. It gathered up into itself all that was worst in the history of the past. It was a shadowing forth of what should be worst in the coming time. The apostles announced that the accursed ambition of the Jews would be utterly disappointed. They said that a new age was at hand---the universal age, the age of the Son of man, which would be preceded by a great crisis that would shake not earth only, but also heaven: not that only which belonged to time, but also all that belonged to the spiritual world, and to man's relations with it. They said that this shaking would be that it might be seen what there was which could not be shaken---which must abide.

'I have tried thus to show you what St. John mean by *the last time*, if he spoke the same language as our Lord spoke, and as the other apostles spoke. I cannot tell what physical changes he or they may have looked for. Physical phenomena are noticed at that time,---famines, plagues, earthquakes. Whether they, or any of them, supposed that these indicated more alteration in the surface or the substance of the earth than they did indicate, I cannot tell; these are not the points upon which I look for information if they gave it. That they did not anticipate the passing away of the *earth*,---what we call the destruction of the earth,---is clear from this, that the new kingdom they spoke of was to be a kingdom on earth as well as a kingdom of heaven. But their belief that such a kingdom had been set up, and would make its power felt as soon as the old nation was scattered, has, I think, been abundantly verified by fact. I do not see how we can understand modern history properly till we accept that belief.'

1. The Epistles of St. John, by F.D. Maurice, M.A., Lect. ix.

Part Three - The Parousia in the Apocalypse.

'The book of Revelation will probably never now admit of a wholly luminous exposition, in consequence of the histories we have of the times to which it refers not corresponding to the magnified scale of its prophecies. But the direction in which it is most wise to seek for a solution of its enigmas is from that standing-point which considers that it was written before the destruction of Jerusalem, to encourage those whose hearts were then failing them for fear of those things which were then speedily coming upon the earth; that is, taken up primarily and principally with events with which its first readers only were immediately interested; that it displays a series of pictures doubtfully chronological, and perchance partly contemporaneous, of events all shortly to come to pass.'---Catholic Thoughts on the Bible and Theology, chap. xxxv. p. 361.

INTERPRETATION OF THE APOCALYPSE.

We come now to the consideration of the most difficult and obscure part of divine Revelation, and we may well pause on the threshold of a region so shrouded in mystery and darkness. The conspicuous failures of the wise and learned men who have too confidently professed to decipher the mystic scroll of the apocalyptic Seer warn us against presumption. We might even feel justified in declining altogether a task which has baffled so many of the ablest and best interpreters of the Word of God. But, on the other hand, do we honour the book by refusing to open it, and pronouncing it hopelessly obscure? Are we justified in so treating any portion of the Revelation which God has given us? Is the book to be virtually handed over to diviners and charlatans, to be the sport of their fantastic speculations? No; we cannot pass it by. The book holds us, whether we will or no, and insists upon being heard. After all, it must have a meaning, and we are bound to do our best to understand that meaning. Wonderful book! that, after ages of misinterpretation and perversion, has still the power to command the attention and fascinate the interest of every reader. It refuses to be made the laughing-stock of imposture and folly; it cannot be degraded even by the ignorance and presumption of fanatics and soothsayers; it can never be other than the Word of God, and is therefore to be held in reverence by us.

But is it intelligible? The answer to this is, Was it written to be understood? Was a book sent by an apostle to the churches in Asia Minor, with a benediction on its readers, a mere unintelligible jargon, an inexplicable enigma, to them? That can hardly be true. Yet if the book were meant to unveil the secrets of distant times, must it not of necessity have been unintelligible to its first readers---and not only unintelligible, but even irrelevant and useless. If it spake, as some would have us believe, of Huns and Goths and Saracens, of mediaeval emperors and popes, of the Protestant Reformation and the French Revolution, what possible interest or meaning could it have for the Christian churches of Ephesus, and Smyrna, and Philadelphia, and Laodicea? Especially when we consider the actual circumstances of those early Christians,---many of them enduring cruel sufferings and grievous persecutions, and all of them eagerly looking for an approaching hour of deliverance which was now close at hand,---what purpose could it have answered to send them a document which they were urged to read and ponder, which was yet mainly occupied with historical events so distant as to be beyond the range of their sympathies, and so obscure that even at this day the shrewdest critics are hardly agreed on any one point? Is it conceivable that an apostle would mock the sufferings and persecuted Christians of his time with dark parables about distant ages? If this book were really intended to minister faith and comfort to the very persons to whom it was sent, it must unquestionably deal with matters in which they were practically and personally interested. And does not this very obvious consideration suggest the true key to the Apocalypse? *Must if not of necessity refer to matters of contemporary history?* The only tenable, the only reasonable, hypothesis is that it was intended to be understood by its original readers; but this is as much as to say that it must be occupied with the events and transactions of their own day, and these comprised within a comparatively brief space of time.

LIMITATION OF TIME IN THE APOCALYPSE.

This is not a mere conjecture, it is certified by the express statements of the book. If there be one thing which more than any other is explicitly and repeatedly affirmed in the Apocalypse it is the *nearness* of the events which it predicts. This is stated, and reiterated again and again, in the beginning, the middle, and the end. We are warned that 'the time is *at hand;*' 'These things must *shortly* come to pass,' 'Behold, I come *quickly;*' 'Surely I come *quickly.*' Yet, in the face of these express and oft-repeated declarations, most interpreters have felt at liberty to ignore the limitations of time altogether, and to roam at will over ages and centuries, regarding the book as a syllabus of church history, an almanac of politico-ecclesiastical events for all Christendom to the end of time. This has been a fatal and inexcusable blunder. To neglect the obvious and clear definition of the time so constantly thrust on the attention of the reader by the book itself is to stumble on the very threshold. Accordingly this inattention has vitiated by far the greatest number of apocalyptic interpretations. It may truly be said that the key has all the while hung by the door, plainly visible to every one who had eyes to see; yet men have tried to pick the lock, or force the door, or climb up some other way, rather than avail themselves of so simple and ready a way of admission as to use the key made and provided for them.

As this is a point of highest importance, and indispensable to the right interpretation of the Apocalypse, it is proper to bring forward the proof that the events depicted in the book are comprehended within a very brief period of time.

The opening sentence, containing what may be called the *title* of the book, is of itself decisive of the nearness of the events to which it relates:---

CHAP. i. 1.---'The Revelation of Jesus Christ, which God gave unto him, to shew unto his servants what things must *shortly come to pass.'*

And in case it might be supposed that this limitation does not extend to the whole prophecy, but may refer only to the introductory, or some other, portion, the same statement recurs, in the same words, at the conclusion of the book. (See chap. xxii. 6.)

CHAP. i. 3.---'Blessed is he that readeth, and they that hear the words of this prophecy, and keep those things which are written therein: *for the time is at hand.'*

The reader will not fail to notice the significant resemblance between this note of time and the watchword of the early Christians. To say o kairoz egguz (the time is at hand) was indeed the same thing in effect as to say o kusioz egguz (the Lord is at hand), Phil. iv. 5. No words could more distinctly affirm the nearness of the events contained in the prophecy.

CHAP i. 7.---'Behold, he cometh with clouds; and every eye shall see him, and they also which pierced him: and all the tribes of the land shall wail because of him. Even so, Amen.'

'Behold, he is coming' [Idou, ercetai], corresponds to 'Behold, I am coming quickly' [Idou, ercomai], in Rev. xxii. 7. This may be called the keynote of the Apocalypse; it is the thesis or text of the whole. To those who can persuade themselves that there is no indication of time in such a declaration as 'Behold, he is coming,' or that it is so indefinite that it may apply equally to a year, a century, or a millennium, this passage may not be convincing; but to every candid judgment it will be decisive proof that the event referred to is imminent. It is the apostolic watch word, 'Maran-atha!' 'the Lord is coming' (1 Cor. xvi. 22). There is a distinct allusion also to the words of our Lord in Matt. xxiv. 30, 'All the tribes of the land shall mourn,' etc., plainly showing that both passages refer to the same period and the same event.

CHAP i. 19.---'Write the things which thou hast seen, and the things which are, and the things which shall be hereafter.'

The last clause does not adequately express the sense of the original; it should be 'the things which are *about to happen after these'* [a mellei genesqai meta tauta].

CHAP. iii. 10.---'I will keep thee from the hour of temptation [trial], which shall come [*is about to come*] upon all the world, to try them that dwell upon the earth.'

Indicative of the near approach of a season of violent persecution, shortly before the breaking out of which the Apocalypse must have been written.

CHAP. iii. 11.---'Behold, I come quickly.'

This warning not is repeated again and again throughout the Apocalypse. Its meaning is too evident to require explanation.

CHAP. xvi. 15.---'Behold, I come as a thief.'

This figure is already known to us in connection with the Parousia. St. Peter declared 'the day of the Lord will come as a thief' [in the night] (2 Pet. iii. 10). St. Paul wrote to the Thessalonians, 'Yourselves know perfectly that the day of the Lord so cometh as a thief in the night' (1 Thess. v. 2). And both these passages look back to our Lord's own words Matt. xxiv. 42-44, in which He inculcated watchfulness by the parable of 'the thief coming in the night.' Here, again, the time and the event referred to are the same in all the passages, and were declared by our Lord to lie within the limits of the generation then existing.

CHAP. xxi. 5, 6.---'And he that sat upon the throne said, Behold, I make all things new.... And he saith unto me, It is done.'

These expressions are evidently indicative of events hastening rapidly to their accomplishment; there was to be no long interval between the prophecy and its fulfilment.

CHAP. xxii. 10.---'And he saith unto me, Seal not the sayings of the prophecy of this book: for the time is at hand.'

This is only the repetition in another form of the declaration in the preceding statement. How can it be possible to attach a non-natural sense to language so express and decisive?

CHAP. xxii. 6.---'And he said unto me, These sayings are faithful and true; and the Lord God of the holy prophets sent his angel to shew unto his servants the things which must shortly be done.'

This passage, which repeats the declaration made at the commencement of the prophecy (chap. i. 1), covers the whole field of the Apocalypse, and conclusively establishes the fact that it alludes to events which were almost immediately to take place.

CHAP. xxii. 7.---'Behold, I come quickly.'

CHAP. xxii. 12.---'Behold, I come quickly.'

CHAP. xxii. 20.---'Surely I come quickly.'

This threefold reiteration of the speedy coming of the Lord, which is the theme of the whole prophecy, distinctly shows that that event was authoritatively declared to be at hand.

Thus we have an accumulation of evidence of the most direct and positive kind that the whole of the Apocalypse was to be fulfilled within a very brief period. This is its own testimony, and to this limitation we are absolutely shut up, if the book is to be permitted to speak for itself.

DATE OF THE APOCALYPSE.

If the foregoing conclusions are well founded, they virtually decide the much-debated questions respecting the date of the Apocalypse. Perhaps it may be admitted that the weight of authority, such as it is, inclines to the side of the late date: that is, that it was written after the destruction of Jerusalem; but the internal evidence seems to us overwhelming on the side of its early date. That the Apocalypse contemplates the Parousia as imminent is surely an incontrovertible proposition. That the Parousia is always represented as coincident with the judgment of the guilty city and nation is no less undeniable. Those who cannot find the Parousia, the destruction of Jerusalem, the judgment of Israel, and the end of the age [sunteleia tou aionos] in the Apocalypse, as in all the rest of the New Testament, and find them also as impending events, must be blind indeed. What other tremendous crisis was approaching at that period to which the Apocalypse could refer? Or what event could be more worthy to be described in the sublime and awful imagery of the Apocalypse than the final catastrophe of the Jewish dispensation, and the unparalleled woes by which it was accompanied?

1. That the Apocalypse was written before the destruction of Jerusalem will follow as a matter of course if it can be shown that that event forms in great measure the subject of its predictions. This, we believe, can be done so as to satisfy any reasonable mind. We appeal to chap. i. 7: 'Behold he cometh with clouds; and every eye shall see him, and they also which pierced him: and all the tribes of the land shall wail because of him.' 'The tribes of the land' can only mean the people of Israel, as is proved by the original prophecy in Zech. xii. 10-14, and still more by the language of our Saviour in Matt. xxiv. 30. There cannot be the shadow of a doubt that the 'coming' referred to is the Parousia, the precursor of judgment, terrible to those 'who pierced him,' and always declared by our Lord to lie within the limits of the existing generation.

2. After the fullest consideration of the remarkable expression th kuriakh hmera [the Lord's day], in Rev. i. 10, we are satisfied that it cannot refer to the first day of the week, but that those interpreters are right who understand it to refer to the period called elsewhere 'the day of the Lord.' There is no example in the New Testament of the first day of the week [Sunday] being called 'the Lord's day,' or 'the day of the Lord;' but the latter phrase is appropriated and restricted by usage to the great judicial period which is constantly represented in Scripture as associated with the Parousia. There is no difference whatever between h hmera kuriakh and h hmera tou kuriou. Nothing could be more violent than to refer to one phrase to one period or day, and the other to a totally different one. There is no evidence that the phrase, 'the day of the Lord,' had a fixed and definite meaning in the apostolic churches. (See 1 Cor. i. 8, v. 5; 2 Cor. i. 14; 2 Thess. ii. 2, v. 2; 2 Pet. iii. 10.) Notwithstanding Alford's objection on the score of grammar, we hold that there is nothing ungrammatical in the construction which regards th kuriakh hmera as 'the (great) day of the Lord.' On the contrary, we prefer the construction, on the score of the grammar, 'I was in spirit in the day of the Lord.' That is to say, the Parousia is the stand-point of the Seer in the Apocalypse: a fact which is amply borne out by the contents.

3. In Rev. iii. 10 we are informed that a season of severe trial was then imminent, viz. a bitter persecution of those who bore the Christian name, extending over the whole world [oikoumenh---or the Roman Empire]. Now the first general persecution of Christians was that which took place under Nero, A.D. 64. We infer that this was the persecution then impending, and therefore that the Apocalypse was written prior to that date.

4. That the book was written before the destruction of Jerusalem appears from the fact that the city and temple are spoken of as still in existence. (See chap. xi. 1, 2, 8.) It is scarcely probable that if Jerusalem had been a heap of ruins the apostle would have received a command to measure the temple; should represent the Holy City as about to be trodden down by the Gentiles; or that he should see the witnesses lie unburied in its streets.

5. But, in truth, the Apocalypse itself is the great argument for its having been written prior to the destruction of Jerusalem. To suppose its prophetical character, and make it bear the same relation to the great consummation called in the New Testament 'the end of the age' that the Iliad bears to the siege of Troy. It may be safely affirmed that on this hypothesis it is incapable of interpretation: it must continue to be what is has so long been, the material for arbitrary

and fanciful speculation; ever changing with the changing aspect of the political and ecclesiastical world. But we venture to think that if the views advocated in this volume are correct, the interpretation of the Apocalypse becomes possible, and that such interpretation will carry with it its own evidence, commending itself by its consistency and fitness to every fair and candid judgment. A true interpretation speaks for itself; and as the right key fits the lock, and so demonstrates its adaptation, so a true interpretation will prove its correctness by satisfactorily showing the correspondence between the historical fact and the prophetical symbol:

THE TRUE SIGNIFICANCE OF THE APOCALYPSE.

We are now better prepared to grapple with the question, What is the real meaning of the Apocalypse? The fact that, by its own showing, the action of the book must necessarily be comprehended within a very short space of time, and the knowledge (approximately) of the date of its composition, are important aids to a correct apprehension of its object and scope. To regard it as a revelation of the distant future, when it expressly declares that it treats of things which must shortly come to pass; and to look for its fulfilment in mediaeval or modern history, when it affirms that the time is at hand, is to ignore its plainest teaching, and to ensure misconception and failure. We are absolutely shut up by the book itself to the contemporary history of the period, and that, too, within very narrow limits.

And here we find an explanation of what must have struck most thoughtful readers of the evangelic history as extremely singular, namely, the total absence in the Fourth Gospel of that which occupies so conspicuous a place in the Synoptical Gospels,---the great prophecy of our Lord on the Mount of Olives. The silence of St. John in his gospel is the more remarkable that he was one of the four favoured disciples who listened to that discourse; yet, in his gospel we find no trace of it whatever. How is this to be accounted for? It may be said that the full reports of that prophecy by the other evangelists rendered any allusion to it by St. John unnecessary; yet, remembering the intense interest of the subject to every Jewish heart, and its bearing upon the apostolic churches generally, it does seem unaccountable that no notice should be taken of so important a prediction by the only one of its original auditors who left a record of the discourses of Christ. But the difficulty is explained if it should be found that *the Apocalypse is nothing else than a transfigured form of the prophecy on the Mount of Olives.* And this we believe to be the fact. The Apocalypse contains our Lord's great prophecy expanded, allegorised, and, if we may so say, dramatised. The same facts and events which are predicted in the Gospels are shown in the Revelation, only clothed in a more figurative and symbolical dress. They pass before us like scenes exhibited by the magic lantern, magnified and illuminated, but not on that account the less real and truthful. In this view the Apocalypse becomes the supplement to the gospel, and gives completeness to the record of the evangelist.

This may at first sight appear a gratuitous and fanciful hypothesis, but the more it is considered the more probable it will be found. We cordially subscribe to the following words of Dr. Alford:---

'The close connection between our Lord's prophetic discourse on the Mount of Olives, and the line of apocalyptic prophecy, cannot fail to have struck every student of Scripture. If it be suggested that such connection may be merely apparent, and we subject it to the test of more accurate examination, our first impression will, I think, become continually stronger that the two (being revelations from the same Lord concerning things to come, and those things being, as it seems to me, bound by the fourfold epcou, which introduces the seals, to the same reference to Christ's coming) must, corresponding as they do in order and significance, answer to one another in detail; and thus the discourse in Matt. xxiv. becomes, as Mr. Isaac Williams has truly named it, *"the anchor of apocalyptic interpretation;"* and, I may add, the touchstone of apocalyptic systems.'

Even a slight comparison of the two documents, the prophecy and the Apocalypse, will suffice to show the correspondence between them. The *dramatis personae,* if we may so call them,---the symbols which enter into the composition of both,---are the same. What do we find in our Lord's prophecy? First and chiefly the Parousia; then wars, famines, pestilence, earthquakes; false prophets and deceivers; signs and wonders; the darkening of the sun and moon; the stars falling from heaven; angels and trumpets, eagles and carcases, great tribulation and woe; convulsions of nature; the treading down of Jerusalem; the Son of man coming in the clouds of heaven; the gathering of the elect; the reward of the faithful; the judgment of the wicked. And are not these precisely the elements which compose the Apocalypse? This cannot be accidental resemblance,---it is coincidence, it is identity. What difference there is in the treatment of the subject arises from the difference in the method of the revelation. The prophecy is addressed to the ear, and the Apocalypse to the eye: the one is a discourse delivered in broad day, amid the realities of actual life,---the other is a vision, beheld in a state of ecstasy, clothed in gorgeous imagery, with an air of unreality as in objects seen in a dream; requiring it to be translated back into the language of everyday life before it can be intelligible as actual fact.

STRUCTURE AND PLAN OF THE APOCALYPSE.

As commonly interpreted nothing can be more loose and unconnected than the arrangement of the Apocalypse. It seems an intricate maze, without any intelligible plan, ranging through time and space, and forming a chaos of heterogeneous ages, nations, and incidents. In reality there is no literary composition more regular in its structure, more methodical in its arrangement, more artistic in its design. No Greek tragedy is composed with greater art or more strict attention to dramatic laws. It is no exaggeration to say with the learned Henry More, 'There never was any book penned with that artifice as this of the Apocalypse, as if every word were weighed in a balance before it was set down.' Yet the plan of its construction is simple, and almost self-evident. The number *seven* governs it throughout. The most unobservant reader cannot fail to notice four of its great divisions which are distinguished by this mystic number,---the seven churches, the seven seals, the seven trumpets, and the seven vials. As every division has certain marked characteristics by which its beginning and ending are distinctly indicated, it is not difficult to draw the lines between the several divisions. In addition to the four already specified we find other three visions, viz. the vision of the sun-clad woman, the vision of the great harlot, and the vision of the bride. These complete the mystic number seven, and form the clear and well-defined arrangement into which the contents of the Apocalypse naturally fall. It would be difficult indeed to invent any other. There are also a preface, or prologue, at the commencement of the book, and an epilogue, at the conclusion; so that the whole arrangement stands as follows:---

Prologue	Chap. i. 1-8
1. Vision of the Seven Churches	Chap. i. ii. iii.
2. Vision of the Seven Seals	Chap. iv. v. vi. vii.
3. Vision of the Seven Trumpets	Chap. viii. ix. x. xi.
4. Vision of the Sun-clad Woman	Chap. xii. xiii. xiv.
5. Vision of the Seven Vials	Chap. xv. xvi.
6. Vision of the Great Harlot	Chap. xvii. xviii. xix. xx.
7. Vision of the Bride	Chap. xxi. xxii. 1-5
Epilogue	Chap. xxii. 8-21

Such is the natural self-arrangement of the book, so far as its great leading divisions are concerned; there are also several subordinate divisions, or episodes as they may be called, which fall under one or other of the great divisions. We shall find that in the different visions there is a common structural resemblance, and that, more particularly, each division concludes with a *finale*, or catastrophe, representing an act of judgment or a scene of victory and triumph.

But the most remarkable feature in the Apocalypse, so far as its structure is concerned, remains to be noticed. It is that the several visions may be described as only *varied representations of the same facts or events;* re-arrangements and new combinations of the same constituent elements. This is obviously the case with two of the great divisions, viz. the vision of the seven trumpets and that of the seven vials. These are almost counterparts of each other; and though the resemblance between the other visions is not so marked, yet it will be found that they are all *different aspects of the same great event.* If we may venture to use such an illustration we should say that the visions are not *telescopic,* looking at the distant; but *kaleidoscopic,*---every turn of the instrument producing a new combination of images, exquisitely beautiful and gorgeous, while the elements which compose the picture remain substantially the same. As Pharoah's dream was *one,* though seen under *two* different forms, so the visions of the Apocalypse are *one,* though presented in seven different aspects. The reason of the repetition is probably in both cases the same. 'For that the dream was doubled unto Pharoah twic, it is because the thing is established by God, and God will shortly bring it to pass''(Gen. xli. 32). In like manner the events foreshadowed in the Apocalypse are declared by their sevenfold repetition to be *sure* and *near.*

THE NUMBER SEVEN IN THE APOCALYPSE.

Every reader of the Apocalypse must be struck by the manner in which certain numerals are employed, not so much in an arithmetical sense as in a symbolical. The numbers three, four, seven, ten, and twelve, the half of seven, and the square of twelve, are used in this significant manner. Of all those mystic numbers, as they may be called, *seven* is the dominant one, which we find continually recurring from beginning to end of the book. That it is invariably used in a symbolical, and never in a literal and arithmetical, sense we will not venture to assert, but that it is frequently, if not generally, so employed must be apparent to every thoughtful reader. It was the number of dignity among the Jews, the symbol of totality or perfection, and signifies *all* of the species, or the highest kind of the species, to which it refers. It is not necessary where this number occurs to require the full tale of units to be made up; it simply means completeness or excellence. Thus we have seven churches, seven seals, seven trumpets, seven vials, seven spirits, seven lamps, seven horns, seven eyes, seven stars, seven mountains, seven kings. It would be absurd to require the exact arithmetical value in all these instances, though it would be rash to affirm that in every one of them the number is symbolical. Still, even in the instance which at first seems the most manifestly literal, viz. the seven churches which are particularly enumerated, it is possible that there may be an underlying symbolism. It can scarcely be supposed that there were only seven churches in all Asia Minor; there may have been seven times seven; but doubtless these seven stand as representatives of the whole number, not in Asia only, but everywhere else. What the Spirit said to them He said to all. It will be found of no small importance to the correct interpretation of the Apocalypse to bear in mind the symbolic character which belongs to the numbers most frequently employed in it.

THE THEME OF THE APOCALYPSE.

We have already endeavoured to show that the Apocalypse is essentially one with the prophecy on the Mount of Olives; that is to say, the subject of both is the same great catastrophe, viz. the Parousia, and the events accompanying it. The Apocalypse announces its great theme in the opening sentence of the book, after the preface or prologue. That opening sentence is the seventh verse of the first chapter:---

'Behold, he cometh with clouds; and every eye shall see him, and they also which pierced him; and all the tribes of the land shall wail because of him. Even so, Amen.'

This is the thesis of the whole discourse; the first prophetic utterance in the book, and also the last; the key to the whole revelation.

It will be seen that these words are the echo of our Lord's prediction in Matt. xxiv. 30:---

'Then shall appear the sign of the Son of man in heaven: and then shall all the tribes of the land mourn, and they shall see the Son of man coming in the clouds of heaven with power and great glory.'

There is no possibility of mistaking the reference in these words; there is no ambiguity or uncertainty as to *whose* coming or *what* coming is intended. The *time* and the *manner* of the coming are plainly indicated: it is *near:* 'Behold, he is coming.' It is in *glory:* 'He is coming with clouds.' The two predictions are in fact identical. The time of its fulfilment was now drawing nigh, for the standpoint of the Seer was in 'the day of the Lord.' That which our Saviour declared to be within the limits of the generation then existing was now, at the close of some thirty or forty years, on the very eve of accomplishment. The knell of doom was just about to sound: 'Behold, he is coming.'

Not less clearly indicated is the *scene* of the coming catastrophe. *It is the land of Israel.* This is plain from the express statement of both passages, in the Apocalypse and in the gospel: 'All the tribes of the land' [pasai ai fulai thz ghz]. The loose way in which this phrase is sometimes taken as referring to all the nations of the globe cannot be sufficiently reprobated. The original source of the expression (Zech. xii. 12), 'the families of the land,' shows that the land of Israel, and *especially the city of Jerusalem* are intended; and a similar limitation is required in the citations both in the gospel and in the Apocalypse. The allusion to the crucifixion strongly confirms this conclusion---'they also who pierced him.' The crucifiers of the Lord of glory are specially 'particularised among the mass that see with dread the tokens of an approaching avenger.'

The First Vision

THE MESSAGES TO THE SEVEN CHURCHES.
Chap. i. 10-20; ii. iii.

Notwithstanding what has been said respecting the imagery and symbolism of the Apocalypse, it is not to be forgotten that underlying these symbols there is everywhere a substratum of fact and reality. We have only to read the messages to the seven churches to discover that we are in a region of actual fact and intense reality. There is such individuality of character in the graphic delineations of the spiritual state of the several churches, that we cannot doubt that they are accurate and truthful portraits of the Christian communities which they describe. There is indeed a strange commingling of figure and fact; but there is no difficulty in discriminating between the one and the other; or, rather, they so admirably blend and harmonise that each lends vividness and force to the other. The explanation, also, of the symbols (ver. 20) converts them into real existences,---'The seven stars are the angels of the seven churches; and the seven candlesticks which thou sawest are the seven churches.'

It is scarcely necessary to say that there is not the slightest foundation for the preposterous theory which represents these delineations of the spiritual condition of the seven churches as typical of successive states or phases of the Christian church in so many future ages of time. Such a hypothesis is incompatible with the express limitations of time laid down in the context, as well as inconsistent with the distinctive individuality of the several churches addressed. Everything shows that it is of the present, and the immediate future, that the Apocalypse treats. The first readers of these epistles must have felt that they came expressly to them, and not to other people, in other times. It is, no doubt, true that these epistles describe types of character which may be repeated, and are repeated continually, in successive generations; but this does not alter the fact that they had a direct and personal application to the churches specified, which they can never have to any other.

Let us endeavour, then, to place ourselves in the situation of those primitive churches in Ephesus, and Smyrna, and Pergamos, and Thyatira, and Sardis, and Philadelphia, and Laodicea. Let us call up the prominent features and actors of the time, and consider the hopes and fears, the dangers and difficulties, which occupied and agitated their minds. Is it not obvious that these things must necessarily constitute the elements which go to the composition of the whole book? If not, it is not easy to see what special interest or concern it could have for its original readers, whose blessedness it was pronounced to be to read, or hear, and keep its words. What, then, do we find in those early days? Suffering and persecuted Christians; malignant and blaspheming Jews; stern Roman magistrates; a brutal and capricious tyrant on the Imperial throne; among themselves false teachers, apostates from the faith; wide-spread degeneracy and defection. In addition to all this we find a general expectation of a great crisis at hand; the conviction that at length the time was come for which all Christians had been taught to wait and hope; the hour of deliverance for the persecuted faithful; the day of retribution and judgment for the enemy and the oppressor. The watchword was passed from man to man, from church to church,---'Maranatha! The Lord is at hand. Behold, he is coming. He will not tarry.' We know certainly that this thought burned in the hearts of the first Christians, for they had been taught to cherish it by the instructions of the apostles and by the promise of the Master. Their hope was not the hope of Christians now,---to live on the earth as long as possible, and to die at a good old age, and then go to heaven, there to await a full and final glorification in some distant period. Their hope was not to die at all, but to live to welcome their returning Lord, to be clothed upon with their heavenly investiture; to be caught up into the clouds to meet the Lord in the air; and so to be for ever with the Lord.

Such unquestionably were the circumstances, expectations, and attitude of the Christian people who received these messages from the coming deliverer by His servant John. It will be obvious how exactly the contents of these epistles correspond with the circumstances of the churches. There is a striking common resemblance in the structure of the epistles, as if cast in the same mould or formed on the same plan. They are all naturally divisible into seven parts:-

1. The superscription.
2. The style or title of the writer.
3. A judicial declaration of the state or character of the church addressed.
4. An expression of commendation or of censure.
5. An exhortation to penitence, or to perseverance.
6. A special promise to 'him that overcometh.'
7. A proclamation to all to hear what the Spirit said to each.

The chief point, however, which concerns us in these epistles to the churches is that we find in each of them a distinct allusion to a great and imminent crisis, when reward or punishment is to be meted out to each according to his work. No one can fail to be struck with the indications that an expected catastrophe is at hand. To Ephesus it is said, 'I will come unto thee quickly' (chap. ii. 5); to Smyrna, 'Thou shalt have tribulation ten days' (chap. ii. 10); to Pergamos, 'I will come unto thee quickly' (chap. ii. 16); to Thyatira, 'Hold fast till I come' (chap. ii. 25); to Sardis, 'I will come on thee as a thief' (chap. iii. 3); to Philadelphia, 'Behold, I come quickly' (chap. iii. 2); to Laodicea, 'Behold, I stand at the door, and knock' (chap. iii. 20). It is impossible to conceive that these urgent warnings had no special meaning to those to whom they were addressed; that they meant no more to them than they do to us; that they refer to a consummation which has never yet taken place. This would be to deprive the words of all significance. What can be more evident than that in these sharp, short, epigrammatic utterances all is intensely urgent, pressing, vehement, as if not a moment were to be lost, and negligence or delay might be fatal? But how could such passionate urgency be consistent with a far-off consummation, which might come in some distant period of time, which after eighteen hundred years is still in the future? Why resort to such an unnatural and unsatisfactory explanation when we know that there was a predicted and expected consummation which was to take place in the days when these churches flourished? We therefore conclude that the period of recompense and retribution referred to in all these epistles to the churches was the approaching 'day of the Lord'---the Parousia, which the Saviour declared would take place before the passing away of the generation which witnessed His miracles and rejected His message.

The Second Vision

THE SEVEN SEALS, CHAPS. IV. V. VI. VII. VIII. 1.
Introduction to the vision, chaps. iv. v.

The real difficulties of apocalyptic exposition now begin. We seem to pass into a different region, where all is visionary and symbolical. The prophet is summoned by the trumpet-voice, which had previously spoken to him, to ascend into heaven, there to be shown *'the things which must take place hereafter'* [*after these*] (chap. iv. 1).

There is a manifest reference in these words to the direction given to the Seer in chap. i. 19, 'Write the things which thou sawest and what they signify, *and the things which are about to happen after these.*' It is these last which the prophet is now to have revealed to him; the phrase, 'the things which must happen after these', being evidently synonymous with 'the things which are about to happen', the latter expression clearly indicating that the time of their fulfilment is close at hand.

We must pass by the magnificent description of the heavenly majesty, in which we are reminded of the sublime visions of Isaiah and Ezekiel, and come to the scene in which the prophet beholds, 'in the right hand of him that sat on the throne, a book, or roll, written within and without, and sealed with seven seals.' A strong angel proclaims with a loud voice, 'Who is worthy to open the book, and to loose the seals thereof?' When none is found equal to the task, and the Seer is overwhelmed with grief because the mystic roll must remain unopened, he is comforted by the announcement made to him by one of the elders, that 'the Lion of the tribe of Juda, the Root of David, hath prevailed to open the book, and to loose the seven seals thereof.' Accordingly, amid the adoring worship of the heavenly host, and of the whole created universe, the Lion-Lamb advances to the throne, takes the book from the right hand of Him that sat thereon, and proceeds to break in succession the seals by which it is fastened.

Nothing can be more vivid and dramatic than the scenes which are successively exhibited as the Lamb opens the seals. The four cherubs that guard the throne, one after another announce the breaking of the first four seals, with a loud cry of 'Come!' And as each is opened the Seer beholds a visionary figure pass across the field of view, emblematic of the contents of that portion of the scroll which is unrolled. It will be observed that there is a manifest gradation in the character of these emblematic representations, which rise in intensity and terror from the first to the last.

What, then, do these symbols represent? It needs only a glance to see their general nature and character. Everywhere it is WAR, and the concomitants of war,---blood, famine, and death, all leading up to and terminating in one dread and final catastrophe, in which the elements of nature seem to be dissolved in universal ruin --- *the great day of wrath'* (chap. vi.).

Of what events does the prophet speak? Some would have us believe that this is a compendium of universal history; that we have here the conquests of Imperial Rome for three hundred years, down to the establishment of Christianity as the religion of the Empire by Constantine. We are sent to the volumes of Gibbon to wander through the ages in search of events to correspond with these symbols. But this is just what the seven churches of Asia had no power to do. Would it not have been a mockery to invite them to study and comprehend such visions, which even with the aid of Gibbon are not luminous to us? Surely, the interpreters who propound such solutions must have closed their eyes against the express teachings of the book itself. We are precluded by the terms of the prophecy from all such vague excursions into general history; we are shut up to the *near,* the *imminent,* the *immediate;* to things which must *shortly* come to pass; to events which intensely concern the original readers of the Apocalypse: 'for *the time is at hand.'* With this light in our hand all becomes clear. We have only to place ourselves in the time and circumstances of those primitive churches, and these visionary symbols shape themselves into historical facts before our eyes. The Seer stands on the verge of the long-predicted, long-expected crisis, for the coming of which in their own day the Saviour had before His departure prepared His disciples. As the prophecy which He delivered on the Mount of Olives commences with wars and rumours of wars, and goes on the speak of 'Jerusalem compassed about with armies,' and 'the abomination of desolation standing in the holy place,' till it culminates in the seeming wreck of universal nature, and 'the coming of the Son of man in the clouds of heaven,' so the prophecy in the Apocalypse proceeds in the same method.

Here, then, the vision is representative of the approaching destruction of Jerusalem and judgment of the guilty land. It is 'the last time;' and the beloved disciple, who hear the prophecy on the Mount, now sees its fulfilment in vision. His heart is filled with one thought, his eye with one scene. The storm of vengeance is gathering over his own land; his own nation --- the city and temple of God. The armies are mustering for the conflict; and, as seal after seal is broken, he beholds the successive waves of that tremendous deluge of wrath which was about to overwhelm the devoted land of Israel. This we believe to be the significance of the symbolic vision of the seven seals. It is only another form of the selfsame catastrophe foretold by our Saviour to His disciples; but now the hour is come; the close of the aeon is at hand, and the ministers of the divine wrath are let loose upon the guilty nation.

OPENING OF THE FIRST SEAL.

Chap. vi. 1, 2---'And I saw when the Lamb opened one of the seven seals, and I heard one of the four living creatures saying, as [with] a voice of thunder, Come. And I saw, and behold a white horse: and he that sat on him had a bow; and a crown was given to him: and he went forth conquering, and to conquer.'

It will be seen that we regard this vision as emblematic of the Jewish war, which was introductory to the great final event of the Parousia. Upon the opening of the first seal we behold the first act in the tragic drama. It is announced by one of the four mystic beings, represented as guarding the throne of God, exclaiming, with a voice of thunder, 'Come!' and behold, an armed warrior, seated on a white horse, and holding in his hand a bow, passes across the field of vision. A crown is bestowed upon the warrior, who goes forth conquering, and to conquer.

This is a most vivid representation of the first scene in the tragic drama of the Jewish war which commenced in the reign of Nero, A.D. 66, under the conduct of Vespasian. In the first scene we see the Roman invader advancing to the combat. As yet the war has not actually begun; the warrior rides upon a *white* horse; he holds in his had a bow, a weapon used at a distance. It is fanciful to see in the *crown* given to the horseman a presage that the diadem was to be placed on the head of Vespasian, or is it only the token of victory? However this may be, the whole imagery, as Alford observes, speaks of victory,---'He went forth conquering and to conquer.'

OPENING OF THE SECOND SEAL.

Chap. vi. 3, 4.---'And when he opened the second seal, I heard the second living creature say, Come. And there went out another horse that was red: and power was given unto him that sat thereon to take peace from the earth [land], and that they should kill one another: and there was given unto him a great sword.'

This symbol also speaks for itself. Hostilities have now commenced; the white horse is succeeded by the red---the colour of blood. The bow gives place to the sword. It is a great sword, for the carnage is to be terrible. Peace flies from the land: all is strife and bloodshed. It is a *civil* as well as a *foreign* war,---'they kill one another.'

All this fitly represents the historical fact. The Jewish war, under Vespasian, commenced at the furthest distance from Jerusalem in Galilee, and gradually drew nearer and nearer to the doomed city. The Romans were not the only agents in the work of slaughter that depopulated the land; hostile factions among the Jews themselves turned their arms against one another, so that it might be said that 'every man's hand was against his brother.' The exchange of the bow for the sword indicates that the combatants had now closed, and fought hand to hand: it is another act in the same tragedy.

It is worthy of notice that the language of the fourth verse not obscurely indicates the scene of war. Peace is taken from *the land* [ek thz ghz]. Stuart has accurately interpreted this circumstance: 'Here, not the whole earth, but *the land of Palestine* is especially denoted.'

THE OPENING OF THE THIRD SEAL.

Chap. vi. 5, 6.---'And when he opened the third seal, I heard the third living creature say, Come. And I beheld, and lo a black horse; and he that sat on him had a pair of balances in his hand. And I heard as it were a voice in the midst of the four living creatures, saying, A measure of wheat for a denarius, and three measures of barley for a denarius; and see thou hurt not the oil and the wine.'

This symbol also is not difficult of interpretation. It signifies the deepening horrors of the war. Famine follows on the heels of war and slaughter. Food is now scarce in Judea, especially in the beleaguered cities, and most of all in Jerusalem, after its investment by Titus. Wheat and barley are at famine prices, for the daily wage of a labouring man (a denarius) suffices to buy only a single measure of wheat (a choenix, or less than a quart), and three times that quantity of inferior grain. This is significant of terrible privation among the crowded masses in the besieged city.

Turning from prophecy to history the pages of Josephus furnish us with a fearful commentary on this passage. He is speaking of the scarcity of food in Jerusalem during the period of the siege:---

'Many privately exchanged all they were worth for a single measure of wheat, if they were rich; of barley, if they were poor. Then, shutting themselves up in the most retired recesses of their houses, some, from extremity of hunger, would eat the grain unprepared; others would cook it according as necessity and fear dictated. A table was nowhere spread, but snatching the dough half-baked from the fire, they tore it in pieces.'

But what means injunction, 'See thou hurt not the oil and the wine'? This has greatly perplexed commentators, for such a command seems not to accord with the prevalence of famine. If we are not mistaken, Josephus will enable us to reconcile this apparent incongruity.

After stating that John of Gischala, one of the partisan leaders who tyrannised over the miserable people in the last days of Jerusalem, seized and confiscated the sacred vessels of the temple, Josephus goes on to relate another act of sacrilege committed by the same chief, which seems to have aroused the deepest indignation and horror in the mind of the historian:---

'Accordingly, drawing the sacred wine and oil, which the priests kept for pouring on the burnt-offerings, and which was deposited in the inner temple, he distributed them among his adherents, who consumed without horror more than a hin in anointing themselves and drinking. And here I cannot refrain from expressing what my feelings suggest. I am of opinion that had the Romans deferred the punishment of these wretches, either the earth would have opened and swallowed up the city, or it would have been swept away by a deluge, or have shared the thunderbolt of the land of Sodom. For it produced a generation far more ungodly than those who were thus visited; for through the desperate madness of these men the whole nation was involved in their ruin.'

This serves to explain the use of the word adikhshz [deal unjustly with] in this injunction: 'See thou deal not unjustly with the oil and the wine.' Mr. Elliott, in opposition to Dean Alford, contends for the sense 'do not *commit injustice* in respect to the oil,' etc. Rinck, as quoted by Alford, renders it 'waste not,' etc. The incident related by Josephus shows how the word adikhshz suits every variety of rendering. The act of John was adikia in the sense of wanton waste.

OPENING OF THE FOURTH SEAL.

Chap. vi. 7, 8.---'And when he had opened the fourth seal, I heard the voice of the fourth living creature saying, Come. And I looked, and behold a pale horse; and his name that sat on him was Death, and Hell followed with him. And power was given unto them over the fourth part of the earth [land], to kill with sword, and with famine, and with death, and by the beasts of the earth.'

The scene here is evidently the same, only with all the horrors and miseries of the war intensified. The ghastly spectres of Death and Hades now follow in the train of famine and war. The 'four sore judgments of God,' which Ezekiel saw commissioned to destroy the land of Israel, 'the sword, and the famine, and the noisome beast, and the pestilence,' are again let loose upon the land, and by them the fourth part of its population is doomed to perish. Never was there such a glut of mortality as in the war which terminated in the siege and capture of Jerusalem. The best commentary on this passage is to be found in the records of Josephus, as the following description will show:---

'All egress being now intercepted, every hope of safety to the Jews was utterly cut off; and famine, with distended jaws, was devouring the people by houses and families. The roofs were filled with women and babes in the last stage; the streets with old men already dead. Children and youths, swollen up, huddled together like spectres in the market-places, and fell down wherever the pangs of death seized them. To inter their relations they who were themselves affected had not strength; and those still in health and vigour were deterred by the multitude of the dead and by the uncertainty that hung over themselves. For many expired while burying others, and many repaired to the cemeteries ere the fatal hour arrived.

'Amidst these calamities there was neither lamentation nor wailing: famine overpowered the affections. With dry eyes and gaping mouths the slowly-dying gazed on those who had gone to their rest before them. Profound silence reigned through the city, and a night pregnant with death, and the brigands more dreadful still than these. For, bursting open the houses, as they would a sepulchre, they plundered the dead, and, dragging off the coverings from the bodies, departed with laughter. They even tried the points of their swords in the carcases, and to prove the temper of their blades would run them through some of those who were stretched still breathing on the ground; others, who implored them to lend them their hand and sword, they abandoned disdainfully to the famine. They all expired with their eyes intently fixed on the temple, averting them from the insurgents whom they left alive. These at first, finding the stench of the bodies insupportable, ordered that they should be buried at the public expense; but afterwards, when unequal to the task, they threw them from the walls into the ravines below.

'But why need I enter into any partial details of their calamities, when Mannoeus, the son of Lazarus, who at this period took refuge with Titus, declared, that from the fourteenth of the month Xanthicus, the day on which the Romans encamped before the walls, until the new moon of Panemus, there were carried through that one gate, which had been entrusted to him, a hundred and fifteen thousand eight hundred and eighty corpses. This multitude was all of the poorer class; nor had he undertaken the charge himself, but having been entrusted with the distribution of the public fund, he was obliged to keep count. The remainder were buried by their relations. The interment, however, consisted merely in bringing them forth and casting them out of the city.

'After him many of the higher ranks escaped; and they brought word that full six hundred thousand of the humbler classes had been thrown out through the gates. Of the others it was impossible to ascertain the number. They stated, moreover, that when they had no longer strength to carry out the poor they piled the carcases in the largest houses and shut them up: and that a measure of wheat had been sold for a talent; and that still later, when it was no longer possible to gather herbs, the city being walled round, some were reduced to such distress that they searched the sewers and the stale ordure of cattle, and ate the refuse; and what they would formerly have turned away from with disgust then became food.'---Traill's Josephus, Jewish War, bk. v. chap. xii. § 3; chap. xiii. § 7.

OPENING OF THE FIFTH SEAL.

Chap. vi. 9-11.---'And when he had opened the fifth seal, I saw under the altar the souls of them that were slain for the word of God, and for the testimony which they held: and they cried with a loud voice, saying, How long, O Lord, holy and true, dost thou not judge and avenge our blood on them that dwell on the earth [land]? And a white robe was given unto every one of them; and it was said unto them, that they should rest yet for a little season, until their fellow-servants also and their brethren, that should be killed as they were, should be fulfilled.'

This passage may be regarded as a crucial test of any interpretation of the Apocalypse. It may be truly said that anything more unsatisfactory, uncertain, and conjectural than the explanation given by those interpreters who find in the Apocalypse a syllabus of ecclesiastical history can scarcely be imagined. But if our guiding principle be correct, it will lead us to such an interpretation as will demonstrate by its self-evidence that it is the true one.

The scene now changes from the battle-field, and the scenes of carnage and blood in the besieged and famished city, to the temple of God. But it is still Jerusalem. The Christian martyrs whom Jerusalem had slain are represented as crying aloud from under the altar, and appealing to the justice of God no longer to delay the vindication of their cause, and the avenging of their blood 'on them that dwell in the land.' This is a new and important scene in the tragic drama, but one that is in perfect keeping with the teaching of the New Testament. Our Lord forewarned the Jews that 'upon them should come all the righteous blood shed upon the earth, from the blood of righteous Abel, unto the blood of Zacharias son of Barachaias, whom ye slew between the temple and the altar. Verily I say unto you, All these things shall come upon *this generation'* (Matt. xxiii. 35, 36). In like manner He forewarned His disciples that some of them would fall victims to Jewish enmity: 'Then shall they deliver you up to be afflicted, and shall kill you' (Matt. xxiv. 9). All this was to precede 'the end' (Matt. xxiv. 13). Our Lord also declared that Jerusalem was deepest in the guilt of shedding innocent blood: she was the murderess of the prophets; and upon her the most signal punishment was to fall (Matt. xxiii. 31-39).

Here, then, we have the chief elements of the scene before us. But this is not all. It is impossible not to be struck with the marked resemblance between the vision of the fifth seal and our Lord's parable of the unjust judge (Luke xviii. 1-8): 'And shall not God avenge his own elect, which cry day and night unto him, though he bear long with them? I tell you that he will avenge them speedily. Nevertheless, when the Son of man cometh, shall he find faith in the land?' This is more than resemblance: it is identity. In both we find the same complanants,---the elect of God; they appeal to Him for redress; in both we find the response to the appeal, 'He will avenge them speedily;' in both we find the scene of their sufferings laid in the same place---*'in the land'*---*i.e.* the land of Judea. The vision and the parable also mutually supplement one another. The vision tells us the cause of the cry for vengeance, and who the appellants are, viz. the martyred disciples of Jesus who have sealed their testimony with their blood. The parable suggests the time when the retribution would arrive,---'when the Son of man cometh;' and likewise the mournful fact that when the Parousia took place it would find Israel still impenitent and still unbelieving.

The vision of the fifth seal likewise elucidates an obscure passage which has hitherto baffled all attempts to solve its meaning. In 1 Peter iv. 6 we find the following statement: 'For, for this cause was the gospel preached also to them that are dead, that they might be judged according to men in the flesh, but live according to God in the spirit.' Referring the reader back to the remarks made upon this passage at page 307, etc., it will suffice here to recapitulate the conclusion there reached. The statement really is, 'For, for this cause a comforting message was brought even to the dead, that they, though condemned in the flesh by man's judgment, should live in the spirit by the judgment of God.' This evidently points to the vindication of those who had by the unrighteous judgment of men suffered death for the truth of God; it declares that they had been comforted after death by the tidings that they should, by the divine judgment, enjoy eternal life. There is no allusion anywhere to be found in Scripture to any such transaction, except in the passage before us,---the vision of the fifth seal. This, however, precisely meets all the requirements of the case. Here we find 'the dead,'---the Christian martyrs, who had died for the faith; they had been condemned in the flesh by the unrighteous judgment of man. It is manifestly implied that they had appealed to the righteous judgment of God. In response to their appeal 'a comforting message' [euaggelion] had been communicated to them; they are told to rest *a little while* until their brethren and fellow-servants who are to be killed like them shall join them; while 'white robes,' the tokens of innocence and emblems of victory, are given to them. We think it must be obvious that this scene under the fifth seal exactly corresponds with the allusion of St. Peter and the parable of our Lord. It is important also to observe the place which this scene occupies in the tragic drama. It is after the outbreak, but before the conclusion, of the Jewish war; it precedes by a little while the final catastrophe of the sixth seal. It is the impatient cry of the martyred saints, 'How long, O Lord, how long?' It calls for just retribution on those who had shed their blood; and it distinctly specifies who they are by describing them as 'them that dwell in *the land.'* And all this is immediately antecedent to the final catastrophe under the next seal, which depicts the wrath of God coming upon the guilty land 'to the uttermost.' Here, then, we have a body of evidence so varied, so minute, and so cumulative that we may venture to call it demonstration.

OPENING OF THE SIXTH SEAL.

Chap. vi. 12-17.---'And I beheld when he opened the sixth seal, and lo, there was a great earthquake; and the sun became black as sackcloth of hair, and the moon became as blood; and the stars of heaven fell unto the earth, even as a fig-tree casteth her untimely figs, when she is shaken of a mighty wind. And the heaven departed as a scroll when it is rolled together; and every mountain and island were moved out of their places. And the kings of the earth [land], and the great men, and the rich men, and the chief captains, and the mighty men, and every bondman, and every free man, hid themselves in the dens and in the rocks of the mountains; and said to the mountains and rocks, Fall on us, and hide us from the face of him that sitteth on the throne, and from the wrath of the Lamb: for the great day of his wrath is come; and who shall be able to stand?'

We now come to the last act of this awful tragedy: the catastrophe which closes the second vision. It may excite surprise that the catastrophe occurs under the sixth seal, and not under the seventh, as we might have expected. But the seventh seal is made the link of connection between the second and the third visions, and is most artistically employed to introduce the next series of seven, viz. the vision of the seven trumpets. We may here observe that each of the visions culminates in a catastrophe, or signal act of divine judgment, bringing destruction on the wicked, and salvation to the righteous.

No one can fail to observe that nearly every feature in this awful scene occurs in our Lord's prophecy on the Mount of Olives with reference to the coming judgments on the city and nation of Israel. There is, therefore, no room for a moment's uncertainty as to the meaning of the vision of the sixth seal; but the more closely that every symbol is studied, the more distinctly will be seen its relation to the great catastrophe. This is the 'dies irae'---the hmera kuriakh---'the great and terrible day of the Lord' predicted by Malachi, by John the Baptist, by St. Paul, by St. Peter, and, above all, by our Lord in His apocalyptic discourse on the Mount of Olives. It is the expected consummation for which the apostolic church was watching and waiting,---the day of the judgment for the guilty nation, and, as we shall presently see, the day of redemption and reward for the people of God.

It will be proper, first, to note the correspondence between the symbols in the vision and those in our Lord's prophetic discourse:---

THE SIXTH SEAL.	THE PROPHECY ON OLIVET.
'And lo, there was a great earthquake.'	'And there shall be earthquakes in divers places' (Luke xxi. 11; Matt. xxiv. 7).
'And the sun became black as sackcloth of hair.'	'Immediately after the tribulation of those days shall the sun be darkened.'
'And the moon became as blood.'	'And the moon shall not give her light.'
'And the stars of heaven fell unto the earth.'	'And the stars shall fall from heaven.'
'And the heavens departed as a scroll when it is rolled together.'	'And the powers of the heavens shall be shaken' (Matt. xxiv. 29).
'And the kings, etc., hid themselves, . . . and said to the mountains and rocks, Fall on us, and hide us,' etc.	'Then shall they begin to say to the mountains, Fall on us: and to the hills, Cover us' (Luke xxiii. 30).

The comparison of these parallel passages must satisfy every reasonable mind that they both refer to one and the same event. What that event is our Lord's words decisively determine: 'Verily I say unto you, This generation shall not pass till all these things be fulfilled' (Matt. xxiv. 34). The only passage which does not come within the discourse on the Mount of Olives is the address to the women who followed our Lord in the way to Calvary, yet even there the limitation of the time is clearly indicated: 'Daughters of Jerusalem, weep not for me, but weep for *yourselves* and *for your children;'* implying that the calamities which He predicted would come in the lifetime of themselves and their children. The same nearness of the time is marked by the phrase, 'Behold, the days are coming' (Luke xxiii. 29).

No doubt it will appear an objection to this explanation that the destruction of Jerusalem, awful as it was, appears inadequate as the antitype of the imagery of the sixth seal. The object applies equally to our Lord's prophecy where His own authority determines the application of the signs. Indeed it applies to all prophecy: for prophecy is poetry, and Oriental poetry also, in which gorgeous symbolical imagery is the vesture of thought. Besides, the objection is based upon an inadequate estimate of the real significance and importance of the destruction of Jerusalem. That event is not simply a tragical historical incident; it is not to be looked at as in the same category with the siege of Troy or the destruction of Tyre or of Carthage. It was a grand providential epoch; the close of an aeon; the winding up of a great period in the divine government of the world. The material catastrophe was but the outward and visible sign of a mighty crisis in the realm of the unseen and the spiritual.

At the same time it is to be observed that the historical facts underlying these symbols are sufficiently real and tangible. The consternation and terror here depicted as seizing on 'the kings of the land, the great men,' etc., are in perfect accord with the scenes in the last days of Jerusalem as described by Josephus. Premising that by 'the kings of the land' [basileiz thz ghz] are meant *the rulers of Judea,* as we shall be able to show, we find the prophetic description wonderfully correspondent with the historical facts. First, the scene in the vision is evidently laid in a country abounding in rocky caverns and hiding-places, which, it is well known, are characteristic of Judea. The limestone hills of that country are literally honeycombed with caverns, which have been the dens of robbers and the shelter of fugitives from time immemorial. Ewald acknowledges 'that there is here a special reference to the peculiarities of Palestine as to its rocks and caves, which afford places of shelter for fugitives.' (Quoted by Stuart, Apocalypse, *in loc.)* These two notes, the land, and its geological character, fix the *locale* of the scene. Secondly, it is a fact attested by Josephus that the last hiding-places of the infatuated citizens of Jerusalem were the rocky caverns and the subterranean passages into which they fled for refuge after the capture of the city:---

'The last hope,' says Josephus, 'that buoyed up the tyrants and their brigand bands lay in the subterranean excavations, in which, should they take refuge, they expected that no search would be made for them, and purposed, after the final overthrow of the city, when the Romans should have withdrawn, to come forth and seek safety in flight. But this was after all a mere dream, for they were unable to hide themselves from the observation either of God, or of the Romans.'

Still more striking, if possible, is the fact mentioned by Josephus, that Simon, one of the chiefs of the rebellion, secreted himself after the capture of the city in one of these subterranean hiding-places. The incident is thus related by the Jewish historian:---

'This Simon, during the siege of Jerusalem, had occupied the upper town; but when the Roman army had entered within the walls and was laying the whole city waste, accompanied by the most faithful of his friends, and some stone-cutters with the iron tools required by them in their trade, and with provisions sufficient for many days, he let himself down with all his party into one of the secret caverns, and advanced through it as far as the ancient excavations permitted. Here, being met by firm ground, they mined it, in hope of being able to proceed farther, and, emerging in a place of safety, thus effect their escape. But the result of the operations proved the hope fallacious. The miners advance slowly and with difficulty, and the provisions, though husbanded, were on the point of failing.

'Thereupon Simon, thinking that he might pass a cheat upon the Romans by the effect of terror, dressed himself in white tunics, and buttoning a purple cloak over them, rose up out of the earth at the very spot where the temple formerly stood. At first indeed, the beholders were seized with amazement, and stood fixed to the spot; but afterwards, approaching nearer, they demanded who he was. This Simon refused to tell them, but directed them to call the general; on which they ran quickly to Terentius Rufus, who had been left in command of the army. He accordingly came, and after hearing from Simon the whole truth, he kept him in irons, and acquainted Caesar with the particulars of his capture . . . . His ascent out of the ground, however, led at that period to the discovery, in other caverns, of a vast multitude of the other insurgents. On the return of Caesar to the maritime Caesarea, Simon was brought to him in chains, and he ordered him to be kept for the triumph which he was preparing to celebrate in Rome.'

EPISODE OF THE SEALING OF THE SERVANTS OF GOD.

Chap. vii. 1-17.---'After this, I saw four angels standing on the four corners of the earth, holding the four winds of the earth, that the wind should not blow on the earth, nor on the sea, nor on any tree. And I saw another angel ascending from the east, having the seal of the living God; and he cried with a loud voice to the four angels, to whom it was given to hurt the earth and the sea, saying, Hurt not the earth, neither the sea, nor the trees, till we have sealed the servants of our God on their foreheads. And I heard the number of them which were sealed; and there were sealed an hundred and forty and four thousand of all the tribes of the children of Israel,' etc.

In the very crisis of the catastrophe the action is suddenly suspended until the safety of the servants of God is assured. The four destroying angels who are commissioned to let loose the elements of wrath upon the guilty land are commanded to stay the execution of the sentence until 'the servants of our God have been sealed on their foreheads.' Accordingly an angel, having 'the seal of the living God,' sets marks upon the faithful, the nationality and number of whom are distinctly declared,---'an hundred and forty and four thousand from every tribe of the children of Israel.' In addition to these, an innumerable multitude, 'of all nations, and kindreds, and people, and tongues,' are seen standing before the throne, clothed with white robes and with palms of victory in their hands, ascribing praise and glory to God amid the felicity and splendours of heaven.

This representation is generally regarded as an episode, or digression from the main action of the piece. No doubt it is so; but at the same time it is essential to the completeness of the catastrophe, and in fact an integral part of it.

It will be seen that in every catastrophe in this book of visions,---and every vision ends in a catastrophe,---there are two parts, viz. the judgment inflicted upon the enemies of Christ and the blessedness conferred upon His servants.

Now, under the sixth seal, where the catastrophe of the vision is placed, we have already seen the first part described, viz. the judgment of the enemies of God; but the other part, the deliverance of the people of God, is represented in the chapter before us. The progress of judgment is even arrested until the safety of the servants of Christ is secured.

What, then, is the meaning of this episode?

In the predictions relating to the 'end of the age' we invariably find a promise of safety and blessedness to the disciples of Christ, coupled with declarations of coming wrath upon their enemies. To give two or three examples out of many: in our Lord's prophecy on the Mount of Olives, of which the Apocalypse is the echo and expansion, He warns His disciples to make their escape from Judea when they saw 'Jerusalem compassed about with armies' (Luke xxi. 20), 'and the abomination of desolation standing in the holy place' (Matt. xxiv. 15). He assures them that 'there should not an hair of their head perish;' that when the signs of His coming began to appear, then they should look up, and lift up their heads, because their redemption was drawing nigh (Luke xxi. 18-28). That the Son of man would send His angels with a great sound of a trumpet, and would 'gather together His elect from the four winds, from one end of heaven to the other' (Matt. xxiv. 31). That in the great judgment day, which was to follow the destruction of Jerusalem, the wicked should 'go away into everlasting punishment, but the righteous into everlasting life' (Matt. xxv. 46).

In harmony with these declarations we find the apostles teaching the churches that when 'the day of the Lord' came, 'sudden destruction would overtake the enemies of God, while Christians would obtain salvation' (1 Thess. v. 2, 3, 9); that when the Lord Jesus was 'revealed from heaven with his mighty angels, in flaming fire, to take vengeance on them that know not God,' His faithful people would enter into 'rest,' and would 'be counted worthy of the kingdom of God' (2 Thess. i. 5-9).

It is this deliverance and salvation promised to the disciples of Christ which is symbolically shadowed forth in the episode to the sixth seal. The imagery by which it is described is evidently taken from the scene beheld in vision by the prophet Ezekiel (chap. ix.), where 'the men that sigh, and that cry for all the abominations of Jerusalem,' have 'a mark set upon their foreheads,' which was to ensure their safety when the executioners of divine justice went forth to slay the inhabitants of the city.

It is worthy of remark that Jerusalem is the scene of judgment alike in the prophecy of Ezekiel and in the Apocalypse; and the allusion by St. Peter to this very transaction in Ezekiel's vision, as about to be repeated in the Jerusalem of his own day, is very significant. (1 Pet. iv. 17.)

But the fullest light is thrown upon this episode by the words of our Lord: 'The Son of man shall send his angels with a great sound of a trumpet, and shall gather together his elect from the four winds, from one end of heaven to the other' (Matt. xxiv. 31). This episode is the representation of the accomplishment of that promise. While wrath to the uttermost is being poured upon the land; while the tribes of the land are mourning; while the enemies of God are fleeing to hide in the dens and caves; in that dread hour the angel's trumpet convokes the faithful remnant of the people of God, 'that they may be hid in the day of the Lord's anger.' The time was now full come; for all this, it must be remembered, was to be witnessed by the apostles themselves, or at least by some of them; for our Lord's own generation was not to pass till all these things were fulfilled.

Accordingly it was the cherished hope of the Christians of the apostolic age that they should escape the general doom, and enter into the possession of immortality by the instantaneous change which should come over them at the appearing of the Lord. St. Paul reassured the Christians of Thessalonica by telling them that they which were alive, and remained unto the coming of the Lord, should not take precedence of those who had departed in the faith previous to the Lord's coming. He declares to them, by the word of the Lord, that 'the Lord himself shall descend from heaven with a shout, with the voice of the archangel, and with the trump of God: and, first, the dead in Christ shall rise; then we, the living, who remain behind, shall be caught up all together with them, in the clouds, to meet the Lord in the air. And so shall we ever be with the Lord' (1 Thess. iv. 15-17). He alludes again to this same confident expectation in 2 Thess. ii. 1, where he says, 'Now we beseech you, brethren, *by the coming of our Lord Jesus Christ,* and by *our gathering together* unto him,' etc. This peculiar expression, 'our gathering together', would be scarcely intelligible but for the light thrown upon it in Matt. xxiv. 31 and in Rev. vii. The same period, the same transaction, are referred to in our Lord's prophecy, in St. Paul's epistle, and in the episode before us. Here is the great consummation, and the assuring of the safety of the people of God when destruction overtakes the impenitent and unbelieving. All this belongs to the great crisis at the end of the aeon,---that is, at the close of the Jewish dispensation. The finger of the Lord has defined the limits beyond which we may not go in determining the period of this transaction: 'Verily I say unto you, This generation shall not pass till all these things are fulfilled.' Whatever our opinion may be as to the extent or the manner of the fulfillment of the prediction, uttered alike by our Lord, by St. Paul, and by St. John, of one thing can be no doubt,---the Scriptures are irrevocably committed to the assertion of the fact.

It will be remarked that there are two classes, or divisions, of 'the people of God' who are specified in this episode. The first class belongs to a particular nation,---'the hundred and forty and four thousand out of every tribe of the children of Israel.' These must of necessity represent the *Jewish Christian church* of the apostolic period. But in addition to these there is a multitude which no man could number, belonging to all nationalities; that is to say, not Israelites but Gentiles. This class, therefore, must of necessity represent the *Gentile church* of the apostolic period; the 'uncircumcision,' who were admitted into the privileges of the covenant people, called to be 'fellow-heirs, and of the same body, and partakers of God's promise in Christ by the gospel,' along with the Jewish believers. This representation implies that the danger and deliverance symbolised by the sealing of the servants of God were not confined to Judea and Jerusalem. The religion of Jesus of Nazareth was a proscribed and persecuted faith over the whole Roman Empire before the outbreak of the Jewish war and the abrogation of the Jewish economy. Accordingly the redeemed in the vision, the 'white-robed multitude,' are said to come out of *great tribulation:* an expression which gives us a clue to the determination of the *time* and the *persons* here referred to. Our Lord, when predicting the season of unparalleled affliction that was to precede the catastrophe of Jerusalem and Juda, says, 'Then shall be *great tribulation* [qliyiz megalh], such as was not since the beginning of the world,' etc. (Matt. xxiv. 21). Now in the statement in the episode, 'These are they that came out of *great tribulation,*' there is an unquestionable allusion to our Lord's words. The proper rendering, as Alford points out, is,---'These are they that came out of *the great tribulation*', the definite article being most emphatic, and *the tribulation* plainly in allusion to the prediction in Matt. xxiv. 21.

We are thus brought, by the guidance of the word of God itself, to one and the same conclusion; and it is impossible not to be impressed by the concurrence of so many different lines of argument leading to one result. We are justified, therefore, in concluding that the episode of the sealing of the servants of God represents the safety and deliverance of the faithful in the fearful time of judgment which, at the Parousia, overtook the guilty city and land of Israel.

The Third Vision - The Seven Trumpets, Chaps. VIII. IX. X. XI.

We have now reached the close of the second vision, and it might be supposed that the catastrophe by which it was concluded is so complete and exhaustive that there could be no room for any further development. But it is not so. And here we have again to call attention to one of the leading features in the structure of the Apocalypse. It is not a continuous and progressive sequence of events, but a continually recurring representation of substantially the same tragic history in fresh forms and new phases. Dr. Wordsworth, almost alone among the interpreters of this book, has comprehended this characteristic of its structure. At the same time every new vision enlarges the sphere of our observation and heightens the interest by the introduction of new incidents and actors.

OPENING OF THE SEVENTH SEAL.

CHAP. viii. 1.---'And when he had opened the seventh seal, there was silence in heaven about the space of half an hour.'

The seventh seal, strictly speaking, belongs to the former vision; but it will be observed that the catastrophe of that vision occurs under the sixth seal, and that the seventh becomes simply the connecting link between the second vision and the third,---between the seals and the trumpets. This no doubt intimates the close relation subsisting between them. We cannot conceive of the events denoted by the seven trumpets as subsequent in point of time to the events represented as taking place at the opening of the sixth seal, for that would involve inextricable confusion and incongruity. It appears the most reasonable supposition that we have here, in the vision of the seven trumpets, a fresh unfolding of the desolating judgments which were about to overwhelm the doomed land of Judea. Dr. Wordsworth observes: 'The seven trumpets do not differ in *time* from the seven seals, but rather synchronise with them.' We doubt whether this is the correct way of stating the synchronism. We think the whole vision of the trumpets forms part of the catastrophe under the sixth seal.

THE FIRST FOUR TRUMPETS.

CHAP. viii. 7-12.---'The first angel sounded, and there followed hail and fire mingled with blood, and they were cast upon the earth' [land], etc.

The vision opens with a proem, or introduction, according to the usual structure of the apocalyptic visions. The standpoint of the Seer is still heaven, though the scene on which the main action of the piece is take to place is the earth, or rather the land. It cannot be too carefully borne in mind that it is Israel,---Judea, Jerusalem,---on which the prophet is gazing. To roam over the breadth of the whole earth, and to bring into the question all time and all nations, is not only to bewilder the reader in a labyrinth of perplexities, but wholly to miss the point and purport of the book. 'The Doom of Israel; or, the Last Days of Jerusalem,' would be no unsuitable title for the Apocalypse. The action of the piece, also, is comprised within a very brief space of time,---for these things were 'shortly to come to pass.'

To return to the vision. After an awful pause on the opening of the seventh seal, significant of the solemn and mournful character of the events which are about to take place, seven angels, or rather *the* seven angels who stand before God, receive seven trumpets, which they are commissioned successively to sound. Before they begin, however, an angel presents to God the prayers of the saints, along with the smoke of much incense from a golden censer, at the golden altar which was before the throne. This is usually regarded as symbolical of the acceptableness of Christian worship through the intercession and advocacy of the Mediator. But observe the effects of the prayers. The angel takes the censer which had perfumed the prayers of the saints, fills it with fire from the altar, and hurls it upon *the land:* and immediately voices, thunderings, lightnings, and an earthquake follow. Strange answers to prayer. But if we regard these prayers of the saints as the appeals of the suffering and persecuted people of God, whom we have seen represented in the former visions as crying aloud, 'How long, O Lord, how long?' all becomes clear. The Lord will avenge the blood of His servants; His wrath is kindled; swift retribution is at hand. The censer which censed the prayers becomes the vehicle of judgment, and is cast upon the land, filled with the fury of the Lord,---the fire from the altar before the throne.

Now, the seven angels prepared to sound, and each blast is the signal for an act of judgment. It will be observed that the first four trumpets, like the first four seals, differ from the remaining three. They have a certain indefiniteness, and the symbols, though sublime and terrible, do not seem susceptible of a particular historical verification. Probably they correspond with those phenomenal perturbations of nature to which our Lord alludes in His prophecy on the Mount of Olives as preceding the Parousia: 'There shall be signs in the sun, and in the moon, and in the stars; and upon the earth [land] distress of nations, with perplexity: the sea and the waves roaring' (Luke xxi. 25). These are the very objects affected by the first four trumpets, viz. the earth, the sea, the sun, the moon, the stars. Without endeavouring, then, to find a specific explanation of these portents, it is enough to regard them as the outward and visible signs of the divine displeasure manifested towards the impenitent and unbelieving; symptoms that the natural world was agitated and convulsed on account of the wickedness of the time; emblems of the general dislocation and disorganisation of society which preceded and portended the final catastrophe of the Jewish people.

The last three trumpets, however, are of a very different character from the first four. They are indeed symbolical, like the others, but the symbols are less indefinite and seem more capable of a historical interpretation. The judgments under the first four trumpets are marked by what we may call an *artificial* character; they affect the *third part* of every thing,---the third part of the trees, the third part of the grass, the third part of the sea, the third part of the fish, the third part of the ships, the third part of the rivers, the third part of sun, the third part of the moon, the third part of the stars, the third part of the day, the third part of the night. It would be preposterous to require a historical verification of such symbols. But the remaining trumpets appear to enter more into the domain of reality and of history; and accordingly we shall find great light thrown upon them by the Scriptures and by the contemporaneous history. That a special importance is attached to these last trumpets is evident from the fact that they are introduced by a note of warning:---

CHAP. viii. 13.---'And I beheld, and heard an eagle flying through the midst of heaven, saying with a loud voice, Woe, woe, woe, to the inhabiters of the land by reason of the other voices of the trumpet of the three angels, which are yet to sound.'

This introductory note to the three woe-trumpets requires some observations.

First, the reader will perceive that the true reading of the text is *eagle,* not *angel.* 'I heard an eagle flying through the midst of heaven.' This is the symbol of war and rapine. There is a striking parallel to this representation in Hosea viii. 1: 'Set the trumpet to thy mouth. He shall come as an eagle against the house of the Lord, because they have transgressed my covenant.' In the Apocalypse the eagle comes on the same mission, announcing woe, war, and judgment.

Secondly, the reader will observe the persons on whom the predicted woes are to fall,---'the inhabiters of the land.' As in chap. vi. 10, so here, *gh* must be taken in a restricted sense, as referring to the land of Israel. The rendering of *gh* by *earth,* instead of *land,* and of *aiwn* by *world,* instead of *age,* have been most fruitful sources of mistake and confusion in the interpretation of the New Testament. With singular inconsistency our translators have rendered *gh* sometimes *earth*, sometimes *land,* in almost consecutive verses, greatly obscuring the sense. Thus in Luke xxi. 23, they render *gh* by *land*: 'there shall be great distress in the land' [epi thzghz], being compelled to restrict the meaning by the next clause,---'And wrath upon *this* people.' But in the next verse but one, where the very same phrase recurs,--- 'distress epi thz ghz,'---they render it *'upon the earth.'* In the passage now before us the woes are to be understood as denounced, not upon the inhabitants of the globe, but of the *land*, that is, of Judea.

THE FIFTH TRUMPET.

CHAP. ix. 1-12.---'And the fifth angel sounded, and I saw a star fallen from heaven unto the earth: and to him was given the key of the pit of the abyss. And he opened the pit of the abyss; and there arose a smoke out of the pit, as the smoke of a great furnace; and the sun and the air were darkened by reason of the smoke of the pit . . . And unto them was given power, as the scorpions of the earth have power . . . And they have a king over them which is the angel of the abyss, whose name in the Hebrew tongue is Abaddon, and in the Greek tongue he hath his name Apollyon. One woe is past; behold there come two woes more after this.'

On this symbolical representation Alford well observes,---'There is an endless Babel of allegorical and historical interpretation of these locusts from the pit; 'but while clearing the ground of the heap of romantic speculation by which it has been encumbered, he abstains from putting anything better in its place.

Without assuming to have more insight than other expositors, we cannot but feel that the principle of interpretation on which we proceed, and which is so obviously laid down by the Apocalypse itself, gives a great advantage in the search and discovery of the true meaning. With our attention fixed on a single spot of earth, and absolutely shut up to a very brief space of time, it is comparatively easy to read the symbols, and still more satisfactory to mark their perfect correspondence with facts.

Whatever obscurity there may be in this extraordinary representation, it seems quite clear that it cannot refer to any *human* army. On the contrary everything points to what is infernal and demoniac. Considering the origin, the nature, and the leader of this mysterious host, it is impossible to regard it in any other light than as a symbol of the irruption of a baleful demon power. It is exactly as it is represented to be, *the host of hell swarming out upon the curse-stricken land of Israel.* We have before us a hideous picture of a historic reality, the utterly demoralised and, so to speak, demon-possessed condition of the Jewish nation towards the tragic close of its eventful history. Have we any ground for believing that the last generation of the Jewish people was really worse than any of its predecessors? Is it reasonable to suppose that this degeneracy had any connection with Satanic influence? To both these questions we answer, Yes. We have a very remarkable declaration of our Lord on these two points, which, we venture to affirm, gives the key to the true interpretation of the symbols before us. In the twelfth chapter of St. Matthew He compares the nation, or rather the generation then existing, to a demoniac out of whom an unclean spirit had been expelled. There had been a temporary moral reformation wrought in the nation by the preaching of the second Elias, and by our Lord's own labours. But the old inveterate unbelief and impenitence soon returned, and returned in sevenfold force:---

'When the unclean spirit is gone out of a man, he walketh through dry places seeking rest, and findeth none. Then he saith, I will return unto my house from whence I came out; and when he is come he findeth it empty, swept, and garnished. Then goeth he, and taketh with himself seven other spirits more wicked than himself, and then enter in and dwell there: and the last state of that man is worse than the first. *Even so shall it be unto this wicked generation*' (Matt. xii. 43-45).

The closing sentence is full of significance. The guilty and rebellious nation, which had rejected and crucified its King, was, in its last stage of impenitence and obduracy, to be given over to the unrestrained dominion of evil. The exorcised demon was at the last to return reinforced by a legion.

We have abundant evidence in the pages of Josephus of the truth of this representation. Again and again he declares that the nation had become utterly corrupt and debased. 'No generation,' says he, 'ever existed more prolific in crime.'

'I am of opinion,' he says again, 'that had the Romans deferred the punishment of these wretches, either the earth would have opened, and swallowed up the city, or it would have been swept away by a deluge, or have shared the thunderbolts of the land of Sodom. For it produced a race far more ungodly than those who were thus visited.'--- Josephus, bk. v. chap. xiii.

Let us now look at the symbols of the fifth trumpet in the light of these observations. There can be no question as to the identity of the 'star fallen from heaven, to whom the key of the abyss is given.' It can only refer to Satan, whom our Lord beheld 'as lightning fall from heaven' (Luke x. 18); 'How art thou fallen from heaven, O Lucifer, son of the morning!' (Isa. xiv. 12.) The cloud of locusts issuing from the pit of the abyss---locusts commissioned not to destroy vegetation, but to torment men---points not obscurely to malignant spirits, the emissaries of Satan. The place from which they proceed, the abyss, is distinctly spoken of in the gospels as the abode of the demons. The legion cast out of the demoniac of Gadara besought our Lord 'that he would not command them to go out into the abyss' (Luke viii. 31). The locusts in the vision are represented as inflicting grievous torments on the bodies of men; and this is in accordance with the statements of the New Testament respecting the physical effect of demoniac possession---'grievously vexed with a devil' (Matt. xv. 22). It need cause no difficulty that unclean spirits should be symbolised by locusts, seeing they are also compared to frogs, Rev. xvi. 13. As to the extraordinary appearance of the locusts, and their power limited to five months' duration, the best critics seem agreed that these features are borrowed from the habits and appearance of the natural locust, whose ravages, it is said, are confined to five months of the year, and whose appearance in some degree resembles horses. (See Alford, Stuart, De Wette, Ewald, etc.) It is enough, however, to regard such minutiae rather as poetical imagery than symbolical traits. Finally, their king, 'the angel of the abyss,' whose name is Abaddon, and Apollyon, the Destroyer, can be no other than 'the ruler of the darkness of this world;' 'the prince of the power of the air;' 'the spirit that worketh in the children of disobedience.' The malignant and infernal dominion of Satan over the doomed nation was now established. Yet his time was short, for 'the prince of this world' was soon to be 'cast out.' Meanwhile his emissaries had no power to injure the true servants of God, 'but only those men which had not the seal of God in their foreheads.'

Such is the invasion of this infernal host; all hell, as it were, let loose upon the devoted land, turning Jerusalem into a pandemonium, a habitation of devils, the hold of every foul spirit, and a cage of every unclean and hateful bird. (Rev. xviii. 2).

THE SIXTH TRUMPET.

CHAP. ix. 13-21.---'And the sixth angel sounded, and I heard a voice from the four horns of the golden altar which is before God, saying to the sixth angel which had the trumpet, Loose the four angels which are bound on the great river Euphrates. And the four angels were loosed, which had been prepared for the hour, and day, and month, and year, for to slay the third part of men. And the number of the army of the horsemen was two myriads of myriads: and I heard the number of them,' etc.

The sixth trumpet is introduced by the announcement,---'The first woe is past, behold, there are coming two woes still after these things;'---indicating that their arrival is near: they are on the way---'they are coming' [ercetai].

There is a certain resemblance between the vision here depicted and the preceding. Both refer to a great and multitudinous host let loose to punish men; in both the host is unlike any actual beings *in rerum natura,* and yet both seem in some points to come within the region of reality, and to be susceptible, in part at least, of a historical verification. The first incident which follows the sounding of the sixth trumpet is the command to 'loose the four angels which are bound on the great river Euphrates.' Of this passage Alford says: 'The whole imagery here has been a crux interpretum as to who these angels are, and what is indicated by the locality here described.' It is in these crucial instances, which defy the dexterity of the most cunning hand to pick the lock, that we prove the power of our master-key. Let us fix first upon that which seems most literal in the vision,---'the great river Euphrates.' That, at least, can scarcely be symbolical. There are said to be four angels bound, not *in* the river, but *at,* or *on,* the river. The loosing of these four angels sets free a vast horde of armed horsemen, with the strange and unnatural characteristics described in the vision. What is the *real* and *actual* that we may gather out of this highly wrought imagery? How is it that these horsemen come from the region of the Euphrates? How is it that four angels are bound on that river? Now it will be remembered that the locust invasion came from *the abyss* of hell; this invading army comes from the *Euphrates.* This fact serves to unriddle the mystery. The invading army that followed Titus to the siege and capture of Jerusalem was actually drawn in very great measure from the region of the Euphrates. That river formed the eastern frontier of the Roman Empire, and we know as a matter of fact that it was kept by four legions, which were regularly stationed there. These *four legions* we conceive to be symbolised by the *four angels* bound *at,* or *on,* the river. The 'loosing of the angels' is equivalent to the *mobilising of the legions,* and we cannot but think the symbol as poetical, as it is historically truthful. But, it will be said, Roman legions did not consist of cavalry. True; but we know that along with the legionaries from the Euphrates there came to the Jewish war auxiliary forces drawn from the very same region. Antiochus of Commagene, who, as Tacitus tells us, was the richest of all the kings who submitted to the authority of Rome, sent a contingent to the war. His dominions were on the Euphrates. Sohemus, also, another powerful king, whose territories were in the same region, sent a force to co-operate with the Roman army under Titus. Now the troops of these Oriental kings were, like their Parthian neighbours, mostly cavalry; and it is altogether consistent with the nature of allegorical or symbolical representation that in such a book as the Apocalypse these fierce foreign hordes of barbarian horsemen should assume the appearance presented in the vision. They are multitudinous, monstrous, fire-breathing, deadly; and so, no doubt, they seemed to the wretched 'inhabiters of the land' which they were commissioned to destroy. The invasion may be fitly described in the analogous language of the prophet Isaiah: 'The Lord of hosts mustereth the host of the battle. They come from a far country, from the end of heaven, even the Lord, and the weapons of his indignation, to destroy the whole land' (Isa. xiii. 4. 5).

It is in favour of this interpretation that there is a manifest congruity in the invasion of the devoted land, first by a malignant demon-host, and then by a mighty earthly army. Each fact is vouched for by decisive historical evidence. Strip the vision of its drapery, and there is a solid kernel of substantial fact. The dramatic unities of time, place, and action are also preserved, and we are gradually conducted nearer and nearer to the catastrophe under the seventh trumpet. But this is to anticipate.

An objection may be taken to this explanation of the vision of the sixth trumpet, on account of the Euphratean hordes being commissioned to destroy *idolaters.* Undoubtedly, the gross idolatry described in the twentieth verse was not the national sin of Israel at that period, though it had been in former ages. But there is too much reason for believing that very many Jews did conform to heathenish practices both in the days of Herod the Great and his descendents. We think, however, that in the sequel it will be satisfactorily proved that in the Apocalypse the sin of idolatry is imputed to those who, though not guilty of the literal worship of idols, were the obstinate and impenitent enemies of Christ. (See exposition of chap. xvii.)

Finally, the true rendering of ver. 15 removes an obscurity which has been the occasion of much perplexity and misconception. The four angels bound at the Euphrates, and loosed by the angel of the sixth trumpet, are declared to have been prepared,---not for *an* hour, and *a* day, and *a* month, and *a* year, but for *the* hour, and day, and month, and year: that is to say, destined by the will of God for a special work, at a particular juncture; and at the appointed time they were let loose to fulfil their providential mission. 'The third part of men' does not mean that the third part of the human race, but the third part of 'inhabitants of the land' (chap. viii. 13), on whom the woes are about to fall.

Episode of the Angel and the Open Book.

I. We might have expected that now the seventh trumpet would have sounded; but as in the vision of the seven seals, so here, the action is interrupted for the introduction of episodes which afford space for fresh matter which does not come strictly into the main current of the narrative.

CHAP. x. 1-11.---'And I saw another mighty angel come down from heaven, clothed with a cloud: and a rainbow was upon his head, and his face was as it were the sun, and his feet as pillars of fire; and he had in his hand a little book open: and he set his right foot upon the sea, and his left foot on the earth, and cried with a loud voice, as when a lion roareth: and when he had cried, seven thunders uttered their voices,' etc.

1. It is natural that we should be disposed at first to regard this mighty angel, who appears as the interlocutor in this and the following episode, as one of the 'ministering spirits' that do the bidding of the Most High. But a fuller consideration precludes this supposition. The attributes with which this angel is invested so closely resemble those ascribed to our Lord in the first chapter, that the majority of interpreters agree in the opinion that it is no other than the Saviour Himself who is here intended. The *glory-cloud* with which he is clothed is a customary symbol of the divine presence; the *'rainbow* about his head' corresponding with the rainbow round about the throne (chap. iv. 3); 'his *face as it were the sun;'* 'his *feet as pillars of fire;'* his 'voice as when a lion-roareth;' all these so exactly resemble the de-

scription in chap. i. 10-16 that it is scarcely possible to come to any other conclusion than that this is a manifestation of the Lord Himself.

2. But here is a further remarkable correspondence between the appearance and action of this 'might angel' and St. Paul's description of the archangel in 1 Thess. iv. 16: 'For the Lord himself shall descend from heaven with a shout, with the voice of the archangel, and with the trump of God.' There is certainly here a very singular coincidence. 1. The glorious angel of the Apocalypse seems undoubtedly to be 'the Lord himself.' 2. Both are said to 'descend from heaven.' 3. In each case he is represented as descending with a *'shout'*. 4. In each case it is the voice of *'the archangel.'* 5. In each case the appearance of the angel, or Saviour, is associated with a *trumpet.* 6. The *time* also of this appearing appears to be the same: in the Apocalypse it is on the eve of the sounding of the last trumpet, when 'the mystery of God shall be finished;' while in the epistle it is on the eve of the 'great consummation,' or 'the day of the Lord' (1 Thess. v. 2).

3. It may be objected that the title *'angel'* or even *'archangel,'* is incompatible with the supreme dignity of the Son of God. But there can be no question that the name *angel* is given in the Old Testament to the Messiah, Isa. lxiii. 9; Mal. iii. 1. The name *archangel* is equivalent to 'prince of the angels,' the very phrase by which the Syriac version renders the word in 1 Thess. iv. 16; in fact it would be more reasonable to object to the title 'archangel' being given to any other than a divine person. It is in harmony with other names confessedly belonging to Christ, as Arch, Arcwn, Archgoz, Arciereuz, Arcipoimhn, so that there is a strong presumption that the title Arcaggeloz also belongs to Christ.

4. Hengstenberg maintains, and with much probability, that there is only *one* archangel, and that he is possessed of a divine nature. This archangel is named *'Michael'* in St. Jude, ver. 9; but in the Book of Daniel *Michael* is expressly identified with the Messiah (Dan. xii. 1). Therefore archangel is a proper title of Christ.

5. It deserves notice that St. Paul speaks, not of the voice of *an* archangel, but of *the* archangel, as if he were referring to that which was well known and familiar to the persons to whom he was writing. But where in the Scriptures do we find any allusion to 'the voice of the archangel and the trump of God'? Nowhere except in this very passage in the Apocalypse. We infer that the Apocalypse was known to the Thessalonians, and that St. Paul alluded to this very description.

6. Again, in the Epistles to the Thessalonians the voice of the archangel is represented as awakening the sleeping saints. But whose voice is that which calls the dead out of their graves? The voice of the Son of God. 'The hour is coming in the which they that are in the graves shall *hear his voice,* and shall come forth' (John v. 25-29). The voice of the archangel, therefore, is the voice of the Son of God. It will be observed, also, that the sounding of the seventh trumpet is said to be 'the time of the dead, that they should be judged' (Rev. xi. 18).

7. Lastly, that the mighty angel of Rev. x. 1 is a divine person, and no other than the Lord Jesus Christ, seems decisively proved by chap. xi. 3: '*I* will give power to *my* two witnesses,' etc., where the speaker is evidently a divine person, yet the same 'mighty angel' whom the prophet beheld descend from heaven.

We therefore conclude that the 'mighty angel' of the Apocalypse is identical with 'the archangel' of 1 Thessalonians, and is no other than 'the Lord himself.'

II. We come next to consider the utterance of the mighty angel.

At first we might suppose that what the angel uttered was kept a secret. We are told that at his shout seven thunders uttered their voices; but when the Seer was proceeding to write their purport he was forbidden so to do: 'Seal up those things which the seven thunders uttered, and write them not' (ver. 5).

The prophet, however, goes on to record what the angel did and said. Standing with his right foot on the sea and his left foot on the land, he lifts up his hand to heaven, and swears by Him that liveth for ever and ever that there shall be no more time or respite. That is to say, 'The end is come; the long-suffering of God can no longer wit; the day of grace is about to close; and no longer respite will be given.'

That this is the meaning of the declaration is evident from what follows, ver. 7:---

'But in the days of the voice of the seventh angel, when he is about to sound, then the mystery of God is accomplished, according to his comforting announcement to his servants the prophets.'

In other words, the seventh and last trumpet, which is just about to sound, will bring the great predicted consummation. This intimate connection between the appearing of the archangel and the sounding of the seventh trumpet (which ushers in the consummation) is most suggestive, and gives strong confirmation to all that has been advanced respecting the correspondence of the scene before us with the description in 1 Thess. iv. 16.

But this seventh verse supplies also a singular and most satisfactory confirmation of the views which have been already expressed with regard to what is erroneously called 'the preaching of the gospel to the dead' (1 Pet. iv. 6). The reader will remember that in the passage referred to the expression employed is 'nekroiz euhggelisqh' (literally, *it was evangelised* to the dead, *i.e.* comforting announcement was made to the dead).

In the passage now before us (chap. x. 7) we discover the original source of this peculiar expression 'evangelised' [enhggelisen], and on more minute consideration we find an allusion, clear and distinct, to the very same communication made to the dead which is referred to by St. Peter. The angel in the vision swears---

'that there shall be no longer delay or respite . . . but in the days of the voice of the seventh angel, when he is about to sound, then the mystery of God is completed, as he *evangelised* his servants the prophets.'

In other words, 'as *he declared by a comforting announcement* to his servants the prophets.'

Here the question presents itself, When was this comforting announcement made? Alford correctly answers this question. In his note upon this verse he says---

'*that time should no longer be, i.e.* should no more intervene; in allusion to the answer given to the cry of the souls of the martyrs, chap. vi. 11. This whole series of trumpet judgments has been an answer to the prayers of the saints, and now the vengeance is about to receive its entire fulfilment: the appointed delay is at an end. That this is the meaning is shown by the all en taiz hmeraiz etc., which follows.'

Next, to whom was this comforting announcement made? The answer is, 'to his servants the prophets.' This clearly refers to those who, in chap. vi. 9, are represented as 'the souls of them that were slain for the word of God, and for the testimony which they bore.' For what is the function of a prophet? Is it not to declare the word of the Lord, and to bear testimony for the truth? In chap. vi. they are described as 'having been slain,' the fate which Jesus predicted for His servants. 'Wherefore, behold, I send unto you *prophets*: and some of them ye shall kill and crucify' (Matt. xxiii. 34). Jerusalem was notoriously the murderess of the prophets. 'O Jerusalem, Jerusalem, thou that killest the prophets' (Matt. xxiii. 37). 'It cannot be that a prophet perish out of Jerusalem' (Luke xiii. 32). It was the blood of these martyrs that was to be required of 'that generation,' and now the time was come.

Lastly, observe the period indicated in this comforting announcement. It is 'in the days of the voice of the seventh angel that the mystery of God shall be finished.' Turn to chap. xi. 18, which describes the result of the sounding of the seventh trumpet, and what do we find? It is declared there, 'Thy wrath is come, *and the time of the dead, that they should be judged, and that thou shouldest give reward unto thy servants the prophets.*' How perfectly this coincides with the statements in 1 Pet. iv. 6, as well as in Rev. vi. 9-11, and how obviously they refer to the same period and the same event, hardly needs to be pointed out. It raises probability to certainty, and demonstrates the truth of the explanation already given, by a subtle and recondite correspondence which will bear the most minute and critical inspection.

III. The open book in the hand of the angel (chap. x. 8-11). The mighty angel is represented as holding in his hand a little book open. Of its contents we are not informed, but we are greatly assisted in the interpretation of the symbol by the manifest correspondence between the scene in the Apocalypse and that described in Ezekiel ii. iii. In fact, they seem counterparts of one another. The roll in Ezekiel corresponds with 'the little book.' In the prophecy it is *'the Lord'* who holds in His hand the roll, and gives it to the prophet; an additional confirmation of the argument that it is *the Lord* who in the Apocalypse holds the little book in His hand. In both the prophecy and the Apocalypse the roll or book is *open*. In both, the roll or book is *eaten* by the prophets; in both it is in the mouth 'as honey for sweetness.' The Apocalypse alone states that it was afterwards *bitter* to the taste; but we may infer that the same characteristic equally applies to Ezekiel's roll. All these remarkable correspondences sufficiently prove that the scene in the prophecy of Ezekiel is the prototype of the vision in the Apocalypse. But the chief point to be noticed is the *character of the contents* of the little book, and this we are enabled to determine by its parallel in the prophecy. The roll which Ezekiel saw 'was written within and without; and there was written therein lamentations, and mourning, and woe' (Ezek. ii. 10). We infer, therefore, that in both the contents were *bitter*, for St. John, like Ezekiel, was the messenger of coming woe to Israel, and this very vision belongs to the woe-trumpets which sounded the signal of judgment.

The Measurement of the Temple.

CHAP. xi. 1, 2.---'And there was given to me a reed like unto a rod: and the angel stood, saying, Rise, and measure the temple of God, and the altar, and them that worship therein. But the court which is without the temple leave out, and measure it not; for it is given unto the Gentiles: and the holy city shall they tread under foot forty and two months.'

If anything were wanting to prove that in these apocalyptic visions we are dealing with contemporary history, with facts and things extant in the days of St. John, it would be supplied by the passage before us. Here we have distinct and decisive evidence with respect to *time* and *place*. The vision speaks of *the city* and *temple* of Jerusalem; the literal city and the literal temple. They were therefore in existence when the Apocalypse was written, for the vision before us predicts their destruction.

What can be more forced and unnatural, what more uncritical and groundless than to interpret a statement like this as symbolical of the Protestant Reformation and the Church of Rome? Such interpretations are indeed a humiliating proof of the extravagance and credulity of some good men; but they do incalculable mischief by setting an example of rash handling of the Word of God, and passing off the fantastic speculations of men for the true sayings of God. We have no right whatever to suppose that anything more or anything else is intended here than the literal city of Jerusalem and the literal temple of God.

The interlocutor in this vision is still the same 'mighty angel' whose identity with 'the archangel,' 'the Lord himself,' we have endeavoured to establish. The Seer receives a measuring rod or staff, and is commanded to measure the temple of God, the altar, and the worshippers. We naturally revert to the scene in Ezekiel xl., where the prophet sees an angel with a line of flax and a measuring reed taking the dimensions of the temple that was about to be built. But it is plain that in this apocalyptic vision it is not construction that is intended by the symbol, but demolition and destruction.

It is important always to keep in mind that the whole action of the Apocalypse is hastening on to a great catastrophe, now not far off. Israel and Jerusalem are never for a moment out of sight. Two woe-trumpets have already sounded the doom of the apostate nation, and the final consummation only waits the blast of the third. The archangel has already declared that 'no more time shall be given,' and the Seer has tasted the bitterness of the *'libel,'*---the little book which contains the indictment and punishment of that wicked generation.

In such circumstances nothing but coming destruction can be the theme. That the measuring-rod or line is employed in Scripture as an emblem of destruction is indisputable, more frequently indeed than of construction. A few instances must suffice. In Lamentations ii. 7, 8, we find a passage which might well be the interpretation of this apocalyptic vision: 'The Lord hath cast off his altar; he hath abhorred his sanctuary; he hath given up into the hands of the enemy the walls of her palaces. The Lord hath purposed to destroy the wall of the daughter of Zion: *he hath stretched out a line;* he hath not withdrawn his hand from destroying.' Again, in the prophecy of Isaiah concerning the destruction of Babylon (chap. xxxiv. 11) we read, 'The cormorant and the bittern shall possess it; and *he shall stretch out upon it the line of confusion,* and the stones of emptiness.' The prophet Amos also uses the same emblem (Amos vii. 6-9): 'Thus he shewed me: and, behold, the Lord stood by a wall made by a plumbline, with a plumbline in his hand. And the Lord said unto me, Amos, what seest thou? And I said, A plumbline. Then said the Lord, Behold, *I will set a plumbline in the midst of my people Israel:* I will not again pass by them any more: *and the high places of Isaac shall be desolate,* and the *sanctuaries of Israel shall be laid waste,'* etc. Another very suggestive passage occurs in 2 Kings xxi. 12, 13: 'Behold, I am bringing such evil upon Jerusalem and Judah, that whosoever heareth of it both his ears shall tingle. And *I will stretch over Jerusalem the line of Samaria, and the plummet of the house of Ahab.'* (See also Psalm lx. 6; Isaiah xxviii. 17.)

But not only is the measuring line or rod used as a symbol of the destruction of *places*, but, what is more singular, of *persons* also. There is a curious passage in 2 Samuel viii. 2 illustrative of this fact: And David 'smote Moab, and *measured them with a line, casting them down to the ground; even with two lines measured he to put to death, and with one full line to keep alive.'* There is some obscurity in the passage, but the meaning appears to be that the captives being ordered to lie down, a certain portion was measured off, equal to two-thirds of the whole, who were appointed to death, while the remaining third was spared. This explains, what would otherwise be almost unintelligible, why in the vision the worshippers are measured as well as the temple and the altar. We think it is plain, then, that the command to measure 'the temple, the altar, and them that worship therein' is significant of the impending destruction which was about to overwhelm the most sacred places of Judaism and the unhappy people themselves.

It will be remarked that one portion of the temple precincts, 'the court which is without the temple,' is excepted from the measurement: and for this a reason is assigned,---'for it is given unto the Gentiles.' The passage reads thus: 'The court which is without the temple *cast out,* and measure it not,' etc. There is some obscurity in this statement. We know that there was a portion of the temple precincts called 'the court of the Gentiles;' but that can hardly be the place alluded to here, for it would be strange to speak of the court of the Gentiles being given to the Gentiles. It is evident also that this abandonment of the outer court to the Gentiles is referred to as something sacrilegious, being coupled with the statement, 'And the holy city shall they tread under foot forty and two months.' The reason, therefore, for the exemption of the outer court from measurement may probably be that the place was *already desecrated;* it was therefore *'cast out,'* rejected, as being no longer a holy place; it was profane and unclean, being in the hands, and even under the feet, of the Gentiles.

Is there anything answering to these facts in the history of the last days of Jerusalem? For that is the true problem which we have to solve. Here the Jewish historian throws a vivid light upon the whole scene described in the vision. Josephus tells us how, on the breaking out of the Jewish war, the temple became the citadel and fortress of the insurgents; how the different factions struggled for the possession of this vantage ground; and how John, on of the rebel chiefs, held the temple with his crew of brigands called the Zealots, while Simon, another and rival leader, occupied the city. He tells us also how the Idumean force, which may properly be regarded as belonging to the Gentiles, effected an entrance into the city under cover of night, during the distraction caused by a terrific storm, and were admitted by the Zealots, their confederates, within the sacred precincts of the temple. It would appear that all through the period of the siege the city and temple courts were in the possession of these wild and lawless men of Edom, who carried rapine and bloodshed wherever they came. It was by them, and on this occasion, that Ananus and Joshua, tow of the most eminent and venerable among the high priests, were foully murdered, a crime to which Josephus ascribes the subsequent capture of Jerusalem and the overthrow of the Jewish commonwealth. (See Traill's Josephus, bk. iv. chap. v. sec. 2.)

Have we not here all the conditions of the problem fully satisfied? The violent and sacrilegious invasion of the temple by the Zealots and Idumeans, and the masterful occupation of the city by these banditti, who trode it down under their feet during the period of the siege, seems to us precisely to meet the requirements of the description. Surely it will not be said that the Idumeans were not Gentiles? It is important to observe that this phrase *the Gentiles,* or *the nations*, so frequently occurring in the New Testament, generally refers to the immediate neighbours of the Jews, many of them dwelling with them, or beside them, in the land of Palestine. Samaria was an eqnoz: so was Idumea, so was Batanaea, so was Galilee, so were the Tyrians and Sidonians; and the phrase 'all the nations,' or 'all the Gentiles,' is often employed in this limited sense as referring to the Palestinian nationalities. When our Lord sent forth the twelve on their first missionary tour, and charged them not to go into the way of the Gentiles, nor to enter into any city of the Samaritans, but to go rather to the lost sheep of the house of Israel, He did not mean by the Gentiles the Greeks and the Romans, the Egyptians and the Persians, but the home-Gentiles, as we may call them, whom the disciples could find without overpassing the limits of Palestine. We are in danger sometimes of being misled by the application of our modern geographical and ethnological ideas to the thought and speech of our Lord's time. The ideas of the Jews were rather provincial than ecumenical: their world was Palestine, and to them *'the nations,'* or *'the Gentiles,'* often meant no more than their nearest neighbours, dwelling on the borders, and sometimes within the borders, of their own land.

The passage which we are now considering throws light also upon our Lord's prediction in Luke xxi. 24: 'And Jerusalem shall be trodden down of the Gentiles, until the times of the Gentiles shall be fulfilled.' Our Lord, it is to be observed, is here speaking of the siege and capture of Jerusalem, the very theme of the apocalyptic vision. It cannot be questioned that our Lord's reference to Jerusalem being trodden down by the Gentiles is identical in meaning with the language in the vision,---'The holy city shall they [the Gentiles] tread under foot.' Both passages must refer to the same act and the same time: whatever is meant by the one is meant by the other. Since, then, the allusion in the Apocalypse is to the violent and sacrilegious occupation of Jerusalem and the temple by the hordes of Zealots and Edomites, we conclude that our Lord, in His prediction, alludes to the same historical fact.

But if so, what are we to understand by *'the times of the Gentiles'* in our Saviour's prediction? It has been generally supposed that this expression refers to some mystic period of unknown duration, extending, it may be, over centuries and aeons, and still rolling on its uncompleted course. But if this non-natural interpretation of words is to be applied to Scripture, it is difficult to see what use there is in specifying any periods of time at all. Surely, it is much more respectful to the Word of God to understand its language as having some definite meaning. What, then, if 'forty and two months' should really mean *forty-two months,* and nothing more? The times of the Gentiles can only mean the time during which Jerusalem is in their occupation. That time is distinctly specified in the Apocalypse as forty-two months. Now this is a period repeatedly spoken of in this book under different designations. It is the 'thousand two hundred and sixty days' of the next verse, and the 'time, times and half a time' of chap. xii. 14, that is to say, *three years and a half.* Now it is evident that such a space of time in the history of nations would be an insignificant point; but for a tumultuous and lawless rabble to domineer over a great city for such a period would be something portentous and terrible. The occupation of such a city by an armed mob is not likely to continue over ages and centuries: it is an abnormal state of things which must speedily terminate. Now this is exactly what happened in the last days of Jerusalem. During the three years and an half which represent with sufficient accuracy the duration of the Jewish war, Jerusalem was actually in the hands and under the feet of a horde of ruffians, whom their own countryman describes as 'slaves, and the very dregs of society, the spurious and polluted spawn of the nation.' The last fatal struggle may be said to have begun when Vespasian was sent by Nero, at the head of sixty thousand men, to put down the rebellion. This was early in the year A.D. 67, and in August A.D.70 the city and the temple were a heap of smoking ashes.

It is scarcely possible to conceive a more complete and striking correspondence between prophecy and history than this, which needs no dexterous manipulation and no non-natural interpretation, but the simple noting of facts registered in the annals of the time.

The following observations of Professor Moses Stuart on this passage are most important:---

"'Forty and two months." After all the investigation which I have been able to make I feel compelled to believe that the writer refers to a literal and definite period, although not so exact that a single day, or even a few days, of variation from it would interfere with the object he has in view. It is certain that the invasion of the Romans lasted just about the length of the period named, until Jerusalem was taken. And although the city was not besieged so long, yet the metropolis in this case, as in innumerable others in both Testaments, appears to stand for the country of Judea. During the invasion of Judea by the Romans the faithful testimony of the persecuted witnesses for Christianity is continued, while at last they are slain. The patience of God in deferring so long the destruction of the persecutors is displayed by this, and especially His mercy in

continuing to warn and reprove them. This is a natural, simple, and easy method of interpretation, to say the least, and one which, although it is not difficult to raise objections against it, I feel constrained to adopt.

Episode of the Two Witnesses.

CHAP. xi. 3-13.-'And I will give [power] unto my two witnesses, and they shall prophesy a thousand two hundred and threescore days, clothed in sackcloth. These are the two olive trees, and the two candlesticks standing before the Lord of the earth. And if any man willeth to hurt them, fire proceedeth out of their mouth, and devoureth their enemies: and if any man willeth to hurt them, he must in this manner be killed. These have power to shut heaven, that it rain not in the days of their prophecy: and have power over the waters to turn them to blood, and to smite the earth [land] with every plague, as often as they will. And when they have finished their testimony, the beast that ascendeth out of the abyss shall make war against them, and overcome them, and kill them. And their dead body shall lie in the [broad] street of the great city, which spiritually is called Sodom and Egypt, where also their Lord was crucified. And they of the people and kindreds and tongues and nations shall see their dead bodies three days and an half, and shall not suffer their dead bodies to be put in graves. And they that dwell upon the earth shall rejoice over them, and make merry, and shall send gifts one to another; because these two prophets tormented them that dwelt upon the earth. And after three days and an half the Spirit of life from God entered into them, and they stood upon their feet; and great fear fell upon them which saw them. And they heard a great voice from heaven saying unto them, Come up hither. And they ascended up to heaven in a cloud; and their enemies beheld them. And the same hour was there a great earthquake, and the tenth part of the city fell, and in the earthquake were slain of men seven thousand: and the remnant were affrighted, and gave glory to the God of heaven.'

We now enter upon the investigation of one of the most difficult problems contained in Scripture, and one which has exercised, we may even say baffled, the research and ingenuity of critics and commentators up to the present hour. Who are the two witnesses? Are they mythical or historical persons? Are they symbols or actual realities? Do they represent principles or individuals? The conjectures, for they are nothing more, which have been propounded on this subject form one of the most curious chapters in the history of Biblical interpretation. So complete is the bewilderment, and so unsatisfactory the explanation, that many consider the problem insoluble, or conclude that the witnesses have never yet appeared, but belong to the unknown future.

It is one of the tests of a true theory of interpretation that it should be a good working hypothesis. When the right key to the Apocalypse is found it will open every lock. If this prophetic vision be, as we believe it to be, the reproduction and expansion of the prophecy on the Mount of Olives; and if we are to look for the *dramatis personae* who appear in its scenes within the limits of the period to which that prophecy extends, then the area of investigation becomes very restricted, and the probabilities of discovery proportionately increased. In the inquiry respecting the identity of the two witnesses we are shut up almost to a point of time. Some of the data are precise enough. It will be seen that the *period* of their prophesying is antecedent to the sounding of the seventh trumpet, that is, just previous to the catastrophe of Jerusalem. The *scene* of their prophesying also is not obscurely indicated: it is 'the great city, which spiritually is called Sodom and Egypt, where also their Lord was crucified.' Nothwithstanding Alford's objections, which appear to have really no weight, there can be no reasonable doubt that *Jerusalem* is the place intended, according to the general consent of almost all commentators and the obvious requirements of the passage. The question then is, What two persons living in the last days of the Jewish commonwealth and in the city of Jerusalem, can be found to answer the description of the two witnesses as given in the vision? That description is so marked and minute that their identification ought not to be difficult. There are seven lending characteristics:---

1. They are witnesses of Christ.
2. They are two in number.
3. They are endowed with miraculous powers.
4. They are symbolically represented by the two olive trees and two candlesticks seen in the vision of Zechariah. (Zech. iv.)
5. They prophesy in sackcloth, *i.e.* their message is one of woe.
6. They die a violent death in the city, and their dead bodies are treated with ignomiry.
7. After three days and a half they rise from the dead, and are taken up to heaven.

Before proceeding further in the inquiry it may be well to notice the following remarks of Dr. Alford on the subject, with which we cordially agree:---

'The two witnesses, etc. No solution has ever been given of this portion of the prophecy. Either the two witnesses are literal,---two individual men,---or they are symbolical,---two individuals taken as the concentration of principles and characteristics, and this either in themselves, or as representing men who embodied those principles and characteristics. . . . The article toiz seems as if the two witnesses were well known, and distinct in their individuality. The dusin is essential to the prophecy, and is not to be explained away. No interpretation can be right which does not, either in individuals, or in characteristic lines of testimony, retain and bring out this dualism.'

On the statement 'clothed in sackcloth' (in token of need of repentance and of approaching judgment), Alford says:--

'Certainly this portion of the prophetic description strongly favours the individual interpretation. For, first, it is hard to conceive how whole bodies of men and churches could be thus described; and, secondly, the principal symbolical interpreters have left out, or passed very slightly, this important particular. One does not see how bodies of men who lived like other men (their being the victims of persecution in another matter) can be said to have prophesied *clothed in sackcloth.'*

Again, on the fifth verse:---

'This whole description is most difficult to apply on the allegorical interpretation; as it that which follows, and, as might have been expected, the allegorists halt and are perplexed exceedingly. The double announcement here seems to stamp the literal sense, and the ei tiz and dei autun apoktanqhnai are decisive against any mere national application of the words. *Individuality* could not be more strongly indicated.'

Again, on the miraculous powers ascribed to the witnesses:---

'All this points out the spirit and power of Moses, combined with that of Elias. And, undoubtedly, it is in these two directions that we must look for the two witnesses, or lines of witnesses. The one impersonates the law, the other the prophets. The one reminds us of the prophet whom God should raise up like unto Moses; the other of Elias the prophet, who should come before the great and terrible day of the Lord.'

Entirely concurring in these observations, which state the problem fairly, and conclusively set aside any allegorical interpretation as incompatible with the plain requirements of the case, we now proceed to search for the two witnesses of Christ who testified for their Lord and sealed their testimony with their blood, in Jerusalem, in the last days of the Jewish polity, *and we have no hesitation in naming St. James and St. Peter* as the persons indicated.

1. St. James

We know as a matter of fact and of history that in the last days of Jerusalem there lived in that city a Christian teacher eminent for his sanctity, a faithful witness of Christ, endowed with the gifts of prophecy and miracles, who prophesied in sackcloth, and who sealed his testimony with his blood, being murdered in the streets of Jerusalem towards the closing days of the Jewish commonwealth. This was 'James, a servant of God, and of the Lord Jesus Christ.'

Let us see how this name fulfills the requirements of the problem. It is impossible to conceive a more adequate representation of the old prophets and the law of Moses than the Apostle James. That he was a faithful witness of Christ in Jerusalem is unquestionable. His habitual, if not his fixed, residence was there: his relation to the church of Jerusalem makes this all but certain. No man of that day had a better title to be called an Elijah. No silken courtier, no prophesier of smooth things, but ascetic in his habits, stern and bold in his denunciation of sin,---a man whose knees were callous, like those of a camel, with much prayer; whose unflinching integrity and primitive sanctity won for him even in that wicked city the appellation of *the Just*: was not this the manner of man to 'torment them that dwelt in the land,' and to answer to the description of a witness of Christ? We can still hear the echo of those stern rebukes which galled the proud and covetous men who 'oppressed the hireling in his wages,' and which predicted the swiftly-coming wrath which was now so near,---'Go to, ye rich men, weep and howl for your miseries which are coming on. Ye heaped up treasures in the last days.' Who can with greater probability be named as one of the two prophet witnesses of the last days than James of Jerusalem, 'the Lord's brother'?

Concerning the exact time and manner of the martyrdom of this witness there may be some doubt, but of the fact itself, and of its having taken place in the city of Jerusalem, there can be none. Thus far, at all events, St. James, in the manner of his life and of his death, answers with remarkable fitness to the description of the witnesses given in the Apocalypse.

The following observations by Dr. Schaff place in a striking light the life and work of St. James of Jerusalem, and are eminently appropriate to the subject under discussion:---

'There was a necessity for the ministry of James. If any could win over the ancient covenant people it was he. It pleased God to set so high an example of the Old Testament piety in its purest form among the Jews, to make conversion to the Gospel, even at the eleventh hour, as easy as possible for them. But when they would not listen to the voice of this last messenger of peace, then was the measure of the divine patience exhausted, and the fearful and long-threatened judgment broke forth. And thus was the mission of James fulfilled. He was not to outlive the destruction of the Holy City and the temple. According to Hegesippus, he was martyred in the year before that event, viz. A.D. 69.'

2. St. Peter.

But who is the other witness? Here we seem to be left wholly in the dark. Stuart indeed suggests that we may regard the number *two* as merely symbolical; but this seems an unwarrantable supposition. Besides, as the Old Testament prototypes of the witnesses, 'the two anointed ones' of Zechariah's vision, were two persons, Zerubbabel and Joshua, it is only congruous that the witnesses of the Apocalypse should be two persons. Undoubtedly the second witness, like the first, must be sought among the apostles. They were pre-eminently Christ's witnesses, and possessed in the highest degree the miraculous endowments ascribed to the witnesses in the Apocalypse.

Now, what other apostle besides St. James had a recognised connection with the church of Jerusalem; dwelt stately in that city; lived up to the eve of the dissolution of the Jewish polity; died a martyr's death; and suffered in Jerusalem? It may seem to some a wild conjecture to suggest the name of *St. Peter*, as we venture to do; but it is by no means a random guess, and we solicit a candid consideration of the arguments in favour of the suggestion.

If it should appear that the habitual or fixed residence of St. Peter was in Jerusalem; that there was an intimate, if not an official, connection between him and the church of that city; and that St. Peter was in Jerusalem on the eve of the Jewish revolt: all these circumstances would lend great probability to the supposition that St. Peter was the other witness associated with St. James.

What, then, are the facts of the case as shown in the New Testament?

1.   We find St. Peter the most prominent person at the original founding of the church of Jerusalem on the day of Pentecost.

2.   We find St. Peter summoned before the Sanhedrin as the representative of the Christians in Jerusalem (Acts iv. 8; v.29).

3.   When the church of Jerusalem was dispersed after the death of Stephen, St. Peter, with the other apostles, continued in Jerusalem (Acts viii. 1).

4.   St. Peter was delegated, along with St. John, to visit the Samaritans converted by the preaching of Philip. After fulfilling their mission they returned to Jerusalem (Acts viii. 25).

5.   When St. Peter was called by a divine revelation to Caesarea to preach the Gospel to Cornelius we find that he returned from Caesarea to Jerusalem (Acts xi. 2).

6.   It was in Jerusalem that St. Peter was apprehended and imprisoned by Herod Agrippa I. after the martyrdom of St. James 'the brother of John' (Acts xii. 3).

7.   On St. Paul's conversion we are told that 'he did not go up to Jerusalem to them which were apostles before him' (Gal i. 17): which implies that there were apostles residing in that city.

8.   Three years after his conversion St. Paul goes up to Jerusalem. For what purpose? 'To see Peter;' and he adds,---'I abode with him fifteen days,' implying that St. Peter's stated abode was in Jerusalem. On this occasion St. Paul saw only one other apostle, viz. 'James, the Lord's brother' (Gal. i. 18, 19).

9.   Fourteen years afterwards St. Paul again visits Jerusalem. Whom does he find there? *'James, Cephas,* and John, who seemed to be pillars' (Gal. Ii. 1, 9).

10.   When Paul and Barnabas were deputed by the church of Antioch to go to Jerusalem to consult the apostles and elders respecting the imposition of the Jewish ritual upon the Gentile converts, what apostles did they find in Jerusalem on that occasion? St. Peter and St. James. (Acts xv. 2, 7, 13.)

11.   We find St. Peter and St. James taking a leading part in the discussion of the question referred to them by the church of Antioch; no other apostles being named as present. (Acts xv. 6-22.)

12.   That St. Peter and St. James had an official and recognised connection with the church of Jerusalem is presumable from the terms of the letter addressed to the Gentile churches in Antioch, etc. The document is styled 'the decrees of the apostles and elders which are in Jerusalem, implying their fixed abode there. (See Steiger on 1 Peter v. 31.)

13.   Judas and Silas, having delivered the epistle to the church of Antioch, returned to Jerusalem, *'unto the apostles'* (Acts xv.33).

14.   We infer that St. Peter was associated with St. James in the church of Jerusalem from the fact that St. Peter, when miraculously brought out of prison, sent a special message to St. James and the brethren,---'Go, shew these things unto James, and to the brethren' (Acts xii. 17).

15.   St. Peter (in 1 Peter v. 13) sends a salutation from 'his son Marcus.' If this means John surnamed Mark, as is most probable, we know that his home was in Jerusalem, where his mother had a house. (Acts xii. 12.)

16.   If it shall appear (as we hope to show) that the Babylon of 1 Peter v. 13 is really Jerusalem, it will be a decisive proof that St. Peter's habitual place of residence was in that city. The complete evidence, however, of the identity of Babylon with Jerusalem must be reserved until we come to the consideration of Rev. xvi. xvii.

17.   A comparison of the epistles of St. James and St. Peter shows that both are addressed to the same class of persons, viz. Jewish believers of the dispersion. (James i. 1; 1 Peter i. 1.) It is very suggestive, in connection with this inquiry, to find these two apostles dwelling in the same city, officially connected with the same church, associated in the same work, addressing the believing Jews in foreign lands, and bearing witness to the same great truths in advanced age, almost at the close of their life, and on the eve of that great catastrophe which buried the city, the temple, and the nation in one common ruin.

18.   Finally, it may be affirmed that, whether these probabilities amount to demonstration or not, no man could be named more answerable to the character of a witness for Christ in the last days of Jerusalem than St. Peter. Of course,

we reject as unhistorical and incredible the lying legends of tradition which assign to him a bishopric and a martyrdom in Rome. The imposture has received only too respectful treatment at the hands of critics and commentators. It is more than time that it should be relegated to the limbo of fable, with other pious frauds of the same character. That St. Peter's stated abode was in Jerusalem is, we think, proved. That he lived up to the verge of the Jewish revolt and war is evident from his epistles. That he died a martyr's death we know from our Lord's prediction; and in his case we may well say that the proverb would hold good, 'It cannot be that a prophet perish out of Jerusalem.' As we read his epistles, and view them as the testimony of one of the two apostolic witnesses of Christ in the doomed city, a new emphasis is imparted to his mysterious utterance which anticipates his own and his country's fate, 'The time is come when judgment must begin at the house of God: and if it first begin at *us!*' How appalling the description of the evil times and evil men, as he saw them in the last days, with his own eyes, in Jerusalem! While the last chapter might be the final testimony of the prophet-witness to the guilty land and city; the last warning-cry before the fiery storm of vengeance burst: 'The day of the Lord *will come* as a thief in the night,' etc. (2 Pet. iii. 10).

Let us now see how far the requirements of the apocalyptic description are met by this identification of the two witnesses as St. James and St. Peter.

They are two in number: 'Individual men, well known, and distinct in their individuality,' as Alford truly says they must be. They are more than this,---they are fellow-servants and brethren in Christ, associated in the same work, the same church, the same city. The *dualism*, which Alford says is essential to the right interpretation, is perfect. Still more than this,---'The one impersonates the law, the other the prophets.' Who could be a better representative of the law than St. James? though he does not the less impersonate the prophets. St. James indeed strongly reminds us of Elias, who might have been his model; the stern ascetic, whose mighty achievements in prayer he commemorates in his epistle. St. Peter also, who may be called the founder of the Jewish Christian church, reminds us of Moses, the founder of the ancient Jewish church. What the old prophets were to Israel, St. James and St. Peter were to their own generation, and especially to Jerusalem, the chief scene of their life and labours. The period of their prophecy is also remarkable; it is for the space of a thousand two hundred and threescore days, or three years and a half, representing the duration of the Jewish war. They prophecy in sackcloth: that is, their message is of coming judgment; the denunciation of the wrath of God. They are likened to the two olive-trees and the two candlesticks seen in the vision of Zechariah: that is, they are 'the two anointed ones' on whom the unction of the Spirit has been poured, the feeders and lights of the Christian church, as Zerubbabel and Joshua were the feeders and lights of Israel in their day. They are endowed with miraculous powers, a characteristic which must not be explained away, and which will apply only to apostolic witnesses. They are to seal their testimony with their blood, and thus far we find St. James and St. Peter perfectly fulfil the conditions of the problem. We are sure that they were both martyrs of Christ, and that too in the last days of the Jewish commonwealth. As regards the place where St. James's blood was shed we have credible historical evidence that it was in Jerusalem. But here the light fails us, and henceforth we are compelled to grope and feel our way. Of the death of St. Peter we possess no record; but the very silence is suggestive. That the two chief persons in the church of Jerusalem should fall victims to a suspicious government, or to popular fury, at the moment when revolution was on the point of breaking out, or had already broken out, is only too probable; that their dead bodies should lie unburied is in accordance with what actually occurred in many instances during that fearful period of lawless barbarity which preceded the fall of Jerusalem: but though we can go thus far we can go no farther. They martyred witnesses are raised again to life after three days and a half; they stand up on their feet, to the consternation of their enemies and murderers; they ascend to heaven in a cloud, in view of those who exulted over their dead bodies. If we are asked, Did this miracle take place with respect to the martyred witnesses of Christ, ST. James and St. Peter? we can only answer, We do not know. There is no evidence one way or another. We only know that it was a distinct promise of Christ that at His coming the living saints should be caught up to meet the Lord in the air. If such a thing might take place on the large scale of tens of thousands, and hundreds of thousands, there is no difficulty in supposing that it might take place in the case of two individuals. If the ascension of Christ Himself is a credible fact, it is not easy to see why the ascension of His two witnesses may not also be a literal fact. But we do not dogmatise on the subject: the facts are before us, and must be left to make their own impression on the mind of the reader. It does not seem possible to resolve the whole into allegory. Where we have found so much already of substantial fact and credible history, it seems inconsistent and unreasonable to sublimate the conclusion into mere metaphor and symbol. We therefore quit the subject with this one observation: Four-fifths at least of the description in the Apocalypse suit the known history of St. James and St. Peter, and no one can allege that the remainder may not be equally appropriate.

There remains, however, one circumstance to which we have not adverted, viz. the enemy by whom the witnesses are slain. We read in ver. 7, 'And when they shall have finished their testimony, the wild beast that cometh up from the abyss shall make war upon them, and shall overcome them, and kill them.' This is the first mention made of a being that occupies a large space in the subsequent part of the Book of Revelation---'the wild beast from the abyss.' Here he is introduced proleptically, that is by anticipation. We shall have much to say respecting this portentous being in the sequel, and only now allude to the subject in order to note the fact that, whatever the symbol may mean, it points to a powerful and deadly antagonist to Christ and His people; and that to the agency of this monster the death of the two witnesses is ascribed.

The ascension of the martyred witnesses to heaven is immediately followed by an act of judgment inflicted on the guilty city in which their blood was shed:---

Chap. xi. 13.---'And in the same hour there was a great earthquake, and the tenth part of the city fell, and there were slain in the earthquake seven thousand men, and the remnant were affrighted, and gave glory to the God of heaven.'

It is difficult to see how this can be regarded as merely symbolical. It is a remarkable fact that we find in Josephus an account of an incident which occurred during the Jewish war which in many respects bears a striking resemblance to the events described in this passage. On that fatal occasion, when the Idumean force was treacherously admitted into the city by the Zealots, a fearful earthquake took place, and in the same night a great massacre of the inhabitants of the city was perpetrated by these brigands. The statement of Josephus is as follows:---

'During the night a terrific storm arose; the wind blew with tempestuous violence, and the rain fell in torrents; the lightnings flashed without intermission, accompanied by fearful peals of thunder, and the quaking earth resounded with mighty bellowings. The universe, convulsed to its very base, appeared fraught with the destruction of mankind, and it was easy to conjecture that these were portents of no trivial calamity.'

Taking advantage of the panic caused by the earthquake, the Idumeans, who were in league with the Zealots, who occupied the temple, succeeded in effecting an entrance into the city, when a fearful massacre ensued. 'The outer court of the temple,' says Josephus, 'was inundated with blood, and the day dawned upon eight thousand five hundred dead.'

We do not quote this as the fulfilment of the scene in the vision, although it may be so; but to show how much the symbols resemble actual historical facts.

So ends the vision of the sixth seal with these impressive words, 'The second woe is past; behold, the third woe cometh quickly.'

THE SEVENTH TRUMPET.

Catastrophe of the Trumpet Vision.

Chap. xi. 15-19.---'And the seventh angel sounded; and there were great voices in heaven, saying, The kingdom of the world is become our Lord's and his Christ's, and he shall reign for ever and ever. And the four and twenty elders, which sat before God on their thrones, fell upon their faces, and worshipped God, saying, We give thee thanks, O Lord God Almighty, which art, and wast [and art to come]; because thou hast taken thy great power, and hast reigned. And the nations were angry, and thine anger came, and the time of the dead to be judged, and to give their reward to thy servants the prophets, and to the saints, and to them that fear thy name, both small and great; and to destroy the destroyers of the earth [land]. And the temple of God was opened in heaven, and the ark of his covenant was seen in his temple: and there were lightnings, and voices, and thunderings, and an earthquake, and a great hail.'

We now reach the last of the trumpet visions, and, as in every other instance, we find that the vision culminates in a catastrophe---an act of judgment inflicted on the enemies of God; and, on the other hand, the triumph and felicity of His people. We have great pleasure in quoting here the remarks of Dean Alford, who correctly apprehends the plan and structure of the successive visions:---

'All this,' he says, 'forms strong ground for inference that the three series of visions---the seals, trumpets, and vials---are not continuous, but resumptive; not indeed going over the same ground with one another, either of time or of occurrence, but each evolving something which was not in the former, and putting the course of God's Providence in a different light. It is true that the seals involve the trumpets, the trumpets the vials; but it is not in mere temporal succession: the involution and inclusion are far deeper,' etc.

This is an important admission, and had the learned critic carried the same principle of *resumption* into all the visions, it would have given tenfold value to his apocalyptic exposition. The principle itself is so legibly stamped upon the book that the marvel is how any one can miss it.

As for the symbols in the seventh trumpet-vision they are exceedingly clear, and almost self-evident. Observe, it is *'the last trumpet'* which now sounds, and the events which follow are such as we might expect at so great a consummation.

The first result is *the proclamation of the kingdom of God.* This is the grand finale towards which, in one form or another all the action of every vision tends. It is the theme of all prophecy; the *terminus ad quem* of the gospels, the epistles, and the Apocalypse. The period of the coming of the kingdom is most distinctly marked throughout the New Testament; it is always associated with the 'end of the age,' or close of Jewish dispensation, the resurrection, and the judgment. The seventh trumpet is the signal that 'the end' is come, and that 'the mystery of God' is finished; it is therefore the time for the proclamation that the kingdom of God has come. Messiah reigns; 'He hath put all enemies under his feet.'

We may here remark the singular consistency and harmony between representations so unconnected and widely dissimilar as they may appear, as the teachings of St. Paul and the visions of the Apocalypse. In the fifteenth chapter of the First Epistle to the Corinthians, St. Paul, speaking of this very period, *'the end,'* and the sounding of *'the last trumpet,'* intimates that it is the time when *the kingdom of God* shall come, and when Christ shall 'deliver up the kingdom to God, even the Father.' This appears to be the very transaction represented in the scene before us. Messiah has overcome; He has put down all rule, and all authority, and all power, *i.e.* the hostile and malignant Jewish antagonism which has been the bitter enemy of His cause. But He has conquered the kingdom that His Father may be supreme. Accordingly the chorus of elders before the throne celebrate the resumption of the kingdom by the Father, saying, 'We give thee thanks, O Lord God Almighty, which art, and wast, because *thou hast taken thy great might, and hast reigned.'* This is a coincidence so subtle, and, if we may so say, undesigned, as to give the force of demonstration to the views which have been propounded.

The next result of the last trumpet is the declaration that the time of *the judgment of the dead* is come, bringing recompense to the people of God and retribution to His enemies (ver. 18).

We have here condensed into a few brief sentences the essence of the eschatology of the New Testament. The wrath that so often was declared to be *coming* is now *come.* It is the time of judgment for the dead: which supposes their resurrection; it is the time for the vindication of the martyrs of Christ, whose expostulation was heard in Rev. vi. 9, and for the rewarding of all the faithful, both small and great; and it is the time of retribution for the enemies of Christ, the destroyers of the land. In fact, the whole catastrophe represents a time and an act of judgment, and the scene of that judgment is the guilty land of Israel, and the time is 'the end of the age,' the termination of the Jewish economy.

The verse which we have just considered is in remarkable correspondence with the second Psalm. 'The nations were angry' is an allusion to 'Why do the nations rage?' They are represented as in revolt against the King of Zion, and are exhorted to make their submission, lest He be angry, and they perish in His wrath. In the vision His wrath is come, and the destroyers of the land perish in that wrath. How accurately all this represents the judgment on the guilty rulers and people of Israel it would be superfluous to point out. The scene is definitely localised by the expression thn ghn---that is to say, 'the land of Israel.'

The symbolical representation in the last verse (ver. 19) seems susceptible of a satisfactory explanation. At the very moment of the doom of Jerusalem, when city and temple perish together,---when all the ceremonial and ritual of the earthly and transitory are swept away, the temple of God in heaven is opened, and the ark of His covenant is seen in the temple. That is as much as to say, the local and temporary passes, but is succeeded by the heavenly and eternal; the earthly and figurative is superseded by the spiritual and the true. We have in this representation a fine comment on the words of the Epistle to the Hebrews, 'The way into the holiest of all was not yet made manifest, while as the first tabernacle was yet standing.' But no sooner is the 'first tabernacle' swept away than the temple in heaven is opened, and even the sacred ark of the covenant, the shrine of the divine Presence and Glory, is revealed to the eyes of men. Access into the holiest of all is no longer forbidden, and 'we have boldness to enter into the holiest by the blood of Jesus.'

So, amidst portentous manifestations of wrath and judgment on the wicked,---'lightnings, and thunders, and earthquake, and hail,' the recognised concomitants in the Old Testament of the divine presence and power,---the vision of the seven trumpets closes.

The Fourth Vision

VISION OF THE SEVEN MYSTIC FIGURES.
Chaps. xii. xiii. xiv.

The catastrophe of the trumpet vision lands us in the very same crisis as the catastrophe of the seven seals. They are both different representations of the same great event. But there is still room for fresh representations; and the next vision ushers in a completely different set of symbols, though belonging to the same period and relating to the same events. Its place, between the seven trumpets and the seven vials, enables us very distinctly to define its limits; and it closes, like the other visions, with a very marked catastrophe. It differs from them, however, in not being so expressly characterised by the number *seven*, though it is not difficult to see that it really consists of that number of principal figures or characters, all of them being symbolical representations. These are,---1. The woman clothed with the sun; 2. The great red dragon; 3. The man-child; 4. The beast from the sea; 5. The beast from the land; 6. The Lamb on Mount Sion; 7. The Son of man on the cloud. We call this vision, therefore, *the vision of the seven mystic figures.* It occupies the next three chapters---chaps. xii. xiii. xiv. It is of the utmost consequence for the correct interpretation of these apocalyptic visions that we keep stedfastly in mind the limits of the area to which we are restricted by the terms of the Book. It is only a point in historical time and geographical space,---the consummation of the Jewish age. The theatre of action, and the greater number of *dramatis personae*, must always be sought at the central spot, where is the focus of the interest,---Jerusalem and Judea. It is rarely that we have to travel beyond this region, although occasionally remoter elements are introduced, when they have a special relation to the principal theme.

1. *The Woman clothed with the Sun.*

CHAP. xii. 1, 2.---'And there appeared a great wonder [sign] in heaven; a woman clothed with the sun, and the moon under her feet, and upon her head a crown of twelve stars: and she being with child cried, travailing in birth, and pained to be delivered.'

CHAP.xii. 5.---'And she brought forth a man child, who shall rule all the nations with a rod of iron: and her child was caught up unto God, and to his throne.'

It is not surprising that this representation of the woman who brings forth a man child destined to rule all the nations, who is caught up to God and to His throne, etc., should at the first view suggest the Virgin Mother and her Son, who was no sooner born than He was persecuted by the murderous jealousy of Herod, 'who sought the young child to destroy him;' and who ascended to the throne of God. Nevertheless, such an interpretation at once breaks down, being wholly incompatible with the subsequent representations in the vision. There is nothing in the history of Mary corresponding to the persecution of the woman by the dragon; to her flight into the wilderness after the ascension of her Son; to the flood of water cast out by the serpent to destroy her; and to the war made upon 'the remnant of her seed.'

There is another objection which is fatal to this interpretation. It is outside the bounds which the Apocalypse itself expressly draws around its scene and time of action. It is not among the things 'which must shortly come to pass.' If we were taken back to look at symbolical representations of the birth of Christ, we should not be upon apocalyptic ground. To leave this ground is to travel out of the record, to forsake the *terra firma* of historical fact, and to launch out upon a shoreless sea of conjecture, without a compass or a guiding star.

We have no difficulty, therefore, in accepting the common opinion that the woman clothed with the sun is representative of the Christian church. But his alone is too vague a statement. It is the *persecuted* church, the apostolic church, *the church of Judea,* that is here symbolised. That is to say, it is the Hebrew-Christian church in the closing days of the Jewish age.

The emblems with which the woman is adorned will not seem incongruous or extravagant when we remember the lofty language in which the prophet Isaiah addresses Israel: 'Arise, shine, for thy light is come, and the glory of the Lord is risen upon thee,' etc. (Isa. lx.) That the apostolic church should be resplendent as the sun, that the moon should be beneath her feet, is only in keeping with all that is spoken in the New Testament of the dignity and glory of the bride of Christ.

But that which identifies the woman in the vision as the Hebrew-Christian church is the crown of twelve stars upon her head. That this is emblematic of the twelve tribes of the children of Israel seems beyond question; and it therefore fixes the reference of the vision to the church of Judea.

2. *The great Red Dragon.*

CHAP. xii. 3, 4.---'And there appeared another wonder in heaven: and behold a great red dragon, having seven heads and ten horns, and seven diadems upon his heads. And his tail drew the third part of the stars of heaven, and did cast them to the earth: and the dragon stood before the woman which was ready to be delivered, for to devour her child as soon as it was born.'

There is no possibility of doubt respecting the identity of this symbol. The dragon is 'that old serpent, called the Devil, and Satan,'---the ancient and inveterate foe of God and of His people. He is represented as possessing vast authority and power; 'having seven heads and ten horns, and seven diadems upon his heads;' for he is 'the god of this world,' 'the prince of the power of the air;' 'the accuser of the brethren;' 'the deceiver of the whole world.' This malignant enemy of the cause of Christ stands ready to devour the child of which the woman is about to be delivered.

3. *The Man Child.*

CHAP. xii. 5.---'And she brought forth a man child, who shall soon rule all the nations with a rod of iron: and her child was caught up to God and to his throne.'

Alford affirms that 'the man child is the Lord Jesus Christ, *and none other.*' He further says that 'the exigencies of this passage require that the birth should be understood literally and historically of that birth of which all Christians know.' And yet he holds that the mother is 'the church;' that 'the Blessed Virgin cannot possibly be intended.' These two suppositions are incompatible, and mutually destructive. It seems indeed natural at first sight to assume that Christ must be intended, but further consideration will show that it cannot be so. The church is never said to be the mother of Christ, nor Christ to be the Son of the church. The church is the bride, the wife, the body, the house of Christ, but never the mother. Christ is the King, the Head, the Husband of the church, but never the Son or Child. He is the Son of God, and the Son of man; but never the Son of the church. There would be an incongruity and impropriety in such a figure from which the sense of fitness revolts.

We believe the key to this symbol is to be found in the sixty-sixth chapter of Isaiah, which is the original source from which the figures are derived. Jerusalem is there represented as a woman in travail, who is delivered of a man child (vers. 7, 8): 'Before she travailed, she brought forth; before her pain came, she was delivered of a man child. Who hath heard such a thing? who hath seen such things? Shall the earth be made to bring forth in one day? or shall a nation be born at once? for as soon as Zion travailed, she brought forth her children.' It is impossible to believe that the resemblance between these passages is merely casual; and we are therefore greatly assisted in the interpretation of the vision by the analogous representations in the prophecy. As the man child, or the children of Zion, in the prophecy, signify the faithful in the land, or in Jerusalem, so the man child born of the persecuted woman in the Apocalypse denotes the *faithful disciples of Christ in Judea, or even in Jerusalem itself.* This explanation harmonises the seeming incongruities of the passage, and gives an intelligible and reasonable sense to the whole representation. The Hebrew-Christian church is personified as the persecuted parent of a persecuted offspring; she gives birth to a man child, but a man child that is also a nation, according to the words of the prophet. This man child is destined 'to rule the nations with a rod of iron, and is caught up unto God, and to his throne.' These are statements which seem to many only applicable to the Son of God Himself; but they are in truth affirmed in the Apocalypse to be the privilege and reward of every faithful disciple: 'To him that overcometh will *I give power over the nations,* and *he shall rule them with a rod of iron'* (chap. ii. 26, 27); 'To him that overcometh will I grant *to sit with me in my throne'* (chap. iii. 21). It is therefore not unwarrantable to apply these expressions, lofty as they are, to the faithful disciples of Christ.

The safety of her offspring being thus secured, provision for the persecuted mother is made by God.

CHAP. xii. 6.---'And the woman fled into the wilderness, where she hath a place prepared of God, that they should feed her there a thousand two hundred and threescore days.'

This anticipatory of the fuller statement in vers. 13-16, where we are told that 'to the woman were given the two wings of the great eagle, that she might fly into the wilderness, into her place, where she is nourished for a time, and times, and half a time, from the face of the serpent.'

This allusion to the period of time during which the woman is preserved furnishes a clue to the interpretation of this part of the vision. It will be seen that it is the same space of time during which Jerusalem is trodden under foot by the Gentiles, and during which the two witnesses utter their prophecy. That is to say, these different designations of time,---forty-two months, a thousand two hundred and threescore days, and a time, and times, and half-a-time, are all equivalent to three years and a half, which is known to have been the duration of the Jewish war. It is reasonable to conclude, therefore, that these different events coincide with the period of the Jewish war, and cover the same duration, being contemporaneous events. Is there then, it may be asked, any historical fact corresponding to the symbols in the vision, namely, the persecuted woman, the mother of the man child, fleeing into the wilderness from the face of the dragon, and preserved in safety there during a space of time equal to three years and a half? We think there is; and we shall endeavour to present the veritable facts which, as we believe, answer to the symbolic representation.

Our Lord distinctly forewarned His disciples that when they saw certain specified signs of the approaching catastrophe, especially when they saw 'Jerusalem compassed about with armies,' and 'the abomination of desolation standing in the holy place,' they should, without loss of time, escape from the doomed city, and 'flee to the mountains.' So hasty was to be their flight that they were even to disregard their property, and only care for personal preservation (Matt. xxiv. 15-18). We have the testimony of Josephus also that many of the Jews at the commencement of hostilities with Rome abandoned Jerusalem as they would a sinking ship. It is presumable that the Christian population, who had been so expressly warned of what was coming, would quit the city; and there appears to be no reason to question the fact that as a body they did retire, and sought refuge in Peraea, beyond the Jordan, a district which we are informed by Josephus is generally desert, and might therefore be properly styled 'the wilderness.'

This, then, is how the symbols shape themselves into history. The church of Jerusalem, the *mother church* as it may well be called, and the fruitful mother of a multitude of spiritual children, is subjected to severe and grievous persecution, stirred up by Satan, the malignant adversary of Christ and of His people. Whether the man child caught up to God and to His throne symboloses the martyred sons of the church referred to in ver. 11, who, 'though condemned by men in the flesh, were justified and crowned by God with life eternal in their spirit' (1 Peter iv. 6), we will not decide, though we think it probable. The mother church, however, though deprived of her first-born, is still persecuted by the dragon. Never was the persecution hotter than when the period of the Jewish revolt arrived and the army of Rome appeared before the gates of Jerusalem. Warned of God, the church of Jerusalem abandoned the city, and fled as on eagle's wings into the wilderness beyond the Jordan, where a safe retreat was found during the period of the war and the siege. Baffled in his attempt to crush the cause of Christ in Jerusalem, the dragon vents his rage by discharging a flood of malignant wrath after the fugitive Christians,---which, however, does them no harm,---and then turns to molest and persecute 'the remnant of the woman's seed,' or disciples in other parts of the earth or the land.

If it be said that there is an incongruity in representing the persecuted Christians of the church of Jerusalem by the double figure of the woman and the man child, one of whom is caught up into heaven, while the other flies for refuge to the wilderness, we answer, that it is an incongruity inseparable from the use of such symbols. Zion and her children in the prophecy of Isaiah are virtually identical; and the same is true of the woman and the man child. We speak of

England and her people when we really mean the same thing by both expressions; and it would be an over-fastidious criticism that would object to such language, which, if not logically correct, adds greatly to the dramatic and poetical effect of the description.

Alford, although he feels quite perplexed about the interpretation of the vision as a whole, gives his opinion in favour of our explanation of a very important part of the symbols. His words are,---

'I own than, considering the analogies and the language used, I am much more disposed to interpret the persecution of the woman by the dragon of the various persecutions by Jews which followed the ascension, and her flight into the wilderness of the gradual withdrawal of the church and her agency from Jerusalem and Judea, finally consummated by the flight to the mountain on the approaching siege, commanded by our Lord Himself.'

Strange that, having found one historical fact that so well corresponded with the symbol, the critic did not seek in the same quarter for more, which would no doubt have resulted in a luminous exposition of the whole; but he is led away by the *ignis fatuus* of a syllabus of universal church history in the Apocalypse, unaccountably ignoring the express statements of the book itself with reference to the very restricted period within which its visions must be fulfilled.

We come next to the conflict between the dragon and the champion who appears in defence of the persecuted woman:---

Chap. xii. 7-9.---'And there was war in heaven: Michael and his angels fought against the dragon; and the dragon fought and his angels, and prevailed not; neither was their place found any more in heaven. And the great dragon was cast out, that old serpent, called the Devil, and Satan, which deceiveth the whole world: he was cast out into the earth, and his angels were cast out with him.'

It does not appear that this transaction,---the conflict between Michael and the dragon,---was represented to the Seer in *vision*. It is not introduced by the usual formula in such cases, 'And I saw, and behold', but related more in the manner of a historian. Nor are we informed of the particular time or occasion of the conflict being fought. Indeed, the whole transaction is mysterious, and outside the range of earthly things; the scene of it is 'in heaven;' the combatants are spiritual beings,---'the principalities and powers in heavenly places;' although it is reasonable to suppose that the event has an intimate bearing upon the history of the apocalyptic period which is the subject of the vision. It is evidently introduced to explain the intense hostility of the dragon against the church of Christ; and this circumstance seems to imply that the casting out of Satan here referred to took place shortly before the outbreak of persecution against the Christians. It is important to remember that 'Michael' is in all probability to be identified with the Son of God. The reader is referred to the satisfactory proof of this identity adduced by Hengstenberg.

We are not to conceive of this conflict as one of physical force, like Milton's battles in 'Paradise Lost,' but rather as a moral and spiritual victory gained by truth over error, by light over darkness, by the Gospel over sin and unbelief. Probably there is an intimate connection between the casting out of Satan here referred to and the words of our Lord to His disciples when they brought back the report of their successful mission as evangelists,---'I beheld Satan as lightning fall from heaven' (Luke x. 18); and, again, 'Now is the judgment of this world, now shall the prince of this world be cast out' (John xii. 31); and, again, 'For this purpose the Son of God was manifested, that he might destroy the works of the devil' (1 John iii. 8). Translating the symbols into common language, they appear to signify that the progress of Christianity in the land aroused the hostility of Satan and his emissaries, and led to more active persecution of the disciples of Christ.

The victory Michael and his angels is celebrated by a triumphant proclamation in heaven, which does come within the purview of the vision.

Chap. xii. 10, 11.---'And I heard a great voice in heaven saying, Now is come salvation, and strength, and the kingdom of our God, and the power of his Christ; for the accuser of our brethren is cast out, which accused them before our God day and night. And they overcame him by the blood of the Lamb, and by the word of their testimony; and they loved not their lives unto the death.'

In all this we have the expression of the general truth that, in the long and deadly conflict with Jewish enmity, intensified by satanic malice, Christ fought for His persecuted disciples and foiled the attacks of their adversaries. How distinctly St. Paul recognised the presence and activity of an infernal power in the malignant hostility which opposed the Gospel may be seen in his remarkable words, 'We wrestle not with flesh and blood, but against principalities, against powers, against the rulers of the darkness of this world, against spiritual wickedness in high places' (Ephes. vi. 12). Divested of its symbolical imagery, the vision shows that the efforts of Satan to crush the truth of God were foiled and defeated, and only led to the more signal and decisive triumph of the kingdom of Christ.

Satan, baulked of his prey and knowing that 'he hath but a little while,' for the consummation is now very near, departs, as we have seen, to make war with the remnant of the woman's seed, 'who keep the commandments of God, and have the testimony of Jesus' (ver. 17).

4. *The First Wild Beast.*

Chap. xiii. 1-10.---'And he stood upon the sand of the sea. And I saw a wild beast coming up out of the sea, having ten horns and seven heads, and upon his horns ten diadems, and upon his heads names of blasphemy. And the beast which I saw was like unto a leopard, and his feet were as the feet of a bear, and his mouth as it were the mouth of a lion: and the dragon gave him his power, and his throne, and great authority. And I saw one of his heads as it were wounded to death; and his deadly wound was healed: and all the world [land] wondered after the beast. And they worshipped the dragon because he gave the power unto the beast: and they worshipped the beast, saying, Who is like unto the beast? Who is able to make war with him? And there was given unto him a mouth speaking great things and blasphemies; and power was given unto him to continue forty and two months. And he opened his mouth in blasphemy against God, to blaspheme his name, and his tabernacle, and them that dwell in heaven. And it was given unto him to make war with the saints, and to overcome them: and power was given him over all kindreds, and tongues, and nations. And all that dwell upon the earth shall worship him, whose names are not written in the book of life of the Lamb slain from the foundation of the world. If any man have an ear, let him hear. He that leadeth into captivity shall go into captivity: he that killeth with the sword must be killed with the sword. Here is the patience and the faith of the saints.'

We now enter upon an investigation full of interest, but also full of difficulty; though that difficulty is greatly mitigated by the known limits of the area within which we are restricted, and where we must look for the personage now introduced upon the scene, and who plays so important a part in the sequel.

The true reading of the first verse is now admitted to be estaqh [he stood], namely, the dragon. This is not unimportant. The dragon, foiled in his attempt to destroy the woman and her seed, stations himself on the sands of the sea, looking out for a potent auxiliary enlisted in his service.

Nor is he long in making his appearance. A portentous monster is beheld coming up out of the sea,---he is designated qhrion [a wild beast], already named by anticipation in chap. xi. 7. The description of this monster is very minute, so that his identification ought to be easy. Let us note the particulars of the description:---

1. The beast comes from the sea.
2. He has seven heads, and ten horns, with ten diadems upon his horns.
3. He bears names of blasphemy upon his heads.
4. He unites the characteristics of all the beasts seen by Daniel (chap. vii.).
5. He is invested by the dragon with his delegated power.
6. One of his heads is mortally wounded; but the deadly would is healed.
7. He receives the homage of the whole world.
8. Divine honours are paid to him.
9. He blasphemes God, and wars against the saints.
10. The duration of his power is limited to forty-two months.
11. His number is 'the number of a man,' and is declared to be 'six hundred threescore and six.' (In chap. xvii. other particulars are added, which complete the description of the beast, although it must be confessed they do not tend to make the discovery of his identity easier.)
12. He was, and is not, and shall again come (chap. xvii. 8).
13. He ascends out of the abyss, and goes into perdition (chap. xvii. 8).
14. He is a king: one of seven, and yet the eighth (chap. xvii. 11).

It would be strange if such a number of marked and peculiar characteristics could be applicable to more than one individual, or if such an individual could be so obscure as not to be immediately recognised. He must be sought among the greatest of the earth; he must be the foremost of his day, the observed of all observers; he must fill the highest throne and rule the mightiest empire. His period, too, is fixed: it is in the last days of the Jewish polity, close upon the final catastrophe. The mystery stands revealed even by its own self-solution. This portentous wild beast, this potentate of the world, this plenipotentiary of Satan, can be no other than the master of the world, the Emperor of Rome, 'the man of sin,'---NERO

Let us now see how the particulars of the description agree with the character of Nero.
1. None will dispute his claim to the title 'wild beast.' If ever man deserved that name it was the brutal monster that disgraced humanity by his infamous cruelties and crimes. St. Paul gives him a similar designation: 'I was delivered out of the mouth of the *lion*' (2 Tim. iv. 17).
2. By his rising out of the sea is probably meant that the beast is a *foreign* power. We are to regard him from a Jewish point of view; and in Judea Nero would of course be a transmarine sovereign.
3. The seven heads and ten crowned horns of the beast are the symbols of his plenary power and universal dominion.
4. The names of blasphemy inscribed upon his heads signify the assumption of the prerogatives of deity.
5. The union of the characteristics of the four beasts in Daniel's vision indicates that the dominion of the beast embraces the kingdoms represented in that vision.

169

6.   The possession of the delegated power of the dragon implies the subserviency of the beast to the interests of Satan. He is the dragon's legate.

7.   One of his heads being wounded to death implies the violent end of the individual symbolised by the beast.

8.   As a matter of course, it would be true of the Roman emperor that he received the homage of the whole world, and idolatrous worship would be paid to him.

9.   History tells us that Nero was the first of the emperors who persecuted Christians.

10.   The duration of that first and bitter persecution accords with the period of forty and two months, or three years and a half, mentioned in the vision. (If we adopt the reading of the Codex Sinaiticus, 'it was given unto him to do what he will for forty and two months,' it would evidently imply that his cruel policy of persecution would be limited to that period. Now, as a matter of fact, the persecution by Nero began in November A.D.64, and ended with his death in June A.D.68, that is as nearly as possible three years and a half.)

Postponing for the moment the consideration of the next and crucial question,---'the number of the beast,' we may here pause to observe how precisely all this tallies with the character of Nero. We might, at first, be disposed to think, with Bossuet, that the visionary beast signifies 'the Roman Empire, or more properly Rome herself, the mistress of the world,---Rome pagan, and the persecutor of the saints.' But as we proceed we are satisfied that it is not an abstraction, but a real person, that is here described, or, at least, the Imperial power embodied in the most ferocious and brutal of its representatives, the Emperor Nero. Every point of the description identifies the criminal. It was this execrable tyrant who first let loose the hell-hounds of persecution on the unoffending Christians of Rome. More like a wild beast than a man, he glutted his bloodthirsty propensities with the murder of his brother, his mother, and his wife. The incendiary of his own capital, he falsely imputed his crime to the innocent Christians, whom he put to death in vast numbers and with unheard-of barbarities. Wielding the mightiest power on earth, he used it for the indulgence of the basest vices, and made himself the slave of the most brutal passions. He arrogated to himself the prerogatives of deity, and claimed and received the worship due to God. His inordinate vanity made him greedy of admiration; it led him to perform as an actor on the stage, to drive as a charioteer in the circus, to contend in the Olympic games. 'The world wondered after the beast.' We are told that he received no less than eighteen hundred crowns for his victories. Dio Cassius relates that he entered Rome in triumph, and was hailed with acclamations by the senate and people, who offered him the most abject adulation. He was greeted with shouts of 'Victories Olympic! Victories Pythian! Thou August! Thou August! Nero the Hercules! Nero the Apollo! Sacred Voice! Eternal One!'

Much more obscure is the apparently paradoxical statement respecting the deadly wound of the beast which was nevertheless healed. Of course, if it was healed it was not deadly; and if it was deadly it could not really be healed. To require a literal fulfillment of an impossibility would manifestly be unreasonable, yet the explanation ought to reconcile the seeming contradiction. Now, it is a curious fact that a plausible explanation of the paradox has been given. Nero died a violent death,---died by a wound from a sword, inflicted either by his own hand or by that of an assassin. It is needless to say that the wound was mortal; but there was undoubtedly a very general belief at the time that he did not die, but was somewhere in concealment, and would ere long reappear, and recover his former power. Tacitus alludes to the popular belief (History, chap. ii. 8), as does also Suetonius (Nero, chap. lvii.). There is nothing improbable in the supposition that such a note of identity, embodying the general belief, might be employed as it is in the vision; at all events, no other explanation supplies so reasonable and satisfactory a solution of the problem.

The Number of the Beast.

We now come to the question which has exercised the ingenuity of critics and commentators almost since the day it was first propounded, and which even yet can hardly be said to be solved, viz. the name or number of the beast. Without wasting time on the various answers that have been given, it may suffice to make one or two preliminary remarks on the conditions of the problem.

1.   It is evident that the writer considered that he was giving sufficient data for the identification of the person intended. It is also presumable that he meant not to puzzle, but to enlighten, his readers.

2.   It is equally evident that the explanation does not lie on the surface. It requires wisdom to understand his words: it is only the man 'who hath understanding' that is competent to solve the problem.

3.   It is plain that what he intends to convey to his readers is the name of the person symbolised by the beast. His *name* expresses a certain *number;* or, the letters which form his name, when added together, amount to a certain numerical value.

4.   The name or number is that of a *man,---i.e.* it is not a beast, nor an evil spirit, nor an abstraction, but a person, a living *man.*

5.   The number which expresses the name is, in Greek characters, c e z, or in numerical value six hundred three-score and six.

We have already, on entirely independent grounds, arrived at the conclusion that by the apocalyptic beast is intended the reigning emperor, Nero. It is his name, therefore, that ought to fulfill, not indeed obviously, nor without some research, yet satisfactorily and conclusively, all the conditions of the problem. That emperor's name would be written in three ways, according as it was expressed in one or other of the three languages, the Latin, the Greek, or the Hebrew: in Latin, *Nero Caesar;* in Greek, *Nerwn Kaisar;* in Hebrew, rsq nwrn.

St. John was not writing to Romans, nor in the Latin tongue, so that the first form may be at once set aside. He was writing, however, in Greek, and to readers well acquainted with Greek, though most of them probably of Jewish blood. It is probable that most of them would at once, and instinctively, pronounce the dreaded name. If so they would feel at a loss, for the Greek letters *N e r w n K a i s a r* would not make up the numbers required.

But if this had been all that was necessary, the name would have lain upon the surface, patent and palpable to the dullest apprehension. It would have required neither wisdom nor understanding to read the riddle. The reader must try another method. St. John was a Hebrew, and though he wrote in Greek characters, his thoughts were Hebrew, and the Hebrew form of the Imperial name and title was familiar to him and to his Hebrew-Christian friends both in Asia Minor and Judea. It might not unnaturally occur to the reflecting reader to calculate the value of the letters which expressed the emperor's name in Hebrew. And the secret would stand disclosed:---

N = 50	Q = 100	
R = 200	S = 60	
W = 6	R = 200	
N = 50		
306	+360	= 666.

Here, then, is a number which expresses a *name;* the name of a *man,* of *the* man who, of all then living, best deserved to be called a wild beast: the head of the Empire, the master of the world; claiming to be a god, receiving divine honours, persecuting the saints of the Most High; in short, answering in every particular to the description in the apocalyptic vision. If it should be asked, Why should the prophet wrap up his meaning in enigmas? Why should he not expressly name the individual he means? First, the Apocalypse is a book of symbols: everything in it is expressed in imagery, which requires translation into ordinary language. But, secondly, it would not have been safe to speak more plainly. To have openly stated the name of the tyrant, after describing and designating him in the manner employed in the Apocalypse, would have been rash and imprudent in the extreme. Like St. Paul when describing 'the man of sin,' St. John veils his meaning under a disguise, which the heathen Greek or Roman would probably fail to penetrate, but which the instructed Christian of Judea or Asia Minor would readily see through.

It is a strong confirmation of the accuracy of this interpretation that we have another enigmatical description of the very same personage from the hand of St. Paul. We have already seen the proof that 'the man of sin' delineated in 1 Thess. ii. is no other than Nero, and the comparison of the two portraitures shows how striking is their resemblance to one another and to the original. This correspondence cannot be a curious coincidence merely; it can only be accounted for by the supposition that both apostles had the same individual in view.

5. *The Second Wild Beast.*

Chap. xiii. 11-17.---'And I saw another wild beast coming up out of the earth [land]; and he had two horns like a lamb, and he spake as a dragon. And he exerciseth all the power of the first beast in his presence, and causeth the land and them which dwell therein to worship the first beast, whose deadly wound was healed. And he worketh great wonders, so that he even maketh fire to come down from heaven to the earth in the sight of men, and he deceiveth them that dwell in the land by means of those miracles which he had power to work in the presence of the beast; saying to them that dwell in the land, that they should make an image to the beast, which had the wound by a sword, and did live. And he had power to give life [breath] to the image of the beast, that the image of the beast should even speak, and cause that as many as would not worship the image of the beast should be slain. And he causeth all, both small and great, rich and poor, free and bond, to receive a mark in their right hand, or on their forehead; and that no men might buy or sell, save he that had the mark, or the name of the beast, or the number of his name.'

If our conclusions respecting the identity of the first beast are correct, it ought not to be difficult to discover who is intended by the second beast. It will be observed that in many respects there is a strong resemblance between them: they are of the same nature, though one is supreme and the other subordinate; but there are also points of difference. It will be proper, however, in this case also, to bring into one view the various particular characteristics which assist to identify the individual intended:---

1. The second beast rises up from the land.
2. He has only two horns, and they are like a lamb's.
3. He speaks like a dragon.
4. He is clothed with the delegated authority of the first beast.
5. He compels men to pay homage, or worship, to the beast.
6. He pretends to exercise miraculous powers.
7. He rules with tyrannical force and cruelty.

8. He excludes from civil rights all who refuse abject submission to the beast.

Looking at these characteristics it becomes at once perfectly clear that we must seek the antitype to this symbolic figure in a man kindred character with the monster Nero himself. He is evidently the *alter ego* of the emperor, though his proportions are drawn on a smaller scale.

1. His rising out of the land, while the first beast rises out of the sea, denotes that the second beast is a *domestic* or home authority, ruling in Judea; while the other is a *foreign* power.

2. His having two horns like a lamb, while the first beast has ten, denotes that his sphere of government is small, and his power limited, compared with the other.

3. That he speaks as a dragon, or serpent, denotes his crafty and deceitful character.

4. His being clothed with the authority of the first beast indicates that he is the official representative and delegate of Nero in Judea.

At this point the individual is revealed to us. He can be no other than the Roman procurator or governor of Judea under Nero, and the particular governor must be sought at or near the outbreak of the Jewish war; and here the history of the time throws a flood of light upon the inquiry.

There are two names which may vie with each other for the bad pre-eminence of the original of this picture of the second beast,---Albinus and Gessius Florus. Each was a monster of tyranny and cruelty, but the latter outdid the former. Before Gessius Florus came into office the Jews counted Albinus the worst governor who had ever ground them by his oppression. After Gessius Florus came they thought Albinus almost a virtuous man in comparison. Florus was a miscreant worthy to stand by the side of Nero: a fit servant of such a master.

The reader will find in the pages of Josephus the story of the enormous and incredible profligacy, fraud, treachery, and tyranny of this last and worst of all the governors who represented the Imperial authority in Judea, and will see how the historian traces to the misrule of this infamous man the ruin that fell upon the nation. It was his intolerable and Draconic oppression that goaded the unhappy Jews into rebellion, and was the proximate cause of the war which ended in the utter overthrow of Jerusalem and her people. Josephus, indeed, has not preserved all the facts, which, if we had them, would no doubt vividly illustrate all the particulars in the apocalyptic portraiture of the second beast. But we scarcely need them. Force, fraud, cruelty, imposture, tyranny, are attributes which too certainly might be predicated of such a procurator as Florus. Perhaps the traits most difficult to verify are those which relate to the compulsory enforcement of homage to the emperor's statue and the assumption of miraculous pretensions. Yet even here all we know is in favour of the description being true to the letter. Dean Milman observes:---

'The image of the beast is clearly the statue of the emperor;' and he adds: 'The test by which the martyrs were tried was to adore the emperor, to offer incense before his statue, and to invoke the gods.' (See Review of Newman's Development of Christian Doctrine.)

Dean Alford's remarks are also deserving of notice:---

'The Seer is now describing facts which history substantiates to us in their literal fulfillment. The image of Caesar was everywhere that which men were made to worship: it was before this that the Christian martyrs were brought to the test, and put to death if they refused the act of adoration ...

'If it be said, as an objection to this, that it is not an image of the emperor, but of the best itself, which is spoken of, the answer is very simple,---that as the Seer himself, in chap. xvii. 11, does not hesitate to identify one of the "seven kings" with the beast itself, so we may fairly assume that the image of the beast, for the time being, would be the image of the reigning emperor.'

To the same effect are the following observations of Dean Howson, which are the more striking as being written without any reference to the passage before us:---

'The image of the emperor was at that time [under the Empire] the object of religious reverence: he was a deity on earth ('Das aequa potestas'---Juv. iv. 71), and the worship paid to him was a real worship. It is a striking thought that in those times (setting aside effete forms of religion) the only two genuine worships in the civilised world were the worship of a Tiberius or a Nero, on the one hand, and the worship of *Christ* on the other.'

We are now in a position to ask the verdict of every candid and judicial mind on the question of identity which has been argued, as well as the complete congruity and correspondence in all points between the symbols in the vision and the historical personages whom, in our opinion, they represent. The time, the place, the scene, the circumstances, and the *dramatis personae* are all in full accord with the requirements of the Apocalypse. It is the eve of the great catastrophe, the final ruin of the Judaic polity. The predicted persecution of the people of God, which was to usher in the end, has broken out. A terrible triumvirate of evil is in league against Christ and His cause. The dragon, the beast from the sea, and the beast from the land,---Satan, the Emperor, and the Roman procurator, are in active hostility against 'the woman and the remnant of her seed.' Their time, however, is short; the hour of retribution is at hand; and the very next scene discovers the champion and avenger of the faithful, and shows the security and blessedness of His people.

6. *The Lamb on Mount Sion.*

Chap. xiv. 1-13.---'And I saw, and behold, the Lamb stood on the mount Sion, and with him an hundred and forty and four thousand, having his name, and the name of his Father, written in their foreheads,' etc.

This portion of the vision scarcely needs an interpreter; it speaks for itself. There is a striking contrast between the wild beast that rules as vicegerent of the dragon and the Lamb that governs in His Father's name. There can be no doubt that the hundred and forty and four thousand, having the name of Christ and the Father inscribed on their foreheads, are identical with the hundred and forty and four thousand out of all the tribes of the children of Israel, who have the seal of God on their foreheads, who are alluded to in chap. vii. They are the elect Hebrew-Christian church of Judea, possibly of Jerusalem, and are represented as standing with the Lamb on the Mount Sion, redeemed, triumphant, glorified; no longer exposed to danger and death, but gathered into the fold of the Great Shepherd. Of course the representation is proleptic---an anticipation of what was now imminent; in fact, a repetition of the glorious scene described in chap. vii. 9-17. Is it possible to believe that the writer of the Epistle to the Hebrews had not this vision in his thoughts when he wrote that noble passage, "Ye are come unto mount Sion, the city of the living God, the heavenly Jerusalem," etc.? The points of resemblance are so marked and so numerous that it cannot possibly be accidental. The scene is the same,---Mount Sion; the *dramatis personae* are the same,---'the general assembly and church of the first-born, which are written in heaven,' corresponding with the hundred and forty and four thousand who bear the seal of God. In the epistle they are called 'the church of the *first-born;*' the vision explains the title,---they are 'the *first-fruits* unto God and to the Lamb;' the first converts to the faith of Christ in the land of Judea. In the epistle they are designated 'the spirits of just men made perfect;' in the vision they are 'virgins undefiled, in whose mouth was found no guile; for they are without fault before the throne of God.' Both in the vision and the epistle we find 'the innumerable company of angels' and 'the Lamb,' by whom redemption was achieved. In short, it is placed beyond all reasonable doubt that since the author of the Apocalypse cannot be supposed to have drawn his description from the epistle, the writer of the epistle must have derived his ideas and imagery from the Apocalypse.

Events are now hastening rapidly towards the consummation. The Seer beholds three angels fly in succession across the field of vision, each bearing a prophetic announcement of the approaching catastrophe. The first, who is charged with the proclamation of the everlasting Gospel, in the first instance to them that dwell in the land, and next to every nation, and kindred, and tongue, and people, crises with a loud voice, 'Fear God, and give glory to him; because the hour of his judgment is come' (ver. 7). There is a manifest allusion here to the fact predicted by our Lord that, before the coming of 'the end,' the Gospel of the kingdom would first be preached in all the world 'for a witness to all the nations' (Matt. xxiv. 14). This symbol, therefore, indicates the near approach of the catastrophe of Jerusalem,---the arrival of the hour of Israel's judgment.

A second angel swiftly follows, and proclaims the fall of Babylon, as if it had already taken place, saying, 'Babylon the great is fallen, is fallen, which made the all nations drink of the wine of the wrath of her fornication.' This is plainly another declaration of the same impending catastrophe, only more distinctly indicating the doom of the guilty city---the great criminal about to be brought to judgment. We shall presently have occasion to discuss the identity of the great city here and elsewhere designated as Babylon.

A third messenger succeeds, who denounces, in awful language, the wrath of God upon all idol worshippers:---

Chap. xiv. 9-11.---'If any man worship the beast and his image, or receive his mark in his forehead, or in his hand, the same shall drink of the wine of the wrath of God, which is poured out without mixture into the cup of his indignation, and he shall be tormented with fire and brimstone in the presence of the holy angels and in the presence of the Lamb,' etc.

In striking contrast to this is the message which a heavenly voice brings to the faithful disciples of Christ 'who keep the commandments of God and the faith of Jesus.'

Chap. xiv. 13.---'And I heard a voice from heaven saying unto me, Write, Blessed are the dead which die in the Lord from henceforth: Yea, saith the Spirit, that they may rest from their labours; and their works do follow them.'

All this is clearly indicative of the near approach of the final catastrophe. There is one expression, however, in the last quotation which calls for explanation, viz. the announcement respecting the blessedness of the dead who die in the Lord *from henceforth.* This 'henceforth' is the emphatic word in the sentence, and must have an important significance. It is not simply that the dead in Christ are safe or happy, but that, from and after a certain specified period, a peculiar blessedness belongs to all those who thenceforth die in the Lord.

It is not unreasonable in itself, and it appears, moreover, to be the distinct teaching of Holy Scripture, that the great consummation which closed the Jewish age had an important bearing upon the condition of all who subsequently to that period, 'die in the Lord.' We have seen (Remarks on Heb. xi. 40) that previously to the redemptive work of Christ the state of the pious dead was not perfect. They had to await the accomplishment of that great event which constituted the foundation of their everlasting felicity. The saints of the old dispensation 'obtained not the promise.' They died in *faith*, but did not possess the inheritance. 'God provided something better for *us,* that they without us should not be made perfect.' So wrote the author of the Epistle to the Hebrews on the verge of the great consummation. The plain meaning of this is that the *Parousia* marked the introduction of a new epoch in the condition of the departed saints and the prospects of all who after that epoch commenced should die in the Lord. 'Blessed are such' *from henceforth.* That is to say, they should not have to wait, as their predecessors had, the arrival of the period when the promise should be fulfilled. They should enter *at once* into 'the rest which remaineth for the people of God.' The way into the holy place has now been made manifest; there is immediate rest and reward for the faithful departed; 'they rest from their labours; for their works do follow them.'

This important passage would be totally inexplicable but for the light thrown upon it by Heb. iv. 1-11; xi. 9, 10, 13, 39, 40.

7. *The Son of Man on the Cloud.*

Chap. xiv. 14-20.---'And I saw, and behold a white cloud, and upon the cloud one sitting like unto the Son of man, having on his head a golden crown, and in his hand a sharp sickle. And another angel came out of the temple, crying with a loud voice to him that sat on the cloud, Thrust in thy sickle and reap: because the time to reap is come; because the harvest of the land is ripe. And he that sat on the cloud cast his sickle on the land; and the land was reaped.

'And another angel came out of the temple which is in heaven, he also having a sharp sickle. And another angel came out from the altar, which had power over the fire; and cried with a loud cry to him that had the sharp sickle, saying, Thrust in thy sharp sickle, and gather the clusters of the vine of the land; for her grapes are fully ripe. And the angel cast his sickle on the land, and gathered the vine of the land, and cast it into the great wine-press of the wrath of God. And the wine-press was trodden outside the city, and blood came out of the wine-press, even to the bits of the horses, for a thousand six hundred furlongs.'

We now come to the seventh and last of the mystic figures of which this fourth vision consists, and to the *denoument,* where we may expect to find the catastrophe of the whole. Nor are we disappointed; for nothing can be more distinctly marked than the catastrophe under this symbol, the interpretation being so self-evident that it can hardly be misunderstood.

The scene opens with the apparition of 'one like unto the Son of man seated on a white cloud,' wearing a golden crown on his head and holding a sharp sickle in his hand. The weapon which he holds is the emblem of the transaction which is about to take place. It is the time of harvest, for 'the harvest of the land is ripe; and he that sat on the cloud cast his sickle on the land; and the land was reaped.'

There can be no misunderstanding this act. We have the original draught of the picture in our Lord's parable of the wheat and the tares. 'In the time of harvest [the end of the age, sunteleia tou aiwnoz], I will say to the reapers, Gather ye together first the tares, and bind them in bundles to burn them; but gather the wheat into my barn' (Matt. xiii. 30).

The parable of the tares and the wheat is also followed in the vision in the separation of this final judicial transaction into two parts---the wheat harvest and the vintage, except only in the transposition of the order of the events. The harvest corresponds with the reaping of the wheat and its safe gathering into the barn; in the other words, it is the fulfillment of the prediction, 'The Son of man shall send his angels, and they shall gather together his elect from the four winds' (Matt. xxiv. 31-34), an event which was to take place before the passing away of that generation. The destruction of the tares corresponds with the 'vintage of the land.' It will be observed that the vintage is wholly of a destructive character. As the 'harvest of the land' denotes the salvation of the faithful people of God, so the 'vintage of the land' denotes the destruction of His enemies. It is worthy of remark that while the Son of man is represented as the reaper, the angel in the vision is the agent in the cutting down of the vine. It is scarcely necessary to point out the peculiar fitness of the imagery employed in the latter impressive scene. 'The vine of the land' is Israel, according to the well-known emblem in Psalm lxxx. 8, 'Thou hast brought a vine out of Egypt,' etc. The vintage is now come, for 'her grapes are fully ripe;' that is to say, the nation is ripe for judgment. The angel commissioned to destroy does not gather the clusters, but cuts down the vine itself, and casts it altogether into the 'great wine-press of the wrath of God.' The wine-press is trodden; and this is represented as taking place outside the city, as the sin-offering was burned outside the camp, and as the criminal was executed outside the gate, being accursed (Heb. xiii. 11-13). Blood comes out of the wine-press, and in such torrents that it is like a river in flood, rising to the horse-bridles, and reaching a distance of 'a thousand and six hundred furlongs.'

This is terrible in symbol, yet almost literal in its historic truth. It was a people that was thus 'trampled' in the fury of divine wrath. Where was there ever such a sea of blood as was shed in the exterminating war of Vespasian and of Titus? The carnage, as related by Josephus, exceeds all that is recorded in the sanguinary annals of warfare. Jerusalem, and her children within her, were trodden in the great wine-press of the wrath of God. Then were fulfilled the words of the prophet Jeremiah, 'The Lord hath trodden the virgin, the daughter of Judah, as in a wine-press' (Lam. i. 15). There is fact as well as figure in the ghastly scene which represents the invading cavalry as swimming in blood up to the horses' bits; and there is probably an allusion to the geographical extent of Palestine in the 'thousand and six hundred furlongs,' so that we may regard the symbolical description as equivalent to the statement that from one end to the other the land was deluged with blood.

In all this the prophecy and the history fit each other like lock and key; and if we had not the testimony of an eye-witness, who certainly could have no interest in exaggerating the ruin of his people or defaming their character, it would scarcely be possible to believe that these symbols were not overcharged. But no one can read that tragic story without recognising there the transactions which are here written in symbol, and which amply attest the reality and truth of the prophecy.

Such is the distinctly marked catastrophe of the vision of the seven mystic figures. Like the other catastrophes it is an act of judgment, presenting the great consummation in a different aspect. If any doubt should still be felt as to the principle which underlies our whole system of interpretation, viz. that the Apocalypse is a sevenfold representation of the same great providential drama, it must be dispelled by the next series of visions, which conclusively demonstrates this feature of the book.

The Fifth Vision

THE SEVEN VIALS, Chaps. xv. xvi.

Chap. xv. 1.---'And I saw another sign in heaven, great and marvelous, seven angels having the seven last plagues; for in them is completed the wrath of God,' etc.

This vision opens, like the first, second, and third, with a prologue or preamble. The scene is laid in heaven, where the Seer beholds seven angels, charged with the infliction of seven plagues, which are called *the last,* as being the completion of the divine wrath upon the guilty nation. The imagery in this introductory scene is conceived in a style of the loftiest sublimity. The seven ministers of vengeance receive from on of the living creatures or cherubim, seven golden vials full of the wrath of God, and are commissioned to begin at once the execution of their mission, which is, to pour out their vials on the land.

It will at once be seen that there is a marked correspondence between the vision of the seven vials and that of the seven trumpets. The vials, indeed, are simply a repetition and abridgment of the trumpets, followed the same order and taking substantially the same form. There are, it is true, additional circumstances introduced into the vision of the seven vials, but still the resemblance between the two visions is so striking as to force the conviction on the mind that they both refer to the same historical events.

The subjoined parallel will show the correspondence between the two visions more distinctly:---

THE TRUMPETS	THE VIALS
1. Plagues poured upon the land.	1. Plagues poured upon the land.
2. Affects the sea, which becomes as blood.	2. Affects the sea, which becomes as blood.
3. Affects the rivers and fountains of waters.	3. Affects the rivers and fountains of waters.
4. Affects the sun, moon, and stars.	4. Affects the sun.
5. The abyss (the seat of the beast) opened. Men tormented.	5. Poured on the seat of the beast (the abyss). Men tormented.
6. The angels at the great river Euphrates loosed. Muster of hordes of cavalry.	6. Poured on the great river Euphrates. Hosts muster for the battle of the great day.
7. Catastrophe; judgment; the kingdom proclaimed. Terrible natural phenomena---voices, thunderings, and an earthquake.	7. Catastrophe; proclamation of the end. Terrible natural phenomena---voices, thunderings, and an earthquake.

This cannot be mere casual coincidence: it is *identity,* and it suggests the inquiry, For what reason is the vision thus repeated? It cannot be merely for the sake of symmetry, to complete the sevenfold plan of the construction, for the marvellous affluence of the book makes the suggestion of poverty of invention, or repetition for the sake of filling up, utterly preposterous. More probable is the explanation that the vision of the vials is introduced not only to reaffirm the judgments about to come upon the land, but especially to prepare the way for the bringing in of the great criminal, the hour of whose judgment is come. The last of the seven vials represents *Babylon the great* as coming in remembrance before God; yet in the catastrophe of the vision her judgment is suspended, because it is to form the material of a separate vision, viz. the sixth.

It will now be proper to pass in brief review the successive vials of the seven angels.

The first four vials (chap. xvi. 2-9), like the first four trumpets, affect the natural world,---the earth or land, the sea, the rivers, the sun. These are all smitten with distemper and plague,---the frame of nature is out of joint, and the inanimate creation sickens and groans on account of the wickedness of men. This may be said to be a figure of speech, though enough in Scripture; how far it expresses any historical facts it is impossible to say, but it is remarkable that the language of our Lord in speaking of this very period comes very near the symbols of the Apocalypse: 'There shall be signs in the sun, and in the moon, and in the stars; and upon the earth [land] distress of the nations, with perplexity; the sea and the waves roaring; men's hearts failing them for fear, and for looking after those things which are coming upon the land: for the powers of heaven shall be shaken' (Luke xxi. 25, 26). If the testimony of Josephus is to be relied on, the destruction of Jerusalem was preceded by portents of the most alarming kind. It is to be observed that the area affected by these plagues is 'the land,' that is Judea, the scene of the tragedy. The local and national character of the transactions represented in the vision is distinctly brought out in ver. 6. When the third angel turns the rivers into blood, the angel of the waters is heard acknowledging the retributive justice of this plague,---'For they shed the blood of saints and prophets, and thou has given them blood to drink; they are worthy.' This 'killing of the prophets' was the very sin of Israel, and of Jerusalem, nor is there any other city or nation against which this particular crime can be alleged as its peculiar characteristic. This impeachment decisively fixes the allusion in the vision to the Jewish people, and to that fearful period in their history when it might truly be said that their rivers ran with blood.

The fifth vial (chap. xvi. 10, 11) corresponds with the fifth trumpet. It is poured out on the seat or throne of the beast, which seems to be identical with 'the abyss' of the trumpet vision. The abyss is the region from which the beast is said to ascend (chap. xi. 7); and that this was the name given to the abode of evil spirits appears from the fact that the demons cast out of the possessed Gadarene besought Jesus 'that he would not command them to go away into *the abyss*' (Luke viii. 31). The seat of the beast, therefore, is the same as the abyss,---the kingdom of the power of darkness. What historical facts are signified by the symbols of terror and misery here employed it is impossible to say, though they point not obscurely to the agonies of distress and suffering which preceded and portended the final consummation.

The sixth vial, like the sixth trumpet, takes effect upon the great river Euphrates (ver. 12), the water of which is dried up, that 'the way of the kings of the east may be prepared.' We now approach the catastrophe. In the vision of the sixth trumpet we see an innumerable host mustered for the great battle; in the vision of the sixth vial we see 'three unclean spirits like frogs come out of the mouth of the dragon, and out of the mouth of the beast, and out of the mouth of the false prophet;' the emissaries of the powers of darkness go forth to muster the armies of the 'kings of the whole world,' to gather them to the great war of 'the great day of God Almighty.' Translated into historical terms this symbol represents the mobilising of the forces of the Empire and of the kings of the neighbouring nations for the Jewish war. The drying up of the Euphrates seems plainly to signify its being crossed with ease and speed; and this, taken in connection with the corresponding symbol under the sixth trumpet, viz. the loosing of the four angels bound at the Euphrates, points to the drawing of troops from that quarter for the invasion of Judea. This we know to be a historical fact. Not only Roman legions from the frontier of the Euphrates, but auxiliary kings whose dominions lay in that region, such as Antiochus of Commagene and Sohemus of Sophene, most properly designated 'kings from the east,' followed the eagles of Rome to the siege of Jerusalem. The name given to the approaching conflict decisively determines the event to which reference is made:---it is 'the battle,' or 'war of that great day of God Almighty'---an expression equivalent to 'the great and terrible day of the Lord.' That this day was now at hand is plainly intimated by the warning in ver. 15, 'Behold, I come as a thief.' The scene of the conflict also, 'Armageddon,'---a name that is associated with one of the darkest and most disastrous days in the history of Israel, the field of Megiddo, the emblem of defeat and slaughter, lies in Jewish territory. That name of evil omen was meet to be the type of that final field of blood on which Israel as a nation was doomed to perish.

The seventh vial, like the seventh trumpet, brings the catastrophe of the vision, accompanied by the same portents of 'voices, and thunderings, and lightnings, and an earthquake, and great hail.' A voice from the temple, a voice from the throne itself, proclaims the consummation, 'It is done! Tegonen! Actum est! All is over!' That is to say, the catastrophe of the vision, and that which it symbolises, is come; for it will be observed that every catastrophe lands us in virtually the same conclusion. An earthquake of unparalleled violence shatters 'the cities of the nations' and divides *the great city* itself, the city which is pre-eminently the theme of these visions, into three parts. 'Babylon the great' (which is clearly meant to be the name of the city just referred to) 'was remembered before God, to give her the cup of the wine of the fierceness of his wrath;' her sins cry for vengeance, and now her judgment is come, and the wine-cup of the fierce wrath of God is filled for her to drink.

That all this refers indubitably and exclusively to *Jerusalem* is surely self-evident, and it is capable of the clearest demonstration as the sequel will show.

One incident in this grad and awful catastrophe deserves special attention. In both the visions, the seventh trumpet and the seventh vial, particular mention is made of the *great hail* which falls upon men. In the seventh vial the hail is more fully dwelt upon, and every stone is said to be about the weight of a talent. There is something so extraordinary, and yet so specific, in this statement that it arrests the attention and suggests the inquiry, Is this wholly symbol, or is it in any degree fact? Of course, we cannot conceive literal hail of which every stone should be of the weight of a talent; yet the language is so precise and definite that we are almost compelled to suppose that it is not mere hyperbole. Now, it is a remarkable fact that in Josephus we seem to get the explanation of this apparently unintelligible symbol. He informs us that at the siege of Jerusalem the tenth legion constructed balistae of enormous magnitude and power, which discharged vast stones into the city. The whole description which Josephus gives of these engines is of such extraordinary interest it is well worthy of quotation:---

'Admirable as were the engines constructed by all the legions, those of the tenth were of peculiar excellence. Their scorpions were of greater power and their stone-projectors larger, and with these they not only kept in check the sallying parties, but those also on the ramparts. *The stones that were thrown were of the weight of a talent,* and had a range of two furlongs and more. The shock, not only to such as first met it, but even to those beyond them for a considerable distance, was irresistible. The Jews, however, at the first, could guard against the stone; for its approach was intimated, not only to the ear by its whiz, but also, being white, to the eye by its brightness. Accordingly they had watchmen posted on the towers, who gave warning when the engine was discharged and the stone projected, calling out in their native language, "The son is coming," on which those towards whom it was directed would separate, and lie down before it reached them. Thus it happened that, owing to these precautions, the stone fell harmless. It then occurred to the Romans to blacken it; when, taking a more successful aim, as it was no longer equally discernible in its approach, they swept down many at a single discharge.'---Josephus, Jewish Wars, bk. v. chap. vi. 3.

Is this only a fanciful coincidence, or is it a signal instance of the exact fulfillment of prophecy? We confess that we incline to the latter alternative, for it is perfectly congruous to represent such a mode of assault as a storm or hail of projectiles, while the specific allusion to the enormous weight of each stone seems to bring the statement within the domain of fact and history.3

1. Jewish Wars, bk. vi. chap. v. section 3, 4.

2. See Josephus, Jewish Wars, bk. iii. chap. iv. paragraph 2; bk. v. chap. i. paragraph 6.

3 There is another curious circumstance connected with this passage in Josephus. Whiston has the following not upon it:---

'What should be the meaning of this signal or watchword when the watchman saw a stone coming from the engine, *"The son cometh,"* or what mistake there is in the reading, I cannot tell. The MSS., both Greek and Latin, all agree in this reading; and I cannot approve of any groundless conjectural alteration of the text from nioz to ioz, that not the son, or a stone, but that the *arrow* or *dart* cometh, as hath been made by Dr. Hudson, and not corrected by Havercamp. Had Josephus written even his first edition of these books of the war in pure Hebrew, or had the Jews then used the pure Hebrew at Jerusalem, the Hebrew word for a son is so like that for a stone,---Ben and Eben, that such a correction might have more easily been admitted. But Josephus wrote his former edition for the use of the Jews beyond the Euphrates, and so in the Chaldee language, as he did this second edition in the Greek language; and Bar was the Chaldee word for son, instead of the Hebrew Ben, and was used not only in Chaldaea, but in Judea also, as the New Testament informs us. Dio also informs us that the very Romans in Rome pronounced the name of Simon the son of Gioras, Bar-Poras for Bar-Gioras, as we learn from Hiphiline, p. 217. Reland observes that "many will here look for a mystery, as though the meaning were that the Son of God came now to take vengeance on the sins of the Jewish nation," which is indeed the truth of the fact, but hardly what the Jews could now mean, unless, possibly, by way of derision of Christ" threatening so oft that He would come at the head of the Roman army for their destruction. But even this interpretation has but a very small degree of probability. If I were to make an emendation by mere conjecture, I would read petroz, instead of nioz, though the likeness is not so great as in ioz, because that is the word used by Josephus just before, as already been noted on this very occasion; while ioz, an arrow or dart, is only a poetical word, and never used by Josephus elsewhere, and is indeed no way suitable to the occasion, this engine not throwing arrows or darts, but great stones at this time.'---Whiston's Josephus, bk. v. chap. vi. paragraph 3, Note.

Dr. Traill makes the following observations on this passage:---

'"The son is coming." O nioz is the reading of all the MSS. and of Rufinus; and it is not easy to conceive how such a singular reading should be found in all if were not the true one. Nor are the alterations proposed at all satisfactory. O ioz would give the "arrow," not the "stone." O liqoz is without authority. Cardwell proposes outoz,---"here it comes." Reland's explanation is probably not far from the truth, viz. that the cry was **wba ab** = "the stone is coming," but that some, deceived by the similarity of sound, took it to be **wbh ab** = "the son is coming." From such a mistake as this, or from some other cause, the term "the son" might come to be applied as a nickname.'---Traill's Josephus, Critical Notes, p. clx.

We are disposed to think that none of these suggestions give a satisfactory explanation, though some of them come near the truth. It could not but be well known to the Jews that the great hope and faith of the Christians was the speedy coming of the Son. It was about this very time, according to Hegesippus, that St. James, the brother of our Lord, publicly testified in the temple that 'the Son of man was about to come in the clouds of heaven,' and then sealed his testimony with his blood. It seems highly probable that the Jews, in their defiant and desperate blasphemy, when they saw the white mass hurtling through the air, raised the ribald cry, 'The Son is coming,' in mockery of the Christian hope of the Parousia, to which they might trace a ludicrous resemblance in the strange appearance of the missile.

The Sixth Vision

THE HARLOT CITY, Chaps. xvii. xviii. xix xx.

We now approach a part of our investigation in which we are about to make great demands upon the candour and impartiality of the reader, and must ask for a patient and unbiased weighing of the evidence that shall be brought before him. Possibly we may run counter to many prepossessions, but if the seat of judgment be occupied by an impartial love of truth, we do not fear an adverse decision.

It may be convenient at the outset to take a general view of this vision as a whole, occupying as it does a larger space than any in the book, and thus indicating the pre-eminent importance of its contents.

It is introduced by a short preface or prologue (chap. xvii. 1, 2). One of the vial-angels invites the Seer to come and behold the judgment of 'the great harlot that sitteth on many waters.' The vision is seen in 'the wilderness.' The prophet sees a woman sitting upon a scarlet-coloured wild beast, full of names of blasphemy, and having seven heads and ten horns. The woman is gorgeously arrayed in a robe of purple and scarlet, and decked with gold and precious stones, and holds in her hand a golden cup 'full of abominations and filthiness of her fornication.' On the forehead of this visionary figure is an inscription, 'Mystery, Babylon the great, the mother of harlots and abominations of the earth.' She is, moreover, said to be 'drunk with the blood of the saints, and with the blood of the martyrs of Jesus.' The angel-interpreter then proceeds to disclose to the wondering prophet the meaning of the apparition. He identifies the wild beast in this vision with the first beast described in chap. xiii., whose number is six hundred and sixty-six, adding additional particulars to the description, some of them of a very obscure character. The woman, or harlot, he declares to be 'that great city which reigneth over the kings of the earth.' In the next chapter (xviii.) the fall of Babylon the great, or the harlot city, is described in language of great power and beauty. This is followed in chap. xix. by the celebration in heaven of the triumph over Babylon, which gives occasion to introduce by anticipation the approaching nuptials of the Lamb; after which there is a description of the victory of the divine Champion, whose name is the Word of God, over 'the beast, the false prophet, and the kings of the earth.' In chap. xx. the dragon, the head of the great confederacy against the cause of truth and of God, is bound and shut up in the abyss for a period of a thousand years. The vision then closes in a grand catastrophe, a solemn act of judgment, in which the dead, small and great, stand before God, and are judged according to their works. Such is a rapid sketch of the outlines of this magnificent vision.

The question of greatest importance and difficulty which we have here to deal with is, What city is signified by the woman sitting on the scarlet beast, and designated 'Babylon the great'?

By the great majority of interpreters it has been, and is, received as an undoubted and almost self-evident proposition that the Babylon of the Apocalypse is, and can be, no other than *Rome*, the empress of the world in the days of St. John, and since his time the seat and centre of the most corrupt form of Christianity and the most overshadowing spiritual despotism that the world has ever seen. That there is much to favour this opinion may be inferred from the fact of its general acceptance. It may even be thought to be placed beyond question by the apparent identification of the harlot in the vision, as the 'city of the seven hills,' and 'the great city which reigneth over the kings of the earth.'

It will seem presumptuous as well as hazardous to challenge a decision which has been pronounced by such high authority, and which has ruled so long among Protestant theologians and commentators, and he who ventures to do so enters the lists at a great disadvantage. Nevertheless, in the interests of truth, and with all reverence and loyalty to the teaching of the divine Word, it may not only be permitted, but may even be imperative, to show cause why the popular interpretation of this symbol should be rejected as untenable and untrue.

1.   There is an *a priori* presumption of the strongest kind against Rome being the Babylon of the Apocalypse. The improbability is great with regard even to Rome pagan, but far greater with regard to Rome papal. The very design of the book excludes the possibility of Rome being represented as one of its *dramatis personae*. The fundamental idea of the Apocalypse, as we have endeavoured to prove, is the approaching Parousia and the accompanying judgment of the guilty nation. Rome, Heathen or Christian, lies altogether outside the apocalyptic field of view, which is restricted to 'things which must shortly come to pass.' To wander into all ages and countries in the interpretation of these visions is absolutely forbidden by the express and fundamental limitations laid down in the book itself.

2.   On the other hand, it is to be expected *a priori* that great prominence should be given in the Apocalypse to *Jerusalem.* This is fact, if our view of the design and subject of the book be correct, ought to be the central figure in the picture. If the Apocalypse is only the reproduction and expansion of our Lord's prophecy on the Mount of Olives, which is mainly occupied with the approaching judgment of Israel and of Jerusalem, we may expect to find the same thing in

the Apocalypse; and it is as unreasonable to look for Rome in the Apocalypse as it would be to look for it in our Lord's prophecy on the Mount.

3.   It deserves particular attention that in the Apocalypse there are two cities, and only two, that are brought prominently and by name into view by symbolic representation. Each is the antithesis of the other. The one is the embodiment of all that is good and holy, the other the embodiment of all that is evil and accursed. To know either, is to know the other. These two contrasted cities are the *new Jerusalem* and *Babylon the great.*

There can be no room for doubt as to what is signified by the *new Jerusalem*: it is the city of God, the heavenly habitation, the inheritance of the saints of light. But what, then, is the proper antithesis to the *new Jerusalem?* Surely, it can be no other than the *old Jerusalem.* In fact, this antithesis between the old Jerusalem and the new is drawn out for us so distinctly by St. Paul in the Epistle to the Galatians, that he puts into our hand a key to the interpretation of this symbol in the Apocalypse. The apostle contrasts the Jerusalem 'which now is' with the Jerusalem which was to be: the Jerusalem which is in *bondage* with the Jerusalem which is *free:* the Jerusalem which is *beneath* with the Jerusalem which is *above* (Gal. iv. 25, 26). We have a similar antithesis in the Epistle to the Hebrews, where 'the city which hath foundations' is contrasted with the 'not-continuing city; the city 'whose builder is God' with the city of human creation; 'the city of the living God,' or the 'heavenly Jerusalem,' with the earthly Jerusalem (Heb. xi. 10, 16; xii. 22). In like manner we have the antithesis between these two cities distinctly and broadly presented to us in the Apocalypse the one being the harlot, the other the bride, the Lamb's wife.

These parallels or contrasts have only to be presented to the eye to speak for themselves:---

The New Jerusalem	The Old Jerusalem
The heavenly Jerusalem	The earthly Jerusalem
The city which hath the foundations	The non-continuing city
The city whose builder is God	The city whose builder is man
The Jerusalem which is to come	The Jerusalem which now is
The Jerusalem which is above	The Jerusalem which is beneath
The Jerusalem which is free	The Jerusalem which is in bondage
The holy city	The wicked city
The bride	The harlot

The real and proper antithesis, therefore, to the new Jerusalem is the old Jerusalem: and since the city contrasted with the new Jerusalem is also designated Babylon, we conclude that Babylon is the symbolic name of the wicked and doomed city, the old Jerusalem, whose judgment is here predicted.

4. If it be objected that other symbolic names have already been appropriated by the old Jerusalem,---that she is designated 'Sodom and Egypt,'---that is no reason why she may not be also styled Babylon. If she passes under one pseudonym, why not under another, provided it be descriptive of her character? All these names, Sodom, Egypt, Babylon, are alike suggestive of evil and of ungodliness, and proper designations of the wicked city whose doom was to be like theirs.

5. It deserves notice that there is a title which, in the Apocalypse, is applied to one particular city *par excellence.* It is the title 'the great city' [h poliz h megalh]. It is clear that it is always the same city which is so designated, unless another be expressly specified. Now, the city in which the witnesses are slain is expressly called by this title, 'that great city;' and the names Sodom and Egypt are applied to it; and it is furthermore particularly identified as the city 'where also our Lord was crucified' (chap. xi. 8). There can be no reasonable doubt that this refers to ancient Jerusalem. If, then, 'the great city' of chap. xi. 8 means ancient Jerusalem, it follows that 'the great city' of chap. xvi. 8, styled also Babylon, and 'the great city' of chap. xvi. 19, must equally signify Jerusalem. By parity of reasoning, 'that great city' in chap. xvii. 18, and elsewhere, must refer also to Jerusalem. It is a mere assumption to say, as Dean Alford does, that Jerusalem is never called by this name. There is no unfitness, but the contrary, in such a distinctive title being applied to Jerusalem, It was to an Israelite the royal city, by far the greatest in the land, the only city which could properly be so designated; and it ought never to be forgotten that the visions of the Apocalypse are to be regarded from a Jewish point of view.

6. In the catastrophe of the fourth vision (that of the seven mystic figures) the judgment of Israel is symbolised by the treading of the wine-press. We are told also that 'the wine-press was trodden *without the city*' (chap. xiv. 20). Since the vine of the land represents Israel, as it undoubtedly does, it follows that 'the city' outside which the grapes are trodden must be Jerusalem. The only city mentioned in the same chapter is Babylon the great (ver. 8), which must therefore represent Jerusalem. It is inconceivable that the vine of Judea should be trodden outside the city of Rome.

7. In chap. xvi. 19 it is stated that 'the great city' was divided into *three parts* by the unprecedented earthquake mentioned in ver. 18. What great city? Evidently great Babylon, which is said to come in remembrance before God. Possibly the division of the city may have no special significance beyond the illustration of the disastrous effect of the

earthquake; but more probably it is an allusion to the figure employed by the prophet Ezekiel in describing the siege of Jerusalem. (Ezek. v. 1-5). The prophet is commanded to take the hairs of his head and beard, and, dividing them into three parts, to burn one part with fire, to cut another with a knife, and to scatter the third to the four winds, drawing out a sword after them; while only a few hairs were to be preserved, and bound in the skirt of his garment. Then follows the emphatic declaration,---'Thus saith the Lord God, *This is Jerusalem.*' It is fitting that in a prophecy so full of symbols as that of Ezekiel we should look for light on the symbols of the Apocalypse. How vividly this tripartite division of the city represents the fate of Jerusalem in the siege of Titus it is needless to say. It is scarcely possible to imagine a more truthful description of the actual historical fact than that which is summed up in the twelfth verse of the same chapter:---'A third part of thee shall die by the pestilence, and with famine shall they be consumed in the midst of thee; and a third part shall fall by the sword round about thee; and I will scatter a third part into all the winds, and I will draw out a sword after them.'

But whether this be the allusion in the vision or not, the language is wholly unintelligible if applied to any other city than Jerusalem. In what reasonable sense could Rome be said to be divided into three parts? Is it Rome that comes into remembrance before God? Is it to Rome that the cup of the wine of the fierceness of the wrath of God is given? This last figure ought to have suggested to commentators the true interpretation. It is a symbol appropriated to Jerusalem. 'Awake, awake, stand up, O Jerusalem, which hast drunk at the hand of the Lord the cup of his fury; thou hast drunken the dregs of the cup of trembling, and wrung them out' (Isa. li. 17).

8. But a weightier argument, and one that may be considered decisive against Rome being the Babylon of the Apocalypse, and at the time proving the identity between Jerusalem and Babylon, is that which is derived from the name and character of the woman in the vision. We have seen that the woman represents a city; a city styled 'the great city, which spiritually is called Sodom and Egypt, where also our Lord was crucified' (chap. xi. 8). This woman or city is also styled *a harlot,* 'that great harlot,' 'the mother of harlots and abominations of the land.' Now, this is an appellation familiar and well known in the Old Testament, and one that is utterly inappropriate and inapplicable to Rome. Rome was a heathen city, and consequently incapable of that great and damning sin which was possible, and, alas, actual, for Jerusalem. Rome was not capable of violating the covenant of her God, of being false to her divine Husband, for she never was the married wife of Jehovah. This was the crowning guilt of Jerusalem alone among all the nations of the earth, and it is *the sin* for which all through her history she is arraigned and condemned. It is impossible to read the graphic description of the great harlot in the Apocalypse without instantly being reminded of the original in the Old Testament prophets. All through their testimony this is *the sin,* and this is *the name,* which they hurl against Jerusalem. We hear Isaiah exclaiming, 'How is the faithful city become an harlot!' (Isa. i. 21.) 'Thou hast discovered thyself to another than me, and art gone up; thou hast enlarged thy bed, and made thee a covenant with them' (Isa. lvii. 8). Still more emphatically does the prophet Jeremiah stigmatise Jerusalem with this reproachful epithet, 'Go, and cry in the ears of Jerusalem, saying, Thus saith the Lord: I remember thee, the kindness of thy youth, the love of thine espousals; '---but, 'upon every high hill and under every green tree thou wanderest, playing the harlot' (Jer. ii. 2, 20). 'Thou hast played the harlot with many lovers;' 'thou hast polluted the land with thy whoredoms and with thy wickedness;' 'thou hadst a whore's forehead, thou refusedst to be ashamed.' 'She is gone up upon every high mountain and under every green tree, and there hath played the harlot.' 'Turn, O backsliding children, saith the Lord; for I am married unto you.' 'Surely as a wife treacherously departeth from her husband, so have ye dealt treacherously with me, O house of Israel, saith the Lord' (Jer. iii. 1, 2, 3, 6, 14, 20). 'Though thou clothest thyself with crimson, though thou deckest thee with ornaments of gold, though thou rentest thyself with painting, in vain shalt thou make thyself fair; thy lovers will despise thee, they will seek thy life' (Jer. iv. 30). 'What hath my beloved to do in mine house, seeing she hath wrought lewdness with many?' (Jer. xi. 15.) 'I have seen thy adulteries, and thy neighings, the lewdness of thy whoredom, and thine abominations on the hills in the fields. Woe unto thee, O Jerusalem, wilt thou not be made clean? When shall it once be?' (Jer. xiii. 27.)

Passing by the other prophets, it is in Ezekiel that we find the figure elaborated to the fullest extent. In the sixteenth chapter the whole history of Israel, personified by Jerusalem, is related in an allegorical and poetical style, and it will be sufficient here to quote the table of contents of that chapter in the words prefixed by our translators.

EZEKIEL XVI.---Contents

1. *Under the similitude of a wretched infant is shewed the natural state of Jerusalem.* 6. *God's extraordinary love towards her.* 15. *Her monstrous whoredom.* 35. *Her grievous judgment.* 44. *Her sin, matching her mother, and exceeding her sisters, Sodom and Samaria, calleth for judgments.* 60. *Mercy is promised her in the end.*

We think it is scarcely possible for any candid and intelligent mind to compare the allegories of Ezekiel in the sixteenth, twenty-second, and twenty-third chapters, with the description of the harlot in the Apocalypse, without being convinced that we find in the prophecy the original and prototype of the vision, and that both portray the same individual, viz. Jerusalem.

We have thus decisive evidence that the characteristic guilt of Jerusalem was that sin which is known in Scripture as spiritual adultery; an offence which could not be imputed to Rome, because it did not hold the same relation to God as Jerusalem did. It is to Jerusalem, and Jerusalem alone, that the disgraceful epithet is, with melancholy uniformity, applied, as peculiarly and pre-eminently *'the harlot city'.*

It will of course be urged as an objection to this identification of Jerusalem as the apocalyptic Babylon, that the topographical description of 'the great city' is so exactly applicable to Rome that it is impossible that any other city should be meant. For example, the ninth verse states, 'Here is the mind that hath wisdom. The seven heads are seven mountains, on which the woman sitteth.' This must be Rome, and can be no other; for she is notoriously the 'urbs septicollis,' the seven-hilled city.

Yet the objector might have surmised that if the identity of the city were so self-evident, it would scarcely have been proper to preface the explanation with the significant words, 'Here is the mind that hath wisdom;' that is to say, it requires wisdom to understand the interpretation of the vision. This explanation is too superficial to be correct.

In the interpretation of a symbolic book an excessive literality may be a source of error. Especially the symbolic number *seven* is least of all to be taken in a strictly arithmetical sense. There are many examples in the Apocalypse of the use of this symbolic number, in which no interpreter with common sense would dream of counting the units. We have seven heads, seven eyes, seven lamps, seven stars, seven thunders, seven spirits. It would be a manifest absurdity to insist upon the full numerical tale of such objects, why, then, should *seven* be understood arithmetically when predicated of *mountains?* Is it not much more congruous with the nature of such a symbol that it should have a *moral,* or *political,* rather than a *topographical* sense, indicating the pre-eminence of the city in power or in privilege? Like Capernaum, Jerusalem was 'exalted to heaven,' and like her was to be 'brought down to hell.'

But granting that the expression, 'sitting on seven mountains,' has a topographical significance, this feature is adequately represented in the situation of Jerusalem. It was really far more a mountain-city than Rome herself. 'His foundation is in the holy mountains' (Ps. lxxxvii. 1); 'God is greatly to be praised in the city of our God, in the mountains of his holiness' (Ps. xlviii. 1, 2). Jerusalem was 'a city set upon a hill.' To this day the traveller is struck with this peculiarity of its site.

'The city itself is superbly placed, *like a queen upon the mountains,* with the deep valleys and mountains around to guard her.'

Should, however, the literalist still require that the mystical Babylon shall have the full tale of hills, Jerusalem has as good a claim as Rome to sit upon seven mountains. In addition to the well-known hills Zion, Moriah, Acra, Bezetha, and Ophel, the castle of Antonia stood upon another height, and there was another rocky eminence or ridge on which the towers of Hippicus, Phasaelus, and Mariamne were built by Herod the Great. (See Zuellig on The Revelation, *Stud. und Krit.* for 1842.) It is possible, therefore, to find seven hills in Jerusalem; though it must be admitted that Josephus speaks only of four, or at most five. We consider, however, that the symbol refers to the elevated situation of the city, or to its political pre-eminence. Another objection, still more formidable, will be alleged in the declaration of ver. 18, 'The woman which thou sawest is that great city which reigneth over the kings of the earth.' This, it will be said, cannot apply to Jerusalem, and can apply only to Rome. Jerusalem never was an imperial city, with vassal nations and tributary kings subject to her authority; whereas Rome was the mistress and monarch of the world.

So far as the title 'the great city' is concerned we have shown that it is actually applied to Jerusalem in several passages in the Apocalypse (chap. xi. 8, 13; xiv. 8, 20; xvi. 19). To the Jew it was a great city, and with good reason. There is a remarkable passage in Josephus, where he gives a report of the speech of Eleazar, the brave defender of the fortress of Masada, inciting his men to destroy themselves with their wives and children rather than surrender to the Romans:---

'Where now,' said he, 'is *that great city,* the metropolis of the whole nation of Jews, protected by so many encircling walls, secured by so many forts, and by the vastness of its towers, which could with difficulty contain its munitions of war, and which was garrisoned by so many myriads of defenders? What has become of that city of ours in which it was believed God Himself was a dweller? Uprooted from its foundation, it has been swept away, one memorial of it alone remaining,---the camp of its destroyers still planted upon its ruins.'

Such a passage disposes at once of the objection that the title of 'that great city' is not applicable to Jerusalem.

With regard to the phrase, 'which reigneth over the kings of the earth,'---the fallacy which has misled many is the mistranslation 'kings of the *earth*'. A very fruitful source of confusion and error in the interpretation of the New Testament is the capricious and uncertain way in which gh is rendered in our Authorised Version. Sometimes, though rarely, it has its proper meaning, *the land;* but more frequently it is translated *the earth,* and our translators never seem to have given themselves any trouble to inquire whether the word should be taken in its widest or in a more restricted sense. With incredible carelessness they render pasai ai fulai thz ghz, 'all the kindreds of the earth,' instead of 'all the tribes of the land;' and h ampeloz thz ghz, 'the vine of the earth,' instead of 'the vine of the land.' so in the passage before us (chap. xvii. 18), the 'kings of the earth' should be 'kings of the land,' *i.e.* Judea or Palestine. This very phrase is used in the New Testament in the restricted sense of 'the rulers of the land,' by St. Peter in Acts iv. 26, 27, 'Of a truth against thy holy child Jesus, whom thou hast anointed, both Herod and Pontius Pilate, with the Gentiles, and the people of Israel were gathered together in this city,' etc. and he recognises this fact as the fulfilment of the prediction in the second Psalm, 'Why did the heathen rage, and the people imagine vain things? *The kings of the land* stood up, and the rulers were gathered together against the Lord, and against his anointed.' The 'kings of the land,' therefore, are identified by the apostle Peter as the confederate rulers who put the Son of God to death in the city of Jerusalem. So also in Rev. vi. 15, where 'the kings of the land' are represented as hiding themselves from the face of Him that sitteth on the throne, in the great day of His wrath. The phrase, therefore, is equivalent to 'the ruling authorities in the land of Judea,' or of Palestine.

We have already pointed out the correspondence between the passage just referred to (Rev. vi. 15, 16) and the original draught of the scene as described in the prophecy of Isaiah (chap. ii. 10-22; iii. 1-3). It is, therefore, unnecessary here to do more than call attention to the obvious correspondence between 'the kings of the land' in the vision, and 'the mighty men, and the men of war,' etc., in the prophecy. We are, therefore, not merely warranted, but compelled to regard the phrase 'kings of the earth' as equivalent to 'rulers of the land.'

Thus interpreted, the description of Babylon the great as 'reigning over the rulers of the land' becomes perfectly appropriate to Jerusalem. This appears from the language in which both the Scriptures and other Hebrew writings speak of the authority and pre-eminence enjoyed by that city. For example, the prophet Jeremiah describes Jerusalem as 'she that was great among the nations, and *princess of the provinces*' (Lam. i. 1), language fully equivalent to 'that great city which beareth rule over the rulers of the land.' Again, if so small a city as Bethlehem might be styled 'not the least amount the princes of Judah' (Matt. ii. 6), surely the metropolitan city might without impropriety be said to 'reign over the princes, or rulers, of the land.' But the language which Josephus employs on this subject is a full justification of the apocalyptic description of Jerusalem.

'Judea,' he tells us, 'reaches in breadth from the river Jordan to Joppa. In its very centre lies the city of Jerusalem; for which reason some, not inaptly, have styled that city "the navel" of the country. It [Judea] is divided into eleven allotments (toparchies), whereof *Jerusalem, as the seat of royalty, is supreme, exalted over all the adjacent region, as the head over the body.'*

This is language which is tantamount to the expression, 'that great city which reigneth over the kings, or rulers, of the land.'

It may possibly be felt to be a difficulty that the Jerusalem of the apostolic age could not with propriety be styled 'the harlot city,' since that name implies *idolatry, i.e.* spiritual adultery; whereas the Jews of that period were intensely monotheistic, and actually threatened to rise in rebellion rather than permit the temple to be desecrated by the introduction of the statue of the emperor. This is undoubtedly true in the letter; yet, as St. Paul intimates (Rom. ii. 22), the Jews of his time, while abhorring idols, were guilty of sacrilege. It has been well said by Dr. Hodge:---

'The essence of idolatry was profanation of God: of this the Jews were in a high degree guilty. They had made His house a den of thieves.'

They had as truly apostatised from God as if they had set up the worship of Baal or of Jupiter. In rejecting the Messiah they had definitively broken the covenant of their God. Our Lord expressly declared that that generation summed up in itself the crimes and guilt of all its predecessors. It was the child and heir of all the evil generations that had gone before, and filled up the measure of its ancestors:---'That upon you may come all the righteous blood shed upon the land,' etc. 'Verily I say unto you, All these things shall come upon this generation' (Matt. xxiii. 35, 36).

One more argument for the identity of Jerusalem with the apocalyptic Babylon, and one which we consider conclusive, is to be found in the character ascribed to the city as the persecutor and murderer of the prophets and saints: 'I beheld the woman drunken with the blood of the saints, and with the blood of the martyrs of Jesus' (chap. xvii. 6); 'And in her was found the blood of the prophets, and of saints, and of all that were slain in the land' (chap. xviii. 24); 'Rejoice over her, thou heaven, and ye holy apostles and prophets, for God hath avenged you on her' (chap. xviii. 20). Who can fail to recognise in this description the distinctive characteristics of the Jerusalem of 'that generation'? Who is it that kills the prophets and stones them that are sent unto her? Jerusalem. What is the city out of which it cannot be that a prophet should perish---that enjoys an infamous monopoly of murdering the messengers of God? Jerusalem. The blood of the saints and of prophets is the immemorial stain upon Jerusalem; the brand of the murderer stamped upon her brow; and the generation that crucified Christ is described by Him as 'the children of them that killed the prophets,' and so 'filled up the measure of their fathers' (Matt. xxiii. 30-32).

It is impossible to mistake the bearer of this conspicuous and distinctive indictment inscribed upon the front of Jerusalem, long before stigmatized by the prophet Ezekiel as 'the bloody city' (Ezek. xxii. 2; xxiv. 6-9).

It is not without cause, therefore, that the apostles and prophets are invited to rejoice over the fall of their relentless persecutor and murderer. The souls under the altar had long cried, 'How long, O Lord, holy and true, dost thou not judge and avenge our blood on them that dwell in the land?' They had been comforted with the message 'that they should rest for *a little season,* until their fellow-servants and brethren, that should be killed as they were, should be fulfilled,' then 'God would speedily avenge his own elect.' And now the day of vengeance, the year of His redeemed, is come.

Can any proof be more conclusive that it is Jerusalem, the murderess of the prophets, which is here described---that Jerusalem is the Babylon of the Apocalypse? How exact is the correspondence between our Lord's prediction in Luke xi. 49-51 and its fulfillment in Rev. xviii. 24:---

'Therefore also said the wisdom of God, I will send them prophets and apostles, and some of them they shall slay and persecute; that the blood of all the prophets which was shed from the foundation of the world may be required of *this generation.'*	'And in her was found the blood of prophets and of saints, and of all that were slain in the land.'

Having thus endeavoured to identify the woman in the vision, we proceed next to investigate the mystery of the beast upon which she is seated.

THE MYSTERY OF THE SCARLET BEAST.

Chap. xvii. 3, 7-11.---'And I saw a woman sitting upon a scarlet beast, full of names of blasphemy, having seven heads and ten horns . . . I will tell thee the mystery of the woman, and of the beast that carrieth her, which hath the seven heads and the ten horns. The beast that thou sawest was, and is not; and is about to ascend out of the abyss, and goeth into perdition: and they that dwell upon the land shall wonder, whose name is not written in the book of life from the foundation of the world, when they behold the beast that was, and is not, and shall come. Here is the mind that hath wisdom. The seven heads are seven mountains, on which the woman sitteth. And there [they] are seven kings: five are fallen, and one is, and the other is not yet come: and when he cometh, he must continue a short space. And the beast that was and is not, even he is the eighth, and is of the seven, and goeth into perdition.'

There can be no reasonable doubt that the beast [qhrion] here described is identical with that in chap. xiii. The name, the description, and the attributes of the monster plainly point to the same individual. There are, however, additional particulars in this second description which at first seem rather to obscure than elucidate the meaning. The *scarlet* colour, indeed, may easily be recognised as the symbol of Imperial dignity; but what can be said of the apparent paradoxes, 'he was, and is not, and shall come again'? and 'he is the eighth [king], and is of the seven, and goeth into perdition'?

We have already been led to the conclusion that the wild beast (chap. xiii.) signifies Nero. The paradox or enigma which represents him as 'the beast which was, and is not, and shall appear,' is a puzzle which at first sight seems inexplicable. It is evidently a contradiction in terms, and can only be true in some peculiar sense. That it should actually be true, in any sense of Nero, is one of the most extraordinary facts in history, and brings home to him this symbolic description with all the force of demonstration. It seems established by the clearest evidence that at the death of Nero there was a popular and wide-spread belief that the tyrant was still alive, and would shortly reappear. We have the express testimony of Tacitus, Suetonius, and other historians to the existence of such a persuasion. It has been objected that this explanation of the paradox virtually imputes equivocation to the Scriptures. What can be more frivolous than such an argument? Any explanation of what is a contradiction in terms must be in some degree unnatural and equivocal; but it is absurd in dealing with a book of symbols to demand literal truth. Must it be shown that Nero had ten horns?

It was surely competent for the prophet-seer to indicate a person, whom he dared not name, by any symbolic representation which would lead to his recognition. What could be more distinctive of the particular person intended than this very fact of his expected reappearance after death? Of how few persons in the world could such an opinion be entertained? That it should be historically true that such a popular delusion prevailed respecting Nero we regard as a singular and conclusive proof that he is the individual denoted by the symbol.

THE SEVEN KINGS.

It is more difficult to unriddle the enigma of the seven kings, of whom the beast is one, and yet the eighth. The seven heads of the monster seem to be emblematic, not only of the seven hills upon which the woman sits, but also of seven kings who have a twofold relation, viz. to the woman and to the beast. The antitype of the symbol ought, therefore, to sustain this double relation, though one would expect, as being connatural with the monster, that their relation to him would be the most intimate. Of these seven kings, 'five,' it is stated, 'are fallen, and one is, and the other is not yet come; and when he cometh, he must continue a short space; and the beast that was, and is now, he is the eighth, and is of the seven, and goeth into perdition.'

We have already seen that in general, the number seven being a symbolic number, is not to be taken as standing for so many units, but as indicating perfectness or totality. There are occasions, however, when it seems necessary to take it in an arithmetical sense, as, for example, when it stands in close connection with other numbers. In the instance before us, where we read of seven kings, five of whom are fallen, and one is, and the seventh is not yet come, while a mysterious eighth is hinted at, it is difficult to understand the number seven in any other than the literal numerical sense.

Where, then, are we to look for these seven kings or heads? It is presumable that they also are where the mountains are, in the place where the scene is laid. If the harlot means Jerusalem we should expect to find the kings there also. Where, then, are seven kings, and a mysterious eighth, to be found in Jerusalem? The kings of the Herodian line have been suggested, viz. 1. Herod the Great; 2. Archelaus; 3. Philip; 4. Herod Antipas; 5. Agrippa I.; 6. Herod of Chalcis; 7. Agrippa II. This is the suggestion of Dr. Zuellig, and deserves the praise of ingenuity; but there are two fatal objections to it: first, they cannot all be said to have been kings or rulers in Jerusalem, or even in Judea; and, secondly, they do not all belong to the apocalyptic period, the close of the Jewish age, or the last days of Jerusalem, which is an indispensable condition.

We venture to propose another solution, which we think will be found to answer in every particular the requirements of the problem. Bearing in mind what has already been proved, that the title *'kings'* is often used as synonymous with rulers or governors, we submit that the basileiz here alluded to are no other than the Roman procurators of Judea under Claudius and Nero. It was in the reign of Claudius that Judea became for the second time a Roman province. This fact is expressly stated by Josephus, and also the reason why the change was made. On the death of Herod Agrippa I., on whom Caligula had conferred the sovereignty of the entire kingdom, his son Agrippa II. was considered by Claudius too young to fill his father's throne. Judea was therefore reduced to the form of a province. Cuspius Fadus was sent into Judea as the first of this second series of procurators.

These procurators were really viceroys, and answer well to the title basileiz in the vision. Their number also exactly tallies with that given in the Apocalypse. From the appointment of Cuspius Fadus to the outbreak of the Jewish war, there were seven governors who bore supreme rule in Jerusalem and Judea. These were: 1. Cuspius Fadus; 2. Tiberius Alexander; 3. Ventidius Cumanus; 4. Antonius Felix; 5. Portius Festus; 6. Albinus; 7. Gessius Florus.

Here, then, we have a well-defined period, falling within the apocalyptic limits as to time, occupying apocalyptic ground as to place, and corresponding with the apocalyptic symbol as to the number, character, and title. These viceroys sustain the double relation required by the symbol; they were related to the beast as Romans and as deputies; and they are related to the woman as governing powers.

It is now easy to see how Nero himself, the beast from the sea, or foreign tyrant, may be said to be the eighth, and yet of the seven. He was the supreme head, and these procurators were his deputies, the representatives of the emperor in Judea and Jerusalem. Thus he might be said to be of them, and yet distinct from them,---the eighth, and yet of the seven. This gives a natural and fitting propriety to the apparently enigmatical and paradoxical language of the symbolic representation, and solves the riddle without violent torture or dexterous manipulation.

THE TEN HORNS OF THE BEAST.

There is much obscurity also in the next symbol in chap. xvii. 12:---

'And the ten horns which thou sawest are ten kings, which have received no kingdom as yet; but they receive authority as kings one hour [or *at one hour,---contemporaneously*] with the beast.'

It will be observed that these 'ten kings' have the following characteristics:---

1. They are satellites or tributaries of the beast, i.e. subject to Rome.
2. They are confederate with the beast against Jerusalem.
3. They are hostile to Christianity.
4. They are hostile to the harlot, and active agents in her destruction.
5. When the apostle wrote these kings were not yet invested with power.
6. Their power was to be contemporaneous with that of the beast.

On the whole, we conclude that this symbol signifies the auxiliary princes and chiefs who were allies of Rome and received commands in the Roman army during the Jewish war. We know from Tacitus and Josephus that several kings of neighbouring nations followed Vespasian and Titus to the war. Allusion has already been made to some of these auxiliaries: Antiochus, Sohemus, Agrippa, and Malchus. There were no doubt others, but it is not incumbent to produce the exact number of *ten*, which, like seven, appears to be a mystic or symbolic number. They are represented as animated by a bitter hostility to Jerusalem, the harlot city: 'These shall hate the whore, and shall make her desolate and naked, and shall eat her flesh, and burn her with fire. For God hath put into their heart to fulfill his will, and to agree, and give their kingdom unto the beast, until the words of God shall be fulfilled' (Rev. xvii. 16, 17). Tacitus speaks of the bitter animosity with which the Arab auxiliaries of Titus were filled against the Jews, and we have a fearful proof of the intense hatred felt towards the Jews by the neighbouring nations in the wholesale massacres of that unhappy people perpetrated in may great cities just before the outbreak of the war. The whole Jewish population of Caesarea were massacred in one day. In Syria every city was divided into two camps, Jews and Syrians. In Scythopolis upwards of thirteen thousand Jews were butchered; in Ascalon, Ptolemais, and Tyre, similar atrocities took place. But in Alexandria the carnage of the Jewish inhabitants exceeded all the other massacres. The whole Jewish quarter was deluged with blood, and fifty thousand corpses lay in ghastly heaps in the streets. This is a terrible commentary on the words of the angel-interpreter: 'The ten horns which thou sawest upon the beast, these shall hate the whore,' etc.

It only remains to notice one other feature in the vision. The woman is represented as 'sitting upon many waters,' and in the fifteenth verse these waters are said to signify 'peoples, and multitudes, and nations, and tongues.' The mystical Babylon, like her prototype the literal Babylon, is said to 'sit upon many waters.' The prophet Jeremiah thus addresses ancient Babylon: 'O thou that dwellest upon many waters' (Jer. li. 12), and this description appears to be equally appropriate to Jerusalem.

The influence exercised by the Jewish race in all parts of the Roman Empire previous to the destruction of Jerusalem was immense; their synagogues were to be found in every city, and their colonies took root in every land. We see in Acts ii. the marvellous ramifications of the Hebrew race in foreign countries, from the enumeration of the different nations which were represented in Jerusalem on the day of Pentecost: 'There were dwelling in Jerusalem Jews, devout men, out of every nation under heaven, . . . Parthians, and Medes, and Elamites, and the dwellers in Mesopotamia, and in Judea, and Cappadocia, in Pontus and Asia, Phrygia, and Pamphylia, in Egypt, and in the parts of Libya about Cyrene, and strangers of Rome, Jews and proselytes, Cretes and Arabians.' Jerusalem might truly be said to 'sit upon many waters,' that is, to exercise a mighty influence upon 'peoples, and multitudes, and nations, and tongues.'

Such is the vision of 'the harlot city,' the fate of which is the great theme of our Lord's prophecy on Olivet as well as of the Apocalypse. That it is Jerusalem, and Jerusalem alone, which is here portrayed must, we think be abundantly clear to every unbiased and candid mind; and any other subject would be utterly foreign to the whole purpose and end of the Apocalypse.

NOTE ON REVELATION XVII. - IDENTITY OF THE BEAST OF THE APOCALYPSE WITH THE MAN OF SIN IN 2 THESSALONIANS II.

Before quitting this chapter it will be proper to point out the remarkable correspondence between the 'man of sin' delineated by St. Paul in 2 Thess. ii. and the wild beast described by St. John in Rev. xiii. and xvii. It will be observed that neither of the apostles *names* the formidable personage at whom he points; and doubtless for the same reason. This circumstance alone might suffice to suggest who is intended. There could be very few persons whose name it would not be safe to utter, probably not more than one, and that one the mightiest in the land. We cannot suppose that the name is suppressed merely for the sake of mystification: there must have been an adequate motive; that motive must have been a prudential one; and if prudential, then, no doubt, political, viz. to avoid incurring the suspicion of disaffection towards the government.

In addition to this there is a correspondence so minute and so manifold between 'the man of sin' of St. Paul and 'the beast' of St. John as to render it all but certain that they both refer to the same individual. We have already, on independent grounds and treating each subject separately, arrived at the conclusion that the Emperor Nero is intended by both apostles, and when we come to the place the two portraitures side by side this conclusion is decisively established. It is only necessary to glance at the parallel descriptions in order to be convinced that they depict the same individual, and that individual the monster Nero:---

THE MAN OF SIN, 2 THESS. II.	THE WILD BEAST, REVE. XIII. XVII.
'The man of sin' (ver. 3).	'Upon his heads names of blasphemy' (chap. xiii. 1).
	'Full of names of blasphemy' (chap. xvii. 3).
'The son of perdition' (ver. 3).	'He shall go into perdition' (chap. xvii. 8).
	'He goeth into perdition' (chap. xvii. 11).
'The lawless one' (ver. 8).	'Power was given unto him *to do what he will*' (chap. xiii. 5).
'Who opposeth and exalteth himself above all that is called God, or that is worshipped' (ver. 4).	'There was given to him a mouth speaking great things, . . . and he opened his mouth in blasphemy against God (chap. xiii. 5, 6)
'So that he as God sitteth in the temple of God, showing himself that he is God' (ver. 4).	'And they worshipped the beast, saying, Who is like unto the beast? . . . And all that dwell in the land shall worship him' (chap. xiii. 4, 8).
'Whom the Lord shall consume with the spirit of his mouth, and shall destroy with the brightness of his coming' (ver. 8).	These shall make ware with the Lamb, and the Lamb shall overcome them' (chap. xvii. 14).
	'And the beast was taken, and with him the false prophet . . . These both were cast alive into the lake of fire burning with brimstone' (chap. xiv. 20).
'Whose coming is after the working of Satan' (ver. 9).	'And the dragon gave him his power' (chap. xiii. 2).
'With all power and signs and lying wonders' (ver. 9).	'And he doeth great wonders, so that he maketh fire come down from heaven in the sight of men' (chap. xiii. 13).

'And with all deceivableness of unrighteousness in them that perish' (ver. 10).

'And for this cause God shall send them strong delusion, that they should believe a lie' (ver. 11).

'That they all might be condemned who believe not the truth' (ver. 12).

'And deceiveth them that dwell in the land by means of those miracles which he had power to do in the sight of the beast' (chap. xiii. 14).

'If any man worship the beast and his image, . . . the same shall drink of the wine of the wrath of God' etc. (chap. xiv. 9, 10).

THE FALL OF BABYLON.

The next scene of the vision represents the fate of the harlot city, which occupies the whole of chap. xvii. First, a mighty angel, whose glory lightens the earth, proclaims with a loud voice, in nearly the same words as in chap. xiv. 8, 'Babylon the great is fallen, is fallen.' Her doom is the consequence of her sin, and at this supreme moment her moral degradation and debasement are most emphatically declared: 'She is become the habitation of demons, and a hold of every unclean spirit, and a hold of every unclean and hated bird,' etc. How true this description of Jerusalem in her decadence is the pages of Josephus testify:---

'That period,' he tells us, 'had somehow become so prolific in iniquity of every description among the Jews, that no work of evil was left unperpetrated, . . . so universal was the contagion both in public and private, and such the emulation to surpass each other in acts of impiety towards God and of injustice towards their neighbours.'

'No generation ever existed more prolific in crime.'

'I am of opinion that had the Romans deferred the punishment of these wretches, either the earth would have opened and swallowed up the city, or it would have been swept away by a deluge, or have shared the thunderbolts of the land of Sodom.'

Next, a voice is heard from heaven calling upon the people of God to come out of the doomed city,---'Come out of her, my people, that ye be not partakers of her sins, and that ye receive not of her plagues.' We observe here how the final catastrophe is kept suspended,---again and again it seems as if the end had actually come, and then we find new circumstances interposed, and the blow apparently arrested when in the very act of falling. This feature of the Apocalypse greatly heightens the dramatic effect and powerfully stimulates the interest in the action. It might have been supposed that all the faithful had long before this abandoned the doomed city; but we are not to look for the same strict consistency and sequence in a poetical and figurative description as in a historical narrative. Besides, the imagery is partly derived from the prophetic description of the fall of ancient Babylon as set forth by Jeremiah (chap. li.), where we find this very call to 'come out of her' (ver. 45).

After this follows a solemn and pathetic dirge, if it may be so called, over the fallen city, whose last hour is now come. The kings or rulers of the land, the merchant-traders and the seamen who knew her in the plentitude of her power and glory, now lament over her fall. The royal city, the mart of trade and wealth, is wrapt in flames, and the mariners and merchants who were enriched by her traffic stand afar off, beholding the smoke of her burning, and crying, 'What city is like unto this great city?' The description given in this chapter of the wealth and luxury of the mystic Babylon might seem scarcely appropriate to Jerusalem were it not that we have in Josephus ample evidence that there is no exaggeration even in this highly-wrought representation. More than once the Jewish historian speaks of the magnificence and vast wealth of Jerusalem. It is very remarkable that the inventory of the spoils taken from the treasury of the temple contains almost every one of the articles enumerated in this lamentation over the fallen city,---'Gold, silver, precious stones, purple, scarlet, cinnamon, odours, ointments, and frankincense.'

No less striking is the description given by Josephus of the spoils of the captured city, which were carried in procession through the streets of Rome in the triumph of Vespasian and Titus, and which fully justify the picture of profusion and magnificence drawn in the Apocalypse.

The last scene in the tragedy of the harlot city follows. A mighty angel takes up a stone, like a great millstone, and casts it into the sea, saying, 'Thus with violence shall that great city Babylon be thrown down, and shall be found no more at all' (ver. 21). Her desolation is now complete: her glory is departed; she is left to silence and solitude, for 'in one hour her judgment is come,' 'in one hour she is made desolate.'

This it may be said is poetry, and no doubt it is; but it is also history. So total was the destruction of Jerusalem that Josephus says 'there was no longer anything to lead those who visited the spot to believe that it had ever been inhabited.'

We have already commented on the concluding words of the chapter, which furnish decisive evidence of the identity of the harlot city: 'In her was found the blood of the prophets, and of saints, and of all that were slain in the land' (ver. 24). To no other city than Jerusalem will these words apply, and they conclusively demonstrate that she is the subject of the whole visionary representation. She was pre-eminently the 'murderer of the prophets,' and of her their blood was to be required, according to the prediction of our Lord,---'That upon you may come all the righteous blood shed in the land' (Matt. xxiii. 35).

We might suppose that we had now reached the catastrophe of the vision, since the judgment of the great harlot is complete, and she disappears from the scene; but the theme is still continued through the next two chapters, which are mainly occupied with acts of judgment on the other enemies of Christ and of His church.

First, however, we have a song of triumph in heaven over the fallen and condemned criminal whose fearful judgment has been consummated (chap. xix. 1-5). It is a Hallelujah chorus of a great multitude, whose voice is like the voice of many waters, and as the voice of mighty thunderings, ascribing glory to God for the justice executed on the harlot city, and the avenging of the blood of His servants at her hand. Now is fulfilled the promise of God that He would speedily avenge His elect, who cried to Him day and night. Now, also, the kingdom of God is come: the long-predicted, long-expected consummation for which the prayers of the saints have ceaselessly ascended to heaven--- 'Thy kingdom come.' Messiah's great victory is won; His kingdom has reached its full development; He surrenders His delegated authority to His Father; and a burst of acclamation resounds through all heaven, 'Alleluia! for the Lord God omnipotent reigneth.'

But the coming of the kingdom is associated with other events, one of the chief of which is 'the marriage of the Lamb,' for which the note of preparation is now given, though the details of the event are reserved for the seventh and last vision. The nuptials of the Lamb are evidently announced proleptically, in accordance with the frequent usage of the Apocalypse. This public and solemn union of Christ and His church is what is shadowed forth in the parables of the marriage feast (Matt. xxii.) and of the ten virgins (Matt. xxv.). It is the marriage supper of the great King, to which the first invited guests refused to come, and shamefully treated and slew the king's messengers. Now judgment has overtaken them: 'The king sent forth his armies, and destroyed those murderers, and burned up their city' (Matt. xxii. 7).

But before this happy consummation takes place, acts of judgment have to be executed. Mystical Babylon has been judged, but the other enemies of the King---the beast, his legate the false prophet, and the dragon---have yet to receive condign punishment.

JUDGMENT OF THE BEAST AND HIS CONFEDERATE POWERS.

Chap. xix. 11-21---'And I saw heaven opened, and behold a white horse; and he that sat upon him was called Faithful and True, and in righteousness he doth judge and make war. His eyes were as a flame of fire, and on his head were many crowns; and he had a name written, that no man knoweth, but he himself. And he was clothed in a vesture dipped in blood: and his name is called the Word of God. And the armies which are in heaven followed him upon white horses, clothed in fine linen, white and clean. And out of his mouth goeth a sharp sword, that with it he should smite the nations: and he shall rule them with a rod of iron: and he treadeth the wine-press of the fierceness and wrath of Almighty God. And he hath upon his vesture and on his thigh a name wirtten, KING OF KINGS, AND LORD OF LORDS. And I saw an angel standing in the sun; and he cried with a loud voice, saying to all the fowls that fly in the midst of heaven, Come and gather yourselves together unto the supper of the great God; that ye may eat the flesh of kings, and the flesh of captians, and the flesh of mighty men, and the flesh of horses, and of them that sit on them, and the flesh of all men, both free and bond, both small and great. And I saw the beast, and the kings of the earth, and their armies, gathered together to make war against him that sat on the horse, and against his army. And the beast was taken, and with him the false prophet that wrought miracles before him, with which he deceived them that had received the mark of the beast, and them that worshipped his image. These both were cast alive into a lake of fire burning with brimstone. And the remnant were slain with the sword of him that sat upon the horse, which sword proceeded out of his mouth; and all the fowls were filled with their flesh.'

This magnificent passage is descriptive of the great event which occupies so prominent a place in the New Testament prophecy, the Parousia, or coming in glory of the Lord Jesus Christ. He comes from heaven; He comes in His kingdom; 'on his head are many crowns;' he comes with His holy angels; 'the armies of heaven follow him;' He comes to execute judgment on His enemies; He comes in glory. It may be said, Why is the Parousia placed after the judgment of the harlot city, and not before? It must be remembered that it is a poem rather than a history that we are now reading; a drama, rather than a journal of transactions, and that there is no book in which poetical and dramatic effect is more studied than in the Apocalypse. These episodical visions are often taken out of their strict chronological order that they may be displayed in fuller detail and make an adequate impression on the mind of the reader. At the same time we do not admit that there is an anachronism in the place which the Parousia occupies. If we examine the prophetic discourse on the Mount of Olives we shall find the same order of events. It is immediately *after* the great tribulation that the sign of the Son of man appears in heaven, and they 'see the Son of man coming in the clouds of heaven with power and great glory' (Matt. xxiv. 29, 30). The scene represented in this vision is that very event. The Lord Jesus is 'revealed from heaven with his mighty angels, in flaming fire taking vengeance on them that know not God, and that obey not the gospel of our Lord Jesus Christ' (2 Thess. i. 7, 8).

The sequel of the chapter relates the victory of the Lamb over the enemies of His cause. An angel standing in the sun summons all the fowls of heaven to prey upon the carcasses of the slain in the coming conflict. The armies of the beast and his confederate powers are marshalled to make war upon the Messiah. The two hosts engage, and the enemies of Christ are routed. The beast is taken prisoner, and with him his false prophet that ruled in his name. 'These two were cast alive into the lake of fire which burneth with brimstone,' while their followers perish, 'slain with the sword of him that sitteth on the horse, whose sword goeth out of his mouth.

If it be asked, What do these symbols represent? the answer is, Assuredly no literal conflict with carnal weapons. It is not on any battle-field on earthly ground that the glorified Redeemer and His heavenly legions confront the banded hosts of earth and hell. We cannot go to the pages of Josephus or Tacitus, or any other historian, for the events which correspond with these symbols. We read in them two great truths: Christ must conquer; His enemies must perish. Nevertheless, there is a kernel of historical fact in this symbolism. Jus as in the symbolic representation of the great harlot we find the historical fact of the destruction of Jerusalem, so in this capture and execution of the wild beast and his congener we find the historical fact of the destruction of Nero and his lieutenant, or deputy, in Judea. This is the core of historic fact at the centre of the vision. Jerusalem, the harlot city, perished in fire and blood. Nero, the beast king, the sanguinary persecutor of the Christians; and Gessius Florus, the tyrant who goaded the unhappy Jews into revolt, both perished by a violent death. These events were really divine judgments, foreseen and predicted long before their occurrence, and written in lurid characters on the page of history, visible and legible for ever. These are the historical facts set forth in all the pomp and splendour of symbolical imagery in the Apocalypse. The symbols were worthy of the facts, and the facts are worthy of the symbols. No doubt there is here something of an anachronism. The death of Nero is placed in the vision subsequent to the judgment of Jerusalem, whereas it actually preceded that event by two years or more. As we have before remarked, something must be conceded to poetic license. In an epic, a drama, or a vision, it is unreasonable to require strict chronological sequence. Now the Apocalypse is composed with consummate art. As Henry More long ago remarked, 'There never was any book penned with that artifice as this of the Apocalypse, as if every word were weighed in a balance before it was set down.' The dramatic effect is certainly greatly heightened by the capture and punishment of the beast being placed where they are. The first and most prominent place is naturally given to the harlot city, and the Seer having begun with her judgment carries it on to its final consummation. He then returns to the beast, and depicts his fate; and, lastly, in the twentieth chapter, proceeds to describe the punishment inflicted on the third hostile power, the dragon.

There is, however, another answer to the charge of anachronism. It deserves consideration whether this whole scene of the great battle and victory of Christ the King, and the punishment of the beast and his armies, may not be properly conceived as taking place in the spirit, not in the flesh? That is, whether it may not be the representation of transactions in the unseen state; the judgment of the dead, and not of the living. An earthly transaction it certainly is not; and if we regard it as the symbolic representation of the judgment and condemnation of the enemies of the Lamb in the spirit-world---a glimpse of that great judicial scene which is depicted in Matt. xxv., 'when the Son of man shall come in his glory, and before him shall be gathered all the nations,'---this would relieve the vision of any anachronism and abundantly satisfy all the requirements of the case. The probability of this view is strongly confirmed by the fact that this punishment of the beast and his armies follows the allusion to the marriage supper of the Lamb, an event which is certainly supposed to take place in the spiritual and eternal state.

THE JUDGMENT OF THE DRAGON.

Chap. xx. 1-3.---'And I saw an angel coming down from heaven, having the key to the abyss and a great chain in his hand. And he laid hold on the dragon, that old serpent, which is the Devil, and Satan, and bound him a thousand years, and cast him into the abyss, and shut him up, and set a seal upon him, that he might deceive the nations no more, till the thousand years should be fulfilled: and after that he must be loosed a little season.'

We now approach a portion of the Apocalypse which is involved in much obscurity, and which, from the very nature of the case, passes beyond the limits which, by the express declarations of the writer, again and again repeated, circumscribe the rest of the prophecy of this book.

The fact that such a protracted period as a thousand years is embraced in the visions of the Apocalypse is considered by many an incontrovertible proof that the fulfillment of the predictions which it contains is not to be restricted to a brief period. Dean Alford, for example, says:---

'The en tacei [shortly] confessedly contains, among other periods, a period of a thousand years. On what principle are we to affirm that it does not embrace a period vastly greater than this in its whole contents?'

That which appears so insurmountable an objection in the eyes of Dean Alford is regarded as none at all by Moses Stuart, who says,---

'The portion of the book which contains this [reference to a distant period] is so small, and that part of the book which was speedily fulfilled is so large, that no reasonable difficulty can be made concerning the declaration before us. 'En tacei, i.e. *speedily,* did the things, on account of which the book was principally written, in fact take place.'

Some interpreters indeed attempt to get over the difficulty by supposing that the thousand years, being a symbolic number, may represent a period of very short duration, and so bring the whole within the prescribed apocalyptic limits; but this method of interpretation appears to us so violent an unnatural that we cannot hesitate to reject it. The act of binding and shutting up the dragon does indeed come within the 'shortly' of the apocalyptic statement, for it is co-incident, or nearly so, with the judgment of the harlot and the beast; but the term of the dragon's imprisonment is distinctly stated to be for a thousand years, and thus must necessarily pass entirely beyond the field of vision so strictly and constantly limited by the book itself. We believe, however, that this is the solitary example which the whole book contains of this excursion beyond the limits of 'shortly;' and we agree with Stuart that no reasonable difficulty can be made on account of this single exception to the rule. We shall also find as we proceed that the events referred to as taking place after the termination of the thousand years are predicted as in a prophecy, and not represented as in a vision. Indeed the passage, chap. xx. 5-10, seems evidently introduced parenthetically, interrupting the continuity of the narrative, which is again resumed, as we shall see, at ver. 11.

The overthrow and punishment of the enemies of Christ would evidently be incomplete without a similar act of judgment on the chief instigator and head of the confederacy, the dragon, or Satan. Accordingly his time has now come: he is seized, chained, and cast into the abyss, which is sealed over him, and he is sentenced to be imprisoned there for a period called 'a thousand years.'

This act of seizing, chaining, and casting into the abyss is represented as taking place under the eye of the Seer, being introduced by the usual formula, 'And I saw.' It is an act contemporaneous, or nearly so, with the judgments executed on the other criminals, the harlot and the beast. This part of the vision, then, falls within the proper limits of apocalyptic vision, and is an integral part of the series of great events connected with the Parousia.

Are we, then, to suppose that anything equivalent to this symbol, the binding and imprisoning of Satan, has actually taken place, and took place at the time indicated, viz. the close of the Jewish dispensation? We have no hesitation in answering in the affirmative, and we think there is the clearest warrant both in Scripture and in history for this conclusion.

1.   No one will contend that the symbols in the vision require a literal or physical chaining of the dragon. Common sense will teach that all that is meant is *the repression and restriction of satanic power* during the period indicated. Now there seems no reason to doubt that before and during our Saviour's incarnation there was an energy and activity of moral evil existing in the earth far exceeding anything that is now known among men. It is not unreasonable to suppose that the period of our Lord's earthly life was a season of intense and unparalleled activity among the powers of darkness. If they knew that the champion of God, the Redeemer of mankind, was come in order 'that he might destroy the works of the devil,' there was cause for their alarm; and our Lord's temptations in the wilderness, and the malignant opposition to Christ and His cause, everywhere ascribed in the New Testament to Satan, reveal both the knowledge of the adversary respecting the Saviour's mission and his unceasing efforts to counteract it. In addition to this, the remarkable prevalence of the mysterious phenomenon of demoniacal possession in the time of Christ is a decisive proof of the presence and activity of a malefic spiritual influence, in a form and degree which to us is unknown, and to many even incredible. Unless, then, we are prepared to give up the reality of that mysterious influence, and resolve it into mere popular ignorance or delusion, we must admit that there has been a marked and decisive check to the power of Satan over men since the time of Christ. The same may be said respecting the prevalence of moral evil in that age of the world. Let any one consider what Rome was in the days of Nero, and what Jerusalem was in the closing period of the Jewish commonwealth, and he will at once concede the undeniable fact of an abnormal and portentous development of wickedness such as to us appears incredible. Juvenal and Tacitus will bear witness of Rome, and Josephus of Jerusalem; and it is not contrary to reason, while wholly agreeable to Revelation, to infer that such enormous and colossal vice betrays the operation of a satanic influence.

2.   It deserves, further, to be considered that the sin of idolatry, with all its mimicry of supernatural and divine power,---a system which the Scriptures recognise as pre-eminently the work of the devil,---was in our Saviour's time in full and undisturbed possession of nearly the entire world. When we remember what Greece was, and what Rome was, in respect of their national religion, in the apostolic age; the authority, antiquity, and popularity of their gods, and the way in which their worship had entwined itself around every act of public and private life, it seems astonishing that a system so time-honoured and inveterate should have withered away so as to wholly disappeared from the face of the earth. No one can be at a loss to account for this remarkable change: it is entirely due to the influence of Christianity; and but for this new element in civilisation there is no reason to think that the ancient superstitions of Heathenism would have died out or given place to something better.

3.   It is no less certain that this marvellous revolution must be dated from the time when the Gospel began to be preached in the apostolic age. We have the most convincing proofs that the change is not to be explained by the advancement of knowledge, or science, or philosophy, nor by the natural progress of human society, but that it was predicted and expected from the very birth of Christianity as the effect of the redemptive work of Christ. Nothing can be more explicit than our Lord's declarations on this subject. When the seventy disciples returned with joy to report how even the devils were subject to them through their Master's name, Jesus said to them, 'I beheld Satan as lightning fall from heaven' (Luke x. 18). It is absurd to explain this as an allusion to Satan's original expulsion from heaven, before

the creation of the world; it is evidently a figurative declaration that in the success of His messengers our Lord recognised and foresaw the coming overthrow of the power of Satan:---

'Before the intuitive glance of His spirit lay open the results which were to flow from His redemptive work after His ascension into heaven. He saw, in spirit, the kingdom of God advancing in triumph over the kingdom of Satan.'

To the same effect is our Lord's saying,---'*Now* is the judgment of this world: *now* shall the prince of this world be *cast out*' (John xii. 31). What meaning can be attached to these significant words if they do not imply that a powerful check was about to be given to the influence of Satan over the minds of men; a check arising wholly from the death of Christ upon the cross?

But it is in this apocalyptic vision that we see the actual representation of this curbing of Satan's power. It is here evidently defined as to the time of its commencement, and associated with the downfall of Jerusalem, and the consequent abrogation of the Jewish dispensation. Nor is there any absurdity in accepting this date. The abolition of Judaism was the removal of the most formidable obstacle to the progress of Christianity; but, besides this, we have the most express assurance in the New Testament that this was the period of the consummation of the Messianic kingdom, and of Christ's putting down all hostile rule, and authority, and power (1 Cor. xv. 24).

We conclude, therefore, that at 'the end of the age' a marked and decisive check was given to the power of Satan; which check is symbolically represented in the Apocalypse by the chaining and imprisoning of the dragon in the abyss. It does not follow from this that error and evil were banished from the earth. It is enough to show that this was, as Schlegel says,---

'the decisive crisis between ancient and modern times; ' and that the introduction of Christianity 'has changed and regenerated not only government and science, but the whole system of human life.'

There was an hour when the tide of human wickedness began to turn: it was at the very period when that tide was in flood; ever since that time it has been ebbing, and we have no difficulty in recognising the first abatement of the power of evil as corresponding in time with the event here designated the binding of Satan and his imprisonment in the abyss.

Respecting the duration of this restriction of satanic power it is not easy to determine; but it seems, on the whole, most in consonance with the symbolic character of the Apocalypse to understand the thousand years as significant of a long but indefinite period. When we have high numbers stated in the Apocalypse they are usually, if not invariably, to be understood indefinitely. For example, it is not to be supposed that the hundred and forty and four thousand of the sealed signify that number, and no more and no less. It would be absurd to say that there were exactly twelve thousand, to a man, saved out of each of the twelve tribes of the children of Israel. The conception is appropriate in a vision, but incredible in a historical statement. In like manner the army of the horsemen in chap. ix. 16 is set down as two hundred millions; but no sane commentator ever ventured to assign to this a precise and literal signification. Following these analogies we are disposed to regard the thousand years as a definite for an indefinite period, covering doubtless more than that space of time, but how much more none can tell.

THE REIGN OF THE SAINTS AND MARTYRS.

Chap. xx. 4-6.---'And I saw thrones, and they sat upon them, and judgment was given to them; and I saw the souls of them that were beheaded for the witness of Jesus, and for the word of God, and whosoever had not worshipped the beast, neither his image, neither had received his mark upon their foreheads, or in their hands; and they lived and reigned with Christ a thousand years. [But the rest of the dead lived not again until the thousand years were finished. This is the first resurrection. Blessed and holy is he that hath part in the first resurrection: on such the second death hath no power, but they shall be priests of God and of Christ, and shall reign with him a thousand years.]

We approach with the greatest diffidence this mysterious passage, carefully avoiding guesses and conjectural explanations, as well as any attempt to force in any way the natural signification of the words.

The first thing which we note is, that the vision now described falls within the apocalyptic period. It is introduced by the formula 'And I saw,' which marks that which comes under the personal observation of the Seer.

Next, it is to be remarked that there is an evident antithesis between this scene and the act of judgment executed on the beast and his followers. It is the usual method of the Apocalypse thus to place in striking contrast the reward of the righteous and the retribution of the wicked.

We further observe that there is a manifest allusion in this passage to the promise of our Lord to His disciples, 'Verily I say unto you, That ye which have followed me, in the regeneration when the Son of man shall sit in the throne of his glory, ye also shall sit upon twelve thrones, judging the twelve tribes of Israel' (Matt. xix. 28). That period has now arrived. The paliggenesia, or *regeneration,* when the kingdom of the Messiah was to come, is now regarded as present, and the disciples are glorified with their glorified Master: 'judgment is given unto them;' they 'sit upon thrones judging the twelve tribes of Israel.' We are to conceive of the multitude of the redeemed from the land---the hundred and forty and four thousand out of all the tribes of the children of Israel---as forming the kingdom, or subjects, placed under the spiritual government of the apostolic brotherhood.

In addition to these the Seer beholds 'the souls of them that were beheaded for the witness of Jesus, and for the word of God,' and also (for the word oitinez appears to indicate that this is another class who are specified) 'whosoever had not worshipped the beast, nor his image;' these also 'live and *reign* with Christ,' an expression which implies that they too had 'thrones' and 'judgment' given to them. It is impossible not to recognise in the 'souls of them that were beheaded' the same martyred saints whom the Seer beheld, in the vision of the sixth seal, lying under the altar and crying for vengeance on their murderers. They were comforted with the message that in a little while, when their fellow-servants who were about to suffer as they had done had joined them, their prayer should be answered. Now that time is come; their enemies have perished, and they live and reign with Christ.

This vision looks back also on the remarkable passage in 1 Peter iv. 6. These martyrs are the dead to whom the comforting message came [euhggelisqh]. They had been condemned by the judgment of men while in the flesh, but now they *live* in their spirit by the judgment of God, which has vindicated and crowned them. What a new light is thrown upon the words of St. Peter, zwsin de kata qeon pneumati, by the language of the Apocalypse, ezhsan kai ebasileusan. This is one of those subtle coincidences which are often the surest tests of a true interpretation.

These witnessing and suffering souls are represented as enjoying a privilege and a distinction not accorded to others: 'They lived and reign with Christ a thousand years: while the rest of the dead live not again until the thousand years are finished.' This is the crux of the passage, and presents a very formidable difficulty. The only quarter in which we can discern any ray of light is in the direction of the inquiry, Who are 'the rest of the dead'? Are they the rest of the pious dead, or the wicked dead, or both the righteous and the wicked alike? The judgment revolts from the idea that they are the pious dead. if they were to be excluded from participation in the blessedness of heaven for a vast period, how could it be said, 'Blessed are the dead which die in the Lord *from henceforth'?* We are compelled, therefore, to imagine the possibility of the other alternative, and that the passage speaks of the wicked dead, though such a supposition is not without its difficulties. in this case *'the first* resurrection' includes only *the dead in Christ;* and this may be the true interpretation, for the next verse certainly intimates that *all* who have a part in *'the first resurrection'* are blessed and holy, and enjoy the high privilege and honour of 'reigning with Christ.'

One thing more to note, and that is, that the reign of the suffering and witnessing saints, and of all who have part in the *first resurrection,* is not said to be *on earth.* They live and reign *'with Christ;'* they are 'with him where he is, beholding his glory.'

Thus far we have endeavoured to feel our way in a region 'dark with excessive bright,' but we do not pretend to feel any confidence in the latter portion of our exegesis.

THE LOOSING OF SATAN AFTER THE THOUSAND YEARS.

Chap. xx. 7-10.---['And when the thousand years are expired, Satan shall be loosed out of his prison, and shall go out to deceive the nations which are in the four corners of the earth [land], God and Magog, to gather them together to the battle: the number of whom is as the sand of the sea. And they went up on the breadth of the earth [land], and compassed the camp of the saints about, and the beloved city: and fire came down out of heaven, and devoured them. And the devil that deceived them was cast in to the lake of fire and brimstone, where also the beast and the false prophet are, and they shall be tormented day and night for ever and ever.']

The mystery and obscurity which hang over a portion of the preceding context become still deeper, if possible, here. There are, however, certain points which seem determinable.

1.   It is evident that this passage is *direct prophecy,* and not a visionary representation taking place before the eyes of the Seer. It is not introduced by the usual formula in such cases, 'And I saw,' but in the style of prophetic prediction.

2.   It is evident that the prediction of what is to take place at the close of a thousand years does not come within what we have ventured to call 'apocalyptic limits.' These limits, as we are again and again warned in the book itself, are rigidly confined within a very narrow compass; the things shown are *'shortly* to come to pass.' It would have been an abuse of language to say that the events at the distance of a thousand years were to come to pass *shortly;* we are therefore compelled to regard this prediction as lying outside the apocalyptic limits altogether.

3.   We must consequently regard this prediction of the loosing of Satan, and the events that follow, as still future, and therefore unfulfilled. We know of nothing recorded in history which can be adduced as in any way a probably fulfillment of this prophecy. Westein has hazarded the hypothesis that possibly it may symbolise the Jewish revolt under Barcochebas, in the reign of Hadrian; but the suggestion is too extravagant to be entertained for a moment.

4.   There is an evident connection between this prophecy and the vision in Ezekiel concerning Gog and Magog (chaps. xxxviii. xxxix.), which is equally mysterious and obscure. In both the scene of conflict is laid in the same place, the land of Israel; and in both the enemies of God meet with a signal and disastrous overthrow.

5.   The result of the whole is, that we must consider the passage which treats of the thousand years, from ver. 5 to ver. 10, as an intercalation or parenthesis. The Seer, having begun to relate the judgment of the dragon, passes in ver. 7 out of the apocalyptic limits to conclude what he had to say respecting the final punishment of 'the old serpent,' and the fate that awaited him at the close of a lengthened period called 'a thousand years.' This we believe to be the sole

instance in the whole book of an excursion into distant futurity; and we are disposed to regard the whole parenthesis as relating to matters still future and unfilfilled. The broken continuity of the narration is joined again at ver. 11, where the Seer resumes the account of what he beheld in vision, introducing it by the familiar formula 'And I saw.'

THE CATASTROPHE OF THE SIXTH VISION.

Chap. xx. 11-15.---'And I saw a great white throne, and him that sat on it, from whose face the earth and the heaven fled away; and there was found no place for them. And I saw the dead, small and great, stand before God; and the books were opened: and another book was opened, which is the book of life: and the dead were judged out of those things which were written in the books, according to their works. And the sea gave up the dead which were in it; and death and Hades gave up the dead which were in them: and they were judged, every man according to their works. And death and Hades were cast into the lake of fire. This is the second death. And whosoever was not found written in the book of life was cast into the lake of fire.'

These verses bring us to the catastrophe of the sixth vision. Like the other catastrophes which have preceded it, it is a solemn act of judgment, or rather the same great judicial transaction presented in a new aspect. The Seer now resumes the narration which had been interrupted by the digression respecting the thousand years, taking up the thread which was dropped at the close of ver. 4. We are therefore brought back to the same standpoint as in the first and fourth verses. This catastrophe naturally and necessarily belongs to the 'same series of events as have been represented in the vision of the harlot city, and falls within the prescribed apocalyptic limits, being among the things 'which must shortly come to pass.'

As to the catastrophe itself, there can be no question that it represents a solemn judicial investigation on the vastest scale. It is the great consummation, or one aspect of it, towards which all the action of the Apocalypse moves, and which is reached, in one form or another, at the close of each successive vision. There are, however, special features in every catastrophe which distinguish it from the others, notwithstanding that they refer to the same great event. A comparison with the preceding catastrophes will show how much the present has in common with them and what is peculiar to itself. In the catastrophe of the vision of the seven seals, for example, we have the very same imagery of the heaven departing, and the mountains and islands being moved out of their places (chap. vi. 14). In the catastrophe of the vision of the seven vials the same image is repeated (chap. xvi. 20). In the catastrophe of the seventh trumpet it is declared that 'the time of the dead, that they should be judged, is come,' etc. (chap. xi. 18); and in the catastrophe of the seven mystic figures we see 'a white cloud, and on the cloud one sitting, like unto the Son of man' (chap. xiv. 14), corresponding with 'the great white throne, and him that sat on it,' in the passage now before us. There are some features, however, peculiar to this catastrophe,---the books of judgment; the sea, death, and Hades, yielding up their dead; and the casting of death and Hades into the lake of fire.

There is no reason to doubt that the judgment scene depicted here is identical with that described by our Lord in Matt. xxv. 31-46. We have the same 'throne of glory,' the same gathering of all the nations, the same discrimination of the judged according to their works, and the same 'everlasting fire prepared for the devil and his angels.'

But if the judgment scene described in this passage be identical with that in Matt. xxv., it follows that it is not 'the end of the world' in the sense of its being the dissolution of the material fabric of the globe and the close of human history, but that which is so frequently predicted as accompanying the sunteleia tou aiwnoz,---the end of the age, or termination of the Jewish dispensation. That great consummation is always represented as a judgment-epoch. It is the time of the Parousia, the coming of Christ in glory to vindicate and reward His faithful servants, and to judge and destroy His enemies. There is a remarkable unity and consistency in the teachings of Scripture on this subject; and whether it be in the gospels, or in the epistles, or in the visions of the Apocalypse, we find one harmonious and concurrent scheme of doctrine, all parts mutually confirming and sustaining one another,---a proof of their common origin in the same divine fountain of inspiration and truth.

The Seventh Vision

THE HOLY CITY, OR THE BRIDE. Chaps. xxi. xxii. 1-5.

This vision is the last of the series, and completes the mystic number of *seven*. It is the grand *finale* of the whole drama, the triumphant consummation and climax of the apocalyptic visions. It stands in striking antithesis of the vision of the harlot city; it is the new Jerusalem in contrast to the old; the bride, the Lamb's wife, in contrast with the foul and bloated adulteress whose judgment has passed before our eyes.

The structure of the vision may detain us for a moment. It is introduced by a preface or prologue, extending from the first verse of chap. xxi. to the eighth. At the ninth verse the vision of the bride opens in the same manner as the vision of the harlot, by 'one of the seven angels, which had the seven vials, full of the seven last plagues,' inviting the

Seer to come and behold 'the bride, the Lamb's wife.' The vision reaches its climax or catastrophe at the fifth verse of chap. xxii. The remainder forms the conclusion, or epilogue, not of this vision only, but of the Apocalypse itself.

PROLOGUE TO THE VISION.

Chap. xxi. 1-8.---'And I saw a new heaven and a new earth: for the first heaven and the first earth were passed away, and there is no more sea. And I saw the holy city, new Jerusalem, coming down out of heaven from God, prepared as a bride adorned for her husband. and I heard a great voice out of the throne saying, Behold, the tabernacle of God is with men, and he shall dwell with them, and they shall be his people, and God himself shall be with them, and be their God. And God shall wipe away every tear from their eyes; and there shall be no more death, neither sorrow, nor crying, neither shall there be any more pain: for the former things are passed away. And he that sat upon the throne said, Behold, I make all things new. And he said unto me, Write: for these words are true and faithful. And he said unto me, It is done. I am Alpha and Omega, the beginning and the end. I will give unto him that is athirst of the fountain of the water of life freely. he that overcometh shall inherit all things; and I will be his God, and he shall be my son. But the fearful, and unbelieving, and the abominable, and murderers, and whoremongers, and sorcerers, and idolaters, and all liars, shall have their part in the lake which burneth with fire and brimstone: which is the second death.'

Although this section may be regarded as introductory to the actual vision described from the ninth verse onwards, yet it is really an integral part of the representation, and covers the very same ground as the subsequent description. It is as if the Seer, full of the glorious object revealed to his eyes, began to tell its wonders and splendours before he could stay to explain the circumstances which had led to his being favoured with the manifestation. The passage now before us is really an abridgment or outline of what is developed in fuller detail in the subsequent part of this and the first five verses of the following chapter.

We now find ourselves surrounded by scenery so novel and so wonderful that it is not surprising that we should be in doubt where we are. Is this earth, or is it heaven? Every familiar landmark has disappeared; the old has vanished, and given place to the new: it is a new heaven above us; it is a new earth beneath us. New conditions of life must exist, for 'there is no more sea.' Plainly we have here a representation in which symbolism is carried to its utmost limits; and he who would deal with such gorgeous imagery as with prosaic literalities is incapable of comprehending them. But the symbols, though transcendental, are not unmeaning. 'They serve unto the example and shadow of heavenly things;' and all the pomp and splendour of earth are employed to set forth the beauty of moral and spiritual excellence.

It is impossible to regard this picture as the representation of any social condition to be realised upon earth. There are, indeed, certain phrases which at first seem to imply that earth is the scene where these glories are manifested: the holy city is said to 'come down out of heaven;' the tabernacle of God is said to be 'with men;' 'the kings of the earth' are said to 'bring their glory and honour into it; ' but, on the other hand, the whole conception and description of the vision forbid the supposition of its being a terrestrial scene. In the first place, it belongs to 'the things which must shortly come to pass;' it falls strictly within apocalyptic limits. It is, therefore, no vision of the future; it belongs as much to the period called 'the end of the age' as the destruction of Jerusalem does; and we are to conceive of this renovation of all things,---this new heaven and new earth, as contemporaneous with, or in immediate succession to, the judgment of the great harlot, to which it is the counterpart or antithesis.

Secondly, What is the chief figure in this visionary representation? It is the holy city, new Jerusalem. But the new Jerusalem is always represented in the Scriptures as situated in heaven, not on earth. St. Paul speaks of the Jerusalem which is *above,* in contrast with the Jerusalem *below.* How can the Jerusalem which is *above* belong to earth? There cannot be a reasonable doubt that the city which is here depicted in such glowing colours is identical with that which is referred to in Heb. xii. 22, 23: 'Ye are come unto mount Sion, and unto the city of the living God, the heavenly Jerusalem, and to an innumerable company of angels; to the general assembly and church of the first-born, which are written in heaven, and to God the Judge of all, and to the spirits of just men made perfect.' Clearly, therefore, the holy city is the abode of the glorified; the inheritance of the saints in light; the mansions of the Father's house, prepared for the home of the blessed.

Once more, this conclusion is certified by the representation of its being the dwelling-place of the Most High Himself: 'The Lord God Almighty and the Lamb are the temple of it;' 'the throne of God and of the Lamb shall be in it;' 'his servants shall serve him, and they shall see his face.' In fact, this vision of the holy city is anticipated in the catastrophe of the vision of the seals, where the hundred and forty and four thousand out of all the tribes of the children of Israel, and the great multitude that no man could number, are represented as enjoying the very same glory and felicity, in the very same place and circumstances, as in the vision before us. The two scenes are identical; or different aspects of one and the same great consummation.

We therefore conclude that the vision sets forth the blessedness and glory of the heavenly state, into which the way was fully opened at the 'end of the age,' or sunteleia tou aiwnoz, according to the showing of the Epistle to the Hebrews.

Having thus arrived at the conclusion that the heavenly state is here signified, we shall not be guilty of the presumption and folly of entering into any detailed explanation of the symbols themselves. There is an apparent confusion of the figures by which the new Jerusalem is represented, being sometimes described as a city. the same double figure is employed in the description of the harlot, or old Jerusalem, which is sometimes represented as a woman and sometimes as a city. In the seventh vision the figure of the bride is dropped almost as soon as it is introduced., and the whole of the remaining description is occupied with the details of the architecture, the wealth, and splendour, and glory of the city. Some of the features are evidently derived from the visionary city beheld by Ezekiel; but there is this remarkable difference, that whereas the temple and its elaborate details occupy the principal part of the Old Testament vision, no temple at all is seen in the apocalyptic vision,---perhaps for the reason that where all is most holy no one place has greater sanctity than another, or because where God's presence is fully manifested, the whole place becomes one great temple.

There is one point, however, which deserves particular notice, as serving to identify the city called the new Jerusalem. In Hebrews xi. 10 we meet with the remarkable statement that the patriarch Abraham sojourned as a stranger in the very land which had been promised to him as his own possession, and that he did so because he had faith in a larger and higher fulfillment of the promise than any mere earthly and human city could have bestowed. 'He looked for *the* city which hath *the* foundations, whose builder and maker is God.' What is this but the very city described in the Apocalypse---the city which has *twelve foundations,* inscribed with the names of the twelve apostles of the Lamb; the city which is built by no mortal hands; 'the city of the *living God,'* the *heavenly Jerusalem?* This is a decisive proof, first, that the writer of the èpistle had read the Apocalypse, and, secondly, that he recognised the vision of the new Jerusalem as a representation of the heavenly world.

The Epilogue

Chap. xxii. 6-21.---'And he said unto me, These sayings are faithful and true: and the Lord God of the spirits of the prophets sent his angel to shew unto his servants the things which must shortly be done. And, behold, I come quickly: blessed is he that keepeth the sayings of the prophecy of this book.

'And I John heard these things, and saw them. And when I had heard and seen, I fell down to worship before the feet of the angel which shewed me these things. Then saith he unto me, See thou do it not: for I am thy fellow-servant, and [the fellow-servant] of thy brethren the prophets, and of them which keep the sayings of this book: worship God. And he said unto me, Seal not the sayings of the prophecy of this book: for the time is at hand. He that is unjust, let him be unjust still: and he that is filthy, let him be filthy still: and he that is righteous, let him be righteous still: and he that is holy, let him be holy still. Behold, I come quickly; and my reward is with me, to give every man according as his work shall be. I am the Alpha and Omega, the first and the last, the beginning and the end. Blessed are they that wash their robes, that they may enter through the gates into the city. For without are dogs, and sorcerers, and whoremongers, and murderers, and idolaters, and whosoever loveth and maketh a lie.

'I Jesus have sent mine angel to testify unto you these things in the churches. I am the root and the offspring of David, and the bright and morning star. And the Spirit and the bride say, Come. And let him that heareth say, Come. And let him that is athrist come. And whosoever will, let him take the water of life freely.

'For I testify unto every man that heareth the sayings of the prophecy of this book, If any man shall add unto these things, God shall add unto him the plagues that are written in this book: and if any man shall take away from the sayings of the book of this prophecy, God shall take away his part from the tree of life, and from the holy city, which are written in this book.

'He which testifieth these things saith, Surely I come quickly! Amen. Come, Lord Jesus.

'The grace of the Lord Jesus Christ be with you all. Amen.'

This epilogue at the conclusion of the book corresponds with the prologue at the commencement, and exemplifies the structural symmetry of the composition. Still more remarkable are the emphasis and frequency with which the approaching fulfillment of the contents of the prophecy is affirmed and reiterated. Seven times over it is declared, in one form or another, that all is on the point of being accomplished. The statement with which the book opens is repeated at this close, that the angel of the Lord has been commissioned 'to shew unto his servants *things which must shortly come to pass.'* The monitory announcement, *'Behold, I come quickly,'* is thrice made into this concluding section. The Seer is commanded not to seal the book of the prophecy, because *'the time is at hand.'* So imminent is the end that it is intimated that now it is too late for any alteration in the state or character of men; such as they are so must they continue: *'He hat is unjust, let him be unjust still.'* The invocation addressed by the four living creatures to the expected Son of man, *'Come!'* (chap. vi. 1, 3, 5, 7), is repeated by the Spirit and the bride; while all that hear are invited to join in the cry: and, lastly, the final expression of the whole book is the fervent utterance of the prayer, 'Amen! *Come, Lord Jesus.'* All these are indications, which cannot be misunderstood, that the predictions contained in the Apocalypse were not to be slowly evolved as ages roll on, but were on the eve of almost instant accomplishment. The whole prophecy, from the first to last, relates to the immediate future, with the solitary exception of the six verses of chap. xx. 5-10. Nineteen-twentieths of the Apocalypse, we might almost say ninety-nine hundredths, belong, according to its own showing, to the very days then present, the closing days of the Jewish age. The coming of the Lord is its grand theme: with this it opens, with this it closes, and from beginning to end this event is contemplated as just about to take place. Whatever else may be dark or doubtful, this at least is clear and certain. The interpreter who does not apprehend and hold fast this guiding principle is incapable of understanding the words of this prophecy, and will infallibly lose himself and bewilder others in a labyrinth of conjecture and vain speculation.

So ends this wonderful book; so elaborate in its construction, so magnificent in its diction, so mysterious in its imagery, so glorious in its revelations. More than any other book in the Bible it has been sealed and shut to the intelligent apprehension of its readers, and this mainly on account of the strange neglect of its own unambiguous directions for its right understanding. Herder, who brought his poetical genius rather than his critical faculty to the elucidation of the Apocalypse, asks,---

'Was there a *key* sent with the book, and has this been lost? Was it thrown into the sea of Patmos, or into the Maeander?'

'No!' answers an able and sagacious critic, Moses Stuart, whose labours have done much to prepare the way for a true interpretation,---

'No key was sent, and none was lost. The primitive readers---I mean of course the men of intelligence among them---could understand the book; and were we for a short time in their place we might dispense with all the commentaries upon it, and the theological romances which have grown out of it, that have made their appearance from the time of John's exile down to the present hour.' 1

But perhaps a better answer may be given. The key *was* sent along with the book, and it has been allowed to lie rusty and unused, while all kinds of false keys and picklocks have been tried, and tried in vain, until men have come to look upon the Apocalypse as an unintelligible enigma, only meant to puzzle and bewilder. The true key has all along been visible enough, and the attention of men has been loudly called to it in almost every page of the book. That key is the declaration so frequently made that *all is on the point of fulfillment.* If the original readers were competent, as Stuart contends, to understand the Apocalypse without an interpreter, it could only be because *they recognised its connection with the events of their own day.* To suppose that they could understand or feel the slightest interest in a book that treated of Papal councils, Protestant reformation, French revolutions, and distant events in foreign lands and far-off ages, would be one of the wildest fancies that ever possessed a human brain. From first to last the book itself bears decisive testimony to the immediate fulfillment of its predictions. It opens with the express declaration that the events to which it refers 'must shortly come to pass,' and it closes with the reiteration of the same statement,---'The Lord God hath sent his angel to shew unto his servants the things which must shortly come to pass.' 'The time is at hand.'

The only luminous interpretation of the vision of the Apocalypse has been given by critics who have consented to use this authentic and divine key to its mysteries. Yet it is remarkable that very few, if any, have done so consistently and throughout. It is surprising and mortifying to find such an expositor as Moses Stuart, after proceeding with courage and success a certain way, suddenly falter, drop the key which had done such good service, and then stagger blindly and helplessly on, groping and guessing through the Egyptian fog which surrounds him. Yet no theologian of our time has contributed so much to the true interpretation of the Apocalypse. By his own admirable commentary he has laid all students of this wonderful book under the highest obligation, and conferred a lasting benefit on the whole church of Christ. Unhappily, by failing to carry out his own principles consistently to the end, he missed the honour of conducting his followers into the promised land of a true exegesis.

As for the majority of interpreters, it is scarcely possible to conceive a more absolute and reckless disregard to the express and manifold directions contained in the book itself than that which they have exhibited in their arbitrary speculations. Of willful perverseness no one will accuse them; but it seems unaccountable that scholarly and reverent students of divine revelation should either overlook or set aside the explicit declarations of the book itself with regard to its speedily approaching fulfillment; that they should, in spite of those plain assertions to the contrary, lay it down as an axiom that the Apocalypse is a syllabus of civil and ecclesiastical history to the end of time; and that they should then, in defiance of all grammatical laws, proceed to invent a non-natural method of interpretation, according to which *'near'* becomes *'distant,'* and *'quickly'* means *'ages hence,'* and *'at hand'* signifies *'afar off.'* All this seems incredible, yet it is true. Language serves only to mislead, words have no meaning, and interpretation has no laws, if the express and repeated declarations of the Apocalypse do not plainly teach the speedy and all but immediate fulfillment of its predictions.

It ought to have occurred to the interpreters of the Apocalypse that it was an overwhelming *a priori* presumption against their method that it required an immense *apparatus criticus,* vast stores of historical information, the lapse of many ages, and 'something like prophetic strain,' to produce an exposition satisfactory even to themselves. Of what value such 'revelation' could be to the primitive believers, who with trembling hearts obeyed the injunction that sent them to the baffling task of studying its pages, it is not easy to see. Nor is it much more value to the mass of modern readers, who must have a high critical faculty to be able to discern the fitness and truthfulness of the interpretation offered, and to decide between conflicting interpretations. It is no wonder that, occupying such a false position, the defenders of divine revelation laid themselves open to the assaults of such sceptics as Strauss and 'the destructive school of criticism,' and, taking refuge in non-natural interpretation, endangered the very citadel of the faith. It must be acknowledged that a culpable negligence of the 'true sayings of God' on the part of Christian expositors has often given a vantage ground to the enemies of revelation of which they have not been slow to avail themselves.

Without undue presumption it may be claimed for the scheme of interpretation advocated in these pages that it is marked by extreme simplicity, by agreement with historical facts, and by exact correspondence with the symbols. There is no wresting of Scripture, no perversion or accommodation of history, no manipulation of facts. The only indispensable *apparatus criticus* is Josephus and the Greek grammar. The guiding and governing principle is implicit and unwavering deference to the teachings of the book itself. The apocalyptic data have been the sole landmarks regarded, and it is believed that they have not been insufficient. To assume that no mistakes have been made would be preposterous; but succeeding travellers by the same route will soon correct what is proved to be erroneous, and confirm what is shown to be right.

It has been the object of the writer to demonstrate that the Apocalypse is really the reproduction and expansion, in symbolical imagery adapted to the nature of a vision, of our Lord's prophetic discourse spoken on the Mount of Olives. That discourse, as we have shown, is one continuous and homogeneous prediction of events which were to take place in connection with the Parousia, the coming in His kingdom of the Son of man, an event which He declared would happen before the passing away of the existing generation, and which some of the disciples would live to witness. Similarly, the Apocalypse is a revelation of the events accompanying the Parousia, but entering far more into detail, and displaying far more of the glory and felicity of 'the kingdom.'

Eighteen centuries ago, as the Seer gazed on the glorious vision of the city whose walls were of jasper, and its gates of pearl, and its streets of pure gold, he was assured again and again that 'these things must *shortly* be done,' and that 'the time was *at hand.'* Standing on the verge of the long-expected Parousia, listening for the footfall of the coming King, knowing that 'the end of the age' must be imminent, and looking eagerly for 'the day of the Lord,' how could it be otherwise than that St. John and his fellow-disciples should believe themselves on the point of witnessing the fulfillment of their cherished hopes? How could it be otherwise, when the Lord Himself, giving His own personal attestation to the assurance of His almost immediate advent, declared thrice over, in the most explicit terms, 'Behold I come quickly;' 'Behold, I come quickly;' 'Yea, I come quickly'?

We are thus led to the conclusion, alike from the teaching of the Apocalypse and the rest of the New Testament scriptures, that in the days of St. John the Parousia was universally believed by the whole Christian church to be close at hand. It was the promise of Christ, the preaching of the apostles, the faith of the church. We are also taught the significance of that great event. It marked a new epoch in the divine administration. Until that event took place the full blessedness of the heavenly state was not open to the souls of believers.

The Epistle to the Hebrews teaches that until the arrival of the great consummation something was wanting to the full perfection of them who had 'died in faith.' The same thing is taught in the Apocalypse. Until the 'harlot city' was judged and condemned, the 'holy city' was not prepared as the habitation of the saints. We are given to understand also that the close of the Jewish dispensation, the abrogation of the legal economy, and the destruction of the city and temple of Jerusalem, indicating the dissolution of the peculiar relation between Jehovah and the nation of Israel. The nation had rejected its King, and the King had judged the nation; and the Messianic mission, both for mercy and for judgment, was then fulfilled. The faithful remnant were gathered into the kingdom, or 'the new Jerusalem,' and the whole frame and fabric of Judaism were shattered and destroyed for ever. The kingdom of God was now come, and He who for so long a period had conducted its administration, its Mediator and Chief, now that He has crowed the edifice, resigns His official character and 'delivers up the kingdom' into the Father's hands. His work as Messiah is accomplished; He is no longer 'a minister of the circumcision;' the local and limited gives place to the universal, 'that God may be All in all.' This does not mean that the relation between Christ and humanity ceases, but that His mission as *King of Israel* is fulfilled; the *covenant-nation* no longer exists; there are no longer Jews and Gentiles, circumcised and uncircumcised; the Israel of God is wider and greater than Israel after the flesh; Jerusalem which is above is not the mother of *Jews,* but is *'the mother of us all.'*

It was in the full view of that glorious day, which was about to 'open the kingdom of heaven to all believers,' that the beloved disciple made response to his Lord's announcement of His speedy coming, 'Amen! Come, Lord Jesus!'

1 Stuart on the Apocalypse, sect. 12

Summary and Conclusion

We have now reached a point in our investigation where it is possible to take a complete and connected survey of the whole field which we have traversed, and to observe the unity and consistency of the prophetic system developed in the New Testament.

1. We find that the Gospel dispensation does not come upon us as an independent and isolated scheme,—a new beginning in the divine government of the world,—but that it implies and assumes the relation of God to Israel in past ages. The whole philosophy of Jewish history is condensed into a single phrase, 'the kingdom of God;' and it is this kingdom which, first John the Baptist, as the herald of the coming king, and next the King Himself, the Lord Jesus Christ, proclaimed as being 'at hand.'

2. We find that John the Baptist adopts the warnings of Old Testament prophecy, especially of the last of the prophets, Malachi, and predicts that the coming of the kingdom would be the coming of wrath upon Israel. He declares that 'the axe is already laid to the root of the tree;' his cry is, 'Flee from the coming wrath,' plainly intimating that a time of judgment was fast approaching.

3. Our Lord affirms the same speedy coming of judgment upon the land and people of Israel; and He further connects this judgment with His own coming in glory,—the Parousia. This event stands forth most prominently in the New Testament; to this every eye is directed, to this every inspired messenger points. It is represented as the nucleus and centre of a cluster of great events; the end of the age, or close of the Jewish economy; the destruction of the city and temple of Jerusalem; the judgment of the guilty nation; the resurrection of the dead; the reward of the faithful; the consummation of the kingdom of God. All these transactions are declared to be coincident with the Parousia.

4. It is demonstrable by the express testimony of our Lord, the uniform and concurrent teaching of His apostles, and the universal expectation of the church of the apostolic age, that the Parousia and its accompanying events were represented as nigh at hand; and not only so, but as about to happen within the limits of a given period; that is to say, in the time of the apostles and their contemporaries; so that many or most of them might expect to witness the great consummation. This is the main point of the whole question, and must be decided by the authority of the Scriptures themselves. While the proof ought to be rigorously demanded, and the evidence thoroughly sifted, it ought also to be dispassionately considered, without resorting to non natural interpretation, uncritical and unfair evasion, or violent wresting of the plain sense of words.

5. Without going over the ground already traversed it may suffice here to appeal to three distinct and decisive declarations of our Lord respecting the time of His coming, each of them accompanied with a solemn affirmation:—

(1) 'Verily I say unto you, Ye shall not have gone over the cities of Israel, till the Son of man be come' (Matt. 10:23).
(2) 'Verily I say unto you, there be some standing here, which shall not taste of death, till they see the Son of man coming in his kingdom' (Matt. 16:28).
(3) 'Verily I say unto you, This generation shall not pass, till all these things be fulfilled' (Matt. 24:34).

The plain grammatical meaning of these statements has been fully discussed in these pages. No violence can extort from them any other sense than the obvious and unambiguous one, viz. that our Lord's second coming would take place within the limits of the existing generation.

6. The doctrine of the apostles with regard to the coming of the Lord is in perfect harmony with this. Nothing can be more evident than that they all believed and taught the speedy return of the Lord. From the first speech of St. Peter on the day of Pentecost to the last utterance of St. John in the Apocalypse, this conviction is clearly and constantly expressed. To say that the apostles were themselves ignorant of the time of their Lord's return, and therefore could have no belief on the subject,—could not teach what they did not know,—is to contradict their own express and reiterated assertions. True, they did not know, and did not teach, 'that day and that hour;' they did not say that He would come in a particular month of a particular year, but they assuredly did give the churches to understand that He was coming quickly; that they might soon expect to see Him; and they never ceased to exhort them to maintain the attitude of constant watchfulness and preparation.

It is not necessary to do more than advert to some of the leading testimonies borne by the apostles to the speedy coming of the Lord:—

(1) St. Paul gives great prominence in his epistles to this cherished hope of the Christian church.

a. In the First Epistle to the Thessalonians he implies the possibility of the Lord's coming in his and their lifetime,— 'We which are alive and remain unto the coming of the Lord.' He also prays that 'their spirit, soul, and body may be preserved blameless unto the coming of our Lord Jesus Christ.'

b. In the Second Epistle to the Thessalonians (which is often erroneously understood to teach that the coming of Christ was not at hand, but which teaches precisely the contrary doctrine) he comforts the suffering believers with the promise that they would obtain rest from their present sufferings 'when the Lord Jesus was revealed from heaven,' etc. (2 Thess. 1:7).

c. In the First Epistle to the Corinthians the apostle speaks of believers as 'waiting for the coming of the Lord Jesus Christ.' He warns them that 'the time is short;' that 'the end of the age,' or ' ends of the ages,' are come upon them; that 'the Lord is at hand.'

d. In the Second Epistle to the Corinthians St. Paul expresses his confidence that though he might die before the coming of the Lord, yet God would raise him from the dead, and present him along with those who survived to that period.

e. In the Epistle to the Romans St. Paul speaks of 'the glory about to be revealed;' of the whole creation waiting for the manifestation of the Son of God; of salvation being near, 'nearer than when they first believed;' that 'it is now high time to awake out of sleep;' that 'the night is far spent, and the day at hand;' that 'God will bruise Satan under their feet shortly.'

f. In the Epistles to the Ephesians, Philippians, and Colossians the apostle speaks of 'the day of Christ' as the period of hope, perfection, and glory to which they were looking forward, and he declares emphatically, 'The Lord is at hand.'

g. In like manner, in the Epistles to Timothy and Titus the expectation of the Parousia is conspicuous. Timothy is exhorted to keep the commandment inviolate 'until the appearing of our Lord Jesus Christ.' 'He is about to judge the living and the dead at his appearing, and his kingdom.' Christians are exhorted to be looking 'for that blessed hope, even the glorious appearing of the great God and our Saviour, Jesus Christ.'

(2) St. James represents the coming of the Lord as just at hand. 'The last days' are come. Suffering Christians are exhorted to 'be patient unto the coming of the Lord.' They are assured that 'it is drawing nigh;' that the Judge standeth before the door.'

(3) St. Peter, like St. Paul, gives great prominence to the Parousia and its related events.

a. On the day of Pentecost he declared that those were 'the last days' predicted by the prophet Joel, introductory to 'the great and terrible day of the Lord.'

b. In his First Epistle he affirms that it was 'the last time;' that God was 'ready to judge the living and the dead;' 'that the end of all things was at hand;' that 'the time had come when judgment was to begin at the house of God.'

c. In his Second Epistle he exhorts Christians to be 'looking for and hasting unto the coming of the day of God;' and depicts the approaching dissolution of 'heaven and earth.'

(4) The Epistle to the Hebrews speaks of 'the last days' as now present; it is 'the end of the age;' the day is seen to be 'approaching;' 'Yet a little, little while, and he that is coming will come, and will not tarry.'

(5) St. John confirms and completes the testimony of his fellow-apostles; it is 'the last time;' 'antichrist has come;' 'he is already in the world.' Christians are exhorted so to live that they may not be ashamed before Christ at His coming.

Finally, the Apocalypse is full of the Parousia: 'Behold, he cometh with clouds;' 'The time is at hand;' 'Behold, I come quickly.'

Such is a rapid sketch of the apostolic testimony to the speedy coming of the Lord. It would have been strange if, with such assurances and such exhortations, the apostolic churches had not lived in constant and eager expectation of the Parousia. That they did so we have the clearest evidence in the New Testament, and we can conceive the mighty influence which this faith and hope must have had upon Christian life and character.

But, admitting, what cannot well be denied, that the apostles and early Christians did cherish these expectations, and that their belief was founded on the teaching of our Lord, the question arises, Were they not mistaken in their expectation? This is practically to ask, Were the apostles permitted to fall into error themselves, and to lead others into a like delusion, with respect to a matter of fact which they had abundant opportunities of knowing; which must frequently have been the subject of conversation and conference among themselves; which they never failed to keep before the attention of the churches, and about which they were all agreed?

There are critics who do not scruple to affirm that the apostles were mistaken, and that time has proved the fallacy of their anticipations. They tell us that either they misunderstood the teaching of their Master, or that He too was under an erroneous impression. This is of course to set aside the claims of the apostles to speak authoritatively as the inspired messengers of Christ, and to undermine the very foundations of the Christian faith.

There are others, more reverential in their treatment of Scripture, who acknowledge that the apostles were indeed mistaken, but that this mistake was, for wise reasons, permitted,—that, in fact, the error was highly beneficial in its results: it stimulated hope, it fortified courage, it inspired devotion." *

(* 'For ages the world's hope has been the second advent. The early church expected it in their own day,—"We which are alive and remain unto the coming of the Lord." The Saviour Himself had said, "This generation shall not pass till all these things be fulfilled." Yet the Son of man has never come. In the first centuries the early Christians believed that the millennial advent was close; they heard the warning of the apostle, brief and sharp, "The time is short." Now, suppose that instead of this they had seen all the dreary page of church history unrolled; suppose that they had known that after two thousand years the world would have scarcely spelled out three letters of the meaning of Christianity,

198

where would have been those gigantic efforts, that life spent as on the very brink of eternity, which characterize the days of the early church?—F. W. Robertson, Sermon on the Illusiveness of Life.)

'If the Christians of the first centuries,' says Hengstenberg, 'had foreseen that the second coming of Christ would not take place for eighteen hundred years, how much weaker an impression would this doctrine have made upon them than when they were expecting Him every hour, and were told to watch because He would come like a thief in the night, at an hour when they looked not for Him!' (Hengstenberg, Christology, vol. iv. p. 443.)

But neither can this explanation be accepted as satisfactory. Unquestionably the first Christians did receive an immense impulse to their courage and zeal from their firm belief in the speedy advent of the Lord; but was this a hope that after all made them ashamed? Must we conclude that the indomitable courage and devotion of a Paul rested mainly on a delusion? Were the martyrs and confessors of the primitive age only mistaken enthusiasts? We confess that such a conclusion is revolting to all our conceptions of Christianity as a revelation of divine truth by the instrumentality of inspired men. If the apostles misunderstood or misrepresented the teaching of Christ in regard to a matter of fact, respecting which they had the most ample opportunities of information, what dependence can be placed upon their testimony as to matters of faith, where the liability to error is so much greater? Such explanations are fitted to unsettle the foundations of confidence in apostolic teaching; and it is not easy to see how they are compatible with any practical belief in inspiration.

There is another theory, however, by which many suppose that the credit of the apostles is saved, and yet room left for avoiding the acceptance of their apparent teaching on the subject of the coming of Christ. This is, by the hypothesis of a primary and partial fulfillment of their predictions in their own time, to be followed and completed by an ultimate and plenary fulfillment at the end of human history. According to this view, the anticipations of the apostles were not wholly erroneous. Something really did take place that might be called 'a coming of the Lord,' 'a judgment day.' Their predictions received a quasi fulfillment in the destruction of Jerusalem and in the judgment of the guilty nation. That consummation at the close of the Jewish age was a type of another and infinitely greater catastrophe, when the whole human race will be brought before the judgment seat of Christ and the earth consumed by a general conflagration. This is probably the view which is most commonly accepted by the majority of expositors and readers of the New Testament at the present day. The first objection to this hypothesis is, that it has no foundation in the teaching of the Scriptures. There is not a scintilla of evidence that the apostles and primitive Christians had any suspicion of a twofold reference in the predictions of Jesus concerning the end. No hint is anywhere dropped that a primary and partial fulfillment of His sayings was to take place in that generation, but that the complete and exhaustive fulfillment was reserved for a future and far distant period. The very contrary is the fact. What can be more comprehensive and conclusive than our Lord's words, 'Verily I say unto you, This generation shall not pass, till ALL these things be fulfilled'? What critical torture has been applied to these words to extort from them some other meaning than their obvious and natural one! How has γενεά been hunted through all its lineage and genealogy to discover that it may not mean the persons then living on the earth! But all such efforts are wholly futile. While the words remain in the text their plain and obvious sense will prevail over all the glosses and perversions of ingenious criticism. The hypothesis of a twofold fulfillment receives no countenance from the Scriptures. We have only to read the language in which the apostles speak of the approaching consummation, to be convinced that they had one, and only one, great event in view, and that they thought and spoke of it as just at hand.

This brings us to another objection to the hypothesis of a double, or even manifold, fulfillment of the predictions in the New Testament, viz. that it proceeds from a fundamentally erroneous conception of the real significance and grandeur or that great crisis in the divine government of the world which is marked by the Parousia. There are not a few who seem to think that if our Lord's prophecy on the Mount of Olives, and the predictions of the apostles of the coming of Christ in glory, meant no more than the destruction of Jerusalem, and were fulfilled in that event, then all their announcements and expectations ended in a mere fiasco, and the historical reality answers very feebly and inadequately to the magnificent prophecy. There is reason to believe that the true significance and grandeur of that great event are very little appreciated by many. The destruction of Jerusalem was not a mere thrilling incident in the drama of history, like the siege of Troy or the downfall of Carthage, closing a chapter in the annals of a state or a people. It was an event which has no parallel in history. It was the outward and visible sign of a great epoch in the divine government of the world. It was the close of one dispensation and the commencement of another. It marked the inauguration of a new order of things. The Mosaic economy,—which had been ushered in by the miracles of Egypt, the lightnings and thunderings of Sinai, and the glorious manifestations of Jehovah to Israel,—after subsisting for more than fifteen centuries, was now abolished. The peculiar relation between the Most High and the covenant nation was dissolved. The Messianic kingdom, that is, the administration of the divine government by the Mediator, so far, at least, as Israel was concerned, reached its culminating point. The kingdom so long predicted, hoped for, prayed for, was now fully come. The final act of the King was to sit upon the throne of His glory and judge His people. He could then 'deliver up the kingdom to God, even the Father.' This is the significance of the destruction of Jerusalem according to the showing of the Word of God. It was not an isolated fact, a solitary catastrophe,—it was the centre of a group of related and coincident events, not only in the material, but in the spiritual world; not only on earth, but in heaven and in hell; some of them being cognisable by the senses and capable of historical confirmation, and others not.

Perhaps it may be said that such an explanation of the predictions of the New Testament, instead of relieving the difficulty, embarrasses and perplexes us more than ever. It is possible to believe in the fulfillment of predictions which take effect in the visible and outward order of things, because we have historical evidence of that fulfillment; but how can we be expected to believe in fulfillments which are said to have taken place in the region of the spiritual and invisible when we have no witnesses to depose to the facts? We can implicitly believe in the accomplishment of all that was predicted respecting the horrors of the siege of Jerusalem, the burning of the temple, and the demolition of the city, because we have the testimony of Josephus to the facts; but how can we believe in a coming of the Son of man, in a resurrection of the dead, in an act of judgment, when we have nothing but the word of prophecy to rely upon, and no Josephus to vouch for the historical accuracy of the facts?

To this it can only be said in reply, that the demand for human testimony to events in the region of the unseen is not altogether reasonable. If we receive them at all, it must be on the word of Him Who declared that all these things would assuredly take place before that generation passed away. But, after all, is the demand upon our faith in this matter so very excessive? A large portion of these predictions we know to have been literally and punctually fulfilled; we recognize in that accomplishment a remarkable proof of the truth of the Word of God and the superhuman prescience that foresaw and foretold the future. Could anything have been less probable at the time when our Lord delivered His prophetic discourse than the total destruction of the temple, the razing of the city, and the ruin of the nation in the lifetime of the existing generation? What can be more minute and particular than the signs of the end enumerated by our Lord? What can be more precise and literal than the fulfillment of them?

But the part which confessedly has been fulfilled, and which is vouched for by uninspired history, is inseparably bound up with another portion which is not so vouched for. Nothing but a violent disruption can detach the one part of this prophecy from the other. It is one from beginning to end—a complete whole. The finest instrument cannot draw a line separating one portion which relates to that generation from another portion which relates to a different and distant period. Every part of it rests on the same foundation, and the whole is so linked and concatenated that all must stand or fall together. We are justified, therefore, in holding that the exact accomplishment of so much of the prophecy as comes within the cognisance of the senses, and is capable of being vouched for by human testimony, is a presumption and guarantee in favour of the exact fulfillment of that portion which lies within the region of the invisible and spiritual, and which cannot, in the nature of things, be attested by human evidence. This is not credulity, but reasonable faith, such as men fearlessly exercise in all their worldly transactions.

We conclude, therefore, that all the parts of our Lord's prediction refer to the same period and the same event; that the whole prophecy is one and indivisible, resting upon the same foundation of divine authority. Further, that all that was cognisable by the human senses is proved to have been fulfilled, and, therefore, we are not only warranted, but bound to assume the fulfillment of the remainder as not only credible, but certain.

As the result of the investigation we are landed in this dilemma: either the whole group of predictions, comprehending the destruction of Jerusalem, the coming of the Lord, the resurrection of the dead, and the rewarding of the faithful, did take place before the passing away of that generation, as predicted by Christ, taught by the apostles, and expected by the whole church; or, else, the hope of the church was a delusion, the teaching of the apostles an error, the predictions of Jesus a dream.

There is no other alternative consistent with the fair grammatical interpretation of the words of Scripture. We may not tear the prophecy of Christ asunder, and arbitrarily decide, this is past, and that is future; this is fulfilled, and that unfulfilled. There is no pretext for such a division in the record of that discourse; like the seamless robe worn by Him who uttered it, it is all of one piece, 'woven from the top throughout.' The grammatical structure and the historical occasion alike imply the unity of the whole prophecy. Neither is there any 'verifying faculty' by which it is possible to distinguish between one part and another as belonging to different periods and epochs. Every attempt to draw such lines of distinction has proved a complete failure. The prophecy refuses to be so manipulated, and asserts its unity and homogeneity in spite of critical artifice or violence. We are compelled, therefore, by all these considerations, and chiefly by regard for the authority of Him whose word cannot be broken, to conclude that the Parousia, or second coming of Christ, with its connected and concomitant events, did take place, according to the Saviour's own prediction, at the period when Jerusalem was destroyed, and before the passing away of 'that generation.'

Here we might pause, for Scripture prophecy guides us no further. But the close of the æon is not the end of the world, and the fate of Israel teaches us nothing respecting the destiny of the human race. Whether we will or no, we cannot help speculating about the future, and forecasting the ultimate fortunes of a world which has been the scene of such stupendous displays of divine judgment and mercy. It will probably be felt by some to be an unwelcome conclusion that the Apocalypse is not that syllabus of civil and ecclesiastical history which a mistaken theory of interpretation supposed it to be. It will seem to them that the extinction of those false lights, which they took for guiding stars, leaves them in total darkness about the future; and they will ask in perplexity, Whither are we tending? What is to be the end and consummation of human history? Is this earth, with its precious freight of immortal and eternal interests, advancing towards light and truth, or hurrying into regions of darkness and distance from God?

Where nothing has been revealed it would be the height of presumption to prognosticate the future. 'It is not for us to know the times and the seasons which the Father hath put in his own power.' It has been said that 'the uninspired prophet is a fool,' and many instances approve the saying. Yet thus much it may be permitted us to conclude: there is no reason to despair about the future. There are some who tell us that as Judaism was a failure, so Christianity will be a failure also. We are not persuaded of this; we regard it rather as an impeachment of the divine wisdom and goodness. Judaism was never constituted to be a universal religion; it was essentially limited and national in its operation; but Christianity is made for man, and has proved its adaptation to every variety of the human family. It is indeed too true that the progress of Christianity in the world has been lamentably slow; and that, after eighteen centuries, it has not succeeded in banishing evil from the world, nor even from the regions where its influence has been most powerfully felt. Yet, after every allowance for its shortcomings, it still remains the mightiest moral force ever called into operation for purifying and ennobling the character of men. It is Christianity that differentiates the new world from the old; the modern from the ancient civilisation. This is the new factor in human society and history which may claim the largest share in the beneficent reformations of the past and to which we may look for still greater results in the future. The philosophic historian recognizes in Christianity a new power, which 'from its very origin, and still more in its progress, entirely renovated the face of the world.' * (Schlegel, Philosophy of History, Lect. x.)

Nor is there any symptom of decrepitude or exhaustion in the religion of Jesus after all the ages and conflicts, and revolutions of opinion through which it has come. It has stood the brunt of the most malignant persecution, and come off victorious. It has endured the ordeal of the most searching and hostile criticism, and come out of the fire unscathed. It has survived the more perilous patronage of pretended friends who have corrupted it into a superstition, perverted it into a policy, or degraded it into a trade. While the enemies of the Gospel predict its speedy extinction, it enters on a new career of conflict and victory. There is a perpetual tendency in Christianity to renew her youth, to regain the ideal of her pristine purity, and defecate herself from the impurities and accretions which are foreign to her nature. Never since the apostolic age were there greater vitality and vigour in the religion of the Cross than today. This is the age of Christian missions; and while all the other religions of the world have ceased to proselytise, and therefore to grow, Christianity goes forth to every land and nation, with the Bible in her hand and the proclamation of the glad tidings in her mouth, 'Believe in the Lord Jesus Christ and thou shalt be saved.'

The true interpretation of New Testament prophecy, instead of leaving us in darkness, encourages hope. It relieves the gloom which hung over a world which was believed to be destined to perish. There is no reason to infer that because Jerusalem was destroyed the world must burn; or, because the apostate nation was condemned, the human race must be consigned to perdition. All this sinister anticipation rests upon an erroneous interpretation of Scripture; and, the fallacies being cleared away, the prospect brightens with a glorious hope. We may trust the God of Love. He has not forsaken the earth, and He governs the world on a plan which He has not indeed disclosed to us, but which we may be well assured will finally evolve the highest good of the creature and the brightest glory of the Creator.

It may, indeed, seem strange and unaccountable that we should now be left without any of those divine manifestations and revelations which in other ages God was pleased to vouchsafe to men. We seem in some respects farther off from heaven than those ages were when voices and visions reminded men of the nearness of the Unseen. We may say, with the Jews of the captivity, 'We see not our signs: there is no more any prophet: neither is there among us any that knoweth how long ' Ps. 74:9).

Eighteen hundred years have rolled away since a voice was heard upon earth saying, 'Thus saith the Lord.' It is as if a door had been shut in heaven, and the direct intercourse of God with man were cut off; and we seem at a disadvantage as compared with those who were favoured with 'visions and revelations of the Lord.' Yet, even in this we may not judge correctly. Doubtless it is better as it is. The presence of the Holy Spirit with the disciples was declared by our Lord to be more than a compensation for His own absence. That Spirit dwells with us, and in us, and it is His office 'to take of Christ's, and to shew it unto us.' We have also the written Word of God, and in this we enjoy an incalculable superiority over the former days. Better the written Word than the living prophet. But should it be needful for the welfare and guidance of mankind that God should again manifest Himself, there is no presumption against further revelations. Why should it be thought that God has spoken His last word to men? But it is for Him to choose, and not for us to dictate. It may well be that even now, in ways unsuspected by us, He is speaking to man. 'God fulfils himself in many ways, and human history is as full of God today as in the ages of miracle and prophecy. Far from us be that incredulity which despairs of Christianity and of man. Surely, it was not in vain that Jesus said, 'I am the Light of the World.' 'God sent not his Son into the world to condemn the world, but that the world might be saved.' 'I, if I be lifted up from the earth, will draw all men unto myself.'

That favoured apostle who more than any other seems to have comprehended 'the breadth, and length, and depth, and height of the love of Christ,' suggests to us ideas of the extent and efficiency of the great redemption which our latent incredulity can scarcely receive. He does not hesitate to affirm that the restorative work of Christ will ultimately more than repair the ruin wrought by sin. 'As by one man's disobedience the many were made sinners, so by the obedience of One shall the many be made righteous.' There would be no point in this comparison if 'the many' on the one side of the equation bore no proportion to 'the many' on the other side. But this is not all: the redemptive work of Christ does more than redress the balance: it outweighs, and that immeasurably, the counterpoise of evil. 'Where sin abounded, grace did beyond measure abound: that as sin reigned in death, even so might grace reign in righteousness unto eternal life through Jesus Christ our Lord' (Rom. 5:19-21).

It does not fall within the scope of this discussion to argue on philosophical grounds the natural probability of a reign of truth and righteousness on the earth; we are happy to be assured of the consummation on higher and safer grounds, even the promises of Him who has taught us to pray, 'Thy will be done in earth, as it is done in heaven.' For every God-taught prayer contains a prophecy, and conveys a promise. This world belongs no more to the devil, but to God. Christ has redeemed it, and will recover it, and draw all men unto Him. Otherwise it is inconceivable that God would have taught His people in all ages to utter in faith and hope that sublime prophetic prayer:—

'God be merciful unto us, and bless us;
And cause his face to shine on us;
That thy way may be known upon earth,
Thy saving health among all nations.
Let the people praise thee, O God;
Let all the people praise thee.
O let the nations be glad and sing for joy:
For Thou shalt judge the people righteously,

And govern the nations upon earth.
Let the people praise thee, O God;
Let all the people praise thee.
Then shall the earth yield her increase;
And God, even our own God, shall bless us.
God shall bless us;
And all the ends of the earth shall fear him.'
(PSALM 67)

Appendix to Part Three

NOTE A.
Reuss on 'the Number of the Beast.' **(Rev. xiii. 18.)**

'It would form a very singular history were we to recount all that has been said by theologians with reference to the number 666 in the Revelation. This is not, however, the place to do so, and it is generally mere waste of time to refute palpable errors and absurd hallucinations. Our texts are so clear to those who have eyes to see and comprehend, that the simple statement of their true meaning ought at once to dissipate the clouds gathered round them by dogmatic prejudices, interested imaginations, and political pre-constructions.

'The number of the beast, 666, is the number of a man, ariqmoz, anqrwpou, says the prophet. It is the number of a name, he says again, and that name is written on the forehead of those who are the loyal subjects and worshippers of the beast. But the beast itself is a personal being---Antichrist, and does not stand for some abstract idea. From this it follows that the number 666 does not represent a period of ecclesiastical history, as is maintained in the interpretation of orthodox Protestant theologians and of pietistic chiliasts of the school of Bengel. Nor does it stand for a common name, and to characterise a power, an empire, as, for example, Roman Paganism, as Irenaeus sought to show with his Aateinoz, which has been adopted by all subsequent interpreters who have failed to invent anything more inadmissible still, and which Protestants have eagerly made use of in the interest of their anti-papal polemics. The terms "Latium," "Latini," had no existence in the first century but in the poetry and local geography of the Campagna of Rome, and, as the name of a language, was utterly unknown in any form within apostolic sphere (Luke xxiii. 38; John xix. 20).

'The number 666 must, then, contain a proper name, the name of the political and historical personage who was to play the part of Antichrist in all the great revolutions awaiting the Judaeo-Christian world. After reading Daniel and the Second Epistle to the Thessalonians we know *what* is the subject. Our author finally proceeds to tell us of *whom* he speaks.

'Here, then, is the difficulty (if difficulty it be) which has most often misled even those who have approached the problem with a spirit free from prejudice and illusion. The beast of the thirteenth chapter is not an individual, but the Roman Empire, regarded as a power. The writer himself tells us (chap. xvii.) that the seven heads of the beast represent the seven hills on which his capital is built; and again, seven kings who have reigned, or still reign, there. This is quite true, but he tells us quite as plainly that this beast is at the same time one of the seven heads, a combination apparently inconceivable and more than paradoxical, but at the same time very natural, and even necessary. The idea of a power, especially of a hostile influence, always tends to assume a concrete form, to personify itself in the popular mind. The ideal monster becomes an individual; the principle assumes a distinct human shape, and under this personal form ideas become popularised, till individuals come in their turn to be the permanent representatives of ideas and influences which outlive themselves. To most men a proper name conveys more than a definition, and is more apt to excite warm and living feeling. The pagan power, idolatry, blasphemy, persecution, all that stirs the lawful antipathies of the church, all that inspires it with horror, and wrings from it the cry of woe, would naturally be individualised and concentrated in the person of him who, a few years before the destruction of Jerusalem, had filled up the measure of his crimes. The beast is, then, at once the Empire and the Emperor, and the name of the latter is on the lips of the thoughtful reader before we utter it. Let us, however, cast upon it all the light of historic science.

'An attentive reading of chap. xi. will have already brought us to the conviction that this book was written before the destruction of Jerusalem. The temple and its inner court, with the great altar, are the measured---destined, that is to say, to be preserved (Zech. ii.), while the rest of the city is given up to the Pagans and devoted to sacrilege. These passages could not have been framed in view of the state of things which existed after the year 70. But the indications given in chap. xvii. are still more decisive. We shall maintain that Rome is here spoken of till it can be shown that in the age of the apostles there existed another city built upon seven hills, *urbem septicollem,* in which the blood of the witnesses of Christ had been shed in torrents (vers. 6, 9). This city, or this empire, has seven kings. The revelations of Daniel, of Enoch, and of Esdras follow the same chronological plan, all counting successions of kings to put the reader upon the track of the dates. Of those seven kings five are already dead (ver. 10), the sixth is reigning at this very time. The sixth emperor of Rome was Galba, an old man, seventy-three years of age at his accession. The final catastrophe, which was to destroy the city and the empire, was to take place in three years and a half, as has already been noted. For this one simple reason the series of emperors will include only one after the then reigning monarch, and he will reign but a little while. The writer does not know him, but he knows the relative duration of his reign, because he knows that Rome will, in three years and a half, perish finally, never to rise again.

'There shall come an eighth emperor, he is one of the seven, and is at the same time the beast that *was,* but at the moment, is not. This must refer, then, to one of the previous emperors, who is to come again a second time, but as Antichrist, that is, invested with all the power of the devil, and for the special end of fighting against the Lord. As it is said that, at the time the vision is written, he is not, but has already been, he must be one of the first five emperors. He has been already wounded to death (chap. xiii. 3), so that there is something miraculous in his reappearance. It cannot, then, be Augustus, Tiberius, or Claudius, who none of them came to a violent end, and who are further place out of the question by the fact that none of these stood in hostile relations to the church. This reason will also exclude Caligula. There remains only Nero; but everything concurs to point him out as the personage thus mysteriously designated. So long as Galba reigned, and even long after that, the people did not believe Nero to be dead; they supposed him hidden somewhere, and ready to return and avenge himself on his enemies. The Messianic ideas of the Jews, which had become vaguely diffused through the West (as we learn from Tacitus and Suetonius), blending with these popular notions, suggested to the credulous the idea that Nero would come again from the East, to regain his throne by the aid of the Parthians. Many false Neros appeared. These popular fancies spread also among Christians. Visions were of common occurrence, and the Fathers of the church perpetuate the same tradition through several centuries later.

'Lastly, that nothing may be wanting to the full evidence, our book names Nero, so to speak, in every character. The name Nero is contained in the number 666. The mechanism of the problem is based upon one of the cabalistic artifices in use in Jewish hermeneutics, which consisted in calculating the numerical value of the letters composing a word. this method, called *ghematria,* or geometrical, that is, mathematical, and used by the Jews in the exegesis of the Old Testament, has given much trouble to our learned men, and has led them into a maze of errors. All ancient and modern alphabets have been placed under contribution, and all imaginable combinations of figures and letters have been tried in turn. It has been made to yield almost all the historical names of the past eighteen centuries,---Titus Vespasian and Simon Gioras, Julian the Apostate and Genseric, Mohomet and Luther, Benedict IX. and Louis XV., Napoleon I. and the Duke de Reichstadt,---and it would not be difficult for any of us, on the same principles, to read in it one another's names. In truth, the enigma was not so hard, though it has only been solved by exegesis in our own days. It was so little insoluble that several contemporary scholars found the clue simultaneously, and without knowing anything of one another's labours. The *ghematria* is a Hebrews ar. The number has to be deciphered by the Hebrew Alphabet: rsq nwrn reads "Nero Caesar":---

$$\mathbf{נ}=50 \quad \mathbf{ר}=200 \quad \mathbf{ו}=6 \quad \mathbf{נ}=50 \quad \mathbf{ק}=100 \quad \mathbf{ס}=60 \quad \mathbf{ר}=200$$

thus:

$$\text{נְרוֹן קֵסָר} = 666$$

'The most curious point is that there exists a very ancient reading which gives 616. This might be the work of a Latin reader of the Revelation who had found the solution, but who pronounced Nero like the Romans, while the writer of the Revelation pronounced it like the Greeks and Orientals. The removal of the final n gives fifty less.'

NOTE B.

Dr. J. M. Macdonald's Life and Writings of St. John.

This volume was ready for the press before the author had an opportunity of consulting the elaborate work of Dr. Macdonald of the Life and Writings of St. John. Though it cannot be said that Dr. Macdonald does for St. John what Conybeare and Howson have done for St. Paul, yet there is much that is valuable in his work. It is especially gratifying to the author to find that, on the difficult question of *'the two witnesses,'* Dr. Macdonald has arrived at a conclusion almost identical with his own. It would seem, however, to be with Dr. Macdonald only a *happy guess.* Paley says, *'He discovers who proves;'* and Dr. Macdonald has not gone deeply into the investigation of the problem.

On the question of the *date of the Apocalypse* Dr. Macdonald unhesitatingly pronounces for the early date; and his remarks on this subject are weighty and powerful. He sees, what indeed is obvious enough, that the internal evidence settles the question beyond all controversy.

But Dr. Macdonald has failed, as so many expositors have failed, to find the true key to the Apocalypse. He follows Moses Stuart closely in the interpretation of the latter portion of the Revelation, and sees in *the harlot city,* not Jerusalem, but Rome. There is an inconsistency in his statements respecting Babylon (the city on the Euphrates) which amounts to self-contradiction. At page 138 he represents the literal Babylon as a large and populous city in the time of St. Peter, and quotes with approval from J. D. Michaelis and D. F. Bacon to show that it had a large Jewish population and offered a most desirable field for the labours of that apostle. At page 225, however, he says: 'The literal Babylon was no more. The prophecies in regard to it uttered by Isaiah had long since been fulfilled.' Both these statements cannot be correct. We have the clearest evidence that in the apostolic age Babylon was a deserted city. Probably the *province,* Babylonia, is confounded with the *city,* Babylon.

The following extracts are interesting and valuable:---

Date of the Apocalypse.

'The external evidence seems, on the whole, to be of comparatively little value in deciding the true date of the Apocalypse. The main reliance, it is clear, must be upon the argument from internal evidence. When it has been made to appear that Irenaeus says nothing respecting the time when the Book of Revelation was written, and that Eusebius ascribes its authorship to another John than the apostle, it is sufficiently evident that the remaining testimony of antiquity, conflicting as it is, or about evenly balanced between the earlier and later date, is of little account in deciding the question. And when we open the book itself, and find inscribed on its very pages evidence that at the time it was written Jewish enemies were still arrogant and active in the city in which our Lord was crucified, and that the temple and altar in it were still standing, we need no date from early antiquity, nor even from the hand of the author himself, to inform us that he wrote before that great historical even and prophetic epoch, the destruction of Jerusalem.'---Pp. 171, 172.

The Two witnesses. (Rev. xi.)

'If we had a Christian history extant, as we have a Pagan one by Tacitus and a Jewish one by Josephus, giving an account of what occurred within that devoted city during that awful period of its history, then we might trace out more distinctly the prophesying of the two witnesses. The great body of Christians, warned by the signs given them by their Lord, according to ancient testimony, appear to have left Palestine on its invasion by the Romans . . . . But it was the will of God that a competent number of witnesses for Christ should remain to preach the Gospel to the very last moment to their deluded, miserable countrymen. It may have been part of their work to reiterate the prophecies respecting the destruction of the city, the temple, and commonwealth. During the time the Romans were to read down the Holy Land and the city, they were to prophecy. Their being clothed in sackcloth intimates the mourningful character of their mission. In their designation as the two olive-trees, and the two candlesticks or lamps standing before God, there is an allusion to Zechariah iv., where these two symbols are interpreted of the two anointed ones, Joshua the high priest, and Zerubbabel the prince, founder of the second temple. The olive-trees, fresh and vigorous, keep the lamps constantly supplied with oil. These witnesses, amidst the darkness which has settled round Jerusalem, give a steady and unfailing light. They possess the power of working miracles as wonderful as any of those performed by Moses and Elijah. What is here predicted must have been fulfilled before the close of the miraculous or apostolic age. All who find here a prediction of the state of the church during the ascendancy of the Papacy, or at any period subsequent to the age of the apostles, are of course under the necessity of explaining away all this language which attributes miraculous power to the witnesses. They were at length to fall victims to the war, or to the same power that waged the war, and their bodies were to lie unburied three days and a half in the streets of the city where Christ was crucified. Their resurrection and ascension to heaven must be interpreted literally; although, as in the case of the miracles they performed, there is no historical record of the events themselves. If these two prophets were the only Christians in Jerusalem, as both were killed, there was no one to make a record or report in the case; and we have here therefore an example of a prophecy which contains at the same time the only history or notice of the events by which it was fulfilled. The wave of ruin which swept over Jerusalem, and wafted them up to heaven, erased or prevented every human memento of their work of faith, their patience of hope, and labour of love. The prophecy that foretold them is their only history, or the only history of the part they were to take in the closing scenes of Jerusalem. We conclude, then, that these witnesses were two of those apostles who seem to be so strangely lost to history, or of whom no authentic traces can be discovered subsequent to the destruction of Jerusalem. May not James the Less, or the second James (in distinction from the brother of John), commonly styled the Bishop of Jerusalem, have been one of them? Why should he not remain faithful at his post to the last? According to Hegesippus, a Jewish Christian historian, who wrote about the middle of the second century, his monument was still pointed out near the ruins of the temple. Hegesippus says that he was killed in the year 69, and represents the apostle as bearing powerful testimony to the Messiahship of Jesus, and pointing to His second coming in the clouds of heaven, up to the very moment of his death. There seems to be a peculiar fitness in these witnesses for Christ, men endowed with the highest supernatural gifts, standing to the last in the forsaken city, prophesying its doom, and lamenting over what was once so dear to God.'---Pp. 161, 162.

SUPPLEMENTARY NOTE.

Bishop Warburton on 'Our Lord's Prophecy on the Mount of Olives,' and on 'The Kingdom of Heaven.'

The following observations by the learned author of 'The Divine Legation' are in remarkable accord with the opinions expressed in this work:---

'The prophecy of Jesus concerning the approaching destruction of Jerusalem by Titus is conceived in such high and swelling terms, that not only the modern interpreters, but the ancient likewise, have supposed that our Lord interweaves into it a direct prediction of His second coming to judgment. Hence arose a current opinion in those times that the consummation of all things was at hand; which hath afforded a handle to an infidel objection in these, insinuating that Jesus, in order to keep His followers attached to His service, and patient under sufferings, flattered them with the near approach of those rewards which completed all their views and expectations. To which the defenders of religion have opposed this answer: That the distinction of short and long, in the duration of time, is lost in eternity; and with the Almighty, "a thousand years are but as yesterday," etc.

'But the principle both go upon is false; and if what hath been said be duly weighed, it will appear that this prophecy doth not respect Christ's second coming to judgment, but His first; in the abolition of the Jewish polity and the establishment of the Christian,---that kingdom of Christ which commenced on the total ceasing of the Theocracy. For as God's reign over the Jews entirely ended with the abolition of the temple service, so the reign of Christ, "in spirit and in truth," had then its first beginning. This was the true establishment of Christianity, not that effected by the conversion or donations of Constantine. Till the Jewish law was abolished, over which the "Father" presided as King, the reign of the "Son" could not take place; because the sovereignty of Christ over mankind was that very sovereignty of God over the Jews transferred and more largely extended.

'This, therefore, being on of the most important eras in the economy of grace, and the most awful revolution in all God's religious dispensations, we see the elegance and propriety of the terms in question to denote so great an event, together with the destruction of Jerusalem, by which it was effected; for in the whole prophetic language, the change and fall of principalities and powers, whether spiritual or civil, are signified by the shaking of heavens and earth, the darkening of the sun and moon, and the falling of the stars; as the rise and establishment of new ones are by processions in the clouds of heaven, by the sound of trumpets, and the assembling together of hosts and congregations.'

Afterword

The author avails himself of this opportunity to make a few observations on several points which have come under his notice since the first publication
of this volume.

DOLLINGER ON "The Man of Sin"

It is with great satisfaction that he finds himself in substantial agreement with the distinguished ecclesiastical historian and theologian, Dr. Dollinger, of Munich, in his interpretation of St. Paul's prediction in 2 Thessalonians. (1) Dr. Dollinger distinctly identifies the "Man of Sin" with Nero, a conclusion now so generally accepted by the highest authorities, that it may be regarded as a settled point. (2) He clearly distinguishes between the "Man of Sin" and "the Apostasy," so frequently confounded by the mass of interpreters. Dollinger shows that the former is a person, the latter a heresy. (3) He recognizes "the Beast" of the Apocalypse as the Emperor, and therefore identical with the "Man of Sin." (4) The miracles wrought by the "Second Beast" (the Beast from the earth) he regards as a representation derived from our Lord's prophecy on the Mount of Olives.
"Magical and theurgic arts are inseparable from Heathenism."

The whole of Dr. Dollinger's observations on this subject are most important, but as they are too lengthy for quotation here, the reader is referred to the "First Age of the Church," vol. 2. pp. 79-96. It is only fair to add that Dollinger seems to hold a personal Antichrist, and a twofold or typical fulfillment of prophecy.

THE BABYLON OF THE APOCALYPSE

The belief that Rome is the Babylon of the Apocalypse is so firmly established in most minds, that nothing but the clearest evidence to the contrary will be able to dislodge it. Yet some of the ablest critics long since suspected that Babylon was a pseudonym of ancient Jerusalem. The illustrious Herder in his Commentary on the Book of Revelation affirms -

"Rome was not in the circle of the prophet's vision, nor is Rome in coincidence with the symbols and metaphors; but the resemblance to Jerusalem is as perfect as the case can be supposed to furnish" (p. 153).

The well-known commentator, John David Michaelis, shrewdly conjectured that Babylon is identical with Jerusalem. Speaking of the place from which the First Epistle of Peter was written, he says:

"If I could only find a single authority for calling Jerusalem by the name of Babylon, I would rather follow Cappellus and Harduin who take Jerusalem to have been the place; which was also, according to Cyril of Alexandria, meant by Isaiah when he is speaking of Babylon. For the contents of this Epistle are not so well suited to any time as to that soon after the Council of Jerusalem, whilst Peter continued in that city. It is not impossible that St. Peter might call Jerusalem by the name of Babylon after she had begun to persecute the Church; and the expression of the elected church at Babylon seems to imply a paradox which would be removed had Jerusalem itself been named. It is therefore not improbable that St. Peter might in an epistle make use of this figurative and opprobrious name to signify Jerusalem. . . . Add to this that St. Peter sends a salutation from Mark, and this Mark, who was also called John, was returned to Jerusalem, not long before the said Council (Acts 13:13) All circumstances thus concurring, and it being never more necessary to the Gentile converts that they should 'stand in the true grace of God,' it appears to me, whilst I am writing, probable in the highest degree, that this Epistle was written at Jerusalem soon after the Council, i.e., in the year of Christ 49. . . . I am the less influenced by the testimony of the ancients to the contrary, as the matter depends not upon the historical question, whether St. Peter ever was at Rome, but upon the critical question, whether he calls Rome by the name of Babylon?"

Michaelis has placed this title in the margin -

"The First Epistle of St. Peter was written at Jerusalem at the time of the first council" (See Introd. Lect. to the "Sacred Books of the New Testament," by J. D. Michaelis, § 148).

JERUSALEM A SEVEN-HILLED CITY

It has been supposed that the description of the "great city" in the Apocalypse, as seated on seven city hills, is conclusive evidence that Rome is here intended. The reader will see how this point is dealt with in its proper place. The author has shown how Zullig enumerates seven hills or mountains in Jerusalem. Herder also remarks -

"The seven heads of the Beast are said to be seven mountains; assuming the woman to be a city founded upon seven mountains. Such was the situation of Jerusalem." (Comm., Herder, p. 156)

As Herder does not stay to prove his assertion, it may be well to supplement it with evidence of a confirmatory kind. Dr. Lange, in his discussion respecting the site of Golgotha, observes -

"Jeremiah predicts (Jer. 31:36-40) that the city should in future times extend beyond the north wall (the second wall) and inclose Gibeat Gareb, or the Leper's Hill, and Gibeat Goath, or the Hill of Death (of roaring, groaning). The position of Gareb can correspond only with Under Bezetha, and the position of Goath only with Upper Bezetha where Golgotha rose. Both of these elevations were inclosed by Agrippa, as parts of the new city, and lay inside the third wall. From the context we learn that Gareb and Goath were unclean places, but, being measured in with the holy city, became sanctified. That the Goath hill of Jeremiah is identical with the Golgotha of the Evangelists, is more than probable. The wall of Agrippa was built around Bezetha by Herod Agrippa, the grandson of Herod the Great" (Lange on Matt. 27:33).

A sketch-plan of ancient Jerusalem, showing Mount Gareb and Mount Goath is given in "Palestine Explored," by the Rev. James Neil, M.A., formerly incumbent of Christ Church, Jerusalem. Mr. Neil enumerates the seven hills on which the city was built, Mount Zion, Mount Ophel, Mount Moriah, Mount Bezetha, Mount Acra, Mount Gareb, and Mount Goath.

THE CRUCIAL QUESTION

Doubtless most readers will shrink from the demand made upon their faith, when they are asked to believe that the predictions of our Lord in Matt. 24, and the kindred prophecy of St. Paul in 1 Thess. 4., had a veritable accomplishment. Many will regard it as an extravagance which refutes itself. Let them consider whether this demand is not made by the most express affirmations of Inspiration. These predictions are bounded by certain limits of time. The time is explicitly declared to fall within the period of the then existing generation. No artifice of logic, no violence of interpretation, can evade or gainsay this undeniable fact. credible or incredible, reasonable or unreasonable, the authority of Scripture is committed to the affirmation. And why should it be thought incredible? The reply will be, "Because there is no historical evidence of the fact."

This, however, is an assumption. It deserves consideration whether we have not all the evidence which the nature of the case admits. What evidence, for example, may be reasonably required that the most seemingly incredible event predicted in Matt. 24:31, and in 1 Thess. 4:17, commonly denominated "the rapture of the saints," actually took place?

The principal, if not the only, portion that seems to come within the cognizance of human sense, is the removal of a great multitude of the disciples of Christ from this earthly scene. We might expect, therefore, that there should be some trace in history of this sudden disappearance of so vast a body of believers. It surely must have made a blank in history; a failure, at the least, in the continuity of the records of Christianity. Admitting that the predictions do not require an absolute and universal removal of the whole body of the faithful (for it is manifest that there is a clear distinction made between the watchful and the unwatchful, the ready and the unready, and that as many might be shut out of the kingdom as those who went in), yet the language of the prophecy certainly implies the sudden and simultaneous removal of a very great number of the faithful. Is there, then, any vestige in history of such a blank? Most certainly there is, and just such an indication as we might expect. A silence which is expressive. Silence where, a moment before, all was life and activity. The ecclesiastical historian will tell you that the light suddenly fails him. The Christian Church of Jerusalem, of which an apostle could say, "Thou seest, brother, how many myriads there are among the Jews which have believed," suddenly dwindles into two wretched sects of Ebionites and Nazarenes. Where are the many myriads of St. James? Where are the hundred and forty and four thousand" whom St. John saw, with the seal of God on their foreheads, and standing with the Lamb on the Mount Zion? Did they perish in the siege of Jerusalem? Certainly not; for it is universally agreed that, forewarned by their Divine Master, they retired from the doomed city to a place of safety. Yet they seem to disappear and leave no trace behind. Ask the ecclesiastical historian to put his finger on the spot where the records of early Christianity are most obscure, and he will unhesitatingly point to the period when the Acts of the Apostles end. Of this period the learned Neander says that, "We have no information, nor can the total want of sources for this part of Church history be at all surprising." And, again, he speaks of "the age immediately succeeding the Apostolic," of which we have unfortunately so few authentic memorials ("Planting and Training," chaps. v. and x.). Hiudekoper, a Dutch theologian, in his work entitled, "Christ's Descent to the Under-world," remarks that "On leaving the Apostolic age we almost lose sight of the Christians in a historical chasm of sixty or eighty years."

Archdeacon Farrar more emphatically dwells upon the fact and probable cause of this unaccountable eclipse - "Although we are so fully acquainted with the thoughts and feelings of the early Christians, yet the facts of their corporate history, and even the closing details in the biographies of their very greatest teachers are plunged in entire uncertainty. When, with the last word in the Acts of the Apostles, we lose the graphic and faithful guidance of St. Luke, the torch of Christian history is for a time abruptly quenched. We are left, as it were, to grope among the windings of the Catacombs. Even the final labors of the life of St. Paul are only so far known as we may dimly infer from the casual allusions of the Pastoral Epistles. For the details of many years in the life of St. Peter, we have nothing on which to rely, except slight and vague allusions, floating rumors, and false impressions, created by the deliberate fictions of heretical romance.

"It is probable that this silence is in itself the result of the terrible scenes in which the apostles perished. It was indispensable to the safety of the whole community that the books of the Christians, when given up by the unhappy weakness of 'traditores,' or discovered by the keen malignity of informers, should contain no compromising matter. But how would it have been possible for St. Luke to write in a manner otherwise than compromising, if he had detailed the horrors of the Neronian persecution? It is a reasonable conjecture that the sudden close of the Acts of the Apostles may have been due to the impossibility of speaking without indignation and abhorrence of the Emperor and the Government, which, between A.D. 64 and 68, sanctioned the infliction upon innocent men and women, of atrocities which excited the pity of the very Pagans. The Jew and the Christians who entered on such themes, could only do so under the disguise of a cryptograph, hiding his meaning from all but the initiated few, in such prophetic symbols as those of the Apocalypse. In that book alone we are enabled to hear the cry of horror which Nero's brutal cruelties wrung from Christian hearts." ("The Early Days of Christianity," vol. 2. pp. 82, 83)

Still more vividly and forcibly, if possible, the case is put by the able reviewer of Renan's "St. Paul" in the pages of "The Edinburgh Review," April, 1870 - "This volume ["The Life of St. Paul"] takes us through the whole period of, what we may call, the ministry of the great apostle, embracing those all-important fifteen or sixteen years (A.D. 45-61), during which his three missionary journeys were undertaken, and the infant Church, with four bold strides, advanced from Jerusalem to Antioch, from Antioch to Ephesus, from Ephesus to Corinth, and from Corinth to Rome. Once arrived there, once securely planted in that central and commanding position, strange to say, the Church, with all its dramatis personae, suddenly vanishes from our view. The densest clouds of obscurity immediately gather round its history, which our eager curiosity in vain attempts to penetrate. It is gone, amid a wreath of smoke, as completely as when a train plunges into a tunnel. In the words of M. Renan - 'The arrival of St. Paul at Rome, owing to the decision taken by the author of the "Acts" to close his narrative at that point, marks for the history of the origin of Christianity the commencement of a profound night, illuminated only by the lurid fire of Nero's horrible festivities, and by the lightning flash of the Apocalypse.' The causes of this sudden and confounding disappearance have not, to this day, been thoroughly investigated. . . . The history of St. Paul's life, and the history of the Apostolic age, together abruptly end. Black darkness falls upon the scene, and a grim and brooding silence - like the silence of impending storm - holds in hushed expectation of the 'day of the Lord' the awe-struck, breathless Church. No more books are written, no more messengers are sent, the very voice of tradition is still. One voice alone, from amid the silence and the dread, breaks upon the straining ear; it is the Apocalyptic vengeance-cry from Patmos, 'Babylon the Great is fallen, is fallen! Rejoice over her, thou heaven! and ye holy apostles and prophets! for God hath avenged you on her: she shall be utterly burned with fire, for strong is the Lord God who judgeth her.' " (Rev.18:20)

THE TRUE SOLUTION

It remains for the reader to consider, whether the causes suggested in the preceding quotations furnish an adequate explanation of this singular phenomenon; or whether the solution of the problem is not to be found in the actual occurrence of the events predicted by our Lord and His apostles. There, in the written record of Inspiration, stand the ineffaceable words which foretell the speedy return of the Son of Man to judge the guilty nation and avenge His own elect. His coming was indissolubly connected with that same generation. The attendant circumstances of His coming are set forth with marked precision. Everything points to a sudden, swift, far-reaching catastrophe, analogous to that which took place "in the days of Noah when the flood came, and took them all away," or in the days of Lot, when the tempest of wrath overwhelmed Sodom and Gomorrah. These are the very images used by our Lord to describe the suddenness and swiftness of His appearing. No wonder that there should be a "total blank" in contemporary history; that there should be a solution of continuity in the records of the Christian Church; that the pen of St. Mark should be arrested in the midst of an unfinished sentence; that St. Luke should abruptly break off his narrative of the life and labors of St. Paul. Grant that there is no failure in the predictions of Christ; that His words had a veritable accomplishment; and all is explained. There is an adequate cause for the otherwise unaccountable hiatus which occurs in the Christian history of the time, and for the total obscuration of the Church, and all its greatest luminaries. Is it unreasonable to ask that the plainest declarations of the Lord Himself, and of His inspired witnesses should obtain a candid hearing, and a cordial belief, from all who own Him as Lord and Master? Surely that robust faith is not utterly extinct, which once could say, "Let God be true, and every man a liar."

This postscript may close with the impressive caution of a great critic and theologian of the last century, which, though it has special reference to the Apocalypse, is equally applicable to the whole prophetical portion of the New Testament.

"If it be objected that the prophecies in the Apocalypse are not yet fulfilled, that they are therefore not fully understood, and that hence arises the difference of opinion in respect to their meaning, I answer, that if the prophecies are not yet fulfilled, it is wholly impossible that the Apocalypse should be a Divine work; since the author expressly declares (Rev. 1:1) that the things which it contains 'must shortly come to pass.' Consequently, either a great part of them, I will not say all, must have been fulfilled, or the author's declaration, that they should shortly be completed, is not consistent with fact. It is true that to the Almighty a thousand years are but as one day, and one day as a thousand years; but if we therefore explain the term 'shortly,' as denoting a period longer than that which has elapsed since the Apocalypse was written, we sacrifice the love of truth to the support of a preconceived opinion. For when the Deity condescends to communicate information to mankind, He will of course use such language as is intelligible to mankind; and not name a period short which all men consider as long, or the communication will be totally useless. Besides, in reference to God's eternity, not only seventeen hundred but seventeen thousand years are nothing. But the author of the Apocalypse himself has wholly precluded any such evasion, by explaining (Rev. 1:3) what he meant by the term 'shortly,' for he there says, 'Blessed is he that readeth, and they that hear the words of this prophecy, and keep those things which are written therein; for the time is at hand.' According, therefore, to the author's own declaration, the Apocalypse contains prophecies with which the very persons to whom it was sent were immediately concerned. But if none of these prophecies were designed to be completed till long after their death, those persons were not immediately concerned with them, and the author would surely not have said that they were blessed in reading prophecies of which the time was at hand, if those prophecies were not to be fulfilled till after the lapse of many ages" (J. D. Michaelis, "Introduction to the New Testament," vol. 4. pp. 503, 504).